African Americ
First segregationist Jim Cr
Battle of Little
Reconstruction fails

1880

Russian Jewish immigration
Chinese Exclusion Act
American Federation of Labor
Statue of Liberty dedicated
Dawes Act grants Indians land if they renounce tribal holdings
Geronimo fights restrictions on Indians

1883 Emma Lazarus: "The New Colossus"

1890

Battle of Wounded Knee
Spanish-American War
Dawes Commission extinguishes tribal lands
U.S. acquires Puerto Rico

1895 Thomas Bailey Aldrich: "Unguarded Gates"

1900

Panama Canal begun
NAACP formed

1900 Arnold Genthe: "The Balloon Man" *(photo)*
1903 W. E. B. Du Bois: "Of Our Spiritual Strivings"
1906–1910 Lewis Hine: "Picturing the Immigrant" *(photo essay)*
1906–1914 Isaac Metzker: "A Bintel Brief: Letters from the Lower East Side to the *Jewish Daily Forward*"
1907 Alfred Stieglitz: "The Steerage" *(photo)*

1910

Jim Crow laws throughout South
World War I
8-hour workday gradually adopted
Russian Revolution
U.S. Attorney General Palmer prosecutes disloyal Americans

1912 James Weldon Johnson: *The Autobiography of an Ex-Colored Man*

1920

Women vote
League of Nations
Jewish state established in Palestine
Child labor prohibited
Lindbergh's solo flight across the Atlantic

1925 Anzia Yezierska: "College"
1926 E. E. Cummings: "next to of course god america i"

1930

Prohibition repealed
Great Depression
Social Security Act
Fair Labor Standards Act
New Deal

1938 Berenice Abbott: "Snuff Shop, 113 Division Street, Manhattan" *(photo)*
1938–1939 Ann Banks: "Immigrant Lives: Oral Histories Collected by the W.P.A. Federal Writers Project"
1938 Langston Hughes: "Let America Be America Again"

(Continued on inside back cover)

Inventing America

Readings in Identity and Culture

GABRIELLA IBIETA
DREXEL UNIVERSITY

MILES ORVELL
TEMPLE UNIVERSITY

ST. MARTIN'S PRESS
New York

For Our Children, Ariana and Dylan

EDITOR: Nancy Lyman
DEVELOPMENT EDITOR: Kristin Bowen
MANAGER, PUBLISHING SERVICES: Emily Berleth
PUBLISHING SERVICES ASSOCIATE: Meryl Perrin
PROJECT MANAGEMENT: Books By Design, Inc.
PRODUCTION SUPERVISOR: Scott Lavelle
TEXT DESIGN: Anna George
COVER DESIGN: Patricia McFadden
COVER ART: Fred Otnes

Library of Congress Catalog Card Number: 95-67066

Manufactured in the United States of America.

0 9 8 7 6
F E D C B A

For information, write:
St. Martin's Press, Inc.
175 Fifth Avenue
New York, NY 10010

ISBN: 0-312-10307-7

Acknowledgments
Acknowledgments and copyrights are continued at the back of the book on pages 595–597, which constitute an extension of the copyright page.

Contents

Preface

To understand America, one must know where Americans have come from. That is the assumption underlying *Inventing America: Readings in Identity and Culture,* and it rests on a conviction that who we are is always related to the place or places where we grow up, to who our parents are, and where they came from. And yet, as much as our sense of American identity is rooted in this notion of the past, it is also rooted, and just as strongly, in the concept of constant change. American society has always engaged in a ceaseless reinvention of itself, both on a collective and an individual level. Americans have an indispensable ability to change and remake themselves, and this ability gives American culture a remarkable and unique character of mobility and self-invention. Americans have always had this double characteristic: while connected to the past, they are also strongly motivated to change themselves.

Inventing America is designed to inquire into this process of self-invention, providing a double perspective for the college student, first by providing a basis for understanding his or her own place in American culture and society, and second by providing the grounds for understanding the perspectives of other social groups.

Thematic Organization

The collection comprises sixty-four selections representing a wide variety of genres, ranging from poetry, fiction, and autobiography, to essays, letters, oral histories, and visual texts. Organized thematically, the chapters include both historical selections and contemporary discussions of ethnic and cultural identity that often challenge one another, offering students the opportunity to think critically, to engage in dialogue with the texts, and to explore issues of identity from different perspectives.

The eight chapters begin with immigrants' first experiences of different cultures, "Encountering Others," and then take up the ambivalence experienced with deracination in "Exiled Voices." The reinvented identity that results from the complex process of assimilation is next considered in "The Multicultural Self" and "Border Crossings." And that process of crossing over, whether into mainstream American culture or into marginalized cultures within it, is explored in the following two chapters, "In the World of Letters" and "Cross-Cultural Impersonations." Next, "Representing Ethnicity" explores how ethnicity and identity are constructed in ads, in photographs, and in our culture's discourse generally. The final chapter, "The Politics of Ethnicity," addresses the issues of harmony and dissonance as they have been played out in politics, education, and other cultural institutions, both in theory and in practice.

FEATURES

- **A historical and cultural focus** provides a broader perspective missing from most other multicultural readers. Each chapter begins with historical readings, many of them primary sources, and includes contemporary discussions of American culture, helping students see the ways identities have been constructed for different groups and individuals throughout American history.
- **A timeline** on the front and back endpapers provides additional historical and cultural context.
- **Many visual texts** help students recognize and analyze visual representations of culture, including such sources as magazines, photo essays, advertisements, and store signs. The five selections that include photographs and other images provide crucial visual evidence and a literal look at the way cultures are represented. The photographs that open each chapter not only illuminate its theme, they are active "texts" as well, with accompanying questions at the end of each chapter. The Reader's Introduction includes guidelines for analyzing visual texts.
- **A balance of writers from many different ethnic groups,** including strong coverage of Latino, Italian American, and Jewish American writers, who are often neglected in multicultural anthologies.
- **An apparatus that promotes critical thinking,** with carefully crafted chapter introductions and individual headnotes, discussion questions, and writing assignments for each selection. End-of-chapter questions encourage students to relate the readings in a chapter to each other and to readings in other chapters. A list of further readings accompanies each selection, thus providing students with the opportunity to explore issues on their own.
- **The Instructor's Manual** provides additional cultural and historical background material, along with teaching suggestions and opportunities for further research.

A Note on Language

A potential subject of controversy, in this anthology and in general, is the use of language that attempts to define people ethnically and racially. One of the problems that we encountered when trying to refer to various groups is the changing nature of terminology, which is defined historically, culturally, and even economically. In *Inventing America,* the selections themselves exemplify this phenomenon. For example, earlier in our century, and as late as the 1950s, African Americans usually described themselves and were described by others as Negroes, and Native Americans were commonly called Indians. Of course, selections have not been edited to reflect current usage, but we would like to offer our rationale for the terms used in the chapter introductions, headnotes, and study questions.

The term Amerindian is used to describe the native inhabitants of the Americas when we refer to selections related to the discovery of the New World, whereas we prefer the term Native American when referring to the native peoples of what is now the United States. We also use the term Indian as it appears in a particular selection, and similarly we use the term Negro or black when referring to a selection in which these terms are used. Although some people prefer the term African American, others still use black; we have used both terms as occasion demands in the apparatus. Likewise, we have followed each author's preference when using the umbrella terms Hispanic and Latino to define peoples whose ethnicity is Latin American. When referring to Americans of Mexican descent, we have used the term Mexican American, and have used Chicano only when a particular author has done so.

Some other language we have used seems self-explanatory, such as Asian American, Cuban American, Italian American, or Jewish American. The term hyphenated American is commonly used to describe foreign-born citizens of the United States, but we prefer our own nonhyphenated usage, which seems more broadly suggestive, allowing the two components of identity a more flexible quality, perhaps more separate, but still joined.

Acknowledgments

A book of this sort is of necessity an enterprise of cooperation and collaboration. Ultimately, it grew out of our own independent and more or less hybridized identities, one of us a Cuban American, the other a Jewish American, and it grew out of a will to share, and to bridge, our differences. We would first like to acknowledge the difficulties, as well as the joys, of collaborating on this project as a common goal when we also share the more demanding common bonds of marriage and parenthood. We have had many good times in pursuit of this goal and also—let's be honest—some fairly awful times regarding such petty issues as division of labor and scheduling. But we have survived, proof that difference can be the grounds for a stronger union.

We want to thank the many friends and relatives who have followed with interest, support, and encouragement the gestation, development, and publication of our book. To our students, who have taught us about cultures throughout our many years in the classroom, we offer our gratitude and our hopes for a world in which the ability to tolerate and to appreciate differences among peoples continues to grow and develop.

A special thanks to all of our reviewers for their generous comments and suggestions: Bonne August, Kingsborough Community College, City University of New York; Nancy K. Barry, Luther College; Sara Blake, El Camino Community College; Catherine Cavanaugh, College of St. Rose; Dulce M. Cruz, George Mason University; Hugh English, Rutgers University; Marshall K. Hattori, Santa Barbara City College; Doug Hesse, Illinois State University; Deepika Karle, Bowling Green State University; Dan Moshenberg, George Washington University; Gary Olsen, University of South Florida; Arthur Ritas, Macomb Community College; Matilda Delgado Saenz, North Lake College; Todd Taylor, University of South Florida; and Linda Woodson, University of Texas at San Antonio.

We have been fortunate, from the beginning, to be working with a staff at St. Martin's Press that has provided moral support, intellectual understanding, and expert assistance at every stage of our progress. Kristin Bowen, development editor, took over the project at an early stage and saw it carried through to the end with calm, thoughtfulness, and intelligent assurance, and deserves our warmest thanks. We are grateful to Joyce Hinnefeld, who provided thorough and indispensable editorial support; to Griff Hansbury for her able assistance; to Emily Berleth for her cool guidance, turning manuscript into bound book; to Nancy Benjamin at Books By Design for managing the project; and to Sandy Schechter, permissions editor, who maintained her humor and perseverance in the face of almost daily challenges. Our warm thanks also to Cathy Pusateri, with whom we initiated this project. And last (but in no way least) we thank Nancy Lyman, acquisitions editor, who assumed the role of Godmother and conscience at a crucial point in our journey and encouraged us to unfurl our sails and voyage on toward *Inventing America.*

A READER'S INTRODUCTION

Identity and Ethnicity

"Who are you?"

That's a simple question, but try for a moment now to jot down a list of answers.

Probably your list would add up to a complex set of information, including what your name is, how old you are, where you live, who your parents are, what religious beliefs you might hold, what school you attend, what you like to do, what work you have done, and so on. In trying to answer the question "Who are you?" you're writing about your identity, the things that make you yourself.

One aspect of identity that you may have included in your list is ethnicity. Perhaps you don't think of yourself as "ethnic" at all. You are simply an American. But think back to your parents, grandparents, or great-grandparents: someone, somewhere along the way, emigrated from somewhere to America. If you think of yourself with this category in mind you might list: African American, Irish American, Italian American, Jewish American, Latino, Mexican American or Chicano, Polish American, Russian American; maybe you would list Asian American, or more specifically Korean American, Chinese American, or Vietnamese American. All of these "ethnicities" are what used to be called "hyphenated Americans," identities that comprise two "nationalities," an old and a new. But perhaps you are Native American, considered "native" to the United States, with ancestors here before there was a United States or even an "America" to talk about. Or perhaps you were born in another country.

The experience of arrival in a strange land is a part of every American's "ethnic" experience, a part of your history that may affect you still. In fact, many aspects of your identity—who you are—may be strongly affected by your ethnic character: the way weddings and birthdays are celebrated in your family, the foods you eat, where you live, the objects surrounding you in your home, the religious holidays you observe, the language you or your relatives speak, the songs and movies you like, and so on. We can see ethnicity as a defining part of our identity; or as something relatively minor that we relegate to the past.

Looking at the nation's population as we move toward the twenty-first century, we see the United States becoming more and more ethnic in its composition. Approximately 25 to 30 percent of the U.S. population can now be counted as "minorities," with the prediction that after the year 2000 a *majority* of the school-aged population will be members of "minorities." Within these figures, the fastest-growing immigrant groups are now Asian and Latin American, replacing the European immigrants who were the majority of the incoming population until about 1960. By the year 2020, about 30 percent of the U.S. population will be nonwhite. Our whole idea of what is minority and majority seems, in this context, to be shifting.

In *Inventing America* the term *ethnic* encompasses people from all four conventionally distinguished racial groups—Asian, black, white, and American Indian. But the main concern throughout this anthology is the social construction of race and ethnicity, that is, how certain groups have come to be regarded or have come to regard themselves in the context of American society. These differences are based in part on visible appearances, but it is worth noting, anthropologists now agree, that the demarcations of racial differences are not absolute biological realities. In various categories of physical traits—skin color, hair, blood types, bones, teeth, inner organs, genes—there simply are no sure guarantees of racial identity. Yet socially, the "typical" characteristics tend to dominate, even overwhelm, the individual, so that in some situations the slightest visible trace of an ethnic trait can serve as the basis for a prejudicial reaction to the individual. And, conversely, ethnicity can also have alluringly positive connotations in the marketplace.

The word *ethnic* has undergone some interesting shifts in meaning and context. Originally it comes from a Greek word, *ethnikos,* which was used to translate the Hebrew *goyim,* meaning non-Israelite. During the Christian Era in western Europe, from the fourteenth to the nineteenth centuries, it came to mean "heathen" (pagan, non-Christian), once again pointing a finger at the "outsider." By the later nineteenth century, *ethnic* came to take on its current connotation, meaning "peculiar to a race or nation." But always, an ethnic is an *other,* and thus ethnicity is something that is defined in terms of cultural difference and is always relative to some starting point: what is not "us" is ethnic. Still, that negative connotation has, in the twentieth century, been changed at times to a positive one, with a resurgence of pride, especially in the last twenty years, in one's ethnicity. You may have seen people wearing buttons that say "Kiss Me I'm Irish" or Italian, and so on, but ethnicity can also run more than skin deep, with many active community associations keeping alive traditions that help define collective and individual identity.

AMERICAN SOCIETY AND ETHNICITY

The history of America has always been, from the beginning, a history of arrivals. (Even "Native Americans" arrived here from somewhere else, probably from Asia.) So, to some extent, efforts to separate "ethnic" experiences from those of the "mainstream" are misguided to begin with. As Oscar Handlin wrote at the start of his prize-winning history of immigration, *The Uprooted,* "Once I thought to write a history of the immigrants in America. Then I discovered that the immigrants *were* American history. . . . As I worked, the conviction grew upon me that adequately to describe the course and effects of immigration involved no less a task than to set down the whole history of the United States." But even if the "whole history of the United States" is unavoidably a history of immigration and ethnicity, it seems no less true that it is a history of boundaries being drawn and redrawn to separate those who have been here a generation or more from those who have just come. And with those boundaries have always been shifting tensions and even at times bloody conflicts between groups.

The tendency of one group to band together and label another group as "outsider" or "ethnic" may be a long-held habit of human societies; but as long as "others" are regarded with suspicion or hostility, the future is bound to hold conflict. Against this tradition of hostility there is another human characteristic that is universally present in human societies (and, as some research has shown, in advanced primates as well): empathy. Empathy is the ability of the human being to feel with, to understand, what another person is going through, to wince involuntarily when someone we see trips on a sidewalk or gets a finger caught in a door. We may wince and empathize in the same way when we read in the newspapers about swastikas being painted on a Jewish synagogue or about an African American arrested out of a crowd just because of his skin color. American language is filled with ethnic slurs that have been used for a century to denigrate and insult those who are different from "us": kike, wop, nigger, spic, mick, polack, hunkie. If, individually and as a society, we develop our ability to empathize and to imagine what it is like to be from an ethnic group different from ours, we will be working toward building a society that does not condone injustice toward the stranger in our midst.

For at least the first half of the twentieth century, an unofficial yet generally agreed on social goal was to diminish cultural differences among immigrants as they melted into society. (African Americans were a notable exception to this general policy.) The price of prosperity and success in America, it was believed, was assimilation: losing one's accent, removing one's "old world" dress, dropping one's native customs, and learning to speak American English. *E pluribus unum*—out of many, one—is the governing ethos and the motto still imprinted on our dollar bills. But beginning in the 1960s, popular consideration of ethnicity and race began to take on a more positive tone. Ethnicity was no longer something to be ashamed of but rather—as patriotic celebrations of the Bicentennial of 1976 made clear—something to be proud of. Around the same time, ethnicity became the basis, more divisively, for "identity politics" that sought to organize racial and ethnic groups around distinctly self-interested programs. We seem to have gained, in the last decades, an awareness of our culturally diverse society, but perhaps at the expense of social coherence.

The belief that guided the writing of *Inventing America* is that the common social task of our time is to build a society in which differences are recognized, acknowledged, and respected, without its individual members being coerced into a single homogenized amalgamation. Yet it is also our shared task to build a coherent society in which mutual respect can lead to productive dialogue. The book's goal is not to strengthen any divisive identity politics, but to encourage readers to look beyond the self to a kind of society that can be broadly tolerant of differences, a society that values multiculturalism for its own sake. As Robert Hughes, an Australian critic now living in America, eloquently put it in his book *The Culture of Complaint:*

> Multiculturalism asserts that people with different roots can co-exist, that they can learn to read the image-banks of others, that they can and should look across the frontiers of race, language, gender and age without prejudice or illusion, and learn to think against the background of a hybridized society. It proposes—modestly enough—that some of the most interesting things in history and culture happen at the interface between cultures. It wants to study border situations, not only because they are fascinating in themselves, but because understanding them may bring with it a little hope for the world.

INVENTING AMERICA: THE STRUCTURE OF THE BOOK

The title of this collection, *Inventing America: Readings in Identity and Culture,* needs a word of explanation. In what sense is America "invented"? one might naturally ask. The title is meant to suggest our sense that the culture of the United States was not, and is not now, a "finished" product, that it is, on the contrary, something that is ever changing in ways that are not always predictable. It is a human invention, as all cultures and nations are, even as it invokes certain divine authorities from time to time. The title also suggests that the process is ongoing and that to some extent, therefore, it is an invention that is within our own powers to shape through our actions and ideas. The selections in this reader look at questions about identity within the context of ethnicity, but within the larger framework that assumes that our culture is not given once and for all to us, but is an artifact of historical creation that is still going on.

The eight chapters in *Inventing America* are interrelated around the central issue of how we have come to terms, as a culture, with the experience of cultural difference. That is, given that we all have come ultimately from different parts of the world and have brought with us different cultural baggage, how have we managed to survive as a coherent political and cultural entity? This question is answered throughout not by statistics or general characterizations but through the lenses of individual perception and experience, looking at the way individual identities are formed within the framework of the national experience. And throughout, cultural difference is considered in terms of ethnicity *and* race, for even though African Americans did not arrive on this continent as part of a voluntary migration, their experience here has in many respects paralleled the immigrant experience and is certainly of no less importance when taking stock of the "invention" of America as a whole.

Inventing America begins with the experiences of immigrants first arriving in their new country, encountering strange cultures, inevitably, with a sense of shock. For many, the dominant feeling was one of exile, and the losses and gains they experienced are the subject of the next chapter. The formation of identity in a multicultural society is explored next in a series of chapters that focus on "The Multicultural Self" and its sense of manifold identity; the crossing over from a minority culture to the larger majority culture ("Border Crossings"); the significance of books and libraries to the forging of new identities ("In the World of Letters"); and the attractions of "Cultural Impersonation," in which an alien identity might be "tried on"—for a variety of reasons. The volume concludes with two chapters that offer a larger perspective on social identity: "Representing Ethnicity" deals with stereotyped images of the ethnic or racial other in popular media; and "The Politics of Ethnicity" examines how the promise of a multicultural society has at times been transgressed, and how it can be fulfilled.

Reading the Texts

Within each chapter of *Inventing America,* the reader will find selections in a variety of genres illustrating different aspects of the topic. Many selections were written in the last twenty years or so, and they address issues that are very much a part of our present culture. But each chapter begins with several historical readings, which provide a sense of perspective on current issues, suggest a longer view of the problem at hand, and frame our own concerns within the larger picture of American history. These historical issues cannot be thoroughly portrayed through one or two such selections, but may still offer a valuable perspective for understanding culture today and a starting point for interested readers who wish to look beyond this collection to other sources.

Each chapter includes a variety of materials from different types and genres of writing: nonfiction, fiction, letters, poems, and journals. The type of writing best represented in this anthology is the essay, the type of writing you will do most often in college. The authors of these essays assume a variety of rhetorical purposes—to *explain* or *describe* some situation or set of facts; to *analyze* and account for the reasons for something; to *argue* or *persuade* us of a particular point of view. And sometimes these essays may do several things at once—define, analyze, and persuade, for example. The essays illustrate different types of expository writing, including *personal narratives, autobiographies, cultural criticism, scholarly essays, journals;* and they can also act as catalysts for your own writing.

In addition to nonfiction writing, this book includes examples of fiction writing, to demonstrate how writers can use language to evoke feelings and situations that can move us deeply; imaginative writing, with its freedom to invent and organize events, appeals to us in ways that an argument or essay may not. But the reverse may be true as well: the essay can ask us to think in ways that fiction sometimes does not. And some types of writing found in this book seem to fit somewhere between fiction and nonfiction, as in the personal narratives and autobiographical writings, where memory and invention both play a large role in the construction of the prose.

You will also find in this collection some examples of writing that don't fit into these categories. For example, reprinted in Chapter 3 are several letters to the editor from earlier in this century ("A Bintel Brief: Letters from the Lower East Side to the *Jewish Daily Forward*") that, as you will see, seem to border at times on fiction. Also reprinted are edited versions of interviews ("Immigrant Lives"), which recreate the spontaneous voice of the speaker, filtered through an editor's written transcription; and a dialogue ("Friend and Foe"), which conveys the opposition between two points of view more clearly than another type of writing might do. These selections too might serve as models for types of writing you can attempt.

Some of the poems in this collection, might be startlingly familiar—the poem on the base of the Statue of Liberty ("Give me your tired, your poor, / your huddled masses yearning to breathe free") and a poem we're more used to singing than reading ("My country, 'tis of thee, / Sweet land of liberty, / of thee I sing"). Reading landmark poems in an unusual context makes them interestingly unfamiliar and analytically engaging. There are a total of six poems, in three different pairings, so that in each case two poems speak to one another and play off of one another in your reading.

Some readers may be provoked, even possibly offended, by some of the selections in *Inventing America* —in particular the poems by Aldrich and Ginsberg. But the whole premise of this collection is that writing can move us, anger us, excite us, inform us, teach us—above all, make us think critically about ourselves and others.

Reading Visual Images

In addition to the writings in this volume, visual materials are reproduced as well. Each chapter begins with a photograph, to provide a concrete, visual point of access to the materials that follow. Other illustrations give additional depth to a chapter's theme, either in connection with a written selection or standing by themselves as "visual essays" on a given subject. We're surrounded by images in our everyday lives—newspapers and magazines, posters and billboards, ads and artworks—so that many readers will be quite at home "reading" them, especially when there is an accompanying text or caption.

In the case of photographs, we tend to assume that because the image was taken by a camera it is in some sense "true." And that is indeed the case for most of the images presented in this volume, which come out of the documentary tradition. But even documentary photographs—pictures of the real world, presumably—can be posed by the photographer to illustrate the idea of the picture more clearly. And some other photographs (as in the selection by Guillermo Gómez-Peña and Coco Fusco in Chapter 1) are "true" records of "fictional" events, and are in that sense not really documentary at all. When a photographer happens to be at the right place at the right time, catching a moment in real life that seems to sum up a whole set of social events or attitudes, then we realize the power of the image to illuminate simply and economically the way we see the world.

Reading a photograph is somewhat different from reading language, of course, because the medium is pictures and not words, but in both cases the author has to frame his or her subject clearly so as to make a particular point. In both visual and written media, details have to be observed for their significance. But there are differences. The first thing to determine as you look at a picture is whether the image was taken as a candid image, or whether it was in some way set up or posed. In either case, look at what might have caused the photographer to take the image. What special quality in the person or subject motivated the photographer's reaction? Every photograph is the record of a photographer's strong reaction to a subject, his or her desire to preserve it for us to look at too. What are we supposed to feel? Are we supposed to be astonished? amused? informed? angered? moved to empathy? Some purpose—we might call it the picture's motivation—exists in every image.

Reading and Writing Actively

A goal of this anthology is to raise questions about cultural differences, to question some common assumptions, letting the reader expand his or her experiences by developing an awareness of others that can be the basis for a kind of imaginative empathy. An additional goal is to foster a kind of critical thinking about culture that will allow the reader to engage in informed debate on issues that affect our social lives. But a main premise of this volume is that developing our empathy and developing our critical abilities require the active participation of the reader. Your goal should be to avoid reading these texts passively: in that case, nothing much will happen. But if you engage actively with this collection of readings, many interesting things could happen.

To help create that active engagement with the texts, we have provided a framework for your reading and thinking about them. Each chapter begins with a general introduction to the subject, and each individual reading is prefaced by a brief headnote, which includes some orientation and background to the selection that follows. These materials provide a cultural context to facilitate your reading, so that you'll be already primed with some sense of how this particular selection fits into the topic that the chapter is exploring. Since these readings are really just the tip of the iceberg when it comes to the complex issues that they cover, we've included a brief list of further readings at the end of each chapter that can lead you to explore in greater depth the topics featured in each selection.

At the end of each reading, you'll find a set of questions, divided into two types: the first set of questions concentrates on the text and is designed to raise controversial issues for you to think about and also to discuss in class with your colleagues. Group questions are also included here, since discussions with your peers will sharpen your sense of what you are thinking: hearing what others think, you may agree or disagree, or even change your mind about things.

The second set of questions concentrates on the writing process. Some questions ask you to make a list of characteristics or details in a text, as a way of calling your attention to some aspect of the writing; others ask you to write a few paragraphs, a personal response, or a brief essay that analyzes particular aspects of the text. At times you will be asked to write in a voice other than your own, often as one of the text's speakers, for such imitation can lead to better writing through practice. And some questions relate to the issues of the text but encourage you to think and write about them in personal terms; for example: How does your own life connect with these issues?

Whether or not you identify yourself in any particular racial or ethnic way, we all live in a world that is strongly and continually affected by issues relating to ethnic, racial, and cultural differences. These issues matter intensely in our lives, and our own attitudes can make a huge difference, not only to ourselves but to others. In the end, *you* are the subject of this collection, and the goal of *Inventing America* is to provide occasions for you to explore your own thoughts and to develop your own base of experience and information as you deal with some of these issues in your own life, with yourself, and with others.

QUESTIONS

1. Write an essay on your name. Where does it come from? How do people react to it? What is it like to have your name? What does it mean to you?
2. Write an essay on your family from the point of view of a stranger. Describe characteristics in general, and individually, that might relate to ethnicity or the lack of it.
3. Write a profile of your class, in which you describe the degree to which people seem to be alike or different from one another. Assuming you don't know your classmates personally yet, what are the signs of ethnicity or cultural difference that you can see?
4. The cover for *Inventing America* features a photograph of a shadow box, constructed by artist Fred Otnes. In the various compartments, he has placed a number of objects and memorabilia—photographs, medals, flags, advertisements, toys, and so on. What do you think is the point of bringing all these diverse things together? How do these objects relate to one another? What aspects of American life and culture do you think they evoke? Write a brief essay describing the shadow box and what you think it says about American identity and culture.

FURTHER READING

Goldberg, Vicki and Arthur Ollman, eds. *A Nation of Strangers.* Albuquerque: University of New Mexico Press, 1995.

Krupat, Arnold. *Ethnocriticism: Ethnography, History, Literature.* Berkeley: University of California Press, 1992.

Sollors, Werner. *Beyond Ethnicity: Consent and Descent in American Culture.* New York: Oxford University Press, 1986.

———, ed. *The Invention of Ethnicity.* New York: Oxford University Press, 1989.

Takaki, Ronald. *A Different Mirror: A History of Multicultural America.* Boston: Little, Brown, 1993.

The Balloon-Man *(photograph by Arnold Genthe), c. 1896. Genthe was a German-born doctor of philosophy, newly arrived in the United States to serve as tutor to a wealthy family, when he discovered San Francisco's Chinatown. He was fascinated by the Chinese community there and spent the next ten years photographing street scenes, including this image of Chinese children buying balloons from a street vendor (one of the balloons has an American flag on it). The children are surrounded by a mix of Americans and Chinese.* (Library of Congress)

1

Encountering Others

Columbus lived and acted within a World in which America, unforeseen and unforeseeable, was at best a mere possibility, but a possibility of which neither he nor anyone else had any idea, nor was such an idea possible.

- EDMUNDO O'GORMAN
The Process of Invention

Guillermo Gómez-Peña and Coco Fusco, impersonating Amerindians from the fictional island of Guatinaui, spent three days in a golden cage (placed at Columbus Plaza in Madrid). They were fed through the bars and taken to the bathroom on leashes.

- GUILLERMO GÓMEZ-PEÑA AND COCO FUSCO
Two Undiscovered Amerindians Visit Spain

Here at our sea-washed, sunset gates shall stand
A mighty woman with a torch, whose flame
Is the imprisoned lightning, and her name
Mother of Exiles. . . .

- EMMA LAZARUS
The New Colossus

O Liberty, white Goddess! is it well
To leave the gates unguarded?

- THOMAS BAILEY ALDRICH
Unguarded Gates

Even though Chinese working men were excluded from most facets of American society and their lives were left unrecorded, their labors bespoke their existence. . . . The evidence of women's lives seems less tangible.

- CONNIE YOUNG YU
The World of Our Grandmothers

Americans formed their impressions of Italy and Italians largely on the basis of negative newspaper reportage and contact with immigrants of humble origin. When they encountered an Italian of middle-class bearing and education . . . they registered surprise and confusion.

- MICHAEL LA SORTE
Italians and Americans

Sometimes you don't fit in.

- PIRI THOMAS
Alien Turf

While we were wondering whether to force a window, a young negro couple came past up the road. Without appearing to look either longer or less long, or with more or less interest, than a white man might care for, and without altering their pace, they made thorough observation of us. . . .

- JAMES AGEE
Near a Church

The first thing you do is to forget that i'm Black.
Second, you must never forget that i'm Black.

- PAT PARKER
For the white person who wants to know how to be my friend

As Arnold Genthe's photograph of San Francisco's Chinatown suggests, America has always been the scene of encounters between different cultures and different peoples. Such encounters can be filled with curiosity, expectation, and delight, or they can be charged with fear, deception, and terror. Especially in first encounters between different cultural groups, questions are often raised about cultural "superiority," about who has the "right" to be here and who doesn't. While it seems logical to assume that the "Native Americans" were "native" to North and South America, in fact they too were once immigrants to this new world. They probably came from Asia, having crossed the Bering Strait from what is now Russia to what is now Alaska.

The first nonnatives to encounter these Native Americans were probably Viking sailors who landed in what is now Canada and New England. *Inventing America* begins where the written record begins, with the European "discovery" of a new continent, peopled by "Indians." This can be called a discovery only from the European point of view, however, since the Indians had already discovered the American continent. The Europeans who gave the name Indians to these inhabitants of the "New World" thought, because of an error in geography, that they were sailing to the Far East, specifically to India. And they would have been right—had they not underestimated the circumference of the globe and failed to realize that there was a whole continent between Europe and the Far East. Thus the settlement of America was, from the very beginning, mired in confusion, error, and presumption.

Every immigrant arriving in America for the first time discovers it anew and experiences the strangeness of moving into an unknown territory that is already populated. In that sense, the process of immigration is always a reenactment of the history of America—a history of first encounters, of one person meeting another person, of one group encountering another group. The readings in this chapter trace various encounters of this kind, beginning with the earliest recorded meetings of peoples from different cultures. While selections in the first half of the chapter focus primarily on encounters with Indians, subsequent selections provide examples of such meetings from much later in American history, closer to our own time. As the later selections demonstrate, more recent waves of immigrants have reenacted some of the earliest encounters experienced in this new land.

The first reading, from Edmundo O'Gorman's *The Invention of America,* places the reader in a time before the concept of America even existed, in order to reimagine the first European encounters with the New World. It illustrates one key assumption of this text: that America is an invented place, where people have constructed their culture out of a combination of old inheritances and new encounters. Virtually all the early narratives of such meetings between Europeans and Native Americans were written by Europeans. The extremely negative images of Native Americans (who are portrayed as cruel savages, cannibals, and heathens) in these narratives served to justify the cruelties and injustices that Native Americans experienced. Only recently have writers and artists begun to think about the relationship between white Europeans and Indians as an exchange or a dialogue, rather than simply a monologue on the part of Europeans. A contemporary example is the work of Mexican artist Guillermo Gómez-Peña and his collaborator Coco Fusco, which satirizes the presumptuousness of the colonizers and raises many questions about the so-called cultural gifts that were bestowed and taken in the exchanges between natives and settlers.

The readings in the rest of the chapter move beyond the white-Indian dialogue to look at encounters between other ethnic groups within the American system, where cultural differences have often been accentuated by the weight of prejudice. By the late nineteenth century, Americans had begun to develop two quite different attitudes toward immigrant newcomers. Officially, the United States held out an open and generous hand, as suggested by Emma Lazarus's poem "The New Colossus," inscribed on the base of the Statue of Liberty. But many Americans, who considered themselves established owners of America, were often selective in their welcome of later newcomers. Indeed, many Americans were suspicious and fearful of immigrants, who were judged to be too different, as the poem "Unguarded Gates" by Thomas Bailey Aldrich makes clear.

Immigrants to the United States from the nineteenth century onward arrived in a country that immediately stigmatized them. Suddenly made conscious of their ethnic and minority status, immigrants often found their first encounter with people in more powerful, established positions in this country to be a painful one. Consider, for example, the reception given on the West Coast, at the Angel Island Immigration Center, to entering Chinese immigrants, as described by Connie Young Yu. This narrative, "The World of Our Grandmothers," describes Yu's effort across a gap of several generations to recover her own family history, beginning with the first arrival of her relatives at Angel Island. Writing from a less personal perspective, the sociologist Michael La Sorte describes the typical experiences of one group, the Italians, who came to the United States and found themselves working at the bottom of the social ladder and experiencing prejudice in a variety of forms. The excerpt from Piri Thomas's novel *Down these Mean Streets* then provides an interesting counterpoint to La Sorte. Thomas describes the similar experiences—of feeling alienated and despised as the new arrivals in the American city—of Puerto Rican immigrants. In this case, the immigrants encounter prejudice in particular from their predecessors—the already entrenched Italians.

The chapter concludes with two selections about encounters across the line of color difference. Like many encounters across the ethnic divide, racial encounters can be fraught with suspicion and prejudice, all of which must be overcome, or at least acknowledged, if the gap is to be closed. In "Near a

Church," James Agee describes his encounter with an African American couple in the South in 1936. During this encounter Agee becomes acutely aware of the social and even legal distance between the couple and himself: he is white, privileged, presumed to hold power in any social exchange, while they are presumed to have little power or privilege, even if it is Agee who is asking permission and advice of them. The tables are turned in the final reading, when Pat Parker, in a poem called "For the white person who wants to know how to be my friend," speaks from the African American point of view, insisting on the need for difference to be *acknowledged* before it can be overcome.

EDMUNDO O'GORMAN

The Process of Invention

In this excerpt from The Invention of America: An Inquiry into the Historical Nature of the New World and the Meaning of Its History *(1948), Edmundo O'Gorman presents the concept of America as something created and molded by Europeans.*

To obtain financial backing for his explorations from the Spanish monarchs, Columbus needed to believe that the territory on which he landed on October 12, 1492, and in subsequent trips was not far from the rich land of Cipangu (Japan). Columbus's early letters and diaries thus reflected his attempt to adapt the reality of the American continent to a preconceived notion of Asia, formed by previous historical and literary accounts.

One central assumption held by those who colonized the New World was that the native inhabitants had to adopt the culture, language, and religion of the conquerors—to become civilized subjects—in order to serve the interests of the conquering nation. To achieve this purpose, a massive effort to convert the Amerindians to Christianity was undertaken, with the stated objective of saving them. The end result was to deprive these native peoples of their cultures and identities—in effect, to enslave them.

Born in Mexico in 1906, Edmundo O'Gorman taught philosophy for many years at the National University of Mexico and played an important role as a theoretician of the colonial history of Latin America. His many works on these subjects, published mainly during the 1940s and 1950s, challenged preconceived notions of how we think about our invented continent, America.

I

Within the picture of the universe and of the World . . . , lived and experienced as a scientific and religious truth at the close of the fifteenth century, there is no entity to be found to which the being of America may be assigned, nothing that can have that peculiar meaning or significance. America, as such, literally does not exist, even though a mass of land exists which, in due course, will be endowed with that meaning, with that being. Columbus lived and acted within a world in which America, unforeseen and unforeseeable, was at best a mere possibility, but a possibility of which neither he nor anyone else had any idea, nor was such an idea possible.

The project that Columbus submitted to the kings of Spain did not, therefore, concern America, nor indeed did his four famous voyages. Let us not make the mistake, now that we are about to accompany Columbus on his great adventure, of assuming, as is commonly done, that although he was not aware of it, he "really" crossed the Atlantic in quest of America and that the shores at which he arrived were "really" those of the American continent. The voyages which Columbus undertook were not, nor could they have been, *voyages to America,*[1] since the interpretation of the past is not retroactive. To believe the contrary is to deprive history of the light which it sheds on its own unfolding, and also to deprive events of their profound human drama, of their intimate personal truth. In complete opposition, therefore, to the attitude adopted by all historians in that they start out with a ready-made, fully constituted America in sight, we shall start out from a void, from a not-yet-existing America. Possessed by this idea and by the sense of mystery that accompanies all truly original and creative adventure, let us proceed to examine Columbus' project.

II

Columbus' project was of Doric[2] simplicity: he intended to cross the Ocean toward the west with the purpose of reaching, from Spain, the far eastern shores of the Island of the Earth and thus connect Europe with Asia.[3] We already know that there was no novelty in this idea or in the notions on which its feasibility was based. It is worth while, however, to recall them briefly.

The fundamental premise is the spherical form of the great mass of water and earth. Since the earth is a globe, it was possible, in theory, to reach the east of the *Orbis Terrarum*[4] by sailing west. The only problem, therefore, was the practical possibility of such a voyage. At this time the size of the globe and the breadth of the Island of the Earth were highly debatable questions.[5] Columbus was able to persuade himself that the earth was much smaller than was commonly supposed, and that the Island of the Earth was much larger than anyone thought. The greater the breadth of the Island of the Earth and the smaller the circumference of the globe, the shorter the intervening distance which he would have to cover.

Neither of these assumptions could be classed at the time as scientific nonsense. But Columbus, in his effort to convince himself and to convince everyone else, reduced the size of the globe so much that he hindered rather than helped his project. For the well-informed man of the period, the only thing that deserved careful and serious attention was the possible proximity of the Atlantic coasts of Europe and Asia, but to make Columbus' project

---

[1]Such, however, is the usual way in which all modern historians speak of them. For instance, Morison, *Admiral of the Ocean Sea,* Vol. I, p. 201; Vol. II, p. 47.

[2]*Doric:* bold and rugged, like the Dorians of ancient Greece (*Ed.*)

[3]We are fully aware of the long polemical discussion over whether Columbus' objective was to reach Asia by sailing west. Many years of debate have piled up overwhelming evidence that such was the case. The issue is of little importance to us, since for our purposes it matters not if Columbus believed he had reached Asia after having found land, as the contrary thesis holds.

[4]*Orbis Terrarum:* (Latin) the globe of the earth (*Ed.*)

[5]See above, Part Two, III, 1, 2.

plausible, the size of the Island of the Earth had to be expanded to an apparently preposterous degree. It is clear, then, why the Portuguese chose the eastern route, in spite of the risk that the coasts of Africa might extend beyond the equator.[6]

This explains the resistance which Columbus met everywhere in his efforts to find someone to sponsor his enterprise. It is not too difficult, however, to understand the motives that finally decided the Catholic kings in its favor. One was rivalry with the Portuguese, whose success in rounding the Cape of Good Hope worked in Columbus' favor. It seems obvious that Ferdinand and Isabella acceded to Columbus' insistent petitions from motives not unlike those of a gambler who, hoping for an extraordinary stroke of luck, decides to accept a risky wager. There was very little that they could lose, and a great deal that might be gained. This explains why the Crown, once it had decided to gamble, agreed to Columbus' exorbitant demands for remuneration.

Another argument for sponsoring the enterprise was the possibility of obtaining for Spain one or several of the many islands which medieval cartography placed in the Atlantic, and which, of course, had nothing to do with the archipelago that was supposed to lie off the coast of Asia.[7] This seems to provide at least a partial explanation of why in the Capitulations signed by the Crown and Columbus (Santa Fe de Granada, April 17, 1492) the enterprise appears only as an oceanic exploration, which, of course, did not preclude the Asiatic objective.[8] This famous and much discussed document also points to another motive that helps to explain the decision of the Spanish kings and to which sufficient attention has not been given: the desire on the part of the Crown to exercise an act of sovereignty on the Ocean. Indeed, the extraordinary thing about the Capitulations is not so much that they make no specific mention of the Asiatic objective of the voyage, as that they contain an express declaration in favor of Spanish seignoralty and lordship over the Ocean, which was, as we have indicated, something unusual if not unprecedented.[9]

These observations are not made with any intention of taking sides in one of the most rancorous debates in American historiography, which, as such, has no bearing on our work.[10] They indicate, however, the contrast between Columbus' position and that of the Crown, which obviously did not share his blind faith in the success of his enterprise. We begin to be aware of a discrepancy that will explain the development of future events.

The project is now under way, full of unknown possibilities, like a shaft in a drawn bow. Two highly interested parties are regarding it from stand-

---

[6]*Ibid.*, IV, 1.

[7]*Ibid.*, IV, 3.

[8]Navarrete, *Collection,* Vol. II, no. v.

[9]See above, Part Two, V, 4. In the *Capitulaciones* (Navarrete, *Collection,* II, v) Ferdinand and Isabella allow themselves to be called "lords of the aforesaid Ocean Seas," and they dispatch Columbus to explore them with the promise of making him admiral of them.

[10]See note 3 above.

points which only partially coincide. Once the shaft is loosed, the knot of possibilities will start to unravel, but the two parties will understand its effects in somewhat different ways. The dialogue begins, and bit by bit, amid coincidence and dissidence, illusions and disillusion, a new and startling vision of the event will take shape. Now it is Columbus' turn to take the floor.

III

In the ancient and dazzling history of geographical exploration, the voyage undertaken by Columbus in 1492 shines out with particular splendor. Not only have the daring, the immense ability, and determination of this celebrated sailor excited just admiration, but the spectacular dénouement has added such luster to the voyage that it has become one of the best known of all historical events. One fine day, so the story is told, by reason of some never explained premonition, magic, or miracle, this modern rival of Ulysses, this prince of navigators and discoverers, revealed the existence of the immense and hitherto unknown continent of America—even though it is admitted that neither Columbus nor anyone else knew or could know at the time that that was what happened. Historical events do not occur in that fashion. Notwithstanding the bibliographical mountain under which it is buried, Columbus' voyage has not yet been properly described. But the temptation to try fortune in this field must wait for a better occasion. Here we need only consider the historical significance of the famous undertaking from the viewpoint of our problem. Let us then examine Columbus' opinion concerning the land which he found at the time of his finding it and also the attitude that he held through the entire exploration. Let us try to understand the meaning which Columbus himself gave to the event and not the meaning which historians have seen fit to assign to it.

When Columbus sighted land in the course of the night between the 11th and 12th of October, 1492, he was certain that he had arrived at Asia, that is, that he had reached the far eastern shores of the Island of the Earth. To be sure, it was only a small island, but he thought it belonged to the archipelago lying off the coast of the *Orbis Terrarum* that had been described by Marco Polo, where, says Columbus, the men of the Great Khan, the Emperor of China, come to collect slaves; not far off, surely, from the celebrated Cipangu (Japan), rich in gold and precious stones, which Columbus set out to locate the day following his arrival.[11] In brief, without any evidence beyond the fact that the island where he made his landfall was inhabited—and this is the important point—Columbus convinced himself that he had reached Asia.

What is extraordinary is not that Columbus should have been convinced that he was close to Asia when, from his flagship, he saw the emerald beach of the first island emerging from the ocean, but that he maintained this belief throughout all his explorations, although he found nothing of what he

---

[11] *Journal for the First Voyage.*

expected, or anything that could provide unquestionable evidence in its favor. There is no need to burden the reader with textual evidence, for the fact is well established: wherever he turned, whatever he saw, Columbus felt certain that he had reached the far eastern extremity of Asia, those remote regions of the *Orbis Terrarum* which an age-old tradition depicted in such glowing colors, and which the cupidity of the navigator endowed so liberally with undreamed of wealth in gold, precious stones, spices, and other natural products of great price and value. The coarseness and nudity of the natives, the absence of the great cities and gilded palaces that he had expected to find, the fact that gold was only to be heard of in the fallacious words of the Indians, the repeated failure of his attempts to locate Cipangu and, later, to establish contact with the Great Khan, did nothing to shake his faith: he had reached Asia, he was in Asia, and it was from Asia that he returned. No one, nothing, to the day of his death, ever made him relinquish this cherished conviction.

Whatever he saw during the course of his exploration was interpreted by Columbus as empirical evidence of this fixed belief. For a less impassioned man, the total absence of all that his reading had led him to expect would, at least, have raised some doubt. But nothing could shake Columbus' faith. When, for instance, he was disappointed at not having found the opulent city which, according to his expectations, was sure to be on the other side of the cape which he had sighted from afar, no disillusionment possessed his soul, but rather the renewed hope of finding it round the next cape, and when the search turned out to be hopeless he immediately found a comforting explanation that left his belief intact. Under the sway of his desire reality was transfigured. Bartolomé de las Casas[12] well describes this situation when, astonished at the credulity of the Admiral, he remarks "how marvellous a thing it is how whatever a man strongly desires and has firmly set in his imagination, all that he hears and sees at each step he fancies to be in its favor."[13] Such was the great dream of Columbus' life; such was the spiritual climate that guided all his future activity and nourished the high hopes of wealth and fame which he conceived on that October day when, having sighted the small island named by him San Salvador, he convinced himself, once and forever, of his victory.

IV

Now that we know what Columbus thought concerning the lands he had found, we should try to determine the meaning of his attitude, in other words, the meaning of the 1492 voyage.

If Columbus was able to persuade himself that he had reached regions 15 belonging to the far eastern end of the Island of the Earth, not on any direct

[12]*Bartolomé de las Casas* (1474–1566): Spanish missionary in the West Indies who denounced oppression of the Amerindians by the Spanish colonizers in his writing (*Ed.*)

[13]Las Casas, *History*, Book I, Chapter 44.

evidence, but merely on the ground that he had found inhabited land where he had found it, it seems clear that his idea was no more than an assumption, a hypothesis. What was the basis for such a hypothesis? Why could Columbus assume that he had reached Asiatic regions simply because he had found inhabited land? The answer is obvious: Columbus was able to do so because of the previous picture he had in his mind concerning the breadth of the Island of the Earth and the distance separating its two extremities. We are dealing, therefore, with an *a priori* hypothesis, that is, an assumption based, not on empirical or *a posteriori* evidence, but on a previous or *a priori* idea.

Columbus' hypothesis is not only not based on evidence offered by experience, but he does not allow experience the benefit of a doubt. His assumption is invulnerable to data provided by experience. Columbus' idea about the excessive breadth of the Island of the Earth has imposed itself upon him as an unquestionable truth. Instead of being free to change his opinion according to data provided by experience, he is obliged to adjust these data so that they conform to his opinion, using interpretations as extreme or as arbitrary as the occasion demands.

The Admiral's assumption, then, is not only a hypothesis but a *belief*. Here we have the truly decisive aspect of his attitude.

This way of thinking is all too common. Anyone who has been in love has had a similar experience, for, as women know only too well, love implies a blind belief in all that the loved one says and does. Hence the profound meaning to be found in Stendhal's[14] story about the woman who, surprised by her lover with another man in a highly compromising situation, excuses herself by denying the fact. But since the lover seems unconvinced in the face of what he is witnessing, the woman resentfully replies with an injured air: "I well see that you no longer love me, because you prefer to believe what you perceive rather than what I tell you." "Facts," says Marcel Proust,[15] "do not penetrate into the world wherein our beliefs live, and since they did not give them birth, they cannot kill them; they may belie them constantly without weakening them, and a torrent of misfortunes or illnesses which, one after the other, afflict a family will not make it doubt in the goodness of its God or in the skill of its physician."

Columbus not merely *thinks* he has arrived at the eastern shores of the *Orbis Terrarum*, but he *believes* it. What, then, is the meaning of the famous voyage?

If we remember that things are in themselves nothing in particular, but that their being depends on the meaning we give them, it becomes evident that Columbus' belief implies that he endowed the lands found by him with a specific being, that of a portion of the Island of the Earth, in the same way that a man who believes in the geocentric system of the universe endows the sun and the moon with the being of being planets. Hence the historical meaning

20

---

[14]*Stendhal* (1783–1842): French novelist (*Ed.*)
[15]*Marcel Proust* (1871–1922): French novelist (*Ed.*)

of the 1492 voyage, from an ontological viewpoint, is that the lands found by Columbus were given the being of belonging to the *Orbis Terrarum,* as it was then conceived, and that they were thus endowed by means of an *a priori* and unconditional hypothesis.

This is the historical fact, which is not to be considered an "error" only because, at a later period, these lands were invested with a different being. This fact must be our point of departure in tracing the process by which, eventually, these lands were endowed with a different being—the process that we have called the invention of America. 21

DISCUSSING THE TEXT

1. What kind of "encounter" (or "encounters") is described in this selection?
2. How has this reading affected your own notions about the "invention" of America? Can you think of any analogies between the process of invention described in this selection and the "invention" of other historical or contemporary events in American culture?
3. Get together with a group of four or five students to discuss the following quotation from O'Gorman's essay: "The voyages which Columbus undertook were not, nor could they have been, *voyages to America,* since the interpretation of the past is not retroactive" (par. 2). What does O'Gorman mean by this statement? Can you think of other situations in which current assumptions or ideas affect interpretations of the past? Take brief notes as you work with your group on this assignment, and be prepared to discuss your opinions with the class.
4. What do you think of O'Gorman's use of literary examples, and of the example of the experience of falling in love, in section IV of the selection? Do these examples help or hinder his arguments about Columbus and the invention of America?

WRITING ABOUT THE TEXT

5. Look up the verb *invent* in the dictionary. Then reread section I of this selection. Write a paragraph discussing the significance of O'Gorman's use of the word *invention.*
6. Describe, in your own words, the difference between an *a priori* idea and *a posteriori* evidence, drawing on O'Gorman's discussion in section IV of this selection.
7. Write a brief essay discussing the roles of faith and of the imagination in Columbus's obsessive belief that the territories he had encountered were part of Asia. What were Columbus's motives in choosing to believe that he had reached Asia, even in the absence of empirical evidence?
8. Imagine yourself a sailor on one of Columbus's ships, and write a diary entry that speculates on the possibility that the land you have reached is not, as your captain assumes, the coast of Asia. Give reasons supporting your point of view.

GUILLERMO GÓMEZ-PEÑA and COCO FUSCO

Inventing Cultural Encounters

As 1992 approached, many contemporary artists and writers produced works that commented on the "discovery" of America five hundred years before, and on the ensuing cultural encounters between Europeans and Amerindians. This selection consists of two photographs recording the work of performance artists Guillermo Gómez-Peña and Coco Fusco.

The first work, "Authentic Cuban Santera and El Aztec High-Tech Welcome Columbus with Ritual Offerings," was part of the project "Norte/Sur" (Mexican Museum, San Francisco 1990). It offers an ironic interpretation of the encounter between Columbus and two "natives." Fusco's persona (on the left) is a priestess in the Afro-Cuban religion of santería, *which combines Christian and African beliefs; this religion evolved in Cuba after African slaves were brought to the island in the sixteenth century. Gómez-Peña's character refers us to the Aztecs, the native inhabitants of central Mexico. In this performance piece, the artists offer a twist on historical accounts of offerings and exchanges between the conquerors and the conquered. The manipulation of chronology, the insertion of such modern U.S. cultural icons as a bottle of Coca-Cola, and the project's title, "Norte/Sur" (which means "North/South"), allude to the cultural borders between Mexico and the United States.*

The second photograph documents a live performance of a work titled "Two Undiscovered Amerindians Visit Spain," which took place at Columbus Plaza in Madrid, Spain, in 1992. The work was performed at other locations in the United States and Europe as well. It recreates the experience of many native inhabitants of the Americas who were transported by ship to the strange land of their conquerors, where they were exhibited as exotic objects of curiosity and savagery. Columbus himself exported several Indians to Spain under these conditions. In doing so he hoped to prove to the Spanish monarchs, Ferdinand and Isabella, that the enormously costly financing of his exploratory voyages was worthwhile; for the natives were considered valuable objects, part of the mercantile economy that was the basis of European colonization. According to Columbus's reasoning, these so-called savages were capable of being civilized through Christianity. Once they were civilized, these natives would become "subjects"—people who could be used to sustain the economic necessities of the Spanish crown. In reality, however, hard labor, mistreatment, and illness nearly caused their complete demise.

Gómez-Peña and Fusco, impersonating Amerindians from the fictional island of Guatinaui, spent three days in a golden cage. They were fed through the bars and taken to the bathroom on leashes; they performed "authentic" dances and told stories in their "native" language.

Born in Mexico in 1955, Gómez-Peña defines himself as a "border artist." His essays, poems, and performance pieces challenge preconceived notions of nationality, assimilation, and identity, and offer an uncompromising, often disturbing vision of cultural encounters. His performance pieces have been featured in many museums in the United States and Europe and are recorded in the collection Warrior for Gringostroika *(1993). Gómez-Peña's collaborator in the projects presented here, Coco Fusco, is a media artist and writer. Her most recent book is* English Is Broken Here: Notes on Cultural Fusion in the Americas *(New Press, 1995).*

1990 "Authentic Cuban Santera and El Aztec High-Tech Welcome Columbus with Ritual Offerings." *The collaborations of Gómez-Peña and Fusco explore notions of "authenticity" and the artificial construction of ethnic identity by the mainstream.* (From the project "Norte/Sur," Mexican Museum, San Francisco. Photo by Christina Taccone.)

1992 "Two Undiscovered Amerindians Visit Spain." *Fusco and Gómez-Peña lived for three days in a golden cage placed at Columbus Plaza in Madrid as "Amerindians from the (fictional) island of Guatinaui." They were taken to the bathroom on leashes and hand-fed through the bars. Audience members could ask for an "authentic dance," a "story in Guatinaui," or a Polaroid. This piece was also performed at Covent Gardens, London; the Walker Art Center, Minneapolis; the Smithsonian Institution, Washington, D.C.; the Museum of Natural History, Sydney, Australia; the Field Museum, Chicago; the Whitney Museum of American Art, New York; and at other locations.* (Photo by Nancy Lytle.)

DISCUSSING THE TEXT

1. The "ritual offerings" depicted in the first performance piece are contemporary products from the United States. What do you think the artists are trying to communicate through these offerings? Do you think they are also saying something about relations between North and South America?
2. In a group of four or five students, discuss the performance piece recorded in the second photograph, "Two Undiscovered Amerindians Visit Spain." What are some of the details that make this piece effective (or ineffective)? What is the purpose of using props such as sunglasses and sneakers in

recreating a sixteenth-century event? Why is it significant that this piece was originally performed in Spain?

WRITING ABOUT THE TEXT

3. Write a brief personal reaction to each photograph.
4. In an early diary entry describing the Amerindians, Columbus wrote: "They never refuse anything that is asked for. They even offer it themselves, and show so much love that they would give their very heart." Write a response to this statement from the point of view of the Cuban santera and El Aztec High-Tech. (Feel free to use humor, as Gómez-Peña and Fusco do.)
5. Gómez-Peña and Fusco are trying to use humor to convey some very serious points. Do you think humor adds to or takes away from treatments of such subjects? Write a paragraph explaining your viewpoint. Try to imagine performance pieces that would address these issues *without* the use of humor. Write a brief essay (two to three pages) in which you argue for or against the use of humor in performance art that addresses serious concerns.

EMMA LAZARUS

The New Colossus[1]

Emma Lazarus (1849–1887) was born into a wealthy Jewish family of Portuguese descent who had come to this country in the seventeenth century. She published poems, translations, and a novel while still in her twenties, but she is best remembered for the poem reprinted here. "The New Colossus," written a few years earlier, was inscribed at the base of the Statue of Liberty in 1886. Lazarus had not previously written as a poet with a cause, but the Russian pogroms of 1881 and 1882—organized massacres in which many Jews were killed—inspired her. These pogroms led to the subsequent migration of many thousands of Jews to the United States.

Read Lazarus's poem and then read "Unguarded Gates" by Thomas Bailey Aldrich (see p. 28). These poems reflect two opposing attitudes Americans had toward immigration in the late nineteenth century.

Not like the brazen giant of Greek fame,
With conquering limbs astride from land to land;
Here at our sea-washed, sunset gates shall stand
A mighty woman with a torch, whose flame
Is the imprisoned lightning, and her name 5

[1]*Colossus:* in antiquity, a statue of a very great size; the Colossus of Rhodes, a statue of the sun god, Helios, stood in the harbor of Rhodes (*Ed.*)

Mother of Exiles. From her beacon-hand
Glows world-wide welcome; her mild eyes command
The air-bridged harbor that twin cities frame.
"Keep, ancient lands, your storied pomp!" cries she
With silent lips. "Give me your tired, your poor, 10
Your huddled masses yearning to breathe free,
The wretched refuse of your teeming shore.
Send these, the homeless, tempest-tost to me,
I lift my lamp beside the golden door!"

DISCUSSING THE TEXT

1. In the opening lines of "The New Colossus," Lazarus specifically contrasts the Statue of Liberty and the Colossus of Rhodes, a large bronze statue of the Greek sun god, Helios. What are the differences between these two images, and how are these differences symbolic of the differences between Old World and New World?
2. When the Statue of Liberty speaks, in Lazarus's poem, it welcomes immigrants from the Old World. What kind of people seem to be addressed in the last six lines of the poem? How does the speaking statue characterize the immigrant to America?

WRITING ABOUT THE TEXT

3. Does the attitude portrayed in Lazarus's poem still reflect U.S. sentiment toward immigration? Why or why not? Write an essay in which you provide contemporary examples to support your views.
4. Read "Unguarded Gates" by Thomas Bailey Aldrich (p. 28). Write a two- or three-page essay comparing the attitudes toward America and toward immigration that are expressed in Lazarus's and Aldrich's poems. Remember to address any similarities you might see, as well as differences between the two.

THOMAS BAILEY ALDRICH

Unguarded Gates

Thomas Bailey Aldrich (1836–1907) was one of the most influential literary figures of his day. Editor of the Atlantic Monthly *from 1881 to 1890 and friend of the socially exclusive Boston literary set (which included Henry Wadsworth Longfellow, Oliver Wendell Holmes, and other prominent figures), Aldrich wrote fiction, poetry, and essays. Speaking for the established interests of his day and for the feelings of more conservative Americans, he voiced some of the fears Americans had as they saw the new immigrants arriving from distant lands. Aldrich seems to write this poem to warn of the risks in welcoming these newcomers.*

Wide open and unguarded stand our gates,
Named of the four winds, North, South, East, and West;
Portals that lead to an enchanted land
Of cities, forests, fields of living gold,
Vast prairies, lordly summits touched with snow, 5
Majestic rivers sweeping proudly past
The Arab's date-palm and the Norseman's pine—
A realm wherein are fruits of every zone,
Airs of all climes, for lo! throughout the year
The red rose blossoms somewhere—a rich land, 10
A later Eden planted in the wilds,
With not an inch of earth within its bound
But if a slave's foot press it sets him free.
Here, it is written, Toil shall have its wage,
And Honor honor, and the humblest man 15
Stand level with the highest in the law.
Of such a land have men in dungeons dreamed,
And with the vision brightening in their eyes
Gone smiling to the fagot[1] and the sword.

Wide open and unguarded stand our gates, 20
And through them presses a wild motley throng—
Men from the Volga and the Tartar steppes,
Featureless figures of the Hoang-Ho,
Malayan, Scythian, Teuton, Kelt, and Slav,[2]
Flying the Old World's poverty and scorn; 25
These bringing with them unknown gods and rites,
Those, tiger passions, here to stretch their claws.
In street and alley what strange tongues are loud,
Accents of menace alien to our air,
Voices that once the Tower of Babel knew! 30

O Liberty, white Goddess! is it well
To leave the gates unguarded? On thy breast

---

[1]*fagot:* a bundle of sticks, used to burn heretics alive (*Ed.*)

[2]*Volga:* a region in Russia; *Tartar* (or Tatar): peoples from East Central Asia who overran parts of Asia and Europe in the thirteenth century; *Hoang-Ho:* the Yellow River in China; *Malayan:* people from Malay, in Southeast Asia; *Scythian:* nomadic conquerors and horsemen who ruled Southern Europe and the Middle East (Palestine) during the seventh century; *Teuton:* early name for present-day Germans; *Kelt* (or Celts): peoples of Ireland, Scotland, and Brittany, the coast of France; *Slav:* large group of peoples in Eastern Europe and Russia, briefly united in the ninth and tenth centuries (*Ed.*)

Fold Sorrow's children, soothe the hurts of fate,
Lift the down-trodden, but with hand of steel
Stay those who to thy sacred portals come 35
To waste the gifts of freedom. Have a care
Lest from thy brow the clustered stars be torn
And trampled in the dust. For so of old
The thronging Goth and Vandal trampled Rome,
And where the temples of the Caesars stood[3] 40
The lean wolf unmolested made her lair.

DISCUSSING THE TEXT

1. In "Unguarded Gates," Aldrich describes the United States in the opening section of the poem as an "enchanted land." What are the physical characteristics he ascribes to America? What are America's political virtues, as Aldrich celebrates them?
2. In the second stanza of "Unguarded Gates," Aldrich depicts immigrants to the United States around the time of the poem's composition in the early 1890s. Working with other students, point to specific words and phrases that indicate his attitude toward those immigrants.

WRITING ABOUT THE TEXT

3. Does Aldrich's attitude toward American immigrants (as expressed in the second half of his poem) square with his celebration of America's political virtues in the preceding lines? Discuss this question in a group of four or five students; take careful notes during your exchange and prepare paragraphs that express your opinions for presentation to the class.
4. Drawing on the list of words and phrases you prepared in response to question 2, write a short essay about how Aldrich's language influences the way you react (or are supposed to react) to his poem.

---

[3]*Goth* (or Visigoths): ancient Germanic tribe, menaced the Roman empire after the fourth century; *Vandal:* ancient Germanic tribe, invaded Gaul (France) in the fifth century; *Caesars:* ruling family of Rome, first century B.C. (*Ed.*)

CONNIE YOUNG YU

The World of Our Grandmothers

In this moving narrative about her Chinese family, Connie Young Yu interweaves personal and historical details. She describes how her grandmother's story was passed down to her within the family, and she analyzes the events in her grandmother's life from the point of view of a contemporary Chinese American woman. By juxtaposing the weight of Chinese family traditions with the culture shock experienced by the new immigrants, the author confronts us with important questions about identity and assimilation.

Yu makes a crucial distinction between textbook history and oral history. The implication here is that history books are not written by people who have actually experienced the events of history (in this case, Chinese immigrants), but by professional historians who are looking at that particular history from the outside. Yu bridges the gap between textbook history and oral history by looking at Chinese immigration—particularly the immigration of Chinese women—from the inside. In her search for materials to reconstruct a historical context for her grandmother's story, Yu realized that Chinese women officially had a very limited role within the historical context of Chinese immigration. Yet not until Chinese women began settling with their families in California during the nineteenth century did a Chinese American society begin to establish itself.

Connie Young Yu has written extensively on Chinese American history and culture. Among her publications are Profiles in Excellence *(1986), a collection of Chinese American biographies, and an anthology of women's writings.*

In Asian America there are two kinds of history. The first is what is written about us in various old volumes on immigrants and echoed in textbooks, and the second is our own oral history, what we learn in the family chain of generations. We are writing this oral history ourselves. But as we research the factual background of our story, we face the dilemma of finding sources. Worse than burning the books is not being included in the record at all, and in American history—traditionally viewed from the white male perspective—minority women have been virtually ignored. Certainly the accomplishments and struggles of early Chinese immigrants, men as well as women, have been obscured.

Yet for a period in the development of the West, Chinese immigration was a focus of prolonged political and social debate and a subject of daily news. When I first began searching into the background of my people, I read this nineteenth-century material with curious excitement, grateful for any information on Chinese immigration.

Looking for the history of Chinese pioneer women, I began with the first glimpses of Chinese in America—newspaper accounts found in bound volumes of the *Alta California* in the basement of a university library. For Chinese workers, survival in the hostile and chaotic world of Gum San, or Gold Mountain, as California was called by Chinese immigrants, was perilous and a constant struggle, leaving little time or inclination for reflection or diary writing. So for a look into the everyday life of early arrivals from China, we have only the impressions of white reporters on which to depend.

The newspapers told of the comings and goings of "Chinamen," their mining activities, new Chinese settlements, their murders by claim-jumpers, and assaults by whites in the city. An item from 17 August 1855, reported a "disgraceful outrage": Mr. Ho Alum was setting his watch under a street clock when a man called Thomas Field walked up and deliberately dashed the timepiece to the pavement. "Such unprovoked assaults upon unoffending Chinamen are not of rare occurrence. . . ." On the same day the paper also reported the suicide of a Chinese prostitute. In this item no name, details, or commentary were given, only a stark announcement. We can imagine the tragic story behind it: the short miserable life of a young girl sold into slavery by her impoverished parents and taken to Gum San to be a prostitute in a society of single men.

An early history of this period, *Lights and Shades in San Francisco* by B. E. Lloyd (1878), devoted ten chapters to the life of California Chinese, describing in detail "the subjects of the Celestial Kingdom." Chinese women, however, are relegated to a single paragraph: 5

> Females are little better than slaves. They are looked upon as merchantable property, and are bought and sold like any other article of traffic, though their value is not generally great. A Chinese woman never gains any distinction until after death. . . . Considering the humble position the women occupy in China, and the hard life they therefore lead, it would perhaps be better (certainly more merciful) were they all slain in infancy, and better still, were they never born.[1]

Public opinion, inflamed by lurid stories of Chinese slave girls, agreed with this odious commentary. The only Chinese women whose existence American society acknowledged were the prostitutes who lived miserable and usually short lives. Senate hearings on Chinese immigration in 1876 resounded with harangues about prostitutes and slave girls corrupting the morals of young white boys. "The Chinese race is debauched," claimed one lawyer arguing for the passage of the Chinese Exclusion Law: "They bring no decent women with them." This stigma on the Chinese immigrant woman remained for many decades, causing unnecessary hardship for countless wives, daughters, and slave girls.

Chinese American society finally established itself as families appeared, just as they did in the white society of the forty-niners who arrived from the East Coast without bringing "decent women" with them. Despite American laws intended to prevent the "settlement" of Chinese, Chinese women did

[1]B. E. Lloyd, *Lights and Shades in San Francisco* (San Francisco: San Francisco Press, 1878).

make the journey and endured the isolation and hostility, braving it for future generations here.

Even though Chinese working men were excluded from most facets of American society and their lives were left unrecorded, their labors bespoke their existence—completed railroads, reclaimed lands, and a myriad of new industries. The evidence of women's lives seems less tangible. Perhaps the record of their struggles to immigrate and overcome discriminatory barriers is their greatest legacy. Tracing that record therefore becomes a means of recovering our history.

Our grandmothers are our historical links. As a fourth-generation Chinese American on my mother's side, and a third-generation on my father's, I grew up hearing stories about ancestors coming from China and going back and returning again. Both of my grandmothers, like so many others, spent a lot of time waiting in China.

My father's parents lived with us when I was growing up, and through them I absorbed a village culture and the heritage of my pioneer Chinese family. In the kitchen my grandmother told repeated stories of coming to America after waiting for her husband to send for her. (It took sixteen years before Grandfather could attain the status of merchant and only then arrange for her passage to this country.)[2] She also told stories from the village about bandits, festivals, and incidents showing the tyranny of tradition. For example, Grandma was forbidden by her mother-in-law to return to her own village to visit her mother: A married woman belonged solely within the boundaries of her husband's world. 10

Sometimes I was too young to understand or didn't listen, so my mother—who knew all the stories by heart—told me those stories again later. We heard over and over how lucky Grandpa was to have come to America when he was eleven—just one year before the gate was shut by the exclusion law banning Chinese laborers. Grandpa told of his many jobs washing dishes, making bricks, and working on a strawberry farm. Once, while walking outside Chinatown, he was stoned by a group of whites and ran so fast he lost his cap. Grandma had this story to tell of her anger and frustration: "While I was waiting in the immigration shed,[3] Grandpa sent in a box of *dim sum*.[4] I was still waiting to be released. I would have jumped in the ocean if they decided to deport me." A woman in her position was quite helpless, but she still had

[2]Under the Chinese Exclusion Act of 1882, Chinese laborers could no longer immigrate to America. Until the act was repealed in 1943, only merchants, diplomats, students, and visitors were allowed to enter.

[3]Between 1910 and 1940 Chinese immigrants arriving in the port of San Francisco were detained at the Angel Island Immigration Station to await physical examinations and interrogation to determine their right to enter this country. Prior to 1910 immigrants were detained in a building on the wharf known as "the shed."

[4]Chinese pastries.

her pride and was not easily pacified. "I threw the box of *dim sum* out the window."

Such was the kind of history I absorbed. I regret deeply that I was too young to have asked the questions about the past that I now want answered; all my grandparents are now gone. But I have another chance to recover some history from my mother's side. Family papers, photographs, old trunks that have traveled across the ocean several times filled with clothes, letters, and mementos provide a documentary on our immigration. My mother—and some of my grandmother's younger contemporaries—fill in the narrative.

A year before the Joint Special Committee of Congress to investigate Chinese immigration met in San Francisco in 1876, my great-grandmother, Chin Shee, arrived to join her husband, Lee Wong Sang, who had come to America a decade earlier to work on the transcontinental railroad. Chin Shee arrived with two brides who had never seen their husbands. Like her own, their marriages had been arranged by their families. The voyage on the clipper ship was rough and long. Seasick for weeks, rolling back and forth as she lay in the bunk, Chin Shee lost most of her hair. The two other women laughed, "Some newlywed you'll make!" But the joke was on them as they mistakenly set off with the wrong husbands, the situation realized only when one man looked at his bride's normal-sized feet and exclaimed, "But the letter described my bride as having bound feet!"[5] Chin Shee did not have her feet bound because she came from a peasant family. But her husband did not seem to care about that nor that the back of her head was practically bald. He felt himself fortunate just to be able to bring his wife to Gum San.

Chin Shee bore six children in San Francisco, where her husband assisted in the deliveries. They all lived in the rear of their grocery store, which also exported dried shrimp and seaweed to China. Great-Grandma seldom left home; she could count the number of times she went out. She and other Chinese wives did not appear in the streets even for holidays, lest they be looked upon as prostitutes. She took care of the children, made special cakes to sell on feast days, and helped with her husband's work. A photograph of her shows a middle-aged woman with a kindly, but careworn face, wearing a very regal brocade gown and a long, beaded necklace. As a respectable, well-to-do Chinese wife in America, married to a successful Chinatown merchant, with children who were by birthright American citizens, she was a rarity in her day. (In contrast, in 1884 Mrs. Jew Lim, the wife of a laborer, sued in federal court to be allowed to join her husband, but was denied and deported.)

15 In 1890 there were only 3,868 Chinese women among 103,620 Chinese males in America. Men such as Lee Yoke Suey, my mother's father, went to China to marry. He was one of Chin Shee's sons born in the rear of the grocery

---

[5]*bound feet:* It was the traditional practice among aristocratic Chinese to bind the feet of female babies so that they would remain small, a sign of uselessness and cultural superiority. (*Ed.*)

store, and he grew up learning the import and export trade. As a Gum San merchant, he had money and status and was able to build a fine house in Toishan. Not only did he acquire a wife but also two concubines. When his wife became very ill after giving birth to an infant who soon died, Yoke Suey was warned by his father that she was too weak to return to America with him. Reminding Yoke Suey of the harsh life in Gum San, he advised his son to get a new wife.

In the town of Foshan, not far from my grandfather's village, lived a girl who was recommended to him by his father's friend. Extremely capable, bright, and with some education, she was from a once prosperous family that had fallen on hard times. A plague had killed her two older brothers, and her heart-broken mother died soon afterwards. She was an excellent cook and took good care of her father, an herb doctor. Her name was Jeong Hing Tong, and she was pretty, with bound feet only three and a half inches long. Her father rejected the offer of the Lee family at first; he did not want his daughter to be a concubine, even to a wealthy Gum San merchant. But the elder Lee assured him this girl would be the wife, the one who would go to America with her husband.

So my maternal grandmother, bride of sixteen, went with my grandfather, then twenty-six, to live in America. Once in San Francisco, Grandmother lived a life of confinement, as did her mother-in-law before her. When she went out, even in Chinatown, she was ridiculed for her bound feet. People called out mockingly to her, "*Jhat!*" meaning bound. She tried to unbind her feet by soaking them every night and putting a heavy weight on each foot. But she was already a grown woman, and her feet were permanently stunted, the arches bent and the toes crippled. It was hard for her to stand for long periods of time, and she frequently had to sit on the floor to do her chores. My mother comments: "Tradition makes life so hard. My father traveled all over the world. There were stamps all over his passport—London, Paris—and stickers all over his suitcases, but his wife could not go into the street by herself."

Their first child was a girl, and on the morning of her month-old "red eggs and ginger party" the earth shook 8.3 on the Richter scale. Everyone in San Francisco, even Chinese women, poured out into the streets. My grandmother, babe in arms, managed to get a ride to Golden Gate Park on a horse-drawn wagon. Two other Chinese women who survived the earthquake recall the shock of suddenly being out in the street milling with thousands of people. The elderly goldsmith in a dimly lit Chinatown store had a twinkle in his eye when I asked him about the scene after the quake. "We all stared at the women because we so seldom saw them in the streets." The city was soon in flames. "We could feel the fire on our faces," recalls Lily Sung, who was seven at the time, "but my sister and I couldn't walk very fast because we had to escort this lady, our neighbor, who had bound feet." The poor woman kept stumbling and falling on the rubble and debris during their long walk to the Oakland-bound ferry.

That devastating natural disaster forced some modernity on the San Francisco Chinese community. Women had to adjust to the emergency and makeshift living conditions and had to work right alongside the men. Life in America, my grandmother found, was indeed rugged and unpredictable.

20 As the city began to rebuild itself, she proceeded to raise a large family, bearing four more children. The only school in San Francisco admitting Chinese was the Oriental school in Chinatown. But her husband felt, as did most men of his class, that the only way his children could get a good education was for the family to return to China. So they lived in China and my grandfather traveled back and forth to the United States for his trade business. Then suddenly, at the age of forty-three, he died of an illness on board a ship returning to China. After a long and painful mourning, Grandmother decided to return to America with her brood of now seven children. That decision eventually affected immigration history.

At the Angel Island immigration station in San Francisco Bay, Grandmother went through a physical examination so thorough that even her teeth were checked to determine whether she was the age stated on her passport. The health inspector said she had filariasis, liver fluke, a common ailment of Asian immigrants which caused their deportation by countless numbers. The authorities thereby ordered Grandmother to be deported as well.

While her distraught children had to fend for themselves in San Francisco (my mother, then fifteen, and her older sister had found work in a sewing factory), a lawyer was hired to fight for Grandmother's release from the detention barracks. A letter addressed to her on Angel Island from her attorney, C. M. Fickert, dated 24 March 1924, reads: "Everything I can legitimately do will be done on your behalf. As you say, it seems most inhuman for you to be separated from your children who need your care. I am sorry that the immigration officers will not look at the human side of your case."

Times were tough for Chinese immigrants in 1924. Two years before, the federal government had passed the Cable Act, which provided that any woman born in the United States who married a man "ineligible for citizenship" (including the Chinese, whose naturalization rights had been eliminated by the Chinese Exclusion Act) would lose her own citizenship. So, for example, when American-born Lily Sung, whom I also interviewed, married a Chinese citizen she forfeited her birthright. When she and her four daughters tried to re-enter the United States after a stay in China, they were denied permission. The immigration inspector accused her of "smuggling little girls to sell." The Cable Act was not repealed until 1930.

The year my grandmother was detained on Angel Island, a law had just taken effect that forbade all aliens ineligible for citizenship from landing in America.[6] This constituted a virtual ban on the immigration of all Chinese, including Chinese wives of U.S. citizens.

---

[6]The Immigration Act of 1924 affected all Asians who sought to immigrate to the United States. Congress repealed the law as to Chinese in 1943, and then in 1952 through the McCarran-Walter Act as to other Asian ethnic groups.

Waiting month after month in the bleak barracks, Grandmother heard many heart-rending stories from women awaiting deportation. They spoke of the suicides of several despondent women who hanged themselves in the shower stalls. Grandmother could see the calligraphy carved on the walls by other detained immigrants, eloquent poems expressing homesickness, sorrow, and a sense of injustice. 25

Meanwhile, Fickert was sending telegrams to Washington (a total of ten the bill stated) and building up a case for the circuit court. Mrs. Lee, after all, was the wife of a citizen who was a respected San Francisco merchant, and her children were American citizens. He also consulted a medical authority to see about a cure for liver fluke.

My mother took the ferry from San Francisco twice a week to visit Grandmother and take her Chinese dishes such as salted eggs and steamed pork because Grandmother could not eat the beef stew served in the mess hall. Mother and daughter could not help crying frequently during their short visits in the administration building. They were under close watch of both a guard and an interpreter.

After fifteen months the case was finally won. Grandmother was easily cured of filariasis and was allowed—with nine months probation—to join her children in San Francisco. The legal fees amounted to $782.50, a fortune in those days.

In 1927 Dr. Frederick Lam in Hawaii, moved by the plight of Chinese families deported from the islands because of the liver fluke disease, worked to convince federal health officials that the disease was noncommunicable. He used the case of Mrs. Lee Yoke Suey, my grandmother, as a precedent for allowing an immigrant to land with such an ailment and thus succeeded in breaking down a major barrier to Asian immigration.

My most vivid memory of Grandmother Lee is when she was in her seventies and studying for her citizenship. She had asked me to test her on the three branches of government and how to pronounce them correctly. I was a sophomore in high school and had entered the "What American Democracy Means To Me" speech contest of the Chinese American Citizens Alliance. When I said the words "judicial, executive, and legislative," I looked directly at my grandmother in the audience. She didn't smile, and afterwards, didn't comment much on my patriotic words. She had never told me about being on Angel Island or about her friends losing their citizenship. It wasn't in my textbooks either. I may have thought she wanted to be a citizen because her sons and sons-in-law had fought for this country, and we lived in a land of freedom and opportunity, but my guess now is that she wanted to avoid any possible confrontation—even at her age—with immigration authorities. The bad laws had been repealed, but she wasn't taking any chances. 30

I think a lot about my grandmother now and can understand why, despite her quiet, elegant dignity, an aura of sadness always surrounded her. She suffered from racism in the new country, as well as from traditional cruelties in the old. We, her grandchildren, remember walking very slowly with her, escorting her to a family banquet in Chinatown, hating the stares of tourists at her tiny feet. Did she, I wonder, ever feel like the victim of a terrible hoax, told as a small weeping girl that if she tried to untie the bandages tightly binding her feet she would grow up ugly, unwanted, and without the comforts and privileges of the wife of a wealthy man?

We seemed so huge and clumsy around her—a small, slim figure always dressed in black. She exclaimed once that the size of my growing feet were "like boats." But she lived to see some of her granddaughters graduate from college and pursue careers and feel that the world she once knew with its feudal customs had begun to crumble. I wonder what she would have said of my own daughter who is now attending a university on an athletic scholarship. Feet like boats travel far?

I keep looking at the artifacts of the past: the photograph of my grandmother when she was an innocent young bride and the sad face in the news photo taken on Angel Island. I visit the immigration barracks from time to time, a weather-beaten wooden building with its walls marked by calligraphy bespeaking the struggles of our history. I see the view of sky and water from the window out of which my grandmother gazed. My mother told me how, after visiting hours, she would walk to the ferry and turn back to see her mother waving to her from this window. This image has been passed on to me like an heirloom of pain and of love. When I leave the building, emerging from the darkness into the glaring sunlight of the island, I too turn back to look at my grandmother's window.

DISCUSSING THE TEXT

1. Why is it important for Connie Young Yu to tell the story of her Chinese family in her own words? How does she manage to make connections between personal events within her family and larger political realities?
2. Yu writes, "I regret deeply that I was too young to have asked the questions about the past that I now want answered" (par. 12). What do you think are some of the questions Yu regrets not having asked? What kinds of questions would you like to ask—or have you asked—your own grandparents about the past?
3. Get together in a group of students and discuss the plight of Yu's grandmother in terms of her physical and economic dependence on her husband. Focus on the following observation made by Yu's mother: "Tradition makes life so hard. My father traveled all over the world . . . but his wife could not go into the streets by herself" (par. 17). Take notes on the ways in which the fact that Yu's grandmother was a woman contributed to her struggles. Be prepared to share your thoughts with the class.

WRITING ABOUT THE TEXT

4. How did Grandmother Lee's detention at the Angel Island immigration center in San Francisco affect U.S. law? Write two paragraphs explaining

how her experience constitutes an example of the intersection between personal experience and historical events.

5. Yu speculates on why her grandmother decided to become a U.S. citizen in her seventies. What do you think her grandmother's motivation might have been? Write a letter from Yu's grandmother's point of view, explaining her reasons to her granddaughter.
6. Toward the beginning of her essay, Yu discusses nineteenth-century newspaper articles on Chinese immigration. How do these accounts reflect the racial prejudices of that time? Using the resources of your school or local library, look in recent magazines or newspapers for an article that you feel is biased in its presentation of a particular ethnic group. Then write a brief essay comparing the issues that it presents with those that Yu addresses.

MICHAEL LA SORTE

Italians and Americans

Like other ethnic minorities in the United States, Italian Americans have experienced discrimination and exploitation. In this excerpt from his book LaMerica: Images of Italian Greenhorn Experience, *Michael La Sorte (b. 1931) applies his training as a sociologist, discussing not only personal details but also socioeconomic and cultural factors in the lives of Italian immigrants in the United States at the turn of the century. The reader gets a vivid picture of real people such as Totonno, Rossi, Cianfarra, and others (men La Sorte interviewed as part of his research for this book). At the same time, however, La Sorte helps his reader to place these people's experiences of prejudice and social injustice within a broader historical context.*

But if American citizens misunderstood and distorted the Italian immigrants' culture, some Italians also expressed rather narrow views of their adopted land; La Sorte writes that in the eyes of some Italian immigrants, "Americans . . . looked toward work as the Great American Savior and were motivated to action by their love of money. Cold and heartless, emotion had no place in their lives, but money did" (par. 17). La Sorte's concern in representing ethnic stereotypes of Italian immigrants in the early 1900s should be read in contrast with other depictions of the conflicts between established and marginalized groups, such as the conflict between assimilated Italian Americans and socially marginalized Puerto Ricans during the 1950s, described by Piri Thomas in the next selection, "Alien Turf" (p. 47).

Michael La Sorte has taught at Hofstra University and at the State University of New York College at Brockport; he has published a book and several articles on marriage and family relationships.

"Even a simpleton can see that they do not like us."
- IMMIGRANT COAL MINER

An Italian was not an Italian. He was a wop, dago, duke, gin, tally, ghini, macaroni or spaghetti or spaghetti bender. He was also Hey Boy or Hey

Youse, or he was given a generic name: Joe, Pete, Tony, Carlo, Dino, Gumba.[1] "Do you know why most Italians are called Tony?" "No." "Because when they land in New York they have cards on their caps that say: To NY."

Most of the terms were obviously meant to dehumanize and to degrade. Others were simply ways of addressing a worker by someone who felt no need to indicate individual identity. Sometimes they were used by the Italians themselves; visitors from Italy noted that the immigrants called each other "ghini." The most common terms were "wop" and "dago." H. L. Mencken accepted "wop" as the institutionalized term for Italians because of its widespread use. The Italian consul in New York received a letter one day with the salutation: "Dear consul of Dagoland." "Dago" was used freely in print, even in leading newspapers, although not without protest. This statement appeared in *L'Italia* (in English) in response to an article in the *Chicago Tribune:* "DAGO: The above appellation as applied to Italians is considered by them as a gross insult. In last Thursday's *Tribune* we notice that a reporter used this term in speaking of an Italian. Anyone pretending to be a gentleman would not use this term."[2]

The language applied to the Italian immigrant signified his status in the society, one of cultural, economic, and moral inferiority. The attitude of Americans toward Italians was expressed succinctly by an Italian editor:

> What has impeded the moral and material development of the immigrant Italians? The Italians are viewed by the Americans as so much meat to be consumed. Italians are maltreated, mocked, scorned, disdained, and abused in every way. The inferiority of the Italians is believed to be almost that of the Asiatics.[3]

The Yellow Peril on the west coast had its counterpart in the Italian Peril on the east coast. The worst part of the American experience, Margariti observed, was the "harsh, negative, uncompromising attitudes of the members of the Celtic race who are convinced that we were of a lower social order and treat us accordingly."[4] D'Angelo had no delusions about his status. "I was a poor laborer, a dago, a wop or some such creature—in the eyes of the world."[5] In his youthful innocence, William Murray accepted the nickname "woppo" from his schoolmates without complaint, but Ventresca knew an insult when he heard it: on the playground "a certain boy named Ralph called me a dago. I gave him one on the jaw right there, and he never indulged in derogatory

---

[1]L. Berrey and M. Vandenbark, *The American Thesaurus of Slang* (New York: Macmillan, 1945), 361. *Gumba* is a dialect version of *compare.*

[2]*L'Italia* (Chicago), Nov. 8, 1886. See also Amy A. Bernardy, *Italia randagia attraverso gli Stati Uniti* (Torino: Fratelli Bocca, 1913), 245; H. L. Mencken, *The American Language,* 4th ed. (New York: Knopf, 1936); Salvatore La Gumina, *WOP! A Documentary History of Anti-Italian Discrimination in the United States* (San Francisco: Straight Arrow Books, 1973).

[3]*La Tribuna* (Detroit), June 5, 1909.

[4]Antonio Margariti, *America! America!* (Salerno: Galzerano, 1980), 75.

[5]Pasquale D'Angelo, *Son of Italy* (New York: Macmillan 1924), 138.

names after that."[6] Maurino, a greenhorn in Boston in 1911, was stopped on the street by two men. "Are you a wop?" they asked. "No, I'm Italian." "Get off the sidewalk!" they shouted, and pushed him violently to the ground.[7]

A day did not pass that the Italian was not vilified in one manner or another. The Americans laughed at his speech, his clothes, his customs, and where and how he lived. Such treatment caused Italians to be wary of all Americans. Broughton Brandenburg, a native American, lived for a brief time with Italians in New York, but there were those who spurned his offers of friendship. He would be confronted by Italians who wanted to know what he and his wife were doing in their midst: "Who are you? What do you want of us?" One man who had been very hostile said to him later by way of explanation and apology, "You know American mans ain't good to Eyetalyuns on'y he make de graft."[8] A policeman whom Totonno had met when his store was robbed tried to befriend him. The policeman wanted Totonno to teach him Italian, and went so far as to suggest that Totonno, who was a large, well-built, and confident man, might join the department as a member of the Italian Squad. Totonno was very suspicious of the man's motives, and agreed to act as his teacher only because of the officer's persistence.

Totonno had every reason to be on his guard; he had been a victim of corruptive police practices when he was fresh off the boat. His diary for June 1906 describes his two-day encounter with the American system of justice: 5

> The afternoon was slow and I had nothing to do. On impulse, I jumped on a bike parked in front of the store and pedaled rapidly up to 154th Street, then circled back and was returning at a brisk pace. At the corner of 152nd a streetcar came alongside, and in my attempt to keep clear of its wheels, I veered to the right. I did not see the two kids who were jostling each other in the road until I struck one of them head on. We both fell and the bike flipped over against the streetcar. The car stopped, a crowd quickly gathered, and before I knew it I was taken into custody by a policeman who escorted me into a grocery store to make sure I did not escape. The boy's leg was twisted and bleeding, he was screaming, and the crowd was getting larger and more boisterous. I understood nothing. An ambulance arrived to take the boy away. Meanwhile, the boy's father came on the scene and the policeman asked him whether he wanted me arrested. Certainly, he replied, and with that the policeman led me out of the store, pushed through the crowd, and placed me in the police wagon. My *paesani*[9] clamored on board, as did the father and one of the boy's cousins, and down to the Police Station we went.

---

[6]William Murray, *Italy: The Fatal Gift* (New York: Dodd, Mead, 1982); Francesco Ventresca, *Personal Reminiscences of a Naturalized American* (New York: Rueson, 1937), 41.
[7]Ferdinand Maurino, *Cavo delle mani* (Cosenza: Pellegrini, 1968).
[8]Brandenburg Broughton, *Imported Americans* (New York: Stokes, 1903).
[9]*paesani:* fellow countrymen (*Ed.*)

> The interrogation continued at the station. To satisfy the father who insisted that I be jailed, they put me into a cell and slammed the door. I looked around and found myself in a steel cage about two meters long and 1.5 meters wide. On one side was an iron bunk and on the other a toilet. I paid twenty-five cents for a pillow and stretched out on the bunk. I was frightened and full of shame. How could I face my *paesani* after this disgrace? The policeman laughed and told me he would take care of things. He knew it was not my fault.
>
> The next morning we went to the courthouse where we were placed in a steel cage with other prisoners to await our trials. One by one each prisoner was called and a short time later would return. Some of them were chained and led into other cells. When I saw that, I could hear my heart pounding and I began to tremble. My legs were jerking so much I could barely stand. When my name was announced I was escorted upstairs to the court. I was relieved to see my friends sitting there. One of them came forward to translate. It all happened very fast. I was found not guilty. The judge told me that if I felt my rights had been violated, I could take the case to civil court.
>
> The policeman took me out the back door to the tram stop. He wanted me to pay him for his testimony. How much? I asked. Five dollars. Sisto and Turiangelo joined us on the tram. We stopped at a bar. I bought a round of beer for twenty-five cents and Sisto gave the policeman the five dollars.

The Americans formed their impressions of Italy and Italians largely on the basis of negative newspaper reportage and contact with immigrants of humble origin. When they encountered an Italian of middle-class bearing and education who did not fit their conception, they registered surprise and confusion. The middle-class Italians were alarmed by the American attitude. They were fiercely proud of their country and their noble Italian heritage, and did not care to defend themselves before every anti-Italian critic when they felt no defense should be necessary. In their desire for respect, some would carefully distinguish themselves from the "wop class," but by doing so, they were admitting to Italian inferiority. The common immigrants had to endure insults much more frequently, but the barbs were suffered more acutely by middle-class Italians, who felt compelled to argue for their honor and the honor of their nation. Those of the "wop class" often did not feel this compulsion; they had been at the bottom of the social ladder in Italy and consequently had acquired an imperviousness to harsh treatment.

Touring Italian artists quickly learned what Americans thought about Italy and the immigrants. The actor Tommaso Salvini was outraged at a depiction of Italy in the 1872 Mardi Gras carnival procession in New Orleans. The float had Pope Pius IX blessing two brigands, who were kneeling before him with knives between their teeth. Naively, Salvini demanded and fully expected an apology from the city officials. His written protest—which said, in part, "Every good person rejects the insult to a nation, which from antiquity to the present merits the respect and admiration of a civilized world"—went 10 unanswered.[10] Giuseppe Giacosa, a celebrated Italian actor of the day, met the impresario of a Philadelphia music hall where he was to perform. The man approached Giacosa, smiled, and remarked in an affirmative tone, "You're French." "No," Giacosa replied, "Italian." The impresario was incredulous. "He looked at me again, taking in my full person, undoubtedly asking himself how this well-dressed, obvious gentleman before him could be one of those macaroni, an organ grinder, a degos, terms of insult that are used for all Italians in America."[11]

While living in Boston, Reverend Gaetano Conte and his wife were visiting some American friends when they were introduced to a proper Bostonian couple. The host presented Conte as a person who was interested in the "Italian Question." The woman immediately exclaimed, "Oh, I do not like those Italians!" After a few moments of conversation she realized that the Contes were Italian. "Well," she said, "no one would ever think that such respectable people as you would belong to that race. Italians are ignorant and illiterate." Conte assured her that there were schools in Italy. After conceding that possibility, she added that, even so, "English is not taught." The fact that the Contes were speaking English seemed to escape her attention.[12]

Rossi saw the Americans as bullheaded and hopelessly provincial. He was appalled at their distorted and superficial knowledge of anything outside of the United States. Every day in New York he had to listen to statements that summed up Italians in terms of stiletto, macaroni, brigand, and vendetta; all Italians had dark eyes and hot blood, and were musically inclined. He rarely ate macaroni, he would tell them; he could not sing or play an instrument, he would insist, and at that moment was not concealing a knife in his pocket. But his arguments fell on deaf ears.[13]

Those Italians who stepped outside their colonies with the intention of "making it" in the world of the Americans frequently had a rude awakening. Robert Ferrari went to Columbia College at the turn of the century at a time when few foreigners were admitted and those few were barely tolerated. "In my day," the handful of Italians "who made the attempt to enter the schools were met with curious glances, a stormy reception, deliberate animosity, and discouragement." When he was examined for a teaching position in English in the New York schools, he answered the questions correctly but was never called to teach. An Italian was not allowed to teach English, or any other subject, to American students. Ferrari eventually found a post teaching Italians.[14]

The Americans considered Italians much the same as gypsies. The Italians lived in groups under the guidance of a "head man," they cooked communally, and their dress and personal hygiene left much to be desired. While walking with his friends, D'Angelo noticed that Americans kept their distance

---

[10]Tommaso Salvini, *Ricordi, aneddotti ed impressioni* (Milano: Dumolard, 1895), 285.

[11]Giuseppe Giacosa, *Impressioni di America* (Milano: Cogliati, 1908).

[12]Gaetano, Conte. *Dieci anni in America: Impressioni e ricordi.* Conferenze riguardanti l'emigrazione Italiana nell'America del Nord (Palermo: Spinnato, 1903).

[13]Adolfo Rossi, *Italiano in America* (Treviso: Buffetti, 1907), 171–75.

[14]Robert Ferrari, "Autobiography" (University of Minnesota, Immigration History Research Center), 96.

on the streets and would make slurring remarks about unkempt and dirty foreigners. When Brandenburg boarded a New York streetcar with some newly arrived Italians, he heard a woman say "Oh, what dirty, dirty wretches," and a stout gentleman exclaimed, "I don't see why they let those lousy dagoes ride on the same cars other people have to use." Later in the day, Brandenburg was turned away from a hotel by the desk clerk, who remarked to his colleague, "Well, what do you think of that nerve. That dago coming in here with a push like that trying to get rooms."[15] Rossi heard immigrants called "those dirty Italians" because when they thronged from the ships, it was said, "they send out a stink that can be detected several meters away. Washing is unknown to them, and a bathtub is a strange object. They do not even change shirts once every fifteen days."[16] Even some Italians agreed with this assessment. Cianfarra had this to say about the "wop class": "For the Americans the Italian is of necessity filthy. It is part of his nature. After all, what can one expect? We created this reputation of being worse than pigs and of illiteracy. Some time must pass before we will be able to eliminate that image."[17] In a country claiming to consider cleanliness next to godliness, sloppy personal habits such as children being sent to school unwashed and unbrushed were intolerable. One teacher sent a note home informing the mother that her daughter had a bad odor and her hair needed washing. The teacher received this reply: "Mary is not a rose. Do not smell her, teach her."[18]

For the Americans, the Italians exemplified the Lombrosian concept of the born criminal: impulsive, primitive, violent. Behavior associated exclusively with the Italian, especially the private vendetta and the "Code of Honor" (the honor of the family must be protected by any means), evoked a sense of disgust, and the fighting tactics of the Italians were considered cowardly and ungentlemanly. The newspapers at the turn of the century gave full exposure to accounts of street fights in which the stiletto was always in evidence. Many Americans would have agreed with the comments of a first-class passenger as he watched the steerage travelers aboard ship:

> These Italians are the worst of the lot. They are a dangerous element. Stick a knife in you in a minute. Look at the villainous-looking fellow standing right there on the box, smoking a cigar. Why, criminal instinct is written in every line of his head and face. See the bravado in the way he holds his shoulders and the nasty look in his uneasy eyes.[19]

Nevertheless, Italians were highly valued by many American employers as toilers who took pride in their work. Mosso visited the owner of a shoe factory who left no doubt of his respect for Italian labor. "I will take any Italian I can hire. America has much work for unskilled laborers. There are railroads to be built as

[15]Brandenburg, *Imported Americans;* D'Angelo, *Son of Italy,* 225.

[16]Rossi, *Italiano in America,* 90.

[17]Camillo Cianfarra, *Diario di un emigrante* (New York: L'Araldo Italiano, 1900), 51.

[18]Domenico Siciliani, *Fra gli Italiani degli Stati Uniti d'America* (Roma: Stabilimento per l'Ammistrazione della Guerra, 1922), 31.

[19]Brandenburg, *Imported Americans,* 105.

well as highways, bridges, canals, and seaports. Italians are models of temperance. They never get drunk and lose a day's work. You can be sure that we will never close the door to the Italian. He is crucial to our economic progress."[20]

The factory owner might have added to his list of positive attributes that the Italian would work at any job for long hours at low pay with few complaints. He was pliable; he knew how to take orders; he was passive. These characteristics irritated Louis Adamic, a Slovene immigrant writer, who for a time labored with pick and shovel. His Italian coworkers were "short, squat, illiterate" men who spoke English sparingly if at all. "I felt, successively, sorry for and disgusted with them. The bosses had them cowed. Their wages were low, but they would have worked for even less. At the end of the day they trudged home, silent, uninspired, a heavy smell of hopelessness about them. They did not belong in America. They knew nothing of the country, nor had the ability or the desire to learn about it. They lived from day to day, from hand to mouth, driven by narrow selfishness."[21] Good workers, but not the stuff of American citizenship. Gherardo Ferreri maintained that the very characteristics that made the Italian a good worker also made him, in the eyes of the Americans, unwanted. To be taken seriously by Americans, Ferreri continued, Italians must not be timid and pliant, uncouth and ignorant, or their destiny would be to occupy a permanent underclass in the society. Ferreri concluded that arrogance must be met with arrogance, that respect and advancement come only from a position of strength.[22]

The Italians gave as much criticism as they received. Many immigrants considered American cultural priorities to be perverted. Italian culture emphasized simplicity, beauty, temperance, love of family, a spirit of economy—values that transcend the individual, and time and place. Americans were concerned with the here and now. They looked toward work as the Great American Savior and were motivated to action by their love of money. Cold and heartless, emotion had no place in their lives, but money did. America was infected by the accursed greed for gain. Money was the only topic of conversation, Carlo Tresca concluded after his first few days in New York: "Money, money, money. Everybody talked of money. I went home thinking of money. 'If I had money.' 'I must make money.' Money, money, money. These words began to haunt me. I asked my brother, 'Where are the Christians in America?'"[23] A person was defined in America not by his individuality but by his money. The man who could turn a profit was admired by his fellows. The businessman, the symbol of America, worshiped at the shrine of the Almighty Dollar. "The Dollar is King in America," Totonno wrote in his diary, "and truly represents the life in this country." Totonno was fascinated by the

[20]Angelo Mosso, *Vita moderna degli Italiani* (Milano: Fratelli Trevesa, 1906), 113.

[21]Louis Adamic, *Laughing in the Jungle* (New York: Harper, 1932), 113.

[22]Gherardo Ferreri, *Gli Italiani in America* (Roma: Farro, 1907), 14.

[23]Carlo, Tresca. "Autobiography." (University of Minnesota, Immigrant History Research Center. Copy at New York Public Library.), 92.

glitter of America; later he realized that behind the glitter was much ugliness. Cianfarra was forewarned by his teacher in Italy, who said to him on the eve of his departure, "You will see some nice things, but don't rush to judgment, because in no country do appearances deceive as in America."[24]

To be sure, the Italians were intrigued by the prospect of wealth; after all, that is why they had come to America. But this American obsession with the dollar was difficult to comprehend. Margariti felt that Americans were of "another world, another race." The lust for money had pinched them dry. Make money! The American child was raised to revere the father who could attract dollars to his billfold. A condition of poverty was examined as if it were the symptom of a terminal disease. Only good flowed from the constant acquisition of wealth, and only bad could come from a failure to do so. Work was the path to salvation, and the immigrants were enjoined to work and work and work. America was a nation of pragmatists; unless what one did made the cash register ring, it was not worth the effort. Talking about construction projects in America, Ventresca complained that while Italians emphasized the aesthetic side of an artifact, the Americans would say, "Never mind your art, we want efficiency," which meant the greatest return for the least outlay.[25]

The person who worked hard was held in high esteem, while anyone who refused to put in a good day's work for his day's pay was considered of no value to the community. The immigrants were expected to labor, to put their backs to the job, and to think of nothing else. Those who did not meet the expectations of the American Work Ethic, which demanded that the immigrant sweat, were called "bums" and "loafers." The Italians looked at the notion of physical labor differently. It was not viewed as a higher calling nor was it always considered dignified, as Iannace recognized:

> The most important difference between the American and non-American involves the concept of work as a worthy and ennobling activity. Coming to America, one enters a new dimension if, consciously, one accepts the concept of work as the vital source of human expression, as a hymn of life, as a way of making contact with one's being, and as the central means by which one interacts with others and the society. Work is viewed in another manner in Italy. Italians believe that work debilitates man, it reduces him to the status of a beast. Especially when one is forced to work for others, in particular for the State.[26]

The Americans were incapable of enjoying life; life for them was not a romp but a crusade pursued with design and calculation. "Americans are joyless, for joy is a fruit that the Americans eat green." They are a people "who had been pickled in the sour juices of Puritanism." To the Italians, America lacked diversity and Americans were without imagination. "*L'America, donne senza*

---

[24]Cianfarra, *Diario,* 10.

[25]Margariti, *America! America!,* 20; Ventresca, *Personal Reminiscences,* 28.

[26]Carmine Iannace, *La scoperta dell'America* (Padova: Rebellato, 1971), 106.

colore e frutta senza sapore."[27] "To my people," Pietro Di Donato wrote, "the Americans were colorless, unsalted, baloney munchers and 'gasoline' drinkers without culture, who spoke with a vocabulary limited to repetitive, four-lettered words, listened to caterwauling, imbecilic music, and all looked more or less alike."[28] The Italians were most struck by the coldness of Americans, their inability or unwillingness to display public emotion. "They will go to a funeral of their best friend and keep a straight face. I believe they are ashamed if in a moment of forgetfulness they've turned to look at a flower or a beautiful sunset."[29] During his early years in America, Constantine Panunzio did not meet one American whom he could like or respect, but only rough and uncouth "persons who knew no refinement of language, of bearing or of manners; who mocked order; who defied and openly broke the law. Dignity had no place in life."[30] Panunzio could trust no one, and he was deceived repeatedly, especially when money was involved.

The Italians were not free of their own brand of greed and rapaciousness. "Bisinissi" was one of the first words the immigrants learned, and it was a term used to cover a multitude of sins. America was a golden opportunity for those Italians with capitalistic intent. There was money to be made in America, and those sharp business practices that were good enough for the Americans certainly suited Italian greed. Italian businessmen would cheat their fellow countrymen while invoking the tenets of the American business creed. Rossi watched one day as an Italian businessman in New York cheated an immigrant rag collector by fixing the scale so that it showed ten pounds less than the actual weight. When Rossi asked the man why he had purposely cheated the poor ragpicker, who was full of innocent trust, out of a few pennies, he smiled and said triumphantly, "That is business, you know."[31] Cianfarra once worked for a man who "would cut your soul out in order to sell it." Cianfarra was selling cigars door to door, and when he returned to the tobacco firm at the end of the day, his Boss would go to great lengths to cheat him out of every possible penny—with obvious relish. Why? Cianfarra finally asked. "*E' cosi' che fanno gli affari gli Americani*" (That's the way the Americans do it).[32] 20

DISCUSSING THE TEXT

1. Why do you think La Sorte opens this section of his book with a list of derogatory terms for Italians ("wop, dago, duke, gin," and so on)? What effect does this opening have on you as a reader?

[27]"America: women without substance and fruit without character" (Carnevali, *Autobiography,* 160–70).

[28]Pietro Di Donato, *Three Circles of Light* (New York: Messner, 1960), 32.

[29]D'Angelo, *Son of Italy,* 80.

[30]Constantine Panunzio, *The Soul of an Immigrant* (New York: Macmillan, 1921), 129.

[31]Rossi, *Italiano in America,* 84.

[32]Cianfarra, *Diario,* 115.

2. La Sorte observes that Italian immigrants were divided among themselves by issues of socioeconomic class and education (for instance, some middle-class Italians made a point of distinguishing themselves from what they referred to as the "wop class"). What does this pattern say about the nature of prejudice?
3. Get together in a group of four or five students. Discuss with your group the concepts of work and money from the point of view of (a) the Italian immigrants and (b) the American employers depicted in La Sorte's account. Can you find any similarities or contradictions? Take brief notes as you work on this assignment and be prepared to discuss your opinions with the class.

WRITING ABOUT THE TEXT

4. Write an imaginary profile of the Italian immigrant mother who replied to a teacher's complaint that her daughter was unkempt with the message "Mary is not a rose. Do not smell her, teach her" (par. 14). What are some traits that you would expect a woman like this to possess? Where might she have lived? What might her life have been like?
5. To what extent have attitudes toward Italian Americans in American society at large changed since the turn of the century (the time La Sorte describes in this excerpt)? Drawing on a recent film, television show, or book that you have seen or read, write a one- or two-page essay arguing for or against this statement: Today, Italian Americans are no longer perceived as the stereotypical "born criminals" that La Sorte describes (see par. 15).
6. Who were the "members of the Celtic race" that Margariti refers to (in par. 3)? Do some research into the question of who the Celtic peoples were; then write an essay that addresses the question of when, if ever, any of these Celtic peoples experienced any form of prejudice or discrimination.

PIRI THOMAS

Alien Turf

The world of Piri Thomas's childhood, New York City during the 1940s, is portrayed in his autobiography, Down These Mean Streets *(1967), from which this selection is taken. Thomas's objective in writing the book, which he started while serving a prison term for armed robbery during the 1950s, was to depict the world of violence, drug abuse, and racial prejudice in which he grew up as a multiracial Puerto Rican.*

In this selection, Thomas recreates the ethnic prejudice that he experienced when his family moved to an Italian American neighborhood. The confrontations between the young Piri and the Italian American boys are characterized by racial and ethnic stereotypes on both sides. Language here becomes a weapon, and the verbal sparring between the groups serves as a kind of metaphor for the real blows that will follow.

Thomas balances his portrait of both Puerto Ricans and Italian Americans by refusing to portray himself as a victim or as free from prejudice himself. Instead, he points to similarities between Hispanic and Italian cultures in terms of family values and notions of manhood. Critic Nelson Aldrich notes that Thomas's "achievement is to have so thoroughly taken the measure of his individuality that he adds significantly to our sense of the richness and shame of being an American."

Piri Thomas (b. 1928) has done volunteer work in prison and drug rehabilitation programs, and has been a trustee of the Community Film Workshop Council and of the American Film Institute. Among his publications are the autobiographical volumes Saviour, Saviour, Hold My Hand *(1972) and* Seven Long Times *(1974).*

Sometimes you don't fit in. Like if you're a Puerto Rican on an Italian block. After my new baby brother, Ricardo, died of some kind of germs, Poppa moved us from 111th Street to Italian turf on 114th Street between Second and Third Avenue. I guess Poppa wanted to get Momma away from the hard memories of the old pad.

I sure missed 111th Street, where everybody acted, walked, and talked like me. But on 114th Street everything went all right for a while. There were a few dirty looks from the spaghetti-an'-sauce cats, but no big sweat. Till that one day I was on my way home from school and almost had reached my stoop when someone called: "Hey, you dirty fuckin' spic."

The words hit my ears and almost made me curse Poppa at the same time. I turned around real slow and found my face pushing in the finger of an Italian kid about my age. He had five or six of his friends with him.

"Hey, you," he said. "What nationality are ya?"

I looked at him and wondered which nationality to pick. And one of his friends said, "Ah, Rocky, he's black enuff to be a nigger. Ain't that what you is, kid?" 5

My voice was almost shy in its anger. "I'm Puerto Rican," I said. "I was born here." I wanted to shout it, but it came out like a whisper.

"Right here inna street?" Rocky sneered. "Ya mean right here inna middle of da street?"

They all laughed.

I hated them. I shook my head slowly from side to side. "Uh-uh," I said softly. "I was born inna hospital—inna bed."

"Umm, *paisan*[1]—born inna bed," Rocky said. 10

I didn't like Rocky Italiano's voice. "Inna hospital," I whispered, and all the time my eyes were trying to cut down the long distance from this trouble to my stoop. But it was no good; I was hemmed in by Rocky's friends. I couldn't help thinking about kids getting wasted for moving into a block belonging to other people.

"What hospital, *paisan?*" Bad Rocky pushed.

---

[1]*paisan:* a fellow countryman (*Ed.*)

"Harlem Hospital," I answered, wishing like all hell that it was 5 o'clock instead of just 3 o'clock, 'cause Poppa came home at 5. I looked around for some friendly faces belonging to grown-up people, but the elders were all busy yakking away in Italian. I couldn't help thinking how much like Spanish it sounded. Shit, that should make us something like relatives.

"Harlem Hospital?" said a voice. "I knew he was a nigger."

15 "Yeah," said another voice from an expert on color. "That's the hospital where all them black bastards get born at."

I dug three Italian elders looking at us from across the street, and I felt saved. But that went out the window when they just smiled and went on talking. I couldn't decide whether they had smiled because this new whatever-he-was was gonna get his ass kicked or because they were pleased that their kids were welcoming a new kid to their country. An older man nodded his head at Rocky, who smiled back. I wondered if that was a signal for my funeral to begin.

"Ain't that right, kid?" Rocky pressed. "Ain't that where all black people get born?"

I dug some of Rocky's boys grinding and pushing and punching closed fists against open hands. I figured they were looking to shake me up, so I straightened up my humble voice and made like proud. "There's all kinds of people born there. Colored people, Puerto Ricans like me, an'—even spaghetti-benders like you."

"That's a dirty fuckin' lie"—*bash,* I felt Rocky's fist smack into my mouth—"you dirty fuckin' spic."

20 I got dizzy and then more dizzy when fists started to fly from everywhere and only toward me. I swung back, *splat, bish*—my fist hit some face and I wished I hadn't, 'cause then I started getting kicked.

I heard people yelling in Italian and English and I wondered if maybe it was 'cause I hadn't fought fair in having hit that one guy. But it wasn't. The voices were trying to help me.

"Whas'sa matta, you no-good kids, leeva da kid alone," a man said. I looked through a swelling eye and dug some Italians pushing their kids off me with slaps. One even kicked a kid in the ass. I could have loved them if I didn't hate them so fuckin' much.

"You all right, kiddo?" asked the man.

"Where you live, boy?" said another one.

25 "Is the *bambino* hurt?" asked a woman.

I didn't look at any of them. I felt dizzy. I didn't want to open my mouth to talk, 'cause I was fighting to keep from puking up. I just hoped my face was cool-looking. I walked away from that group of strangers. I reached my stoop and started to climb the steps.

"Hey, spic," came a shout from across the street. I started to turn to the voice and changed my mind. "Spic" wasn't my name. I knew that voice, though. It was Rocky's. "We'll see ya again, spic," he said.

I wanted to do something tough, like spitting in their direction. But you gotta have spit in your mouth in order to spit, and my mouth was hurt dry. I just stood there with my back to them.

"Hey, your old man just better be the janitor in that fuckin' building."

Another voice added, "Hey, you got any pretty sisters? We might let ya stay onna block." 30

Another voice mocked, "Aw, fer Chrissake, where ya ever hear of one of them black broads being pretty?"

I heard the laughter. I turned around and looked at them. Rocky made some kind of dirty sign by putting his left hand in the crook of his right arm while twisting his closed fist in the air.

Another voice said, "Fuck it, we'll just cover the bitch's face with the flag an' fuck er for old glory."

All I could think of was how I'd like to kill each of them two or three times. I found some spit in my mouth and splattered it in their direction and went inside.

Momma was cooking, and the smell of rice and beans was beating the smell of Parmesan cheese from the other apartments. I let myself into our new pad. I tried to walk fast past Momma so I could wash up, but she saw me. 35

"My God, Piri, what happened?" she cried.

"Just a little fight in school, Momma. You know how it is, Momma, I'm new in school an' . . ." I made myself laugh. Then I made myself say, "But Moms, I whipped the living——outta two guys, an' one was bigger'n me."

"*Bendito,* Piri, I raise this family in Christian way. Not to fight. Christ says to turn the other cheek."

"Sure, Momma." I smiled and went and showered, feeling sore at Poppa for bringing us into spaghetti country. I felt my face with easy fingers and thought about all the running back and forth from school that was in store for me.

I sat down to dinner and listened to Momma talk about Christian living without really hearing her. All I could think of was that I hadda go out in that street again. I made up my mind to go out right after I finished eating. I had to, shook up or not; cats like me had to show heart. 40

"Be back, Moms," I said after dinner. I'm going out on the stoop." I got halfway to the stoop and turned and went back to our apartment. I knocked.

"Who is it?" Momma asked.

"Me, Momma."

She opened the door. "*Qué pasa?*"[2] she asked.

"Nothing, Momma, I just forgot something," I said. I went into the bedroom and fiddled around and finally copped a funny book and walked out the door again. But this time I made sure the switch on the lock was open, just in case I had to get back real quick. I walked out on that stoop as cool as could be, feeling braver with the lock open. 45

There was no sign of Rocky and his killers. After awhile I saw Poppa coming down the street. He walked like beat tired. Poppa hated his pick-and-shovel job with the WPA.[3] He couldn't even hear the name WPA without getting

---

[2]*Qué pasa:* What's happening? (*Ed.*)

[3]*WPA:* Works Projects Administration; established in 1935 by President Franklin Delano Roosevelt, it created jobs for millions when unemployment was widespread (*Ed.*)

a fever. *Funny,* I thought, *Poppa's the same like me, a stone Puerto Rican, and nobody in this block even pays him a mind. Maybe older people get along better'n us kids.*

Poppa was climbing the stoop, "Hi, Poppa," I said.

"How's it going, son? Hey, you sure look a little lumped up. What happened?"

I looked at Poppa and started to talk it outta me all at once and stopped, 'cause I heard my voice start to sound scared, and that was no good.

"Slow down, son," Poppa said. "Take it easy." He sat down on the stoop 50 and made a motion for me to do the same. He listened and I talked. I gained confidence. I went from a tone of being shook up by the Italians to a tone of being a better fighter than Joe Louis and Pedro Montanez lumped together, with Kid Chocolate[4] thrown in for extra.

"So that's what happened," I concluded. "And it looks like only the beginning. Man, I ain't scared, Poppa, but like there's nothin' but Italianos on this block and there's no me's like me except me an' our family."

Poppa looked tight. He shook his head from side to side and mumbled something about another Puerto Rican family that lived a coupla doors down from us.

I thought, *What good would that do me, unless they prayed over my dead body in Spanish?* But I said, "Man! That's great. Before ya know it, there'll be a whole bunch of us moving in, huh?"

Poppa grunted something and got up. "Staying out here, son?"

"Yeah, Poppa, for a little while longer." 55

From that day on I grew eyes all over my head. Anytime I hit that street for anything, I looked straight ahead, behind me and from side to side all at the same time. Sometimes I ran into Rocky and his boys—that cat was never without his boys—but they never made a move to snag me. They just grinned at me like a bunch of hungry alley cats that could get to their mouse anytime they wanted. That's what they made me feel like—a mouse. Not like a smart house mouse but like a white house pet that ain't got no business in the middle of cat country but don't know better 'cause he grew up thinking he was a cat—which wasn't far from wrong 'cause he'd end up as part of the inside of some cat.

Rocky and his fellas got to playing a way-out game with me called "One-finger-across-the-neck-inna-slicing-motion," followed by such gentle words as "It won't be long, spico." I just looked at them blank and made it to wherever I was going.

I kept wishing those cats went to the same school I went to, a school that was on the border between their country and mine, and I had *amigos* there—and there I could count on them. But I couldn't ask two or three *amigos* to break into Rocky's block and help me mess up his boys. I knew 'cause I had asked them already. They had turned me down fast, and I couldn't blame them. It would have been murder, and I guess they figured one murder would be better than four.

---

[4]*Joe Louis, Pedro Montanez, Kid Chocolate:* great boxers of the 1930s (*Ed.*)

I got through the days trying to play it cool and walk on by Rocky and his boys like they weren't there. One day I passed them and nothing was said. I started to let out my breath. I felt great; I hadn't been seen. Then someone yelled in a high, girlish voice, "Yoo-hoo . . . Hey, *paisan* . . . we see yoo . . ." And right behind that voice came a can of evaporated milk—whoosh, clatter. I walked cool for ten steps then started running like mad.

This crap kept up for a month. They tried to shake me up. Every time they threw something at me, it was just to see me jump. I decided that the next fucking time they threw something at me I was gonna play bad-o and not run. That next time came about a week later. Momma sent me off the stoop to the Italian market on 115th Street and First Avenue, deep in Italian country. Man, that was stompin' territory. But I went, walking in the style which I had copped from the colored cats I had seen, a swinging and stepping down hard at every step. Those cats were so down and cool that just walking made a way-out sound. 60

Ten minutes later I was on my way back with Momma's stuff. I got to the corner of First Avenue and 114th Street and crushed myself right into Rocky and his fellas.

"Well-l, fellas," Rocky said. "Lookee who's here."

I didn't like the sounds coming out of Rocky's fat mouth. And I didn't like the sameness of the shitty grins spreading all over the boys' faces. But I thought, *No more! No more! I ain't gonna run no more.* Even so, I looked around, like for some kind of Jesus miracle to happen. I was always looking for miracles to happen.

"Say, *paisan,*" one guy said, "you even buying from us *paisans,* eh? Man, you must wantta be Italian."

Before I could bite that dopey tongue of mine, I said, "I wouldn't be a guinea on a motherfucking bet." 65

"Wha-at?" said Rocky, really surprised. I didn't blame him; I was surprised myself. His finger began digging a hole in his ear, like he hadn't heard me right. "Wha-at? Say that again?"

I could feel a thin hot wetness cutting itself down my leg. I had been so ashamed of being so damned scared that I had peed on myself. And then I wasn't scared any more; I felt a fuck-it-all attitude. I looked real bad at Rocky and said, "Ya heard me. I wouldn't be a guinea on a bet."

"Ya little sonavabitch, we'll kick the shit outta ya," said one guy, Tony, who had made a habit of asking me if I had any sen-your-ritas for sisters.

"Kick the shit outta me yourself if you got any heart, you motherfuckin' fucker," I screamed at him. I felt kind of happy, the kind of feeling that you get only when you got heart.

Big-mouth Tony just swung out, and I swung back and heard all of Momma's stuff plopping all over the street. My fist hit Tony smack dead in the mouth. He was so mad he threw a fist at me from about three feet away. I faked and jabbed and did fancy dance steps. Big-mouth put a stop to all that with a punch in my mouth. I heard the home cheers of "Yea, yea, bust that spic wide open!" Then I bloodied Tony's nose. He blinked and sniffed without putting his hands to his nose, and I remembered Poppa telling me, "Son, if 70 you're ever fighting somebody an' you punch him in the nose, and he just blinks an' sniffs without holding his nose, you can do one of two things: fight like hell or run like hell—'cause that cat's a fighter."

Big-mouth came at me and we grabbed each other and pushed and pulled and shoved. *Poppa,* I thought, *I ain't gonna cop out. I'm a fighter, too.* I pulled away from Tony and blew my fist into his belly. He puffed and butted my nose with his head. I sniffed back. *Poppa, I didn't put my hands to my nose.* I hit Tony again in that same weak spot. He bent over in the middle and went down to his knees.

Big-mouth got up as fast as he could, and I was thinking how much heart he had. But I ran toward him like my life depended on it; I wanted to cool him. Too late, I saw his hand grab a fistful of ground asphalt which had been piled nearby to fix a pothole in the street. I tried to duck; I should have closed my eyes instead. The shitty-gritty stuff hit my face, and I felt the scrappy pain make itself a part of my eyes. I screamed and grabbed for two eyes with one hand, while the other I beat some kind of helpless tune on air that just couldn't be hurt. I heard Rocky's voice shouting, "Ya scum bag, ya didn't have to fight the spic dirty; you could've fucked him up fair and square!" I couldn't see. I heard a fist hit a face, then Big-mouth's voice: "Whatta ya hittin' me for?" and then Rocky's voice: "*Putana!* I ought ta knock all your fuckin' teeth out."

I felt hands grabbing at me between my screams. I punched out. *I'm gonna get killed,* I thought. Then I heard many voices: "Hold it, kid." "We ain't gonna hurt ya." "Je-*sus,* don't rub your eyes." "Ooooohhhh, shit, his eyes is fulla that shit."

You're fuckin' right, I thought, *and it hurts like* coño.

I heard a woman's voice now: "Take him to a hospital." And an old man asked: "How did it happen?" 75

"Momma, Momma," I cried.

"Comon, kid," Rocky said, taking my hand. "Lemme take ya home." I fought for the right to rub my eyes. "Grab his other hand, Vincent," Rocky said. I tried to rub my eyes with my eyelids. I could feel hurt tears cutting down my cheeks. "Come on, kid, we ain't gonna hurt ya," Rocky tried to assure me. "Swear to our mudders. We just wanna take ya home."

I made myself believe him, and trying not to make pain noises, I let myself be led home. I wondered if I was gonna be blind like Mr. Silva, who went around from door to door selling dish towels and brooms, his son leading him around.

"You okay, kid?" Rocky asked.

"Yeah," what was left of me said. 80

"A-huh," mumbled Big-mouth.

"He got much heart for a nigger," somebody else said.

A *spic,* I thought.

"For anybody," Rocky said. "Here we are, kid," he added. "Watch your step."

I was like carried up the steps. "What's your apartment number?" Rocky asked. 85

"One-B—inna back—ground floor," I said, and I was led there. Somebody knocked on Momma's door. Then I heard running feet and Rocky's voice yelling back, "Don't rat, huh, kid?" And I was alone.

I heard the door open and Momma say, "*Bueno,* Piri, come in." I didn't move. I couldn't. There was a long pause; I could hear Momma's fright. "My God," she said finally. "What's happened?" Then she took a closer look. "Ai-eeee," she screamed. "*Dios mío!*"

"I was playing with some kids, Momma," I said, "an' I got some dirt in my eyes." I tried to make my voice come out without the pain, like a man.

"*Dios eterno*—your eyes!"

"What's the matter? What's the matter?" Poppa called from the bedroom. 90

"*Está ciego!*" Momma screamed. "He is blind!"

I heard Poppa knocking things over as he came running. Sis began to cry. Blind, hurting tears were jumping out of my eyes. "Whattya mean, he's blind?" Poppa said as he stormed into the kitchen. "What happened?" Poppa's voice was both scared and mad.

"Playing, Poppa."

"Whatta ya mean, 'playing'?" Poppa's English sounded different when he got warm.

"Just playing, Poppa." 95

"Playing? Playing got all that dirt in your eyes? I bet my ass. Them damn Ee-ta-liano kids ganged up on you again." Poppa squeezed my head between the fingers of one hand. "That settles it—we're moving outta this damn section, outta this damn block, outta this damn shit."

Shit, I thought, *Poppa's sure cursin' up a storm.* I could hear him slapping the side of his leg, like he always did when he got real mad.

"Son," he said, "you're gonna point them out to me."

"Point who out, Poppa? I was playin' an'—"

"Stop talkin' to him and take him to the hospital!" Momma screamed. 100

"*Pobrecito,* poor Piri," cooed my little sister.

"You sure, son?" Poppa asked. "You was only playing?"

"Shit, Poppa, I said I was."

Smack—Poppa was so scared and mad, he let it out in a slap to the side of my face.

"*Bestia!* Ani-*mul!*" Momma cried. "He's blind, and you hit him!" 105

"I'm sorry, son, I'm sorry," Poppa said in a voice like almost-crying. I heard him running back into the bedroom, yelling, "Where's my pants?"

Momma grabbed away fingers that were trying to wipe away the hurt in my eyes. "*Caramba,* no rub, no rub," she said, kissing me. She told Sis to get a rag and wet it with cold water.

Poppa came running back into the kitchen. "Let's go, son, let's go. Jesus! I didn't mean to smack ya, I really didn't," he said, his big hand rubbing and grabbing my hair gently.

"Here's the rag, Momma," said Sis.

"What's that for?" asked Poppa. 110

"To put on his eyes," Momma said.

I heard the smack of a wet rag, *blapt,* against the kitchen wall. "We can't put nothing on his eyes. It might make them worse. Come on, son," Poppa said nervously, lifting me up in his big arms. I felt like a little baby, like I didn't hurt so bad. I wanted to stay there, but I said, "Let me down, Poppa, I ain't no kid."

"Shut up," Poppa said softly. "I know you ain't, but it's faster this way."

"Which hospeetal are you taking him to?" Momma asked.

"Nearest one," Poppa answered as we went out the door. He carried me through the hall and out into the street, where the bright sunlight made a red hurting color through the crap in my eyes. I heard voices on the stoop and on the sidewalk: "Is that the boy?" 115

"A-huh. He's probably blinded."

"We'll get a cab, son," Poppa said. His voice loved me. I heard Rocky yelling from across the street, "We're pulling for ya, kid. Remember what we . . ." The rest was lost to Poppa's long legs running down to the corner of Third Avenue. He hailed a taxi and we zoomed off toward Harlem Hospital. I felt the cab make all kinds of sudden stops and turns.

"How do you feel, *hijo?*" Poppa asked.

"It burns like hell."

"You'll be okay," he said, and as an afterthought added, "Don't curse, son." 120

I heard cars honking and the Third Avenue el roaring above us. I knew we were in Puerto Rican turf, 'cause I could hear our language.

"Son."

"Yeah, Poppa."

"Don't rub your eyes, fer Christ sake." He held my skinny wrists in his one hand, and everything got quiet between us.

The cab got to Harlem Hospital. I heard change being handled and the door opening and Poppa thanking the cabbie for getting here fast. "Hope the kid'll be okay," the driver said. 125

I will be, I thought. *I ain't gonna be like Mr. Silva.*

Poppa took me in his arms again and started running. "Where's emergency, mister?" he asked someone.

"To your left and straight away," said a voice.

"Thanks a lot," Poppa said, and we were running again. "Emergency?" Poppa said when we stopped.

"Yes, sir," said a girl's voice. "What's the matter?" 130

"My boy's got his eyes full of ground-up tar an'—"

"What's the matter?" said a man's voice.

"Youngster with ground tar in his eyes, doctor."

"We'll take him, mister. You just put him down here and go with the nurse. She'll take down the information. Uh, you the father?"

"That's right, doctor." 135

"Okay, just put him down here."

"Poppa, don't leave me," I cried.

"Sh, son, I ain't leaving you. I'm just going to fill out some papers, an' I'll be right back."

I nodded my head up and down and was wheeled away. When the rolling stretcher stopped, somebody stuck a needle in me and I got sleepy and started thinking about Rocky and his boys, and Poppa's slap, and how great Poppa was, and how my eyes didn't hurt no more . . .

I woke up in a room blind with darkness. The only lights were the ones inside my head. I put my fingers to my eyes and felt bandages. "Let them be, sonny," said a woman's voice. 140

I wanted to ask the voice if they had taken my eyes out, but I didn't. I was afraid the voice would say yes.

"Let them be, sonny," the nurse said, pulling my hand away from the bandages. "You're all right. The doctor put the bandages on to keep the light out. They'll be off real soon. Don't you worry none, sonny."

I wished she would stop calling me sonny. "Where's Poppa?" I asked cool-like.

"He's outside, sonny. Would you like me to send him in?"

I nodded, "Yeah." I heard walking-away shoes, a door opening, a whisper, and shoes walking back toward me. "How do you feel, *hijo?*" Poppa asked. 145

"It hurts like shit, Poppa."

"It's just for awhile, son, and then off come the bandages. Everything's gonna be all right."

I thought, *Poppa didn't tell me to stop cursing.*

"And son, I thought I told you to stop cursing," he added.

I smiled. Poppa hadn't forgotten. Suddenly I realized that all I had on was a hospital gown. "Poppa, where's my clothes?" I asked. 150

"I got them. I'm taking them home an'—"

"Whatta ya mean, Poppa?" I said, like scared. "You ain't leavin' me here? I'll be damned if I stay." I was already sitting up and feeling my way outta bed. Poppa grabbed me and pushed me back. His voice wasn't mad or scared any more. It was happy and soft, like Momma's.

"Hey," he said, "get your ass back in bed or they'll have to put a bandage there too."

"Poppa," I pleaded. "I don't care, wallop me as much as you want, just take me home."

"Hey, I thought you said you wasn't no kid. Hell, you ain't scared of being alone?" 155

Inside my head there was a running of *Yeah, yeah, yeah,* but I answered, "Naw, Poppa, it's just that Momma's gonna worry and she'll get sick an' everything, and—"

"Won't work, son," Poppa broke in with a laugh.

I kept quiet.

"It's only for a couple days. We'll come and see you an' everybody'll bring you things."

I got interested but played it smooth. "What kinda things, Poppa?" 160

Poppa shrugged his shoulders and spread his big arms apart and answered me like he was surprised that I should ask. "Uh . . . fruits and . . . candy and ice cream. And Momma will probably bring you chicken soup."

I shook my head sadly. "Poppa, you know I don't like chicken soup."

"So we won't bring chicken soup. We'll bring what you like. Goddammit, whatta ya like?"

"I'd like the first things you talked about, Poppa," I said softly. "But instead of soup I'd like"—I held my breath back, then shot it out—"some roller skates!"

Poppa let out a whistle. Roller skates were about $1.50, and that was rice and beans for more than a few days. Then he said, "All right, son, soon as you get home, you got 'em." 165

But he had agreed too quickly. I shook my head from side to side. Shit, I was gonna push all the way for the roller skates. It wasn't every day you'd get hurt bad enough to ask for something so little like a pair of roller skates. I wanted them right away.

"Fer Christ sakes," Poppa protested, "you can't use 'em in here. Why, some kid will probably steal 'em on you." But Poppa's voice died out slowly in a "you win" tone as I just kept shaking my head from side to side. "Bring 'em tomorrow," he finally mumbled, "but that's it."

"Thanks, Poppa."

"Don't ask for no more."

My eyes were starting to hurt like mad again. The fun was starting to go outta the game between Poppa and me. I made a face. 170

"Does it hurt, son?"

"Naw, Poppa. I can take it." I thought how I was like a cat in a movie about Indians, taking it like a champ, tied to a stake and getting like burned toast.

Poppa sounded relieved. "Yeah, it's only at first it hurts." His hand touched my foot. "Well, I'll be going now . . ." Poppa rubbed my foot gently and then slapped me the same gentle way on the side of my leg. "Be good, son," he said and walked away. I heard the door open and the nurse telling him about how they were gonna move me to the ward 'cause I was out of danger. "Son," Poppa called back, "you're *un hombre*."

I felt proud as hell.

"Poppa." 175

"Yeah, son?"

"You won't forget to bring the roller skates, huh?"

Poppa laughed. "Yeah, son."

I heard the door close.

DISCUSSING THE TEXT

1. How does Thomas react when he is called a spic? How would you relate this incident to the adage "Sticks and stones may break my bones, but words will never hurt me"?
2. Find references to being "cool" in this selection. What do you think Thomas's attitude toward coolness and toughness is here? Do you share his attitude?

3. Find examples of language that seems dated to you in this piece (such as the verb "to dig"). Does such language add or detract from the power of this piece? Why?
4. Get together in a group of four or five students and discuss the following points: How would you compare Thomas's experience in the 1940s with that of young people living in neighborhoods torn by racial and ethnic strife today? In what ways has the violence escalated in recent years? Make a list of possible ways to foster better relations among young people in different ethnic groups.

WRITING ABOUT THE TEXT

5. Write a brief personal response to the phrase "alien turf." What does this phrase mean to you? Have you ever found yourself in a situation similar to the one Thomas describes here? Do you know anyone who has?
6. Write a paragraph discussing the concept of a *border,* as it is addressed by Thomas in paragraph 58: "I kept wishing those cats went to the same school I went to, a school that was on the border between their country and mine, and I had *amigos* there—and there I could count on them."
7. Although Piri Thomas wrote his autobiography as an adult, this selection shows his skill in describing situations through the eyes, and in the language, of a child. Write two paragraphs about an experience you had as a child; like Thomas, try to incorporate the dual perspective of the adult you are now and of the child you once were.
8. Choose two passages in the text that reflect or describe racial and ethnic prejudice toward Puerto Ricans and toward Italian Americans. Make a list of words that denote biases. Then find passages in Michael La Sorte's "Italians and Americans" (p. 38) that reflect or describe ethnic prejudice toward Italian immigrants and toward Americans. Write a brief essay comparing and contrasting the two selections in terms of the specific theme of prejudice.

JAMES AGEE

Near a Church

What rules and conventions govern the random meeting of a black person and a white person in the Deep South during the time of racially discriminatory Jim Crow laws[1] *and lynching? James Agee (1909–1955) implicitly answers this question, and raises many others, in this excerpt from a long narrative about the South,* Let Us Now Praise Famous Men *(1941). Agee wrote the book after his trip to Alabama during*

[1]*Jim Crow laws:* The South during the 1930s was still enforcing laws enacted beginning in the post–Civil War period that legalized segregation and ensured white supremacy. Under these discriminatory laws, African Americans suspected of violating racial boundaries were subject to violence, including lynching, by ad hoc bands of whites. (*Ed.*)

the summer of 1936 with photographer Walker Evans. The two were on assignment for Fortune *magazine, researching a piece on southern sharecroppers and tenant farmers. During the 1930s a number of photographers and writers were funded by the U.S. government to document conditions of poverty in the rural South and elsewhere, and Evans was on loan to* Fortune *from one of the government agencies. Although what Agee and Evans eventually produced proved unsuitable for* Fortune, *it has become a unique and irreplaceable record of the South during the depression, one of the great nonfiction works of our century, and a book that inspired many civil rights activists during the 1960s.*

In this selection, from near the beginning of Let Us Now Praise Famous Men, *Agee describes his encounter, first of all, with a rural church. Walker Evans, considered by many people the greatest photographer of the 1930s, accompanies Agee, and they both understand immediately that they must have a picture of this structure. Although they consider going inside to photograph the interior, when they see a black couple passing by they feel ashamed of their intrusive intentions; Agee goes to ask the couple where they can find the minister of the church to let them inside. In the encounter that follows, Agee dramatizes this moment and the unspoken assumptions about white and black behavior and obligations in the South at that time.*

It was a good enough church from the moment the curve opened and we saw it that I slowed a little and we kept our eyes on it. But as we came even with it the light so held it that it shocked us with its goodness straight through the body, so that at the same instant we said *Jesus*. I put on the brakes and backed the car slowly, watching the light on the building, until we were at the same apex, and we sat still for a couple of minutes at least before getting out, studying in arrest what had hit us so hard as we slowed past its perpendicular.

It lost nothing at all in stasis, but even more powerfully strove in through the eyes its paralyzing classicism: stood from scoured clay, a light lift above us, no trees near, and few weeds; every grain, every nailhead, distinct; the subtle almost strangling strong asymmetries of that which has been hand wrought toward symmetry (as if it were an earnest description, better than the intended object): so intensely sprung against so scarcely eccentric a balance that my hands of themselves spread out their bones, trying to regiment on air between their strengths its tensions and their mutual structures as they stood subject to the only scarcely eccentric, almost annihilating stress, of the serene, wild, rigorous light: empty, shut, bolted, of all that was now withdrawn from it upon the fields the utter statement, God's mask and wooden skull and home stood empty in the meditation of the sun: and this light upon it was strengthening still further its imposal and embrace, and in about a quarter of an hour would have trained itself ready, and there would be a triple convergence in the keen historic spasm of the shutter.

I helped get the camera ready and we stood away and I watched what would be trapped, possessed, fertilized, in the leisures and shyness which are a phase of all love for any object: searching out and registering in myself all its lines, planes, stresses of relationship, along diagonals withdrawn and approached, and vertical to the slightly off-centered door, and broadside, and at several distances, and near, examining merely the ways of the wood, and the nails, the three new boards of differing lengths that were let in above the left of the door, the staring small white porcelain knob, the solesmoothed stair-lifts, the wrung stance of thick steeple, the hewn wood stoblike spike at sky, the old hasp and new padlock, the randomshuttered windowglass whose panes were like the surfaces of springs, the fat gold fly who sang and botched against a bright pane within, and within, the rigid benches, box organ, bright stops, hung charts, wrecked hymnals, the platform, pine lectern doilied, pressed-glass pitcher, suspended lamp, four funeral chairs, the little stove with long swan throat aluminum in the hard sober shade, a button in sun, a flur of lint, a torn card of Jesus among children:

While we were wondering whether to force a window, a young negro couple came past up the road. Without appearing to look either longer or less long, or with more or less interest, than a white man might care for, and without altering their pace, they made thorough observation of us, of the car, and of the tripod and camera. We spoke and nodded, smiling as if casually; they spoke and nodded, gravely, as they passed, and glanced back once, not secretly, nor long, nor in amusement. They made us, in spite of our knowledge of our own meanings, ashamed and insecure in our wish to break into and possess their church, and after a minute or two I decided to go after them and speak to them, and ask them if they knew where we might find a minister or some other person who might let us in, if it would be all right. They were fifty yards or so up the road, walking leisurely, and following them, I watched aspects of them which are less easily seen (as surrounding objects are masked by looking into a light) when one's own eyes and face and the eyes and face of another are mutually visible and appraising. They were young, soberly buoyant of body, and strong, the man not quite thin, the girl not quite plump, and I remembered their mild and sober faces, hers softly wide and sensitive to love and to pleasure, and his resourceful and intelligent without intellect and without guile, and their extreme dignity, which was as effortless, unvalued, and undefended in them as the assumption of superiority which suffuses a rich and social adolescent boy; and I was taking pleasure also in the competence and rhythm of their walking in the sun, which was incapable of being less than a muted dancing, and in the beauty in the sunlight of their clothes, which were strange upon them in the middle of the week. He was in dark trousers, black dress shoes, a new-laundered white shirt with lights of bluing in it, and a light yellow, soft straw hat with a broad band of dark flowered cloth and a daisy in the band; she glossy-legged without stockings, in freshly whited pumps, a flowered pink cotton dress, and a great sun of straw set far back on her head. Their swung hands touched gently with their walking, stride by stride, but did not engage. I was walking more rapidly than they but quietly; before I had gone ten steps they turned their heads (toward each other) and looked at me briefly and impersonally, like horses in a field, and faced front again; and this, I am almost certain, not through having heard sound of me, but through a subtler sense. By the time I raised my hand, they had looked away, and did not see me, though nothing in their looking had been quick with abruptness or surreption. I walked somewhat faster now, but I was overtaking them a little slowly for my patience; the light would be right by now or very soon; I had no doubt Walker would do what he wanted whether we had "permission" or not, but I wanted to be on hand, and broke into a trot. At the sound of the twist of my shoe in the gravel, the young woman's whole body was jerked down tight as a fist into a crouch from which immediately, the rear foot skidding in the loose stone so that she nearly fell, like a kicked cow scrambling out of a creek, eyes crazy, chin stretched tight, she sprang forward into the first motions of a running not human but that of a suddenly terrified wild animal. In this same instant the young man froze, the emblems of sense in his wild face wide open toward me, his right hand stiff toward the girl who, after a few strides, her consciousness overtaking her reflex, shambled to a stop and stood, not straight but sick, as if hung from a hook in the spine of the will not to fall for weakness, while he hurried to her and put his hand on her flowered shoulder and, inclining his head forward and sidewise as if listening, spoke with her, and they lifted, and watched me while, shaking my head, and raising my hand palm outward, I came up to them (not trotting) and stopped a yard short of where they, closely, not touching now, stood, and said, still shaking my head (*No; no; oh, Jesus, no, no, no!*) and looking into their eyes; at the man, who was not knowing what to do, and at the girl, whose eyes were lined with tears, and who was trying so hard to subdue the shaking in her breath, and whose heart I could feel, though not hear, blasting as if it were my whole body, and I trying in some fool way to keep it somehow relatively light, because I could not bear that they should receive from me any added reflection of the shattering of their grace and dignity, and of the nakedness and depth and meaning of their fear, and of my horror and pity and self-hatred; and so, smiling, and so distressed that I wanted only that they should be restored, and should know I was their friend, and that I might melt from existence: "I'm *very sorry!* I'm *very* sorry if I scared you! I didn't mean to scare you at all. I wouldn't have done any such thing for anything."

They just kept looking at me. There was no more for them to say than for me. The least I could have done was to throw myself flat on my face and embrace and kiss their feet. That impulse took hold of me so powerfully, from my whole body, not by thought, that I caught myself from doing it exactly and as scarcely as you snatch yourself from jumping from a sheer height: here, with the realization that it would have frightened them still worse (to say nothing of me) and would have been still less explicable; so that I stood and looked into their eyes and loved them, and wished to God I was dead. After a little the man got back his voice, his eyes grew a little easier, and he said without conviction that that was all right and that I hadn't scared her. She shook her head slowly, her eyes on me; she did not yet trust her voice. Their faces were secret, soft, utterly without trust of me, and utterly without understanding; and they had to stand here now and hear what I was saying, because in that country no negro safely walks away from a white man, or even appears not to listen while he is talking, and because I could not walk away abruptly, and relieve them of me, without still worse a crime against nature than the one I had committed, and the second I was committing by staying, and holding them. And so, and in this horrid grinning of faked casualness, I gave them a better reason why I had followed them than to frighten them, asked what I had followed them to ask; they said the thing it is usually safest for negroes to say, that they did not know; I thanked them very much, and was seized once more and beyond resistance with the wish to clarify and set right, so that again, with my eyes and smile wretched and out of key with all I was able to say, I said I was awfully sorry if I had bothered them; but they only retreated still more profoundly behind their faces, their eyes watching mine as if awaiting any sudden move they must ward, and the young man said again that that was all right, and I nodded, and turned away from them, and walked down the road without looking back.

DISCUSSING THE TEXT

1. How does James Agee describe why he and Walker Evans need to have a photograph of this particular rural church? How does Agee's language give us a visual picture of it? What does his description make us see or understand?
2. What does Agee mean, in paragraph 4, by the idea of "a subtler sense" that makes the couple aware of his presence behind them?
3. Reread Agee's description of the young couple (par. 4). What kinds of words does he use to describe them? Does his language support or contradict cultural stereotypes of African Americans? Do you think this sort of description could be written in the 1990s? Why or why not?
4. Agee describes his approach to the couple and their brief verbal exchange in dramatic and very precise terms. Get together with a group of four or five students and discuss your reactions to this passage. Which elements in Agee's description could be defined as objective details? Which elements might be part of a more subjective account of his feelings, connected more with his *imagining* how the couple might feel? Take brief notes as you work on this assignment, and be prepared to discuss your opinions with the class.

WRITING ABOUT THE TEXT

5. Write a description of an encounter you've had with a member (or members) of another race or ethnic group, or perhaps a member of another socioeconomic class, in which there was the possibility of misunderstanding or faulty communication. How did you react to the conflict? Were you both able to resolve the problem? How was this event significant, and what did you learn from it?
6. Agee uses precise and poetic descriptive detail in his depiction of the church. Choose an object that interests you (for example, a building, a car, an article of clothing, a piece of jewelry, a furniture item) and make a list of the details that best describe it. Think about why these details are significant. How do you react to them? What are you trying to communicate to your reader through these details? Once you have recorded your notes, write a quick, detailed description of the object.

7. In paragraph 3, Agee writes of what would be "trapped, possessed, fertilized," in Walker Evans's photograph of the church. Think about the meanings of these verbs. Then consider the whole project of photographing poor people during the depression. Can you see problems with a project of this kind? Drawing on Agee's thoughts as well as your own, write a one- to two-page discussion of the advantages and disadvantages of "documenting" the lives of poor people through photography.
8. Try to assume the point of view of the couple, and to imagine some of their reactions to Agee's approach. Jot down some ideas about how they would discuss the incident between them, and what they might think of Agee. Then read Pat Parker's poem "For the white person who wants to know how to be my friend" (the next selection). Compare your ideas about the couple's reaction to the incident described in "Near a Church" with Parker's poem in a brief essay.

PAT PARKER

For the white person who wants to know how to be my friend

In this poem from the collection Movement in Black *(1978), Parker plays with common stereotypes of African Americans and uses them in an ironic way. Specifically addressed to "whites," the poem establishes a sense of both intimacy and distance by implying that even though interracial friendships are indeed possible, preconceived notions about the "Other" must be overcome.*

Pat Parker (1944–1989) was founder of the Black Women's Revolutionary Council in 1980, and from 1978 to 1987 she served as a board member and medical coordinator at the Oakland Feminist Women's Health Center. Her publications include Child of Myself *(1971),* Womanslaughter *(1978), and* Jonestown and Other Madness *(1985).*

The first thing you do is to forget that i'm Black.
Second, you must never forget that i'm Black.

You should be able to dig Aretha,[1]
but don't play her every time i come over.
And if you decide to play Beethoven—don't tell me 5
his life story. They made us take music appreciation too.

[1] *Aretha Franklin:* popular African American blues and rock singer (*Ed.*)

Eat soul food if you like it, but don't expect me
to locate your restaurants
or cook it for you.

And if some Black person insults you,
mugs you, rapes your sister, rapes you,
rips your house or is just being an ass—
please, do not apologize to me
for wanting to do them bodily harm.
It makes me wonder if you're foolish.

And even if you really believe Blacks are better lovers than
whites—don't tell me. I start thinking of charging stud fees.[2]

In other words—if you really want to be my friend—*don't*
make a labor of it. I'm lazy. Remember.

10

15

DISCUSSING THE TEXT

1. Why do you think Parker uses a lowercase *i* in the word *i'm* in the poem's first two lines?
2. In the first two lines, Parker seems to be contradicting herself. What does this contradiction convey? How does it set the tone of the poem?
3. Parker seems to imply in the fourth stanza that a desire for revenge transcends ethnicity. Discuss your ideas about this passage in a group of four or five students; as a group, come up with one or two contemporary examples that involve issues of race and/or ethnicity and a desire for revenge.
4. What specific African American stereotypes is Parker referring to in the last two stanzas? Do you think these stereotypes are a thing of the past? If not, what evidence do you see of them—perhaps in books, movies, television shows, or movies—today?

WRITING ABOUT THE TEXT

5. Is it possible to "forget" that a person is black and to "never forget" that a person is black at one and the same time? Write a paragraph in response to this question.
6. The poem's second stanza suggests that to play popular black music for an African American guest, or to try to explain the life of a classical white musician to him or her, might be condescending. Write two paragraphs expressing your reactions to Parker's ideas. Do you agree or disagree with her point of view? Can you think of any situations in which this might not be the case?
7. Write a brief poem (two or three stanzas) in Parker's style to a person of another race and/or ethnicity "who wants to know how to be [your] friend."

---

[2]*stud fees:* money paid to owner of a stallion to sire foals (*Ed.*)

MAKING CONNECTIONS

1. Several readings in this chapter depict encounters between culturally different individuals who find themselves to be influenced by stereotypes. Think about an experience you've had in which someone used a stereotype in reference to you, whether ethnic, racial, or some other type (for example, "dumb jock," "country bumpkin," or "bimbo"). How did knowing you'd been stereotyped affect your reactions to that person? How did that person's stereotypical idea of you influence his or her behavior?
2. Think of yourself as a white European explorer of the sixteenth century in America. Write a paragraph expressing your reactions to your encounter with the cultural and racial "other," an Indian. Then think of yourself as a native inhabitant of the Americas in the sixteenth century, and write a paragraph expressing your reactions to an encounter with the cultural and racial "other," a white European. Incorporate your two paragraphs into a brief essay that compares and contrasts the two different points of view and sums up your ideas about cultural encounters.
3. From your own experience, describe an encounter with a "foreign" or somehow different ethnic group or individual. Make a list of some of the preconceptions about the group or individual that you had. What did you learn about your preconceptions? Which ones, if any, were confirmed? Which were proved wrong?
4. Go to the library and find out what you can about the original gift of the Statue of Liberty from France to the United States. How did Emma Lazarus's poem "The New Colossus" end up on the statue's base? How is Lazarus inventing America in this poem, and what kinds of images does she use to communicate her sentiments? Do you think this was a good choice to be included on the Statue of Liberty? Why or why not?
5. Compare and contrast the experience of "encountering the other" in Piri Thomas's "Alien Turf" and James Agee's "Near a Church."
6. In her narrative essay "The World of Our Grandmothers," Connie Young Yu recreates her identity as a Chinese American through her family's oral history, documents and newspapers, and other historical records. How is what she is doing an example of "inventing America"?
7. Study Arnold Genthe's photograph of San Francisco's Chinatown at the beginning of this chapter. Take some notes describing what you see and how it is presented. Then write a brief essay connecting the photograph to this chapter's overall theme of cultural encounters.
8. Choose an ethnic group you are interested in, possibly your own. Visit the library and research the history of this group in America, looking for examples of encounters with other ethnic groups or with already established American citizens. Look particularly for examples of tension between these groups. How was that tension resolved (*if* it was resolved)?
9. Talk with an older member or members of your family, or with friends of an older generation. Ask them to tell you about their experiences with encountering cultural difference, from either side of the power divide. Take notes as you talk, or tape-record your conversations. Record these conversations in writing, either as an oral history (in the voices of the persons you spoke with) or as an essay (in your own voice).

FURTHER READING

Edmundo O'Gorman

Bodmer, Beatriz Pastor. *The Armature of Conquest, Spanish Accounts of the Discovery of America 1492–1589.* Stanford: Stanford University Press, 1992.

Greenblatt, Stephen. *Marvelous Possessions: The Wonder of the New World.* Chicago: University of Chicago Press, 1991.

Joseph, Alvin M., ed. *America in 1492: The World of the Indian Peoples before the Arrival of Columbus.* New York: Knopf, 1991.

Guillermo Gómez-Peña and Coco Fusco

Gómez-Peña, Guillermo. *Warrior for Gringostroika.* St. Paul, Minn.: Graywolf Press, 1993.

Hicks, Emily D. *Border Writing: The Multidimensional Text.* Minneapolis: University of Minnesota Press, 1991.

Anzaldúa, Gloria. *Borderlands: La Frontera-The New Mestiza.* San Francisco: Spinsters/Aunt Lute, 1987.

Emma Lazarus

Higham, John. *Send These to Me: Jews and Other Immigrants to Urban America.* New York: Atheneum, 1975.

Thomas Bailey Aldrich

Higham, John. *Strangers in the Land: Patterns of American Nativism 1867–1925.* New York: Atheneum, 1975.

Connie Young Yu

Asian Women United of California, ed. *Making Waves: An Anthology of Writings by and about Asian American Women.* Boston: Beacon Press, 1989.

Hagedorn, Jessica, ed. *Charlie Chan Is Dead: An Anthology of Contemporary Asian American Fiction.* New York: Penguin Books, 1993.

Michael La Sorte

Mangione, Jerre. *La Storia.* New York: HarperCollins, 1992.

Panella, Vincent. *The Other Side: Growing Up Italian in America.* New York: Doubleday, 1979.

Piri Thomas

Flores, Juan. *Divided Borders: Essays on Puerto Rican Identity.* Houston: Arte Publico Press, 1993.

Rivera, Edward. *Family Installments: Memories of Growing Up Hispanic.* New York: Penguin Books, 1992.

James Agee

Agee, James, and Walker Evans. *Let Us Now Praise Famous Men*. 1941. Reprint, Boston: Houghton Mifflin, 1988.

Bergreen, Laurence. *James Agee: A Life*. New York: Penguin Books, 1985.

Wright, Richard. *Uncle Tom's Children*. 1940. Reprint, New York: Harper and Row, 1965.

Pat Parker

Gates, Henry Louis, ed. *Reading Black, Reading Feminist: A Critical Anthology*. Bloomington, Ill.: Meridian, 1992.

Parker, Pat. *Movement in Black*. Ithaca, N.Y.: Firebrand, 1990.

Ready for Sabbath Eve in a Coal Cellar *(photograph by Jacob Riis), c. 1895. Jacob Riis, himself a Danish immigrant, began photographing on New York's Lower East Side as a way of publicizing, and changing, the living conditions of the immigrants. The Jewish cobbler pictured here has made his home in this space out of desperation, against the efforts of the Board of Health to keep such unsanitary cellars free of habitation.*

(The Jacob A. Riis Collection, Museum of the City of New York)

2

Exiled Voices

When I looked round the ship too, and saw a large furnace of copper boiling, and a multitude of black people of every description chained together, every one of their countenances expressing dejection and sorrow, I no longer doubted of my fate; and, quite overpowered with horror and anguish, I fell motionless on the deck and fainted.

- OLAUDAH EQUIANO
The Life of Olaudah Equiano or Gustavus Vassa the African. Written by Himself

[W]herever the immigrants went, there was one common experience they shared: nowhere could they transplant the European village. Whatever the variations among environments in America, none was familiar.

- OSCAR HANDLIN
The Ghettos

Oh, sometimes I was wishing I was back in *Italia!* But sometimes not too.

- MARIE HALL ETS
Rosa, The Life of an Italian Immigrant

Lourdes misses the birds she had in Cuba. She thinks of joining a bird-watching society, but who would take care of the bakery in her absence? . . . It's a shame, too, because all Lourdes ever sees in Brooklyn is dull little wrens or those filthy pigeons.

- Cristina Garcia
Enough Attitude

Some of our neighbors came from other highly respected Haitian families, but in New York, they were just blacks who took care of other people's children, cleaned other people's apartments, worked in the garment factories around 34th Street or drove cabs.

- Joel Dreyfuss
The Invisible Immigrants

America comes out of Europe, but these people have never seen America, nor have most of them seen more of Europe than the hamlet at the foot of their mountain. Yet they move with an authority which I shall never have; and they regard me, quite rightly, not only as a stranger in their village but as a suspect latecomer, bearing no credentials, to everything they have—however unconsciously—inherited.

- James Baldwin
Stranger in the Village

In order to forget more efficiently we rather avoid any allusion to concentration or internment camps we experienced in nearly all European countries—it might be interpreted as pessimism or lack of confidence in the new homeland.

- Hannah Arendt
We Refugees (January 1943)

Exile is strangely compelling to think about but terrible to experience. It is the unhealable rift forced between a human being and a native place, between the self and its true home: its essential sadness can never be surmounted.

- Edward Said
Reflections on Exile

This chapter takes a closer look at those who have journeyed to America throughout the centuries as slaves, exiles, refugees, or immigrants. Certainly no two experiences in this process of migration have been the same, but many have been shaped by responses to similar kinds of political or economic conditions. The early settlers of the seventeenth and eighteenth centuries came often in pursuit of economic opportunity or religious freedom, as others would continue to do up to the present day. In the nineteenth century, economic conditions in the homeland were the biggest motivators for most immigrants, as in the case of the Irish who came here in great numbers trying simply to survive the potato famine of the 1840s. Survival was a motivating factor for many emigrants in the late nineteenth and early twentieth centuries as well: the Jews from Russia, for example, were in many cases trying to escape the terrible pogroms, in which villages were ransacked and inhabitants killed. Jews fled from the terrors of the Nazi regime in the late 1930s and early 1940s; those unable to flee—some six million—were slaughtered. In the years following World War II, survival has continued to be a prime motivation, whether for economic or political reasons, as with the immigrants from Southeast Asia, Latin America, and Africa, all seeking to escape oppressive conditions at home. Many aspects of life are different: space and living conditions, economic and social status, food and clothing, political structure, language, and family support, to name a few. And on an interpersonal level, the experience of exile almost always involves being perceived as different—as "strange" or "foreign"—by those who already live in the new land.

The readings in this chapter explore the condition of strangeness and dislocation that the new arrival experiences in America. There are, of course, many different situations facing those who arrive here from another land, and different names to describe these varied situations. One can, for example, be forced as an individual to leave one's homeland; one can leave with many others as a result of some political change; one can leave because conditions in the homeland are intolerable; one can leave to seek only a temporary new land. In the last selection in this chapter, Edward Said offers a succinct analysis of the distinctions between, for example, terms like *exile* and *refugee,* or *expatriate* and *émigré.* (You might want to read the selection by Said first, to become acquainted with some of these concepts before your other readings; or you may prefer to read his essay last, as a kind of summary and philosophical reflection on the earlier readings in this chapter.)

In nearly every case, the sense of exile is characterized by a feeling of doubleness, or a sense of having two separate lives: the experience of the present, in the new land, is measured against the remembered experience of the past, in the old country. The exile's sense of the difference between these two lives may cause elation or sadness, but it will inevitably affect his or her sense of self. How well this person adapts to the new land, how much he or she clings to the past—these will depend on the new arrival's age, resources, and resilience.

The first selection in this chapter is an excerpt from the autobiography of a former slave, Olaudah Equiano, who bought his own independence around the same time that the United States was declaring its independence from Britain. Equiano's particular form of exile—that of enslavement—stands at one extreme of the American experience, and reminds us that the United States has historically dictated forced exile and suffering for some, even while others have sought refuge here from hardships in their homelands.

The next selection, Oscar Handlin's "The Ghettos," presents a broad overview of the living conditions faced by those who sought to come to the United States as a place of opportunity, or as a refuge from harsh conditions at home. Handlin, a historian, looks at the living spaces and way of life of the immigrants who came to American cities toward the end of the nineteenth century and the beginning of the twentieth century. What he finds is a pattern of discrimination and suffering that took generations to overcome. If America is the promised land, that promise was slow to be fulfilled for many immigrants. The next selection, an oral history provided by an Italian immigrant named Rosa, retells the story of Handlin's immigrants, this time from a very personal, individual perspective.

The story of exile and dislocation is told yet again from another family's point of view in the selection that follows, an excerpt from Cristina Garcia's novel *Dreaming in Cuban*. Here we find a dramatic portrayal of different reactions to exile within the same family. Where Garcia portrays a generational division within one family, Joel Dreyfuss, in his essay about Haitians, portrays the divisions within the larger group known from the outside as "Haitians." Dreyfuss's essay reminds readers that members of one ethnic group can be quite different in their backgrounds and their attitudes toward their position as exiles.

In "Stranger in the Village," James Baldwin suggests that the issue of identity is enormously complicated for African Americans. Living and writing in Switzerland, Baldwin experiences a double exile: from his American homeland and from his homeland beyond the United States—Africa. Having an identity as a black American *outside* America is, Baldwin notes, different from having the identity of a black American within the United States. His distance from his American home helps to clarify, for Baldwin, the nature of his own rage against American innocence and naivete about these issues.

In her essay "We Refugees," Hannah Arendt maintains that personal, ethnic, and cultural identity is something that cannot be taken for granted. She provides an insider's account of the experience of many Jews who were forced to leave their European homes and seek refuge in new lands during World War II. Arendt, a philosopher, is most interested in the spiritual and psychological effects of *deracination* (the process of uprooting). She emphasizes the cost of this process to the self—the cost, that is, of leaving forever a once secure place in a complex civilization.

Arendt writes from the perspective of a European Jewish refugee from the Nazi Holocaust. Yet she raises the question of whether the experience of the Jews has become a model for the experiences of people throughout the world—the product of the breakdown of cultures everywhere. Similar ground is covered, from yet another perspective, in Edward Said's essay "Reflections on Exile." Writing as an exile himself (from Palestine), Said explores the various kinds of consciousness that can result from the condition of deracination. In doing so, he challenges preconceived notions about the nature of exile and the problems and opportunities that it can bring.

The selections in this chapter all pose questions that are an inevitable part of the exile's experience: What have I left behind? Who am I? How will I change? As you enter into the strange new worlds of the "exiled voices" that follow, try to keep these fundamental questions in mind. Remember, too, that simple psychological answers cannot address all aspects of the exile's experience; broader cultural concerns must be taken into account as well.

OLAUDAH EQUIANO

FROM

The Life of Olaudah Equiano or Gustavus Vassa the African. Written by Himself

*Olaudah Equiano's extraordinary autobiography—*The Life of Olaudah Equiano or Gustavus Vassa the African. Written by Himself.*—illustrates several narrative traditions. First, it is the story of Equiano's captivity as a slave and his struggle to achieve freedom; as such it is one of the first of a long line of slave narratives. Second, Equiano's life story is an autobiography, a story about the fortunate rise in the world of a self-made man; as such it complements Ben Franklin's account in his own* Autobiography, *which was written around the same time. And finally, it is a great adventure story, recounting the perils of Equiano's life and the horrors he witnessed, along with his masterful achievements and his travels around the globe.*

Equiano (1745–1797) learned to read and write while serving various masters on land and on sea. The writing of his life story (characterized by the language and rhythm of a refined eighteenth-century English style) was one way in which Equiano demonstrated to the world that a slave could possess humanity and intelligence. As a spokesperson for black people, Equiano repeatedly affirmed their rights and spoke against the brutality of slavery. He was also personally active in securing the freedom of runaway slaves. He married in 1792 and settled in England, where he died in 1797.

In this chapter from the Life, *Equiano details how it felt to be suddenly uprooted from his life of freedom with his family and kidnapped into slavery. Slaves were commonly held in Nigeria, where Equiano was born, and in fact his father had many slaves himself. But this in no way prepared the eleven-year-old boy for the trauma of separation. Equiano was sold to European slave traders, who eventually took him to what was then the English colony of Virginia.*

Equiano's description of what has become known as the "middle passage" reveals the terrible and dehumanizing ordeal by which human beings were turned into chattel, movable property. Forced into cramped quarters with no adequate sanitary facilities, often chained together for long periods with meager rations, many Africans never made it to America alive. Equiano's astonishing account tells us not only the physical details but also the emotions—anxiety, loneliness, fear, anger—that accompanied this painful exile from his homeland. Equiano's Life *was one of the first accounts of the experience of forced exile from family and home to be narrated by a slave who survived the middle passage and became free. The reading begins with a summary of the narrative, a common format when the book was first published.*

CHAPTER II.

The author's birth and parentage—His being kidnapped with his sister—Their separation—Surprise at meeting again—Are finally separated—Account of the different places and incidents the author met with till his arrival on the coast—The effect the sight of a slave-ship had on him—He sails for the West Indies—Horrors of a slave ship—Arrives at Barbadoes, where the cargo is sold and dispersed.

I hope the reader will not think I have trespassed on his patience in introducing myself to him, with some account of the manners and customs of my country. They had been implanted in me with great care, and made an impression on my mind, which time could not erase, and which all the adversity and variety of fortune I have since experienced, served only to rivet and record; for, whether the love of one's country be real or imaginary, or a lesson of reason, or an instinct of nature, I still look back with pleasure on the first scenes of my life, though that pleasure has been for the most part mingled with sorrow.

I have already acquainted the reader with the time and place of my birth. My father, besides many slaves, had a numerous family, of which seven lived to grow up, including myself and a sister, who was the only daughter. As I was the youngest of the sons, I became, of course, the greatest favorite with my mother, and was always with her; and she used to take particular pains to form my mind. I was trained up from my earliest years in the art of war: my daily exercise was shooting and throwing javelins; and my mother adorned me with emblems, after the manner of our greatest warriors. In this way I grew up till I was turned the age of eleven, when an end was put to my happiness in the following manner:—generally when the grown people in the neighborhood were gone far in the fields to labor, the children assembled together in some of the neighboring premises to play; and commonly some of us used to get up a tree to look out for any assailant, or kidnapper, that might come upon us—for they sometimes took those opportunities of our parents' absence, to attack and carry off as many as they could seize. One day as I was watching at the top of a tree in our yard, I saw one of those people come into the yard of our next neighbor but one to kidnap, there being many stout young people in it. Immediately on this I gave the alarm of the rogue, and he was surrounded by the stoutest of them, who entangled him with cords, so that he could not escape till some of the grown people came and secured him. But, alas! ere long it was my fate to be thus attacked, and to be carried off, when none of the grown people were nigh. One day, when all our people were gone out to their works as usual, and only I and my dear sister were left to mind the house, two men and a woman got over our walls, and in a moment seized us both, and, without giving us time to cry out, or make resistance, they stopped our mouths, and ran off with us into the nearest wood. Here they tied our hands, and continued to carry us as far as they could, till night came on, when we reached a small house, where the robbers halted for refreshment, and spent the night. We were then unbound, but were unable to take any food; and, being quite overpowered by fatigue and grief, our only relief was some sleep, which allayed our misfortune for a short time. The next morning we left the house, and continued travelling all the day. For a long time we had kept the woods, but at last we came into a road which I believed I knew. I had now some hopes of being delivered; for we had advanced but a little way before I discovered some people at a distance, on which I began to cry out for their assistance; but my cries had no other effect than to make them tie me faster and stop my mouth, and then they put me into a large sack. They also stopped my sister's mouth, and tied her hands; and in this manner we proceeded till we were out of sight of these people. When we went to rest the following night, they offered us some victuals, but we refused it; and the only comfort we had was in being in one another's arms all that night, and bathing each other with our tears. But alas! we were soon deprived of even the small comfort of weeping together. The next day proved a day of greater sorrow than I had yet experienced; for my sister and I were then separated, while we lay clasped in each other's arms. It was in vain that we besought them not to part us; she was torn from me, and immediately carried away, while I was left in a state of distraction not to be described. I cried and grieved continually; and for several days did not eat any thing but what they forced into my mouth. At length, after many days travelling, during which I had often changed masters, I got into the hands of a chieftain, in a very pleasant country. This man had two wives and some children, and they all used me extremely well, and did all they could to comfort me; particularly the first wife, who was something like my mother. Although I was a great many days' journey from my father's house, yet these people spoke exactly the same language with us. This first master of mine, as I may call him, was a smith, and my principal employment was working his bellows, which were the same kind as I had seen in my vicinity. They were in some respects not unlike the stoves here in gentlemen's kitchens, and were covered over with leather; and in the middle of that leather a stick was fixed, and a person stood up, and worked it in the same manner as is done to pump water out of a cask with a hand pump. I believe it was gold he worked, for it was of a lovely bright yellow color, and was worn by the women on their wrists and ankles. I was there I suppose about a month, and they at last used to trust me some little distance from the house. This liberty I used in embracing every opportunity to inquire the way to my own home; and I also sometimes, for the same purpose, went with the maidens, in the cool of the evenings, to bring pitchers of water from the springs for the use of the house. I had also remarked where the sun rose in the morning, and set in the evening, as I had travelled along; and I had observed that my father's house was towards the rising of the sun. I therefore determined to seize the first opportunity of making my escape, and to shape my course for that quarter; for I was quite oppressed and weighed down by grief after my mother and friends; and my love of liberty, ever great, was strengthened by the mortifying circumstance of not daring to eat with the free-born children, although I was mostly their companion.

▼ ▼ ▼

Soon after this, my master's only daughter, and child by his first wife, sickened and died, which affected him so much that for some time he was almost frantic, and really would have killed himself, had he not been watched and prevented. However, in short time afterwards he recovered, and I was again sold. I was now carried to the left of the sun's rising, through many dreary wastes and dismal woods, amidst the hideous roarings of wild beasts. The people I was sold to used to carry me very often, when I was tired, either on their shoulders or on their backs. I saw many convenient well built sheds along the road, at proper distances, to accommodate the merchants and travellers, who lay in those buildings along with their wives, who often accompany them; and they always go well armed.

From the time I left my own nation, I always found somebody that understood me till I came to the sea coast. The languages of different nations did not totally differ, nor were they so copious as those of the Europeans, particularly the English. They were therefore, easily learned; and, while I was journeying thus through Africa, I acquired two or three different tongues. In this manner I had been travelling for a considerable time, when, one evening, to my great surprise, whom should I see brought to the house where I was but my dear sister! As soon as she saw me, she gave a loud shriek, and ran into my arms—I was quite overpowered: neither of us could speak; but, for a considerable time, clung to each other in mutual embraces, unable to do any thing but weep. Our meeting affected all who saw us; and, indeed, I must acknowledge, in honor of those sable destroyers of human rights, that I never met with any ill treatment, or saw any offered to their slaves, except tying them, when necessary, to keep them from running away. When these people knew we were brother and sister, they indulged us to be together; and the man, to whom I supposed we belonged, lay with us, he in the middle, while she and I held one another by the hands across his breast all night; and thus for a while we forgot our misfortunes, in the joy of being together; but even this small comfort was soon to have an end; for scarcely had the fatal morning appeared when she was again torn from me forever! I was now more miserable, if possible, than before. The small relief which her presence gave me from pain, was gone, and the wretchedness of my situation was redoubled by my anxiety after her fate, and my apprehensions lest her sufferings should be greater than mine, when I could not be with her to alleviate them. Yes, thou dear partner of all my childish sports! thou sharer of my joys and sorrows! happy should I have ever esteemed myself to encounter every misery for you and to procure your freedom by the sacrifice of my own.—Though you were early forced from my arms, your image has been always rivetted in my heart, from which neither time nor fortune have been able to remove it; so that, while the thoughts of your sufferings have damped my prosperity, they have mingled with adversity and increased its bitterness. To that Heaven which protects the weak from the strong, I commit the care of your innocence and virtues, if they have not already received their full reward, and if your youth and delicacy have not long since fallen victims to the violence of the African trader, the pestilential stench of a Guinea ship, the seasoning in the European colonies, or the lash and lust of a brutal and unrelenting overseer.

I did not long remain after my sister. I was again sold, and carried through a number of places, till after travelling a considerable time, I came to a town called Tinmah, in the most beautiful country I had yet seen in Africa. It was extremely rich, and there were many rivulets which flowed through it, and supplied a large pond in the centre of the town, where the people washed. Here I first saw and tasted cocoa nuts, which I thought superior to any nuts I had ever tasted before; and the trees which were loaded, were also 5 interspersed among the houses, which had commodious shades adjoining, and were in the same manner as ours, the insides being neatly plastered and whitewashed. Here I also saw and tasted for the first time, sugar-cane. Their money consisted of little white shells, the size of the finger nail. I was sold here for one hundred and seventy-two of them, by a merchant who lived and brought me there. I had been about two or three days at his house, when a wealthy widow, a neighbor of his, came there one evening, and brought with her an only son, a young gentleman about my own age and size. Here they saw me; and, having taken a fancy to me, I was bought of the merchant, and went home with them. Her house and premises were situated close to one of those rivulets I have mentioned, and were the finest I ever saw in Africa: they were very extensive, and she had a number of slaves to attend her. The next day I was washed and perfumed, and when meal time came, I was led into the presence of my mistress, and ate and drank before her with her son. This filled me with astonishment; and I could scarce help expressing my surprise that the young gentleman should suffer me, who was bound, to eat with him who was free; and not only so, but that he would not at any time either eat or drink till I had taken first, because I was the eldest, which was agreeable to our custom. Indeed, every thing here, and all their treatment of me, made me forget that I was a slave. The language of these people resembled ours so nearly, that we understood each other perfectly. They had also the very same customs as we. There were likewise slaves daily to attend us, while my young master and I, with other boys, sported with our darts and bows and arrows, as I had been used to do at home. In this resemblance to my former happy state, I passed about two months; and I now began to think I was to be adopted into the family, and was beginning to be reconciled to my situation, and to forget by degrees my misfortunes, when all at once the delusion vanished; for, without the least previous knowledge, one morning early, while my dear master and companion was still asleep, I was awakened out of my reverie to fresh sorrow, and hurried away even amongst the uncircumcised.

Thus, at the very moment I dreamed of the greatest happiness, I found myself most miserable; and it seemed as if fortune wished to give me this taste of joy only to render the reverse more poignant.—The change I now experienced, was as painful as it was sudden and unexpected. It was a change indeed, from a state of bliss to a scene which is inexpressible by me, as it discovered to me an element I had never before beheld, and till then had no idea of, and wherein such instances of hardship and cruelty continually occurred, as I can never reflect on but with horror.

All the nations and people I had hitherto passed through, resembled our own in their manners, customs, and language: but I came at length to a country, the inhabitants of which differed from us in all those particulars. I was very much struck with this difference, especially when I came among a people who did not circumcise, and ate without washing their hands. They cooked also in iron pots, and had European cutlasses and cross bows, which were unknown to us, and fought with their fists among themselves. Their women were not so modest as ours, for they ate, and drank, and slept with their men.

But above all, I was amazed to see no sacrifices or offerings among them. In some of those places the people ornamented themselves with scars, and likewise filed their teeth very sharp. They wanted sometimes to ornament me in the same manner, but I would not suffer them; hoping that I might some time be among a people who did not thus disfigure themselves, as I thought they did. At last I came to the banks of a large river which was covered with canoes, in which the people appeared to live with their household utensils, and provisions of all kinds. I was beyond measure astonished at this, as I had never before seen any water larger than a pond or a rivulet: and my surprise was mingled with no small fear when I was put into one of these canoes, and we began to paddle and move along the river. We continued going on thus till night, and when we came to land, and made fires on the banks, each family by themselves; some dragged their canoes on shore, others stayed and cooked in theirs, and laid in them all night. Those on the land had mats, of which they made tents, some in the shape of little houses; in these we slept; and after the morning meal, we embarked again and proceeded as before. I was often very much astonished to see some of the women, as well as the men, jump into the water, dive to the bottom, come up again, and swim about.—Thus I continued to travel, sometimes by land, sometimes by water, through different countries and various nations, till, at the end of six or seven months after I had been kidnapped, I arrived at the sea coast. It would be tedious and uninteresting to relate all the incidents which befel me during this journey, and which I have not yet forgotten; of the various hands I passed through, and the manners and customs of all the different people among whom I lived—I shall therefore only observe, that in all the places where I was, the soil was exceedingly rich; the pumpkins, eadas, plantains, yams, &c. &c. were in great abundance, and of incredible size. There were also vast quantities of different gums, though not used for any purpose, and every where a great deal of tobacco. The cotton even grew quite wild, and there was plenty of red-wood. I saw no mechanics whatever in all the way, except such as I have mentioned. The chief employment in all these countries was agriculture, and both the males and females, as with us, were brought up to it, and trained in the arts of war.

The first object which saluted my eyes when I arrived on the coast, was the sea, and a slave ship, which was then riding at anchor, and waiting for its cargo. These filled me with astonishment, which was soon converted into terror, when I was carried on board. I was immediately handled, and tossed up to see if I were sound, by some of the crew; and I was now persuaded that I had gotten into a world of bad spirits, and that they were going to kill me. Their complexions, too, differing so much from ours, their long hair, and the language they spoke (which was very different from any I had ever heard) united to confirm me in this belief. Indeed, such were the horrors of my views and fears at the moment, that, if ten thousand worlds had been my own, I would have freely parted with them all to have exchanged my condition with that of the meanest slave in my own country. When I looked round the ship too, and saw a large furnace of copper boiling, and a multitude of black people of every description chained together, every one of their countenances expressing dejection and sorrow, I no longer doubted of my fate; and, quite overpowered with horror and anguish, I fell motionless on the deck and fainted. When I recovered a little, I found some black people about me, who I believed were some of those who had brought me on board, and had been receiving their pay; they talked to me in order to cheer me, but all in vain. I asked them if we were not to be eaten by those white men with horrible looks, red faces, and long hair. They told me I was not: and one of the crew brought me a small portion of spirituous liquor in a wine glass, but, being afraid of him, I would not take it out of his hand. One of the blacks, therefore, took it from him and gave it to me, and I took a little down my palate, which, instead of reviving me, as they thought it would, threw me into the greatest consternation at the strange feeling it produced, having never tasted any such liquor before. Soon after this, the blacks who brought me on board went off, and left me abandoned to despair.

I now saw myself deprived of all chance of returning to my native country, or even the least glimpse of hope of gaining the shore, which I now considered as friendly; and I even wished for my former slavery in preference to my present situation, which was filled with horrors of every kind, still heightened by my ignorance of what I was to undergo. I was not long suffered to indulge my grief; I was soon put down under the decks, and there I received such a salutation in my nostrils as I had never experienced in my life: so that, with the loathsomeness of the stench, and crying together, I became so sick and low that I was not able to eat, nor had I the least desire to taste any thing. I now wished for the last friend, death, to relieve me; but soon, to my grief, two of the white men offered me eatables; and, on my refusing to eat, one of them held me fast by the hands, and laid me across, I think the windlass, and tied my feet, while the other flogged me severely. I had never experienced any thing of this kind before, and although not being used to the water, I naturally feared that element the first time I saw it, yet, nevertheless, could I have got over the nettings, I would have jumped over the side, but I could not; and besides, the crew used to watch us very closely who were not chained down to the decks, lest we should leap into the water; and I have seen some of these poor African prisoners most severely cut, for attempting to do so, and hourly whipped for not eating. This indeed was often the case with myself. In a little time after, amongst the poor chained men, I found some of my own nation, which in a small degree gave ease to my mind. I inquired of these what was to be done with us? they gave me to understand, we were to be carried to these white people's country to work for them. I then was a little revived, and thought, if it were no worse than working, my situation was not so desperate; but still I feared I should be put to death, the white people looked and acted, as I thought, in so savage a manner; for I had never seen among any people such instances of brutal cruelty; and this not only shown towards us blacks, but also to some of the whites themselves. One white man in particular I saw, when we were permitted to be on deck, flogged so unmercifully with a large rope near the foremast, that he died in consequence of it; and they tossed him over the side as they would have done a brute. This made me fear these people the more; and I expected nothing less than to be treated in the same manner. I could not help expressing my fears and apprehensions to some of my countrymen; I asked them if these people had no country, but lived in this hollow place? (the ship) they told me they did not, but came from a distant one. 'Then,' said I, 'how comes it in all our country we never heard of them?' They told me because they lived so very far off. I then asked where were their women? had they any like themselves? I was told they had. 'And why,' said I, 'do we not see them?' They answered, because they were left behind. I asked how the vessel could go? they told me they could not tell; but that there was cloth put upon the masts by the help of the ropes I saw, and then the vessel went on; and the white men had some spell or magic they put in the water when they liked, in order to stop the vessel. I was exceedingly amazed at this account, and really thought they were spirits. I therefore wished much to be from amongst them, for I expected they would sacrifice me; but my wishes were vain—for we were so quartered that it was impossible for any of us to make our escape.

While we stayed on the coast I was mostly on deck; and one day, to my great astonishment, I saw one of these vessels coming in with the sails up. As soon as the whites saw it, they gave a great shout, at which we were amazed; and the more so, as the vessel appeared larger by approaching nearer. At last, she came to an anchor in my sight, and when the anchor was let go, I and my countrymen who saw it, were lost in astonishment to observe the vessel stop—and were now convinced it was done by magic. Soon after this the other ship got her boats out, and they came on board of us, and the people of both ships seemed very glad to see each other.—Several of the strangers also shook hands with us black people, and made motions with their hands, signifying I suppose, we were to go to their country, but we did not understand them. 10

At last, when the ship we were in, had got in all her cargo, they made ready with many fearful noises, and we were all put under deck, so that we could not see how they managed the vessel. But this disappointment was the least of my sorrow. The stench of the hold while we were on the coast was so intolerably loathsome, that it was dangerous to remain there for any time, and some of us had been permitted to stay on the deck for the fresh air; but now that the whole ship's cargo were confined together, it became absolutely pestilential. The closeness of the place, and the heat of the climate, added to the number in the ship, which was so crowded that each had scarcely room to turn himself, almost suffocated us. This produced copious perspirations, so that the air soon became unfit for respiration, from a variety of loathsome smells, and brought on a sickness among the slaves, of which many died—thus falling victims to the improvident avarice, as I may call it, of their purchasers. This wretched situation which was again aggravated by the galling of the chains, now became insupportable; and the filth of the necessary tubs, into which the children often fell, and were almost suffocated. The shrieks of the women, and the groans of the dying, rendered the whole a scene of horror almost inconceivable. Happily perhaps, for myself, I was soon reduced so low here that it was thought necessary to keep me almost always on deck; and from my extreme youth I was not put in fetters. In this situation I expected every hour to share the fate of my companions, some of whom were almost daily brought upon deck at the point of death, which I began to hope would soon put an end to my miseries. Often did I think many of the inhabitants of the deep much more happy than myself. I envied them the freedom they enjoyed, and as often wished I could change my condition for theirs. Every circumstance I met with, served only to render my state more painful, and heightened my apprehensions; and my opinion of the cruelty of the whites.

One day they had taken a number of fishes; and when they had killed and satisfied themselves with as many as they thought fit, to our astonishment who were on deck, rather than give any of them to us to eat, as we expected, they tossed the remaining fish into the sea again, although we begged and prayed for some as well as we could, but in vain; and some of my countrymen, being pressed by hunger, took an opportunity, when they thought no one saw them, of trying to get a little privately; but they were discovered, and the attempt procured them some very severe floggings. One day, when we had a smooth sea and moderate wind, two of my wearied countrymen who were chained together, (I was near them at the time,) preferring death to such a life of misery, somehow made through the nettings and jumped into the sea: immediately, another quite dejected fellow, who, on account of his illness, was suffered to be out of irons, also followed their example; and I believe many more would very soon have done the same, if they had not been prevented by the ship's crew, who were instantly alarmed. Those of us that were the most active, were in a moment put down under the deck, and there was such a noise and confusion amongst the people of the ship as I never heard before, to stop her, and get the boat out to go after the slaves. However, two of the wretches were drowned, but they got the other, and afterwards flogged him unmercifully, for thus attempting to prefer death to slavery. In this manner we continued to undergo more hardships than I can now relate, hardships which are inseparable from this accursed trade. Many a time we were near suffocation from the want of fresh air, which we were often without for whole days together. This, and the stench of the necessary tubs, carried off many.

During our passage, I first saw flying fishes, which surprised me very much; they used frequently to fly across the ship, and many of them fell on the deck. I also now first saw the use of the quadrant; I had often with astonishment seen the mariners make observations with it, and I could not think what it meant. They at last took notice of my surprise; and one of them, willing to increase it, as well as to gratify my curiosity, made me one day look through it. The clouds appeared to me to be land, which disappeared as they passed along. This heightened my wonder; and I was now more persuaded than ever, that I was in another world, and that every thing about me was magic. At last, we came in sight of the island of Barbadoes, at which the whites on board gave a great shout, and made many signs of joy to us. We did not know what to think of this; but as the vessel drew nearer, we plainly saw the harbor, and other ships of different kinds and sizes, and we soon anchored amongst them, off Bridgetown. Many merchants and planters now came on board, though it was in the evening. They put us in separate parcels, and examined us attentively. They also made us jump, and pointed to the land, signifying we were to go there. We thought by this, we should be eaten by these ugly men, as they appeared to us; and, when soon after we were all put down under the deck again, there was much dread and trembling among us, and nothing but bitter cries to be heard all the night from these apprehensions, insomuch, that at last the white people got some old slaves from the land to pacify us. They told us we were not to be eaten, but to work, and were soon to go on land, where we should see many of our country people. This report eased us much. And sure enough, soon after we were landed, there came to us Africans of all languages.

We were conducted immediately to the merchant's yard, where we were all pent up together, like so many sheep in a fold, without regard to sex or age. As every object was new to me, every thing I saw filled me with surprise. What struck me first, was, that the houses were built with bricks and stories, and in every other respect different from those I had seen in Africa; but I was still more astonished on seeing people on horseback. I did not know what this could mean; and, indeed, I thought these people were full of nothing but magical arts. While I was in this astonishment, one of my fellow-prisoners spoke to a countryman of his, about the horses, who said they were the same kind they had in their country. I understood them, though they were from a distant part of Africa; and I thought it odd I had not seen any horses there; but afterwards, when I came to converse with different Africans, I found they had many horses amongst them, and much larger than those I then saw.

We were not many days in the merchant's custody, before we were sold after their usual manner which is this:—On a signal given, (as the beat of a drum,) the buyers rush at once into the yard where the slaves are confined, and make choice of that parcel they like best. The noise and clamor with which this is attended, and the eagerness visible in the countenances of the buyers, serve not a little to increase the apprehension of terrified Africans, who may well be supposed to consider them as the ministers of that destruction to which they think themselves devoted. In this manner, without scruple, are relations and friends separated, most of them never to see each other again. I remember, in the vessel in which I was brought over, in the men's apartment, there were several brothers, who, in the sale, were sold in different lots; and it was very moving on this occasion, to see and hear their cries at parting. O, ye nominal Christians! might not an African ask you—Learned you this from your God, who says unto you, Do unto all men as you would men should do unto you? Is it not enough that we are torn from our country and friends, to toil for your luxury and lust of gain? Must every tender feeling be likewise sacrificed to your avarice? Are the dearest friends and relations, now rendered more dear by their separation from their kindred, still to be parted from each other, and thus prevented from cheering the gloom of slavery, with the small comfort of being together, and mingling their sufferings and sorrows? Why are parents to lose their children, brothers their sisters, or husbands their wives? Surely, this is a new refinement in cruelty, which, while it has no advantage to atone for it, thus aggravates distress, and adds fresh horrors even to the wretchedness of slavery.

DISCUSSING THE TEXT

1. Think of some ideas, or preconceptions, you have had about African life and about the way Africans became slaves. Which of these preconceptions does this chapter from Equiano's *Life* modify or overturn?
2. How does Equiano describe the culture of Africa into which he is born? What was it like to be a child in such a world?
3. Equiano fears being attacked by animals while in Africa, but when he falls into the hands of the slave traders he fears being eaten by them; he sees them as "savages." How do you think Equiano's audience in the late eighteenth century would have reacted to this fear? How do you react now? What does Equiano's fear teach us about cultural encounters? Discuss these issues in a group of four or five students. Take notes, and be prepared to share your opinions with the class.

WRITING ABOUT THE TEXT

4. In paragraph 11, Equiano writes that the slaves on the ship were victims of an "improvident avarice." Write a one-page discussion of what you think Equiano means by the phrase "improvident avarice," drawing on examples from the chapter included here.
5. At times Equiano seems to write from an African sensibility, while at other times he writes like an Anglo-American. What elements of his writing demonstrate these aspects of his voice and identity? Make a list of examples, looking especially at the kinds of things Equiano notices, the words he uses to describe his feelings, allusions, quotations, figures of speech, and so on. When you have completed your list, write a brief essay comparing and contrasting these two sides of Equiano's voice as a writer.
6. Try to imagine what it was like to be a slave on a slave ship. Besides this excerpt from Equiano's *Life,* you might want to look into other accounts of the horrors of the middle passage. Rewrite Equiano's description of the journey here in your own contemporary words.

OSCAR HANDLIN

The Ghettos

The United States, from the moment of its "discovery" by European explorers and settlers, has had the image of a land of great opportunity, and this reputation has drawn millions of people from all over the world. Yet immigrants to this country, arriving with the grandest of hopes, were also exiles from their homelands. As such, they suffered a sense of dislocation. The nineteenth-century immigrants, most often from Britain, the European continent, Scandinavia, Asia, and Russia, came with few resources in education and money. What they discovered as they moved into the major cities of the United States was often a shock to them. The prairies, if they got that far, offered a different kind of shock.

In this chapter from his book The Uprooted, *Oscar Handlin describes the places that immigrants moved into once they arrived in the United States. He also addresses the challenges to the immigrants' survival, and the quality of their lives in these new places. Handlin wrote* The Uprooted *for a general audience, and in it he seeks to find what was common among the experiences of the various immigrant groups, or what the typical immigrant experience was like. Handlin's book provides a description of conditions from around the mid-nineteenth century to the early twentieth century, but you may want to ask how relevant its observations are to contemporary urban life and to the experience of today's immigrants to the United States.*

Oscar Handlin was born in 1915, the son of Jewish immigrants, and was raised in Brooklyn, where he went to Brooklyn College. In 1951 he won the Pulitzer Prize in history for The Uprooted, *one of many honors and prizes awarded him over his long career as a widely respected historian. Handlin has taught at Harvard University for many years.*

The place was important too. Settlement in America had snipped the continuity of the immigrants' work and ideas, of their religious life. It would also impose a new relationship to the world of space about them. In the Old Country setting, the physical scene had been integral with the existence of the men in it. Changes would have explosive repercussions.

In the United States, the newcomers pushed their roots into many different soils. Along the city's unyielding asphalt streets, beside the rutted roads of mill or mining towns, amidst the exciting prairie acres, they established the homes of the New World. But wherever the immigrants went, there was one common experience they shared: nowhere could they transplant the European village. Whatever the variations among environments in America, none was familiar. The pressure of that strangeness exerted a deep influence upon the character of resettlement, upon the usual forms of behavior, and upon the modes of communal action that emerged as the immigrants became Americans.

The old conditions of living could not survive in the new conditions of space. Ways long taken for granted in the village adjusted slowly and painfully to density of population in the cities, to disorder in the towns, and to distance on the farms. That adjustment was the means of creating the new communities within which these people would live.

Although the great mass of immigrants spent out their days in the great cities, there was always an unorganized quality to settlement in such places that left a permanent impress upon every fresh arrival. Chance was so large an element in the course of migration, it left little room for planning. The place of landing was less often the outcome of an intention held at the outset of the journey than of blind drift along the routes of trade or of a sudden halt due to the accidents of the voyage. Consequently the earliest concentrations of the foreign-born were in the chain of Atlantic seaports: Boston, Philadelphia, Baltimore, New Orleans, and most of all New York, the unrivaled mart of Europe's commerce with America. For the same reasons, later concentrations appeared at the inland termini, the points of exchange between rail and river or lake traffic—Cleveland, Chicago, Cincinnati, Pittsburgh, and St. Louis.

In all such places the newcomers pitched themselves in the midst of communities that were already growing rapidly and that were therefore already crowded. Between 1840 and 1870, for instance, the population of New York City mounted by fully 50 per cent every ten years, for every two people at the start of a decade, there were three at its end. (In all, the 312,000 residents of 1840 had become 3,437,000 in 1900.) Chicago's rise was even more precipitate; the 4000 inhabitants there in 1840 numbered 1,700,000 in 1900. Every ten-year interval saw two people struggling for the space formerly occupied by one. 5

These largest cities were representative of the rest. The natural increase through the excess of births over deaths, with the additional increase through the shift of native-born population from rural to urban areas, and with the further increase through overseas immigration, all contributed to the enormous growth of American municipalities. To house all the new city dwellers was a problem of staggering proportions. Facilities simply did not keep pace with the demand.

To house the immigrants was more difficult still. For these people had not the mobility to choose where they should live or the means to choose how. Existing on the tenuous income supplied by unskilled labor, they could not buy homes; nor could they lay out much in payment of rent. Their first thought in finding accommodations was that the cost be as little as possible. The result was they got as little as possible.

The willingness to accept a minimum of comfort and convenience did not, however, mean that such quarters would always be available. Under the first impact of immigration, the unprepared cities had not ready the housing immigrants could afford. The newcomers were driven to accept hand-me-downs, vacated places that could be converted to their service at a profit.

The immigrants find their first homes in quarters the old occupants no longer desire. As business grows, the commercial center of each city begins to blight the neighboring residential districts. The well-to-do are no longer willing to live in close proximity to the bustle of warehouses and offices; yet that same proximity sets a high value on real estate. To spend money on the repair or upkeep of houses in such areas is only wasteful; for they will soon be torn down to make way for commercial buildings. The simplest, most profitable use is to divide the old mansions into tiny lodgings. The rent on each unit will be low; but the aggregate of those sums will, without substantial investment or risk, return larger dividends than any other present use of the property.

Such accommodations have additional attractions for the immigrants. 10 They are close to the familiar region of the docks and they are within walking distance of the places where labor is hired; precious carfare will be saved by living here. In every American city some such district of first settlement receives the newcomers.

Not that much is done to welcome them. The carpenters hammer shut connecting doors and build rude partitions up across the halls; middle-class homes thus become laborers'—only not one to a family, but shared among many. What's more, behind the original structures are grassy yards where children once had run about at play. There is to be no room for games now. Sheds and shanties, hurriedly thrown up, provide living space; and if a stable is there, so much the better: that too can be turned to account. In 1850 already in New York some seven thousand households are finding shelter in such rear buildings. By this time too ingenuity has uncovered still other resources: fifteen hundred cellars also do service as homes.

If these conversions are effected without much regard for the convenience of the ultimate occupants, they nevertheless have substantial advantages. The carpenter aims to do the job as expeditiously as possible; he has not the time to contrive the most thorough use of space; and waste square feet leave luxurious corners. There are limits to the potentialities for crowding in such quarters.

There were no such limits when enterprising contractors set to work devising edifices more suitable for the reception of these residents. As the population continued to grow, and the demand with it, perspicacious owners of real estate saw profit in the demolition of the old houses and the construction, between narrow alleys, of compact barracks that made complete use of every inch of earth.

Where once had been Mayor Delavall's orchard, Cherry Street in New York ran its few blocks to the East River shipyards. At Number 36, in 1853, stood Gotham Court, one of the better barracks buildings. Five stories in height, it stretched back one hundred and fifty feet from the street, between two tight alleys (one nine, the other seven feet wide). Onto the more spacious alley opened twelve doors through each of which passed the ten families that lived within, two to each floor in identical two-room apartments (one room, 9 × 14; one bedroom, 9 × 6). Here without interior plumbing or heat were the homes of five hundred people. Ten years later, there were some improvements: for the service of the community, a row of privies in the basement, flushed occasionally by Croton water.[1] But by then there were more than eight hundred dwellers in the structure, which indeed continued in use till the very end of the century.

That these conditions were not then reckoned outlandish was shown in 15 the model workmen's home put up by philanthropic New Yorkers at Elizabeth and Mott Street. Each suite in this six-story structure had three rooms; but the rooms were smaller (4 × 11, 8 × 7, and 8 × 7). There were gas lights in the halls; but the water closets were in sheds in the alleys. And well over half the rooms had no windows at all.

At the middle of the nineteenth century, these developments were still chaotic, dependent upon the fancy of the individual builder. But the pressure of rising demand and the pattern of property holding gradually shaped a common form for the tenement house. The older barracks still left waste space in alleys, halls, and stair wells; and they did not conform to the uniform city real-estate plot, twenty or twenty-five feet wide and one hundred feet deep. As the cost of land went up, builders were increasingly constrained to confine themselves to those rectangular blocks while pushing their edifices upward and eliminating the interstitial alleys.

Ultimately, the dumbbell tenement lined street after street, a most efficient structure that consumed almost the entire area of the real-estate plot. Attached to its neighbors on either side, it left vacant only a strip, perhaps ten feet deep, in the rear. On a floor space of approximately twenty by ninety feet, it was possible, within this pattern, to get four four-room apartments.

The feat was accomplished by narrowing the building at its middle so that it took on the shape of a dumbbell. The indentation was only two-and-a-half feet wide and varied in length from five to fifty feet; but, added to the similar indentations of the adjoining houses, it created on each side an airshaft five feet wide. In each apartment three of the rooms could present their windows to the shaft, draw from it air and light as well; only one chamber in each suite need face upon the street or rear yard. The stairs, halls, and common water closets were cramped into the narrow center of the building so that almost the whole of its surface was available for living quarters.

These structures were at least six stories in height, sometimes eight. At the most moderate reckoning, twenty-four to thirty-two families could be housed on this tiny space, or more realistically, anywhere from one hundred and fifty to two hundred human beings. It was not a long block that held ten such tenements on either side of the street, not an unusual block that was home for some four thousand people.

There were drastic social consequences to living under these dense con- 20 ditions. The immigrants had left villages which counted their populations in scores. In the Old World a man's whole circle of acquaintances had not taken

---

[1]*Croton water:* a main reservoir in upstate New York providing water to New York City (*Ed.*)

in as many individuals as lived along a single street here. By a tortuous course of adjustments, the newcomers worked out new modes of living in response to their environment. But the cost of those adjustments was paid out of the human energies of the residents and through the physical deterioration of the districts in which they lived.

The tenement flourished most extensively in New York, the greatest point of immigrant concentration. But it was also known in Boston and in the other Atlantic ports. In the interior cities it was less common; there land values were not so rigid and commercial installations not such barriers to the centrifugal spread of population. From the barracklike buildings of the area of first settlement, the immigrants could move out to smaller units where at least the problems of density were less oppressive. Little two-story cottages that held six families were characteristic of places like Buffalo. Elsewhere were wooden three- or four-floor structures that contained a dozen households. Even single homes were to be found, dilapidated shanties or jerry-built boxes low in rent. Yet internally these accommodations were not superior to those of the tenement. In one form or another, the available housing gave the districts to which the immigrants went the character of slums.

Well, they were not ones to choose, who had lived in the thatched peasant huts of home. Nor was it unbearably offensive to reside in the least pleasant parts of the city, in Chicago over against the slaughterhouses, in Boston hemmed in by the docks and markets of the North End, in New York against the murky river traffic of the East Side. Such disadvantages they could survive. The hardship came in more subtle adjustments demanded of them.

Certainly the flats were small and overcrowded. In no room of the dumbbell tenement could you pace off more than eleven feet; and the reforming architects of 1900 still thought of chambers no larger than those of Gotham Court. In addition, the apartments shrank still further when shared by more than one family or when they sheltered lodgers, as did more than half those in New York at the end of the century. But that was not the worst of it.

Here is a woman. In the Old Country she had lived much of her life, done most of her work, outdoors. In America, the flat confines her. She divides up her domain by calico sheets hung on ropes, tries to make a place for her people and possessions. But there is no place and she has not room to turn about. It is true, everything is in poor repair, the rain comes through the ceilings, the wind blows dirt through the cracks in the wall. But she does not even know how to go about restoring order, establishing cleanliness. She breaks her back to exterminate the proliferating vermin. What does she get? A dozen lice behind the collar.

The very simplest tasks become complex and disorganizing. Every day there is a family to feed. Assume she knows how to shop, and can manage the unfamiliar coal stove or gas range. But what does one do with rubbish who has never known the meaning of waste? It is not really so important to walk down the long flight of narrow stairs each time there are some scraps to be disposed of. The windows offer an easier alternative. After all, the obnoxious 25 wooden garbage boxes that adorn the littered fronts of the houses expose their contents unashamed through split sides and, rarely emptied, themselves become the nests of boldly foraging rodents.

The filthy streets are seldom cleaned; the municipality is not particularly solicitous of these, the poorest quarters of the city. The alleys are altogether passed by and the larger thoroughfares receive only occasionally the services of the scavenger. The inaccessible alleys and rear yards are never touched and, to be sure, are redolent of the fact. In the hot summer months the stench of rotting things will mark these places and the stained snow of winter will not conceal what lies beneath. Here and there an unwitting newcomer tries the disastrous experiment of keeping a goat, adds thereby to the distinctive flavor of his neighborhood.

It was the same in every other encounter with the new life. Conveniences not missed in the villages became sore necessities in the city; although often the immigrants did not know their lack till dear experience taught them. Of what value were sunlight and fresh air on the farm? But how measure their worth for those who lived in the three hundred and fifty thousand dark interior rooms of New York in 1900!

There was the rude matter of what Americans called sanitation. Some of the earliest buildings had had no privies at all; the residents had been expected to accommodate themselves elsewhere as best they could. Tenements from midcentury onward had generally water closets in the yards and alleys, no great comfort to the occupants of the fifth and sixth floors. The newest structures had two toilets to each floor; but these were open to the custom of all comers, charged to the care of none, and left to the neglect of all. If in winter the pipes froze in unheated hallways and the clogged contents overflowed, weeks would go by before some dilatory repairman set matters right. Months thereafter a telling odor hung along the narrow hallways.

What of it? The filth was inescapable. In these districts where the need was greatest, the sewage systems were primitive and ineffectual. Open drains were long common; in Boston one such, for years, tumbled down the slope of Jacob's Ladder in the South Cove; and in Chicago the jocosely named Bubbly Creek wended its noisome way aboveground until well into the twentieth century.

With the water supply there had always been trouble at home too: poor wells, shallow, and inconveniently situated. The inconvenience here was not unexpected. Still it was a burden to carry full tubs and jugs from the taps in the alley up the steep stairs. Not till late was city water directly connected with the toilets; it was later still to reach the kitchen sink; and bathrooms had not yet put in an appearance in these quarters. Then, too, the consequences were more painful: city dirt was harder to scrub away, and there was no nearby creek. It could well be, as they came to say, that a man got a good bath only twice in his life: from midwife and undertaker.

All might yet be tolerable were not the confining dimensions of the flat so oppressive. The available space simply would not yield to all the demands made upon it. Where were the children to play if the fields were gone? Where were things to be stored or clothes to be hung? Beds or bedding consumed the bedroom; there was only one living room, and sink and stove left little free of that. The man in the evening, come home from work, found not a niche for rest; the tiny intervals of leisure were wasted for want of a place to spend them. Privacy now was more often sought for than in the Old Country where every person and every thing had its accustomed spot. Yet privacy now was difficult to achieve; there was no simple way of dividing space too small to share. Under pressure of the want, the constricted beings bowed to a sense of strain.

Disorganization affects particularly the life of the home. In these tiny rooms that now are all they call their home, many traditional activities wither and disappear. Not here will the friends be welcomed, festivals commemorated, children taught, and the family unite to share in the warmth of its security. Emptied of the meaning of these occurrences and often crowded with strange lodgers, home is just the feeding and sleeping place. All else moves to the outside.

The street becomes the great artery of life for the people of these districts. Sometimes, the boys and girls play in back in the narrow yards, looking up at the lines of drying clothes that spiderweb the sky above them. More often the crowded street itself is the more attractive playground. They run in games through the moving traffic, find fun in the appearance of some hopeful street musician, or regard with dejected envy the wares of the itinerant vendors of seasonal delicacies, the sweet shaved ice of summer, the steaming potatoes and chestnuts of fall and winter.

The adults too drift out, sit on the steps, flow over onto the sidewalks. The women bring their work outdoors, the men at evening hang about, now and then talk. They begin to be neighborly, learn to be sensitive to each other. That is the good of it.

There is also the bad. The street in its strangeness is the evidence of the old home's disintegration. Why, the very aspect is forbidding: the dear sun never shines brightly, the still air between the high buildings is so saturated with stench it would take a dragon to hold out. These are all signs of the harshness of the physical environment, of the difficulties of living in these quarters, of the disintegration here of old ways. Those children in earnest play at the corner—who controls them, to what discipline are they subject? They do not do the things that children ought. No one does the things he ought. The place prevents it. 35

Almost resignedly, the immigrants witnessed in themselves a deterioration. All relationships became less binding, all behavior more dependent on individual whim. The result was a marked personal decline and a noticeable wavering of standards.

Some of the reactions to the new conditions of living were immediate, direct, and overt. The low level of health and the high incidence of disease were certain products of overcrowding. Residents of the tenements did not need the spotted maps of later students to tell them where tuberculosis hit, a terror of an illness that spread from victim to victim in the stifling rooms. If the cholera came, or smallpox, or diphtheria—and all did in their time—it was impossible to limit their decimating course. Little else by now remained communal; but contagion and infection these people could not help but share with each other.

The mortality rate was an indication of their helplessness against disease. The immigrants were men and women in the prime of life, yet they died more rapidly than the generality of Americans. Everywhere their life expectancy was lower; and, as might be anticipated, it was particularly infants who suffered. In one Chicago precinct at the end of the nineteenth century, three babies of every five born died before they reached their first birthday.

▼ ▼ ▼

There were other means of release, temporary of duration and therefore more subject to control. It was thus possible, for a time, to dissolve in alcohol the least soluble of problems. After a day's effort to hammer happiness out of the unyielding American environment it was good, now and then, to go not to the narrow realities of home but to the convivial places where the glass played the main part. The setting could take a variety of forms: basement shops, combination kitchen-and-bars, little cafés, the Irish grocery of 1850, the German *Bierstube*[2] of 1870, the Italian speakeasy of 1900 to which prohibition would later bring another clientele. But the end was the same, a temporary relaxation of tension. And the end was so clear that some could achieve it alone, in the fastness of their own rooms, with the solitary company of a bottle.

There were immigrants who came to America with the inclination to drunkenness already well established. In Ireland, whisky went farther than bread as a relief from hunger; in Norway, eighteen quarts of alcohol were consumed for every person in the country each year; and elsewhere through Europe the habit of imbibing was well known. There were other newcomers who learned to know the consolations of a dram in the course of the crossing. A bit of grog was the regular prescription for seasickness; if it effected no cure, it dulled the misery.

It was that relief a man needed as much as the eyes in his head. Sometimes he drank away without thought what he had bathed in sweat to earn; but he gained in return an interval free of recollection or anticipation. In the good company, as his burdens lightened, he discovered in himself altogether unexpected but exhilarating powers, acquired daring and self-confidence beyond any sober hope. Well, and sometimes it would lead to a brawl, and the falling clubs of policemen, and the cold awakening of a cell; or, if not that, simply to the next day's throbbing reckoning of costs: what things the money might have bought! But there was none to point the finger of blame; and

---

[2]*Bierstube:* tap-room or bar (*Ed.*)

temptation came again and again. Not a few succumbed in every group of immigrants, though more in some groups than in others.

There was still another way of entering immediately into a realm of hope that shone in bright contrast to the visible dreariness about them. In that realm the evil dame, Chance, was transfigured into a luminous goddess; no longer as in real life did she strike down the lowly, but elevated them. Chance, here, ceased to deal out disaster; instead, conjured up the most heartwarming dreams.

Sometimes the men gambled among themselves, drew cards or lots for little stakes. There was a finger game Italians played, and among eastern Europeans a liking for pinochle. But these were sociable as much as gambling occasions, and had unpleasant disadvantages. The sum of little fortunes around the table hardly made a total worth the winning. One man's gain was another's loss; the joy of one, another's sorrow. Chance had not free rein; skill was as well involved, and the strain of calculation. Most of all, there was not the solitude in which the mind could drift away from time and place and rock itself in the comfort of hope.

Much preferable was some form of the lottery: the stakes were small, the rewards enormous; one might win, but none lost much; and chance was absolute. Lottery took many guises from the informal picks and chances of bar and shop to the highly organized enterprises city-wide in extension. Beneath was the attractiveness of an identical dream.

He can sit with a card, one of scores, in a club or saloon, check the squares, wait the call. Over and over and over again the little cage spins and no one knows when the little cage stops and a little ball hops and the number comes forth for the fortunate man. There's no telling—who knows? This may be when. The word's on his lips; let but chance give the sign and he will rise, *keno, lotto, bingo;* and all will be his. 45

She buys the slip from a policy man, who may be the corner grocer, the mailman, or anyone who in a daily round encounters a constant circle of people. Her number costs what she can spare, a dime, a nickel, just a penny. She chooses by what signs chance may give, a dream, an omen, a sudden intuition; and all day carries hope in her apron.

Did they really think to win who could not afford to lose? Yes, in a way they did, although they knew what odds were against them. But *why not* they? They would grant you that thousands lost for one who won, but could they surrender that one hope too? His hand that holds the card is soft and white, a hand that signs checks and gestures commands, the hand of a man who will drive to the comfort of a decent home. Her slip rests in the pocket of a gown, a gown that rustles leisurely as she walks with shining children up the steps. Indeed they have so often spent the money, and had the pleasure of dreaming it, it hardly mattered that they lost. At the price they paid, such dreams were cheap enough.

▼ ▼ ▼

Without a doubt they wished also to escape from the physical environment itself. As the years went by they got to know that the city held also pleasant tree-shaded streets where yards and little gardens set the houses off from each other. To these green spaces the most daring hearts aspired.

After 1850, cheaper rapid-transit systems brought the suburbs closer to the heart of the city. On the street railway the trolley took the horse's place and was joined by subway and elevated lines. Through these channels, the laboring masses spilled out from the district of first settlement to the surrounding regions. Naturally, this was a selective process; those who had a modicum of well-being, who could afford the higher rents and transportation charges, moved most freely. The poorest were immobilized by their poverty.

Those who went gained by going, but not by any means all they hoped for. Somehow, what they touched turned to dross. The fine house they saw in their mind's vision across the bridge or over the ferry turned out in actuality to have been converted into narrow flats for several families. In the empty spaces, little cottages rose; and long rows of two- and three-story attached buildings shut off the sight of the trees. The trouble was, so many moved that these newer places began to repeat the experience of the area of first settlement. 50

Never mind, for a time at least it was better. There was room to keep a goat, a few chickens; the men could sit at ease in their own front rooms facing the friendly street, while the women visited through the sociable low windows. This was a home to which attachments could grow, a place where deviations were less likely to appear.

And if in time the pressure of mounting population brought here too the tenement, and the spreading slum engulfed this first refuge, then those who could launched upon a second remove. Then a third. Till at last the city was a patchwork of separated districts, the outlines of which were shaped by the transit facilities, by the quality of available housing, and by the prior occupancy of various groups of immigrants. Always in this winnowing process the poorest were left in the older sections; the ability to move outward went with prosperity. Unfortunately it was the outer regions that were the thinnest settled. Least capable of organizing their lives to the new environment, the great mass long clustered at the center.

On the farms, space was too ample, not too little. Emptiness, not overcrowding, was the disorganizing element; and for those whose habits of life were developed in the peasant village, the emptiness of the prairie farm was in its own way as troublesome as the crowding of the city slum.

Here they called them neighbors who lived two or three miles off. Here one could stand on the highest rise of land and see nowhere but in the one farmstead any sign of man's tenancy. Such distances were too great to permit easy adjustment by the newcomers.

The peculiar characteristics of the prairie where the distances were greatest tested the immigrants to the utmost. In the midst of the open places they came by wagon and confronted the problem of shelter. They would live 55 in what they could themselves build, for there was no community to help them; and certainly nothing was ready, awaiting their arrival. If they were fortunate, they found a nearby wood where the stove could rest and they could camp while the men chopped the logs for the cabin.

The cabin, no doubt, had its defects as a residence. It was small, perhaps twelve by fourteen feet in all; and above and below and about was mud, for the floor was as they found it and the spaces in the roof and walls were chinked with clay to keep the weather out.

But the people who settled into such quarters had only to compare situations with those who found no wood nearby, to count their own blessings. The cost of bringing timber in was at first prohibitive. If there were none on the spot, home would be of another material. Some would burrow dugouts into the slopes, return unknowingly to the life of the caves. Many cut the sun-baked surface of the earth, piled the sod in a double wall with dirt between, and in these huts spent a long period of trial.

Often years went by before such farmers advanced to the dignity of a frame house, with separate plastered rooms. There were first a barn and all the appurtenances of agriculture to be acquired. Meanwhile they got on in narrow quarters, felt the wind of winter through the cracks, heard the sides settle in the spring thaw, saw surprised snakes or gophers penetrate the floor.

Under such circumstances, there was an additional depth to their helplessness. No trees shielded them against the blast of winds. They were parched in the dry heat and they perished in the merciless blizzards. Hail and drought came and the clouds of grasshoppers that ate up their crops. On a limited monotonous diet the immigrants sickened, from the sudden shifts in climate the ague[3] got them, from the prevalence of dirt, the itch. No doctors were near and home remedies or self-prescribed cures from bottles put a sad but decisive end to their misery. Alone in these distances they could expect no help.

That was the worst of it. The isolation which all immigrants sensed to some degree, on the farm was absolute; and not only on the prairie but everywhere. In the older Midwestern states, where the newcomers were not the first to settle, they found homes built and clearings made at their arrival; and soil and climate were not so hostile. Still, even there, they were detached, cut off from the company of other men. Each family was thrown in upon itself; every day the same faces round the same table and never the sight of outsiders. To have no familiar of one's own age and sex was a hard deprivation. 60

They would think sometimes of the friendly village ways, of the common tasks lightened for being done in common; they would remember the cheering inn, and the road on which some reassuring known figure could always be seen. At such times, alone in the distance, helpless in their isolation, a vague and disturbing melancholia fell over them. It was easier for them when they added acres and when stocked barns and heavy wagonloads gave

---

[3]*ague:* fever, chills, shaking (*Ed.*)

a sense of substance and achievement to their lives. Still, even then would come regrets for the disorganization wrought in their existence by the place. Insanity appeared among some; others sought solace in alcohol; and most continued to work, under strain, eager for relief.

They would probably have said that it was the mill town made the least demand upon them. This was not so large as a single city ward and here space was not at a premium; yet neither was there here the complete isolation of the farm. The immigrants' round of activities here fell into a unit the size of which they could comprehend.

What pressure there was came from the situation of such communities. Often a single company or at most a single industry supplied the employment for all the residents. Any man who came to work in the mine or factory was altogether dependent upon the sole hirer. He was not free to choose among jobs or to argue long about terms; he could only acquiesce or leave. In that sense, it was a condition of his membership in this community that he cut himself off from the world outside the town.

Confined within the immediate locality, the laborers discovered that there was plenty of space, but not plenty of housing. Despite the low density of population, the available quarters were so restricted there was serious overcrowding. As the workers arrived they found at first only the farm or village buildings, quickly converted to their use. The single men were likely to live in makeshift boarding-houses; those with families in cup-up portions of the old houses. Shortly either the company or individual investors threw up additional facilities. Into the surrounding farm land, narrow alleys were pushed, lined with three-story frame tenements or with tiny two-room cottages. The company which controlled all was hardly interested in increasing the supply of housing to an unprofitable excess over demand; nor was it anxious to go to the expense of providing gas, water, and sewerage. The results matched those of the city slums.

Still, the open fields were not far off, and there was not the same total lack of space. The disorganizing effects of the environment were therefore probably less harsh, the deviations less pronounced. What strain there was, was the product of confinement in the town and of constricted housing. 65

To some degree, these factory town immigrants, like those who went to the cities and those who settled on farms, found the physical conditions of life in America hostile. Nowhere could they recapture the terms of village life; everywhere a difficult adjustment began with the disorganization of the individual, now grown uncertain as to his own proper role. Reorganization would involve first the creation of new means of social action within which the man alone could locate himself.

From the physical as from the religious experience with the New World, the immigrants had gained a deep consciousness of their separateness. It seemed sometimes as if there were only one street in the world, and only a single house on it, and nothing more—only walls and very few people, so that *I am in America and I do not even know whether it is America.* This street was apart as if a ghetto wall defined it. On other streets were other men, deeply different because they had not the burden of this adjustment to bear. This street and those did not run into each other; nor this farm into those. If the immigrants were to achieve the adjustment to their new environment, it had to be within the confines of the ghettos the environment created.

DISCUSSING THE TEXT

1. How does Handlin describe the living conditions in the slums of the big cities that first housed the immigrants? How do these conditions compare with village life in the "Old World"? To what extent does Handlin's description of the slums of the late nineteenth and early twentieth centuries match the urban slums of our own day?
2. In Handlin's account, what factors led to the crowded and unsanitary living conditions of newly arrived immigrants to the cities? Do you think that these contributing factors still affect the living conditions of some people today? If so, which people are affected, and in what ways? If not, what do you think has changed? Discuss these questions with other students in small groups.
3. What were the problems of immigrants who moved to the prairies? How did their lives compare with those of urban immigrants? Can you think of any contemporary situations that replicate this particular pattern of migration?
4. Working in groups of four or five students, try to draw a "blueprint" of one floor in the dumbbell tenement building Handlin describes in paragraphs 16–21. Try to picture the actual space of a tenement apartment by measuring off within your own classroom the dimensions that Handlin provides. How do these spaces compare with spaces in which you have lived?

WRITING ABOUT THE TEXT

5. When home becomes just the "feeding and sleeping place," as Handlin calls it, the street becomes the more active place for social life. How does Handlin evaluate the quality of life on the street? How does he account for the high consumption of alcohol and the attractions of gambling among urban immigrant populations? What needs do these activities reflect? Write a two- to three-page essay addressing these questions.
6. In paragraph 35, Handlin writes that on the street, "No one does the things he ought. The place prevents it." Drawing on your own experience as well as that of people you have known, write an argument for or against the idea that people's behavior is a product of their physical surroundings.
7. Handlin moves back and forth between the past and present verb tenses in this selection. Why do you think he does this? Try to get a sense of the effect of these changes in tense by rewriting a section of the piece; within this section, change all present tense verbs to past tense verbs, and vice versa. What effect do these changes have?
8. Do some research into your state's, or a nearby state's, official lottery. Who usually participates in this lottery? Where does the money spent on lottery tickets go? Compare your findings with the things Handlin says about chance and gambling in paragraphs 42–47. Write a page or two in response to this question: Do lotteries help or hinder the poor?

MARIE HALL ETS

FROM

Rosa, The Life of an Italian Immigrant

In this oral history of an Italian immigrant living in Chicago at the end of the nineteenth century, Marie Hall Ets attempts to capture the poignancy of Rosa's experience by recreating her point of view and her diction. Ets transcribed countless hours of conversation with Rosa and then, over many years, simplified, clarified, and organized the narrative into what appears to be an autobiography. Many texts offered as oral history in fact are often developed as a kind of collaboration between a speaker and an editor, as is the case here. Such narratives are related to ethnographic writing, where an individual, a family, or a group is described in detail, with attention to customs, beliefs, and material lives.

Through this woman's simple, direct narration of her experience, we can read into the horrors of child labor (six-year-old Domenico carrying pails of coal and chopping wood); culture shock (Rosa spending her money on a worthless trip on April Fools' Day); and the internalization of oppression, as family members turn against each other (Gionin's cousin cheating him of his money). Although Rosa's tone here is one of fear and resignation, her strong sense of social injustice and exploitation also comes through (in her recounting of incidents involving the family's landlord, for example). Marie Hall Ets's balance in presenting Rosa's narrative avoids easy sentimentality, providing instead a poignant yet matter-of-fact account of the woman's life.

The real Rosa Cassettari was born in 1866 or 1867 in Italy and met Marie Hall Ets during the 1930s in Chicago. The excerpt here is from the completed narrative, published first in 1970 as Rosa, the Life of an Italian Immigrant. *Marie Hall Ets, born in 1893 in Milwaukee, Wisconsin, attended art school but worked as a social worker in Chicago during the 1920s; for forty years beginning in 1935, she authored and illustrated children's books, many of which won awards.*

Pretty soon after the World's Fair—that Fair of 1893—there came such a hard time. Oh, it was so poor a time! Some people had no room to sleep in, so the city was making a big wooden building to cover them up. Oh, that was a terrible, terrible poor time! There was no work; the men couldn't stay in Chicago. So Gionin he went away too. He pawned his watch and my wedding gold—all that we had he gave that pawn man to get ten dollars for the big boots and the ticket. Then he went to the sawmill in Wisconsin where they saw the trees, and he was taking care for the engine in the nighttime. But he had to go the whole month before he got the ten dollars' wage to send me. Me and my children were home there and starving.

One time I remember I had nothing to eat for three days in the house, and Domenico he came up *so* hungry. He said, "Mamma, Mis' Sibel downstairs, she's got a whole loaf of bread! I came past her door and I see it—she's got a whole loaf of bread on the table and one little piece too!"

I said, "Well, I don't know. You want to ask her for some?"

"No, Mamma," he said. "If I ask her maybe she don't give it. I'll just go in and take that little piece."

"No, no, Domenico," I said. "That's stealing—that's a sin."

That poor little boy he was crying and crying, and *so* hungry. Pretty soon he couldn't stand it anymore. He went down by that lady's door. He was there looking at the bread and waiting for Mis' Sibel to come back. That lady didn't come and didn't come, so Domenico he took that little chunk of bread and ate it up. When he saw Mis' Sibel coming up the stairs, he told her. That woman, she was the wife to the saloon man, she was rich—she had plenty to eat—she didn't care for the little chunk of old bread. When she saw how starving my little boy was she was sorry. Instead of licking him for stealing she took him in her house and gave him that whole loaf of bread to bring home.

In that time I was scrubbing the saloon—all the floors in the saloon downstairs for fifty cents. But I didn't get the fifty cents; the man he kept that for my rent. Then I had to move to the attic on the top floor. We were right under the roof in the really attic, because I could no more pay those six dollars rent we paid on the third floor: I was doing the scrubbing and giving two dollars more. He gave me the attic for the scrubbing—four dollars a month rent. Oh, sometimes I was wishing I was back in *Italia!* But sometimes not too.

In that time the city hall was giving food to the people. The people were standing in line there on Clinton Street where the rope pulled up the streetcar. We used to get for one week a piece of salt pork and some dried peas and the loaf of bread and some coffee or some tea. Sometimes we stood there half the day and when it's our turn they had no more left to give. One day I was standing there early, early in the morning, so I would come in before the food was gone. Us poor women were frozen to death; we didn't have the warm clothes, and there was such a storm with the snow and the wind! Eight o'clock, when the door opened, all the people were pushing to get in. There came the police with their clubs and they were yelling like we were animals. Then one of those police hit the woman next to me on the head with his club. I didn't see her, but I don't think she pushed. The people behind were pushing us, that's all. When I saw that, I said to myself, "Better I starve before I let that policeman hit me!" And I ran home from that line. And I never, never went there again.

Another place the people were waiting in line was the police station. Every day they gave a little pail of soup and a piece of bread for each family. I used to send my Domenico and Visella. But Visella was so little she couldn't stand it—she chewed up half the bread before she came home. We used to get a little coal sometimes from the city—like two bags in one month. We were freezing up there under the roof. When we could find nothing else to burn, Domenico and Visella used to go and find the wood blocks that came loose in the road so we had something to burn in our stove. All the roads were made of those wood blocks in that time. My Domenico, he was six or seven years old, he used to go for five cents a week by one lady and carry the coal and the wood. Every day he carried two pails of coal—big pails—from the basement to the third floor, and he chopped the wood and carried that too. So every Saturday he got one nickel. Oh, how glad he was to come home with that nickel! He gave it to me and we bought the big soup bone and had good soup.

You know in that time the meat was cheap—for five cents you got a big piece; but we didn't have the nickel to buy. Now the women complain the meat is dear, but they've got the fifty cents to buy it.

Once in that poor time I was crying and praying. All the night I was praying. I said, "Oh God, if I can only have a crust of bread for these children! I have not one crumb in the house—not one thing!"

Early in the morning I went down the stairs to empty the dirty water in the basement. There in the snow I thought I saw something shine like money. I put down my pail and went there. I thought probably I mistake—it's a piece of tin—and there I was scared to pick it up. But sure enough, I took it in my hand and it was a quarter! Think of that miracle! I ran to the store without even a shawl on my head. For fifteen cents the lady gave me a whole bag of bread pieces, because they were stale, so I had ten cents for another day. I came home and I hollered, "Children, get up! Get up! I've got a big bag of bread!" Those children, they couldn't believe it—they had to see it for themselves. So then they all jumped up and we had that bread with some tea I had left from the city hall. Three children I had home that time: my Domenico, my Visella, and my Maria. And me, I was in family-way with my first Leo. I no longer had my Francesco. Just after I came in Chicago Mamma Lena sent word for Francesco to come back to Bugiarno with some men who were going. She said she had arranged already to send Francesco to school to make him a priest. And when I knew she wanted to make him a priest I couldn't say no. But he didn't make a priest. After a few years the school said it's no use. Maybe he can be an artist or something else, but not a priest.

That quarter I found when I prayed God for some bread, it was really a miracle! But you know, even when I was so poor, I never wanted to die. I used to suffer and didn't get discouraged because I thought it was supposed to be like that. I had such a strong religion—such a good faith. I thought God wanted it that way and when He wanted different it would be.

One day a beautiful lady came in my house—a beautiful dancer. She said she wanted somebody to wash her clothes and clean her house. She went by those American ladies in the house next door first—Mis' Nelson and Mis' Regan—and they told her about me. I said, "Well, lady, I can wash good, but I don't know to iron. I never did the ironing."

She said, "Oh yes, you can do it—they're all silk things." So I went there with her—far on the north side. We went on the streetcar, because it would take the whole day to walk.

She said, "Here." She gave me just a little bundle of washing—a bunch of handkerchiefs and the silk kimono and the underwear—and she said, "When you get through the washing, you can clean the house." She showed me those three rooms and what to do. Then she said, "When you finish you close the door and leave the house." She put there on the table meat and potatoes; then she gave me one dollar. When I saw those good things to eat and one dollar for such a little work I almost fainted! Then she went—she had to go back to her work in the theater.

So I continued for a long time to do that little work every week and made one dollar. Think how nice—how happy I was! But then one day she said she had to leave—she had to go away with the company. She said, "Rosa, when I come back, the first thing I'm going to find you again."

I came home so sad and so sorry. I met that Mis' Nelson and the other lady and I had tears coming down from my eyes. But I told them that she was going to find me again when she came back.

So it went along and it was April, in that terrible poor year, and a lot of snow. Here came that Mis' Nelson in my house and she said, "Rosa, I got a letter from that dancing lady. She's in the same place and she wrote the letter to tell you to go right away back—today. She thought you wouldn't understand if she wrote to you. You go to that same place."

I had only one nickel in my house to make the supper for my family, but I was so glad. I took that nickel and went on the streetcar; then I had to walk a long piece too. My shoes were all broke open, with my feet cold and freezing, so I had the chill—wet and a chill. But anyway I was happy. I knocked on the door. Here came a lady I never saw before. I said, "Some ladies said I have the letter to come here and wash the clothes for Miss Miller."

She said, "Well, I don't know; I don't think she's coming back. She didn't 20 come back yet. But you come in and get warm. I think I know what those women did to you. Those ladies, they fooled you. Today is the April Fool. But that's no way to do to a poor lady that can't understand! I don't think it's right for the American women to fool a poor lady that doesn't know how to talk English!"

She let me get warm and she gave me a cup of coffee. Then she went to her closet and found some shoes to put on me, and she gave me some stockings too. Me, I wanted to cry—I had even no money to go home. That good lady, she gave me the carfare. But how did I know in America they make the April Fool? I didn't even know what it was. And there I lost that nickel I was saving to make some supper for my children.

Toni, he had no work in the mosaic and he couldn't find no work anywhere. So then he remembered that organ his old father used to carry on the street. He said, "I don't care for me, but those poor children!" He had many meals nothing to eat himself, but he couldn't stand it when he heard my children cry for hunger. So he took that organ on his back and he went the whole day—but far away where there were rich people. I remember he had three or four songs in that organ. He used to play "Rosie O'Grady," and "After the Ball Is Over," and one song it went like this: "Boy and girl together, me and Maimie Morain"—or O'Ryan or something that sounded like that. So he used to go around and pick up a few cents with that organ.

One night he came home after all day and he said, "Here, I made fifteen cents today! Take it and we'll make a polenta!"[1]

We ran out and for three cents we got the bag of cornmeal; then we got some liver. The liver was cheap in that time—they were throwing it to the cats and dogs. (Not like now, huh? Now it's the style to eat liver.) So I cooked that

[1] *polenta:* popular Italian peasant dish made of cornmeal or farina (*Ed.*)

cornmeal with the liver in it and made a nice polenta. My children, when they got that good supper—oh, I wish you had seen it! They thought it was the king's wedding!

He all the time helped us in that hard time, Toni. I guess if he didn't, me and my children would be starved. He had no work, but he carried that hand-organ every day the whole day and picked up a few cents from the rich. What he had he gave to me to make the meal so everybody could eat. After the poor time, Toni got the good job again making the mosaic. Then my husband made his sister come from *Italia,* and Toni married her. But that sister was working in those places to sew the clothes—those dark places where they used to make the clothes—and she got the consumption and died. When their two children got the consumption too, Toni went insane. And he's there now, sitting in the insane house in Kankakee. He doesn't even remember that those two children died. I feel sorry for that good, kind Toni.

When Gionin came home from Wisconsin at the end of that winter he brought for three months the pay—thirty dollars he brought. You were like a millionaire if you had thirty dollars in that time! I got a nice clean cloth and wrapped that money, then I put it under the clothes in the bureau drawer. It was not yet two hours when here came in our house one of those cousins of his. That man said, "Gionin, I've got to have the money. I've got to have! Let me have some money."

My husband said, "Well, I brought just thirty dollars and my wife she needs it. She has no clothes for the children—the children are naked. And it's almost the time for the new baby to be born."

"Give it to me," he said. "Gionin, let me have it and I'll give it back right away on Saturday night."

"You're sure you will give it back Saturday night?"

"Sure! Give it to me! I've got to have it!"

So my husband came to me and said, "Rosa, give me the thirty dollars back."

I said, "No! Why are you going to take it? I need it! I need it!" Then I began to cry.

"Give it to me!" he said.

So there I had to give it to him and I had not one penny left in the house. All the night I was crying, because I lose that thirty dollars. Gionin he couldn't stand it to hear me cry like that. He got up from the bed about nine o'clock and he went. (In that time we were going to bed when it was dark—six o'clock, or what time it got dark. We didn't have no oil to burn and we had no place to go.)

In the morning when I went to the house of Mis' Mill to do the cleaning, she saw that I had been crying so much, and she asked me about it. When I told her, she said, "Well don't cry, Mis' Cavalleri." And she went and found some little stockings and clothes to put on my children.

Gionin, when he saw me crying like that, he went again and again in the night by his cousin and asked him, and begged him, for the thirty dollars back again. But all the time, every night, that cousin had some sad-luck story. After a few weeks my husband got tired and he didn't even ask anymore. He knew he wouldn't get it. And I don't have it yet! But God He helped us, and that cousin of my husband, he stayed a poor man. That's the punishment he got from God. But oh, I was brokenhearted when I had that thirty dollars and lost it.

I don't know if I should tell about that fire we had when we were living over the saloon—that man he's alive yet and he's more religious than anybody now. He all the time goes to the Italian church. Sometimes he looks to me like he wants to say something—but I never speak to that man. He got so religious after his wife died. Well, that time in the poor year, he had a lot of wine in his saloon and it went bad and he wanted to get the insurance. So he chopped up some wood in the basement and made a fire. My husband woke up in the middle of the night and he heard that wood chopping, but he didn't wake up enough. The next thing he woke up and we were all ready to burn up—all smothered with smoke. That saloon man was outside hollering, "Fire! Get out!"

There we had not even time to put a coat on. Some of that family from the second floor were on the stairs. The little girl was falling over in a faint—she said she couldn't go. And that big cat they had was already dead. Visella came down with two shoes in her hand, but that's all the clothes we saved. We came out in the snow with no clothes, and *so* cold. We had to run way down the next block, to our knees in snow, and barefoot, in the middle of the night. Tomaso, the cousin of my husband, he took us in and they made hot coffee with whiskey in, but I got sick from that cold anyway—and my baby not yet born.

When the insurance came to investigate they found out the saloon keeper had his family all moved one block away with all their things—with the clothes and the furniture and all what they had. When they saw he made the fire himself he got not one cent. Our things didn't burn, though; the firemen came and put out the fire before it could reach the attic. Only the windows broke, and they fixed them the next day so we could go back. I guess that man thought he could tell us in plenty of time after the first floor burned. But what did he think we're going to do in the attic if all the underneath burned first? Did he think we could stay up in the air with nothing under?

The night my first Leo was born my husband came home with his first pay—seven dollars for one week. We thought we would jump to the moon when he found that good job in the candy factory with seven dollars' pay for one week! The midwife was gone already when he came home with that pay. He ran out and bought the butter and some bread and made that hot water with the bread and butter in, like us Italian women always drink when we have the baby just born. 40

Then that boss in the candy factory said, "Why do you want to pay the rent? You and your family can come here in these nice rooms behind the factory."

Gionin thought it was nice if we could leave that attic and have the rooms to live in without paying the rent, so he said yes.

But that man, he was not good. He came after me. He said it's such a poor time he's going to buy me the clothes and all the things I want. Then he talked bad—he wanted me to be like a wife. When he came after me like that I got the scare. I told Gionin. Gionin said, "Well, we don't say anything—we will just go away. We're going to get out without the fighting."

So there my husband had that nice job in the hard times and he had to lose it. He was good, no—to go away and lose that good job to save me from the boss? Seven dollars a week in that time was something wonderful! He found three nice light rooms, but far away from those other *Toscani*.[2] We moved to Union Street where there were all the German and Irish and Norwegian. And then Gionin had to go and go and try to find another job. He used to come home with his feet all blisters, trying to find a job. 44

DISCUSSING THE TEXT

1. Ets has written Rosa's oral history in Rosa's own words. What do you think of this method? Does Rosa's English sound authentic to you? Does this method make the selection more credible? Explain why or why not.
2. What might have been Miss Nelson's motivation for tricking Rosa on April Fools' Day? How do you interpret Rosa's reaction? How would you have responded?
3. Of her poverty Rosa says, "I thought God wanted it that way and when he wanted it different it would be." With a small group of students, discuss ways in which religion might help the poor. Are there also ways in which it might hinder them? Be prepared to discuss your group's ideas with the rest of the class.

WRITING ABOUT THE TEXT

4. Make a list of words or phrases in the text that are not considered standard English. Then write one brief paragraph discussing the value of reproducing Rosa's language in this way, and a second brief paragraph discussing possible problems with using this kind of language.
5. Rewrite Rosa's account of the food line at Clinton Street and the policeman's clubbing of one of the women (par. 8) from the point of view of a social reformer writing a newspaper editorial. What different choices might a writer in this situation make?
6. Write a one-page analysis comparing and contrasting Rosa's account of immigrant life with that presented by Oscar Handlin in "The Ghettos."
7. Interview an older person—perhaps a relative or a neighbor—about the experience of being a newcomer, if not to this country maybe to a community, school, or job. Prepare an oral history in which you maintain this person's language choices, speech patterns, and so on.

[2]*Toscani:* natives of Tuscany, in west-central Italy (*Ed.*)

CRISTINA GARCIA

Enough Attitude

Cristina Garcia's first novel, Dreaming in Cuban *(1992), focuses on two main characters: Lourdes, a middle-aged Cuban exile who owns a bakery in Brooklyn, and her daughter Pilar, a visual artist.* Dreaming in Cuban *depicts generational conflict among the different members of the del Pino family, as well as the effects of the Cuban Revolution of 1959 on their lives in the United States.*

Divided into two parts, this excerpt offers a striking contrast between the mother's respectful, noncritical attitude toward the United States, and her daughter's negative "attitude" toward her mother's family values and American society in general. The mother's sense of a fragmented identity and her unabated longing for Cuba give her the voice of an exile. Her daughter, on the other hand, while she does retain aspects of her Cuban identity, sees herself as belonging in the United States; thus she feels confident enough to be critical.

Born in Cuba in 1958, Cristina Garcia came to the United States with her family at age two. She grew up in New York City, attended Barnard College and Johns Hopkins University, and has worked as a correspondent for Time *magazine in San Francisco, Miami, and Los Angeles. Garcia sees Latino writing as a major current within the literature of the United States: "We'll be part of the mainstream not by becoming more like 'them' and less like 'us', but by what it means to be an American in the twenty-first century. This is changing and its definition will be necessarily broader and more inclusive."*

Lourdes Puente is walking her beat. It's a five-block square of Brooklyn with brownstones and linden trees, considered safe as neighborhoods go on this side of Atlantic Avenue. Lourdes is an auxiliary policewoman, the first in her precinct. She scored one hundred on her written test by answering "c" to the multiple-choice questions she wasn't sure of or didn't understand. Captain Cacciola congratulated her personally. He wanted to make sure she was tough enough on crime. Lourdes said she believed drug dealers should die in the electric chair. This pleased the captain, and she was sent on patrol Tuesday and Thursday nights between seven and ten.

Lourdes enjoys patrolling the streets in her thick-soled black shoes. These shoes, it seems to her, are a kind of equalizer. She can run in them if she has to, jump curbs, traverse the buckled, faulted sidewalks of Brooklyn without twisting an ankle. These shoes are power. If women wore shoes like these, she thinks, they wouldn't worry so much about more abstract equalities. They would join the army reserve or the auxiliary police like her, and protect what was theirs. In Cuba nobody was prepared for the Communists and look what happened. Now her mother guards their beach with binoculars and a pistol against Yankees. If only Lourdes had had a gun when she needed it.

It's Thursday, just after nine. There's a full moon out. It hangs fat and waxy in the sky, creased with shadows.

"Every loony in New York comes out of the woodwork on nights like this," the regular beat cop had warned her.

But so far everything's been quiet. It's too cold for loiterers. Lourdes suddenly remembers how her daughter had ridiculed Armstrong's first words on the moon. "He had months to think up something and that's all he could say?" Pilar was only ten years old and already mocking everything. Lourdes slapped her for being disrespectful, but it made no difference to her daughter. Pilar was immune to threats. She placed no value on normal things so it was impossible to punish her. Even now, Pilar is not afraid of pain or of losing anything. It's this indifference that is most maddening. 5

The last of the Jews have moved out of the neighborhood. Only the Kellners are left. The others are on Long Island or in Westchester or Florida, depending on their ages and their bank accounts. Pilar thinks Lourdes is bigoted, but what does her daughter know of life? Equality is just another one of her abstractions. "I don't make up the statistics," she tells Pilar. "I don't color the faces down at the precinct." Black faces, Puerto Rican faces. Once in a while a stray Irish or Italian face looking scared. Lourdes prefers to confront reality—the brownstones converted to tenements in a matter of months, the garbage in the streets, the jaundice-eyed men staring vacantly from the stoops. Even Pilar couldn't denounce her for being a hypocrite.

Lourdes feels the solid ground beneath her solid black shoes as she walks. She breathes in the wintry air, which stings her lungs. It seems to her as if the air were made of crystal filaments, scraping and cleaning her inside. She decides she has no patience for dreamers, for people who live between black and white.

Lourdes slides her hand up and down her wooden nightstick. It's the only weapon the police department will issue her. That and handcuffs. Lourdes has used the stick only once in her two months of patrolling, to break up a fight between a Puerto Rican kid and three Italians down at the playground. Lourdes knows the Puerto Rican's mother. She's the one who worked at the bakery for an afternoon. Lourdes caught her pocketing fifty cents from the sale of two crullers, and threw her out. No wonder her son is a delinquent. He sells plastic bags of marijuana behind the liquor store.

Lourdes's son would have been about the same age as the Navarro boy. *Her* son would have been different. He wouldn't have talked back to her or taken drugs or drunk beer from paper bags like the other teenagers. *Her* son would have helped her in the bakery without complaint. He would have come to her for guidance, pressed her hand to his cheek, told her he loved her. Lourdes would have talked to her son the way Rufino talks to Pilar, for companionship. Lourdes suffers with this knowledge.

Down the street, the trees are imprisoned equidistantly in square plots of dirt. Everything else is concrete. Lourdes remembers reading somewhere about how Dutch elm disease wiped out the entire species on the East Coast except for a lone tree in Manhattan surrounded by concrete. Is this, she wonders, how we'll all survive? 10

It became clear to Lourdes shortly after she and Rufino moved to New York that he would never adapt. Something came unhinged in his brain that would make him incapable of working in a conventional way. There was a part of him that could never leave the *finca*[1] or the comfort of its cycles, and this diminished him for any other life. He could not be transplanted. So Lourdes got a job. Cuban women of a certain age and a certain class consider working outside the home to be beneath them. But Lourdes never believed that.

While it was true that she had grown accustomed to the privileges that came with marrying into the Puente family, Lourdes never accepted the life designated for its women. Even now, stripped of their opulence, crowded into two-bedroom apartments in Hialeah and Little Havana, the Puente women clung to their rituals as they did their engraved silverware, succumbing to a cloying nostalgia. Doña Zaida, once a formidable matriarch who ruled her eight sons by a resolute jealousy, spent long afternoons watching *novelas* on television and perfuming her thickening wrists.

Lourdes knew she could never be this kind of woman. After her honeymoon, she got right to work on the Puente ranch. She reviewed the ledgers, fired the cheating accountant, and took over the books herself. She redecorated the musty, coffer-ceilinged mansion with watercolor landscapes, reupholstered the sofas with rustic fabrics and discarded the cretonne drapes in favor of sliding glass doors that invited the morning light. Out went the ornate bric-a-brac, the austere furniture carved with the family crest. Lourdes refilled the mosaic-lined fountain with sweet water and built an aviary in the garden, stocking it with toucans and cockatoos, parrots, a macaw, and canaries that sang in high octaves. Sometimes at night, she could hear the cries of the quail doves and solitaires interspersed with the songs from the aviary.

When a disgruntled servant informed Doña Zaida about the changes in her country house, she descended on the ranch in a fury and restored the villa to its former state. Lourdes, who defiantly rebuilt the aviary and restocked it with birds, never spoke to her mother-in-law again.

Lourdes misses the birds she had in Cuba. She thinks of joining a bird-watching society, but who would take care of the bakery in her absence? Pilar is unreliable and Rufino can't tell a Danish from a donut. It's a shame, too, because all Lourdes ever sees in Brooklyn is dull little wrens or those filthy pigeons. Rufino has taken to raising pigeons in wire-mesh cages in their backyard the way he saw Marlon Brando do in *On the Waterfront*. He prints messages on bits of paper, slips them through metal rings on the pigeons' legs, then kisses each bird on the head for good luck and lets it loose with a whoop. Lourdes doesn't know or care what her husband is writing, or to whom. By now, she accepts him the way she accepts the weather. What else can she do? 15

Rufino has stopped confiding in her. She hears secondhand snippets about his projects from Pilar, and knows he's trying to develop a super carburetor, one that will get two hundred miles to the gallon. Lourdes knows,

---

[1]*Finca:* (Spanish) farm (*Ed.*)

too, that her husband is still brooding about artificial intelligence. She is not sure what this means although Rufino explained to her once that it would do for the brain what the telephone did for the human voice, take it farther and faster than it could go unassisted. Lourdes cannot understand why this is so difficult. She remembers seeing robots at the World's Fair ten years ago. She and Rufino and Pilar ate in a restaurant observatory shaped like a spaceship. The food was terrible. The view was of Queens.

These days, Lourdes recognizes her husband's face, his thinning reddish hair, and the crepey pouches under his eyes, but he is a stranger to her. She looks at him the way she might look at a photograph of her hands, unfamiliar upon close inspection.

Lourdes is herself only with her father. Even after his death, they understand each other perfectly, as they always have. Jorge del Pino doesn't accompany Lourdes on her beat because he doesn't want to interfere with her work. He is proud of his daughter, of her tough stance on law and order, identical to his own. It was he who encouraged Lourdes to join the auxiliary police so she'd be ready to fight the Communists when the time came. "Look how El Líder[2] mobilizes the people to protect his causes," Jorge del Pino told his daughter. "He uses the techniques of the Fascists. Everyone is armed and ready for combat at a moment's notice. How will we ever win Cuba back if we ourselves are not prepared to fight?"

Pilar makes fun of Lourdes in her uniform, of the way she slaps the nightstick in her palm. "Who do you think you are, Kojak?" she says, laughing, and hands her mother a lollipop. This is just like her daughter, scornful and impudent. "I'm doing this to show you something, to teach you a lesson!" Lourdes screams, but Pilar ignores her.

Last Christmas, Pilar gave her a book of essays on Cuba called *A Revolutionary Society*. The cover showed cheerful, clean-cut children gathered in front of a portrait of Che Guevara.[3] Lourdes was incensed. 20

"Will you read it?" Pilar asked her.

"I don't have to read it to know what's in it! Lies, poisonous Communist lies!" Che Guevara's face had set a violence quivering within her like a loose wire.

"Suit yourself," Pilar shot back.

Lourdes snatched the volume from under the Christmas tree, took it to the bathroom, filled the tub with scalding water, and dropped it in. Che Guevara's face blanched and swelled like the dead girl Lourdes had seen wash up once on the beach at Santa Teresa del Mar with a note pinned to her breast. Nobody ever came to claim her. Lourdes fished Pilar's book out of the tub with barbecue tongs and placed it on the porcelain platter she reserved for her

---

[2]*El Líder:* the leader, a reference to Fidel Castro, head of the Cuban government since 1959 (*Ed.*)

[3]*Che Guevara:* Ernesto Guevara (1928–1967), nicknamed Che, or buddy; popular Argentine-born revolutionary leader associated with Fidel Castro (*Ed.*)

roasted pork legs. Then she fastened a note to the cover with a safety pin. "Why don't you move to Russia if you think it's so great!" And she signed her name in full.

All this she left on Pilar's bed. But it did not provoke her daughter. The next day, the platter was back in the cupboard and *A Revolutionary Society* was drying on the clothesline. 25

Lourdes's walkie-talkie crackles as she works her way along the length of river that forms the western boundary of her territory. The night is so clear that the water reflects every stray angle of light. Without the disruptions of ships and noise, the river is a mirror. It reminds Lourdes of a photograph she saw once of the famous Hall of Mirrors in the Palace of Versailles with its endless ricocheting light.

At the edge of her vision, the darkness shifts. Her spine stiffens and her heart is audible deep inside her ears. She turns and squints but she cannot make out the figure, crouched and still, by the river. Lourdes grips her nightstick with one hand and pulls on her flashlight with the other. When she looks up again, the figure springs across the low fence and jumps into the river, shattering the light.

"Stop!" she shouts, running toward the spot as if chasing a part of herself. Lourdes turns her flashlight on the river, penetrating its rippled surface, then hoists herself over the fence. "Stop!" she shouts again at nothing at all. Lourdes pulls her walkie-talkie from its holster and screams too close to the speaker. She cannot remember what to say, the codes she had carefully memorized. A voice is talking to her now, calm and officious. "Tell us your location," it says, ". . . your location." But Lourdes jumps into the river instead. She hears the sirens wailing as the cold envelops her, numbing her face and her hands, her feet in their thick-soled shoes. The river smells of death.

Only one more fact is important. Lourdes lived and the Navarro boy died.

PILAR

The family is hostile to the individual. This is what I'm thinking as Lou Reed says he has enough attitude to kill every person in New Jersey. I'm at a club in the Village with my boyfriend, Max. I figure I have enough attitude to kill a few people myself, only it never works on the right ones. 30

"I'm from Brooklyn, man!" Lou shouts and the crowd goes wild. I don't cheer, though. I wouldn't cheer either if Lou said, "Let's hear it for Cuba." Cuba. Planet Cuba. Where the hell is that?

Max's real name is Octavio Schneider. He sings and plays bass and harmonica for the Manichaean Blues Band, a group he started back in San Antonio, where he's from. They do Howlin' Wolf and Muddy Waters and lots of their own songs, mostly hard rock. Sometimes they do back-up for this crazy bluesman, the Reverend Billy Hines, who keeps his eyes shut when he sings. Max says that the reverend was a storefront preacher who played the Panhandle years ago and is attempting a comeback. Max himself had a modest hit in Texas with "Moonlight on Emma," a song about an ex-girlfriend who dumped him and moved to Hollywood.

I met Max at a downtown basement club a few months ago. He came over and started speaking to me in Spanish (his mother is Mexican) as if he'd known me for years. I liked him right away. When I brought him around to meet my parents, Mom took one look at his beaded headband and the braid down his back and said, *"Sácalo de aquí."* When I told her that Max spoke Spanish, she simply repeated what she said in English: "Take him away."

Dad was cool, though. "What does your band's name mean?" he asked Max.

"The Manichaeans, see, were followers of this Persian guy who lived in the third century. They believed that hedonism was the only way to get rid of their sins." 35

"Hedonism?"

"Yeah, the Manichaeans liked to party. They had orgies and drank a lot. They got wiped out by other Christians, though."

"Too bad," my father said sympathetically.

Later, Dad looked up the Manichaeans in the encyclopedia and discovered that, contrary to what Max claimed, the Manichaeans believed that the world and all matter were created by nefarious forces, and that the only way to battle them was through asceticism and a pure life. When I told Max about this, he just shrugged and said, "Well, I guess that's okay, too." Max is a tolerant kind of guy.

I just love the way Lou Reed's concerts feel—expectant, uncertain. You never know what he's going to do next. Lou has about twenty-five personalities. I like him because he sings about people no one else sings about—drug addicts, transvestites, the down-and-out. Lou jokes about his alter egos discussing problems at night. I feel like a new me sprouts and dies every day. 40

I play Lou and Iggy Pop and this new band the Ramones whenever I paint. I love their energy, their violence, their incredible grinding guitars. It's like an artistic form of assault. I try to translate what I hear into colors and volumes and lines that confront people, that say, "Hey, we're here too and what we think matters!" or more often just "Fuck you!" Max is not as crazy about the Ramones as I am. I think he's more of a traditionalist. He has a tough time being rude, even to people who deserve it. Not me. If I don't like someone, I show it. It's the one thing I have in common with my mother.

Neither of my parents is very musical. Their entire record collection consists of *Perry Como's Greatest Hits,* two Herb Alpert & the Tijuana Brass albums, and *Alvin and the Chipmunks Sing Their Favorite Christmas Carols,* which they bought for me when I was a kid. Recently, Mom picked up a Jim Nabors album of patriotic songs in honor of the bicentennial. I mean, after Vietnam and Watergate, who the hell wants to hear "The Battle Hymn of the Republic"?

I used to like the Fourth of July okay because of the fireworks. I'd go down by the East River and watch them flare up from the tugboats. The girandoles looked like fiery lace in the sky. But this bicentennial crap is making me crazy. Mom has talked about nothing else for months. She bought a second bakery and plans to sell tricolor cupcakes and Uncle Sam marzipan. Apple pies, too. She's convinced she can fight Communism from behind her bakery counter.

Last year she joined the local auxiliary police out of some misplaced sense of civic duty. My mother—all four feet eleven and a half inches and 217 pounds of her—patrols the streets of Brooklyn at night in a skintight uniform, clanging with enough antiriot gear to quash another Attica. She practices twirling her nightstick in front of the mirror, then smacks it against her palm, steadily, menacingly, like she's seen cops do on television. Mom's upset because the police department won't issue her a gun. Right. She gets a gun and I move out of state fast.

45 There's other stuff happening with her. For starters, she's been talking with Abuelo Jorge since he died. He gives her business advice and tells her who's stealing from her at the bakery. Mom says that Abuelo spies on me and reports back to her. Like what is this? The ghost patrol? Mom is afraid that I'm having sex with Max (which I'm not) and this is her way of trying to keep me in line.

Max likes Mom, though. He says she suffers from an "imperious disposition."

"You mean she's a frustrated tyrant?" I ask him.

"More like a bitch goddess," he explains.

Max's parents split up before he was born and his mother cleans motel rooms for minimum wage. I guess Mom must seem exotic by comparison.

50 But she's really not. Mom makes food only people in Ohio eat, like Jell-O molds with miniature marshmallows or recipes she clips from *Family Circle*. And she barbecues anything she can get her hands on. Then we sit around behind the warehouse and stare at each other with nothing to say. Like this is it? We're living the American dream?

The worst is the parades. Mom gets up early and drags us out on Thanksgiving Day loaded with plastic foam coolers, like we're going to starve right there on Fifth Avenue. On New Year's Day, she sits in front of the television and comments on every single float in the Rose Parade. I think she dreams of sponsoring one herself someday. Like maybe a huge burning effigy of El Líder.

Max flatters me but not in a sleazy way. He says he loves my height (I'm five feet eight inches) and my hair (black, down to my waist) and the whiteness of my skin. His mouth is a little sauna, hot and wet. When we slow-dance, he presses himself against me and I feel his hardness against my thighs. He says I would make a good bass player.

Max knows about Abuela Celia in Cuba, about how she used to talk to me late at night and how we've lost touch over the years. Max wants to go to Cuba and track her down, but I tell him what happened four years ago, when

I ran away to Florida and my plans to see my grandmother collapsed. I wonder what Abuela Celia is doing right this minute.

Most days Cuba is kind of dead to me. But every once in a while a wave of longing will hit me and it's all I can do not to hijack a plane to Havana or something. I resent the hell out of the politicians and the generals who force events on us that structure our lives, that dictate the memories we'll have when we're old. Every day Cuba fades a little more inside me, my grandmother fades a little more inside me. And there's only my imagination where our history should be.

It doesn't help that Mom refuses to talk about Abuela Celia. She gets annoyed every time I ask her and she shuts me up quickly, like I'm prying into top secret information. Dad is more open, but he can't tell me what I really want to know, like why Mom hardly speaks to Abuela or why she still keeps her riding crops from Cuba. Most of the time, he's too busy refereeing the fights between us, or else he's just in his own orbit. 55

Dad feels kind of lost here in Brooklyn. I think he stays in his workshop most of the day because he'd get too depressed or crazy otherwise. Sometimes I think we should have moved to a ranch in Wyoming or Montana. He would have been happy there with his horses and his cows, his land, and a big empty sky overhead. Dad only looks alive when he talks about the past, about Cuba. But we don't discuss that much either lately. Things haven't been the same since I saw him with that blond bombshell. I never said anything to him, but it's like a cut on my tongue that never healed.

▼ ▼ ▼

Mom has decided she wants me to paint a mural for her second Yankee Doodle Bakery.

"I want a big painting like the Mexicans do, but pro-American," she specifies.

"You want to commission *me* to paint something for *you?*"

"*Sí,* Pilar. You're a painter, no? So paint!" 60

"You've got to be kidding."

"Painting is painting, no?"

"Look, Mom, I don't think you understand. I don't *do* bakeries."

"You're embarrassed? My bakery is not good enough for you?"

"It's not that." 65

"This bakery paid for your painting classes."

"It has nothing to do with that, either."

"If Michelangelo were alive today, he wouldn't be so proud."

"Mom, believe me, Michelangelo would definitely *not* be painting bakeries."

"Don't be so sure. Most artists are starving. They don't have all the advantages like you. They take heroin to forget." 70

"Jesus Christ!"

"This could be a good opportunity for you, Pilar. A lot of important people come to my shop. Judges and lawyers from the courts, executives from

Brooklyn Union Gas. Maybe they'll see your painting. You could become famous."

My mother talks and talks, but I block out her words. For some reason I think about Jacoba Van Heemskerck, a Dutch expressionist painter I've become interested in lately. Her paintings feel organic to me, like breathing abstractions of color. She refused to title her paintings (much less do patriotic murals for her mother's bakery) and numbered her works instead. I mean, who needs words when colors and lines conjure up their own language? That's what I want to do with my paintings, find a unique language, obliterate the clichés.

I think about all the women artists throughout history who managed to paint despite the odds against them. People still ask where all the important women painters are instead of looking at what they did paint and trying to understand their circumstances. Even supposedly knowledgeable and sensitive people react to good art by a woman as if it were an anomaly, a product of a freak nature or a direct result of her association with a male painter or mentor. Nobody's even heard of feminism in art school. The male teachers and students still call the shots and get the serious attention and the fellowships that further their careers. As for the women, we're supposed to make extra money modeling nude. What kind of bullshit revolution is that?

"*Mira,* Pilar. I'm asking you as a favor. You could paint something simple, something elegant. Like the Statue of Liberty. Is that too much to ask?" 75

"Okay, okay, I'll paint something," I say deliberately, deciding to play my last card. "But on one condition. You can't see it before the unveiling." This will get her, I think. She'll never agree to this in a million years. She's too much of a control freak.

"That's fine."

"What?"

"I said that's fine, Pilar."

I must be standing there with my mouth open because she pops a macaroon into it and shakes her head as if to say, "See, you always underestimate me." But that's not true. If anything, I overestimate her. It comes from experience. Mom is arbitrary and inconsistent and always believes she's right. It's a pretty irritating combination. 80

Shit. How did I get into this mess?

Our warehouse is only two blocks from the river, and the Statue of Liberty is visible in the distance. I'd been there once when I was a kid, before we settled in Brooklyn. Mom and Dad took me on a ferry and we climbed up behind Liberty's eyes and looked out over the river, the city, the beginning of things.

A Circle Line tour boat is rounding the tip of Manhattan, optimistic as a wedding cake. There's someone on the top deck with a pair of binoculars aimed at Brooklyn. I can imagine what the tour guide is saying: ". . . and on your left, ladies and gentlemen, is the borough of Brooklyn, former home of the

Dodgers and the birthplace of famous 'It' girl Clara Bow. . . ."[4] What they don't say is that nobody ever dies in Brooklyn. It's only the living that die here.

That night, I get to work. But I decide to do a painting instead of a mural. I stretch a twelve-by-eight-foot canvas and wash it with an iridescent blue gouache—like the Virgin Mary's robes in gaudy church paintings. I want the background to glow, to look irradiated, nuked out. It takes me a while to get the right effect.

When the paint dries, I start on Liberty herself. I do a perfect replication of her a bit left of center canvas, changing only two details: first, I make Liberty's torch float slightly beyond her grasp, and second, I paint her right hand reaching over to cover her left breast, as if she's reciting the National Anthem or some other slogan. 85

The next day, the background still looks off to me, so I take a medium-thick brush and paint black stick figures pulsing in the air around Liberty, thorny scars that look like barbed wire. I want to go all the way with this, to stop mucking around and do what I feel, so at the base of the statue I put my favorite punk rallying cry: I'M A MESS. And then carefully, very carefully, I paint a safety pin through Liberty's nose.

This, I think, sums everything up very nicely. *SL-76*. That'll be my title.

I fuss with Liberty another couple of days, more out of nervousness than anything. I keep getting the feeling that Mom is going to spy on my work. After all, her record doesn't exactly inspire confidence. So, before I leave my studio, I set up a booby trap—two tight rows of paint cans on the floor just inside the door. Mom would trip on them if she managed to open the latch and come creeping around late at night. It would serve her right, too, show her that she can't go breaking her promises and invading my privacy any time she damn well pleases.

I'm usually a heavy sleeper but these last nights every little noise makes me jump out of bed. I'd swear I heard her footsteps, or someone picking the lock on my studio. But when I get up to investigate, I always find my mother sound asleep, looking innocent the way chronically guilty people do sometimes. Then I go to the refrigerator, find something to eat, and stare at the cold stub of her cigar on the kitchen table. In the mornings, my paint cans remain undisturbed and there are no suspicious stains on any of Mom's clothing in the hamper. Jesus, I must really be getting paranoid.

Max helps me set the painting up in the bakery the night before the grand opening, and we drape it with sewn-together sheets. My mother, surprisingly, still hasn't even tried to get a glimpse of the work. I can tell she's proud of the blind faith she's placed in me. She's positively aglow in her 90

---

[4]*Clara Bow* (1905–1965): charming silent screen actress best known for her starring comic role in *It* (*Ed.*)

magnanimity. When I come home that night, Mom shows me the full-page ad she took out in the *Brooklyn Express:*

YANKEE DOODLE BAKERY

invites

OUR FRIENDS AND NEIGHBORS

to the

GRAND OPENING

of

OUR SECOND STORE

and the

UNVEILING

of a

MAJOR NEW WORK OF ART

for the

200TH BIRTHDAY OF AMERICA

SUNDAY, 12 NOON

(free food and drinks)

Free food and drinks! This is more serious than I thought. Mom doesn't give anything away if she can help it.

Now I can't sleep all night thinking maybe this time I've gone too far. After all, Mom didn't seem to have any ulterior motives, at least none that I can figure. For once, I think she genuinely wanted to give me a break. I try to calm down by reminding myself that *she* was the one that cornered me into doing this painting. What did she expect?

At five in the morning, I go to my parents' room. They're sleeping back to back, like strange doughy twins. I want to warn her: "Look, I wanted to do it straight but I couldn't, I just couldn't. Do you understand?"

She shifts in her sleep, her plump body curling forward. I reach out to touch her but quickly pull back my hand.

"What's wrong? What's the matter?" Mom is suddenly awake, sitting 95 upright. Her nightgown clings to the soft folds of her breasts, her stomach, the creases in her thighs.

"Nothing, Mom. I only wanted . . . I couldn't sleep."

"You're just nervous, Pilar."

"Yeah, well."

"Don't worry, *mi cielo.*" Mom takes my hand and pats it gently. "Go back to bed."

The next morning, the bakery is hung with flags and streamers and a Dixieland band is playing "When the Saints Go Marching In." Mom is in her new red, white, and blue two-piece suit, a matching handbag stiff on her elbow. She's giving away apple tartlets and brownies and cup after cup of coffee.

"Yes, my daughter created it," I hear her boast, trilling her "r" 's, clipping her vowels even more precisely than usual, as if her accent were partly responsible for the painting. "She is an *artista.* A very brilliant *artista.*" Mom is pointing in my direction and I feel the sweat collecting at the small of my back. Someone from the *Brooklyn Express* snaps my picture. 100

At noon, Mom gingerly balances atop a stepladder on her tiny, size-four feet. The drum rolls endlessly as she pulls on the sheet. There's a stark silence as Liberty, in her full punk glory, glares down at the audience. For a brief moment, I imagine the sound of applause, of people calling my name. But my thoughts stop dead when I hear the hateful buzzing. It's as if the swarm of stick figures have come alive in their background, threatening to fly off the canvas and nest in our hair. The blood has drained from my mother's face and her lips are moving as if she wants to say something but can't form the words. She stands there, immobile, clutching the sheet against her silk blouse, when someone yells in raucous Brooklynese, "Gaaahbage! Whadda piece of gaaahbage!" A lumpish man charges Liberty with a pocketknife, repeating his words like a war cry. Before anyone can react, Mom swings her new handbag and clubs the guy cold inches from the painting. Then, as if in slow motion, she tumbles forward, a thrashing avalanche of patriotism and motherhood, crushing three spectators and a table of apple tartlets.

And I, I love my mother very much at that moment.

DISCUSSING THE TEXT

1. Why is Lourdes so interested in law and order? How is her yearning for power described?
2. Lourdes herself is a member of an immigrant minority. But what is her attitude toward other ethnic minorities? Point to examples in the text. Why do you think she reacts to people in the way that she does?
3. The generational conflict between mother and daughter is a major theme in this selection. Get together in a group of four or five students and discuss some of the conflicts that arise between Lourdes and Pilar. Which problems that mother and daughter experience are magnified by the fact that they are immigrants? Which, if any, problems seem unrelated to their immigrant status? How does the ending point to the resolution of the conflict between mother and daughter?
4. Why is it significant that the narrative voice shifts to first person in the section titled "Pilar"? What effect does this shift have on you as a reader?

WRITING ABOUT THE TEXT

5. Write a brief paragraph explaining your reactions to the title of the first part of this selection, "Enough Attitude."
6. Reread the passage that describes Pilar's painting of the Statue of Liberty, *SL-76* (par. 84–87), and write a list of the details that radically change the statue's original appearance. Then write a brief essay interpreting Pilar's message in her work.
7. In the story's final section, Pilar gets her picture taken by a local newspaper at the bakery's Fourth of July celebration (par. 100). In the voice of the newspaper's editor, write two paragraphs that criticize *SL-76* for being unpatriotic. Then write a response in Lourdes's voice, defending her daughter's ideas.

JOEL DREYFUSS

The Invisible Immigrants

In this essay, which appeared originally in the New York Times Magazine *in 1993, Joel Dreyfuss voices the concerns of the Haitian exile community in terms of their "invisibility" in the United States. Dreyfuss believes that the media's negative attention to the thousands of Haitian immigrants who have arrived in the United States illegally over the past few years has obscured the accomplishments of a previous generation of Haitian Americans, as well as the contributions of the more recent immigrants. Addressing the assimilation of Haitians into American culture, Dreyfuss quotes anthropologist Michel S. Laguerre, who says: "By and large, one can compare the Haitian immigration experience in the United States to that of other, more celebrated, immigrant groups. . . . They are young, aggressive, even pushy, and to that extent, not very different from other immigrants."*

Born in 1945 in Haiti, Dreyfuss emigrated with his family to the United States as a child and grew up in a Haitian neighborhood in New York City. His account of the different waves of Haitian immigration over the past forty years raises important questions about identity, public image, and cultural stereotypes. Dreyfuss notes particularly that issues of class and race have been important in determining how Haitians in the United States look at themselves. For example, he claims that some Haitians think of themselves as "black," and are therefore assimilated into the African American community. Others, however, identify themselves as "Haitian," and thus remain foreign.

Joel Dreyfuss has written for the New York Post, *the* Washington Post, Playboy, *and the* Village Voice. *He is also the author of* The Bakke Case: The Politics of Inequality *(1979). His piece on Haiti was written before the U.S. intervention in Haiti, which resulted in the return of exiled President Aristide to power.*

"Where are you from?" In multiethnic America, the question is a way to classify you: to embrace or dismiss you. For those of us who came to America from Haiti 20 or 30 years ago, the question was usually a signal to brace ourselves. If our interrogators knew anything about our native land just a few hundred miles south of Miami, it was not likely to be very positive. "Aha!" people would say once we had answered, "Voodoo. Poverty. Papa Doc." It was a snapshot that, denying the complexity of our country, imprisoned us in a stereotype. Today the response is "Aha! AIDS. Boat People."

For 12 years, the news media have dutifully reported the thousands of black people packed to the gunwales of leaky boats trying to make their way to Florida or, once there, quarantined because they are H.I.V. positive.

Despite the stereotypes and our having come from the poorest country in the Western Hemisphere, we Haitians have established ourselves in the United States as an industrious, upwardly mobile immigrant group with a strong work ethic. We are cabdrivers and college professors, schoolteachers and police officers, stockbrokers and baby sitters, soldiers and politicians, bankers and factory workers. "By and large, one can compare the Haitian immigration experience in the United States to that of other, more celebrated, immigrant groups," says Michel S. Laguerre, an anthropologist of Haitian origin who teaches at the University of California at Berkeley. "They are young, aggressive, even pushy, and to that extent, not very different from other immigrants."

There were about 290,000 who claimed Haitian ancestry in the 1990 census, but that does not include the tens of thousands who are here illegally or second- and third-generation Haitian-Americans who simply identify themselves as black, Laguerre explains. Even legal immigrants may not want to admit to roots that go back to a Caribbean nation so often associated with superstition and poverty. Laguerre, who has written extensively about Haitians in America, estimates that as many as 1.2 million people in the United States are of Haitian ancestry.

The two largest communities are in southern Florida (300,000) and the New York metropolitan area (500,000), with smaller communities in Boston and Chicago. Yet, for the most part, Haitians are invisible immigrants, hidden by the banality of success. Detailed data from the 1990 census has not yet been released, but experts say that few Haitian immigrants are on welfare. And police say that even fewer get in trouble with the law. 5

This is not to suggest that all is wonderful for Haitians in America. Many are undocumented, trapped in fear and dead-end jobs. Behind the facade of pride and achievement, there is a litany of social problems: battered women, homeless families, economic exploitation. But like most immigrants, Haitians busy themselves in the pursuit of the American dream.

"Even some of those who came on boats are homeowners now," says the Rev. Thomas Wenski, director of the Pierre Toussant Center in the Little Haiti district of Miami. "It's a tribute to the Haitians' resourcefulness and their self-discipline."

My own family settled in New York in the 1950's. The Haitian community was small, consisting mostly of mixed-race members of the so-called elite.

Many could be mistaken easily for white or Hispanic. Back then, when New Yorkers learned we were Haitian, the reaction was mostly bewilderment. Most had never heard of Haiti, and they knew even less about it. "Tahiti?" I was asked more than once. We were proud to tell them about the world's first black republic, about our own struggle for independence and about Alexandre Dumas, the author of "The Three Musketeers" and the son of a Haitian general.

We had to explain that Haiti's middle and upper middle classes had their unique melting pot: Africans, Europeans, Arabs, Asians, Jews. That yes, most light-skinned Haitians were members of the elite, but so were some very dark-skinned Haitians. Status back home was a matter of history and family and circumstance, much more complex than the simplistic racial definitions in the United States. But we had no easy explanation for the sharp disparities of power and income back home, of the even sharper division among social classes—and of the treacherous politics that had forced us to America.

10 My family was typical of the ethnic stew that prevailed in Haiti's middle class. Emmanuel Dreyfuss, a Jew from Amiens, France who had served in the French Army in Indochina, sailed west in the 1880's in a wave of European emigrants and landed in Haiti. He would never confirm any relation to Capt. Alfred Dreyfus, the French officer whose anti-Semitic persecution had outraged the world and bitterly divided France, but my father remembered that mere mention of the case was enough to set his father's pince-nez quivering and his hands shaking. Dreyfuss married into a fair-skinned and class-conscious family of South American and French origin, which traced its roots in Haiti back to the 1700's.

My mother came from an equally haughty black family in Haiti's north, where Henri Christophe, one of the three leaders of the struggle for independence, had ruled. In fact, one of my great-great-grandfathers had helped build the Citadelle, Christophe's mountaintop fortress in the early 1800's, and another, Jean-Baptiste Riché, who had been a general in Christophe's army, served as a president of Haiti in the 1840's. But all that history and all that pride counted for naught in America. I remember well as a 7- or 8-year-old my bewilderment when my mother tried to explain why a cab wouldn't pick us up at the Miami airport because we were "colored." America—at least on matters of race—was a great social leveler.

Our community was centered on the West Side of Manhattan, mostly around 86th Street along Broadway and Amsterdam Avenue (West End Avenue and Riverside Drive landlords would not often rent to blacks—even exotic, light-skinned foreigners with French accents). A number of families managed to congregate at the Bretton Hall on 86th and Broadway and the Oxford Hotel at 88th and Amsterdam. My sisters and I went to the local Catholic schools. As in most families, our parents spoke French to us, Creole to each other, and did their best to preserve the memories of home. The nostalgia was most obvious at the loud Sunday dinners with steaming dishes of our savory foods from home—spicy chicken and goat, rice and djondjon, a dried mushroom—Haitian music, loud arguments in Creole and French and much laughter.

Some of our neighbors came from other highly respected Haitian families, but in New York, they were just blacks who took care of other people's children, cleaned other people's apartments, worked in the garment factories around 34th Street or drove cabs. The weekend gatherings were an opportunity to regain self-respect, to cast off the burden of being black in a white world and to recall what they had lost: privilege, status, servants, warm weather. Few from that old middle and upper class had plans to set down roots in America.

The first hint that our stay might be long came when the nature of the Haitian community began to change in the 1960's. Since François Duvalier had taken power in 1957, many of my parents' friends had expected him to be ousted in a matter of weeks or months. After all, that was the pattern for Haitian presidents. But his regime, swept into office on a vague pattern of black power, became unusually tenacious. Duvalier instituted a reign of terror uncommon even for Haiti. Schoolchildren were bused to public executions. Opponents, real or imagined, were beaten or killed with impunity. Those who had stayed behind lived in daily fear of arbitrary arrest. The Tontons Macoutes, Duvalier's vicious militia, swaggered through the towns and villages in dark glasses and denim suits, with pistols tucked in their belts.

15 New arrivals to our community from Haiti were now politicians and professionals who had finally grasped the scope of Duvalier's brutality. One frequent Sunday guest was a former Senator who had been forced to flee after running afoul of the regime. He came from a prominent political family and he lived for politics. He and his cronies crowded the benches on a Broadway traffic island on weekends, naming each other to hypothetical cabinets and reading position papers out loud in flawless French, waiting for the change of Government. But on weekdays, the Senator pushed a hand truck through the bustling traffic of the garment district. Sharp-tongued Haitians were merciless. "Make way for the Senator," they shouted as he maneuvered down Seventh Avenue. "Make way for Senator Broadway."

After "Papa Doc" Duvalier died in 1971 and his 19-year-old son, Jean-Claude, was placed at the head of the government as "President-for-Life," the exodus accelerated. Many of the new arrivals were working-class Haitians, chased out by the realization that no improvement in their lives was likely under a regime led by a boy more interested in fast cars and women than in public works and budgets. The stream of refugees became a flood, many of them illegals who came on tourist visas. They were not "people we know," the elite sniffed.

The West Side was no longer the Haitian haven. Gentrification had priced the neighborhood out of reach. People began moving to Flushing and Elmhurst, in Queens. The new, poorer arrivals settled around Nostrand and Flatbush avenues in Crown Heights, Florida, with employment opportunities at Miami Beach resorts and weather reminiscent of Haiti's, became a new center of Haitian activity.

"The boat people are a tragic aspect of Haitian life," says one Haitian immigrant. "But most of us are not boat people and we hate being lumped with them." I can understand his anger. The majority of Haitians arrive in the United States by plane. The daily American Airlines Flight No. 658 between Port-au-Prince and Kennedy Airport disgorges passengers who reflect the range of Haitians living in the United States. There are those who are returning from visiting relatives back home: the prosperous upper-middle-class Haitians are deliberately casual in their designer jeans and resort wear; the working-class immigrants wear their Sunday best and carry the bags of food from home that they hope to slip by alert customs officials. Then there are the new arrivals, often shivering in their thin suits and dresses and glancing about with open anxiety for the relatives and friends who are supposed to meet them.

In the Haitian enclaves of New York and Miami, a strong entrepreneurial spirit has spawned grocery stores, barbershops, restaurants, real-estate firms and medical clinics. Bustling shopping districts have taken on a strong Caribbean flavor, laced with Haiti's African-inflected Creole and driven by the best of merengues and compas. Haitian weekly papers report the minutiae of political maneuverings back home. Radio and cable television programs air heated political debates and, increasingly, instructions on coping with life in America. Farther north, the computer boom along Route 128 in Massachusetts has created plenty of factory jobs for Haitians.

The latest wave of Haitian immigrants comes on the bicentennial of the first. Haiti, then called St.-Domingue, was the richest of the French colonies. In the 1790's, the black populace of the island revolted against slavery and there was a panicked exodus. Thousands of whites, free blacks and slaves fled to American seaports, contributing to large French-speaking communities in New Orleans, Norfolk, Va., Baltimore, New York and Boston. 20

Immigrants from Haiti who made their mark in the United States during the 18th and 19th centuries include Jean Baptiste Point du Sable, a trapper who settled on the shore of Lake Michigan and became the founder of the city of Chicago. There was also Pierre Toussaint, whom the Vatican is considering naming the first black saint from the United States. Toussaint, a devout Catholic, came to New York as the slave of a French family in 1787. He became a prominent hairdresser to New York's rich, and a major fund-raiser who helped the sick and the destitute.

France remained the center of the universe for most educated Haitians. Only a few middle-class Haitians chose the United States, which the elite saw through Francophile eyes as a nation bursting with energy but lacking in civilization. My own father was considered something of a rebel when he decided to come to America in 1927 to accept a scholarship to graduate school at Yale. During World War II, with access to Europe cut off by the war, growing numbers of Haitian scholars came here. Felix Morisseau-Leroy, a renowned poet and playwright, lived at the International House on Riverside Drive with a half-dozen men and women who would be Haiti's brightest literary stars in the postwar years. Morisseau-Leroy recalls few racial incidents. "We were treated well," he says. "We had the feeling that the Americans had been told to be nice to us."

The slow migration of Haitians to the United States might have remained unnoticed by most Americans had not the first bodies washed up on the Florida coast in 1979. The very poor were now determined to escape the dictatorship of Baby Doc, which had changed the emphasis of Government from terror to just plain larceny. Blaise Augustin, a native of St. Louis-du-Nord, an impoverished town in Haiti's northwest, saved enough money to take a boat to the Bahamas in 1977. When the newly independent island began expelling Haitians, Augustin headed for Florida. He was one of several dozen Haitians pushed off an overcrowded boat by a panicked smuggler. A woman and her four children drowned. Augustin managed to make it to the Florida shore. The son of peasant farmers, Augustin is a small-boned slim man with an uncanny resemblance to exiled President Jean-Bertrand Aristide. Like many boat people, he has unusual energy.

Policy makers argue about whether the Haitians are economic or political refugees. Augustin's description of the obstacles he faced back home explain why a simple answer is difficult. "If you saved some money and bought some cement blocks to add to your house or opened a small grocery store, everyone noticed," he says. "Sooner or later, the local Tontons Macoutes or chef de section (a regional military chieftain) approached you for a loan. If you refused, he might denounce you as an opponent of the Government and have you arrested.

"In Haiti, it's very hard to move up," says Augustin. "The U.S. is a country with a lot of complications, but if you're smart, you can get ahead." [25]

Today, Augustin is an outreach worker for a Catholic church in Pompano Beach, 20 miles north of Miami. He owns his home and a car. He and his wife have opened a small variety store to serve the town's growing Haitian population. He has taken a course in photography and now takes pictures at weddings and baptisms. The store shares a tiny mall with a sleepy Haitian restaurant and a Haitian doctor's office. It stocks Haitian foods, records and tapes. An employee helps Augustin's wife with the store while he is engaged in church business. "I have a vision of becoming a businessman," says Augustin, modestly.

Augustin's story—and his ambition—are repeated again and again in south Florida. Dr. David Abellard, who lives a few miles farther north along the Florida coast, is a fine example of the immigrant success story Americans like to celebrate. As a boy growing up in a hilltop village, he woke before dawn and walked miles in bare feet to attend school. On Saturdays, he helped his peasant mother sell vegetables in the market. Today, he has a profitable medical practice in Lake Worth, 60 miles north of Miami. A steady stream of affluent patients passes through his waiting room. Abellard has no nostalgia about home. "I had influential friends," he says, citing connections made in high school and at the University of Haiti, where he earned degrees in law and medicine. "I could have been a minister. But it would have been very unstable. I might have been shot."

Little Haiti, which tourist-conscious Miami officials have touted as an example of immigrant entrepreneurship, may have passed its peak. The several blocks of shops, restaurants, travel agencies, community centers, law offices and doctors' clinics that display signs in French, Creole and English seem worse for wear. A bad imitation of Port-au-Prince's famous Iron Market sits seedy and half-empty.

Haitians in New York have also begun to abandon their traditional enclaves in Manhattan, Queens and Brooklyn. The ads in Haiti-Observateur, the largest Haitian paper in the United States, with a circulation of 30,000, are directed to Haitians in northern New Jersey, Spring Valley N.Y., Nassau and Suffolk counties in New York, Boston and Montreal.

Radio and television are the glue that holds these geographically dispersed communities together. Programs like "Moment Creole," which airs every Sunday on WLIB-AM from 10 A.M. to 4 P.M., and "Eddy Publicité" on WNWK-FM, offer a mix of Haitian music, news and a discussion of community issues. There is even a radio "underground," subcarrier stations that require a special radio, but offer freewheeling discussion, call-in shows, news, gossip and nuts-and-bolts services like death announcements. Radio Tropical (50,000 subscribers) and Radio Soleil d'Haiti (10,000 subscribers) both broadcast 24 hours a day over special radios that the stations sell to listeners for between $75 and $120. Several cable television programs have also begun to target Haitian audiences. Some focus on community or health issues—or politics. Others simply show videos made by Haitian performers.

The ability of broadcast media to reach an audience of a half a million interests Wilner Boucicault, 43, whose A & B Furniture & Appliances in Brooklyn is one of the largest Haitian-owned businesses in New York.

He has ambitions to help propel Haitian immigrants to the next important stage in their Americanization—politics. "Haitians are ready," says Boucicault, who came to New York from Haiti at age 19, attended New York University and eventually opened the store with a partner. "Since Aristide, Haitians have developed a political consciousness. They have to organize themselves here." He and other Haitians trace their American political awakening to April 20, 1990. That was the day more than 50,000 Haitians marched across the Brooklyn Bridge to City Hall. They were protesting the most damaging label yet attached to Haitians. The Centers for Disease Control and the American Red Cross had ruled that no Haitians could give blood because all Haitians were AIDS risks. That ruling, the only one ever applied to one nationality, was later rescinded.

The size of the march, and the ability of Haitian leaders to organize it, stunned New York's political establishment—and the organizers themselves. "We told the police we expected 5,000 people, but we hoped 25,000 would turn up," says Fritz Martial, a vice president at Inner City Broadcasting. "When we saw the size of the crowd, we ran to the front of the line in panic." Now Martial, Boucicault and others are looking for a Haitian candidate to back for City Council from Brooklyn, which has the highest concentration of Haitians in New York.

Bringing no historical baggage to their American relationships, Haitians tend to get along with neighbors from different ethnic backgrounds. In Crown

Heights, where American-born blacks and Hasidic Jews have been at odds, Haitians mention Jews as a model of effective political organization. Haitian stores sit side by side with shops owned by Dominicans and British West Indians. On Sundays, neatly dressed Jamaicans and Trinidadians, flow out of Methodist and Evangelical churches, shouting to their children in English patois. On the same streets, Haitians pour out of the Catholic churches, shouting caution in French and Creole to their suited and ribboned children.

Even Haitians like me, who have been in America far longer than in Haiti, retain a close identification with our native land. We agonize over the political turmoil there, and we rage over United States inaction. But while we look for ways to help, we have no plans to go back. Ghislain Gouraiges Jr., 34, and his family left Haiti when he was 8 years old. Gouraiges grew up in Albany, where his father taught at the State University. Today Gouraiges works for Citibank in Miami, where he manages the accounts of multimillionaires and looks the part: well-tailored pinstripes, suspenders, two-tone shirts and gold cufflinks. There is no trace of Haiti in his English and he has no ambition to return there. Yet, "I feel Haitian," he says. "One of the reasons I moved here was to be closer to Haiti."

For those who have difficulties grabbing the first rung of the ladder of American success, a group of self-help programs and social agencies is evolving. Haitian-Americans United for Progress sits in a nondescript storefront on a section of Linden Boulevard in Queens dominated by Haitian businesses. On a Saturday morning, the Haitian-American Women's Advocacy Network is meeting. They have contacted American feminist groups for advice and are drawing up a constitution and a charter. "Many Haitian women need help integrating themselves into American society," says Marie Thérèse Guilloteau, one of the organizers. "They have a different role here."

In Brooklyn, a community organizer, Lola Poisson, just won a $400,000 New York City grant to provide mental health services to Haitians and other Caribbean immigrants. Poisson says she wants to provide an "extended family" for Haitians, who often feel emotionally lost in New York.

At the Haitian Information Center on Flatbush Avenue, the entire staff is unpaid. Daniel Huttinot, one of the founders, says the organization was started to counter misinformation about Haiti and Haitians, but its staff soon learned that Haitians had more pressing needs. They switched gears and now offer help with immigration problems, teaching language classes and courses in computers. In Miami, the Pierre Toussaint Haitian Catholic Center offers literacy classes, Sunday School, preparation for the high-school equivalency exam and help in job placement.

Getting these services is hardly unusual for new immigrants. What is remarkable is the involvement of Haitians, who came from a country where social services and philanthropy are usually left to foreign missionaries. In a way, this charity is a sign of their Americanization.

A subject of ambiguity for Haitians is race. Most are eager to talk about their country's role as the first independent black nation in the modern era. Even middle-class Haitians are now willing to acknowledge the deep African roots of Haitian culture. But they are less sure about the value of being categorized with African-Americans. Most will acknowledge that many of the obstacles they face are racial. "They want to force us to live in black neighborhoods by pricing us out of the white areas," complains Augustin, the young entrepreneur in Pompano Beach. "We need the help of black Americans to help save Haiti, and to help against what whites do to us here."

Yet, almost as quickly, he begins to delineate the differences he perceives between African-Americans and Haitians. "We have a different culture. We are completely different," says Augustin, echoing comments I hear frequently in discussions with Haitians. What these perceived differences are depends on what experience the Haitians have had with black Americans. Those in Miami's Little Haiti, which abuts impoverished Liberty City, often talk in stereotypes. "The blacks" are not clean, they say. They do not work. They don't care about their homes. When pressed, Haitians acknowledge that they have heard about the black middle class. But living near poor black neighborhoods that most successful blacks escaped long ago, many Haitians say they don't know any "good blacks."

Most Haitian-Americans seek a middle ground between assimilation and ethnic isolation. Edeline Léger, 15, and her sister Edna, 13, live in Lincroft, a New Jersey suburb. They were both born in the United States. Their father, Eddy, is a settlements manager for the brokerage firm of Kidder Peabody. Although the two girls have never been to Haiti, they are its staunch defenders. They write book reports in school on Haitian topics and don't hesitate to speak in defense of the country they've never seen. "We're not ashamed of Haiti," Edeline says. "We tell everybody we're Haitian."

I suspect that being Haitian teen-agers in a predominantly white suburb makes them exotic, as we were decades earlier. But I find myself comforted by their self-assertion. Haitians will change in America and they will learn to flex their new economic and political muscle. They are now moving more deeply into the mainstream, away from Little Haiti to the Miami suburbs, from Brooklyn to Westchester, from the West Side to Long Island and New Jersey, from Boston to Newton and Brookline. But they seem in no danger of losing their identity. No one says "Tahiti?" any more when we say Haiti, and even the boat people label and the AIDS label will pass too. Someday the other Americans will even appreciate our role as a new link in the long chain of hyphenated Americans.

DISCUSSING THE TEXT

1. At the beginning of this essay, Dreyfuss suggests that, when posed to a foreigner, the question "Where are you from?" is "a way to classify you: to embrace or dismiss you." Do you agree or disagree with this statement? Have you ever asked anyone this question? If so, what happened? Has anyone asked you a similar question? If so, how did you react?
2. Why do you think Dreyfuss makes a distinction between the more established Haitian immigrant community and the so-called boat people?

3. Near the end of his essay, Dreyfuss says that "Most Haitian-Americans seek a middle ground between assimilation and ethnic isolation." Which, if any, of the people Dreyfuss refers to in this piece would you say have reached this "middle ground"? Why? Do you agree that this is an ideal place for them to be? Why or why not?

WRITING ABOUT THE TEXT

4. Write two paragraphs that address the following questions: Why does Dreyfuss call Haitians "the invisible immigrants"? Do you agree with his observation? Can you think of any other immigrant group that could be defined as "invisible"?
5. Reread the passage in which Dreyfuss discusses the intersection of class and race in the immigrant Haitian community that he grew up in during the 1950s (par. 8–13). Then write a brief essay (two to three pages) addressing the significance of class, race, and gender in the formation of an American immigrant's identity.
6. Dreyfuss concludes by referring to Haitian immigrants as a "new link in the long chain of hyphenated Americans." Do you agree or disagree with this depiction of immigrants to this country as forming a "long chain"? Write a one-page response to this image.
7. Do some research into different "boat people" who have arrived in the state of Florida in the last few years. Write a brief essay reporting on who these people are, where they have come from, how they have been treated, and where they are now. (Articles in newspapers and news magazines over the last year should provide relevant information.)

JAMES BALDWIN

Stranger in the Village

James Baldwin (1924–1987) was born and raised in Harlem, in New York City. He developed his oratorical skills as a teenage preacher in his father's church while at the same time reading voraciously. The early support of Richard Wright (author of Native Son*) confirmed Baldwin's vocation as a writer, and he began to publish essays and stories. Finding American society stifling to his creativity, Baldwin moved to France in 1948; he lived there on and off for the rest of his life.*

During his career, which bridged the periods of segregation and the civil rights struggle, Baldwin produced work that was crucial for both black and white Americans. It gave them a sense of the psychological dimensions of racism and illuminated the nuances of the struggle for identity in a racist society. Again and again, Baldwin called for the necessary acceptance of reality as the foundation for a just society and a mature identity. Although he was sometimes criticized for writing primarily for a white audience, his prophetic denunciations and searching critiques made Baldwin one of the most important writers of the fifties and sixties. He has been called one of the great essayists of the twentieth century.

"Stranger in the Village," from Baldwin's early collection Notes of a Native Son *(1955), begins as do so many of Baldwin's essays, on an autobiographical note. Baldwin is staying in a remote village in the Swiss mountains that offers "no distractions whatever and has the further advantage of being extremely cheap." But in reality, as the essay unfolds, we realize that Baldwin has been much distracted by his anomalous situation. Furthermore, his racial identity as the only black man in a white village has provoked more general thoughts and questions about his identity at home, in the United States. Thus Baldwin presents himself here as an exile in a double sense: from white America and from his African past, which was taken from him by the history of enslavement.*

Central to Baldwin's argument is the notion that white supremacy is a myth of innocence based on an essentially unreal view of the world, a myth that denies blacks their humanity and so fosters their rage. In trying to rationalize the fantasy of white supremacy, Baldwin maintains, white society is "pathological." Although he begins from a point of exile from America and a sense of the profound difference between white and black, Baldwin moves in this essay toward a convergence of the interests, and the futures, of white and black peoples in the world.

From all available evidence no black man had ever set foot in this tiny Swiss village before I came. I was told before arriving that I would probably be a "sight" for the village; I took this to mean that people of my complexion were rarely seen in Switzerland, and also that city people are always something of a "sight" outside of the city. It did not occur to me—possibly because I am an American—that there could be people anywhere who had never seen a Negro.

It is a fact that cannot be explained on the basis of the inaccessibility of the village. The village is very high, but it is only four hours from Milan and three hours from Lausanne. It is true that it is virtually unknown. Few people making plans for a holiday would elect to come here. On the other hand, the villagers are able, presumably, to come and go as they please—which they do: to another town at the foot of the mountain, with a population of approximately five thousand, the nearest place to see a movie or go to the bank. In the village there is no movie house, no bank, no library, no theater; very few radios, one jeep, one station wagon; and, at the moment, one typewriter, mine, an invention which the woman next door to me here had never seen. There are about six hundred people living here, all Catholic—I conclude this from the fact that the Catholic church is open all year round, whereas the Protestant chapel, set off on a hill a little removed from the village, is open only in the summertime when the tourists arrive. There are four or five hotels, all closed now, and four or five *bistros,* of which, however, only two do any business during the winter. These two do not do a great deal, for life in the village seems to end around nine or ten o'clock. There are a few stores, butcher, baker, *épicerie,*[1] a hardware store, and a money-changer—who cannot change travelers'

---

[1]*épicerie:* (French) grocery *(Ed.)*

checks, but must send them down to the bank, an operation which takes two or three days. There is something called the *Ballet Haus,* closed in the winter and used for God knows what, certainly not ballet, during the summer. There seems to be only one schoolhouse in the village, and this for the quite young children; I suppose this to mean that their older brothers and sisters at some point descend from these mountains in order to complete their education—possibly, again, to the town just below. The landscape is absolutely forbidding, mountains towering on all four sides, ice and snow as far as the eye can reach. In this white wilderness, men and women and children move all day, carrying washing, wood, buckets of milk or water, sometimes skiing on Sunday afternoons. All week long boys and young men are to be seen shoveling snow off the rooftops, or dragging wood down from the forest in sleds.

The village's only real attraction, which explains the tourist season, is the hot spring water. A disquietingly high proportion of these tourists are cripples, or semicripples, who come year after year—from other parts of Switzerland, usually—to take the waters. This lends the village, at the height of the season, a rather terrifying air of sanctity, as though it were a lesser Lourdes.[2] There is often something beautiful, there is always something awful, in the spectacle of a person who has lost one of his faculties, a faculty he never questioned until it was gone, and who struggles to recover it. Yet people remain people, on crutches or indeed on deathbeds; and wherever I passed, the first summer I was here, among the native villagers or among the lame, a wind passed with me—of astonishment, curiosity, amusement, and outrage. That first summer I stayed two weeks and never intended to return. But I did return in the winter, to work; the village offers, obviously, no distractions whatever and has the further advantage of being extremely cheap. Now it is winter again, a year later, and I am here again. Everyone in the village knows my name, though they scarcely ever use it, knows that I come from America—though, this, apparently, they will never really believe: black men come from Africa—and everyone knows that I am the friend of the son of a woman who was born here, and that I am staying in their chalet. But I remain as much a stranger today as I was the first day I arrived, and the children shout *Neger! Neger!* as I walk along the streets.

It must be admitted that in the beginning I was far too shocked to have any real reaction. In so far as I reacted at all, I reacted by trying to be pleasant—it being a great part of the American Negro's education (long before he goes to school) that he must make people "like" him. This smile-and-the-world-smiles-with-you routine worked about as well in this situation as it had in the situation for which it was designed, which is to say that it did not work at all. No one, after all, can be liked whose human weight and complexity cannot be, or has not been, admitted. My smile was simply another unheard-of phe-

---

[2]*Lourdes:* town in southwest France with a religious shrine that attracts millions of pilgrims annually who have faith in the curative powers of its water (*Ed.*)

nomenon which allowed them to see my teeth—they did not, really, see my smile and I began to think that, should I take to snarling, no one would notice any difference. All of the physical characteristics of the Negro which had caused me, in America, a very different and almost forgotten pain were nothing less than miraculous—or infernal—in the eyes of the village people. Some thought my hair was the color of tar, that it had the texture of wire, or the texture of cotton. It was jocularly suggested that I might let it all grow long and make myself a winter coat. If I sat in the sun for more than five minutes some daring creature was certain to come along and gingerly put his fingers on my hair, as though he were afraid of an electric shock, or put his hand on my hand, astonished that the color did not rub off. In all of this, in which it must be conceded there was the charm of genuine wonder and in which there was certainly no element of intentional unkindness, there was yet no suggestion that I was human: I was simply a living wonder.

I knew that they did not mean to be unkind, and I know it now; it is necessary, nevertheless, for me to repeat this to myself each time that I walk out of the chalet. The children who shout *Neger!* have no way of knowing the echoes this sound raises in me. They are brimming with good humor and the more daring swell with pride when I stop to speak with them. Just the same, there are days when I cannot pause and smile, when I have no heart to play with them; when, indeed, I mutter sourly to myself, exactly as I muttered on the streets of a city these children have never seen, when I was no bigger than these children are now: *Your* mother *was a nigger.* Joyce[3] is right about history being a nightmare—but it may be the nightmare from which no one *can* awaken. People are trapped in history and history is trapped in them. 5

There is a custom in the village—I am told it is repeated in many villages—of "buying" African natives for the purpose of converting them to Christianity. There stands in the church all year round a small box with a slot for money, decorated with a black figurine, and into this box the villagers drop their francs. During the *carnaval* which precedes Lent, two village children have their faces blackened—out of which bloodless darkness their blue eyes shine like ice—and fantastic horsehair wigs are placed on their blond heads; thus disguised, they solicit among the villagers for money for the missionaries in Africa. Between the box in the church and the blackened children, the village "bought" last year six or eight African natives. This was reported to me with pride by the wife of one of the *bistro* owners and I was careful to express astonishment and pleasure at the solicitude shown by the village for the souls of black folk. The *bistro* owner's wife beamed with a pleasure far more genuine than my own and seemed to feel that I might now breathe more easily concerning the souls of at least six of my kinsmen.

I tried not to think of these so lately baptized kinsmen, of the price paid for them, or the peculiar price they themselves would pay, and said nothing

---

[3]*James Joyce* (1882–1941): Irish author; Baldwin refers here to Joyce's much-quoted line from his novel *Ulysses* (1922): "History is the nightmare from which I am trying to awake."

about my father, who having taken his own conversion too literally never, at bottom, forgave the white world (which he described as heathen) for having saddled him with a Christ in whom, to judge at least from their treatment of him, they themselves no longer believed. I thought of white men arriving for the first time in an African village, strangers there, as I am a stranger here, and tried to imagine the astounded populace touching their hair and marveling at the color of their skin. But there is a great difference between being the first white man to be seen by Africans and being the first black man to be seen by whites. The white man takes the astonishment as tribute, for he arrives to conquer and to convert the natives, whose inferiority in relation to himself is not even to be questioned; whereas I, without a thought of conquest, find myself among a people whose culture controls me, has even, in a sense, created me, people who have cost me more in anguish and rage than they will ever know, who yet do not even know of my existence. The astonishment with which I might have greeted them, should they have stumbled into my African village a few hundred years ago, might have rejoiced their hearts. But the astonishment with which they greet me today can only poison mine.

And this is so despite everything I may do to feel differently, despite my friendly conversations with the *bistro* owner's wife, despite their three-year-old son who has at last become my friend, despite the *saluts* and *bonsoirs* which I exchange with people as I walk, despite the fact that I know that no individual can be taken to task for what history is doing, or has done. I say that the culture of these people controls me—but they can scarcely be held responsible for European culture. America comes out of Europe, but these people have never seen America, nor have most of them seen more of Europe than the hamlet at the foot of their mountain. Yet they move with an authority which I shall never have; and they regard me, quite rightly, not only as a stranger in their village but as a suspect latecomer, bearing no credentials, to everything they have—however unconsciously—inherited.

For this village, even were it incomparably more remote and incredibly more primitive, is the West, the West onto which I have been so strangely grafted. These people cannot be, from the point of view of power, strangers anywhere in the world; they have made the modern world, in effect, even if they do not know it. The most illiterate among them is related, in a way that I am not, to Dante, Shakespeare, Michelangelo, Aeschylus, Da Vinci, Rembrandt, and Racine; the cathedral at Chartres says something to them which it cannot say to me, as indeed would New York's Empire State Building, should anyone here ever see it. Out of their hymns and dances come Beethoven and Bach. Go back a few centuries and they are in their full glory—but I am in Africa, watching the conquerors arrive.

The rage of the disesteemed is personally fruitless, but it is also absolutely inevitable; this rage, so generally discounted, so little understood even among the people whose daily bread it is, is one of the things that makes history. Rage can only with difficulty, and never entirely, be brought under the domination of the intelligence and is therefore not susceptible to any arguments whatever. This is a fact which ordinary representatives of the

Herrenvolk,[4] having never felt this rage and being unable to imagine it, quite fail to understand. Also, rage cannot be hidden, it can only be dissembled. This dissembling deludes the thoughtless, and strengthens rage and adds, to rage, contempt. There are, no doubt, as many ways of coping with the resulting complex of tensions as there are black men in the world, but no black man can hope ever to be entirely liberated from this internal warfare—rage, dissembling, and contempt having inevitably accompanied his first realization of the power of white men. What is crucial here is that, since white men represent in the black man's world so heavy a weight, white men have for black men a reality which is far from being reciprocal; and hence all black men have toward all white men an attitude which is designed, really, either to rob the white man of the jewel of his naïveté, or else to make it cost him dear.

The black man insists, by whatever means he finds at his disposal, that the white man cease to regard him as an exotic rarity and recognize him as a human being. This is a very charged and difficult moment, for there is a great deal of will power involved in the white man's naïveté. Most people are not naturally reflective any more than they are naturally malicious, and the white man prefers to keep the black man at a certain human remove because it is easier for him thus to preserve his simplicity and avoid being called to account for crimes committed by his forefathers, or his neighbors.

▼ ▼ ▼

There is a dreadful abyss between the streets of this village and the streets of the city in which I was born, between the children who shout *Neger!* today and those who shouted *Nigger!* yesterday—the abyss is experience, the American experience. The syllable hurled behind me today expresses, above all, wonder: I am a stranger here. But I am not a stranger in America and the same syllable riding on the American air expresses the war my presence has occasioned in the American soul.

For this village brings home to me this fact: that there was a day, and not really a very distant day, when Americans were scarcely Americans at all but discontented Europeans, facing a great unconquered continent and strolling, say, into a marketplace and seeing black men for the first time. The shock this spectacle afforded is suggested, surely, by the promptness with which they decided that these black men were not really men but cattle. It is true that the necessity on the part of the settlers of the New World of reconciling their moral assumptions with the fact—and the necessity—of slavery enhanced immensely the charm of this idea, and it is also true that this idea expresses, with a truly American bluntness, the attitude which to varying extents all masters have had toward all slaves.

But between all former slaves and slave-owners and the drama which begins for Americans over three hundred years ago at Jamestown, there are at least two differences to be observed. The American Negro slave could not

---

[4]*Herrenvolk:* (German) ruling class (*Ed.*)

suppose, for one thing, as slaves in past epochs had supposed and often done, that he would ever be able to wrest the power from his master's hands. This was a supposition which the modern era, which was to bring about such vast changes in the aims and dimensions of power, put to death; it only begins, in unprecedented fashion, and with dreadful implications, to be resurrected today. But even had this supposition persisted with undiminished force, the American Negro slave could not have used it to lend his condition dignity, for the reason that this supposition rests on another: that the slave in exile yet remains related to his past, has some means—if only in memory—of revering and sustaining the forms of his former life, is able, in short, to maintain his identity.

This was not the case with the American Negro slave. He is unique among the black men of the world in that his past was taken from him, almost literally, at one blow. One wonders what on earth the first slave found to say to the first dark child he bore. I am told that there are Haitians able to trace their ancestry back to African kings, but any American Negro wishing to go back so far will find his journey through time abruptly arrested by the signature on the bill of sale which served as the entrance paper for his ancestor. At the time—to say nothing of the circumstances—of the enslavement of the captive black man who was to become the American Negro, there was not the remotest possibility that he would ever take power from his master's hands. There was no reason to suppose that his situation would ever change, nor was there, shortly, anything to indicate that his situation had ever been different. It was his necessity, in the words of E. Franklin Frazier, to find a "motive for living under American culture or die." The identity of the American Negro comes out of this extreme situation, and the evolution of this identity was a source of the most intolerable anxiety in the minds and the lives of his masters.

For the history of the American Negro is unique also in this: that the question of his humanity, and of his rights therefore as a human being, became a burning one for several generations of Americans, so burning a question that it ultimately became one of those used to divide the nation. It is out of this argument that the venom of the epithet *Nigger!* is derived. It is an argument which Europe has never had, and hence Europe quite sincerely fails to understand how or why the argument arose in the first place, why its effects are so frequently disastrous and always so unpredictable, why it refuses until today to be entirely settled. Europe's black possessions remained—and do remain—in Europe's colonies, at which remove they represented no threat whatever to European identity. If they posed any problem at all for the European conscience, it was a problem which remained comfortingly abstract: in effect, the black man, *as a man,* did not exist for Europe. But in America, even as a slave, he was an inescapable part of the general social fabric and no American could escape having an attitude toward him. Americans attempt until today to make an abstraction of the Negro, but the very nature of these abstractions reveals the tremendous effects the presence of the Negro has had on the American character.

When one considers the history of the Negro in America it is of the greatest importance to recognize that the moral beliefs of a person, or a people, are never really as tenuous as life—which is not moral—very often causes them to appear; these create for them a frame of reference and a necessary hope, the hope being that when life has done its worst they will be enabled to rise above themselves and to triumph over life. Life would scarcely be bearable if this hope did not exist. Again, even when the worst has been said, to betray a belief is not by any means to have put oneself beyond its power; the betrayal of a belief is not the same thing as ceasing to believe. If this were not so there would be no moral standards in the world at all. Yet one must also recognize that morality is based on ideas and that all ideas are dangerous—dangerous because ideas can only lead to action and where the action leads no man can say. And dangerous in this respect: that confronted with the impossibility of remaining faithful to one's beliefs, and the equal impossibility of becoming free of them, one can be driven to the most inhuman excesses. The ideas on which American beliefs are based are not, though Americans often seem to think so, ideas which originated in America. They came out of Europe. And the establishment of democracy on the American continent was scarcely as radical a break with the past as was the necessity, which Americans faced, of broadening this concept to include black men.

This was, literally, a hard necessity. It was impossible, for one thing, for Americans to abandon their beliefs, not only because these beliefs alone seemed able to justify the sacrifices they had endured and the blood that they had spilled, but also because these beliefs afforded them their only bulwark against a moral chaos as absolute as the physical chaos of the continent it was their destiny to conquer. But in the situation in which Americans found themselves, these beliefs threatened an idea which, whether or not one likes to think so, is the very warp and woof of the heritage of the West, the idea of white supremacy.

Americans have made themselves notorious by the shrillness and the brutality with which they have insisted on this idea, but they did not invent it; and it has escaped the world's notice that those very excesses of which Americans have been guilty imply a certain, unprecedented uneasiness over the idea's life and power, if not, indeed, the idea's validity. The idea of white supremacy rests simply on the fact that white men are the creators of civilization (the present civilization, which is the only one that matters; all previous civilizations are simply "contributions" to our own) and are therefore civilization's guardians and defenders. Thus it was impossible for Americans to accept the black man as one of themselves, for to do so was to jeopardize their status as white men. But not so to accept him was to deny his human reality, his human weight and complexity, and the strain of denying the overwhelmingly undeniable forced Americans into rationalizations so fantastic that they approached the pathological.

20 At the root of the American Negro problem is the necessity of the American white man to find a way of living with the Negro in order to be able to live with himself. And the history of this problem can be reduced to the means used by Americans—lynch law and law, segregation and legal acceptance, terrorization and concession—either to come to terms with this necessity, or to find a way around it, or (most usually) to find a way of doing both these

things at once. The resulting spectacle, at once foolish and dreadful, led someone to make the quite accurate observation that "the Negro-in-America is a form of insanity which overtakes white men."

In this long battle, a battle by no means finished, the unforeseeable effects of which will be felt by many future generations, the white man's motive was the protection of his identity; the black man was motivated by the need to establish an identity. And despite the terrorization which the Negro in America endured and endures sporadically until today, despite the cruel and totally inescapable ambivalence of his status in his country, the battle for his identity has long ago been won. He is not a visitor to the West, but a citizen there, an American; as American as the Americans who despise him, the Americans who fear him, the Americans who love him—the Americans who became less than themselves, or rose to be greater than themselves by virtue of the fact that the challenge he represented was inescapable. He is perhaps the only black man in the world whose relationship to white men is more terrible, more subtle, and more meaningful than the relationship of bitter possessed to uncertain possessor. His survival depended, and his development depends, on his ability to turn his peculiar status in the Western world to his own advantage and, it may be, to the very great advantage of that world. It remains for him to fashion out of his experience that which will give him sustenance, and a voice.

The cathedral at Chartres, I have said, says something to the people of this village which it cannot say to me; but it is important to understand that this cathedral says something to me which it cannot say to them. Perhaps they are struck by the power of the spires, the glory of the windows; but they have known God, after all, longer than I have known him, and in a different way, and I am terrified by the slippery bottomless well to be found in the crypt, down which heretics were hurled to death, and by the obscene, inescapable gargoyles jutting out of the stone and seeming to say that God and the devil can never be divorced. I doubt that the villagers think of the devil when they face a cathedral because they have never been identified with the devil. But I must accept the status which myth, if nothing else, gives me in the West before I can hope to change the myth.

Yet, if the American Negro has arrived at his identity by virtue of the absoluteness of his estrangement from his past, American white men still nourish the illusion that there is some means of recovering the European innocence, of returning to a state in which black men do not exist. This is one of the greatest errors Americans can make. The identity they fought so hard to protect has, by virtue of that battle, undergone a change: Americans are as unlike any other white people in the world as it is possible to be. I do not think, for example, that it is too much to suggest that the American vision of the world—which allows so little reality, generally speaking, for any of the darker forces in human life, which tends until today to paint moral issues in glaring black and white—owes a great deal to the battle waged by Americans to maintain between themselves and black men a human separation which could not be bridged. It is only now beginning to be borne in on us—very faintly, it must be admitted, very slowly, and very much against our will—that this vision of the world is dangerously inaccurate, and perfectly useless. For it protects our moral high-mindedness at the terrible expense of weakening our grasp of reality. People who shut their eyes to reality simply invite their own destruction, and anyone who insists on remaining in a state of innocence long after that innocence is dead turns himself into a monster.

24 The time has come to realize that the interracial drama acted out on the American continent has not only created a new black man, it has created a new white man, too. No road whatever will lead Americans back to the simplicity of this European village where white men still have the luxury of looking on me as a stranger. I am not, really, a stranger any longer for any American alive. One of the things that distinguishes Americans from other people is that no other people has ever been so deeply involved in the lives of black men, and vice versa. This fact faced, with all its implications, it can be seen that the history of the American Negro problem is not merely shameful, it is also something of an achievement. For even when the worst has been said, it must also be added that the perpetual challenge posed by this problem was always, somehow, perpetually met. It is precisely this black-white experience which may prove of indispensable value to us in the world we face today. This world is white no longer, and it will never be white again.

DISCUSSING THE TEXT

1. At the beginning of his essay, how does Baldwin portray the Swiss village in which he finds himself? What details does he use to emphasize its strangeness to him? Have you ever been in a similar situation?
2. Baldwin's physical person—his black skin, his hair—seems endlessly fascinating to the Swiss villagers. How does Baldwin portray his own body? How does he react to the villagers' curiosity? How do you think you would react under similar circumstances?
3. Baldwin perceives the tiny Swiss village as a microcosm of white Western civilization; they are the makers of the modern world. Is this a fair characterization? In paragraph 15, he writes that "the American Negro slave . . . is unique among the black men of the world in that his past was taken from him, almost literally, at one blow." Is Baldwin implying that he is himself without history and without culture? Get together in a group of four or five students and discuss these issues; take notes, and be prepared to share your opinions with the class.
4. According to Baldwin, "the American Negro problem is . . . something of an achievement" (par. 24). In what sense does he consider it an achievement?

WRITING ABOUT THE TEXT

5. What are the sources of Baldwin's rage? Is such rage the sole privilege of the black man? Are there others in American society who might feel the similar rage of the "disesteemed"? Write a personal response addressing these issues.

6. Reread the passage in which Baldwin imagines the first meetings of blacks and whites in an African village (par. 13). What point is he trying to make here? How does this passage compare with James Agee's account, from a white point of view, of an encounter with blacks in the American South in "Near a Church" in Chapter 1 (pp. 58–63)? Write a brief essay comparing and contrasting the two different points of view.
7. Baldwin writes that "People are trapped in history and history is trapped in them" (par. 5); he also writes that "no individual can be taken to task for what history is doing, or has done" (par. 8). Write a one-page definition of the term *history* as Baldwin uses it in this essay.
8. Write two paragraphs that summarize Baldwin's opinion about the role of black people in the evolving American culture (par. 23–24). Then write a personal response focusing on the role of black people in American society today. Are there differences between Baldwin's vision of the role of black people and what you perceive that role to be today?

HANNAH ARENDT

We Refugees (January 1943)

Hannah Arendt was a leading political thinker and philosopher of the mid-twentieth century. She was, and is, widely admired (and debated) for her courage in confronting some of the most troubling problems of our century: totalitarianism, exile and identity, mass society, and the nature of evil in the wake of the Holocaust. Her most controversial book, Eichmann in Jerusalem: A Report on the Banality of Evil, *addressed the trial of Adolf Eichmann, who was responsible for the deaths of millions of Jews during the Holocaust. Rather than seeing Eichmann as an aberration, a demon, Arendt presented him as a person essentially like others, arguing that evil can be manifest in relatively commonplace individuals.*

Born in Germany in 1906, Hannah Arendt was awarded a Ph.D. in philosophy from Heidelberg University at the age of twenty-two. She quickly established a reputation as an outstanding essayist on philosophical and political matters, but as a Jew she was forced to flee Nazi Germany for France in 1933. As Nazi troops took over France, Arendt fled Paris for the United States, where she commenced a career in publishing and teaching, with appointments at Princeton, the University of Chicago, and the New School for Social Research in New York City. She died in 1975.

"We Refugees (January 1943)" was published originally in a Jewish journal, The Menorah Journal, *and was included in Arendt's 1978 volume,* The Jew as Pariah. *In this essay she explores, from her personal experience as a refugee, the experience of political exile. Approximately 150,000 German-speaking Jews immigrated to the United States between 1933 and 1945; unlike earlier Jewish immigrants, these individuals came not to better their economic conditions but to save their lives. From generally middle-class backgrounds, they thought of themselves, as Arendt*

makes clear, as Germans and as Jews; they have had a strong cultural influence on American life.

As you read this selection, consider whether Arendt presents the Jews as a special case, or whether their experience might stand for a more universal experience of exile. Although Arendt seems in a sense to celebrate the role of the Jew as pariah, or social outcast, by doing so she manages to use that status as a way of relating Jewish history to the history of "all other nations." As you read this essay, think about whether or not you agree with Arendt. That is, does the history of the Jews in some way prefigure the persecutions and exclusions of various groups in regions of conflict around the world today?

In the first place, we don't like to be called "refugees." We ourselves call each other "newcomers" or "immigrants." Our newspapers are papers for "Americans of German language"; and, as far as I know, there is not and never was any club founded by Hitler-persecuted people whose name indicated that its members were refugees.

A refugee used to be a person driven to seek refuge because of some act committed or some political opinion held. Well, it is true we have had to seek refuge; but we committed no acts and most of us never dreamt of having any radical political opinion. With us the meaning of the term "refugee" has changed. Now "refugees" are those of us who have been so unfortunate as to arrive in a new country without means and have to be helped by Refugee Committees.

Before this war broke out we were even more sensitive about being called refugees. We did our best to prove to other people that we were just ordinary immigrants. We declared that we had departed of our own free will to countries of our choice, and we denied that our situation had anything to do with "so-called Jewish problems." Yes, we were "immigrants" or "newcomers" who had left our country because, one fine day, it no longer suited us to stay, or for purely economic reasons. We wanted to rebuild our lives, that was all. In order to rebuild one's life one has to be strong and an optimist. So we are very optimistic.

Our optimism, indeed, is admirable, even if we say so ourselves. The story of our struggle has finally become known. We lost our home, which means the familiarity of daily life. We lost our occupation, which means the confidence that we are of some use in this world. We lost our language, which means the naturalness of reactions, the simplicity of gestures, the unaffected expression of feelings. We left our relatives in the Polish ghettos and our best friends have been killed in concentration camps, and that means the rupture of our private lives.

Nevertheless, as soon as we were saved—and most of us had to be saved several times—we started our new lives and tried to follow as closely as possible all the good advice our saviors passed on to us. We were told to forget; and we forgot quicker than anybody ever could imagine. In a friendly way we were reminded that the new country would become a new home; and after four weeks in France or six weeks in America, we pretended to be 5

Frenchmen or Americans. The more optimistic among us would even add that their whole former life had been passed in a kind of unconscious exile and only their new country now taught them what a home really looks like. It is true we sometimes raise objections when we are told to forget about our former work; and our former ideals are usually hard to throw over if our social standard is at stake. With the language, however, we find no difficulties; after a single year optimists are convinced they speak English as well as their mother tongue; and after two years they swear solemnly that they speak English better than any other language—their German is a language they hardly remember.

In order to forget more efficiently we rather avoid any allusion to concentration or internment camps we experienced in nearly all European countries—it might be interpreted as pessimism or lack of confidence in the new homeland. Besides, how often have we been told that nobody likes to listen to all that; hell is no longer a religious belief or a fantasy, but something as real as houses and stones and trees. Apparently nobody wants to know that contemporary history has created a new kind of human beings—the kind that are put in concentration camps by their foes and in internment camps by their friends.

Even among ourselves we don't speak about this past. Instead, we have found our own way of mastering an uncertain future. Since everybody plans and wishes and hopes, so do we. Apart from these general human attitudes, however, we try to clear up the future more scientifically. After so much bad luck we want a course as sure as a gun. Therefore, we leave the earth with all its uncertainties behind and we cast our eyes up to the sky. The stars tell us—rather than the newspapers—when Hitler will be defeated and when we shall become American citizens. We think the stars more reliable advisers than all our friends; we learn from the stars when we should have lunch with our benefactors and on what day we have the best chances of filling out one of these countless questionnaires which accompany our present lives. Sometimes we don't rely even on the stars but rather on the lines of our hand or the signs of our handwriting. Thus we learn less about political events but more about our own dear selves, even though somehow psychoanalysis has gone out of fashion. Those happier times are past when bored ladies and gentlemen of high society conversed about the genial misdemeanors of their early childhood. They don't want ghost-stories any more; it is real experiences that make their flesh creep. There is no longer any need of bewitching the past; it is spellbound enough in reality. Thus, in spite of our outspoken optimism, we use all sorts of magical tricks to conjure up the spirits of the future.

I don't know which memories and which thoughts nightly dwell in our dreams. I dare not ask for information, since I, too, had rather be an optimist. But sometimes I imagine that at least nightly we think of our dead or we remember the poems we once loved. I could even understand how our friends of the West coast, during the curfew, should have had such curious notions as to believe that we are not only "prospective citizens" but present "enemy aliens." In daylight, of course, we become only "technically" enemy aliens—all refugees know this. But when technical reasons prevented you from leaving your home during the dark hours, it certainly was not easy to avoid some dark speculations about the relation between technicality and reality.

No, there is something wrong with our optimism. There are those odd optimists among us who, having made a lot of optimistic speeches, go home and turn on the gas or make use of a skyscraper in quite an unexpected way. They seem to prove that our proclaimed cheerfulness is based on a dangerous readiness for death. Brought up in the conviction that life is the highest good and death the greatest dismay, we became witnesses and victims of worse terrors than death—without having been able to discover a higher ideal than life. Thus, although death lost its horror for us, we became neither willing nor capable to risk our lives for a cause. Instead of fighting—or thinking about how to become able to fight back—refugees have got used to wishing death to friends or relatives; if somebody dies, we cheerfully imagine all the trouble he has been saved. Finally many of us end by wishing that we, too, could be saved some trouble, and act accordingly.

10

Since 1938—since Hitler's invasion of Austria—we have seen how quickly eloquent optimism could change to speechless pessimism. As time went on, we got worse—even more optimistic and even more inclined to suicide. Austrian Jews under Schuschnigg were such a cheerful people—all impartial observers admired them. It was quite wonderful how deeply convinced they were that nothing could happen to them. But when German troops invaded the country and Gentile neighbors started riots at Jewish homes, Austrian Jews began to commit suicide.

Unlike other suicides, our friends leave no explanation of their deed, no indictment, no charge against a world that had forced a desperate man to talk and to behave cheerfully to his very last day. Letters left by them are conventional, meaningless documents. Thus, funeral orations we make at their open graves are brief, embarrassed and very hopeful. Nobody cares about motives, they seem to be clear to all of us.

I speak of unpopular facts; and it makes things worse that in order to prove my point I do not even dispose of the sole arguments which impress modern people—figures. Even those Jews who furiously deny the existence of the Jewish people give us a fair chance of survival as far as figures are concerned—how else could they prove that only a few Jews are criminals and that many Jews are being killed as good patriots in wartime? Through their effort to save the statistical life of the Jewish people we know that Jews had the lowest suicide rate among all civilized nations. I am quite sure those figures are no longer correct, but I cannot prove it with new figures, though I can certainly with new experiences. This might be sufficient for those skeptical souls who never were quite convinced that the measure of one's skull gives the exact idea of its content, or that statistics of crime show the exact level of national ethics. Anyhow, wherever European Jews are living today, they no longer behave according to statistical laws. Suicides occur not only among the panic-stricken people in Berlin and Vienna, in Bucharest or Paris, but in New York and Los Angeles, in Buenos Aires and Montevideo.

On the other hand, there has been little reported about suicides in the ghettos and concentration camps themselves. True, we had very few reports at all from Poland, but we have been fairly well informed about German and French concentration camps.

At the camp of Gurs, for instance, where I had the opportunity of spending some time, I heard only once about suicide, and that was the suggestion of a collective action, apparently a kind of protest in order to vex the French. When some of us remarked that we had been shipped there "*pour crever*"[1] in any case, the general mood turned suddenly into a violent courage of life. The general opinion held that one had to be abnormally asocial and unconcerned about general events if one was still able to interpret the whole accident as personal and individual bad luck and, accordingly, ended one's life personally and individually. But the same people, as soon as they returned to their own individual lives, being faced with seemingly individual problems, changed once more to this insane optimism which is next door to despair.

We are the first non-religious Jews persecuted—and we are the first ones who, not only *in extremis,* answer with suicide. Perhaps the philosophers are right who teach that suicide is the last and supreme guarantee of human freedom: not being free to create our lives or the world in which we live, we nevertheless are free to throw life away and to leave the world. Pious Jews, certainly, cannot realize this negative liberty; they perceive murder in suicide, that is, destruction of what man never is able to make, interference with the rights of the Creator. *Adonai nathan veadonai lakach* ("The Lord hath given and the Lord hath taken away"); and they would add: *baruch shem adonai* ("blessed be the name of the Lord"). For them suicide, like murder, means a blasphemous attack on creation as a whole. The man who kills himself asserts that life is not worth living and the world not worth sheltering him.

Yet our suicides are no mad rebels who hurl defiance at life and the world, who try to kill in themselves the whole universe. Theirs is a quiet and modest way of vanishing; they seem to apologize for the violent solution they have found for their personal problems. In their opinion, generally, political events had nothing to do with their individual fate; in good or bad times they would believe solely in their personality. Now they find some mysterious shortcomings in themselves which prevent them from getting along. Having felt entitled from their earliest childhood to a certain social standard, they are failures in their own eyes if this standard cannot be kept any longer. Their optimism is the vain attempt to keep head above water. Behind this front of cheerfulness, they constantly struggle with despair of themselves. Finally, they die of a kind of selfishness.

---

[1] *pour crever:* (French) to die (*Ed.*)

If we are saved we feel humiliated, and if we are helped we feel degraded. We fight like madmen for private existences with individual destinies, since we are afraid of becoming part of that miserable lot of *schnorrers* whom we, many of us former philanthropists, remember only too well. Just as once we failed to understand that the so-called *schnorrer* was a symbol of Jewish destiny and not a *shlemihl,*[2] so today we don't feel entitled to Jewish solidarity; we cannot realize that we by ourselves are not so much concerned as the whole Jewish people. Sometimes this lack of comprehension has been strongly supported by our protectors. Thus, I remember a director of a great charity concern in Paris who, whenever he received the card of a German-Jewish intellectual with the inevitable "Dr." on it, used to exclaim at the top of his voice, "Herr Doktor, Herr Doktor, Herr Schnorrer, Herr Schnorrer!"

The conclusion we drew from such unpleasant experiences was simple enough. To be a doctor of philosophy no longer satisfied us; and we learnt that in order to build a new life, one has first to improve on the old one. A nice little fairy-tale has been invented to describe our behavior; a forlorn émigré dachshund, in his grief, begins to speak: "Once, when I was a St. Bernard . . ."

Our new friends, rather overwhelmed by so many stars and famous men, hardly understand that at the basis of all our descriptions of past splendors lies one human truth: once we were somebodies about whom people cared, we were loved by friends, and even known by landlords as paying our rent regularly. Once we could buy our food and ride in the subway without being told we were undesirable. We have become a little hysterical since newspapermen started detecting us and telling us publicly to stop being disagreeable when shopping for milk and bread. We wonder how it can be done; we already are so damnably careful in every moment of our daily lives to avoid anybody guessing who we are, what kind of passport we have, where our birth certificates were filled out—and that Hitler didn't like us. We try the best we can to fit into a world where you have to be sort of politically minded when you buy your food.

Under such circumstances, St. Bernard grows bigger and bigger. I never can forget that young man who, when expected to accept a certain kind of work, sighed out, "You don't know to whom you speak; I was Section-manager in Karstadt's [a great department store in Berlin]." But there is also the deep despair of that middle-aged man who, going through countless shifts of different committees in order to be saved, finally exclaimed, "And nobody here knows who I am!" Since nobody would treat him as a dignified human being, he began sending cables to great personalities and his big relations. He learnt quickly that in this mad world it is much easier to be accepted as a "great man" than as a human being.

20

---

[2]*schnorrer:* (Yiddish) a beggar, cheapskate; *shlemihl:* (Yiddish) a foolish person, simpleton (*Ed.*)

The less we are free to decide who we are or to live as we like, the more we try to put up a front, to hide the facts, and to play roles. We were expelled from Germany because we were Jews. But having hardly crossed the French borderline, we were changed into "boches."[3] We were even told that we had to accept this designation if we really were against Hitler's racial theories. During seven years we played the ridiculous role of trying to be Frenchmen—at least, prospective citizens; but at the beginning of the war we were interned as "boches" all the same. In the meantime, however, most of us had indeed become such loyal Frenchmen that we could not even criticize a French governmental order; thus we declared it was all right to be interned. We were the first *"prisonniers volontaires"* history has ever seen. After the Germans invaded the country, the French government had only to change the name of the firm; having been jailed because we were Germans, we were not freed because we were Jews.

It is the same story all over the world, repeated again and again. In Europe the nazis confiscated our property; but in Brazil we have to pay 30% of our wealth, like the most loyal member of the *Bund der Auslandsdeutschen.* In Paris we could not leave our homes after eight o'clock because we were Jews; but in Los Angeles we are restricted because we are "enemy aliens." Our identity is changed so frequently that nobody can find out who we actually are.

Unfortunately, things don't look any better when we meet with Jews. French Jewry was absolutely convinced that all Jews coming from beyond the Rhine were what they called *Polaks*—what German Jewry called *Ostjuden.* But those Jews who really came from eastern Europe could not agree with their French brethren and called us *Jaeckes.* The sons of these *Jaecke*-haters—the second generation born in France and already duly assimilated—shared the opinion of the French Jewish upper classes. Thus, in the very same family, you could be called a *Jaecke* by the father and a *Polak* by the son.

Since the outbreak of the war and the catastrophe that has befallen European Jewry, the mere fact of being a refugee has prevented our mingling with native Jewish society, some exceptions only proving the rule. These unwritten social laws, though never publicly admitted, have the great force of public opinion. And such a silent opinion and practice is more important for our daily lives than all official proclamations of hospitality and good will.

Man is a social animal and life is not easy for him when social ties are cut off. Moral standards are much easier kept in the texture of a society. Very few individuals have the strength to conserve their own integrity if their social, political and legal status is completely confused. Lacking the courage to fight for a change of our social and legal status, we have decided instead, so many of us, to try a change of identity. And this curious behavior makes matters much worse. The confusion in which we live is partly our own work.

Some day somebody will write the true story of this Jewish emigration from Germany; and he will have to start with a description of that Mr. Cohn

[3]*boches:* (French) Germans (*Ed.*)

from Berlin who had always been a 150% German, a German super-patriot. In 1933 that Mr. Cohn found refuge in Prague and very quickly became a convinced Czech patriot—as true and as loyal a Czech patriot as he had been a German one. Time went on and about 1937 the Czech Government, already under some nazi pressure, began to expel its Jewish refugees, disregarding the fact that they felt so strongly as prospective Czech citizens. Our Mr. Cohn then went to Vienna; to adjust oneself there a definite Austrian patriotism was required. The German invasion forced Mr. Cohn out of that country. He arrived in Paris at a bad moment and he never did receive a regular residence-permit. Having already acquired a great skill in wishful thinking, he refused to take mere administrative measures seriously, convinced that he would spend his future life in France. Therefore, he prepared his adjustment to the French nation by identifying himself with "our" ancestor Vercingetorix.[4] I think I had better not dilate on the further adventures of Mr. Cohn. As long as Mr. Cohn can't make up his mind to be what he actually is, a Jew, nobody can foretell all the mad changes he will still have to go through.

A man who wants to lose his self discovers, indeed, the possibilities of human existence, which are infinite, as infinite as is creation. But the recovering of a new personality is as difficult—and as hopeless—as a new creation of the world. Whatever we do, whatever we pretend to be, we reveal nothing but our insane desire to be changed, not to be Jews. All our activities are directed to attain this aim: we don't want to be refugees, since we don't want to be Jews; we pretend to be English-speaking people, since German-speaking immigrants of recent years are marked as Jews; we don't call ourselves stateless, since the majority of stateless people in the world are Jews; we are willing to become loyal Hottentots,[5] only to hide the fact that we are Jews. We don't succeed and we can't succeed; under the cover of our "optimism" you can easily detect the hopeless sadness of assimilationists.

With us from Germany the word assimilation received a "deep" philosophical meaning. You can hardly realize how serious we were about it. Assimilation did not mean the necessary adjustment to the country where we happened to be born and to the people whose language we happened to speak. We adjust in principle to everything and everybody. This attitude became quite clear to me once by the words of one of my compatriots who, apparently, knew how to express his feelings. Having just arrived in France, he founded one of these societies of adjustment in which German Jews asserted to each other that they were already Frenchmen. In his first speech he said: "We have been good Germans in Germany and therefore we shall be good Frenchmen in France." The public applauded enthusias-

---

[4]*Vercingetorix* (d. 46 B.C.): leader of the Gauls in revolt against Romans in 52 B.C., captured by Julius Caesar (*Ed.*)

[5]*Hottentots:* natives of South Africa, related to the Bushmen, metaphor here of the extreme adaptability of the Jews (*Ed.*)

tically and nobody laughed; we were happy to have learnt how to prove our loyalty.

If patriotism were a matter of routine or practice, we should be the most patriotic people in the world. Let us go back to our Mr. Cohn; he certainly has beaten all records. He is that ideal immigrant who always, and in every country into which a terrible fate has driven him, promptly sees and loves the native mountains. But since patriotism is not yet believed to be a matter of practice, it is hard to convince people of the sincerity of our repeated transformations. This struggle makes our own society so intolerant; we demand full affirmation without our own group because we are not in the position to obtain it from the natives. The natives, confronted with such strange beings as we are, become suspicious; from their point of view, as a rule, only a loyalty to our old countries is understandable. That makes life very bitter for us. We might overcome this suspicion if we would explain that, being Jews, our patriotism in our original countries had rather a peculiar aspect. Though it was indeed sincere and deep-rooted. We wrote big volumes to prove it; paid an entire bureaucracy to explore its antiquity and to explain it statistically. We had scholars write philosophical dissertations on the predestined harmony between Jews and Frenchmen, Jews and Germans, Jews and Hungarians, Jews and . . . Our so frequently suspected loyalty of today has a long history. It is the history of a hundred and fifty years of assimilated Jewry who performed an unprecedented feat: though proving all the time their non-Jewishness, they succeeded in remaining Jews all the same.

The desperate confusion of these Ulysses-wanderers who, unlike their great prototype, don't know who they are is easily explained by their perfect mania for refusing to keep their identity. This mania is much older than the last ten years which revealed the profound absurdity of our existence. We are like people with a fixed idea who can't help trying continually to disguise an imaginary stigma. Thus we are enthusiastically fond of every new possibility which, being new, seems able to work miracles. We are fascinated by every new nationality in the same way as a woman of tidy size is delighted with every new dress which promises to give her the desired waistline. But she likes the new dress only as long as she believes in its miraculous qualities, and she will throw it away as soon as she discovers that it does not change her stature—or, for that matter, her status. 30

One may be surprised that the apparent uselessness of all our odd disguises has not yet been able to discourage us. If it is true that men seldom learn from history, it is also true that they may learn from personal experiences which, as in our case, are repeated time and again. But before you cast the first stone at us, remember that being a Jew does not give any legal status in this world. If we should start telling the truth that we are nothing but Jews, it would mean that we expose ourselves to the fate of human beings who, unprotected by any specific law or political convention, are nothing but human beings. I can hardly imagine an attitude more dangerous, since we actually live in a world in which human beings as such have ceased to exist for quite a while; since society has discovered discrimination as the great social weapon by which one may kill men without any bloodshed; since passports or birth certificates, and sometimes even income tax receipts, are no longer formal papers but matters of social distinction. It is true that most of us depend entirely upon social standards; we lose confidence in ourselves if society does not approve us; we are—and always were—ready to pay any price in order to be accepted by society. But it is equally true that the very few among us who have tried to get along without all these tricks and jokes of adjustment and assimilation have paid a much higher price than they could afford: they jeopardized the few chances even outlaws are given in a topsy-turvy world.

The attitude of these few whom, following Bernard Lazare, one may call "conscious pariahs," can as little be explained by recent events alone as the attitude of our Mr. Cohn who tried by every means to become an upstart. Both are sons of the nineteenth century which, not knowing legal or political outlaws, knew only too well social pariahs and their counterpart, social parvenus.[6] Modern Jewish history, having started with court Jews and continuing with Jewish millionaires and philanthropists, is apt to forget about this other trend of Jewish tradition—the tradition of Heine, Rahel Varnhagen, Sholom Aleichem, of Bernard Lazare, Franz Kafka or even Charlie Chaplin.[7] It is the tradition of a minority of Jews who have not wanted to become upstarts, who preferred the status of "conscious pariah." All vaunted Jewish qualities—the "Jewish heart," humanity, humor, disinterested intelligence—are pariah qualities. All Jewish shortcomings—tactlessness, political stupidity, inferiority complexes and money-grubbing—are characteristic of upstarts. There have always been Jews who did not think it worth while to change their humane attitude and their natural insight into reality for the narrowness of caste spirit or the essential unreality of financial transactions.

History has forced the status of outlaws upon both, upon pariahs and parvenus alike. The latter have not yet accepted the great wisdom of Balzac's "*On ne parvient pas deux fois*";[8] thus they don't understand the wild dreams of the former and feel humiliated in sharing their fate. Those few refugees who insist upon telling the truth, even to the point of "indecency," get in exchange for their unpopularity one priceless advantage: history is no longer a closed book to them and politics is no longer the privilege of Gentiles. They know that the outlawing of the Jewish people in Europe has been followed closely by the outlawing of most European nations. Refugees driven from country to

---

[6]*parvenus:* (from French) newcomers (*Ed.*)

[7]*Heinrich Heine* (1797–1856): German lyric poet and satirist; *Rahel Vernhagen* (1771–1833): had a famous salon in Berlin, a center of German romanticism; *Sholom Aleichem:* (1859–1916) Yiddish writer, chronicler of European shtetl (village) life; *Bernard Lazare* (1865–1903): French social and literary critic, authored works on Jewish people and anti-Semitism; *Franz Kafka* (1881–1924): born in Prague, Czechoslovakia, wrote in German, author of *The Trial* (1925) and other works; *Charlie Chaplin:* (1889–1977) English-born actor and director, whose film *The Great Dictator* (1940) satirized Nazi regime; Chaplin may have been thought to be Jewish but was not (*Ed.*)

[8]*"On ne parvient . . .":* one does not arrive (succeed) twice (*Ed.*)

country represent the vanguard of their peoples—if they keep their identity. For the first time Jewish history is not separate but tied up with that of all other nations. The comity of European peoples went to pieces when, and because, it allowed its weakest member to be excluded and persecuted.

DISCUSSING THE TEXT

1. Speaking as a member of the larger group of Jews, Arendt argues at the outset that "we don't like to be called 'refugees.'" Why not? What does she feel is betrayed by the label? Have you ever experienced being labeled in any way? If so, how did it make you feel?
2. What does Arendt say the Jew lost in fleeing from his or her home country to a new land of refuge? How does the Jew, newly arrived in his or her new land, look back on the past? Do you think this kind of loss is particularly Jewish? Can you relate it to some other kind of loss portrayed in any other selection in this chapter?
3. In a group of four or five students, discuss the anecdote about the easily assimilating Mr. Cohn, a generalized type (par. 26). Is Arendt blaming Mr. Cohn for his fate? What does she say about the alternative to his behavior—that is, "telling the truth that we are nothing but Jews"? What would you have done if you were Mr. Cohn? Take brief notes as you work on this assignment, and be prepared to share your opinions with the class.

WRITING ABOUT THE TEXT

4. Arendt divides the modern history of the Jews into those who accepted the status of "pariah" (or social outcast) and those who aspired to success within a given society, the "parvenus." What is involved in this distinction? Does Arendt ultimately favor one over the other? Make a list of characteristics that would define the pariah and one that would define the parvenu. Then write a brief paragraph stating which one you would rather be, and why, in a similar situation of exile.
5. What is the message of the "nice little fairy-tale" that Arendt refers to in paragraph 18, the one that begins, "'Once, when I was a St. Bernard . . .'"? In a paragraph or two, try to summarize Arendt's argument in this section of the essay, which she concludes by stating that "it is much easier to be accepted as a 'great man' than as a human being."
6. Arendt employs understatement and irony often in this essay, such as when she mordantly observes that "There are those odd optimists among us who, having made a lot of optimistic speeches, go home and turn on the gas or make use of a skyscraper in quite an unexpected way" (par. 9). What is your reaction to a statement like this? Write a one-page response to this statement; try to frame your remarks both within the context of what we now know about the Holocaust and within the context of your own personal views and beliefs.
7. Write a brief essay in which you compare and contrast this essay with that of Edward Said, "Reflections on Exile."

EDWARD SAID

Reflections on Exile

In this challenging essay, first published in the magazine Granta *in 1984, Edward Said poses difficult questions associated with not only the physical conditions but also the psychological conditions of exile. Said makes important distinctions between* exiles *(which he defines as people who are prevented from returning to their homelands),* expatriates, émigrés, *and* refugees. *In the case of expatriates and émigrés, Said sees the possibility of their having made a choice (for personal, economic, or social reasons) to leave their homelands as a crucial distinguishing factor. He claims that the term* refugee *suggests "innocent and bewildered people requiring urgent international assistance." Although refugees may be temporarily prevented from returning to their country for political reasons, Said argues that a sense of solidarity and community holds them together. The exile, however, experiences isolation and displacement.*

Although Said's tone is philosophical as well as political, he also makes important connections between exile and literature, citing as examples the works of James Joyce and Theodor Adorno. Both writers sought to look at their native countries (Ireland for Joyce and Germany for Adorno, who was Jewish) with detachment. According to Said, each writer found, ultimately, that "the only home . . . though fragile and vulnerable, is in writing."

This last statement applies to Edward Said as well. A Palestinian born in Jerusalem in 1935 and educated in Palestine and Egypt while those countries were under British rule, Said has lived in the United States since the 1950s. He is a professor of English at Columbia University, and among his many critical works, his book Orientalism *(1978) stands out for its analysis of the cultural stereotypes that the West has applied to the East. Said has pursued a similar theme in* Covering Islam *(New York: Pantheon, 1981), and more recently in* Cultural Imperialism *(New York: Knopf, 1993).*

Exile is strangely compelling to think about but terrible to experience. It is the unhealable rift forced between a human being and a native place, between the self and its true home: its essential sadness can never be surmounted. And while it is true that literature and history contain heroic, romantic, glorious, even triumphant episodes in an exile's life, these are no more than efforts meant to overcome the crippling sorrow of estrangement. The achievements of exile are permanently undermined by the loss of something left behind for ever.

Exiles look at non-exiles with resentment. *They* belong in their surroundings, you feel, whereas an exile is always out of place. What is it like to be born in a place, to stay and live there, to know that you are of it, more or less for ever?

Although it is true that anyone prevented from returning home is an exile, some distinctions can be made between exiles, refugees, expatriates and émigrés. Exile originated in the age-old practice of banishment. Once banished, the exile lives an anomalous and miserable life, with the stigma of being an outsider. Refugees, on the other hand, are a creation of the twentieth-century state. The word "refugee" has become a political one, suggesting large herds of innocent and bewildered people requiring urgent international assistance, whereas "exile" carries with it, I think, a touch of solitude and spirituality.

Expatriates voluntarily live in an alien country, usually for personal or social reasons. Hemingway and Fitzgerald were not forced to live in France. Expatriates may share in the solitude and estrangement of exile, but they do not suffer under its rigid proscriptions. Émigrés enjoy an ambiguous status. Technically, an émigré is anyone who emigrates to a new country. Choice in the matter is certainly a possibility. Colonial officials, missionaries, technical experts, mercenaries and military advisers on loan may in a sense live in exile, but they have not been banished. White settlers in Africa, parts of Asia and Australia may once have been exiles, but as pioneers and nation-builders the label "exile" dropped away from them.

5 Much of the exile's life is taken up with compensating for disorienting loss by creating a new world to rule. It is not surprising that so many exiles seem to be novelists, chess players, political activists, and intellectuals. Each of these occupations requires a minimal investment in objects and places a great premium on mobility and skill. The exile's new world, logically enough, is unnatural and its unreality resembles fiction. Georg Lukács, in *Theory of the Novel,* argued with compelling force that the novel, a literary form created out of the unreality of ambition and fantasy, is *the* form of "transcendental homelessness." Classical epics, Lukács wrote, emanate from settled cultures in which values are clear, identities stable, life unchanging. The European novel is grounded in precisely the opposite experience, that of a changing society in which an itinerant and disinherited middle-class hero or heroine seeks to construct a new world that somewhat resembles an old one left behind for ever. In the epic there is no *other* world, only the finality of *this* one. Odysseus returns to Ithaca after years of wandering; Achilles will die because he cannot escape his fate. The novel, however, exists because other worlds *may* exist, alternatives for bourgeois speculators, wanderers, exiles.

No matter how well they may do, exiles are always eccentrics who *feel* their difference (even as they frequently exploit it) as a kind of orphanhood. Anyone who is really homeless regards the habit of seeing estrangement in everything modern as an affectation, a display of modish attitudes. Clutching difference like a weapon to be used with stiffened will, the exile jealously insists on his or her right to refuse to belong.

This usually translates into an intransigence that is not easily ignored. Wilfulness, exaggeration, overstatement: these are characteristic styles of being an exile, methods for compelling the world to accept your vision—which you make more unacceptable because you are in fact unwilling to have it accepted. It is yours, after all. Composure and serenity are the last things associated with the work of exiles. Artists in exile are decidedly unpleasant, and their stubbornness insinuates itself into even their exalted works. Dante's vision in *The Divine Comedy* is tremendously powerful in its universality and detail, but even the beatific peace achieved in the *Paradiso* bears traces of the vindictiveness and severity of judgment embodied in the *Inferno*. Who but an exile like Dante, banished from Florence, would use eternity as a place for settling old scores?

James Joyce *chose* to be in exile: to give force to his artistic vocation. In an uncannily effective way—as Richard Ellmann has shown in his biography—Joyce picked a quarrel with Ireland and kept it alive so as to sustain the strictest opposition to what was familiar. Ellmann says that "whenever his relations with his native land were in danger of improving, [Joyce] was to find a new incident to solidify his intransigence and to reaffirm the rightness of his voluntary absence." Joyce's fiction concerns what in a letter he once described as the state of being "alone and friendless." And although it is rare to pick banishment as a way of life, Joyce perfectly understood its trials.

But Joyce's success as an exile stresses the question lodged at its very heart: is exile so extreme and private that any instrumental use of it is ultimately a trivialization? How is it that the literature of exile has taken its place as a *topos*[1] of human experience alongside the literature of adventure, education or discovery? Is this the *same* exile that quite literally kills Yanko Goorall and has bred the expensive, often dehumanizing relationship between twentieth-century exile and nationalism? Or is it some more benign variety?

Much of the contemporary interest in exile can be traced to the somewhat pallid notion that non-exiles can share in the benefits of exile as a redemptive motif. There is, admittedly, a certain plausibility and truth to this idea. Like medieval itinerant scholars or learned Greek slaves in the Roman Empire, exiles—the exceptional ones among them—do leaven their environments. And naturally "we" concentrate on that enlightening aspect of "their" presence among us, not on their misery or their demands. But looked at from the bleak political perspective of modern mass dislocations, individual exiles force us to recognize the tragic fate of homelessness in a necessarily heartless world. 10

A generation ago, Simone Weil posed the dilemma of exile as concisely as it has ever been expressed. "To be rooted," she said, "is perhaps the most important and least recognized need of the human soul." Yet Weil also saw that most remedies for uprootedness in this era of world wars, deportations and mass exterminations are almost as dangerous as what they purportedly remedy. Of these, the state—or, more accurately, statism—is one of the most insidious, since worship of the state tends to supplant all other human bonds.

Weil exposes us anew to that whole complex of pressures and constraints that lie at the center of the exile's predicament, which, as I have suggested, is as close as we come in the modern era to tragedy. There is the sheer fact of isolation and displacement, which produces the kind of narcissistic masochism that resists all efforts at amelioration, acculturation and com-

---

[1]*topos:* a commonplace or recurring literary formula (*Ed.*)

munity. At this extreme the exile can make a fetish of exile, a practice that distances him or her from all connections and commitments. To live as if everything around you were temporary and perhaps trivial is to fall prey to petulant cynicism as well as to querulous lovelessness. More common is the pressure on the exile to join—parties, national movements, the state. The exile is offered a new set of affiliations and develops new loyalties. But there is also a loss—of critical perspective, of intellectual reserve, of moral courage.

It must also be recognized that the defensive nationalism of exiles often fosters self-awareness as much as it does the less attractive forms of self-assertion. Such reconstitutive projects as assembling a nation out of exile (and this is true in this century for Jews and Palestinians) involve constructing a national history, reviving an ancient language, founding national institutions like libraries and universities. And these, while they sometimes promote strident ethnocentrism, also give rise to investigations of self that inevitably go far beyond such simple and positive facts as "ethnicity." For example, there is the self-consciousness of an individual trying to understand why the histories of the Palestinians and the Jews have certain patterns to them, why in spite of oppression and the threat of extinction a particular ethos remains alive in exile.

Necessarily, then, I speak of exile not as a privilege, but as an *alternative* to the mass institutions that dominate modern life. Exile is not, after all, a matter of choice: you are born into it, or it happens to you. But, provided that the exile refuses to sit on the sidelines nursing a wound, there are things to be learned: he or she must cultivate a scrupulous (not indulgent or sulky) subjectivity.

15 Perhaps the most rigorous example of such subjectivity is to be found in the writing of Theodor Adorno, the German-Jewish philosopher and critic. Adorno's masterwork, *Minima Moralia,* is an autobiography written while in exile; it is subtitled *Reflexionen aus dem beschädigten Leben (Reflections from a Mutilated Life).* Ruthlessly opposed to what he called the "administered" world, Adorno saw all life as pressed into ready-made forms, prefabricated "homes." He argued that everything that one says or thinks, as well as every object one possesses, is ultimately a mere commodity. Language is jargon, objects are for sale. To refuse this state of affairs is the exile's intellectual mission.

Adorno's reflections are informed by the belief that the only home truly available now, though fragile and vulnerable, is in writing. Elsewhere, "the house is past. The bombings of European cities, as well as the labor and concentration camps, merely precede as executors, with what the immanent development of technology had long decided was to be the fate of houses. These are now good only to be thrown away like old food cans." In short, Adorno says with a grave irony, "it is part of morality not to be at home in one's home."

To follow Adorno is to stand away from "home" in order to look at it with the exile's detachment. For there is considerable merit in the practice of noting the discrepancies between various concepts and ideas and what they actually produce. We take home and language for granted; they become nature, and their underlying assumptions recede into dogma and orthodoxy.

The exile knows that in a secular and contingent world, homes are always provisional. Borders and barriers, which enclose us within the safety of familiar territory, can also become prisons, and are often defended beyond reason or necessity. Exiles cross borders, break barriers of thought and experience.

Hugo of St Victor, a twelfth-century monk from Saxony, wrote these hauntingly beautiful lines:

> It is, therefore, a source of great virtue for the practised mind to learn, bit by bit, first to change about invisible and transitory things, so that afterwards it may be able to leave them behind altogether. The man who finds his homeland sweet is still a tender beginner; he to whom every soil is as his native one is already strong; but he is perfect to whom the entire world is as a foreign land. The tender soul has fixed his love on one spot in the world; the strong man has extended his love to all places; the perfect man has extinguished his.

Erich Auerbach, the great twentieth-century literary scholar who spent the war years as an exile in Turkey, has cited this passage as a model for anyone wishing to transcend national or provincial limits. Only by embracing this attitude can a historian begin to grasp human experience and its written records in their diversity and particularity; otherwise he or she will remain committed more to the exclusions and reactions of prejudice than to the freedom that accompanies knowledge. But note that Hugo twice makes it clear that the "strong" or "perfect" man achieves independence and detachment by *working through* attachments, not by rejecting them. Exile is predicated on the existence of, love for, and bond with, one's native place; what is true of all exile is not that home and love of home are lost, but that loss is inherent in the very existence of both.

Regard experiences as if they were about to disappear. What is it that anchors them in reality? What would you save of them? What would you give up? Only someone who has achieved independence and detachment, someone whose homeland is "sweet" but whose circumstances makes it impossible to recapture that sweetness, can answer those questions. (Such a person would also find it impossible to derive satisfaction from substitutes furnished by illusion or dogma.) 20

This may seem like a prescription for an unrelieved grimness of outlook and, with it, a permanently sullen disapproval of all enthusiasm or buoyancy of spirit. Not necessarily. While it perhaps seems peculiar to speak of the pleasures of exile, there are some positive things to be said for a few of its conditions. Seeing "the entire world as a foreign land" makes possible originality of vision. Most people are principally aware of one culture, one setting, one home; exiles are aware of at least two, and this plurality of vision gives rise to an awareness of simultaneous dimensions, an awareness that—to borrow a phrase from music—is *contrapuntal*.[2]

---

[2]*contrapuntal:* in music, playing one idea against another in a contrasting or interweaving manner (*Ed.*)

For an exile, habits of life, expression or activity in the new environment inevitably occur against the memory of these things in another environment. Thus both the new and the old environments are vivid, actual, occurring together contrapuntally. There is a unique pleasure in this sort of apprehension, especially if the exile is conscious of other contrapuntal juxtapositions that diminish orthodox judgment and elevate appreciative sympathy. There is also a particular sense of achievement in acting as if one were at home wherever one happens to be.

This remains risky, however: the habit of dissimulation is both wearying and nerve-racking. Exile is never the state of being satisfied, placid, or secure. Exile, in the words of Wallace Stevens, is "a mind of winter" in which the pathos of summer and autumn as much as the potential of spring are nearby but unobtainable. Perhaps this is another way of saying that a life of exile moves according to a different calendar, and is less seasonal and settled than life at home. Exile is life led outside habitual order. It is nomadic, decentered, contrapuntal; but no sooner does one get accustomed to it than its unsettling force erupts anew. 23

DISCUSSING THE TEXT

1. In paragraph 6 Said writes that "exiles are always eccentrics who *feel* their difference . . . as a kind of orphanhood." What do you think he means by this? In using a term like *orphanhood,* do you think Said is implying that it is impossible for the exile to become completely assimilated, or adapted, to his or her new home? Why or why not?
2. According to Said, what is the difference between political exile and the "voluntary" exile of writers like James Joyce?
3. Get together in a group of four or five students and discuss Hugo of St Victor's assertion (quoted by Said in par. 19), especially the lines: "The man who finds his homeland sweet is still a tender beginner; he to whom every soil is as his native one is already strong; but he is perfect to whom the entire world is as a foreign land." Do the categories established here ("tender beginner," "strong," "perfect") make sense to you? How do they relate to the concept of exile? Take brief notes, and be prepared to share your opinions with the class.
4. What is the difference between "*working through* attachments" and "rejecting them"—the two possibilities Said presents in paragraph 19?

WRITING ABOUT THE TEXT

5. Imagine a situation in which you might be an exile in a new land. Write a letter to a friend describing your feelings about your homeland, your reactions to the new environment, and your plans for the future.
6. Said makes a distinction between the awareness of self and nationality experienced by some exiles and the "strident ethnocentrism" or "worship of the state" that nationalistic projects sometimes promote among some other exiles. Drawing on Said's essay, news reports, or other sources, write two

paragraphs, providing examples that illustrate these two different patterns of exile.

7. Write a one-page definition of the term *contrapuntal* as Said uses it in the concluding paragraphs of this essay.
8. Said quotes a number of well-known writers, critics, and philosophers who were exiles and who wrote about, or out of, the experience of exile. Choose one of these figures and do some research into what brought about that person's own experience of exile. Prepare a written report of your findings.

MAKING CONNECTIONS

1. The exile's sense of loss—of things, or people, or status left behind in the homeland—is acutely experienced in several selections in this chapter. Drawing on two of these selections, describe how people in exile react to this sense of loss psychologically and what strategies for coping, if any, are available to them.
2. Examine the photo at the start of this chapter. What does Jacob Riis's image of a Jewish man celebrating Sabbath in a coal cellar tell us about the struggle to maintain one's religious and social identity in the world of New York just before the turn of the century? What things pictured here signify the man's desire to preserve a sense of home and religion? What hardships—to judge by the environment—must be overcome? Write a one-page description of the image, paying special attention to the cultural meaning of objects.
3. Drawing on two selections from this chapter, write an essay on the difficulties the exile (or refugee) faces in trying to adapt to his or her new country.
4. In this chapter, the exiled voices you've read have taken different forms: fiction (Garcia); oral history (Ets); autobiography (Equiano, Baldwin); personal essay (Arendt, Dreyfuss); scholarly essay (Handlin, Said). Choose two pieces you find particularly effective (making sure to select two from different categories). Write a brief essay that compares and contrasts these pieces in terms of their genre and style, strategies used by their writers, and their overall effectiveness.
5. As described by James Baldwin in "Stranger in the Village," the American Negro "is unique among the black men of the world in that his past was taken from him, almost literally, at one blow." This is different, Baldwin asserts, from the experience of other slaves in exile, who maintained their identity through the continuity of their memory of the past. Do you see evidence of what Baldwin describes in Olaudah Equiano's selection from *The Life of Olaudah Equiano or Gustavus Vassa the African. Written by Himself?* To what extent is the sense of exile from African history true of African American experience today? How would you compare the African American experience with that of other ethnic groups "in exile" in the United States?
6. Both Hannah Arendt in "We Refugees" and Edward Said in "Reflections on Exile" are concerned about the terms that define or describe the experience of people who have left their native country (for example, *immigrant, exile, pariah, refugee*). What are the distinctions between refugees and exiles, as Said explains them? Is Arendt's sense of herself as a refugee consistent with Said's terminology?
7. Reread the passage that describes Pilar's painting of the Statue of Liberty in Cristina Garcia's "Enough Attitude" (p. 114). Then reread Emma Lazarus's poem inscribed at the base of the Statue of Liberty, "The New Colossus," in Chapter 1 (pp. 26–27). What do these two very different images of the statue represent? Are they equally legitimate? Can you think of any other interpretations of this major symbol of America?

FURTHER READING

Olaudah Equiano

Andrews, William L. *To Tell a Story: The First Century of Afro-American Autobiography, 1760–1865.* Urbana: University of Illinois Press, 1986.

Davis, Charles T., and Henry Louis Gates, Jr., eds. *The Slave's Narrative.* New York: Oxford University Press, 1985.

Oscar Handlin

Handlin, Oscar. *Race and Nationality in American Life.* Boston: Little, Brown, 1957.

Riis, Jacob. *How the Other Half Lives.* 1890. Reprint, New York: Dover, 1971.

Marie Hall Ets

Cornelisen, Ann. *Women of the Shadows: A Study of the Wives and Mothers of Southern Italy.* New York: Penguin Books, 1992.

Seller, Maxine, ed. *Immigrant Women.* Philadelphia: Temple University Press, 1981.

Cristina Garcia

Geldof, Lynn. *Cubans: Voices of Change.* New York: St. Martin's Press, 1991.

Medina, Pablo. *Exiled Memories: A Cuban Childhood.* Austin: University of Texas Press, 1990.

Joel Dreyfuss

Danticat, Edwige. *Breath, Eyes, Memory.* New York: Vintage, 1994.

Vehiller, Nina. *Haitian Americans.* New York: Chelsea House, 1991.

James Baldwin

Baldwin, James. *Nobody Knows My Name.* New York: Dell, 1961.

Leeming, David Adams. *James Baldwin: A Biography.* New York: Knopf, 1994.

Hannah Arendt

Arendt, Hannah. *The Origins of Totalitarianism.* New York: Harcourt, 1951.

Cohn, Arthur A., ed. *Arguments and Doctrines: A Reader of Jewish Thinking in the Aftermath of the Holocaust.* New York: Harper, 1970.

Edward Said

Said, Edward. *The World, the Text, and the Critic.* Cambridge: Harvard University Press, 1983.

———. *The Politics of Dispossession: The Struggle for Palestinian Self-Determination, 1969–1994.* New York: Pantheon Books, 1994.

Snuff Shop *(photograph by Berenice Abbott), 1938. Struck by how rapidly the city was changing in the 1930s, Abbott photographed New York neighborhoods. The image here, from* Changing New York, *shows a snuff shop on the Lower East Side of Manhattan that is a meeting point for several cultures: Sandy, the "Scotch Indian," is a symbol of tobacco products; the Yiddish lettering speaks to the neighboring population; the Italian brand name invokes yet another ethnicity.* (Berenice Abbott / Commerce Graphics Ltd., Inc.)

3

The Multicultural Self

To the real question, How does it feel to be a problem? I answer seldom a word.

- W. E. B. Du Bois
Of Our Spiritual Strivings

I can't say when I first noticed my blackness.

- Reginald McKnight
Confessions of a Wannabe Negro

I join all others who marvel at your "Bintel Brief," where almost everyone who has something on his conscience, or a secret, can express himself.

- Isaac Metzker
A Bintel Brief: Letters from the Lower East Side to the Jewish Daily Forward

Hector always felt as if he were in costume, his true nature unknown to others and perhaps even to himself.

- Oscar Hijuelos
Our House in the Last World

A voice from my childhood says: "You are other. You are less than. You are unalterably alien."

- Kesaya E. Noda
Growing Up Asian in America

Gold Mountain was the name of my father's America.

- FAE MYENNE NG
False Gold

The best that immigrants bring to America is diversity. American education should respect diversity, celebrate diversity.

- RICHARD RODRIGUEZ
Asians

I am the quintessential imperfect Latina. I can't dance salsa to save my life, I learned about Montezuma and the Aztecs in sixth grade, and I haven't prayed to the *Virgen de Guadalupe* in years.

- ANNA LISA RAYA
It's Hard Enough Being Me

. . . an American to Mexicans / a Mexican to Americans / a handy token / sliding back and forth . . .

- PAT MORA
Legal Alien

The selections in this chapter attempt to define the "multicultural self." That is, they describe the difficult task of constructing a personal identity that encompasses multiple ethnicities and cultural traditions. The writers represented here are all struggling, in very different ways, with the psychological processes of identity formation. Each of their struggles is articulated from the point of view of an individual who is trying to integrate varying—and often conflicting—ethnic, racial, and cultural elements.

For W. E. B. Du Bois, writing in *The Souls of Black Folk* at the beginning of the twentieth century, the process of identity formation for blacks was split between attitudes and traits associated with being "white" and those associated with being "black." The result, according to Du Bois, was a "double consciousness" on the part of African Americans. But for Reginald McKnight, writing in "Confessions of a Wannabe Negro" ninety years later, the issue is considerably more complicated. McKnight argues that the consciousness of black Americans is more than double—it is "polymorphous." And in some ways, McKnight maintains, *all* Americans are "cultural mulattoes."

The problems of cultural heterogeneity are discussed by McKnight from the vantage point of a contemporary African American. Such problems—revolving around assimilation, ethnicity, class, and gender—are seen as well in the European Jewish experience during the earlier part of the twentieth century, as described in the selections from *A Bintel Brief.* In their letters to the *Jewish Daily Forward,* the newly arrived Jewish immigrants asked for advice on many different issues that were intimately related to the search for a viable identity in a new environment. In a sense, their plight is reminiscent of the double conciousness—the split between black and white—that Du Bois had explored; for these Jewish immigrants, one major challenge was to assimilate, or adapt, to the mainstream culture of America while still retaining their Old World traditions.

For Hector, Oscar Hijuelos's character in the selection excerpted from his novel *Our House in the Last World,* the attempt to discard his Cuban parents' cultural traditions is fraught with pain and self-loathing. Ashamed of his father's poverty, clothing style, and accent, Hector frantically tries to deny his multicultural self. At the same time, his desire and struggles to be like his friends transcend the conflicts experienced by the multicultural self, reflecting the process of identity formation that all adolescents experience.

The essays by Kesaya Noda and Fae Myenne Ng focus on the experience of Asian Americans, a group that is itself extremely varied and multicultural. In "Growing Up Asian in America," Noda discusses the cultural and racial stereotyping that she has experienced as an American of Japanese ancestry, and she describes her efforts to forge a multicultural identity that defies such stereotypes. In "False Gold," Fae Myenne Ng, an American of Chinese ancestry, probes the conflicts of the multicultural self through a narrative that interweaves her parents' experiences in America with her own.

The category "Asians" is also significant in an essay by Mexican American writer Richard Rodriguez, who explores his own experiences as the child of immigrant Mexican parents, some of whose friends and neighbors were Chinese Americans. Rodriguez juxtaposes these memories with accounts of his experiences as a college teacher in Los Angeles, working with Asian students of varying backgrounds. Besides providing cultural comparisons and contrasts between Mexican Americans and Asian Americans, the essay illustrates Rodriguez's controversial position on ethnicity and assimilation, discussed in the introduction to Rodriguez's essay.

The selection by Anna Lisa Raya, a college student originally from Los Angeles, California, expresses the views of a young person at a crucial stage of self-definition and development. Raya stresses the changes in her perception of herself when she began attending Columbia University in New York City, which was in some ways like a foreign country to her. Within this context, the experience of the multicultural self carries with it a certain amount of frustration and impatience for Raya, who felt that the ethnic labels imposed on her from the outside—albeit in a positive way—were too confining.

The poem that ends the chapter, "Legal Alien" by Mexican American poet Pat Mora, reflects yet another view of the multicultural self. The theme of a double consciousness, developed by Du Bois and by several other writers represented in this chapter, is voiced through Mora's experience as "an American to Mexicans / a Mexican to Americans." For this is indeed the fate of the multicultural self in all of its various cultural manifestations: to be conscious of definitions that come from outside the self, and to challenge them; and at the same time to be conscious of one's own definitions of the self, and perhaps to challenge them as well. Integrating these separate elements into a viable identity is part of shaping a truly multicultural self.

W. E. B. DU BOIS

Of Our Spiritual Strivings

One of the most powerful and enduring definitions of the culturally divided self is that of W. E. B. Du Bois (1868–1963) in his classic The Souls of Black Folk *(1903). In this book Du Bois tries to illuminate—from personal experience as well as from the perspectives of history and sociology—the condition of the African American. Such a person is, according to Du Bois, "an American, a Negro; two souls, two thoughts, two unreconciled strivings; two warring ideals in one dark body, whose dogged strength alone keeps it from being torn asunder."*

Although trained as a sociologist, Du Bois was also the author of several novels in which he gave voice to the dilemmas of black identity. The Souls of Black Folk, *generally considered his greatest work, is a blend of nonfiction and fiction in a poetic yet analytic prose style. In it, Du Bois attempts to describe the spiritual core of black experience in a series of essays that explore different aspects of black American character and history, including the legacy of Reconstruction, the mission of education, and the meaning of black spiritual music.*

Du Bois wrote at a time when the disappointments of the post-Reconstruction period in American history were most acute; discriminatory Jim Crow laws were operative in the South and lynchings were not uncommon. Du Bois opposed Booker T. Washington's influential arguments for industrial and agricultural education for blacks, arguing that such education basically accepted social inequality in exchange for limited economic growth. Instead, Du Bois stressed the importance of higher education and cultural recognition for what he termed the "talented tenth" of black Americans, that is, those best equipped to profit from higher education and in turn become teachers and leaders of their fellow African Americans.

In addition to his voluminous output in fiction, poetry, history, and sociology, Du Bois had a long and varied academic career, teaching subjects ranging from Greek and Latin to sociology, history, and economics. From 1910 to 1934 he was director of publicity and research for the National Association for the Advancement of Colored People, and he worked for this organization again during World War II. In his later years, Du Bois declared himself a Communist, arguing that private ownership and free enterprise were leading the world to disaster. To the end of his life he was active in international peace movements and in Pan-African affairs. He died in Ghana at the age of ninety-five.

O water, voice of my heart, crying in the sand,
All night long crying with a mournful cry,
As I lie and listen, and cannot understand
The voice of my heart in my side or the voice of the sea,
O water, crying for rest, is it I, is it I?
All night long the water is crying to me.

Unresting water, there shall never be rest
Till the last moon drop and the last tide fail,
And the fire of the end begin to burn in the west;
And the heart shall be weary and wonder and cry like the sea,

All life long crying without avail,
As the water all night long is crying to me.
—ARTHUR SYMONS

Between me and the other world there is ever an unasked question: unasked by some through feelings of delicacy; by others through the difficulty of rightly framing it. All, nevertheless, flutter round it. They approach me in a half-hesitant sort of way, eye me curiously or compassionately, and then, instead of saying directly, How does it feel to be a problem? they say, I know an excellent colored man in my town; or, I fought at Mechanicsville;[1] or, Do not these Southern outrages make your blood boil? At these I smile, or am interested, or reduce the boiling to a simmer, as the occasion may require. To the real question, How does it feel to be a problem? I answer seldom a word.

And yet, being a problem is a strange experience,—peculiar even for one who has never been anything else, save perhaps in babyhood and in Europe. It is in the early days of rollicking boyhood that the revelation first bursts upon one, all in a day, as it were. I remember well when the shadow swept across me. I was a little thing, away up in the hills of New England, where the dark Housatonic winds between Hoosac and Taghkanic to the sea. In a wee wooden schoolhouse, something put it into the boys' and girls' heads to buy gorgeous visiting-cards—ten cents a package—and exchange. The exchange was merry, till one girl, a tall newcomer, refused my card,—refused it peremptorily, with a glance. Then it dawned upon me with a certain suddenness that I was different from the others; or like, mayhap, in heart and life and longing, but shut out from their world by a vast veil. I had thereafter no desire to tear down that veil, to creep through; I held all beyond it in common contempt, and lived above it in a region of blue sky and great wandering shadows. That sky was bluest when I could beat my mates at examination-time, or beat them at a foot-race, or even beat their stringy heads. Alas, with the years all this fine contempt began to fade; for the worlds I longed for, and all their dazzling opportunities, were theirs, not mine. But they should not keep these prizes, I said; some, all, I would wrest from them. Just how I would do it I could never decide: by reading law, by healing the sick, by telling the wonderful tales that swam in my head,—some way. With other black boys the strife was not so fiercely sunny: their youth shrunk into tasteless sycophancy, or into silent hatred of the pale world about them and mocking distrust of everything white; or wasted itself in a bitter cry, Why did God make

---

[1]*Mechanicsville:* Civil War battle (June 26, 1862), in which Union forces threatened Richmond, Virginia (*Ed.*)

me an outcast and a stranger in mine own house? The shades of the prison-house closed round about us all: walls strait and stubborn to the whitest, but relentlessly narrow, tall, and unscalable to sons of night who must plod darkly on in resignation, or beat unavailing palms against the stone, or steadily, half hopelessly, watch the streak of blue above.

After the Egyptian and Indian, the Greek and Roman, the Teuton and Mongolian, the Negro is a sort of seventh son, born with a veil, and gifted with second-sight in this American world,—a world which yields him no true self-consciousness, but only lets him see himself through the revelation of the other world. It is a peculiar sensation, this double-consciousness, this sense of always looking at one's self through the eyes of others, of measuring one's soul by the tape of a world that looks on in amused contempt and pity. One ever feels his twoness,—an American, a Negro; two souls, two thoughts, two unreconciled strivings; two warring ideals in one dark body, whose dogged strength alone keeps it from being torn asunder.

The history of the American Negro is the history of this strife—this longing to attain self-conscious manhood, to merge his double self into a better and truer self. In this merging he wishes neither of the older selves to be lost. He would not Africanize America, for America has too much to teach the world and Africa. He would not bleach his Negro soul in a flood of white Americanism, for he knows that Negro blood has a message for the world. He simply wishes to make it possible for a man to be both a Negro and an American, without being cursed and spit upon by his fellows, without having the doors of Opportunity closed roughly in his face.

This, then, is the end of his striving: to be a co-worker in the kingdom of culture, to escape both death and isolation, to husband and use his best powers and his latent genius. These powers of body and mind have in the past been strangely wasted, dispersed, or forgotten. The shadow of a mighty Negro past flits through the tale of Ethiopia the Shadowy and of Egypt the Sphinx. Throughout history, the powers of single black men flash here and there like falling stars, and die sometimes before the world has rightly gauged their brightness. Here in America, in the few days since Emancipation, the black man's turning hither and thither in hesitant and doubtful striving has often made his very strength to lose effectiveness, to seem like absence of power, like weakness. And yet it is not weakness,—it is the contradiction of double aims. The double-aimed struggle of the black artisan—on the one hand to escape white contempt for a nation of mere hewers of wood and drawers of water, and on the other hand to plough and nail and dig for a poverty-stricken horde—could only result in making him a poor craftsman, for he had but half a heart in either cause. By the poverty and ignorance of his people, the Negro minister or doctor was tempted toward quackery and demagogy; and by the criticism of the other world, toward ideals that made him ashamed of his lowly tasks. The would-be black *savant*[2] was confronted by the

[2]*savant:* (French) learned person or scholar (*Ed.*)

paradox that the knowledge his people needed was a twice-told tale to his white neighbors, while the knowledge which would teach the white world was Greek to his own flesh and blood. The innate love of harmony and beauty that set the ruder souls of his people a-dancing and a-singing raised but confusion and doubt in the soul of the black artist; for the beauty revealed to him was the soul-beauty of a race which his larger audience despised, and he could not articulate the message of another people. This waste of double aims, this seeking to satisfy two unreconciled ideals, has wrought sad havoc with the courage and faith and deeds of ten thousand thousand people,—has sent them often wooing false gods and invoking false means of salvation, and at times has even seemed about to make them ashamed of themselves.

Away back in the days of bondage they thought to see in one divine event the end of all doubt and disappointment; few men ever worshipped Freedom with half such unquestioning faith as did the American Negro for two centuries. To him, so far as he thought and dreamed, slavery was indeed the sum of all villainies, the cause of all sorrow, the root of all prejudice; Emancipation was the key to a promised land of sweeter beauty than ever stretched before the eyes of wearied Israelites. In song and exhortation swelled one refrain—Liberty; in his tears and curses the God he implored had Freedom in his right hand. At last it came,—suddenly, fearfully, like a dream. With one wild carnival of blood and passion came the message in his own plaintive cadences:—

> "Shout, O children!
> Shout, you're free!
> For God has bought your liberty!"

Years have passed away since then,—ten, twenty, forty; forty years of national life, forty years of renewal and development, and yet the swarthy spectre sits in its accustomed seat at the Nation's feast. In vain do we cry to this our vastest social problem:—

> "Take any shape but that, and my firm nerves
> Shall never tremble!"

The Nation has not yet found peace from its sins; the freedman has not yet found in freedom his promised land. Whatever of good may have come in these years of change, the shadow of a deep disappointment rests upon the Negro people,—a disappointment all the more bitter because the unattained ideal was unbounded save by the simple ignorance of a lowly people.

The first decade was merely a prolongation of the vain search for freedom, the boon that seemed ever barely to elude their grasp,—like a tantalizing will-o'-the-wisp, maddening and misleading the headless host. The holocaust of war, the terrors of the Ku-Klux Klan, the lies of carpet-baggers, the disorganization of industry, and the contradictory advice of friends and foes, left the bewildered serf with no new watch-word beyond the old cry for freedom. As the time flew, however, he began to grasp a new idea. The ideal of liberty demanded for its attainment powerful means, and these the Fifteenth Amendment gave him. The ballot, which before he had looked upon as a visible sign of freedom, he now regarded as the chief means of gaining and perfecting the liberty with which war had partially endowed him. And why not? Had not votes made war and emancipated millions? Had not votes enfranchised the freedmen? Was anything impossible to a power that had done all this? A million black men started with renewed zeal to vote themselves into the kingdom. So the decade flew away, the revolution of 1876[3] came, and left the half-free serf weary, wondering, but still inspired. Slowly but steadily, in the following years, a new vision began gradually to replace the dream of political power,—a powerful movement, the rise of another ideal to guide the unguided, another pillar of fire by night after a clouded day. It was the ideal of "book-learning"; the curiosity, born of compulsory ignorance, to know and test the power of the cabalistic letters of the white man, the longing to know. Here at last seemed to have been discovered the mountain path to Canaan; longer than the highway of Emancipation and law, steep and rugged, but straight, leading to heights high enough to overlook life.

Up the new path the advance guard toiled, slowly, heavily, doggedly; only those who have watched and guided the faltering feet, the misty minds, the dull understandings, of the dark pupils of these schools know how faithfully, how piteously, this people strove to learn. It was weary work. The cold statistician wrote down the inches of progress here and there, noted also where here and there a foot had slipped or some one had fallen. To the tired climbers, the horizon was ever dark, the mists were often cold, the Canaan was always dim and far away. If, however, the vistas disclosed as yet no goal, no resting-place, little but flattery and criticism, the journey at least gave leisure for reflection and self-examination; it changed the child of Emancipation to the youth with dawning self-consciousness, self-realization, self-respect. In those sombre forests of his striving his own soul rose before him, and he saw himself,—darkly as through a veil; and yet he saw in himself some faint revelation of his power, of his mission. He began to have a dim feeling that, to attain his place in the world, he must be himself, and not another. For the first time he sought to analyze the burden he bore upon his back, that dead-weight of social degradation partially masked behind a half-named Negro problem. He felt his poverty; without a cent, without a home, without land, tools, or savings, he had entered into competition with rich, landed, skilled neighbors. To be a poor man is hard, but to be a poor race in a land of dollars is the very bottom of hardships. He felt the weight of his ignorance,—not simply of letters, but of life, of business, of the humanities; the accumulated sloth and shirking and awkwardness of decades and centuries shackled his hands and

[3]*revolution of 1876:* 1876 marked the end of the failed effort at "reconstructing" the South after the Civil War, an effort that had established civil and political rights for African Americans and had embittered many white Southerners. After the disputed election of 1876, Rutherford B. Hayes (Republican) withdrew federal troops from the South and white Southern interests returned to dominance. (*Ed.*)

feet. Nor was his burden all poverty and ignorance. The red stain of bastardy, which two centuries of systematic legal defilement of Negro women had stamped upon his race, meant not only the loss of ancient African chastity, but also the hereditary weight of a mass of corruption from white adulterers, threatening almost the obliteration of the Negro home.

A people thus handicapped ought not to be asked to race with the world, 10 but rather allowed to give all its time and thought to its own social problems. But alas! while sociologists gleefully count his bastards and his prostitutes, the very soul of the toiling, sweating black man is darkened by the shadow of a vast despair. Men call the shadow prejudice, and learnedly explain it as the natural defence of culture against barbarism, learning against ignorance, purity against crime, the "higher" against the "lower" races. To which the Negro cries Amen! and swears that to so much of this strange prejudice as is founded on just homage to civilization, culture, righteousness, and progress, he humbly bows and meekly does obeisance. But before that nameless prejudice that leaps beyond all this he stands helpless, dismayed, and well-nigh speechless; before that personal disrespect and mockery, the ridicule and systematic humiliation, the distortion of fact and wanton license of fancy, the cynical ignoring of the better and the boisterous welcoming of the worse, the all-pervading desire to inculcate disdain for everything black, from Toussaint[4] to the devil,—before this there rises a sickening despair that would disarm and discourage any nation save that black host to whom "discouragement" is an unwritten word.

But the facing of so vast a prejudice could not but bring the inevitable self-questioning, self-disparagement, and lowering of ideals which ever accompany repression and breed in an atmosphere of contempt and hate. Whisperings and portents came borne upon the four winds: Lo! we are diseased and dying, cried the dark hosts; we cannot write, our voting is vain; what need of education, since we must always cook and serve? And the Nation echoed and enforced this self-criticism, saying: Be content to be servants, and nothing more; what need of higher culture for half-men? Away with the black man's ballot, by force or fraud,—and behold the suicide of a race! Nevertheless, out of the evil came something of good,—the more careful adjustment of education to real life, the clearer perception of the Negroes' social responsibilities, and the sobering realization of the meaning of progress.

So dawned the time of *Sturm und Drang:* storm and stress today rocks our little boat on the mad waters of the world-sea; there is within and without the sound of conflict, the burning of body and rending of soul; inspiration strives with doubt, and faith with vain questionings. The bright ideals of the past,—physical freedom, political power, the training of brains and the training of hands,—all these in turn have waxed and waned, until even the last grows dim and overcast. Are they all wrong,—all false? No, not that, but each

---

[4]*François Dominique Toussaint L'Ouverture* (1744–1803): Haitian patriot, leader of slave rebellions and eventual governor of Haiti (1801) until the French captured and imprisoned him (*Ed.*)

alone was oversimple and incomplete,—the dreams of a credulous race-childhood, or the fond imaginings of the other world which does not know and does not want to know our power. To be really true, all these ideals must be melted and welded into one. The training of the schools we need to-day more than ever,—the training of deft hands, quick eyes and ears, and above all the broader, deeper, higher culture of gifted minds and pure hearts. The power of the ballot we need in sheer self-defence,—else what shall save us from a second slavery? Freedom, too, the long-sought, we still seek,—the freedom of life and limb, the freedom to work and think, the freedom to love and aspire. Work, culture, liberty,—all these we need, not singly but together, not successively but together, each growing and aiding each, and all striving toward that vaster ideal that swims before the Negro people, the ideal of human brotherhood, gained through the unifying ideal of Race; the ideal of fostering and developing the traits and talents of the Negro, not in opposition to or contempt for other races, but rather in large conformity to the greater ideals of the American Republic, in order that some day on American soil two world-races may give each to each those characteristics both so sadly lack. We the darker ones come even now not altogether empty-handed: there are to-day no truer exponents of the pure human spirit of the Declaration of Independence than the American Negroes; there is no true American music but the wild sweet melodies of the Negro slave; the American fairy tales and folklore are Indian and African; and, all in all, we black men seem the sole oasis of simple faith and reverence in a dusty desert of dollars and smartness. Will America be poorer if she replace her brutal dyspeptic blundering with light-hearted but determined Negro humility? or her coarse and cruel wit with loving jovial good-humor? or her vulgar music with the soul of the Sorrow Songs?

Merely a concrete test of the underlying principles of the great republic is the Negro Problem, and the spiritual striving of the freedmen's sons is the travail of souls whose burden is almost beyond the measure of their strength, but who bear it in the name of an historic race, in the name of this the land of their fathers' fathers, and in the name of human opportunity.

And now what I have briefly sketched in large outline let me on coming pages tell again in many ways, with loving emphasis and deeper detail, that men may listen to the striving in the souls of black folk.

DISCUSSING THE TEXT

1. What is the so-called veil that Du Bois refers to in paragraph 2? How does it affect the lives of black Americans? How does Du Bois personally react to his discovery of this veil? How do others react? Do you think there is a similar veil shutting out other ethnic or minority groups in the United States today?

2. What are the sources of the double consciousness Du Bois describes (par. 3)? Is this a completely negative condition? A little later Du Bois speaks of the "double-aimed struggle" of the black who is caught between his desire to serve the black community and his awareness of the standards and power of the white community (par. 5). What are the consequences of this dilemma, as Du Bois sees it? Do you share his views?
3. Du Bois is describing a moment in black history when African Americans, freed from slavery forty years before, struggled with the burdens of poverty, ignorance, and the weakened bonds of family. To what extent can one generalize about the condition of *all* African Americans, either historically or today? Would Du Bois's description of "the souls of black folk" be valid today? Would his concept of the divided self apply to other cultural experiences of America? Discuss these issues with a group of four or five other students, and record your ideas and observations for presentation to the rest of the class.

WRITING ABOUT THE TEXT

4. Du Bois notes certain special virtues of black American culture, such as lightheartedness, jovial good humor, and spiritual qualities (par. 12). What contributions does Du Bois predict the black community will make to mainstream American culture as a whole? Do you agree with Du Bois's observations? Can you detect anything in contemporary American culture that illustrates his predictions? Write a personal reaction to this selection that addresses the question of the black community's unique contributions to American culture.
5. What audience do you think Du Bois was writing for—black? white? mixed? Make a list of the passages in the essay that support your position, and then write two paragraphs summing up your argument.
6. Throughout this essay, Du Bois refers repeatedly to the fate of Negro men to make his points. How might his examples have been different if he had drawn on the experiences of African American women? Try rewriting some of Du Bois's examples of African American life at the end of the nineteenth century from the point of view of a woman. See, for example, paragraph 5 and paragraph 9.
7. Du Bois argued strongly for higher education and training of African Americans, and he described vividly the handicaps of Negroes after emancipation (see par. 9). Yet he also argued that blacks must, as far as possible, solve their own social problems. Where do you think Du Bois would have stood on current debates regarding affirmative action, the policy that was instituted initially as an effort to remedy the long-standing suppression of African Americans in education and business? Research the recent debate over affirmative action in the Supreme Court and Congress. Then write a one- or two-page essay, drawing on Du Bois's essay, to describe what his position on affirmative action would be. Do you agree with this position? Why or why not?

REGINALD McKNIGHT

Confessions of a Wannabe Negro

Reginald McKnight's reflections on black American identity take up where W. E. B. Du Bois left off, and in fact McKnight quotes Du Bois's central notion of the double consciousness of the black American as a reference point. But what was relatively simple for Du Bois—the argument that black Americans share a common experience of separation from white America and an identity split between their black experience and their American context—becomes more complicated in McKnight's essay: McKnight goes beyond the simple black-white dichotomy to explore the more complex negotiations of cultural identity that are common to contemporary African Americans.

McKnight incorporates several anecdotes from his own personal history. In this way he emulates the writing strategy of James Baldwin (see "Stranger in the Village," p. 126), who also moves his argument from the personal to the general. McKnight was born in Germany, and he moved to various other places in the United States with his family before attending Colorado College and the University of Denver. All of his work, both fiction and nonfiction, deals with the generation of African Americans who have come of age after the civil rights struggles of the 1950s and 1960s, and who have often lost their "culture"—although not their color—as they have moved into the white mainstream. McKnight is acutely aware of the gains and losses that come from this kind of deracination, as he calls it.

McKnight has won several prizes for his short fiction, collected in Moustapha's Eclipse *(1988). He teaches English at Carnegie-Mellon University and is the author of a novel,* I Get on the Bus, *published in 1990. "Confessions of a Wannabe Negro" originally appeared in Gerald Early's 1993 collection,* Lure and Loathing.

I can't say when I first noticed my blackness. Such things fall upon one like sleep, appear like gray hairs on the head. One moment we are not aware of some aspect of our being, and the next we are saying that we have never known ourselves any different. I do, however, remember the very day I noticed that my blackness made me different. There was this girl named Marsha on whom I had what you could call a crush, young as I was. Her hair was white as sunlight on a web, her eyes were as blue as plums. This was so long ago, thirty years or better, that I can't remember the context within which all of this took place, but I do remember that it happened in school, and I remember that we were indoors, queued next to a row of windows that cast light only on Marsha. I stood in line dead next to her, inhaling her Ivory soap and whole-milk scent, watching the light set fire to that delicate hair. Some kid behind me had been trying to engage me in a conversation for more than five minutes, but I was having little of it. I only wanted to consume Marsha's presence. But, through sheer persistence, the kid broke through. I heard him say, ". . . born in California, just up the road. Where was you born?" "Germany," I answered, and drifted back to Marsha, her elbows, the backs of her knees, the heels of her saddle shoes. Then she turned around . . . to look at me . . . to speak to me . . . to cast her radiance my way. She said, "Coloreds can't be born in Germany." Of course I felt humiliated, embarrassed, angered. My stomach folded in on itself, my hands trembled, my face burned. I couldn't have explained it to you then, but I had never felt this way before, never felt singled out on account of my color, and at first I thought Marsha had misunderstood me, so I replied, "I didn't say I was German, I said I was *born* in Germany." But she stuck to her guns, empty as their chambers were, saying, "You're just a liar! Colored people do not come from Germany." And I told Marsha, as gently as I could, of course, that I most certainly had been born in Germany. Just ask my mother, etc., etc. But the more I asserted my claim, the more incredulous Marsha, and then a growing number of my schoolmates, became. I remember one boy telling me that he was Catholic, and that, ". . . um, in the Catholic Church? um, if you lie? um, you'll, ah go to H.E.L.L." I had only one supporter that morning, a kid whose name I can no longer recall. She tried to defend me by announcing that though she was Chinese she'd been born in Tennessee. Marsha, for some reason, saw no logic in this, and said, "Well, maybe so, but that doesn't mean a colored can be born in Germany."

I was six, I think.

A few years later I remember walking home from school with my neighbors, my friends, the Weatherford kids, Ginny, Kathelynn, and Junior. The Weatherford kids were white, but at the time I didn't think of them as white. If I thought of them in terms of a class, or a type, or a category at all, I thought of them as Southerners, children, friends, and so forth. The afternoon was windless, cool. The bone-dry, yellow, tan, and evergreen of a typical Colorado autumn. We strode down the sidewalk, mindful of little outside the foursquare of ourselves. Junior, as he usually did, boasted about some impressive thing he had done or had thought that day in school. Kathelynn and Ginny bickered about which of them had made the bigger mess that morning in the room they shared. I bounced my Car 54 lunch box off my thigh, pretending to listen to Junior, while giving my full attention to his sisters, and somehow being aware of the magpie-fashion hollering of the flock of boys who walked behind us half a block or so back. Though they themselves drew no nearer to us, their words incrementally became more distinct to me. Dummy in the blue shirt. Dummy in the blue shirt. Dummy in the blue shirt, they were saying, and I knew they were talking about me, even though I was wearing not a blue shirt but a blue sweater. It made no difference that I was the only one of the four of us wearing blue. I would have known even if all four of us had been swathed from collar to ankle in blue. Dummy in the blue shirt. Dummy in the blue shirt. "Hey, Dummy, turn around." "Yeah, look at us, Dummy!" "Hey, look at us!" "Were you too dumb to take a bath this morning, Dummy?" "Yeah, you sure are dirty." "Phew! I can smell you from here."

Of course the Weatherford kids heard this too, and one or two of them told me I ought not turn around. I thought that was a good idea. Junior, my man Junior, turned around, though, and hollered back, "You're the dummies. . . . Shut up!" Then he turned to me and said, "They're the dumb ones, not you." Just then a chunk of feldspar, the size of an eight-year-old's fist, zinged a couple of feet over my head and skittered down the sidewalk several feet ahead of us, and came to rest in the grass. "Hey, Dummy, turn around."

"Just ignore them, Junior," Ginny said.

This nonsense went on for several blocks, ending only when we turned right, heading down our own street. Just before we turned, however, I finally did glance back at the kids. They appeared to be a couple of grades ahead. I didn't recognize any of them. Neither did I expect to.

I said nothing to my family about this, that day, but the following morning I told my mother about the incident while she was knocking a few naps out of my hair with a very small-toothed comb. It wasn't till I was about three quarters of the way through the story that I realized I'd made a mistake. In the first place, my mother has never been a "morning person," and she went about all her morning tasks with great flame and fury even when things were running smoothly. But as my story unfolded I noted she began combing my hair with increasing vehemence. It felt as though some great bird were swooping down on me, clutching my head with its blade-sharp talons, and by degrees, plucking the bone away to get to the meat. Quite honestly, I had expected her to lay the comb aside, set me on her lap, and coo rather than caw. But Mama said, "What were you doing? Were you acting like a dummy?" And I said, "No, ma'am, I was just walking." "Well," she said, combing with still greater heat, "you must've been doing something, boy." I was pretty sure my scalp had begun bleeding. "Hold still, boy," she said. Then, "I tell you *what*—if I *ever* catch you acting the fool at school or anywhere else, I'll skin you alive—you hear me?" And I said, "Yes, ma'am, I did, but I didn't do a thing except walk home from school." "I said hold still, boy! You better not be lying to me, Reginald." I was in tears by this time and all I could manage to say was what I'd already said before, that I'd just been walking, and so forth. Then, in a last-ditch effort for sympathy, I mentioned the rock they'd chucked, and that it had just barely missed hitting me smack on the head. "Well, why didn't you throw one back?" Mama said, and then she said she'd be damned if she was going to raise anybody's sissy. But I heard something catch in her throat, and she laid the comb on the rim of the basin, then rested her hands on my shoulders. I was too ashamed of my tears to look up into the mirror and at her reflection. She turned me about, drew me into her warm bosom, held me, talked about how ignorant some people were, that I shouldn't let a bunch of stupid boys upset me, that the world could sometimes be a tough, mean, petty place and I was just going to have to toughen up right along with it. She said a few more things, which I can no longer remember, but I do remember that her warmth and the sounds that issued from her throat, dozy, lugubrious, made my belly heat up and glow, made my legs tremble, made me want to sleep. But Mama said, "Come on now, son, you got to be strong." She took me by the shoulders again, turned me back around, and resumed working on my hair.

I think I was about eight then.

And by this time I thought I was getting it, thought I had discovered the difference, and what it meant, but in that same year I made a second discovery, something that made it clear to me that I was different, but not different in the way I thought I was. That year my grandfather took ill and the air force granted my father a special two-month leave so my mother and he could go to Waco and tend to family needs. At first I was delighted, for I thought my father's leave meant a leave from school for me and my siblings. I was wrong, of course. One of the very first things my parents did when we got to Waco was enroll my sisters and me in school, and for the first time in my life I attended a segregated school.

For the first two or three days it was quite nice. The teacher seemed to adore me, unlike previous teachers I had had, the majority of whom treated me with a benign indifference. But with this new teacher, Mrs. Wood, it appeared I could do no wrong. She enjoyed having me read aloud, often stopping me midsentence and asking my classmates to mark the way I'd pronounced a particular word. The schoolwork seemed easy to me, and Mrs. Wood would invariably make positive comments on my work as she handed our assignments back to us. To this day I don't know whether I did well in school because the school, as some of my friends have suggested, was substandard, or because, as others have said, for once I'd felt comfortable amid my peers and didn't feel like the usual dummy in the blue shirt. Perhaps it was both. Perhaps it was coincidence. I can't be sure because in those days I was a very quiet kid, very shy. I felt no comfort in the teacher's special attention. I felt no comfort amid my peers, whether black or white, and I don't recall the work being significantly different from what I'd had at previous schools. It was the first school I ever attended, however, that permitted the practice of corporal punishment. Perhaps that made all the difference. 10

In any case, one afternoon, as I was leaving the campus at the end of the school day, two boys jumped me from behind and tried to tackle me to the ground. Not only was I surprised by the attack, but I was surprised by the ineptitude of my attackers. Neither of them attempted to slug me even though several onlookers standing nearby were hollering, "Hit 'im. Hit that white paddy. Hit that boy." One of my attackers, as he gripped me in a headlock, kept saying, "You think you something good, huh? You think you the teacher's pet, huh?" The other one said, "Git his legs, git his legs, git his legs." And he finally decided to get my legs himself and they brought me down, though I had boy number one in the headlock, rather than he me. Boys as small as we were could hardly do one another any harm, but all the dust we kicked up, all the pounding we exchanged, all the yelping of our spectators, not to mention the surprise of the attack, had me extremely agitated. Extremely nonplused too, because I wasn't clear as to whether they were simply playing, Texas style, or really trying to do me harm. While I lay prone, still holding the one boy in the headlock, and as the other boy, rather than slugging me, tried to peel my arms from around his friend's head, my Uncle Bill, who was responsible for picking me up from school each day, approached us and very coolly asked me, "You okay?" I felt the grips of both boys slacken a notch, but as I would not let go, they would not let go.

"I'm okay."

"What y'all fighting about?"

"Don't know. Just jumped me. Just started fighting me."

"Why'd y'all jump him?" 15

"Teacher's pet," said one.

"He think he white," said the other.

"Yeah, he think he something."

Uncle Bill said, "Y'all know this is my sister's boy?"

"Naw," said the first boy as though he didn't care, but I felt him slacken 20 his grip still further, and this allowed me to throw my leg over his belly and straddle him. The other boy then got *me* in a headlock. "Awright," said Uncle Bill, "that's enough. I got some errands to run." Then Bill hoisted me up by my belt, swung me over his shoulder, and carried me to my grandfather's old Willie.

As the Jeep vibrated away from the school, I noticed, after a while, that I had been staring at the backs of my hands, and alternately glancing at the hands of my uncle. After a while I said, "Uncle Bill, do you think I look white?" And without looking at me, he said, "Do you think you look white?"

"Don't look white to me," I said.

"Me neither," he said.

And I didn't. I don't. I'm the color of a well-worn penny, as dark as, or darker than, any of my classmates in that Texas school. What on earth could they have meant? As the old woody rolled down the street, rattling the windows of Piggly Wigglys, hardware stores, barbershops and five-and-dimes, streets in this part of Waco where whitefolk were seldom seen, rarely thought of, I recalled a conversation I'd had just a week or so before with a classmate, this bullet-headed boy who sat two seats in front of me in Mrs. Wood's class. We were at lunch, and I remember being fairly amazed at what his lunch consisted of, rice buried in sugar (sugar?) and milk (milk?), two boiled eggs, and an orange. We were just getting acquainted, and he began by asking me the usual sort of questions: Where you from? Where's that? Why you move here? and so on. Then rather suddenly he asked me—and it seemed so incongruous to the previous questions—"Is your mama white?" And I said no. "Your daddy white?" No, I told him. "Hm," the boy said, "they why you talk so funny?" and he waited for my reply. I really didn't know what to say, but ended up with "I don't know. I don't think I talk funny." Then he asked me, "Why you walk so funny? Walk like you afraid to move, like you Frankenstein. Walk like a whiteboy." He chugged his milk, then wiped his mouth with the heel of his hand. "You act funny, too."

I turned toward my uncle and said, "Uncle Bill, what's a white paddy?" 25 Bill shrugged, shook his head. "Aw, it's a whole lot of things, Reggie. Someone who looks white or acts white. Someone who acts sidicty, you know, like he better than everybody else. Something like that. Those boys are just ignorant, Reggie. They don't know nothing about nothing. Somebody don't act the way they do or look or think the way they do, and they wanna call him white paddy. You take my advice: Don't even study people like that."

But I did study them, as I suppose they studied me. I studied people both black and white, both critical and congratulatory. I studied the buck-toothed, tube-headed, freckle-faced whiteboy named Mike who called me nigger when I struck out in a softball game in the fourth grade. That happened in Colorado. It was the first time anyone ever called me nigger. I studied the two little Waco black girls who tossed rocks at me and my cousin Valencia as they chanted, "White paddy, white paddy." I remember the relief I felt, though it was only momentary, when I thought the girls meant that both Valencia and I were white paddies. It turns out I was mistaken, though. They meant just me. What mystified me at the time was that they hadn't even heard me speak, hadn't seen me walk. What were they seeing? I asked myself. How could I hide it? What was I doing? I studied the Colorado brother who, in school one day, replied to my "What's happ'nin', man?" with "Tom." And he coolly rolled away like mercury on glass, leaving me utterly bamboozled. I didn't know the guy, had never seen the guy before. Another high school acquaintance, a guy named Keith, used to joke with me, from time to time, by calling me Uncle Tunk. I studied him, too, discovering that he sincerely liked me but just thought I acted white. I studied the white boys in Louisiana who called me Charlie Brown, Coony, Nigra, Hippy Nigger, Boy, Monkey, Spade, Jig, who sincerely disliked me, and thought of me as typically black. I studied the six kids who spat on me as I walked past their bus parked in front of the school one day. As I approached the bus, each of them poked his head out the window and chanted, "Fuck a duck. Screw a penny. Nigger's dick's as good as any!" And then they showered me with their poetic residue. I must admit that though I studied the poem I never quite understood the intent. The spittle, though, was as legible as big black lettering on a yellow school bus.

I studied those who said to me, intending kindness, I suppose, "You know, you're really not that colored at all." Or "Were your family ever slaves? I mean, you don't act like other colored folks at all." "You know," a black friend said to me once, "I can't tell whether you're ahead of your time or behind it . . . cause you're one funny black man. You know?" A white friend asked me on a number of occasions whether I would be interested in dating his sister. I asked him, "You've told her I'm black, haven't you, Mike?" "Black," he laughed. "Yeah, right." And I remember the lanky, Dead Head blonde woman, who sat in front of me in a college Linguistics class, asking me whether I could speak like "other blacks." Deciding to forgo the mighty-righteous question "Just what the hell do you mean by like *other* blacks?"—I knew, I knew—I told her I could. "Let's see," she said. I crossed my arms and said, "Whaddaya mean, 'Let's see'? You don't believe me? Anyway, it's a matter of context. I just can't leap into it on command." She smirked, shrugged, and said, "Really, Reg, don't have a cow. It's okay." I felt like sliding from my chair, dropping to one knee, and singing, "I'd walk a million miles / for one o' ya smiles / my M-a-a-a-mmy," or something by the Righteous Brothers, or Joe Cocker. Minstrels. But I didn't because she might not have caught the irony. In fact, she might have said, Wow! That was good, or, Well, I didn't think you could do it—either of which would have left me more deeply flummoxed than I already was.

I think these people have been trying to suggest to me that though I exhibit blackness I perform it rather poorly. I believe they are trying to tell me that there are a limited number of valid ways to express blackness, and that my own expression of it is, at best, shaky. Trey Ellis talks about this sort of thing in his essay "The New Black Aesthetic." Ellis says, "It wasn't unusual for me to be called 'oreo' and 'nigger' on the same day. . . . I realized I was a cultural mulatto."[1] But when I say that I am a cultural mulatto, I don't mean to suggest that the majority of blacks in this country (or anywhere else) have some unwitting propensity toward resisting cross-cultural influences in the same way that a duck's oily feathers resist water. In a certain sense all Americans are mulattoes of one shade or another. But when whites "do blackface," people don't so much as blink (though a few would call them nigger lovers; a few would accuse them of exploiting black art/culture for lucre and fame or power and diversion). I daresay they are looked upon by many with a kind of admiration. They are lauded as hip white cats, down whitegirls, soulful purveyors of the "suchness," if not the substance, of negritude. As for blacks who are influenced by expression that is not, as some would say "preponderantly black," the response is rather more ambiguous. Charlie Pride, for example, or Richie Havens, or Jimi Hendrix, or Tracy Chapman may be praised for their talents, their virtuosity in the "pure" sense, but I know of no one who lauds such artists for their mastery of art forms that could be referred to as decidedly "white," except a handful of rock bands who argue, and quite rightly, that rock is a product of black culture as much as it is of white culture, if not more so. There may or may not be such a thing as "blue-eyed soul," but there is certainly the language for the concept. I know of no such term, however, for blacks who perform, in one way or another, to whatever degree, the white "thing" except for the term "crossover" which applies not only to blacks but to everyone else as well. Why the difference? Are we to conclude that this difference lies in the notion that blackness-as-performance is more neatly extricable from blackness-as-being than whiteness-as-performance is from whiteness-as-being? Is blackness-as-performance somehow regarded as a free-floating entity, belonging to no one in particular, while whiteness-as-performance can, and *should,* only belong to whites? After all, it appears to me that black-influenced whites are very often thought to be deepened and ennobled by such processes, while white-influenced blacks are regarded as weakened, diluted, less black.

Of course, it should come as no surprise that some blacks resent certain other blacks who seem willing to accept Eurocentrism, either in part or wholesale, given our history of having it shoved down our gullets. But I have seen whites reveal the same sort of resentment toward white-influenced blacks, as if blackness-as-performance belongs to anyone who would grasp it, master it, even extend upon and recreate its various forms, while its opposite doesn't or shouldn't belong to anyone but its primary producers. Are we to suspect, as Timothy Maliqalim Simone does, that whites may be engaged in "a new form of parasitism"? Simone asks, "Is the assumption of black ideas and worldviews simply a virulent means of recuperating white identity, so that it may

[1]Ellis, Trey. "The New Black Aesthetic," *Callaloo,* Spring, 1989.

resuscitate a waning confidence in its legitimacy to dominate others?"[2] Both of these questions are exceedingly difficult to answer, largely because I'm not sure we know what we're talking about when we talk about "everybody." And also because, ". . . like it or not," says Henry Louis Gates, Jr., in a recent *New York Times Book Review* essay, "all writers" (and from here I extrapolate musicians, painters, sculptors, etc., as well as a number of individuals who are not artists—black, white, yellow, etc., etc.) "are 'cultural impersonators.'"[3] It almost goes without saying that the nature of being human has a great deal to do with mimesis, adaptability, absorption, shape-shifting, souleating.

Like Ellis I was reared in predominantly white environments for most 30 of my life. Though there were schools I attended where I was the only black person in the class, or my grade, and on one occasion, the entire school, for the most part I went to schools where the ethnic representation reflected national ethnic proportions. The neighborhoods in which I grew up were also integrated, being, most of them, military bases established or demographically reconstituted after 1947, the year that the armed forces were integrated. As a result of my upbringing, I learned quite early that the meaning of being black is always, always, always a matter of context. On the sliding scale of my personal history I have been adjudged to be both an Uncle Tom and a Hippie Nigger Bigot. In a 1988 interview with Bob Edwards of National Public Radio's *Morning Edition,* I described myself as a victim/beneficiary of the Civil Rights movement. Since that time I have heard others use the term (though I'm not here implying that I coined it. Historians have suggested that there are times in certain societies when things reach a critical mass of sorts, and ideas, more or less, invent themselves) and I've no doubt that the term implies a grudging affirmation that the movement succeeded to a certain degree. It also implies its failure. The term "victim/beneficiary," just like the word "mulatto," connotes the tragic, leaves us with the image of the heart and mind shred in two by the exigencies of two parallel but inherently incompatible worlds. Success is the irresistible force, failure, the immovable object. The result is either a new creature, a fresh-born slippery babe, yet half veiled by its own steam, but leaving us breathless with hope and wonder; or it is a mutant bastard, a monster, without a place, without a voice, illegible, indecipherable, not worthy of our trust; or it is nothing, a heartless, brainless wonder worthy of neither hope nor scorn. Has the successful failure, the failed success of the Civil Rights movement, left blackfolk in the same slough, left us with the same "sense of always looking at one's self through the eyes of others, of measuring one's soul by the tape of a world that looks on in amused contempt and pity" that W. E. B. Du Bois speaks of in *The Souls of Black Folk?* Are we still left with that "double-consciousness . . . two souls, two thoughts, two unre-

---

[2]Simone, Timothy Maliqalim. *About Face: Race in Postmodern America.* Autonomedia Brooklyn, 1989.

[3]Gates, Henry Louis, Jr. "'Authenticity,' or the Lesson of Little Tree," *New York Times Book Review,* November 24, 1991. [Reprinted in this text, p. 439 (*Ed.*)]

conciled strivings; two warring ideals in one dark body"? I think it has, I think we are, but with one significant difference, a difference, however, that was not promulgated so much in the Civil Rights era, but in the era of Du Bois himself. As Julius Lester puts it:

> Dissent and disagreement have been the hallmark of black history. Though Booker T. Washington, the most politically powerful black American in history, sought to control the minds of black folk with that power, W. E. B. Dubois [sic], the preeminent intellectual and the founder of the NAACP, fought publicly with him over whether the minds and souls of black folks were better protected by protest and the vote or accommodationism and economic nationalism. Later, Dubois [sic] and Marcus Garvey, the ideological father of today's black separatists, would not even pretend that they liked or respected each other.[4]

The phenomenon Du Bois talks about ought not really be regarded as mere bifurcation, for it is not the nonblack world alone that is engaged in the act of being touchstone and measuring tape of the black world, but we ourselves. The "double-consciousness" of which Du Bois speaks isn't really so much a double-consciousness as it is a poly-consciousness. Someone who's black like me doesn't feel particularly torn between one thing and another, but rather among a multiplicity of things. For the better part of this century, many of our leaders, and a good many of us who have followed them, have insisted on toeing one ideological, aesthetic, political, spiritual, or intellectual line or another. Many of us have assiduously searched for the essence of blackness and again and again returned to the inner self empty-handed. What does one have to be or do or believe to be truly, wholly, monolithically black? Some have suggested to me that the wearing of European clothing is unblack, while others have preached the Black Gospel while dressed like Young Republicans. Others have said that the consumption of pork is unblack, while others have insisted that to eschew pork is to deny one's cultural roots. Some have insisted that marrying a nonblack spouse is unblack, while others have said, When you get down to it, we're all African. Some would judge one's level of blackness as being manifest in one's level of knowledge of the history and culture produced by blacks, while others say that very few products have been invented in a vacuum, that when one straddles the interstices of culture and history one begins to trace all the borrowings, the purchases, the thefts, the loans, the imitations that lead to the artifacts that one group or another claims as theirs, that when we are honest with ourselves, the best we can say is that this thing or that thing is a product of our species.

Many say that the term "black" itself is inadequate, and substitute for it African American, Afro-American, Afrikan, and so on and on. . . . Many say so much, so often, with such fervor and conviction that I can't tell rectitude

---

[4] Lester, Julius. "What Price Unity?," *The Village Voice,* September 17, 1991.

from attitude: *"Hey, man, them shoes ain't black." "Look, here, brother, that ain't the way a brother's supposed to talk to a sister." "Dag, 'B,' brothers don't supposed to read that kinda shit." "Hey, don't talk to me about that Africa stuff, cause I've never been to Africa. I don't know the first thing about the place. I'm an American. Period." "Look here, baby, I don't know what that is you listening to, but it ain't music." "Understand something, little brother, I'm the last black man. That's right. You kids don't know a thing about dancing or walking or thinking or making love under the moon. Don't know about knocking whitey the fuck up the side of his head when he needs it. You kids don't know a thing. When I'm dead, that's it. No more black men."* For a long, long time I've let myself be pulled from joint to joint, pulled by the joint. I've stood up and praised her praise song, cursed his condemnation, then changed places with myself. Weren't they all authorities, all valid, all experts when held up to my pathetic little narrow-behind wavering blackness? My inability to put it all together, find the center, swim away clean, black, and sanctified was my fault, no? I thought so. But all the while in the back of my head I sensed something missing, felt some still and empty point that was always out of reach. I soon discovered, though, that what was missing was my own voice.

The thing that has accounted for at least half of the trouble that the performance of my blackness has brought me is the way I speak. *"Now, listen to the way Reginald* enunciates *when he reads that paragraph again, class. Go ahead, Reginald. Start from the top of the page."* I don't know if Mrs. Wood knew that since the "standard" form of any language is established on political rather than purely elocutionary imperatives, no dialect conveys meaning any better or sounds any better—depending on who's doing the listening—than any other dialect. It's just a matter of which dialect the ruling class chooses to make its own. I know for certain that I didn't know this, way back in second grade. I suppose that to some ears I speak the patois[5] of the ruling class, though to my own ears it is more of an ideolect[6] that has resulted from living in a household in which my father's Alabamese and my mother's rather un-Texaslike East Texas accent, and the various accents of all the places we lived have mixed rather curiously upon my tongue. Nevertheless, people have responded to my use of English as though I were an impostor, a usurper, as if I were puttin' on airs, stubbornly willing myself to speak in a way that wasn't natural to "my kind," and by doing so have marked myself as an adopted (at least adoptable) member of the ruling class.

Some have assumed that I come from a privileged background, upper-middle class, college-educated parents, and so on. And beneath this assumption lies the suspicion that I feel little more than contempt for black people and that I would wish nothing more than to assimilate more deeply into the dominant culture. Well, I would be more than a fiction writer if I say I have never felt anger toward certain black people, or have never admired certain

---

[5]*patois:* dialect or special language of a particular group (*Ed.*)
[6]*ideolect:* language particular to one's own ideas (*Ed.*)

whites, but since I have experienced few constants in terms of my innumerable encounters with members of both groups, there have been few times in my life when I felt any particular way about anyone until I became acquainted with her or him. I have never consciously desired to be white. I have never even imagined what it would be like to be white, outside the confines of what I do as a writer. But there were definitely times I was made to feel I wasn't black enough, and wished somehow that I could get a handle on being so, being properly black. I felt this way, even though, when I want to, I can use my father's dialect, as well as a number of others, that are considered to be more or less black. But I kept silent for a long, long while, not because I had nothing to say, but because I thought I had nothing with which to say it. When I spoke in my own ideolect, I lacked authority. When I borrowed my father's I felt like an impostor, and still lacked authority. Having traveled as much as I have I've acquired a fairly decent ear, but my natural speech is my natural speech, and if I don't fit in because of it, I think that's absurd. And I am beginning to suspect that I am as black as I can possibly be. I don't think it would make any difference, in this respect, if I spoke with an Irish brogue. When I lived in Senegal, a friend who had recently introduced me to his family said to me, "You know, they like you, but they just can't get over the fact that you come from a country where all the black people speak English. English!" I asked him if he had considered the notion that I came from a place where blacks might be just as mystified or surprised as his family that there are countries where nearly everyone speaks (at least some) French. "I see what you're getting at," he said. "But to me, it seems natural for a black person to speak French. But English. Man, that is so strange to them. To me, too, to tell you the truth."

35 From Marsha with the plum-colored eyes to my friend Mike who wanted me to date his sister, people are trying to tell me, as I say above, that there is something essential that I exhibit but poorly perform. At times this poor performance troubles some people, at times it brings others comfort. From southern "rednecks" to northern "rustnecks," from southern "geechees" to northern "Malcolmists," from the privileged to the dispossessed, I had grown up feeling hard-pressed to find a genuine place for myself, a general consciousness upon which to draw. I felt I had no group with whom I was completely at peace or for whom I held unbending antipathy, no permanent correspondences based on culture, color, class, race, sex, gender. Be this as it may, I never believed that I was wholly unique in terms of how I performed my blackness or perceived my position in the black world. But I am not saying that I had or have "risen above" the constraints or the licenses of culture, class, race, and so on. And I don't mean to suggest that the relative isolation I have experienced has given me any special insights into any of the apparent enclaves through which I have traveled and by which I have been shaped. All I know is that it is my responsibility to carve out a "space" for myself in the black world without giving up my individuality. In fact, the whole idea of there being a world in which the individual does not fit seems, to me, to be antithetical to the very idea of a "world." As Julius Lester puts it,

"The intellectual and spiritual health of any group is secured only to the extent that its members are permitted to be themselves and still be accepted as part of the group."[7] It's really very simple, and wholly without climax when you get down to it.

For all I know, there may be some essential blackness, but I tend to think it won't be found within the architecture of any particular ideology. In fact, if it is to be found at all, it will likely be found to be a sort of palimpsest,[8] upon which is written all names, ideas, philosophies, arguments, fears, projections, productions, hopes, extrapolations, histories, even silences. But it ought to be the sort of palimpsest upon which there can be no erasures. I have grown weary of my differentness being used against me, or being used as a lever to force me to the banks of our dark and dusky river of being, when, in actuality, my differentness, my relative uniqueness, expands the black world, makes it more complex, contributes to our wherewithal to survive sudden or gradual changes in the political environment. If we insist on a definition of blackness it will have to be predicated on something other than a set of codified and repeatable performances (though this is not to eschew our traditions), for blackness is a process, ever changing, ever growing. I think only lemmings should move in lockstep.

I am not merely asserting that "We are not all alike." Those who aren't aware of that would not likely read this essay or anything like it. What I am saying is that generalizations from within are every bit as fragmenting as scrutiny from without. From my boyhood I have read and heard all manner of statistical facts and figures about black people. Really, they've told me very little about who I am, let alone who we are. We're too big for that, and as individuals too complex. I'm not so sure we should ever find ourselves in the position of saying this general thing or that general thing about black people, expecting our words to discover the essence of our "true self-consciousness," for when we do, we will be doing no more than talking *about* black people, talking *around* them, never quite getting it right, never pinning us down, never quite turning sound into substance, and never—much like the way sharks course around caged divers—ever able to sink our teeth into flesh.

38 We are, from the bottom to the top, as polymorphous as the dance of Shiva.[9] We are not a race, not a culture, not a society, not a subgroup, not a "breeding group," or a cline, not even simply an agglomeration of individuals. We are, in my mind, a civilization, a collection of cultures, societies, nations, individuals, "races." We are ancient and new, Christian, Muslim, Jew, American, Trinidadian, Zimbabwean, female and male, gay and straight, brilliant and stupid, wealthy and poor, mocha and almond and ripe olive. We are at times a "We" and a "Them," an "Us" and "The Other." Being a civilization

---

[7]Lester, op. cit. (*Ed.*)

[8]*palimpsest:* writing material in which two or three layers of writing may be visible (*Ed.*)

[9]*dance of Shiva:* Shiva, the Preserver, is one of the chief gods in Hinduism. (*Ed.*)

does not mean we will always like one another, agree with one another, or even—though this is not wise—listen to one another. But I hope it means that my name will be written on this great palimpsest, my ideas, my contributions, my voice, right next to yours. Let all be included. Let none be cast aside.

DISCUSSING THE TEXT

1. What do the terms *white* and *black* mean to the children who taunt McKnight (whose skin color is brown)? Why do they call him white?
2. Although black children often saw McKnight as more white than black, he was perceived as "typically black" by white people who observed him. What did it mean, to these people, for someone to be black?
3. McKnight says that all Americans are cultural mulattoes—that is, mixtures of different races and ethnic characteristics (par. 28). Get together with a group of four or five students and discuss this idea. Do you agree with McKnight on this point? Why or why not? Take brief notes as you work on this assignment, and be prepared to share your opinions with the class.

WRITING ABOUT THE TEXT

4. McKnight quotes W. E. B. Du Bois and then revises Du Bois's thesis about the double-consciousness of black people, arguing that what black Americans experience today "isn't really so much a double-consciousness as it is a poly-consciousness" (par. 31). What does McKnight mean by the term *poly-consciousness?*
5. Reread McKnight's discussion of blackness-as-performance, blackness-as-being, whiteness-as-performance, and whiteness-as-being in paragraph 28. Write a one-page response to his suggestion that "black-influenced whites are very often thought to be deepened and ennobled . . . while white-influenced blacks are regarded as weakened, diluted, less black." Try to include examples of performers, both white and black, whose work you are familiar with in your response.
6. McKnight stresses the importance of individuality, and the danger of generalizing about blackness, even from within black identity. What do you think of this argument? Would it hold for other ethnic groups and identities as well? Which is more important, individual identity or loyalty to a group or community? Write a brief essay that addresses these questions.
7. Near the end of his essay, McKnight illustrates his "poly-consciousness," or the many different forms of black identity and attitudes, in a long string of quotations from anonymous voices (par. 32). Think of a situation in which you feel torn between different identities or consciousnesses (such as the values of your parents and the values of your friends). Write a passage in which, like McKnight, you present these different consciousnesses, or attitudes, in the voices of different people who hold them.

ISAAC METZKER

FROM

A Bintel Brief: Letters from the Lower East Side to the *Jewish Daily Forward*

The immigrant's difficult adjustment to a new life in America is clearly and movingly depicted in letters sent to the editor of a Yiddish immigrant newspaper, the Jewish Daily Forward, *in the early 1900s. Forty to fifty letters from people seeking advice would arrive each day, and each was answered by the editor, Abraham Cahan, who was also a novelist and essayist. This feature, started by Cahan in 1906, was called "A Bintel Brief" (meaning "a bundle of letters" in Yiddish), and it became the most popular feature of the* Jewish Daily Forward. *A largely working-class newspaper with a national readership, the* Forward *was published on the Lower East Side of New York City, one of the most densely populated urban spaces in the world, at a time when the Jewish population grew to over two and a half million as a result of the exodus of nearly a third of Europe's Jews by 1925, the great majority of whom settled in New York.*

The Bintel Brief letter became a kind of genre in itself—an often remarkable yet true story that reflected the intimate details of immigrant life. In these letters, one can read the dilemmas of those who had just arrived from the Old Country, as well as note the ways in which a new self was being fashioned. Some letter writers feel the tie to old political movements; others have obligations to parents and families that are difficult to meet; others have to decide how much of their old lives they should keep. The letters also illustrate the personal dilemmas of love and marriage in the New World: old loves resurfacing to make their claims, new loves entering lives unexpectedly and threatening marriages, and the inevitable possibility of a "mixed marriage" to someone outside the faith. Each query was answered in a way that was both practical and empathetic, and that tried to reconcile general ethical and Jewish principles with the requirements of practical life.

Ultimately, these letters served to "Americanize" an immigrant population, fostering the transition from "greenhorn," or newcomer, to "American." They provide a fascinating record of some of the issues and dilemmas that would arise for other immigrant groups as well.

Isaac Metzker, himself a longtime editor of the Jewish Daily Forward *and author of five novels in Yiddish, collected these letters for a volume published in 1971; some of the letters have been shortened or condensed by Metzker, along with most of the editor's replies.*

1906

Esteemed Editor,

I hope that you will advise me in my present difficulty.

I am a "greenhorn," only five weeks in the country, and a jeweler by trade. I come from Russia, where I left a blind father and a stepmother. Before I left, my father asked me not to forget him. I promised that I would send him the first money I earned in America.

When I arrived in New York I walked around for two weeks looking for a job, and the bosses told me it was after the season. In the third week I was lucky, and found a job at which I earn eight dollars a week. I worked, I paid my landlady board, I bought a few things to wear, and I have a few dollars in my pocket.

Now I want you to advise me what to do. Shall I send my father a few dollars for Passover, or should I keep the little money for myself? In this place the work will end soon and I may be left without a job. The question is how to deal with the situation. I will do as you tell me.

–Your thankful reader,
I.M.

ANSWER:
The answer to this young man is that he should send his father the few dollars for Passover because, since he is young, he will find it easier to earn a living than would his blind father in Russia.

1906

Worthy Editor,

We are a small family who recently came to the "Golden Land." My husband, my boy and I are together, and our daughter lives in another city.

I had opened a grocery store here, but soon lost all my money. In Europe we were in business; we had people working for us and paid them well. In short, there we made a good living but here we are badly off.

My husband became a peddler. The "pleasure" of knocking on doors and ringing bells cannot be known by anyone but a peddler. If anybody does buy anything "on time," a lot of the money is lost, because there are some people who never intend to pay. In addition, my husband has trouble because he has a beard,[1] and because of the beard he gets beaten up by the hoodlums.

Also we have problems with our boy, who throws money around. He works every day till late at night in a grocery for three dollars a week. I watch over him and give him the best because I'm sorry that he has to work so hard. But he costs me plenty and he borrows money from everybody. He has many friends and owes them all money. I get more and more worried as he takes here and borrows there. All my talking doesn't help. I am afraid to chase him away from home because he might get worse among strangers. I want to point out that he is well versed in Russian and Hebrew and he is not a child any more, but his behavior is not that of an intelligent adult.

I don't know what to do. My husband argues that he doesn't want to continue peddling. He doesn't want to shave off his beard, and it's not fitting

---

[1]*beard:* It was customary for Orthodox Jews to wear beards, following an injunction in *Leviticus* not to round the corners of one's beard; long curling sideburns (payess) became an obvious symbol of the Jew in America. (*Ed.*)

for such a man to do so. The boy wants to go to his sister, but that's a twenty-five-dollar fare. What can I do? I beg you for a suggestion.

–Your constant reader,
F.L.

ANSWER:
Since her husband doesn't earn a living anyway, it would be advisable for all three of them to move to the city where the daughter is living. As for the beard, we feel that if the man is religious and the beard is dear to him because the Jewish law does not allow him to shave it off, it's up to him to decide. But if he is not religious, and the beard interferes with his earnings, it should be sacrificed.

1906

Dear Editor,

For a long time I worked in a shop with a Gentile girl, and we began to go out together and fell in love. We agreed that I would remain a Jew and she a Christian. But after we had been married for a year, I realized that it would not work.

I began to notice that whenever one of my Jewish friends comes to the house, she is displeased. Worse yet, when she sees me reading a Jewish newspaper her face changes color. She says nothing, but I can see that she has changed. I feel that she is very unhappy with me, though I know she loves me. She will soon become a mother, and she is more dependent on me than ever.

She used to be quite liberal, but lately she is being drawn back to the Christian religion. She gets up early Sundays mornings, runs to church and comes home with eyes swollen from crying. When we pass a church now and then, she trembles.

Dear Editor, advise me what to do now. I could never convert, and there's no hope for me to keep her from going to church. What can we do now?

–Thankfully,
A Reader

ANSWER:
Unfortunately, we often hear of such tragedies, which stem from marriages between people of different worlds. It's possible that if this couple were to move to a Jewish neighborhood, the young man might have more influence on his wife.

1906

Worthy Editor,

I am a workingman from Bialystok, and there I belonged to the Bund.[2] But I had to leave Bialystok, and later came to Minsk where I worked and

---

[2]*Bund:* (Yiddish / German) union or alliance of workers (*Ed.*)

joined the Socialist-Revolutionaries. What convinced me to join this organization is this: in Minsk there was a Bundist demonstration that was attacked by the police. They beat up the demonstrators brutally, and arrested many of them. The prisoners were lashed so severely that many of them became ill. One worker from Dvinsk was sentenced to fifty lashes, which caused him to develop epilepsy and while working in a factory he would suddenly fall in a fit.

When we, his co-workers, saw this, it aroused in us a desire for revenge against Czar Nicholas[3] and his tyrannical police force. But when there was a convention of the Bund at that time, and they declared a policy against revenge, many of our Bund members joined the Socialist-Revolutionaries. I wanted to enter the militant organization, but war was declared against Japan, and since I was a reservist, I began to get mail from home advising me to flee to America. I let myself be talked into it and left.

I have been in the country now two years, and life is not bad. I work in a jewelry store, for good wages. But my heart will not remain silent within me over the blood of my brothers being spilled in Russia. I am restless because of the pogroms[4] that took place in Bialystok, where I left old parents and a sister with three small children. I haven't heard from them since the pogrom and don't know if they're alive. But since they lived in the vicinity of the "Piaskes" where the Jewish defense group was located, it's possible they are alive.

Now I ask your advice. I cannot make up my mind whether to fulfill my duty to my parents and sister and bring them to America, if I hear from them, or to go back to Russia and help my brothers in their struggle.

If I had known what was going to happen there, I would not have gone to America. I myself had agitated that one should not leave for America but stay and fight in Russia till we were victorious. Now I feel like a liar and a coward. I agitated my friends, placed them in the danger of soldiers' guns and bullets. And I myself ran away.

–Respectfully,
M.G.

ANSWER:

If one were to ask us the question before leaving Russia, we would not advise him to leave the revolutionary battlefields. Since the writer of the letter is already here and speaks of his two duties, we would like to tell him that the Assistance Movement in America is developing so rapidly that everyone who wants to be useful will be able to do enough here. He should bring his parents and sister here, and become active in the local movement.

---

[3] *Czar Nicholas:* Nicholas II (1868–1918), the last emperor and czar of Russia (1894–1917), abdicated in 1917 and was executed by the revolutionary government in 1918. *(Ed.)*

[4] *pogroms:* organized massacre and looting of a group of people, usually Jews *(Ed.)*

1906

Dear Editor,

I am a Russian revolutionist and a freethinker. Here in America I became acquainted with a girl who is also a freethinker. We decided to marry, but the problem is that she has Orthodox parents, and for their sake we must have a religious ceremony. If we refuse the ceremony we will be cut off from them forever. Her parents also want me to go to the synagogue with them before the wedding, and I don't know what to do. Therefore I ask you to advise me how to act.

–Respectfully,
J.B.

ANSWER:
The advice is that there are times when it pays to give in to old parents and not grieve them. It depends on the circumstances. When one can get along with kindness it is better not to break off relations with the parents.

1906

Dear Editor,

I am a girl from Galicia[5] and in the shop where I work I sit near a Russian Jew with whom I was always on good terms. Why should one worker resent another?

But once, in a short debate, he stated that all Galicians were no good. When I asked him to repeat it, he answered that he wouldn't retract a word, and that he wished all Galician Jews dead.

I was naturally not silent in the face of such a nasty expression. He maintained that only Russian Jews are fine and intelligent. According to him, the *Galitzianer* are inhuman savages, and he had the right to speak of them so badly.

Dear Editor, does he really have a right to say this? Have the Galician Jews not sent enough money for the unfortunate sufferers of the pogroms in Russia? When a Gentile speaks badly of Jews, it's immediately printed in the newspapers and discussed hotly everywhere. But that a Jew should express himself so about his own brothers is nothing? Does he have a right? Are Galicians really so bad? And does he, the Russian, remain fine and intelligent in spite of such expressions?

As a reader of your worthy newspaper, I hope you will print my letter and give your opinion.

–With thanks in advance,
B.M.

---

[5]*Galicia:* a part of Poland formerly under Austrian rule, where many Jews lived; Galician Jews and Russian Jews were often fierce rivals, each claiming superiority over the other. (*Ed.*)

ANSWER:
The Galician Jews are just as good and bad as people from other lands. If the Galicians must be ashamed of the foolish and evil ones among them, then the Russians, too, must hide their heads in shame because among them there is such an idiot as the acquaintance of our letter writer.

1906

Dear Editor,

I join all the others who marvel at your "Bintel Brief," where almost everyone who has something on his conscience, or a secret, can express himself. I, too, wish to get something off my chest, and I want your advice.

I came to America as a *shokhet*.[6] The ship I was on sank. I was among the lucky ones who were rescued, but my valise with my possessions, including the papers that certified that I am a *shokhet*, was lost.

Since I could no longer be a *shokhet*, I became a shirtmaker. Later I worked my way up and became a cloakmaker. But I was not satisfied because the physical labor and the degradation we had to endure in the shops was unbearable.

Within a few years two of my brothers came from Europe. We stayed together and we all worked in a shirt shop. Several times we tried contracting, but it didn't work out. At that time, white collars for shirts came into fashion. We had to sew on neckbands, to which the white collars were buttoned. This became a nuisance that delayed the work. Imagine having to cut out a band to fit each shirt we made. This wasn't easy, and the boss gave us the job of making the bands at home, as night work.

In short, one of us got an idea. Since the whole trade found the neckbands a problem, why not make the neckbands for all the manufacturers? Said and done! It worked out well. They snatched the bands from our hands and we were very busy. We were the only ones in the line from the start, and we prospered. Later a few more shops opened, but that didn't bother us because the trade grew even bigger.

Now we have a huge factory with our names on a big sign on the front of the building. But the bands that gave us our start are no longer made by us alone. We have many workers but have paid little attention to them since we were so involved with making our fortune.

In time I began to read your newspaper and, out of curiosity, even the "Bintel Brief," to see what was going on in the world. As I read more and more about the troubles, my conscience awoke and I began to think: "Robber, cold-blooded robber." My conscience spoke to me: "Just look at your workers, see how pale and thin and beaten they look, and see how healthy and ruddy your face and hands are."

---

[6]*shokhet:* (Yiddish) authorized slaughterer of animals, according to Jewish dietary custom (*Ed.*)

This conscience of mine has a strong voice. It yells at me just as I yell at my workers, and scolds me for all my offenses against them. It will be enough for me to give just a few samples of my evil deeds: The clock in our shop gets "fixed" twice a day; the hands are moved back and forth. The foreman has on his table a stick like a conductor's baton and when someone says a word during working hours he hears the tick-tock of that stick. Our wages are never under two dollars or over seven dollars a week.

My conscience bothers me and I would like to correct my mistakes, so that I will not have to be ashamed of myself in the future. But do not forget that my brothers do not feel as I do, and if I were to speak to them about all this they would consider me crazy. So what is left for me to do? I beg you, worthy Editor, give me a suggestion.

–Yours sincerely,
B.

ANSWER:
We are proud and happy that through the *Forward* and the "Bintel Brief" the conscience of this letter writer was aroused. We can only say to the writer that he must not muffle the voice of his conscience. He will lose nothing, but will gain more and more true happiness.

1907

Worthy Editor,

I was born in America and my parents gave me a good education. I studied Yiddish and Hebrew, finished high school, completed a course in bookkeeping and got a good job. I have many friends, and several boys have already proposed to me.

Recently I went to visit my parents' home town in Russian Poland. My mother's family in Europe had invited my parents to a wedding, but instead of going themselves, they sent me. I stayed at my grandmother's with an aunt and uncle and had a good time. Our European family, like my parents, are quite well off and they treated me well. They indulged me in everything and I stayed with them six months.

It was lively in the town. There were many organizations and clubs and they all accepted me warmly, looked up to me—after all, I was a citizen of the free land, America. Among the social leaders of the community was in intelligent young man, a friend of my uncle's, who took me to various gatherings and affairs.

He was very attentive, and after a short while he declared his love for me in a long letter. I had noticed that he was not indifferent to me, and I liked him as well. I looked up to him and respected him, as did all the townsfolk. My family became aware of it, and when they spoke to me about him, I could see they thought it was a good match.

He was handsome, clever, educated, a good talker and charmed me, but I didn't give him a definite answer. As my love for him grew, however, I wrote to my parents about him, and then we became officially engaged.

A few months later we both went to my parents in the States and they received him like their own son. My bridegroom immediately began to learn English and tried to adjust to the new life. Yet when I introduced him to my friends they looked at him with disappointment. "This 'greenhorn' is your fiancé?" they asked. I told them what a big role he played in his town, how everyone respected him, but they looked at me as if I were crazy and scoffed at my words.

At first I thought, Let them laugh, when they get better acquainted with him they'll talk differently. In time, though, I was affected by their talk and began to think, like them, that he really was a "greenhorn" and acted like one.

In short, my love for him is cooling off gradually. I'm suffering terribly because my feelings for him are changing. In Europe, where everyone admired him and all the girls envied me, he looked different. But, here, I see before me another person.

I haven't the courage to tell him, and I can't even talk about it to my parents. He still loves me with all his heart, and I don't know what to do. I choke it all up inside myself, and I beg you to help me with advice in my desperate situation.

–Respectfully,
A Worried Reader

ANSWER:
The writer would make a grave mistake if she were to separate from her bridegroom now. She must not lose her common sense and be influenced by the foolish opinions of her friends who divided the world into "greenhorns" and real Americans.

We can assure the writer that her bridegroom will learn English quickly. He will know American history and literature as well as her friends do, and be a better American than they. She should be proud of his love and laugh at those who call him "greenhorn."

1914

Worthy Mr. Editor,

I, an old woman of seventy, write you this letter with my heart's blood, because I am distressed.

In Galicia, I was a respected housewife and my husband was a well-known businessman. God blessed us with three daughters and three sons and we raised them properly. When they grew up, one by one they left home, like birds leaving their nest. Our daughters got married, and later left for America with their husbands. Our oldest son also married but a month after his wedding a misfortune befell us—he went swimming and was drowned.

This tragedy had such a bad effect on my husband that he neglected his business, began to ail, and died. The two younger sons both went to America after that, and I was left alone. I longed for the children and wrote to them that I wanted to come to America, to be with them and the grandchildren. But from the first they wrote me that America was not for me, that they do not keep *kosher*[7] and that I would be better off staying at home.

But I didn't let them convince me, and I went to America. All of my children came to meet me at the boat, and I will never forget that moment when they and my grandchildren hugged me and kissed me. Is there any greater happiness for a mother?

But now a new trouble has fallen on me. A few weeks ago when Austria declared war and we heard that Russia was fighting against Austria, my two sons, who are ardent patriots of Kaiser Franz Josef,[8] announced that they were sailing home to help him in the war. When I heard them, I began to cry and begged them not to rush into the fire because they would be shortening my life. But so far they have not given up the idea of going to fight for the Kaiser.

Worthy Editor, I hope you will voice your opinion on this serious matter. Maybe you can have influence on them to give up the idea of leaving this country and their old mother, and going to war.

–Your reader,
The Suffering Mother

ANSWER:
In the answer it says that the woman's two sons should thank God that they are in America, where they are free and can't be forced to shed their blood for the Austrian Kaiser.

1926

Worthy Editor,

We live in a small town in the country where we are the only Jewish family, and we earn a good living here. So all is well, apparently. But we have four daughters, all of them ready for marriage, and there is no one here with whom to make a match. We wanted to send them to a big city, but they don't want to go without Mother and Father. They want us to give up the business, sell everything, and move to another city. But we have no desire to break up our home and give up our good life. It's not easy, in our declining years, to go seek a living elsewhere, when we have such a good business here.

But what doesn't one do for children? Here it's impossible to marry off a girl, because there are no Jews, only Gentiles. Our daughters are fine girls. They are always in the store and behave decently. The question is, however, how will it end? We beg you to advise us.

–Your Country Readers

---

[7]*kosher:* (Hebrew / Yiddish) fit to eat, because ritually clean according to Jewish dietary laws (*Ed.*)

[8]*Kaiser Franz Josef* (1830–1916): emperor of Austria (1848–1916) and king of Hungary (1867–1916); the assassination of his heir apparent set off World War I, which precipated the dissolution of the empire. (*Ed.*)

ANSWER:
In order to advise them, we would have to be well acquainted with their family life, their circumstances, and the character of the parents and their children. We can only tell them that many Jewish families that are in the same position leave the small towns for the sake of their children. Others, on the other hand, remain where they are.

In such circumstances it is better not to rely on advice of others but on themselves.

DISCUSSING THE TEXT

1. How strong a force is Orthodox religion for the Jewish letter writers? What kinds of difficult decisions does it require of the new American? What are some of the ways in which the letter writers try to integrate this doubleness of experience, or bridge the gap between Old World and New World values?
2. What conflicts arise as these immigrants attempt to rise in social status once they arrive in America? Do they seem able to look back with understanding on where they have come from? Can you discern similar patterns in more recent immigrant groups with which you are familiar?
3. Based on the situations described in these letters, how would you characterize the new American society—as an amalgamation, or melting pot, in which differences are eroded, or as a stew in which the various pieces remain quite separate and distinct in character? Why?
4. A number of the letter writers feel conflicted about staying in the United States and wonder if they should return to their homeland. Why? Can you think of other immigrant groups in the United States who might have experienced similar conflicts, or who might be experiencing them today?

WRITING ABOUT THE TEXT

5. From what you've read in these letters, why is marriage outside the Jewish religion and culture often considered dangerous? Do you think that such feelings still exist as part of immigrant life for newly arrived groups? Do you think they exist for ethnic groups that have been in the United States for several generations? Write two paragraphs that address these questions and that explain your own views on ethnically mixed marriages.
6. Reread the letter by the American-born young woman who brings a "greenhorn" bridegroom to America and begins to lose her appreciation of him, along with the editor's given answer (pp. 188–189). Then write your own response to the problem, offering the woman more concrete advice on how to deal with the situation.
7. Form a correspondence team with another member of your class. Your assignment will be to (a) write a letter to be answered by your teammate, and (b) provide a written response to a letter written by your teammate. In your letter, try to address a dilemma in your own life (or the life of a friend), perhaps one that involves a conflict between school or social issues and family or personal values or attitudes.

8. Based on the kinds of responses he provides to these letters, write a brief character profile of Abraham Cahan, the editor of the *Jewish Daily Forward.* What seem to be his attitudes toward the Old and New Worlds, toward the roles and responsibilities of the new American citizens, toward Jewish culture and religion, and so on? How would you characterize his outlook on the multicultural self ?

OSCAR HIJUELOS

FROM

Our House in the Last World

This brief selection from Oscar Hijuelos's first novel, Our House in the Last World *(1984), poignantly portrays the plight of the multicultural self in an alienating environment. The novel chronicles the lives of a Cuban family who emigrated to the United States in the 1940s. It focuses particularly on the character of the adolescent son, Hector, and his struggles to construct a viable identity.*

In this selection, Hector's attempts to transcend his family's values and to break free from the influence of his loving father, Alejo, take him to some strange places: the world of affluence and drugs of some of his peers and the world of petty theft. Even though the excerpt ends as Hector leaves his family in New York to live with his aunt in Miami, his parting is not final or complete. Hector's identification with his father and everything Cuban, even against his own will, will continue to haunt him as he tries to forge a new identity.

Oscar Hijuelos was born in 1951 in New York City into a working-class Cuban immigrant family, and he studied at City College. He has received many awards for his writing, including a fellowship from the National Endowment for the Arts. The Mambo Kings Sing Songs of Love *(1989), Hijuelos's second novel, won the Pulitzer Prize in literature; his third novel is* The Fourteen Sisters of Emilio Montez O'Brien *(1993).*

Hector was tired, tired of being a Cuban cook's son and hearing people say, "Oh you look just like Alejo!" Look like Alejo? It made him cringe. He felt like a freak, a hunchback, a man with a deformed face. Like Alejo? At least Alejo had his people, the Cubans, his brothers, but Hector was out in the twilight zone, trying to crawl out of his skin and go somewhere else, be someone else. But he could do nothing to change himself to his own satisfaction. Anything he did, like growing his hair long or dressing like a hippy, was an affectation, layered over his true skin like hospital tape. Hector always felt as if he were in costume, his true nature unknown to others and perhaps even to himself. He was part "Pop," part Mercedes; part Cuban, part American—all wrapped tightly inside a skin in which he sometimes could not move.

He would go and get lost. Sometimes down to the rich neighborhoods, West End Avenue and Riverside Drive, and down to the park where he sometimes went with a red-sunburst, cowboy-looking guitar that he had stolen out of a music store window. He had just pulled the guitar off its stand and gone running off with it. If he had been caught, he would have gone to reform school like the deaf mute Mary's kids, but he didn't get caught.

One day, when he was sitting in the park under a tree, strumming a chord, some rich kids who were high on acid came by and asked him if he wanted to come to a party with them, and he said yes. They always had parties when their parents went away on weekends, they said. They would take LSD and eat opium and swallow pills. Hector went into various apartments, with white bearskin rugs, books everywhere, African instruments on the walls, color TVs, and big mirrors at the ends of halls, two bathrooms, maids trying to ignore everything. He took drugs with the others in order to be a friend. Young pretty girls turned into wild flowers and cats. They pulled down their panties and hopped on top of pianos, shook their loins and showed off their parts, while the piano strings hummed up their long slender legs into a softness that gave off scents like perfume from another world. They made him insatiably hungry, until he wanted to eat and taste them, all the beautiful flower children kissing and fucking and eating grapes and ice cream and brownies in the kitchen and in the closets. Fine and naked zombies walking around and fluttering their hands like butterflies. Girls in the corner, naked, braiding their long hair and moaning each time the sunshine warmed their necks and the smalls of their backs.

And Hector would sit there trying to maintain his cool, but all around him corpses were hiding in the closets, their eyes looking out from the dark. He could always hear Mercedes's high-pitched voice calling him: "Hector! Hector!" And he would swear that Alejo was in the next room, even though he was far away. Then there was the problem of his own body, the Cuban-diseased body with its microbios[1] and a heart thumping loudly, ready to burst. Looking in a mirror, he would see Alejo's face and feel the microbios festering inside him, and hear in the halls, children running by like fleeting sprites, like Mercedes, until someone tapped his shoulder and drew his attention away, or some pretty naked girl, with the most concerned expression, passed a rose under his nostrils, as if to bring him back.

Sometimes he came home in this state of mind, and then he would become anxious trying to avoid Alejo who, in those days after leaving the hospital, wanted to win back his friendship. As soon as Hector came home he went to bed. One time there was a knock at his door.

"Who is it?"

"Yo," Alejo said. "It's me."

"Okay, okay, what do you want?"

---

[1]*Cuban-diseased body with its microbios:* Hector imagines his body is "infected" by an obsession with Cuba. (*Ed.*)

"I came to bring you something." Alejo pushed open the door and turned on the light. Holding a box, he looked at Hector most strangely, puzzled. "Is something wrong with you? You never go to sleep this early."

"Nothing." 10

"Well, I've brought you something." And he put the box on the bed. Inside were a pair of white sneakers, just like his.

"These are for you."

"Why?"

"Because you're my son."

"Okay, okay. Thanks, Pop." 15

Then Alejo tried to give him a kiss, but Hector turned away.

After Alejo left, Hector stayed up thinking about him and the sneakers and about looking like him. Hector couldn't sleep.

The rich kids' fathers were doctors and lawyers and book publishers. When they asked about Alejo's occupation, Hector always told them "chef," as Horacio always told people. But he was only a cook, and he smelled of meat. Hector got sneakers, but his friends were given stereos and sent away to resortlike colleges and to Europe. Hector went to Coney Island. So when Alejo asked, "Why don't you look at me? I try to give you things," Hector answered him roughly and demanded more. When he finally graduated from high school, which he had hated, he demanded a cash present, one hundred dollars, which Alejo managed to give him. Then Hector blew it on a girl in a bar. And even that wasn't enough. Nothing could equal the big parties, trips, and cash of his West End and Riverside friends.

Hector came to a point when he paid no attention to Alejo.

"Would you take a walk with me today?" 20

"No Pop, I'm busy."

And yet Alejo continued to try. Each time he went out, he returned with something for Hector. A pair of socks, identical to his own; a T-shirt, a sports shirt, or pants identical to his own.

"Come on, Pop," Hector always said. "I'm my own man."

But he wasn't. He wanted to get out of his skin and go somewhere. He was tired of the neighborhood: the hoods, the racists, the snotty college kids, the dope fiends, the booze, the drugs. He was tired of getting drunk with his neighborhood pals, tired of being high, tired of being like a Cuban Quasimodo.[2] He wanted to go somewhere, but where?

One day in the late spring he started to think about Aunt Buita in Miami. 25 She still sent him presents every Christmas and wrote the same letters each year: "I miss you very much and dream of the days when you will come to see me." So Hector badgered Alejo until he called Buita to arrange a visit that summer.

The very day Hector left for Miami, he said two words to Alejo, and passed much of his time pacing his bedroom, impatient to go. He looked in

---

[2]*Quasimodo:* the name of the deformed bell-ringer of the Paris Cathedral in Victor Hugo's novel *Notre Dame de Paris* (*Ed.*)

the mirror; he was the hip blimp wearing a gray flannel jacket and black turtleneck. "Don't you think you'll be hot in Miami?" asked Alejo.

"No." That was one of the two words.

And he had loaded himself down with a guitar and with a stack of records, rock 'n' roll—"heepie music," as Buita would call it.

"Don't you think you're taking too much?" Alejo asked him.

"So?" And that was the second word. 30

There were kids playing ball in the street and some neighbors waited with Alejo on the stoop when the car came around. Alejo was wearing black pants, a belt that had been stretched very far, so that its holes were like oriental eyes, a T-shirt, and comfortable sneakers that gave him spring when he rushed to the car to get an embrace and kiss from Hector. He rapped at the window. Hector moved inside and waved him away. There were so many people around.

"Come on, I'm your papa," said Alejo, with his head so far inside the car that his slightly bristled cheek was right in front of Hector. "Come on, I'm your papa," he said again. But Hector ignored him, and Alejo went back to the stoop, waving like a mad man as the car finally drove away.

DISCUSSING THE TEXT

1. Why does Hector always feel as if he were "in costume"? What are some of the "costumes" he symbolically tries on? How are they significant in terms of issues of social class and ethnicity?
2. Why do you think Hector's father, Alejo, is always giving him clothes that are identical to his own? What does this tell us about Alejo? How do you interpret Hector's reactions to his father? How would you react under similar circumstances?
3. With a group of four or five other students, discuss Hector's experience of the multicultural self. Why do you think he is so negative about himself and his family? Do you think there is any way in which he could integrate the different parts of himself into a whole? Take some notes as you work on this assignment, and be prepared to share your opinions with the class.

WRITING ABOUT THE TEXT

4. A number of images in this selection, such as the drug-induced visions in paragraph 4, suggest Hector's desire to escape his identity, his family, and his surroundings. Make a list of these images and any other similar images that you notice, trying to think of connections among them. Then write two paragraphs explaining what you think about Hector's fantasies. Do you think they will help him or hinder him in his search for a new identity?
5. Hijuelos writes that "Anything he [Hector] did, like growing his hair long or dressing like a hippy, was an affectation, layered over his true skin like hospital tape" (par. 1). Recall a time when you tried to change (or thought about trying to change) something about your identity by somehow changing the way you looked. Write a brief account of this experience. What were

your reasons for wishing to make such a change? How successful do you think you were in actually changing your identity (or how successful do you think you would have been if you had actually made the changes you considered)? How big a role does appearance play in shaping identity?

6. Try to imagine what happens to Hector when he visits Aunt Buita in Miami. Write a two- to three-page follow-up scene to the selection included here.

KESAYA E. NODA

Growing Up Asian in America

In writing about her experiences as an American woman of Japanese ancestry, Kesaya Noda focuses on the conflicts raised by her three identities: Japanese, Japanese American, and female. Noda describes the experience of thinking of herself from the inside, as rooted in Japanese cultural traditions that she herself accepts, but also from the outside (through images in the media, for example) as an alien presence within American culture and society. Her overall integration of different cultures and traditions reflects pride in her ancestors and a strong sense of self.

As she relates her personal history, Noda places this history in context by providing important details about the fate of Japanese immigrants in the United States. She observes their powerlessness during the nineteenth century, when those who were ineligible for citizenship were not allowed to buy, sell, or lease land. The message to Japanese Americans was clear: they could not lay claim to American territory. Noda also discusses the plight of Japanese Americans in the 1940s, during World War II—a time when people of Japanese ancestry who had been born in the United States were driven from their homes and placed in concentration camps by the U.S. government.

Kesaya Noda was born in California and grew up in New Hampshire. She has lived, studied, and traveled in Japan. Noda is author of The Yamato Colony, *a history of the Japanese American community in California where her parents grew up. "Growing Up Asian in America" first appeared in* Making Waves: Anthology of Writings by and about Asian Women, *edited by Asian Women United of California in 1989.*

Sometimes when I was growing up, my identity seemed to hurtle toward me and paste itself right to my face. I felt that way, encountering the stereotypes of my race perpetuated by non-Japanese people (primarily white) who may or may not have had contact with other Japanese in America. "You don't like cheese, do you?" someone would ask. "I know your people don't like cheese." Sometimes questions came making allusions to history. That was another aspect of the identity. Events that had happened quite apart from the me who stood silent in that moment connected my face with an incomprehensible past.

"Your parents were in California? Were they in those camps during the war?" And sometimes there were phrases or nicknames: "Lotus Blossom." I was sometimes addressed or referred to as racially Japanese, sometimes as Japanese American, and sometimes as an Asian woman. Confusions and distortions abounded.

How is one to know and define oneself? From the inside—within a context that is self defined, from a grounding in community and a connection with culture and history that are comfortably accepted? Or from the outside—in terms of messages received from the media and people who are often ignorant? Even as an adult I can still see two sides of my face and past. I can see from the inside out, in freedom. And I can see from the outside in, driven by the old voices of childhood and lost in anger and fear.

I Am Racially Japanese

A voice from my childhood says: "You are other. You are less than. You are unalterably alien." This voice has its own history. We have indeed been seen as other and alien since the early years of our arrival in the United States. The very first immigrants were welcomed and sought as laborers to replace the dwindling numbers of Chinese, whose influx had been cut off by the Chinese Exclusion Act of 1882. The Japanese fell natural heir to the same anti-Asian prejudice that had arisen against the Chinese. As soon as they began striking for better wages, they were no longer welcomed.

I can see myself today as a person historically defined by law and custom as being forever alien. Being neither "free white," nor "African," our people in California were deemed "aliens, ineligible for citizenship," no matter how long they intended to stay here. Aliens ineligible for citizenship were prohibited from owning, buying, or leasing land. They did not and could not belong here. The voice in me remembers that I am always a *Japanese* American in the eyes of many. A third-generation German American is an American. A third-generation Japanese American is a Japanese American. Being Japanese means being a danger to the country during the war and knowing how to use chopsticks. I wear this history on my face.

I move to the other side. I see a different light and claim a different context. My race is a line that stretches across ocean and time to link me to the shrine where my grandmother was raised. Two high, white banners lift in the wind at the top of the stone steps leading to the shrine. It is time for the summer festival. Black characters are written against the sky as boldly as the clouds, as lightly as kites, as sharply as the big black crows I used to see above the fields in New Hampshire. At festival time there is liquor and food, ritual, discipline, and abandonment. There is music and drunkenness and invocation. There is hope. Another season has come. Another season has gone. 5

I am racially Japanese. I have a certain claim to this crazy place where the prayers intoned by a neighboring Shinto priest (standing in for my grandmother's nephew who is sick) are drowned out by the rehearsals for the pop singing contest in which most of the villagers will compete later that night.

The village elders, the priest, and I stand respectfully upon the immaculate, shining wooden floor of the outer shrine, bowing our heads before the hidden powers. During the patchy intervals when I can hear him, I notice the priest has a stutter. His voice flutters up to my ears only occasionally because two men and a woman are singing gustily into a microphone in the compound, testing the sound system. A prerecorded tape of guitars, samisens, and drums accompanies them. Rock music and Shinto prayers. That night, to loud applause and cheers, a young man is given the award for the most *netsuretsu*—passionate, burning—rendition of a song. We roar our approval of the reward. Never mind that his voice had wandered and slid, now slightly above, now slightly below the given line of the melody. Netsuretsu. Netsuretsu.

In the morning, my grandmother's sister kneels at the foot of the stone stairs to offer her morning prayers. She is too crippled to climb the stairs, so each morning she kneels here upon the path. She shuts her eyes for a few seconds, her motions as matter of fact as when she washes rice. I linger longer than she does, so reluctant to leave, savoring the connection I feel with my grandmother in America, the past, and the power that lives and shines in the morning sun.

Our family has served this shrine for generations. The family's need to protect this claim to identity and place outweighs any individual claim to any individual hope. I am Japanese.

I Am a Japanese American

"Weak." I hear the voice from my childhood years. "Passive," I hear. Our parents and grandparents were the ones who were put into those camps. They went without resistance; they offered cooperation as proof of loyalty to America. "Victim," I hear. And, "Silent."

Our parents are painted as hard workers who were socially uncomfortable and had difficulty expressing even the smallest opinion. Clean, quiet, motivated, and determined to match the American way; that is us, and that is the story of our time here. 10

"Why did you go into those camps," I raged at my parents, frightened by my own inner silence and timidity. "Why didn't you do anything to resist? Why didn't you name it the injustice it was?" Couldn't our parents even think? Couldn't they? Why were we so passive?

I shift my vision and my stance. I am in California. My uncle is in the midst of the sweet potato harvest. He is pressed, trying to get the harvesting crews onto the field as quickly as possible, worried about the flow of equipment and people. His big pickup is pulled off to the side, motor running, door ajar. I see two tractors in the yard in front of an old shed; the flat bed harvesting platform on which the workers will stand has already been brought over from the other field. It's early morning. The workers stand loosely grouped and at ease, but my uncle looks as harried and tense as a police officer trying to unsnarl a New York City traffic jam. Driving toward the shed, I pull my car off the road to make way for an approaching tractor. The front wheels of the car sink luxuriously into the soft, white sand by the roadside and the car slides to a dreamy halt, tail still on the road. I try to move forward. I try to move back. The front bites contentedly into the sand, the back lifts itself at a jaunty angle. My uncle sees me and storms down the road, running. He is shouting before he is even near me.

"What's the matter with you," he screams. "What the hell are you doing?" In his frenzy, he grabs his hat off his head and slashes it through the air across his knee. He is beside himself. "Don't you know how to drive in sand? What's the matter with you? You've blocked the whole roadway. How am I supposed to get my tractors out of here? Can't you use your head? You've cut off the whole roadway, and we've got to get out of here."

I stand on the road before him helplessly thinking, "No, I don't know how to drive in sand. I've never driven in sand."

15 "I'm sorry, uncle," I say, burying a smile beneath a look of sincere apology. I notice my deep amusement and my affection for him with great curiosity. I am usually devastated by anger. Not this time.

During the several years that follow I learn about the people and the place, and much more about what has happened in this California village where my parents grew up. The issei, our grandparents, made this settlement in the desert. Their first crops were eaten by rabbits and ravaged by insects. The land was so barren that men walking from house to house sometimes got lost. Women came here too. They bore children in 114 degree heat, then carried the babies with them into the fields to nurse when they reached the end of each row of grapes or other truck farm crops.

I had had no idea what it meant to buy this kind of land and make it grow green. Or how, when the war came, there was no space at all for the subtlety of being who we were—Japanese Americans. Either/or was the way. I hadn't understood that people were literally afraid for their lives then, that their money had been frozen in banks; that there was a five-mile travel limit; that when the early evening curfew came and they were inside their houses, some of them watched helplessly as people they knew went into their barns to steal their belongings. The police were patrolling the road, interested only in violators of curfew. There was no help for them in the face of thievery. I had not been able to imagine before what it must have felt like to be an American—to know absolutely that one is an American—and yet to have almost everyone else deny it. Not only deny it, but challenge that identity with machine guns and troops of white American soldiers. In those circumstances it was difficult to say, "I'm a Japanese American." "American" had to do.

But now I can say that I am a Japanese American. It means I have a place here in this country, too. I have a place here on the East Coast, where our neighbor is so much a part of our family that my mother never passes her house at night without glancing at the lights to see if she is home and safe; where my parents have hauled hundreds of pounds of rocks from fields and arduously planted Christmas trees and blueberries, lilacs, asparagus, and crab apples; where my father still dreams of angling a stream to a new bed so that he can dig a pond in the field and fill it with water and fish. "The neighbors already came for their Christmas tree?" he asks in December. "Did they like it? Did they like it?"

I have a place on the West Coast where my relatives still farm, where I heard the stories of feuds and backbiting, and where I saw that people survived and flourished because fundamentally they trusted and relied upon one another. A death in the family is not just a death in a family; it is a death in the community. I saw people help each other with money, materials, labor, attention, and time. I saw men gather once a year, without fail, to clean the grounds of a ninety-year-old woman who had helped the community before, during, and after the war. I saw her remembering them with birthday cards sent to each of their children.

I come from a people with a long memory and a distinctive grace. We live our thanks. And we are Americans. Japanese Americans. 20

I Am a Japanese American Woman

Woman. The last piece of my identity. It has been easier by far for me to know myself in Japan and to see my place in America than it has been to accept my line of connection with my own mother. She was my dark self, a figure in whom I thought I saw all that I feared most in myself. Growing into womanhood and looking for some model of strength, I turned away from her. Of course, I could not find what I sought. I was looking for a black feminist or a white feminist. My mother is neither white nor black.

My mother is a woman who speaks with her life as much as with her tongue. I think of her with her own mother. Grandmother had Parkinson's disease and it had frozen her gait and set her fingers, tongue, and feet jerking and trembling in a terrible dance. My aunts and uncles wanted her to be able to live in her own home. They fed her, bathed her, dressed her, awoke at midnight to take her for one last trip to the bathroom. My aunts (her daughters-in-law) did most of the care, but my mother went home from New Hampshire to California each summer to spend a month living with grandmother, because she wanted to and because she wanted to give my aunts at least a small rest. During those hot summer days, mother lay on the couch watching the television or reading, cooking foods that grandmother liked, and speaking little. Grandmother thrived under her care.

The time finally came when it was too dangerous for grandmother to live alone. My relatives kept finding her on the floor beside her bed when they went to wake her in the mornings. My mother flew to California to help clean the house and make arrangements for grandmother to enter a local nursing home. On her last day at home, while grandmother was sitting in her big, overstuffed armchair, hair combed and wearing a green summer dress, my mother went to her and knelt at her feet. "Here, Mamma," she said. "I've polished your shoes." She lifted grandmother's legs and helped her into the shiny black shoes. My grandmother looked down and smiled slightly. She left her house walking, supported by her children, carrying her pocket book, and wearing her polished black shoes. "Look, Mamma," my mom had said, kneeling. "I've polished your shoes."

Just the other day, my mother came to Boston to visit. She had recently lost a lot of weight and was pleased with her new shape and her feeling of good health. "Look at me, Kes," she exclaimed, turning toward me, front and back, as naked as the day she was born. I saw her small breasts and the wide, brown scar, belly button to pubic hair, that marked her because my brother and I were both born by Caesarean section. Her hips were small. I was not a large baby, but there was so little room for me in her that when she was carrying me she could not even begin to bend over toward the floor. She hated it, she said.

"Don't I look good? Don't you think I look good?" 25

I looked at my mother, smiling and as happy as she, thinking of all the times I have seen her naked. I have seen both my parents naked throughout my life, as they have seen me. From childhood through adulthood we've had our naked moments, sharing baths, idle conversations picked up as we moved between showers and closets, hurried moments at the beginning of days, quiet moments at the end of days.

I know this to be Japanese, this ease with the physical, and it makes me think of an old, Japanese folk song. A young nursemaid, a fifteen-year-old girl, is singing a lullaby to a baby who is strapped to her back. The nursemaid has been sent as a servant to a place far from her own home. "We're the beggars," she says, "and they are the nice people. Nice people wear fine sashes. Nice clothes."

If I should drop dead,
bury me by the roadside!
I'll give a flower
to everyone who passes.

What kind of flower?
The cam-cam-camellia [tsun-tsun-tsubaki]
watered by Heaven:
alms water.[1]

The nursemaid is the intersection of heaven and earth, the intersection of the human, the natural world, the body, and the soul. In this song, with clear eyes, she looks steadily at life, which is sometimes so very terrible and sad. I think of her while looking at my mother, who is standing on the red and purple carpet before me, laughing, without any clothes.

I am my mother's daughter. And I am myself.

I am a Japanese American woman. 30

Epilogue

I recently heard a man from West Africa share some memories of his childhood. He was raised Muslim, but when he was a young man, he found

---

[1]Patia R. Isaku, *Mountain Storm, Pine Breeze: Folk Song in Japan* (Tucson, Ariz.: University of Arizona Press, 1981), 41.

himself deeply drawn to Christianity. He struggled against this inner impulse for years, trying to avoid the church yet feeling pushed to return to it again and again. "I would have done *anything* to avoid the change," he said. At last, he became Christian. Afterwards he was afraid to go home, fearing that he would not be accepted. The fear was groundless, he discovered, when at last he returned—he had separated himself, but his family and friends (all Muslim) had not separated themselves from him.

The man, who is now a professor of religion, said that in the Africa he knew as a child and a young man, pluralism was embraced rather than feared. There was "a kind of tolerance that did not deny your particularity," he said. He alluded to zestful, spontaneous debates that would sometimes loudly erupt between Muslims and Christians in the village's public spaces. His memories of an atheist who harangued the villagers when he came to visit them once a week moved me deeply. Perhaps the man was an agricultural advisor or inspector. He harassed the women. He would say:

> "Don't go to the fields! Don't even bother to go to the fields. Let God take care of you. He'll send you the food. If you believe in God, why do you need to work? You don't need to work! Let God put the seeds in the ground. Stay home."

The professor said, "The women laughed, you know? They just laughed. Their attitude was, 'Here is a child of God. When will he come home?'"

The storyteller, the professor of religion, smiled a most fantastic, tender smile as he told this story. "In my country, there is a deep affirmation of the oneness of God," he said. "The atheist and the women were having quite different experiences in their encounter, though the atheist did not know this. He saw himself as quite separate from the women. But the women did not see themselves as being separate from him. 'Here is a child of God,' they said. 'When will he come home?'" 34

DISCUSSING THE TEXT

1. What are some of the connections that Noda establishes among her three identities (Japanese, Japanese American, and woman)?
2. Noda begins her essay with the statement "Sometimes when I was growing up, my identity seemed to hurtle toward me and paste itself right to my face." Is this a feeling you recognize in any way? She goes on to say, in paragraph 4, "I wear this history on my face." What do you think she means by this?
3. Working with a group of four or five other students, take a closer look at the section of Noda's essay in which she considers her identity as a Japanese American *woman* (par. 21–30). Why does she choose to dwell on her grandmother's illness and her mother's naked body? What is the significance of the nursemaid's song at the end of this section? Record your thoughts and ideas, and be prepared to present them to the rest of the class.
4. Why do you think Noda chooses to end her essay with the story told by the West African professor of religion?

WRITING ABOUT THE TEXT

5. Make a list of the Japanese stereotypes that Noda has encountered. Then write two paragraphs addressing the following questions: How does Noda deal with such stereotypes? Why is it important for her to address them?
6. Write two paragraphs in which you compare and contrast Noda's sense of cultural alienation (the ways in which she looks at herself "from the inside and from the outside") with W. E. B. Du Bois's notion of "double-consciousness" in *The Souls of Black Folk* (p. 161).
7. Noda observes that, for the multicultural self, the formation of identity can often be a dual process: "How is one to know and define oneself ? From the inside—within a context that is self defined, from a grounding in community and a connection with culture and history that are comfortably accepted? Or from the outside—in terms of messages received from the media and people who are often ignorant? Even as an adult I can still see two sides of my face and past" (par. 2). Write a brief essay using Noda's method of looking at oneself both from the inside and the outside to explore the problem of identity in your own life.

FAE MYENNE NG

False Gold

In this essay, first published in The New Republic *in 1993, Fae Myenne Ng provides a glimpse at the multicultural self in all its complexity. Speaking out of the fusion of two very different cultures and lifestyles—immigrant Chinese and American—Ng describes the circumstances surrounding her Chinese father's immigration to the United States under an assumed identity and, at the same time, questions the reality of "the American dream" for her family. By doubting the worth of her father's journey to the United States (referred to by the Chinese as "Gold Mountain"), Ng raises important questions about the validity of the American dream. "The question is not how bad it is in China," Ng writes. "The question is how good it can be in America."*

Financial hardship and the establishment of a new identity are important themes in immigrant narratives. Ng adds a new dimension to these central issues by letting us hear her father's perspective on his own life, which he calls "a bitter, no-luck life."

Fae Myenne Ng (b. 1957) is a first-generation Chinese American. Her family's connections to the United States go back to the last century, when her great-grandfather immigrated to California during the gold rush (although he eventually returned to his wife and children in China). As a child, Ng helped her mother with her sewing at the Chinatown sweatshops of San Francisco. Her widely praised first novel, Bone *(1993), narrates her parents' struggles in "Gold Mountain." Since her parents do not read English, the author has told them what it's about: "I tell them that the book celebrates the hard work and living they endured in order to give future generations a better life," she says.*

It's that same old, same old story. We all have an immigrant ancestor, one who believed in America; one who, daring or duped, took sail. The Golden Venture emigrants have begun the American journey, suffering and sacrificing, searching for the richer, easier life. I know them; I could be one of their daughters. Like them, my father took the sacrificial role of being the first to venture. Now, at the end of his life, he calls it a bitter, no-luck life. I have always lived with his question, Was it worth it? As a child, I saw the bill-by-bill payback and I felt my own unpayable emotional debt. Obedience and Obligation: the Confucian curse.

For $4,000 my father became the fourth son of a legal Chinese immigrant living in San Francisco. His paper-father sent him a coaching book, detailing complicated family history. It was 1940; my father paid ninety more dollars for passage on the s.s. *Coolidge.* He had little hand luggage, a change of clothes, herbs and seeds and a powder for soup. To soothe his pounding heart during the fifteen-day voyage he recited the coaching book over and over again. It was not a floating hell. "The food was Chinese. We traveled third-class. A bunk was good enough space." He was prepared for worse. He'd heard about the Peruvian ships that transported Chinese coolies[1] for plantation labor in the 1850s. (Every generation has a model.) One hundred and twenty days. Two feet by six for each man. Were these the first ships to be called floating hells?

Gold Mountain was the name of my father's America. In February, when the Golden Venture immigrants sailed from Bangkok, they were shouting, *Mei Guo! Mei Guo!* "Beautiful Country" was the translation they preferred. America is the land of light and hope. But landing here is only the beginning of a long tale. When I saw the photos of the shipwrecked Chinese on the beach, I was reminded of the men kept on Angel Island, the detention center in the middle of San Francisco Bay. A sea of hats on the deck of the ship. Triple-decked bunkers. Men in loose pants playing volleyball. "Was volleyball fun?" I wanted to know. My father shrugged, "Nothing else to do. It helped pass the day." Our fathers spent months detained on Angel Island. Their name for it was Wooden House. What, I wonder, are the Chinese calling the detention center in Bethlehem, Pennsylvania?

After his release from Angel Island, my father lived at a bachelor hotel on Waverly Place with a dozen other bachelors in one room, communal toilets, no kitchen. He had breakfast at Uncle's Cafe, dinners at the Jackson Cafe, midnight noodles at Sam Wo's. Drinks at the Li Po Bar or Red's Place, where fat burlesque queens sat on his lap. Marriage for duty. Sons for tradition. My father left the hotel but kept the habits. He still eats like a mouse, in the middle of the night, cooking on a hot plate in his room. (I do my version of the same.) He keeps his money under the floorboard. When I have it, I like to have a grip, bill by bill. Like everyone, too little money upsets me; but more money than I can hold upsets me too. I feel obliged to give it away. Is it a wonder that money has a dirty feel? Get it and get it fast. Then get rid of it.

---

[1]*coolie:* (Urdu, hireling) in Asia, an unskilled native worker, employed cheaply (*Ed.*)

I remember this Angel Island photograph. Thirty bare-chested Chinese men are waiting for a medical examination. The doctor, a hunching man with a scraping stare, sits at a small desk, elbows and thick hands over a black book. At his side, a guard in knee-high boots measures a boy's forehead. Arranged by height, baby-eyed boys stand stoop-shouldered on the outer edge. The men, at least a head taller, stand toward the center of the room, staring at the examiner. Those eyes scare me. Bold and angry and revengeful. Eyes that owe. Eyes that will make you pay. Humiliation with a vengeance. 5

As boldly, the Golden Venture men have looked into American cameras. (If they believed a foot on soil would make them legal, a photo in an American newspaper would be as good as a passport.) There was a "See me!" bounce in their faces. They'd arrived, and now they wanted to send their news back home. And back home, a grateful father jumped when he picked out his son as one of the survivors, "He's alive! My son made it."

Another photo. A Golden Venture man looks out from a locked door, his face framed by a tight window. He has a jail-view of the Beautiful Country. How would he describe his new world? I imagine he'd use his own body as a measure. "Window, two head high. Sun on both ears." Can we forget the other "face" photograph taken earlier this century? The sold and smuggled prostitute, demoted from brothel to a crib, a wooden shack with barred windows that barely fits a cot. Looking out from her fenced window, she has the same downcast eyes, the same bitter-strange lips that seem to be smiling as well as trembling. The caption quotes her price: "Lookee two bits, feelee floor bits, doee six bits."

Life was and still is weighed in gold. People buy people. Sons and wives and slaves. There was the imperial edict that forbade Chinese to leave China; there was China's contribution to France during World War I, in which tens of thousands of Chinese lived horrible lives as indentured slaves. I've heard parents threaten to sell children who misbehave. (Mine threatened to throw me into the garbage can where they claimed they found me.) There's the story of Old Man Jeong, the one on Beckett Alley. Lonely after his wife died, fearful no one would care for him in his senile retirement, he went back to his home village and bought himself a wife. A woman born in 1956.

Listen to the animal names. Snakes sneak into America. The Golden Venture was a snake ship. The emigrants are snake cargo; the middleman, a snakehead. In my father's time, a pig was sold to America. A pig gets caught, a pig gets cheated. My father feels cheated, sold, on an easy story.

On a recent visit to my father's house in Guangzhou, I found his original coaching book. I knew it had been untouched since he last held it. In my hand, the loosely bound papers felt like ashes. I thought about how when he committed everything to memory, he became another man's son. There's an elaborate map of the family compound; each page is lined with questions and answers, some marked with red circles. Tedious questions and absurd details. How much money did Second Brother send to Mother? How much farmland did Mother have and what vegetables were harvested? Third Brother's wife's 10 feet, were they big or bound? The book has a musty smell that reaches into my throat.

One out of every four relations let me know they wanted to come to America. At the end of my visit, a distant relation and her 13-year-old daughter followed me into the rice paddies. "I'm selling her," the mother told me.

"What did you say? Say again?" I replied.

She held a palm over her (golden) lower teeth, and said it again, "Don't know what I'm saying? Sell. We sell her."

I stared at her. She laughed some more and then just walked away, back toward the village. The girl followed me, quiet till we got to the river, where she posed for some pictures and then asked for my address. I wrote it on the back of a business card. (I considered giving her my post office box.) I hope never to be surprised. I hope never to see this child at my door holding the card like a legal document.

"Don't add and don't take away" was the advice of an uncle who heard 15 that I wrote things. Stay safe. Keep us safe. How right that "China" is written with the character "middle." Obedience is a safe position. The Golden Venture men trusted the stories they heard. Their clansmen entrusted their dreams to them. The question is not how bad it is in China. The question is how good it can be in America. My father believes the Golden Venturers have only passed through the first hell. In coming to America, he laments (there is no other word) that he trusted too much. Ironic that in Chinese he bought a name that reads, To Have Trust.

DISCUSSING THE TEXT

1. Like many other Chinese immigrants, Ng's father entered the United States under false pretenses, as another man's "paper son." In purchasing his new identity for $4,000, what was the father giving up? Can you justify his actions? Would you ever consider doing something like that? Explain your answer.
2. What is the author's relation to money? Why do you think she describes it as having "a dirty feel" (par. 4)?
3. With a group of four or five other students, discuss the mood, or tone, of Ng's essay, especially the concluding paragraph. Would you characterize it as hopeful? Pessimistic? Something else? What does Ng seem to be saying about the possibilities, for Chinese immigrants, of shaping truly multicultural selves? Provide specific examples from the essay to illustrate your ideas.

WRITING ABOUT THE TEXT

4. Ng writes that for the Chinese, "Life was and still is weighed in gold" (par. 8). The term *gold* has a number of different meanings and associations in this essay, as well as within Ng's own history. Make a list of some of these

meanings and associations. Then write two paragraphs discussing their significance.

5. What does Fae Myenne Ng mean when she tells us "My father feels cheated, sold, on an easy story" (par. 9)? What do you think she means by "an easy story"? Is her father's bitterness justified? Do you think his expectations were false? Write a brief essay addressing these questions.
6. Ng provides several examples to support her view that "Life was and still is weighed in gold." Can you think of examples from contemporary life (and from other cultural or ethnic groups) that confirm this view of the importance of "gold" (or money)? Do you agree with her observation? After taking some notes on these questions, try writing at least two paragraphs that argue *against* Ng's assertion.
7. Ng describes the terms "Obedience and Obligation" as "the Confucian curse" (par. 1). Do some research into the Chinese philosopher Confucius and the basic principles of Confucianism. Then reread Ng's essay, looking for parts that seem to convey her attitudes toward this philosophy. What is your reaction to the attitudes she expresses? Write a two- to three-page essay recording your findings and your views.

RICHARD RODRIGUEZ

Asians

In this essay, from the book Days of Obligation: An Argument with My Mexican Father *(1992), Richard Rodriguez poses difficult questions about the nature of America. More specifically, he addresses the role of immigrants within the nation's structure, and the attempt, within American education, to transmit a sense of a common history to all students in the United States.*

Writing in a highly personal style, Rodriguez combines childhood memories, recollections of his relationship with his father, and reflections on education. He considers different aspects of the identity of Hispanic Americans, comparing them with Asians and with the European immigrant cultures of America, which he in turn contrasts with the Puritan Protestant heritage of the country's founding fathers.

Rodriguez discusses the concepts of individualism, freedom, and choice, which are often considered uniquely American, in terms of their many contradictions within a heterogeneous society. "Americans," Rodriguez claims, "have resorted to the idea of a shared culture only at times of international competition; at times of economic depression; during war; during periods of immigration."

Born into a Mexican family in San Francisco in 1944, Rodriguez studied at Columbia University, Stanford University, and the University of California, Berkeley. His first book, Hunger of Memory: The Education of Richard Rodriguez *(1982), stirred a powerful debate within the Latino intellectual community. In this book Rodriguez identified himself as middle class and assimilated, arguing against bilingualism and affirmative action, which he portrayed as forms of discrimination. In thus arguing the need for a common culture, Rodriguez seems to deny the possibility of sustaining an ethnic identity or a multicultural self.*

For the child of immigrant parents the knowledge comes like a slap: America exists.

America exists everywhere in the city—on billboards; frankly in the smell of burgers and French fries. America exists in the slouch of the crowd, the pacing of traffic lights, the assertions of neon, the cry of freedom overriding the nineteenth-century melodic line.

Grasp the implications of American democracy in a handshake or in a stranger's Jeffersonian "hi." America is irresistible. Nothing to do with choosing.

Our parents came to America for the choices America offers. What the child of immigrant parents knows is that here is inevitability.

A Chinese boy says his high-school teacher is always after him to stand up, speak up, look up. Yeah, but then his father puts him down at home: "Since when have you started looking your father in the eye?" 5

I'd like you to meet Jimmy Lamm. Mr. Lamm was an architect in Saigon. Now he is a cabbie in San Francisco. Stalled in traffic in San Francisco, Jimmy tells me about the refugee camp in Guam where, for nearly two years, he and his family were quartered before their flight to America. A teenager surfs by on a skateboard, his hair cresting in purple spikes like an iron crown, his freedom as apparent, as deplorable, as Huck Finn's.[1]

Damn kid. Honk. Honk.

The damn kid howls with pleasure. Flips us the bird.

Do you worry that your children will end up with purple hair?

Silence. 10

Then Jimmy says his children have too much respect for the struggle he and his wife endured. His children would never betray him so.

On the floor of Jimmy Lamm's apartment, next to the television, is a bowl of fruit and a burning wand of joss.[2]

He means: his children would never *choose* to betray him.

Immigrant parents re-create a homeland in the parlor, tacking up postcards or calendars of some impossible blue—lake or sea or sky.

The child of immigrant parents is supposed to perch on a hyphen, taking only the dose of America he needs to advance in America. 15

At the family picnic, the child wanders away from the spiced food and faceless stories to watch some boys playing baseball in the distance.

---

[1]*Huck Finn:* character in *The Adventures of Huckleberry Finn,* a novel by Samuel Clemens [Mark Twain] considered to be one of the greatest American books of the nineteenth century. Huck is a wily yet sensitive adolescent who lives on the margins of society and who befriends Nigger Jim. Although Jim has in fact been freed, Huck doesn't know it as they float down the Mississippi River on a raft, and he decides to be loyal to his friend rather than turn him in as a runaway slave. (*Ed.*)

[2]*joss:* incense stick (*Ed.*)

My Mexican father still regards America with skepticism from the high window of his morning paper. "Too much freedom," he says. Though he has spent most of his life in this country, my father yet doubts such a place as the United States of America exists. He cannot discern boundaries. How else to describe a country?

My father admires a flower bed on a busy pedestrian street in Zurich—he holds up the *National Geographic* to show me. "You couldn't have that in America," my father says.

When I was twelve years old, my father said he wished his children had Chinese friends—so polite, so serious are Chinese children in my father's estimation. The Spanish word he used was *formal.*

20 I didn't have any Chinese friends. My father did. Seventh and J Street was my father's Orient. My father made false teeth for several Chinese dentists downtown. When a Chinese family tried to move in a few blocks away from our house, I heard a friend's father boast that the neighbors had banded together to "keep out the Japs."

Many years pass.

In college, I was reading *The Merchant of Venice*[3]—Shylock urging his daughter to avoid the temptation of the frivolous Christians on the lido. Come away from the window, Shylock commands. I heard my father's voice:

> Hear you me, Jessica.
> Lock up my doors, and when you hear the drum
> And the vile squealing of the wry-necked fife,
> Clamber not you up to the casements then,
> Nor thrust your head into the public street
> To gaze on Christian fools with varnished faces,
> But stop my house's ears, I mean my casements.
> Let not the sound of shallow foppery enter
> My sober house.

I interview the mother on Evergreen Street for the *Los Angeles Times.* The mother says they came from Mexico ten years ago, and—look—already they have this nice house. Each year the kitchen takes on a new appliance.

Outside the door is Los Angeles; in the distance, the perpetual orbit of traffic. Here old women walk slowly under paper parasols, past the Vietnam vet who pushes his tinkling ice-cream cart past little green lawns, little green

---

[3]*Merchant of Venice* (1596): a "comedy" by William Shakespeare in which a Jewish merchant, Shylock, lends money to a Venetian merchant in temporary need, asking for a pound of flesh if the loan is not paid. In the end, Shylock is not paid his money, but neither is he allowed his pound of flesh; instead, the duke gives half his wealth to the rich merchant who borrowed from him and orders the other half to be given to his daughter Jessica, who has married a Christian and has previously been disinherited by Shylock. In the lines quoted here, Shylock warns his daughter Jessica to beware the Christians on "the lido," a fashionable sea resort near Venice. Shakespeare's depiction of the Jew, Shylock, has been much debated, with some considering it anti-Semitic. (*Ed.*)

lawns, little green lawns. (Here teenagers have black scorpions tattooed into their biceps.)

Children here are fed and grow tall. They love Christmas. They laugh at cartoons. They go off to school with children from Vietnam, from Burbank, from Hong Kong. They get into fights. They come home and they say dirty words. Aw, Ma, they say. Gimme a break, they say. 25

The mother says she does not want American children. It is the thing about Los Angeles she fears, the season of adolescence, of Huck Finn and Daisy Miller.[4]

Foolish mother. She should have thought of that before she came. She will live to see that America takes its meaning from adolescence. She will have American children.

The best metaphor of America remains the dreadful metaphor—the Melting Pot. Fall into the Melting Pot, ease into the Melting Pot, or jump into the Melting Pot—it makes no difference—you will find yourself a stranger to your parents, a stranger to your own memory of yourself.

A Chinese girl walks to the front of the classroom, unfolds several ruled pages, and begins to read her essay to a trio of judges (I am one of her judges).

The voice of the essay is the voice of an immigrant. Stammer and elision approximate naïveté (the judges squirm in their chairs). The narrator remembers her night-long journey to the United States aboard a Pan Am jet. The moon. Stars. Then a memory within a memory: in the darkened cabin of the plane, sitting next to her sleeping father, the little girl remembers bright China. 30

Many years pass.

The narrator's voice hardens into an American voice; her diction takes on rock and chrome. There is an ashtray on the table. The narrator is sitting at a sidewalk café in San Francisco. She is sixteen years old. She is with friends. The narrator notices a Chinese girl passing on the sidewalk. The narrator remembers bright China. The passing girl's face turns toward hers. The narrator recognizes herself in the passing girl—herself less assimilated. Their connective glance lasts only seconds. The narrator is embarrassed by her double—she remembers the cabin of the plane, her sleeping father, the moon, stars. The stranger disappears.

End of essay.

The room is silent as the Chinese student raises her eyes from the text.

One judge breaks the silence. Do you think your story is a sad story? 35

No, she replies. It is a true story.

What is the difference?

(Slowly, then.)

---

[4]*Daisy Miller:* main character in *Daisy Miller* (1878), one of Henry James's most popular novels. Daisy is a charming and innocent girl who comes to a tragic end in the sophisticated society of Europe. (*Ed.*)

When you hear a sad story you cry, she says. When you hear a true story you cry even more.

The U.S. Army took your darling boy, didn't they? With all his allergies and his moles and his favorite flavors. And when they gave him back, the crystals of his eyes had cracked. You weren't sure if this was the right baby. The only other institution as unsentimental and as subversive of American individuality has been the classroom. 40

In the nineteenth century, even as the American city was building, Samuel Clemens[5] romanced the nation with a celebration of the wildness of the American river, the eternal rejection of school and shoes. But in the red brick cities, and on streets without trees, the river became an idea, a learned idea, a shared idea, a civilizing idea, taking all to itself. Women, usually women, stood in front of rooms crowded with the children of immigrants, teaching those children a common language. For language is not just another classroom skill, as today's bilingualists would have it. Language is *the* lesson of grammar school. And from the schoolmarm's achievement came the possibility of a shared history and shared future. To my mind, this achievement of the nineteenth-century classroom was an honorable one, comparable to the opening of the plains, the building of bridges. Grammar-school teachers forged a nation.

A century later, my own teachers encouraged me to read *Huckleberry Finn.* I tried several times. My attempts were frustrated by the dialect voices. (*You don't know about me without you have read . . .*) There was, too, a confidence in Huck I shied away from and didn't like and wouldn't trust. The confidence was America.

Eventually, but this was many years after, I was able to read in Huck's dilemma—how he chafed so in autumn—a version of my own fear of the classroom: Huck as the archetypal bilingual child. And, later still, I discerned in Huck a version of the life of our nation.

This nation was formed from a fear of the crowd. Those early Puritans trusted only the solitary life. Puritans advised fences. Build a fence around all you hold dear and respect other fences. Protestantism taught Americans to believe that America does not exist—not as a culture, not as shared experience, not as a communal reality. Because of Protestantism, the American *ideology* of individualism is always at war with the experience of our lives, our *culture.* As long as we reject the notion of culture, we are able to invent the future.

Lacking any plural sense of ourselves, how shall we describe Americanization, except as loss? The son of Italian immigrant parents is no longer Italian. America is the country where one stops being Italian or Chinese or German. 45

---

[5]*Samuel Clemens* (1835–1910): wrote under the name Mark Twain and set several of his works on the Mississippi River, including *Life on the Mississippi* and *The Adventures of Huckleberry Finn* (*Ed.*)

And yet notice the testimony of thousands of bellhops in thousands of hotel lobbies around the world: Americans exist. There is a recognizable type—the accent, of course; the insecure tip; the ready smile; the impatience; the confidence of an atomic bomb informing every gesture.

When far from home, Americans easily recognize one another in a crowd. It is only when we return home, when we live and work next to one another, that Americans choose to believe anew in the fact of our separateness.

Americans have resorted to the idea of a shared culture only at times of international competition; at times of economic depression; during war; during periods of immigration. Nineteenth-century nativists feared Catholics and Jews would undermine the Protestant idea of America. As the nineteenth-century American city crowded with ragpickers, and crucifix-kissers, and garlic-eaters, yes, and as metaphors of wildness attached to the American city, nativists consoled themselves with a cropped version of America—the small white town, the general store, the Elks Hall, the Congregational church.

To this day, political journalists repair to the "heartland" to test the rhetoric of Washington or New York against true America.

50 But it was the antisociability of American Protestantism which paradoxically allowed for an immigrant nation. Lacking a communal sense, how could Americans resist the coming of strangers? America became a multiracial, multireligious society precisely because a small band of Puritans did not want the world.

The American city became the fame of America worldwide.

In time, the American city became the boast of America. In time, Americans would admit their country's meaning resided in the city. America represented freedom—the freedom to leave Europe behind, the freedom to re-create one's life, the freedom to re-create the world. In time, Americans came to recognize themselves in the immigrant—suitcase in hand, foreign-speaking, bewildered by the city. The figure of the immigrant became, like the American cowboy, a figure of loneliness, and we trusted that figure as descriptive of Protestant American experience. We are a nation of immigrants, we were able to say.

Now "Hispanics and Asians" have replaced "Catholics and Jews" in the imaginations of nativists. The nativist fear is that non-European immigrants will undo the European idea of America (forgetting that America was formed against the idea of Europe).

We are a nation of immigrants—most of us say it easily now. And we are working on a new cliché to accommodate new immigrants: the best thing about immigrants, the best that they bring to America, we say, is their "diversity." We mean they are not us—the Protestant creed.

55 In the late nineteenth century, when much of San Francisco was sand dunes, city fathers thought to plant a large park running out to the edge of the sea. Prescient city fathers. San Francisco would become crowded. Someday there would be the need for a park at the edge of the sea.

Having reached the end of the continent, Americans contemplated finitude. The Pacific Coast was ominous to the California imagination. The Pacific

Coast was an Asian horizon. The end of us was the beginning of them. Old duffers warned, "Someday there will be sampans[6] in the harbor."

With one breath people today speak of Hispanics and Asians—the new Americans. Between the two, Asians are the more admired—the model minority—more protestant than Protestants; so hardworking, self-driven; so bright. But the Asian remains more unsettling to American complacence, because the Asian is culturally more foreign.

Hispanics may be reluctant or pushy or light or dark, but Hispanics are recognizably European. They speak a European tongue. They worship or reject a European God. The shape of the meat they eat is identifiable. But the Asian?

Asians rounded the world for me. I was a Mexican teenager in America who had become an Irish Catholic. When I was growing up in the 1960s, I heard Americans describing their nation as simply bipartate: black and white. When black and white America argued, I felt I was overhearing some family quarrel that didn't include me. Korean and Chinese and Japanese faces in Sacramento rescued me from the simplicities of black and white America.

I was in high school when my uncle from India died, my Uncle Raj, the dentist. After Raj died, we went to a succession of Chinese dentists, the first Asian names I connected with recognizable faces; the first Asian hands. 60

In the 1960s, whole blocks of downtown Sacramento were to be demolished for a redevelopment. The *Sacramento Bee* reported several Chinese businessmen had declared their intention to build a ten-story office building downtown with a pagoda roof. About that same time, there was another article in the *Bee*. Mexican entrepreneurs would turn Sixth and K into a Mexican block with cobblestones, restaurants, colonial façades. My father was skeptical concerning the Mexican enterprise. "Guess which one will never get built?" my father intoned from the lamplight, snapping the spine of his newspaper.

Dr. Chiang, one of our family dentists, had gone to the University of the Pacific. He encouraged the same school for me. Our entire conversational motif, repeated at every visit, was college—his path and my plans.

Then there was Dr. Wang.

Not Dr. Wang! My sister refused. Dr. Wang didn't bother with Novocaine. Dr. Wang's office was a dark and shabby place.

My father said we owed it to Dr. Wang to be his patients. Dr. Wang referred business to my father. 65

Dr. Wang joked about my long nose. "Just like your father." And again: "Just like your father," as he pulled my nose up to open my mouth. Then China entered my mouth in a blast of garlic, a whorl of pain.

The Chinese businessmen built a ten-story office building downtown with a pagoda roof. Just as my father predicted they would.

Americans must resist the coming of fall, the starched shirt, the inimical expectation of the schoolmarm, because Americans want to remain

---

[6]*sampans:* small, flat-bottomed Chinese boats (*Ed.*)

individual. The classroom will teach us a language in common. The classroom will teach a history that implicates us with others. The classroom will tell us that we belong to a culture.

American educators, insofar as they are Americans, share with their students a certain ambivalence, even a resistance, to the public lessons of school. Witness the influence of progressivism on American education, a pedagogy that describes the primary purpose of education as fostering independence of thought, creativity, originality—notions that separate one student from another.

The hardest lesson for me, as for Huck Finn, as for the Chinese kid in the fifth paragraph of this chapter, was the lesson of public identity. What I needed from the classroom was a public life. The earliest necessity for any student is not individuality but something closer to the reverse. With Huck, I needed to learn the names of British kings and dissident Protestants, because they were the beginning of us. I read the writings of eighteenth-century white men who powdered their wigs and kept slaves, because these were the men who shaped the country that shaped my life. 70

Today Huck Finn would emerge as the simple winner in the contest of public education. Today Huck's schoolmarm would be cried down by her students as a tyrannical supremacist.

American educators have lost the confidence of their public institution. The failure represents, in part, an advance for America: the advance of the postwar black civil-rights movement. As America became racially integrated, Americans were less inclined to claim a common identity. It was easier to speak of an American "we" when everyone in the classroom was the same color. And then, as America became integrated, the black civil-rights movement encouraged a romantic secession from the idea of America—Americans competed with one another to claim victimization for themselves, some fence for themselves as minorities.

A second factor undermining the classroom's traditional function has been the large, non-European immigration of the last two decades. It was one thing to imagine a common culture when most immigrants came from Europe. A grammar-school teacher in California may now have students from fifty-four language groups in her class, as does one grammar-school teacher I know. How shall she teach such an assembly anything singular?

Or the college professor who lectures on Shakespeare. Most of his students are Asian. He was grading papers on *The Merchant of Venice* last term when he suddenly realized most of his Asian students had no idea what it meant that Shylock was a Jew.

Teachers and educational bureaucrats bleat in chorus: we are a nation of immigrants. The best that immigrants bring to America is diversity. American education should respect diversity, celebrate diversity. Thus the dilemma of our national diversity becomes (with a little choke on logic) the solution to itself. But diversity is a liquid noun. Diversity admits everything, stands for nothing. 75

There are influential educators today, and I have met them, who believe the purpose of American education is to instill in children a pride in their ancestral pasts. Such a curtailing of education seems to me condescending; seems to me the worst sort of missionary spirit. Did anyone attempt to protect the white middle-class student of yore from the ironies of history? Thomas Jefferson—that great democrat—was also a slaveowner. Need we protect black students from complexity? Thomas Jefferson, that slaveowner, was also a democrat. American history has become a pageant of exemplary slaves and black educators. Gay studies, women's studies, ethnic studies—the new curriculum ensures that education will be flattering. But I submit that America is not a tale for sentimentalists.

If I am a newcomer to your country, why teach me about my ancestors? I need to know about seventeenth-century Puritans in order to make sense of the rebellion I notice everywhere in the American city. Teach me about mad British kings so I will understand the American penchant for iconoclasm. Then teach me about cowboys and Indians; I should know that tragedies created the country that will create me.

Once you toss out Benjamin Franklin and Andrew Jackson, you toss out Navajos. You toss out immigrant women who worked the sweatshops of the Lower East Side. Once you toss out Thomas Jefferson, you toss out black history.

A high-school principal tells me there are few black students in his school, but—oh my!—in the last decade his school has changed its color, changed its accent; changed memory. Instead of Black History Week, his school now observes "Newcomers' Week." But does not everyone in America have a stake in black history? To be an American is to belong to black history.

80 To argue for a common culture is not to propose an exclusionary culture or a static culture. The classroom is always adding to the common text, because America is a dynamic society. Susan B. Anthony, Martin Luther King, Jr., are inducted into the textbook much as they are canonized by the U.S. Postal Service, not as figures of diversity, but as persons who implicate our entire society.

Sherlock Holmes?

I know a lot of teachers. Yet another teacher faces an eighth-grade class of Filipino immigrants. Boy-oh-boy, she would sure like to watch me try to teach her eighth-grade Filipino students to read Conan Doyle.[7]

For example, she says: Meerschaum—a kind of pipe. Well, a pipe—you know, you smoke? Pen knife. Bell pull. Harley Street. Hobnail boots. Dressing gown. Fex. Cockney. Turkish delight. Pall Mall. Wales . . . Well, they know what whales are, she says mordantly. It's too hard. It's too hard for Conan Doyle, that's for damn sure.

But for Shakespeare?

85 A high-school counselor tells me her school will soon be without a football team. Too few whites and blacks are enrolled; Hispanic and Asian kids would rather play soccer. As I listen to her, a thought occurs to me: she hates

---

[7]*Arthur Conan Doyle* (1859–1930): author of the popular series of stories, begun in the 1880s, based on the detective Sherlock Holmes (*Ed.*)

football. She looks for the demise of football. Perhaps what she wants most from Hispanic and Asian children is the same reassurance earlier generations of Americans sought from European immigrants, the reassurance—the hope—that an immigrant can undo America, can untie the cultural knot.

Now the American university is dismantling the American canon in my name. In the name of my father, in the name of Chinese grocers and fry cooks and dentists, the American university disregards the Judeo-Christian foundation of the American narrative. The white university never asked my father whether or not his son should read Milton, of course. Hispanics and Asians have become the convenient national excuse for the accomplishment of what America has always wanted done—the severing of memory, the dismantlement of national culture. The end of history.

Americans are lonely now. Hispanics and Asians represent to us the alternatives of communal cultures at a time when Americans are demoralized. Americans are no longer sure that economic invincibility derives from individualism. Look at Japan! Americans learn chopsticks. Americans lustily devour what they say they fear to become. Sushi will make us lean, corporate warriors. Mexican Combination Plate #3, smothered in mestizo gravy, will burn a hole through our hearts.

No belief is more cherished by Americans, no belief is more typical of America, than the belief that one can choose to be free of American culture. One can pick and choose. Learn Spanish. Study Buddhism. . . . My Mexican father was never so American as when he wished his children might cultivate Chinese friends.

Many years pass.

Eventually I made my way through *Huckleberry Finn.* I was, by that time, a graduate student of English, able to trail Huck and Jim through thickets of American diction and into a clearing. Sitting in a university library, I saw, once more, the American river. 90

There is a discernible culture, a river, a thread, connecting Thomas Jefferson to Lucille Ball to Malcolm X to Sitting Bull. The panhandler at one corner is related to the pamphleteer at the next, who is related to the bank executive who is related to the Punk wearing a FUCK U T-shirt. The immigrant child sees this at once. But then he is encouraged to forget the vision.

When I was a boy who spoke Spanish, I saw America whole. I realized that there was a culture here because I lived apart from it. I didn't like America. Then I entered the culture. I entered the culture as you did, by going to school. I became Americanized. I ended up believing in choices as much as any of you do.

What my best teachers realized was their obligation to pass on to their students a culture in which the schoolmarm is portrayed as a minor villain.

When I taught Freshman English at Berkeley, I took the "F" bus from San Francisco. This was about the time when American educators were proclaiming Asians to be "whiz kids" and Asian academic triumphs fed the feature pages of American newspapers. There were lots of Asians on the "F" bus.

One day, sitting next to a Chinese student on the bus, I watched him study. The way he worried over the text was troubling to me. He knew something about the hardness of life, the seriousness of youth, that America had never taught me. I turned away; I looked out the bus window; I got off the bus at my usual stop. But consider the two of us on the "F" bus headed for Berkeley: the Chinese student poring over his text against some terrible test. Me sitting next to him, my briefcase full of English novels; lucky me. The Asian and the Hispanic. We represented, so many Americans then imagined, some new force in America, a revolutionary change, an undoing of the European line. But it was not so. 95

Immigrant parents send their children to school (simply, they think) to acquire the skills to "survive" in America. But the child returns home as America. Foolish immigrant parents.

By eight o'clock that morning—the morning of the bus ride—I stood, as usual, in a classroom in Wheeler Hall, lecturing on tragedy and comedy. Asian kids at the back of the room studied biochemistry, as usual, behind propped-up Shakespeares. I said nothing, made no attempt to recall them. At the end of the hour, I announced to the class that, henceforward, class participation would be a consideration in grading. Asian eyes peered over the blue rims of their Oxford Shakespeares.

Three Asian students came to my office that afternoon. They were polite. They had come to ask about the final exam—what did they need to know?

They took notes. Then one student (I would have said the most Americanized of the three) spoke up: "We think, Mr. Rodriguez, that you are prejudiced against Asian students. Because we do not speak up in class."

I made a face. Nonsense, I blustered. Freshman English is a course concerned with language. Is it so unreasonable that I should expect students to speak up in class? One Asian student is the best student in class . . . and so forth. 100

I don't remember how our meeting concluded. I recall my deliberation when I gave those three grades. And I think now the students were just. I did have a bias, an inevitable American bias, that favored the talkative student. Like most other American teachers, I equated intelligence with liveliness or defiance.

Another Asian student, a woman, an ethnic Chinese student from Vietnam or Cambodia, ended up with an F in one of my classes. It wasn't that she had no American voice, or even that she didn't know what to make of Thoreau. She had missed too many classes. She didn't even show up for the Final.

On a foggy morning during winter break, this woman came to my office with her father to remonstrate.

I was too embarrassed to look at her. I spoke to her father. She sat by the door.

I explained the five essay assignments. I showed him my grade book, the blank spaces next to her name. The father and I both paused a long time over my evidence. I suggested the university's remedial writing course. . . . *Really, you know, her counselor should never have . . .* 105

In the middle of my apology, he stood up; he turned and walked to where his daughter sat. I could see only his back as he hovered over her. I heard the slap. He moved away.

And then I saw her. She was not crying. She was looking down at her hands composed neatly on her lap.

Jessica! 108

DISCUSSING THE TEXT

1. How does Rodriguez explain his Mexican father's sense of kinship and admiration for Chinese Americans? How have Rodriguez's childhood experiences with Asians framed some of his views about multiculturalism as an adult?
2. Language, according to Rodriguez, is "not just another classroom skill"; it is, he says, "*the* lesson of grammar school" (par. 41). Do you agree or disagree? Why?
3. Rodriguez claims that, despite its multicultural nature, "America exists" (par. 1) as a single entity, connected by "a discernible culture" (par. 91). He provides several examples throughout the essay as he builds up his argument. Get together with a group of four or five students, discuss Rodriguez's argument, and then provide reasons why you agree or disagree with it. Take notes as you work on this assignment, and be prepared to share your opinions with the class.

WRITING ABOUT THE TEXT

4. In this essay, Rodriguez makes a case for assimilation into a unified American culture through education. Summarize his argument by outlining his major points in two or three paragraphs. Conclude by offering your own point of view on this issue.
5. Make a list of some of the differences between Asians and Hispanics that Rodriguez points out. Do you find any stereotypes in his descriptions? Write a one-page essay addressing the issue of stereotypes in relation to this selection.
6. Toward the beginning of the essay, Rodriguez quotes a Shakespeare character in *The Merchant of Venice,* Shylock, as he admonishes his daughter Jessica to stay away from Christians (par. 22). Rodriguez ends the essay with a brief narrative about an Asian immigrant's confrontation with his daughter, a student in Rodriguez's class; he concludes this narrative, and the essay, with a single line: *Jessica!* (par. 108). What point is Rodriguez trying to make by reintroducing the character of Jessica? What kind of analogy, or comparison, is he attempting here? Do you think he is successful in making this analogy? Why or why not? Write a brief essay addressing these questions.
7. According to Rodriguez, "This nation was formed from a fear of the crowd" on the part of the early Puritan settlers (par. 44); "it was the antisociability of American Protestantism," he writes, "which paradoxically allowed for an immigrant nation" (par. 50). Write a two- to three-page essay in which you

present Rodriguez's interpretation of early American history, drawing on his ideas and examples, and then argue *against* Rodriguez's interpretation, presenting a different view of how early American history ties in with today's American "immigrant nation."

ANNA LISA RAYA

It's Hard Enough Being Me

In this selection, Anna Lisa Raya offers a personal view of the identity problems she faced as a multicultural American within the specific context of Columbia University in New York City. Born in the United States of a second-generation Mexican American father and a Puerto Rican mother, Raya grew up in a Mexican neighborhood of Los Angeles. Although she always felt the duality of her cultural background, Raya defined herself as either Mexican or Puerto Rican, depending on where she was at the time, and she saw herself as part of Los Angeles's multicultural majority.

In this essay, which appeared in the magazine Columbia College Today *in 1994, Raya looks at the issue of ethnic labeling, which she sees as having both positive and negative effects when it comes to the construction of an identity. She explains how she feels constrained not only by the term* Latina *but also by the expectations that often accompany it: that she speak Spanish and dance salsa, for example, or that she act politically in line with "minority" interests.*

Raya's frustrations, although focused on her attempts to define a multicultural self, are also universal, directed as they are at reconciling our views of ourselves with the images that are often imposed from the outside.

Anna Lisa Raya majored in English and is a member of the Columbia College class of 1995.

When I entered college, I *discovered* I was Latina. Until then, I had never questioned who I was or where I was from: My father is a second-generation Mexican-American, born and raised in Los Angeles, and my mother was born in Puerto Rico and raised in Compton, Calif. My home is El Sereno, a predominantly Mexican neighborhood in L.A. Every close friend I have back home is Mexican. So I was always just Mexican. Though sometimes I was just Puerto Rican—like when we would visit Mamo (my grandma) or hang out with my Aunt Titi.

Upon arriving in New York as a first-year student, 3000 miles from home, I not only experienced extreme culture shock, but for the first time I had to define myself according to the broad term "Latina." Although culture shock and identity crisis are common for the newly minted collegian who goes away to school, my experience as a newly minted Latina was, and still is, even more complicating. In El Sereno, I felt like I was part of a majority, whereas at the College I am a minority.

I've discovered that many Latinos like myself have undergone similar experiences. We face discrimination for being a minority in this country while also facing criticism for being "whitewashed" or "sellouts" in the countries of our heritage. But as an ethnic group in college, we are forced to define ourselves according to some vague, generalized Latino experience. This requires us to know our history, our language, our music, and our religion. I can't even be a content "Puerto Mexican" because I have to be a politically-and-socially-aware-Latina-with-a-chip-on-my-shoulder-because-of-how-repressed-I-am-in-this-country.

I am none of the above. I am the quintessential imperfect Latina. I can't dance salsa to save my life, I learned about Montezuma and the Aztecs in sixth grade, and I haven't prayed to the *Virgen de Guadalupe* in years.

Apparently I don't even look Latina. I can't count how many times people have just assumed that I'm white or asked me if I'm Asian. True, my friends back home call me *güera* ("whitey") because I have green eyes and pale skin, but that was as bad as it got. I never thought I would wish my skin were a darker shade or my hair a curlier texture, but since I've been in college, I have—many times. 5

Another thing: my Spanish is terrible. Every time I call home, I berate my mama for not teaching me Spanish when I was a child. In fact, not knowing how to speak the language of my home countries is the biggest problem that I have encountered, as have many Latinos. In Mexico there is a term, *pocha,* which is used by native Mexicans to ridicule Mexican-Americans. It expresses a deep-rooted antagonism and dislike for those of us who were raised on the other side of the border. Our failed attempts to speak pure, Mexican Spanish are largely responsible for the dislike. Other Latin American natives have this same attitude. No matter how well a Latino speaks Spanish, it can never be good enough.

Yet Latinos can't even speak Spanish in the U.S. without running the risk of being called "spic" or "wetback." That is precisely why my mother refused to teach me Spanish when I was a child. The fact that she spoke Spanish was constantly used against her: It prevented her from getting good jobs, and it would have placed me in bilingual education—a construct of the Los Angeles public school system that has proved to be more of a hindrance to intellectual development than a help.

To be fully Latina in college, however, I *must* know Spanish. I must satisfy the equation: Latina = Spanish-speaking.

So I'm stuck in this black hole of an identity crisis, and college isn't making my life any easier, as I thought it would. In high school, I was being prepared for an adulthood in which I would be an individual, in which I wouldn't have to wear a Catholic school uniform anymore. But though I led an anonymous adolescence, I knew who I was. I knew I was different from white, black, or Asian people. I knew there was a language other than English that I could call my own if I only knew how to speak it better. I knew there were historical reasons why I was in this country, distinct reasons that make my existence here easier or more difficult than other people's existence. Ultimately, I was content.

Now I feel pushed into a corner, always defining, defending, and proving myself to classmates, professors, or employers. Trying to understand who and why I am, while understanding Plato or Homer, is a lot to ask of myself. 10

A month ago, I heard three Nuyorican (Puerto Ricans born and raised in New York) writers discuss how New York City has influenced their writing. One problem I have faced as a young writer is finding a voice that is true to my community. I was surprised and reassured to discover that as Latinos, these writers had faced similar pressures and conflicts as myself; some weren't even taught Spanish in childhood. I will never forget the advice that one of them gave me that evening: She said that I need to be true to myself. "Because people will always complain about what you are doing—you're a 'gringa' or a 'spic' no matter what," she explained. "So you might as well do things for yourself and not for them."

I don't know why it has taken 20 years to hear this advice, but I'm going to give it a try. *Soy yo* and no one else. *Punto.*[1]

DISCUSSING THE TEXT

1. Even though Raya's father is a second-generation Mexican American from Los Angeles and she did not grow up in Mexico or speak Spanish as a child, she always thought of herself as "just Mexican." How do you explain such a classification? How accurate do you think it is? What does it say about how the Raya family defined itself ?
2. What is Raya's attitude toward bilingual education? How does her attitude compare with that of Richard Rodriguez in "Asians" (p. 207)? What is your response to these writers' views?
3. With a group of four or five students, discuss various ethnic labels that are attached to different groups in the United States. What sorts of images does the term *Latina* (or *Latino*), first encountered by Raya when she arrived in New York, bring to mind? How is this term different from the label *Latin American,* for example? Be prepared to present your ideas to the rest of the class.

WRITING ABOUT THE TEXT

4. Think of yourself as a college classmate of Anna Lisa Raya and write a brief description of her, drawing on what you have learned about her from this selection. Besides her physical characteristics, try to capture aspects of her personality as well.

[1]*Soy yo:* (Spanish) I am myself; *punto:* (Spanish) period, final (*Ed.*)

5. How do you define yourself ethnically? Have you ever been conflicted in terms of your cultural identity? Has there been a discrepancy between how you see yourself ethnically and how others see you? Can you compare yourself to Raya in any way? How do you respond, for example, to her statement that "Trying to understand who and why I am, while understanding Plato or Homer, is a lot to ask of myself" (par. 10). Write a brief essay that addresses these issues.
6. How are Raya's experiences similar to and different from those of the character of Hector in the excerpt from Oscar Hijuelos's *Our House in the Last World* (p. 192), or of Reginald McKnight in "Confessions of a Wannabe Negro" (p. 169)? Write a brief essay comparing Raya's multicultural-identity struggles with those presented in one or both of these earlier selections.

PAT MORA

Legal Alien

*Pat Mora (b. 1942) addresses in this poem the dilemma of the multicultural self by presenting herself as a hyphenated American, someone who is an "alien" both to Mexicans and to Americans. As someone who straddles two cultures, the speaker of the poem also speaks two different languages that define her in different ways: English is the language for business memos, while Spanish is the language for food. Although the poem includes a key phrase in Spanish (*Me'stan volviendo loca, *meaning "They're driving me crazy"), it is important to note that for this writer, English is also the language of poetry: her audience is, evidently, an English-speaking one.*

Pat Mora was born in Texas, into a Mexican American family. She has worked as an instructor and administrator at the University of Texas at El Paso since 1979. Mora has contributed to many literary anthologies and journals and has published several books of poetry, among them Chants *(1984) and* Borders *(1986). She has been the recipient of a Kellogg National Fellowship and a Chicano/Hispanic Faculty and Professional Staff Association award. "Legal Alien" appears in the book* Chants.

Bi-lingual, Bi-cultural,
able to slip from "How's life?"
to "*Me'stan volviendo loca,*"
able to sit in a paneled office
drafting memos in smooth English, 5
able to order in fluent Spanish
at a Mexican restaurant,
American but hyphenated,
viewed by Anglos as perhaps exotic,
perhaps inferior, definitely different, 10
viewed by Mexicans as alien,

(their eyes say, "You may speak
Spanish but you're not like me")
an American to Mexicans
a Mexican to Americans 15
a handy token
sliding back and forth
between the fringes of both worlds
by smiling
by masking the discomfort 20
of being pre-judged
Bi-laterally.

DISCUSSING THE TEXT

1. Mora has titled her poem "Legal Alien," implicitly making a reference to illegal aliens. What do you think is intended here? Does Mora see a difference between "legal" and "illegal" aliens? Do you? What is your position?
2. What does it mean to be "American but hyphenated"? Why does Mora begin and end her poem with terms beginning with the prefix *bi-* (*bi-lingual, bi-cultural, bi-laterally*)?
3. The speaker in the poem refers to herself as "sliding back and forth / between the fringes of both worlds." What does it mean to be on "the fringes" of a given world? Have you ever felt that you were existing on "the fringes"? Have you ever felt that you were "sliding back and forth" between worlds? Describe any such experiences you have had.

WRITING ABOUT THE TEXT

4. Write a brief story about a day in the life of the speaker in this poem. What does she look like? What does she do? How has her ethnicity affected her life? Try giving yourself the additional challenge of avoiding ethnic stereotypes in your narrative.
5. Write a dialogue between Pat Mora and W. E. B. Du Bois (see the selection from *The Souls of Black Folk*, p. 161), or between Pat Mora and Anna Lisa Raya (see "It's Hard Enough Being Me," on p. 219). Have the speakers address various problems encountered by the multicultural self in the United States—both those they have in common and those that are unique to each of them.
6. Drawing on an experience you recalled in response to question 3 above, write a poem recounting your own feelings of "sliding back and forth" between worlds. Use Mora's poem as a model for your own.

MAKING CONNECTIONS

1. How do you situate yourself within American society and within your community? Do you consider yourself to be a multicultural self in any way? Are ethnic elements essential to your identity? Religious elements? Regional elements? Think of the various identifying elements that contribute to the construction of your social identity, and write an essay about yourself, focusing on how these different elements come together or conflict with one another.
2. Study the photograph *Snuff Shop*, by Berenice Abbott, at the beginning of this chapter (p. 156). Write a brief description of the variety of signs that it depicts. How would you characterize these signs? What is your reaction to them? Would you choose to go into this particular shop? What would you expect to find?
3. Choose two selections from this chapter and discuss their authors' concepts of the multicultural self. Identify significant differences and similarities between the authors' concepts, and conclude by relating the accounts presented in these two readings to your own experience.
4. Some of the letters from *A Bintel Brief* depict generational conflicts within the immigrant family, conflicts that were often aggravated by the immigrants' arrival in America. A similar pattern is described in the selection from Oscar Hijuelos's *Our House in the Last World*. Write a brief essay that compares and contrasts the generational conflicts in these two selections. Can you relate these conflicts to your own experience in any way?
5. In "False Gold," Fae Myenne Ng describes her father's bitterness and sense of failure in the United States; in the poem "Legal Alien," Pat Mora presents a speaker who alludes to her own feelings of alienation and her difficulties in straddling two cultures. Do you see any similarities between the situations and ideas expressed in these two texts? How are Ng and the speaker in "Legal Alien" representative of the multicultural self ?
6. Compare and contrast the image of Asians in Richard Rodriguez's "Asians" and Kesaya Noda's "Growing Up Asian in America." How do you think Noda would respond to Rodriguez's images of Asians in his essay? How would you relate Noda's concept of multiculturalism to Rodriguez's?
7. How do immigrants today learn about American society? How, or where, do immigrants receive advice about manners, mores, common practices, or typical problems? How do such individuals come to terms with the experience of the multicultural self ? Speak to one or two recent immigrants, or first-generation Americans, and ask about this process. How would you compare the resources these people describe with those of the Jewish immigrants in the early twentieth century who read the Bintel Brief column?
8. In "Our Spiritual Strivings," W. E. B. Du Bois discusses the concept of identity from the point of view of the marginalized individual. His work reflects his efforts to change people's perceptions of African Americans at the beginning of the twentieth century, a time of great conflict and strife for African Americans. How is Du Bois "inventing America" through his perception of the multicultural self ? Are his ideas still relevant today?

9. Write an imaginary dialogue between Du Bois and Reginald McKnight in which they discuss the concept of a double-consciousness in the life of black Americans.
10. According to Kesaya Noda, "The family's need to protect [their] claim to identity and place outweighs any individual claim to any individual hope" (p. 198). Think back to Reginald McKnight's ideas about the importance of individual differences in "Confessions of a Wannabe Negro" (and perhaps to the essay you wrote in response to question 6 on p. 181). Write a one- to two-page essay comparing and contrasting these two contemporary American writers' attitudes toward the individual and the community, especially as factors shaping the multicultural self.
11. A classic American film dealing with racial identity is *Imitation of Life* (1957), which is available on videotape. After seeing the film, write an essay on the portrayal of African American identity in the film. What is the film trying to say about the position of blacks in American society at that time? Do you think that the problems depicted in the film still exist?
12. Watch a film or video on ethnic and/or racial identity. Prepare a written analysis of connections between the film or video and ideas about the multicultural self that you have encountered in this chapter. The films *Crossing Delancey* (1988), *The Joy Luck Club* (1993), *My Crazy Life* (1994), and *Losing Isaiah* (1994) are a few examples, but there are many other possibilities; check at your local or college library for other suggestions.

FURTHER READING

W. E. B. Du Bois

Hamilton, Virginia. *W. E. B. Du Bois: A Biography.* New York: T. Y. Crowell, 1972.

Paschal, Andrew, ed. *A W. E. B. Du Bois Reader.* New York: Macmillan, 1971.

Rampersad, Arnold. *The Art and Imagination of W. E. B. Du Bois.* Cambridge, Mass.: Harvard University Press, 1976.

Reginald McKnight

McKnight, Reginald. *Moustapha's Eclipse.* Pittsburgh: University of Pittsburgh Press, 1988.

West, Cornel. *Race Matters.* Boston: Beacon Press, 1993.

Williams, Gregory Howard. *Life on the Color Line: The True Story of a White Boy Who Discovered He Was Black.* New York: Dutton, 1995.

Isaac Metzker

Howe, Irving. *Worlds of Our Fathers.* New York: Harcourt, 1976.

Rosten, Leo. *The Joys of Yiddish.* New York: McGraw-Hill, 1968.

Oscar Hijuelos

Hijuelos, Oscar. *The Fourteen Sisters of Emilio Montez O'Brien.* New York: Farrar, Straus and Giroux, 1993.

———. *The Mambo Kings Play Songs of Love.* New York: Farrar, Straus and Giroux, 1989.

Kesaya E. Noda

Isaku, Patia R. *Mountain Storm, Pine Breeze: Folk Song in Japan.* Tucson: University of Arizona Press, 1981.

Kim, Elaine. *Asian American Literature: An Introduction to the Writings and Their Social Contexts.* Philadelphia: Temple University Press, 1982.

Fae Myenne Ng

Bruchac, Carol, and Sylvia Watanabe. *Home to Stay: Asian American Women's Fiction.* Greenfield Center, N.Y.: Greenfield Review Press, 1990.

Kingston, Maxine Hong. *The Woman Warrior.* New York: Vintage, 1977.

Ng, Fae Myenne. *Bone.* New York: HarperPerennial, 1993.

Richard Rodriguez

Rodriguez, Richard. *Days of Obligation: An Argument with My Mexican Father.* New York: Viking Press, 1992.

———. *Hunger of Memory: The Education of Richard Rodriguez.* Boston: Godine, 1982.

Sollors, Werner, ed. *The Invention of Ethnicity.* New York: Oxford University Press, 1989.

ANNA LISA RAYA

Cordova, Teresa, et al., eds. *Chicana Voices: Intersections of Class, Race and Gender.* Austin: Center for Mexican American Studies, 1986.

Mora, M., and A. R. del Castillo, eds. *Mexican Women in the United States: Struggles Past and Present.* Los Angeles: UCLA Chicano Studies Center, 1980.

PAT MORA

Fernandez, Roberta, ed. *In Other Words: Literature by Latinas of the United States.* Houston: Arte Publico, 1994.

Mora, Pat. *Borders.* Austin: Arte Publico, 1986.

———. *Nepantla.* Albuquerque: University of New Mexico Press, 1993.

The Steerage *(photograph by Alfred Stieglitz), 1907. One of the most influential photographers of the century, Alfred Stieglitz used the camera to give everyday moments the feeling of beauty and significance.* The Steerage *is perhaps his most famous image and is often taken as a symbol of immigrant America; in fact, Stieglitz took the photograph on a ship bound to Europe and those pictured here are returning to their homelands. Stieglitz was born in New Jersey into a relatively well-off German Jewish family and devoted his life to the advancement of modern art in America.* (The Metropolitan Museum of Art, Alfred Stieglitz Collection, 1949)

4

Border Crossings

My discontent grew upon me. I was ever on the look-out for means of escape.

- FREDERICK DOUGLASS
Narrative of the Life of Frederick Douglass, An American Slave

My old man come over and my mother and us four boys. Then we send for other people. That's how we all come.

- ANN BANKS
Immigrant Lives: Oral Histories Collected by the W.P.A. Federal Writers Project

I dozed, startled awake, panicked when I didn't know where I was, remembered where we were going, then dozed off again, to repeat the whole cycle, in and out of sleep, between earth and sky, somewhere between Puerto Rico and New York.

- ESMERALDA SANTIAGO
Angels on the Ceiling

What a feast of happenings each day of college was to those other students. . . . I watched the gay goings-on around me like one coming to a feast, but always standing back and only looking on.

- ANZIA YEZIERSKA
College

This was my world, I said to myself, and I shall be in it, and surrounded by it, if it is the last thing I do on God's green dirt-ball.

- ZORA NEALE HURSTON
School Again

As I tried to bridge the wide gap between my Sicilian and American lives, I became increasingly resentful of my relatives for being more foreign than anyone else.

- JERRE MANGIONE
Growing Up Sicilian

On Saturday at exactly two o'clock the man of Maya's dreams floats toward her as lovers used to in shampoo commercials. . . . He is serene, assured, a Hindu god touching down in Illinois.

- BHARATI MUKHERJEE
The Tenant

I need my Salvadoran fiancée here in Los Angeles, even as there is a force that urges me to be back in San Salvador. I need my cities, my families to be one.

- RUBÉN MARTÍNEZ
L.A. Journals

The readings in this chapter continue the exploration of multicultural identity begun in the previous chapter. Here, however, the selections focus on the various borders, both literal and symbolic, that must be crossed in shaping such an identity. The borders that literally encompass our lives—between one country and another, for example—are sometimes crossed easily, and sometimes with enormous difficulty, depending on government policies and immigration laws. Borders between neighborhoods, more easily crossed from a physical point of view, may be quite hard to cross in other ways; people born and raised in a particular ethnic or geographic neighborhood can spend their whole lives within that same sheltered environment. Other borders between social groups can be painfully difficult to cross, or else challenging and liberating: college represents one such border; entering the world of business or the professions can represent others.

The selection that begins this chapter, from Frederick Douglass's autobiography, speaks of literal, geographical borders—dividing South from North.

For Douglass, a former slave writing in the mid-nineteenth century, the act of crossing the line between South and North in the United States gave birth to a new identity. Through an illegal act of border crossing, Douglass's identity changed from that of a slave to that of a free man.

For the European immigrants speaking out in the chapter's second selection, "Immigrant Lives," crossing the border also meant a radical break with the past. For many people who arrived in the United States during the nineteenth or early twentieth century, the thought of going back to their country of origin was, at best, a dream. Economic hardship, family obligations, and long, expensive travel by ship were often insurmountable obstacles. Thus adaptation and assimilation in the new country became, for them, a more acute necessity.

The creation of a new life in a new country, with its required crossing of both real and symbolic borders, cannot be achieved without the pain of loss. The costs of crossing over can indeed be high: What must be given up to create the new self? Must one leave one's old identity entirely? Must one leave one's family? Must one abandon one's former language and culture? These questions, and the unavoidable conflicts that go along with them, are posed in the selection by Esmeralda Santiago, an excerpt from her autobiography *When I Was Puerto Rican.* This book, published simultaneously in English and in Spanish in 1993, records Santiago's experiences as a Puerto Rican—"a foreigner" who is also an American citizen at birth—and the complexities that accompany such a dual identity. Santiago crosses borders by moving back and forth between two cultures, an act that brings feelings of fear and excitement.

Bharati Mukherjee defines herself as a voluntary exile, someone who has "chosen and achieved the right to be an American, rather than just being American by an accident of birth." Born in India, she has lived in Canada and the United States since 1961, crossing borders literally and in her writing many times. In her story "The Tenant," Mukherjee portrays the character of Maya, an Indian scholar whose search for a viable identity leads her to cross geographical, psychological, and cultural borders.

For several writers in this chapter, one way of crossing borders has been through education. For Anzia Yezierska ("College"), Zora Neale Hurston ("School Again"), and Jerre Mangione ("Growing Up Sicilian"), schooling has meant a profound personal change and a way to achieve the American dream. But the act of leaving home and taking up a new identity in a new, educational environment places pressures on the individual that must be confronted. These writers also speak of the gulf between generations that almost inevitably occurs when younger people cross the border between the uneducated and the educated worlds. The pull of the old world—of family, language, traditions, beliefs, and religious practices—can continue to act as a strong force, even as the individual struggles to cross into a new identity.

The chapter ends with a selection from Rubén Martínez's book *The Other Side: Fault Lines, Guerrilla Saints, and the True Heart of Rock and Roll,* in which the borders between various cultures in the United States are presented as fluid, or unstable. For Martínez, this fluidity is the source of an unavoidable dilemma. Born in Los Angeles of a Mexican father and a Salvadoran mother, Martínez does not want to give up what is valuable in *any* of his multicultural lives. He seeks to solve this dilemma by treasuring the different cultures that have created him, even as he searches for a new identity that can include all of them. For Martínez, as for many other Americans, crossing and recrossing the borders between these different cultures becomes a challenging way of life, an ongoing process that is part of the invention of an American identity.

The photograph at the opening of this chapter, Alfred Stieglitz's *The Steerage* (1907), is a well-known image. For many years it was thought to be a poignant representation of the immigrant's arduous journey to the new land, captured during a moment of idleness on board, when thoughts might be free to roam. Many people have also seen the upper and lower decks of the ship in this photograph as symbolic of class divisions within American society. But in fact, Stieglitz was crossing from America to France when he took this picture; these were immigrants who were *returning to their homelands,* as many did during the peak years of immigration for many different reasons. Stieglitz took the photograph from his own more privileged position as a first-class passenger, although paradoxically, when he looked at these returning immigrants, he longed for the freedom and ease that he felt they embodied. *The Steerage* serves as a reminder that, for many, the forging of the multicultural self in America was simply impossible. For these people, the return to the homeland was the only possible response to the extremely difficult challenge of forming a new life, and a new identity, in America. Sometimes, the borders can be too hard to cross.

FREDERICK DOUGLASS

FROM

Narrative of the Life of Frederick Douglass, An American Slave

Frederick Douglass (1817–1895) was one of the most ardent and effective antislavery advocates of the nineteenth century. The son of an unknown white father and a woman who was a slave, Douglass was born into slavery and managed to escape to freedom in his early twenties. After escaping from Maryland to the North, he made his way to New Bedford, Massachusetts, where he began earning his living through a variety of odd jobs. He also began speaking in public, addressing a meeting of the Massachusetts Anti-Slavery Society in 1841. So impressive were his oratorical gifts that he was soon asked to speak to other meetings, and he was employed as an agent of the Anti-Slavery Society. Because people could not believe that someone of his intellect and eloquence had been a slave, Douglass wrote his life story in 1845 as a way of authenticating his identity as a former slave.

In addition to his autobiographical writings, in 1847 Douglass founded an antislavery newspaper called the North Star *in Rochester, New York. One of the most celebrated orators of his age, Douglass advocated women's suffrage, as well as industrial education for African Americans and the use of African American troops during the Civil War.*

In this excerpt, Chapter 11 from his autobiography, Douglass narrates the story of his escape from slavery—a time when he crossed the border from slavery to freedom. But he restrains himself at the outset from telling all *the details, for reasons that he explains in the opening paragraph. Even with some of the details missing, however, Douglass's story has become one of the most important documents of nineteenth-century American culture. It is an exemplary narrative that deepens the meaning of the term* liberty.

CHAPTER XI

I now come to that part of my life during which I planned, and finally succeeded in making, my escape from slavery. But before narrating any of the peculiar circumstances, I deem it proper to make known my intention not to state all the facts connected with the transaction. My reasons for pursuing this course may be understood from the following: First, were I to give a minute statement of all the facts, it is not only possible, but quite probable, that others would thereby be involved in the most embarrassing difficulties. Secondly, such a statement would most undoubtedly induce greater vigilance on the part of slaveholders than has existed heretofore among them; which would, of course be the means of guarding a door whereby some dear brother bondman might escape his galling chains. I deeply regret the necessity that impels me to suppress any thing of importance connected with my experience in slavery. It would afford me great pleasure indeed, as well as materially add to the interest of my narrative, were I at liberty to gratify a curiosity, which I know exists in the minds of many, by an accurate statement of all the facts pertaining to my most fortunate escape. But I must deprive myself of this pleasure, and the curious of the gratification which such a statement would afford. I would allow myself to suffer under the greatest imputations which evil-minded men might suggest, rather than exculpate myself, and thereby run the hazard of closing the slightest avenue by which a brother slave might clear himself of the chains and fetters of slavery.

I have never approved of the very public manner in which some of our western friends have conducted what they call the *underground railroad,* but which, I think, by their open declarations, has been made most emphatically the *upperground railroad.* I honor those good men and women for their noble daring, and applaud them for willingly subjecting themselves to bloody persecution, by openly avowing their participation in the escape of slaves. I, however, can see very little good resulting from such a course, either to themselves or the slaves escaping; while, upon the other hand, I see and feel assured that those open declarations are a positive evil to the slaves remaining, who are seeking to escape. They do nothing towards enlightening the slave, whilst they do much towards enlightening the master. They stimulate him to greater watchfulness, and enhance his power to capture his slave. We owe something to the slaves south of the line as well as to those north of it; and in aiding the latter on their way to freedom, we should be careful to do nothing which would be likely to hinder the former from escaping from slavery. I would keep the merciless slaveholder profoundly ignorant of the means of flight adopted by the slave. I would leave him to imagine himself surrounded by myriads of invisible tormentors, ever ready to snatch from his infernal grasp his trembling prey. Let him be left to feel his way in the dark; let darkness commensurate with his crime hover over him; and let him feel that at every step he takes, in pursuit of the flying bondman, he is running the frightful risk of having his hot brains dashed out by an invisible agency. Let us render the tyrant no aid; let us not hold the light by which he can trace the footprints of our flying brother. But enough of this. I will now proceed to the statement of those facts, connected with my escape, for which I am alone responsible, and for which no one can be made to suffer but myself.

In the early part of the year 1838, I became quite restless. I could see no reason why I should, at the end of each week, pour the reward of my toil into the purse of my master. When I carried to him my weekly wages, he would, after counting the money, look me in the face with a robber-like fierceness, and ask, "Is this all?" He was satisfied with nothing less than the last cent. He would, however, when I made him six dollars, sometimes give me six cents, to encourage me. It had the opposite effect. I regarded it as a sort of admission of my right to the whole. The fact that he gave me any part of my wages was proof, to my mind, that he believed me entitled to the whole of them. I always felt worse for having received any thing; for I feared that the giving me a few cents would ease his conscience, and make him feel himself to be a pretty honorable sort of robber. My discontent grew upon me. I was ever on the look-out for means of escape; and, finding no direct means, I determined to try to hire my time, with a view of getting money with which to make my escape. In the spring of 1838, when Master Thomas came to Baltimore to purchase his spring goods, I got an opportunity, and applied to him to allow me to hire my time. He unhesitatingly refused my request, and told me this was another stratagem by which to escape. He told me I could go nowhere but that he could get me; and that, in the event of my running away, he should spare no pains in his efforts to catch me. He exhorted me to content myself, and be obedient. He told me, if I would be happy, I must lay out no plans for the future. He said, if I behaved myself properly, he would take care of me. Indeed, he advised me to complete thoughtlessness of the future, and taught me to depend solely upon him for happiness. He seemed to see fully the pressing necessity of setting aside my intellectual nature, in order to contentment in slavery. But in spite of him, and even in spite of myself, I continued to think, and to think about the injustice of my enslavement, and the means of escape.

About two months after this, I applied to Master Hugh for the privilege of hiring my time. He was not acquainted with the fact that I had applied to Master Thomas, and had been refused. He too, at first, seemed disposed to refuse; but, after some reflection, he granted me the privilege, and proposed the following term: I was to be allowed all my time, make all contracts with those for whom I worked, and find my own employment; and, in return for this liberty, I was to pay him three dollars at the end of each week; find myself in calking[1] tools, and in board and clothing. My board was two dollars and a half per week. This, with the wear and tear of clothing and calking tools, made my regular expenses about six dollars per week. This amount I was compelled to make up, or relinquish the privilege of hiring my time. Rain or shine, work or no work, at the end of each week the money must be forthcoming, or I must give up my privilege. This arrangement, it will be perceived, was decidedly in my master's favor. It relieved him of all need of looking after me. His money was sure. He received all the benefits of slaveholding without its evils; while I endured all the evils of a slave, and suffered all the care and anxiety of a freeman. I found it a hard bargain. But, hard as it was, I thought it better than the old mode of getting along. It was a step towards freedom to be allowed to bear the responsibilities of a freeman, and I was determined to hold on upon it. I bent myself to the work of making money. I was ready to work at night as well as day, and by the most untiring perseverance and industry, I made enough to meet my expenses, and lay up a little money every week. I went on thus from May till August. Master Hugh then refused to allow me to hire my time longer. The ground for his refusal was a failure on my part, one Saturday night, to pay him for my week's time. This failure was occasioned by my attending a camp meeting[2] about ten miles from Baltimore. During the week,

---

[1]*calking:* or caulking, a substance driven into seams to seal a boat or pipe tight against leaks (*Ed.*)

[2]*camp meeting:* gathering, often in large tents, for a religious meeting (*Ed.*)

I had entered into an engagement with a number of young friends to start from Baltimore to the camp ground early Saturday evening; and being detained by my employer, I was unable to get down to Master Hugh's without disappointing the company. I knew that Master Hugh was in no special need of the money that night. I therefore decided to go to camp meeting, and upon my return pay him the three dollars. I staid at the camp meeting one day longer than I intended when I left. But as soon as I returned, I called upon him to pay him what he considered his due. I found him very angry; he could scarce restrain his wrath. He said he had a great mind to give me a severe whipping. He wished to know how I dared go out of the city without asking his permission. I told him I hired my time, and while I paid him the price which he asked for it, I did not know that I was bound to ask him when and where I should go. This reply troubled him; and, after reflecting a few moments, he turned to me, and said I should hire my time no longer; that the next thing he should know of, I would be running away. Upon the same plea, he told me to bring my tools and clothing home forthwith. I did so; but instead of seeking work, as I had been accustomed to do previously to hiring my time, I spent the whole week without the performance of a single stroke of work. I did this in retaliation. Saturday night, he called upon me as usual for my week's wages. I told him I had no wages; I had done no work that week. Here we were upon the point of coming to blows. He raved, and swore his determination to get hold of me. I did not allow myself a single word; but was resolved, if he laid the weight of his hand upon me, it should be blow for blow. He did not strike me, but told me that he would find me in constant employment in future. I thought the matter over during the next day, Sunday, and finally resolved upon the third day of September, as the day upon which I would make a second attempt to secure my freedom. I now had three weeks during which to prepare for my journey. Early on Monday morning, before Master Hugh had time to make any engagement for me, I went out and got employment of Mr. Butler, at his ship-yard near the drawbridge, upon what is called the City Block, thus making it unnecessary for him to seek employment for me. At the end of the week, I brought him between eight and nine dollars. He seemed very well pleased, and asked me why I did not do the same the week before. He little knew what my plans were. My object in working steadily was to remove any suspicion he might entertain of my intent to run away; and in this I succeeded admirably. I suppose he thought I was never better satisfied with my condition than at the very time during which I was planning my escape. The second week passed, and again I carried him my full wages; and so well pleased was he, that he gave me twenty-five cents, (quite a large sum for a slaveholder to give a slave,) and bade me to make a good use of it. I told him I would.

Things went on without very smoothly indeed, but within there was trouble. It is impossible for me to describe my feelings as the time of my contemplated start drew near. I had a number of warm-hearted friends in Baltimore,—friends that I loved almost as I did my life,—and the thought of being separated from them forever was painful beyond expression. It is my opinion that thousands would escape slavery, who now remain, but for the strong cords of affection that bind them to their friends. The thought of leaving my friends was decidedly the most painful thought with which I had to contend. The love of them was my tender point, and shook my decision more than all things else. Besides the pain of separation, the dread and apprehension of a failure exceeded what I had experienced at my first attempt.[3] The appalling defeat I then sustained returned to torment me. I felt assured that, if I failed in this attempt, my case would be a hopeless one—it would seal my fate as a slave forever. I could not hope to get off with any thing less than the severest punishment, and being placed beyond the means of escape. It required no very vivid imagination to depict the most frightful scenes through which I should have to pass, in case I failed. The wretchedness of slavery, and the blessedness of freedom, were perpetually before me. It was life and death with me. But I remained firm, and, according to my resolution, on the third day of September, 1838, I left my chains, and succeeded in reaching New York without the slightest interruption of any kind. How I did so,—what means I adopted,—what direction I travelled, and by what mode of conveyance,—I must leave unexplained, for the reasons before mentioned.

I have been frequently asked how I felt when I found myself in a free State. I have never been able to answer the question with any satisfaction to myself. It was a moment of the highest excitement I ever experienced. I suppose I felt as one may imagine the unarmed mariner to feel when he is rescued by a friendly man-of-war from the pursuit of a pirate. In writing to a dear friend, immediately after my arrival at New York, I said I felt like one who had escaped a den of hungry lions. This state of mind, however, very soon subsided; and I was again seized with a feeling of great insecurity and loneliness. I was yet liable to be taken back, and subjected to all the tortures of slavery. This in itself was enough to damp the ardor of my enthusiasm. But the loneliness overcame me. There I was in the midst of thousands, and yet a perfect stranger; without home and without friends, in the midst of thousands of my own brethren—children of a common Father, and yet I dared not to unfold to any one of them my sad condition. I was afraid to speak to any one for fear of speaking to the wrong one, and thereby falling into the hands of money-loving kidnappers, whose business it was to lie in wait for the panting fugitive, as the ferocious beasts of the forest lie in wait for their prey. The motto which I adopted when I started from slavery was this—"Trust no man!" I saw in every white man an enemy, and in almost every colored man cause for distrust. It was a most painful situation; and, to understand it, one must needs experience it, or imagine himself in similar circumstances. Let him be a fugitive slave in a strange land—a land

---

[3]*my first attempt:* a few years earlier, in 1835, Douglass had planned an escape with two fellow slaves, but their plans were discovered before the attempt could be made. (*Ed.*)

given up to be the hunting-ground for slaveholders—whose inhabitants are legalized kidnappers—where he is every moment subjected to the terrible liability of being seized upon by his fellowmen, as the hideous crocodile seizes upon his prey!—I say, let him place himself in my situation—without home or friends—without money or credit—wanting shelter, and no one to give it—wanting bread, and no money to buy it,—and at the same time let him feel that he is pursued by merciless men-hunters, and in total darkness as to what to do, where to go, or where to stay,—perfectly helpless both as to the means of defence and means of escape,—in the midst of plenty, yet suffering the terrible gnawings of hunger,—in the midst of houses, yet having no home,—among fellow-men, yet feeling as if in the midst of wild beasts, whose greediness to swallow up the trembling and half-famished fugitive is only equalled by that with which the monsters of the deep swallow up the helpless fish upon which they subsist,—I say, let him be placed in this most trying situation,—the situation in which I was placed,—then, and not till then, will he fully appreciate the hardships of, and know how to sympathize with, the toil-worn and whip-scarred fugitive slave.

Thank Heaven, I remained but a short time in this distressed situation. I was relieved from it by the humane hand of Mr. David Ruggles, whose vigilance, kindness, and perseverance, I shall never forget. I am glad of an opportunity to express, as far as words can, the love and gratitude I bear him. Mr. Ruggles is now afflicted with blindness, and is himself in need of the same kind offices which he was once so forward in the performance of toward others. I had been in New York but a few days, when Mr. Ruggles sought me out, and very kindly took me to his boarding-house at the corner of Church and Lespenard Streets. Mr. Ruggles was then very deeply engaged in the memorable *Darg* case, as well as attending to a number of other fugitive slaves, devising ways and means for their successful escape; and, though watched and hemmed in on almost every side, he seemed to be more than a match for his enemies.

Very soon after I went to Mr. Ruggles, he wished to know of me where I wanted to go; as he deemed it unsafe for me to remain in New York. I told him I was a calker, and should like to go where I could get work. I thought of going to Canada; but he decided against it, and in favor of my going to New Bedford, thinking I should be able to get work there at my trade. At this time, Anna,[4] my intended wife, came on; for I wrote to her immediately after my arrival at New York, (notwithstanding my homeless, houseless, and helpless condition,) informing her of my successful flight, and wishing her to come on forthwith. In a few days after her arrival, Mr. Ruggles called in the Rev. J. W. C. Pennington, who, in the presence of Mr. Ruggles, Mrs. Michaels, and two or three others, performed the marriage ceremony, and gave us a certificate, of which the following is an exact copy:—

---

[4]She was free.

"This may certify, that I joined together in holy matrimony Frederick Johnson[5] and Anna Murray, as man and wife, in the presence of Mr. David Ruggles and Mrs. Michaels.

"JAMES W. C. PENNINGTON.

"New York, Sept. 15, 1838."

Upon receiving this certificate, and a five-dollar bill from Mr. Ruggles, I shouldered one part of our baggage, and Anna took up the other, and we set out forthwith to take passage on board of the steamboat John W. Richmond for Newport, on our way to New Bedford. Mr. Ruggles gave me a letter to a Mr. Shaw in Newport, and told me, in case my money did not serve me to New Bedford, to stop in Newport and obtain further assistance; but upon our arrival in Newport, we were so anxious to get to a place of safety, that, notwithstanding we lacked the necessary money to pay our fare, we decided to take seats in the stage, and promise to pay when we got to New Bedford. We were encouraged to do this by two excellent gentlemen, residents of New Bedford, whose names I afterward ascertained to be Joseph Ricketson and William C. Taber. They seemed at once to understand our circumstances, and gave us such assurance of their friendliness as put us fully at ease in their presence. It was good indeed to meet with such friends, at such a time. Upon reaching New Bedford, we were directed to the house of Mr. Nathan Johnson, by whom we were kindly received, and hospitably provided for. Both Mr. and Mrs. Johnson took a deep and lively interest in our welfare. They proved themselves quite worthy of the name of abolitionists. When the stage-driver found us unable to pay our fare, he held on upon our baggage as security for the debt. I had but to mention the fact to Mr. Johnson, and he forthwith advanced the money.

We now began to feel a degree of safety, and to prepare ourselves for the duties and responsibilities of a life of freedom. On the morning after our arrival at New Bedford, while at the breakfast-table, the question arose as to what name I should be called by. The name given me by my mother was, "Frederick Augustus Washington Bailey." I, however, had dispensed with the two middle names long before I left Maryland so that I was generally known by the name of "Frederick Bailey." I started from Baltimore bearing the name of "Stanley." When I got to New York, I again changed my name to "Frederick Johnson," and thought that would be the last change. But when I got to New Bedford, I found it necessary again to change my name. The reason of this necessity was, that there were so many Johnsons in New Bedford, it was already quite difficult to distinguish between them. I gave Mr. Johnson the privilege of choosing me a name, but told him he must not take from me the name of "Frederick." I must hold on to that, to preserve a sense of my identity.

[5] I had changed my name from Frederick *Bailey* to that of *Johnson.*

Mr. Johnson had just been reading the "Lady of the Lake,"[6] and at once suggested that my name be "Douglass." From that time until now I have been called "Frederick Douglass;" and as I am more widely known by that name than by either of the others, I shall continue to use it as my own.

I was quite disappointed at the general appearance of things in New Bedford. The impression which I had received respecting the character and condition of the people of the north, I found to be singularly erroneous. I had very strangely supposed, while in slavery, that few of the comforts, and scarcely any of the luxuries, of life were enjoyed at the north, compared with what were enjoyed by the slaveholders of the south. I probably came to this conclusion from the fact that northern people owned no slaves. I supposed that they were about upon a level with the non-slaveholding population of the south. I knew *they* were exceedingly poor, and I had been accustomed to regard their poverty as the necessary consequence of their being non-slaveholders. I had somehow imbibed the opinion that, in the absence of slaves, there could be no wealth, and very little refinement. And upon coming to the north, I expected to meet with a rough, hard-handed, and uncultivated population, living in the most Spartan-like simplicity, knowing nothing of the ease, luxury, pomp, and grandeur of southern slaveholders. Such being my conjectures, any one acquainted with the appearance of New Bedford may very readily infer how palpably I must have seen my mistake.

In the afternoon of the day when I reached New Bedford, I visited the wharves, to take a view of the shipping. Here I found myself surrounded with the strongest proofs of wealth. Lying at the wharves, and riding in the stream, I saw many ships of the finest model, in the best order, and of the largest size. Upon the right and left, I was walled in by granite warehouses of the widest dimensions, stowed to their utmost capacity with the necessaries and comforts of life. Added to this, almost every body seemed to be at work, but noiselessly so, compared with what I had been accustomed to in Baltimore. There were no loud songs heard from those engaged in loading and unloading ships. I heard no deep oaths or horrid curses on the laborer. I saw no whipping of men; but all seemed to go smoothly on. Every man appeared to understand his work, and went at it with a sober, yet cheerful earnestness, which betokened the deep interest which he felt in what he was doing, as well as a sense of his own dignity as a man. To me this looked exceedingly strange. From the wharves I strolled around and over the town, gazing with wonder and admiration at the splendid churches, beautiful dwellings, and finely-cultivated gardens; evincing an amount of wealth, comfort, taste, and refinement, such as I had never seen in any part of slaveholding Maryland.

Every thing looked clean, new and beautiful. I saw few or no dilapidated houses, with poverty-stricken inmates; no half-naked children and barefooted women, such as I had been accustomed to see in Hillsborough, Easton, St. Michael's, and Baltimore. The people looked more able, stronger, healthier, and happier, than those of Maryland. I was for once made glad by a view of

---

[6]*Lady of the Lake:* a poem by Sir Walter Scott, published in 1810, in which one of the principal characters is named Lord James of Douglas (*Ed.*)

extreme wealth, without being saddened by seeing extreme poverty. But the most astonishing as well as the most interesting thing to me was the condition of the colored people, a great many of whom, like myself, had escaped thither as a refuge from the hunters of men. I found many, who had not been seven years out of their chains, living in finer houses, and evidently enjoying more of the comforts of life, than the average of slaveholders in Maryland. I will venture to assert that my friend Mr. Nathan Johnson (of whom I can say with a grateful heart, "I was hungry, and he gave me meat; I was thirsty, and he gave me drink; I was a stranger, and he took me in") lived in a neater house; dined at a better table; took, paid for, and read, more newspapers; better understood the moral, religious, and political character of the nation,—than nine tenths of the slave-holders in Talbot county, Maryland. Yet Mr. Johnson was a working man. His hands were hardened by toil, and not his alone, but those also of Mrs. Johnson. I found the colored people much more spirited than I had supposed they would be. I found among them a determination to protect each other from the blood-thirsty kidnapper, at all hazards. Soon after my arrival, I was told of a circumstance which illustrated their spirit. A colored man and a fugitive slave were on unfriendly terms. The former was heard to threaten the latter with informing his master of his whereabouts. Straightway a meeting was called among the colored people, under the stereotyped notice, "Business of importance!" The betrayer was invited to attend. The people came at the appointed hour, and organized the meeting by appointing a very religious old gentleman as president, who, I believe, made a prayer, after which he addressed the meeting as follows: *"Friends, we have got him here, and I would recommend that you young men just take him outside the door, and kill him!"* With this, a number of them bolted at him; but they were intercepted by some more timid than themselves, and the betrayer escaped their vengeance, and has not been seen in New Bedford since. I believe there have been no more such threats, and should there be hereafter, I doubt not that death would be the consequence.

I found employment, the third day after my arrival, in stowing a sloop with a load of oil. It was new, dirty, and hard work for me; but I went at it with a glad heart and a willing hand. I was now my own master. It was a happy moment, the rapture of which can be understood only by those who have been slaves. It was the first work, the reward of which was to be entirely my own. There was no Master Hugh standing ready, the moment I earned the money, to rob me of it. I worked that day with a pleasure I had never before experienced. I was at work for myself and newly-married wife. It was to me the starting-point of a new existence. When I got through with that job, I went in pursuit of a job of calking; but such was the strength of prejudice against color, among the white calkers, that they refused to work with me, and of course I could get no employment.[7] Finding my trade of no immediate benefit, I threw off my calking habiliments, and prepared myself to do any kind of

---

[7] I am told that colored persons can now get employment at calking in New Bedford—a result of anti-slavery effort.

work I could get to do. Mr. Johnson kindly let me have his wood-horse and saw, and I very soon found myself a plenty of work. There was no work too hard—none too dirty. I was ready to saw wood, shovel coal, carry the hod,[8] sweep the chimney, or roll oil casks,—all of which I did for nearly three years in New Bedford, before I became known to the antislavery world.

In about four months after I went to New Bedford, there came a young man to me, and inquired if I did not wish to take the "Liberator." I told him I did; but, just having made my escape from slavery, I remarked that I was unable to pay for it then. I, however, finally became a subscriber to it. The paper came, and I read it from week to week with such feelings as it would be quite idle for me to attempt to describe. The paper became my meat and my drink. My soul was set all on fire. Its sympathy for my brethren in bonds—its scathing denunciations of slaveholders—its faithful exposures of slavery—and its powerful attacks upon the upholders of the institution—sent a thrill of joy through my soul, such as I had never felt before!

17 I had not long been a reader of the "Liberator," before I got a pretty correct idea of the principles, measures and spirit of the anti-slavery reform. I took right hold of the cause. I could do but little; but what I could, I did with a joyful heart, and never felt happier than when in an anti-slavery meeting. I seldom had much to say at the meetings, because what I wanted to say was said so much better by others. But, while attending an anti-slavery convention at Nantucket, on the 11th of August, 1841, I felt strongly moved to speak, and was at the same time much urged to do so by Mr. William C. Coffin, a gentleman who had heard me speak in the colored people's meeting at New Bedford. It was a severe cross, and I took it up reluctantly. The truth was, I felt myself a slave, and the idea of speaking to white people weighed me down. I spoke but a few moments, when I felt a degree of freedom, and said what I desired with considerable ease. From that time until now, I have been engaged in pleading the cause of my brethren—with what success, and with what devotion, I leave those acquainted with my labors to decide.

DISCUSSING THE TEXT

1. Douglass states at the outset why he cannot tell the full story of his escape. How does his announcement of this omission affect your reading of this selection? What does it tell you about his potential audience?
2. It was not an uncommon practice for slaves to hire themselves out for wages, as Douglass did. What do you think was the slaveholder's thinking in granting slaves this freedom? How does Douglass feel about this arrangement?
3. What kinds of things, according to Douglass, kept many people from attempting to escape from slavery?
4. Douglass is surprised by the signs of wealth in New Bedford, including the wealth of free blacks. What are some of the signs of wealth that Douglass

[8] *hod:* a tray with a handle, used to carry mortar on the shoulder (*Ed.*)

describes? How does what he sees alter his thinking about the economics of slavery and the economics of a free society?

WRITING ABOUT THE TEXT

5. At several points in the narrative, Douglass considers the possibility of violence: when he imagines a frightened slaveholder (par. 2), when his master raves at him for not giving him the wages he had earned (par. 4), when a meeting of the black community is held in New Bedford to deal with the presumed "betrayer" of an escaped slave (par. 14). Write two paragraphs interpreting Douglass's reactions to these events. How does he feel about the possibility of violence in these circumstances?
6. Douglass begins paragraph 6 by noting, "I have been frequently asked how I felt when I found myself in a free State." In the rest of this paragraph he attempts to answer that question. Write a one-page analysis of the various strategies Douglass uses in this paragraph to describe the experience of "the toil-worn and whip-scarred fugitive slave" for his readers. How effective are these strategies?
7. Imagine that you are at an antislavery meeting at which Frederick Douglass is a speaker. After hearing Douglass tell the story of his escape from slavery (as it is recounted in this selection), you decide that you must communicate with him. Write a letter to Douglass expressing your ideas and feelings about his speech and about the abolitionist movement.
8. Frederick Douglass's experiences of wonder and strangeness in New Bedford are not unlike some immigrant narratives that you have read in previous chapters (such as "Alien Turf," by Piri Thomas, p. 47, and Marie Hall Ets, "Rosa, The Life of an Italian Immigrant," p. 98). Choose one of these narratives and write a brief essay that discusses similarities and differences between it and Frederick Douglass's account.

ANN BANKS

Immigrant Lives: Oral Histories Collected by the W.P.A. Federal Writers Project

The immigrant arrives in a new place in two senses. First, he or she must arrive on the physical level, enduring what is often an unimaginably harsh crossing to the United States. Second, the immigrant must arrive as a social being, assuming a place in American society that may at first be contested before it is finally recognized.

The three stories included in this selection are all told by immigrants who have come from different ethnic backgrounds—from Russia, Portugal, and Canada—and who occupy different spaces, geographically and economically. Their stories were collected as part of a massive oral history project that recorded the lives of Americans from many different regions and occupations during the Great Depression of the 1930s. Under the larger government-sponsored project called the Federal Writers Project, editors, researchers, and writers were paid to gather information and produce a variety of written narratives. In the case of the oral histories, the writers allowed their subjects to speak, with minimal guidance and editing. This practice allowed the real voices of these immigrants to be filtered through the written narrative of the writer responsible for producing the interview. The name of the writer/interviewer is printed at the end of each life story.

The subjects of these interviews were in their old age in the 1930s, looking back on their beginnings in the United States during the second half of the nineteenth century. They were not asked to be philosophical about their lives, for the most part; they were asked instead to recall incidents that had brought them to where they were in the 1930s. Thus these stories provide an inside glimpse into the anonymous history of immigrants who crossed over into this country and adjusted as well as they could to their new lives. The three lives narrated here—those of Morris Horowitz, Manuel Captiva, and Philippe Lemay (fictional names)—were gathered together, with many others recorded by the Federal Writers Project, in a collection titled First-Person America, *edited by writer Ann Banks (b. 1943) in 1980. Banks arranged the various interviews, from all over the United States, into eleven chapters, each devoted to a different subject; the life stories in this selection are from the chapter "Immigrant Lives." The name of the original W.P.A. editor appears after each life history.*

Morris Horowitz

How did I happen to become a peddler? When I came to Chicago in 1870, there was nothing else to do. I was eighteen years old. I had learned no trade in Russia. The easiest thing to do was to peddle. People coming to America today have a much harder time. There are better houses to live in and nearly everybody has a bathtub, but there are no jobs. In the old days, if you had a few dollars, you could buy some dry goods and peddle. But today you must know a trade or have a profession; otherwise you have no chance.

I went to live with an aunt and uncle when I first came to Chicago. They lived in a small four-room house on Fourth Avenue. They had four children but they managed to rent one room to two roomers. I shared the bed with these two men. The day after I got to Chicago my uncle asked me if I had any money. I told him I had ten dollars. He told me to invest it in dry goods and start peddling. I peddled in Chicago till after the fire of 1871. There were not many stores, so I had no trouble selling my goods. I used to make from six to ten dollars a week. I paid my aunt three dollars a week for food and lodging and I saved the rest. I had the responsibility of bringing my father, two sisters, and two brothers to America.

It was the great fire of 1871 that made me a country peddler. I remember the fire very well. It was in October. We used to go to bed early, because the two roomers had to go to work very early. We were getting ready to go to bed, when we heard the fire bells ringing. I asked the two men if they wanted to see where the fire was.

"Why should I care as long as our house is not on fire," one of the men said. "There is a fire every Monday and Thursday in Chicago." But I wanted to see the fire, so I went out into the street. I saw the flames across the river, but I thought that since the river was between the fire and our house, there was nothing to worry about. I went back to bed. The next thing I knew my two bedfellows were shaking me. "Get up," they cried. "The whole city is on fire! Save your things! We are going to Lincoln Park."

I jumped out of bed and pulled on my pants. Everybody in the house was trying to save as much as possible. I tied my clothes in a sheet. With my clothes under my arm and my pack on my back, I left the house with the rest of the family. Everybody was running north. People were carrying all kinds of crazy things. A woman was carrying a pot of soup, which was spilling all over her dress. People were carrying cats, dogs, and goats. In the great excitement people saved worthless things and left behind good things. I saw a woman carrying a big frame in which was framed her wedding veil and wreath. She said it would have been bad luck to leave it behind.

When we came to Lake Street I saw all the wagons of Marshall Field and Company [the firm was then called Field, Leiter and Company] lined up in front. Men were carrying the goods out of the building and loading everything into the wagons. The merchandise was taken to the streetcar barns on State near Twentieth Street; a couple of weeks later, Marshal Field started doing business there.

No one slept that night. People gathered on the streets and all kinds of reasons were given for the fire. I stood near a minister talking to a group of men. He said the fire was sent by God as a warning that the people were wicked. He said there were too many saloons in Chicago, too many houses of prostitution. A woman who heard this said that a fire started in a barn was a direct warning from God since Jesus was also born in a barn. I talked to a man who lived next door to Mrs. O'Leary, and he told me that the fire started in Mrs. O'Leary's barn. She went out to milk the cow when it was beginning to get dark. The cow kicked the lamp over and that's how the fire started. There were all kinds of songs made up about the fire. Years after, people were still singing songs about it. You remember the song "Hot Time in the Old Town?" Well there was a song made up to that tune. These are the words:

> One moonlit night while the families were in bed,
> Mrs. O'Leary took a lantern to the shed,
> The cow kicked it over, winked her eye and said:
> There'll be a hot time in the old town tonight, my baby.

Since many homes were burned, many people left the city. Some went to live with relatives in other cities. A great many men became country peddlers. There were thousands of men walking from farm to farm with heavy packs on their backs. These peddlers carried all kinds of merchandise, things they thought farmers and their families could use.

There was no rural mail delivery in those days. The farmers very seldom saw a newspaper and were hungry for news. They were very glad to see a peddler from any large city. They wanted to hear all about the great fire. When I told a farmer that I was from Chicago, he was very glad to see me. You see, I was a newspaper and a department store.

The farms were ten, fifteen, twenty, and even thirty miles apart. It would 10 take a day sometimes to walk from one farm to the next. I used to meet peddlers from all over. It was not an easy life, but we made pretty good money. Most of the men had come from Europe and had left their families behind. We were all trying to save enough money to bring relatives to America.

The living expenses of the peddlers were very little. The farmers' wives always gave us plenty of food. I did not eat anything that was not kosher, but I could eat eggs and there were plenty of them. There was fresh milk and bread and butter. The farmers always gave us a place to sleep. In the summer we slept in the hayloft. In the winter, if there was no spare bed, we would sleep on the floor. When the farmer had no extra blankets, we slept with our clothes on to keep warm.

I had a customer in Iowa and I used to get to his farm once a year. He had a nice six-room house, and it was one of the few places where I could have a bed to sleep in. When I got to the place after a year's absence, there was no house. The ground was covered with snow, and I could not even see the place where the house had been. As I was looking around, thinking that I was lost, my friend the farmer came out of a dugout. I asked him what had happened to his house.

"Oh, we had a terrible storm about four months ago, and the house blew away," said the farmer. "We are living in this dugout; it isn't as nice as the house was, but it's safe and warm. Come on in."

I had never been in a dugout and I was surprised to see how nice the farmer and his wife had fixed up this hole in the ground. Seven people were living in this dugout, but they made room for me. The farmers were very lonely during the long winters, and they were glad to have anybody come to their homes.

After carrying the pack on my back for two years, I decided to buy a 15 horse and wagon. Many other peddlers got the same idea. I used to meet the small covered wagons as they drove about the country. I had now been peddling for five years and had saved enough money to bring my father, brothers, and sisters to Chicago. By that time a great many new houses had been built and we rented a four-room house on Maxwell Street. My oldest brother started peddling. One of my sisters started working in a clothing factory, while the other one kept house.

After my father had been in Chicago a few months, he wanted to go to Burlington, Iowa, to see a friend who had been his neighbor in Russia. When he got there, he met this friend's daughter and decided that I ought to marry her. So I went to Burlington, met the girl, and I agreed with my father. The young lady and I were married in 1875. I rented a small house near my father's home and we furnished it. I believe we had the first rug in the neighborhood. We were very proud of our first American home. It was the beginning of a good life. I stayed home for a week with my young wife. It was my first vacation since I had come to America. Then I started off again in my wagon. During the fifty years that I peddled, I always went home for all the Jewish holidays and when a baby was born. I would stay home a week and then was off again.

Many of the men who carried packs on their backs and in covered wagons became very rich. They learned American business ways. Some of them opened small stores which their wives looked after while the men were on the road. When the stores showed a good profit, they would quit peddling. Some of the largest department stores in the country were started by men who peddled with packs on their backs.

I never got rich. My wife and I raised six children. When my sisters and brothers got married, my father came to live with us. Then one of my sisters died and her children came to live with us. Then my wife brought her parents to America and they lived with us. Then we wanted our children to have an education, so we sent them to college. There never was enough money left to start any kind of business. But I feel that we made a good investment.

–*Hilda Polacheck*
Chicago
1939

Manuel Captiva

I wouldn't never be happy without I had a boat under me. In the Old Country, we was all fishermen, me and my brothers. My father fished, and his father too. Some dragging, but mostly with hooks. That's about all they do back there. I could work as good as a man by the time I was fourteen. I come over here when I was nineteen. The way I come, we had folks over here. They write to my father, tell him there was good money over here. My old man come over and my mother and us four boys. Then we send for other people. That's how we all come.

My boy's a good fisherman. Portuguese boys do more like the old man. 20 Some of em get these ideas to go to high school. Don't do em no good, as I can see, but don't do em no harm either. Lots of these Americans tell me their boys is in the city. Got jobs here, got jobs there. Me, I like to have the boy on my boat. Then I know where he is, what he's doing. The boat will be his. It's good for him to know how to handle her.

On land the Portuguese and Americans don't always get on so good. But we fish together all right. It's different out in the boats. There's the same rules for everyone. The rules for a captain and crew are the same everywhere, and we all want the same things: a good catch and a good market. We get on good on the sea.

They find out we're good fishermen. Anybody'll tell you they ain't no men can fish better than the Portuguese. We can always get jobs on the boats. I wouldn't want to work on land all the time. Lots of the men do when they get older, but not me. I wouldn't never be happy unless I had a boat under me. I'm a good fisherman. Maybe I wouldn't do so good with a regular land job.

The Yankees fish to get money enough to go ashore, run shops maybe, or do business. The Portuguese fishes because he wants to, because he doesn't want no boss. One time I had a good job on a yacht. Good pay, the best of everything, but I didn't like it. Rather be independent, not say this "Yes sir" and "No sir" all the time. The Yankees they don't mind. They run stores, they work for bosses, and they don't care.

It's a good life and there used to be big money in it. Not no more, though. Now the middleman gets everything and they don't pay the prices anyhow. Sometimes you might as well throw away the catch. It don't keep forever. Give it away or throw it away if you can't sell it. I think the government don't know the conditions of fishing. We make a big lot of money some seasons, then for a long time we're broke. We got to get good prices.

You won't find many nowadays got much of anything saved. We most of us belong to one of these burial insurance societies. But the widows of most of us wouldn't have much if we went. That's why a man's foolish not to buy a house if he can, even if he has to have a pretty big mortgage. And that's why it's good to own your boat. The Portuguese aren't as good for business as the Yankee fisherman.

I do dragging. We drag with big nets along the bottom. I don't go out nights much no more, but I got accommodations on my boat so's eight men can sleep on board. She's a sloop—that's one mast. My new engine's beautiful. Raises my profit. Used to cost ten, twelve dollars a day to take the boat out. Now costs only two, three.

I got a good crew, too. I'm captain. Then I got engineer, and cook. And my boy fishes. We fish on shares; I get most because the boat's mine. I don't know nothing else, only fishing and the sea. I never think about drowning any mor'n you think about the danger in the streets. Sure, the women worry, I guess. They used to get down on the beach and yell and pray when there was storms and the boat was out late. But the women always worrying about something, anyway.

My wife worries sometimes about the boy. I tell her he's better off at sea than running around with all these wild crowds. Ain't drowned yet, nor I ain't drowned yet. She wouldn't really want me to come ashore. Her people was fishing folks too. She knows I wouldn't be no good on land.

My boat can hold twenty-five thousand pounds. We don't often get that much. Sometimes we do, though. One time we went out seven-thirty, eight o'clock at night. Nine o'clock we come back in—full. Twenty-five thousand pound this silver perch. Made a thousand dollar that one night. We go out nights when we hear the fish are running good. We don't have no regular plan where we go, but no boat ever goes alone. We start out, try all the places where we know fish come sometimes. Then we come back, one boat comes up. The Cap says, "You had a good catch?" If I say, "Yes," then likely he'll say, "Jeeze, I didn't get nothing. I'm coming with you tomorrow." Or if I didn't do so good, next day I go out with a crowd that's got a good catch.

We start about three, four in the morning. It's dark, and boy is it cold! We go outside the harbor, not far—couple of hours, maybe—and start fishing. It's light then and there's coffee on the stove. Everybody feels good. I got a beautiful stove on my boat. We cook chowder, oyster stew, make coffee—everything. And plenty of room.

My great-grandfather he was Spanish, and he was took prisoner by the Moors. After two, three months he escape. He comes to Portugal and settle down in little village near Lisbon. He was young fellow, very handsome, good fisherman. He had scars from Moorish prison. He was brave and also he told big stories, how he escape and kill Moors and everything. So everybody they call him Captiva. That means "prisoner." So that's the name we had since then. People say the Captivas got to be brave because of my great-grandfather. When I first tell the children they won't believe me. But now they do. First they laugh and say, "Some more stories!" The Old Country, she's far away. And they think they know more than their old man.

It's the schools does it. They used to keep sending word home—have so much milk, so much orange juice. Must brush teeth. I never brush my teeth in the Old Country. Nobody did. And I got fine teeth. I send back word to the teacher once. I says, "Tell em I know them when they was little. Their fathers was fishermen just like me. They never had no orange juice and no quarts of milk." But they laugh. Say times is change. I guess so.

The young people over here, they have a good time. Back home the old folks was strict. Too strict. Young people was all the time running away. My kids they bring their friends home. That youngest girl of mine, she's always after me to dance with her, go out places. Kids ain't afraid of the old folks no more. I think that's a good thing. Look at the Fisherman's Ball. It's for the families. My wife was there and my girls. My girl, the youngest one, she likes make me dance with her. She says, "Don't be behind the times, pa." She's a great kid.

We're the Portuguese pilgrims. We made the Cape. We built it up. Us and the American fishermen. We make Gloucester too. I was up there a couple of years. I fished all over, out of Chatham, out of Gloucester, everywhere. When we first come here there wasn't nothing but sand and a few houses and docks and boats. We used to dry the codfish out on the Dunes. There'd be pretty near miles of it spread out. The whole place stunk.

There was fishermen all up and down the Cape then. The old whalers went out then. And fishing off the Grand Banks was a goldmine. You'd get so much you couldn't load it all. Times you'd be up two, three nights cleaning, up to your knees in it and half frozen.

Then the artists come down. They must have painted a hundred miles of nets and boats and docks. And then the writers heard about it, and the summer people. But we started it. Even now they'll ask you to take them out in the boats and they ask questions. Fishing seems exciting to them.

–*Alice D. Kelly*
Cape Cod
1939

PHILIPPE LEMAY

When we landed at Lowell in 1864, there were very few French Canadians. Many more came after the Civil War was over. I was only eight years old, but that didn't stop me from going to work. My first job as a textile worker was in the Lawrence mill, Number Five, where I worked as a doffer [a worker who removes filled bobbins from spindles] for about three years. In 1872, when I was sixteen, our family moved to Manchester.

Here I started in a card room[1] as roping and bobbin boy, but I wanted to be a fly-spinner, making cotton into thread, ready for the weave room. It wasn't until 1875 that I got my chance. How I landed in Number One spinning mill of the Amoskeag, where no French Canadian could be hired before, is a story in itself.

Each spring and fall, it seems, the older immigrants had a touch of homesickness. Most of them still had farms in old Quebec, so they went back to Canada twice a year. They had to make many sacrifices to save up enough money to pay railroad fares and other necessary expenses. While there, they visited friends and relatives, but their principal reason was a serious one. At heart, they were still farmers like their ancestors, and they wanted to get something out of those farms, some of which had been in the family for many generations. In the spring, they attended to ploughing, harrowing, and sowing; in the fall, to the harvesting of the crops.

While they were absent from the mills, other hands had their chance to work. That's how I got into spinning. The overseer was out sick and the second hand hired me. When the boss came back, I was giving all my attention to my work and not losing a minute. But the overseer didn't look pleased when his assistant told him my name. He wanted to know why I had been hired when he didn't want any Frenchman working in his mill. The second hand said he'd discharge me right away and I felt that my dream of becoming a fly-spinner was coming to an end quickly. I kept on working. The boss looked at me, seemed to think twice before he spoke, and then said: "Don't do it now; wait until Smith comes back to work."

Smith did come back and I was out of a job, but not for long. The boss was sorry to let me go, that was plain. He took my address and said he'd let me know as soon as he needed me. He had changed his mind about hiring French Canadians after he had seen one of them work. The very next day he sent for me and after that I had a regular job in the Amoskeag. That same boss hired many of my people, and that is the point I want to bring out in my story.

Later, I was transferred to Number Four mill. One day, another overseer tried to get me, and when I spoke of leaving, the boss of Number Four wouldn't hear of it. To keep me, he offered me extra pay if I would do the

[1]The card is the machine that untangles the cotton or wool fiber in preparation for spinning.

work of a sickly operative who had to loaf at times, and more extra pay if I wanted to take the place of a third hand once in a while. I accepted, and as long as the arrangement lasted I got two dollars a day and a little more. I was finally given a regular job as third hand, quite a promotion for a French Canadian at the time. In 1881 I was made second hand, and in 1901, overseer in Number One spinning mill.

It was a big event when I was appointed overseer of the One and Eight spinning mills. There was to be a vacancy very shortly. I knew about it and, convinced that no one would say a good word for me, I decided to speak for myself. I asked the super if he wouldn't give me the chance. He was so surprised that he couldn't speak for a long time, or so it seemed to me. He was looking at me as if he had been struck by thunder and lightning. What! A Frenchman had the crust to think he could be an overseer! That was something unheard of, absolutely shocking. When he recovered enough to speak, he told me he'd think it over, turned his back on me, and walked off. He was certainly upset.

The next day, he came to me and, with a doubting expression still spread all over his face, said he'd try me for six months. But I didn't want six months, I answered back. I wasn't going to clog up that spinning department. Either I was the man for the job, I said, or I wasn't. One month: that's all I wanted to show what I could do. The super seemed to be wondering again but answered it was all right with him. So I became the overseer of Number One spinning, where I had made my shaky debut in 1875.

That was another step ahead for the French Canadians, but this time it was an awful scandal. The sad news didn't take long to spread. Americans and Irish were mad clean through. The Irish, it seemed, were afraid that we had come to take their jobs away from them in the mills and tried hard to send us back to Canada by making life impossible for us in America. They looked at me and spoke to me only when they were strictly obliged to, but there was no more friendship. I, a Frenchman, had jumped over the heads of others who thought themselves the only ones entitled to the job of overseer. Here was a sin that could not be forgiven, and what was the world coming to, anyway? 45

Later, several other French-Canadian textile workers got well-deserved promotions. One of my own second hands was a boss just three days. Then he came back to his old job with me after telling the superintendent that he'd be happier and healthier that way. "An overseer has too many worries," he said. So my friend had the distinction of being the first French Canadian to refuse an overseer's job.

I liked the people who were with me in the mills and I sympathized with them. I helped them as anybody else would have done in my place. Didn't I, when I was a boss, hide some who weren't quite sixteen, when inspectors visited the mills? If boys and girls were big and strong enough to work, even if they were a little under the legal age, I gave them a chance to keep their jobs. I started working in the Lowell mills when I was only eight years old, and I could understand. Their parents were poor and needed every cent they could get. So I'd tell these younger workers to keep out of sight until the inspector had gone away. There was no harm to anybody in that, and it did a lot of good. Besides, the law wasn't so strict in those days.

That strike of 1922 was really a terrible thing. It lasted nearly ten months and was the worst thing that ever happened. It was bad for the city, its merchants, tenement owners, business in general. It destroyed Amoskeag's trade. The company never recovered from the blow and kept going down until it had to close its doors [in 1936]. But my sympathy goes first to all the workers, for they suffered the most. They lost all their savings, went deep in debt, and lived on canned beans while the hope of winning the fight was kept dangling before their eyes. They were told almost every day by the strike leaders to be patient and tighten their belts because victory was in sight. But there was no victory, only defeat for all concerned.

49 As an overseer, I couldn't join their ranks in the union nor help them in any way, but neither could I be against them. As a boy, a young man, and a middle-aged man with a family, I had worked long hours for anything but high wages. I knew what it meant to be poor, what sacrifices must be made if you want to lay something aside for a rainy day. The workers wanted more pay; I would have given them a living wage if it had been in my power to do so, every worker having a right to that. They wanted shorter hours; I would have given them a reasonable work week if I had anything to say about it. Even as a second hand and an overseer, I never forgot my humble beginning and always considered myself a textile worker. Those strikers were textile workers too, and I was sorry for them.

–*Louis Paré*
Manchester, New Hampshire
n.d.

DISCUSSING THE TEXT

1. Morris Horowitz, the peddler, looks back on his years of hard work and says at one point, "It was the beginning of a good life." What has made it a "good life" for Horowitz? Would you consider his life a good one now?
2. What are the sources of Manuel Captiva's pride as a Portuguese fisherman? How does he describe life on the sea? What advantages does he see in his occupation?
3. What difficulties did Philippe Lemay encounter as a French Canadian in the mills? How did he overcome them? Compare Lemay's experiences with those suffered by Frederick Douglass when he tried to work as a caulker in New Bedford (see *Narrative of the Life of Frederick Douglass,* p. 233).
4. All three speakers describe relationships they formed with other people through the work they did. Working with a group of four or five students, discuss similarities and differences in these three men's experiences with people they encountered through their work. Be prepared to share your ideas with the rest of the class.

WRITING ABOUT THE TEXT

5. There is a sense of pride and accomplishment in the way that these three people talk about their lives as immigrants in the United States. Choose a passage from each narrative that illustrates these proud feelings. Then write a brief essay that compares and contrasts the sources of these men's pride.
6. Two speakers, Morris Horowitz and Manuel Captiva, make passing reference to the experiences of their wives, but neither woman's point of view is presented directly. Based on the information provided in their husbands' narratives, write an imaginary first-person narrative in the voice of one of these women.
7. Suppose plans were made for a new Federal Writers Project. Who should be interviewed for such a project? How should their stories be told? What media should be used? Who should be hired to conduct the project? Write a one- to two-page proposal for a Federal Writers Project for today.

ESMERALDA SANTIAGO

Angels on the Ceiling

Esmeralda Santiago was born and raised in Puerto Rico and came to the continental United States with her family when she was thirteen years old. Her book When I Was Puerto Rican *portrays from a personal perspective the ambiguous social, cultural, and political stance of Puerto Ricans, who are unlike any other immigrant group in the continental United States: they are American citizens with the right to vote, but they are not represented in Congress.*

Santiago's book offers a detailed record of one year in her life, during which she crossed various significant borders: from childhood to adolescence; from a rural area of Puerto Rico to Brooklyn, New York; from junior high in Brooklyn to the High School of Performing Arts in Manhattan. In this excerpt from a chapter titled "Angels on the Ceiling," Santiago recalls her first day in New York, beginning with her arrival at the airport with her mother and sisters and ending as she lies down to sleep in her new home in Brooklyn. For Negi, as the family calls Esmeralda, crossing the border was filled with feelings of strangeness, excitement, and disorientation. As she tries to fall asleep that day, staring at the angels on the ceiling, she tells the reader: "I had no idea where I was, only that it was very far from where I'd been."

Esmeralda Santiago graduated from Harvard College and has a master in fine arts degree from Sarah Lawrence College. Her work has appeared in the New York Times *and the* Boston Globe. When I was Puerto Rican, *Santiago's first book, was published in both English and Spanish in 1993.*

Ahí fué donde la puerca entorchó el rabo.

That's where the sow's tail curled.[1]

Uniformed women with lacquered hair, high heels, and fitted skirts looked down on us, signalled that we should fasten our safety belts, place parcels under the seat in front of us, and sit up.

"Stewardesses," Mami said, admiring their sleek uniforms, pressed white blouses, stiff navy ribbons tied into perfect bows in their hair. None of them spoke Spanish. Their tight smiles were not convincing, did not welcome us. In our best clothes, with hair combed, faces scrubbed, the dirt under our nails gouged out by Mami's stiff brush, I still felt unclean next to the highly groomed, perfumed, unwrinkled women who waited on us.

"Someday," Mami mused, "you might like to be a stewardess. Then you can travel all over the world for free."

The stewardesses minced up and down the narrow aisle, glancing from side to side like queens greeting the masses. I tried to read in their faces where else they'd been, if their travels had taken them to places like Mongolia, Singapore, Timbuktu. That's where I'd want to go if I were a stewardess. Not New York, Paris, or Rome. I'd want to go places so far away that I couldn't even pronounce their names. I'd want to see sights so different that it would show on my face. None of the stewardesses seemed to have been anywhere that exotic. Their noncommittal smiles, the way they seemed to have everything under control was too reassuring, too studied, too managed to make me comfortable. I would have felt better had there been more chaos.

"Do these planes ever just fall from the sky?" I asked Mami, who sat across the aisle from me. 5

The woman sitting in front of her shot me a fearful look and crossed herself. "*Ay, nena,*[2] don't say such a thing," she said in a hoarse whisper. "It's bad luck."

Mami smiled.

We were high over thick clouds, the sky above so bright it hurt my eyes. In the window seat, Edna pressed her face flat against the pane. She looked up, eyes shining. "There's nothing there!" She stretched over my lap and reached out her hand to Mami. "I'm hungry."

"They'll serve us dinner soon," Mami said. "Just wait."

The stewardesses brought us small trays fitted with square plates filled with sauce over chicken, mushy rice, and boiled string beans. It all tasted like salt. 10

The sky darkened, but we floated in a milky whiteness that seemed to hold the plane suspended above Puerto Rico. I couldn't believe we were moving; I imagined that the plane sat still in the clouds while the earth flew below

---

[1] *That's where the sow's tail curled:* meaning "That's where things began to change" (*Ed.*)
[2] *Ay, nena:* (Puerto Rican colloquialism) Oh, baby girl (*Ed.*)

us. The drone of the propellers was hypnotic and lulled us to sleep in the stiff seats with their square white doilies on the back.

"Why do they have these?" I asked Mami, fingering the starched, piqué-like fabric.

"So that people's pomade doesn't stain the seat back," she answered. The man in front of me, his hair slick with brilliantine, adjusted his doily, pulled it down to his neck.

I dozed, startled awake, panicked when I didn't know where I was, remembered where we were going, then dozed off again, to repeat the whole cycle, in and out of sleep, between earth and sky, somewhere between Puerto Rico and New York.

It was raining in Brooklyn. Mist hung over the airport so that all I saw as we landed were fuzzy white and blue lights on the runway and at the terminal. We thudded to earth as if the pilot had miscalculated just how close we were to the ground. A startled silence was followed by frightened cries and *aleluyas*[3] and the rustle of everyone rushing to get up from their seats and out of the plane as soon as possible. 15

Mami's voice mixed and became confused with the voices of other mothers telling their children to pick up their things, stay together, to walk quickly toward the door and not to hold up the line. Edna, Raymond, and I each had bundles to carry, as did Mami, who was loaded with two huge bags filled with produce and spices *del país*.[4] "You can't find these in New York," she'd explained.

We filed down a long, drafty tunnel, at the end of which many people waited, smiling, their hands waving and reaching, their voices mingling into a roar of *hello*'s and *how are you*'s and *oh, my god, it's been so long*'s.

"Over there," Mami said, shoving us. On the fringes of the crowd a tall woman with short cropped hair, a black lace dress, and black open-toed shoes leaned against a beam that had been painted yellow. I didn't recognize her, but she looked at me as if she knew who I was and then loped toward us, arms outstretched. It was my mother's mother, Tata. Raymond let go of Mami's hand and ran into Tata's arms. Mami hugged and kissed her. Edna and I hung back, waiting.

"This is Edna," Mami said, pushing her forward for a hug and kiss.

"And this must be Negi," Tata said, pulling me into her embrace. I pressed against her and felt the sharp prongs of the rhinestone brooch on her left shoulder against my face. She held me longer than I expected, wrapped me in the scratchy softness of her black lace dress, the warmth of her powdered skin, the sting of her bittersweet breath, pungent of beer and cigarettes. 20

Behind her loomed a man shorter than she, but as imposing. He was squarely built, with narrow eyes under heavy eyebrows, a broad nose, and

---

[3]*aleluyas:* (Spanish) Hallelujahs (*Ed.*)
[4]*del país:* (Spanish) from the country (*Ed.*)

full lips fuzzed with a pencil mustache. No one would have ever called him handsome, but there was about him a gentleness, a sweetness that made me wish he were a relative. He was, in a manner of speaking. Mami introduced him as "Don Julio, Tata's friend." We shook hands, his broad, fleshy palm seeming to swallow mine.

"Let's get our things," Mami said, pulling us into a knot near her. "You kids, don't let go of each others' hands. It's crazy here tonight."

We joined the stream of people claiming their baggage. Boxes filled with fruit and vegetables had torn, and their contents had spilled and broken into slippery messes on the floor. Overstuffed suitcases tied with ropes or hastily taped together had given way, and people's underwear, baby diapers, and ratty shoes pushed through the stressed seams where everyone could see them. People pointed, laughed, and looked to see who would claim these sorry belongings, who could have thought the faded, torn clothes and stained shoes were still good enough for their new life in Brooklyn.

"That's why I left everything behind," Mami sniffed. "Who wants to carry that kind of junk around?"

We had a couple of new suitcases and three or four boxes carefully packed, taped at the seams, tied with rope, and labelled with our name and an address in New York that was all numbers. We had brought only our "good" things: Mami's work clothes and shoes, a few changes of playclothes for me, Edna, and Raymond, some of them made by Mami herself, others bought just before we left. She brought her towels, sheets, and pillowcases, not new, but still "decent looking." 25

"I'll see if I can find a taxi," Don Julio said. "You wait here."

We huddled in front of the terminal while Don Julio negotiated with drivers. The first one looked at us, counted the number of packages we carried, asked Don Julio where we were going, then shook his head and drove along the curb toward a man in a business suit with a briefcase who stood there calmly, his right hand in the air as if he were saluting, his fingers wiggling every so often. The second driver gave us a hateful look and said some words that I didn't understand, but I knew what he meant just the same. Before he drove off, Mami mumbled through her teeth "*Charamanbiche.*"[5] Don Julio said it was illegal for a driver to refuse a fare, but that didn't stop them from doing it.

Finally, a swarthy man with thick black hair and a flat cap on his head stopped, got out of his taxi, and helped us load our stuff. He didn't speak Spanish, none of us spoke English, and, it appeared, neither did he. But he gave us a toothy, happy smile, lifted Raymond into Mami's lap, made sure our fingers and toes were inside the taxi before he closed the doors, then got in with a great deal of huffing and puffing, as his belly didn't fit between the seat and the steering wheel. Tata and Don Julio sat in the front seat with the driver, who kept asking questions no one understood.

---

[5]*Charamanbiche:* (Latino slang) son of a bitch (*Ed.*)

"He wants to know where we're from," Mami figured out, and we told him.

"Ah, Porto Reeco, yes, ees hot," he said. "San Juan?"

"Yes," Mami said, the first time I'd ever heard her speak English.

The driver launched into a long speech peppered with familiar words like America and President Kennedy. Mami, Tata, and Don Julio nodded every once in a while, uh-huhed, and laughed whenever the taxi driver did. I wasn't sure whether he had no idea that we didn't understand him, or whether he didn't care.

Rain had slicked the streets into shiny, reflective tunnels lined with skyscrapers whose tops disappeared into the mist. Lampposts shed uneven silver circles of light whose edges faded to gray. An empty trash can chained to a parking meter banged and rolled from side to side, and its lid, also chained, flipped and flapped in the wind like a kite on a short string. The taxi stopped at a red light under an overpass. A train roared by above us, its tiny square windows full of shapes.

"Look at her," Tata laughed from the front seat, "Negi's eyes are popping out of her head."

"That's because the streets are not paved with gold, like she thought," Mami teased.

The taxi driver grinned. I pressed my face to the window, which was fogged all around except on the spot I'd rubbed so that I could look out.

It was late. Few windows on the tall buildings flanking us were lit. The stores were shuttered, blocked with crisscrossed grates knotted with chains and enormous padlocks. Empty buses glowed from within with eerie gray light, chugging slowly from one stop to the next, their drivers sleepy and bored.

Mami was wrong. I didn't expect the streets of New York to be paved with gold, but I did expect them to be bright and cheerful, clean, lively. Instead, they were dark and forbidding, empty, hard.

We stopped in front of a brick building. Here, too, battered trash cans were chained to a black lamppost, only these were filled with garbage, some of which had spilled out and lay scattered in puddles of pulpy hash. The door to the building was painted black, and there was a hole where the knob should have been.

Mami had to wake up Edna and Raymond. Tata picked one up, and Mami the other. Don Julio helped the taxi driver get our stuff.

"This way," Tata said.

We entered a hallway where a bare dim bulb shed faint blue light against green walls. Tata led us past many doors to the other end of the hall, where she pushed against another black door and led us into a cobblestoned courtyard with a tree in front of another, smaller building.

"Watch the puddles," Tata said, too late. Cold water seeped into my right shoe, soaking my white cotton socks. We went in another door without a knob, into a smaller hallway with steps leading up to a landing.

Tata pushed the first door on our left with her foot. We entered a small room with a window giving onto the courtyard. As we came in, a tall man got up from a cot near the window and weaved toward us. His long hair was gray. Round hazel eyes bulged from their sockets; the whites were streaked with red and yellow. He hugged Mami and helped her settle Raymond on the cot he'd just left. Tata lay Edna next to Raymond and tucked a blanket around them.

"So this is Negi," the tall man said. 45

"This is your uncle Chico, Tata's brother," Mami said. "You remember him, don't you?"

I remembered the name, but not this bony scarecrow with the stale smell of sweat and beer.

"She was just a little kid when I last saw her," he said, his hands on my shoulders. "How old are you now?"

"Thirteen," I croaked.

"Thirteen!" He whistled. 50

Don Julio came in. He took a key from a nail by the door and went out again.

"Give me a hand with this stuff, can you, Chico?"

"Oh, of course, of course." He shuffled off after Don Julio.

"How about something to eat?" Tata said. "Or a beer?" Mami shook her head. Tata took a Budweiser from the small refrigerator and opened it. She drank from the can.

"Are you hungry?" Mami asked me. 55

"Yes."

Tata put her beer down and turned on the hot plate next to the refrigerator.

"Chico made some *asopao*.[6] I'll make some coffee."

"Where's the bathroom?" Mami asked.

"Across the hall." Tata pointed to the door. Next to it there was a curtained-off area. On her way out, Mami peeked inside. The curtain hid a large bed and clothes on wire hangers lining the wall. 60

"That's our bedroom," Tata said. "Your apartment is upstairs. Two big rooms. And you don't have to share a bathroom like we do."

"I'll go take a look." Mami stepped out then turned around to find me right behind her. "Negi, you wait right here."

"But I want to see too."

"Have something to eat and keep still. You'll have plenty of time later."

I leaned against the door and watched Tata. 65

Even though she was quite tall, Tata was not cramped by the small room. Her hands, with long tapered fingers and wide nails, grasped pots and cooking spoons from shelves above the stove and placed them soundlessly on the glowing hot-plate burner. Her back was wide, straight, and she carried her head as if she had something on it that she couldn't let fall. Her hair was

---

[6]*asopao:* Puerto Rican dish of chicken and rice (*Ed.*)

black streaked with silver, cut short and curled away from her face. Her large brown eyes were outlined with long black lashes under arched brows. She smiled mischievously as she put a bowl of *asopao* on the table opposite the cot and dragged one of the two chairs from its place against the wall.

"Here you are," she said. "Chico makes good *asopao,* but not as good as mine."

It was delicious, thick with rice and chunks of chicken, cubed potatoes, green olives, and capers. She tore off a chunk of bread from a long loaf on top of the refrigerator, spread it thick with butter, and put the bread on a napkin in front of me.

"Monín told me you like bread. This is fresh from the bakery down the street."

It was crunchy on the outside and soft on the inside, just the way I liked it. 70

Don Julio and Chico came back, followed by Mami, her eyes bright.

"What a great place! Wait till you see it, Negi. It's twice the size of this one, with windows in the front and back. And there's a huge bathtub, and a gas stove with four burners!"

"And your school is only five blocks from here," Don Julio said. "Just beyond *la marketa.*"

"What's a *marketa?*" I asked. Everyone laughed.

"It's a big building with stalls where you can buy anything," Mami said. 75

"Like the plaza in Bayamón," Tata added.

"Only much bigger," Chico said.

"Look at her. She's excited about it already," Tata said, and they all stared at me with broad smiles, willing me to give in to their enthusiasm. I ran into Mami's arms, unable to admit that a part of me was looking forward to the morning, to the newness of our life, and afraid to let the other part show, the part that was scared.

There were angels on the ceiling. Four fat naked cherubs danced in a circle, their hands holding ivy garlands, their round buttocks half covered by a cloth swirling around their legs. Next to me, Mami snored softly. At the foot of the bed, Edna and Raymond slept curled away from each other, their backs against my legs. The bedroom had very high ceilings with braided molding all the way around, ending in a circle surrounded by more braid above the huge window across from the bed. The shade was down, but bright sunlight streaked in at the edges. The cherubs looked down on us, smiling mysteriously, and I wondered how many people they had seen come in and out of this room.

DISCUSSING THE TEXT

1. The incident with the various taxi drivers at the airport, when Negi and her family arrive in New York City (par. 27–32), is the family's first experience

of discrimination in the United States. How does Santiago narrate this incident? What details does she choose to include? What do you think of Don Julio's reactions? What can we infer about the taxi driver who agrees to take them to Brooklyn? Have you ever found yourself in a comparable situation?

2. On sensing Negi's disappointment as she looks at the city from the taxi, her mother teases her by saying that "the streets are not paved with gold, like she thought" (par. 35). What does the expression "streets paved with gold" mean, within the context of the American immigrant experience? What is the source of Negi's disappointment?
3. In a group of four or five classmates, discuss Negi's sense of strangeness and alienation on her arrival. Why is it important for her to describe everything she sees in detail? What do we learn about her environment from the way she describes it? Why do you think she feels so different from the airline stewardesses, for instance? How would you characterize her feelings about her new apartment? Be prepared to share your thoughts and ideas with the rest of the class.

WRITING ABOUT THE TEXT

4. Write two paragraphs in which you compare and contrast Negi's border crossing with that of Morris Horowitz in "Immigrant Lives" (p. 244).
5. On the day she arrives in New York, Negi says that "a part of me was looking forward to the morning, to the newness of our life, and afraid to let the other part show, the part that was scared" (par. 78). In the voice of thirteen-year-old Negi, write a diary entry that elaborates on this quotation, and that describes her conflicted feelings about crossing the various borders between Puerto Rico and Brooklyn.
6. Write a narrative describing your own experience of arriving in a new, and perhaps frightening or bewildering, place. Try to include the kinds of details that Santiago includes as you describe the new place, the people you encountered, and so on.

ANZIA YEZIERSKA

College

Anzia Yezierska (1885?–1970) was born in Russian Poland and immigrated to the United States with her family in 1901. For Yezierska, as for many immigrants to the United States, the clearest route to the promised opportunities of America lay in education. Three years after arriving in the United States—where she studied English at night and worked in a sweatshop during the day—she earned a scholarship to Columbia University, and for several years after graduating she taught "domestic science," that is, cooking, nutrition, sewing, and hygiene.

Much of Yezierska's work draws on her own life experience, including her struggle to break free from her oppressive patriarchal family, in which the woman's role—to serve husband and children—was strictly prescribed. She did achieve that freedom, but not without paying a heavy emotional price. She married twice between 1910 and 1911 and had a daughter by her second husband, but relinquished her familial responsibilities before 1915 to pursue her writing career.

Yezierska's short stories dealing with immigrant Jewish life and the search for happiness in America were very successful. Her 1920 collection Hungry Hearts *was turned into a silent film by Hollywood studio head Samuel Goldwyn. Yezierska herself was offered a large salary to work for motion pictures in Hollywood, but, after trying it for a year, she gave it up to return to New York, the source of her art. There she could write again, and she produced several novels during the 1920s (including* Salome of the Tenements *[1922] and* Children of Loneliness *[1923]) that made her famous. Yezierska wrote about the gap between generations in immigrant families, the yearning for an idealized love, and the tension between Old World customs and the opportunities of a new land. Although she was widely known during the 1920s as a writer of fiction, Yezierska's work disappeared from view for many years until the republication, in 1975, of her most successful novel,* Bread Givers: A Struggle between a Father of the Old World and a Daughter of the New *(1925).*

In this excerpt from Bread Givers, *the heroine, Sara Smolinsky, has broken with her father, who has cursed her for leaving the family home to pursue her life independently. She determines to seek an education: "Knowledge was what I wanted more than anything else in the world," she says. She leaves New York City alone, on a quest for self-fulfillment.*

That burning day when I got ready to leave New York and start out on my journey to college! I felt like Columbus starting out for the other end of the earth. I felt like the pilgrim fathers who had left their homeland and all their kin behind them and trailed out in search of the New World.

I had stayed up night after night, washing and ironing, patching and darning my things. At last, I put them all together in a bundle, wrapped them up with newspapers, and tied them securely with the thick clothes line that I had in my room on which to hang out my wash. I made another bundle of my books. In another newspaper I wrapped up my food for the journey: a loaf of bread, a herring, and a pickle. In my purse was the money I had been saving from my food, from my clothes, a penny to penny, a dollar to a dollar, for so many years. It was not much but I counted out that it would be enough for my train ticket and a few weeks start till I got work out there.

It was only when I got to the train that I realized I had hardly eaten all day. Starving hungry, I tore the paper open. *Ach!* Crazy-head! In my haste I had forgotten even to cut up the bread. I bent over on the side of my seat, and half covering myself with a newspaper, I pinched pieces out of the loaf and ripped ravenously at the herring. With each bite, I cast side glances like a guilty thing; nobody should see the way I ate.

After a while, as the lights were turned low, the other passengers began to nod their heads, each outsnoring the other in their thick sleep. I was the only one on the train too excited to close my eyes.

Like a dream was the whole night's journey. And like a dream mounting 5
on a dream was this college town, this New America of culture and education.

Before this, New York was all of America to me. But now I came to a town of quiet streets, shaded with green trees. No crowds, no tenements. No hurrying noise to beat the race of the hours. Only a leisured quietness whispered in the air: Peace. Be still. Eternal time is all before you.

Each house had its own green grass in front, its own free space all around, and it faced the street with the calm security of being owned for generations, and not rented by the month from a landlord. In the early twilight, it was like a picture out of fairyland to see people sitting on their porches, lazily swinging in their hammocks, or watering their own growing flowers.

So these are the real Americans, I thought, thrilled by the lean, straight bearing of the passers-by. They had none of that terrible fight for bread and rent that I always saw in New York people's eyes. Their faces were not worn with the hunger for things they never could have in their lives. There was in them that sure, settled look of those who belong to the world in which they were born.

The college buildings were like beautiful palaces. The campus stretched out like fields of a big park. Air—air. Free space and sunshine. The river at dusk. Glimmering lights on passing boats, the floating voices of young people. And when night came, there were the sky and the stars.

This was the beauty for which I had always longed. For the first few 10
days I could only walk about and drink it in thirstily, more and more. Beauty of houses, beauty of streets, beauty shining out of the calm faces and cool eyes of the people! Oh—too cool. . . .

How could I most quickly become friends with them? How could I come into their homes, exchange with them my thoughts, break with them bread at their tables? If I could only lose myself body and soul in the serenity of this new world, the hunger and the turmoil of my ghetto years would drop away from me, and I, too, would know the beauty of stillness and peace.

What light-hearted laughing youth met my eyes! All the young people I had ever seen were shut up in factories. But here were young girls and young men enjoying life, free from the worry for a living. College to them was being out for a good time, like to us in the shop a Sunday picnic. But in our gayest Sunday picnics there was always the under-feeling that Monday meant back to the shop again. To these born lucky ones joy seemed to stretch out for ever.

What a sight I was in my gray pushcart clothes against the beautiful gay colours and the fine things those young girls wore. I had seen cheap, fancy style, Five- and Ten-Cent Store finery. But never had I seen such plain beautifulness. The simple skirts and sweaters, the stockings and shoes to match. The neat finished quietness of their tailored suits. There was no show-off in their clothes, and yet how much more pulling to the eyes and all the senses than the Grand Street richness I knew.

And the spick-and-span cleanliness of these people! It smelled from them, the soap and the bathing. Their fingernails so white and pink. Their hands and necks white like milk. I wondered how did those girls get their hair so soft, so shiny, and so smooth about their heads. Even their black shoes had a clean look.

15 Never had I seen men so all shaved up with pink, clean skins. The richest store-keepers in Grand Street shined themselves up with diamonds like walking jewellery stores, but they weren't so hollering clean as these men. And they all had their hair clipped so short; they all had a shape to their heads. So ironed out smooth and even they looked in their spotless, creaseless clothes, as if the dirty battle of life had never yet been on them.

I looked at these children of joy with a million eyes. I looked at them with my hands, my feet, with the thinnest nerves of my hair. By all their differences from me, their youth, their shiny freshness, their carefreeness, they pulled me out of my senses to them. And they didn't even know I was there.

I thought once I got into the classes with them, they'd see me and we'd get to know one another. What a sharp awakening came with my first hour!

As I entered the classroom, I saw young men and girls laughing and talking to one another without introductions. I looked for my seat. Then I noticed, up in front, a very earnest-faced young man with thick glasses over his sad eyes. He made me think of Morris Lipkin, so I chose my seat next to him.

"What's the name of the professor?" I asked.

20 "Smith," came from his tight lips. He did not even look at me. He pulled himself together and began busily writing, to show me he didn't want to be interrupted.

I turned to the girl on my other side. What a fresh, clean beauty! A creature of sunshine. And clothes that matched her radiant youth.

"Is this the freshman class in geometry?" I asked her.

She nodded politely and smiled. But how quickly her eyes sized me up! It was not an unkind glance. And yet, it said more plainly than words, "From where do you come? How did you get in here?"

Sitting side by side with them through the whole hour, I felt stranger to them than if I had passed them in Hester Street. Wasn't there some secret something that would open us toward one another?

25 In one class after another, I kept asking myself, "What's the matter with me? Why do they look at me so when I talk with them?"

Maybe I'd have to change myself inside and out to be one of them. But how?

The lectures were over at four o'clock. With a sigh, I turned from the college building, away from the pleasant streets, down to the shabby back alley near the post office, and entered the George Martin Hand Laundry.

Mr. Martin was a fat, easy-going, good-natured man. I no sooner told him of my experience in New York than he took me on at once as an ironer at fifty cents an hour, and he told me he had work for as many hours a day as I could put in.

I felt if I could only look a little bit like other girls on the outside, maybe I could get in with them. And that meant money! And money meant work, work, work!

Till eleven o'clock that night, I ironed fancy white shirtwaists. 30

"You're some busy little worker, even if I do say so," said Mr. Martin, good-naturedly. "But I must lock up. You can't live here."

I went home, aching in every bone. And in the quiet and good air, I so overslept that I was late for my first class. To make matters worse, I found a note in my mailbox that puzzled and frightened me. It said, "Please report at once to the dean's office to explain your absence from Physical Education I, at four o'clock."

A line of other students was waiting there. When my turn came I asked the secretary, "What's this physical education business?"

"This is a compulsory course," he said. "You cannot get credit in any other course unless you satisfy this requirement."

At the hour when I had intended to go back to Martin's Laundry, I 35 entered the big gymnasium. There were a crowd of girls dressed in funny short black bloomers and rubber-soled shoes.

The teacher blew the whistle and called harshly, "Students are expected to report in their uniforms."

"I have none."

"They're to be obtained at the bookstore," she said, with a stern look at me. "Please do not report again without it."

I stood there dumb.

"Well, stay for to-day and exercise as you are," said the teacher, taking 40 pity on me.

She pointed out my place in the line, where I had to stand with the rest like a lot of wooden soldiers. She made us twist ourselves around here and there, "Right face!" "Left face!" "Right about face!" I tried to do as the others did, but I felt like a jumping-jack being pulled this way and that way. I picked up dumbbells and pushed them up and down and sideways until my arms were lame. Then she made us hop around like a lot of monkeys.

At the end of the hour, I was so out of breath that I sank down, my heart pounding against my ribs. I was dripping with sweat worse than Saturday night in the steam laundry. What's all this physical education nonsense? I came to college to learn something, to get an education with my head, and not monkeyshines with my arms and legs.

I went over to the instructor. "How much an hour do we get for this work?" I asked her, bitterly.

She looked at me with a stupid stare. "This is a two-point course."

Now I got real mad. "I've got to sweat my life away enough only to earn 45 a living," I cried. "God knows I exercised enough, since I was a kid——"

"You properly exercised?" She looked at me from head to foot. "Your posture is bad. Your shoulders sag. You need additional corrective exercises outside the class."

More tired than ever, I came to the class next day. After the dumbbells, she made me jump over the hurdles. For the life of me, I couldn't do it. I bumped myself and scratched my knees on the top bar of the hurdle, knocking it over with a great clatter. They all laughed except the teacher.

"Repeat the exercise, please," she said, with a frozen face.

I was all bruises, trying to do it. And they were holding their sides with laughter. I was their clown, and this was their circus. And suddenly, I got so wild with rage that I seized the hurdle and right before their eyes I smashed it to pieces.

The whole gymnasium went still as death. 50

The teacher's face was white. "Report at once to the dean."

The scared look on the faces of the girls made me feel that I was to be locked up or fired.

For a minute when I entered the dean's grand office, I was so confused I couldn't even see.

He rose and pointed to a chair beside his desk. "What can I do for you?" he asked, in a voice that quieted me as he spoke.

I told him how mad I was, to have piled on me jumping hurdles when I 55 was so tired anyway. He regarded me with that cooling steadiness of his. When I was through, he walked to the window and I waited, miserable. Finally he turned to me again, and with a smile! "I'm quite certain that physical education is not essential in your case. I will excuse you from attending the course."

After this things went better with me. In spite of the hard work in the laundry, I managed to get along in my classes. More and more interesting became the life of the college as I watched it from the outside.

What a feast of happenings each day of college was to those other students. Societies, dances, letters from home, packages of food, midnight spreads and even birthday parties. I never knew that there were people glad enough of life to celebrate the day they were born. I watched the gay goings-on around me like one coming to a feast, but always standing back and only looking on.

▼ ▼ ▼

Never before or since in all my life had I worked as hard as during that first term. I was not only earning a living and getting an education, I was trying to break into this new college world.

Every week, I saved a bit more for a little something in my appearance—a brush for the hair, a pair of gloves, a pair of shoes with stockings to match. And now I began to work still longer hours to save up for a plain felt hat like those college girls wore. And the result of my wanting to dress up was that I was too tired to master my hardest subject. In January, the blow fell. On the bulletin board, where everybody could see, my name was posted as failing in geometry. It meant taking the course all over again. And something still worse. Two weeks later, the bursar sent me a bill for the same old geometry course.

I hurried to his office and pushed myself in ahead of the line of waiting 60 students. "I want my money back for the geometry course that you didn't teach me," I cried. "I paid to learn, not to fail."

The man gaped at me for a moment as if I had gone mad and then paid no more attention to me. His indifference got me into such a rage that I could have broken through the cage and shaken him. But I remembered the smashed hurdle and the kind dean. With an effort, I got hold of myself and went to this more understanding man.

"I didn't smash any hurdles, but I'm ready to smash the world. Why should I pay the college for something I didn't get?" And then I told him how they wanted to cheat me.

This time, even the dean did not understand. And I had no new hat that winter.

I flung myself into the next term's work with a fierce determination to wring the last drop of knowledge from each course. At first, psychology was like Greek to me. So many words about words. "Apperception," "reflex arc," "inhibitions." What had all that fancy book language to do with the real, plain every day?

65 Then, one day, Mr. Edman said to the class: "Give an example from your own experience showing how anger or any strong emotion interferes with your thinking?"

Suddenly, it dawned on me. I jumped to my feet with excitement. I told him about Zalmon the fish-peddler. Once I saw him get so mad at a woman for wanting to bargain down a penny on a pound of fish that in his anger he threw a dollar's worth of change at her.

In a flash, so many sleeping things in my life woke up in me. I remembered the time I was so crazy for Morris Lipkin. How I had poured out all my feelings without sense. That whole picture of my first mad love sprang before my eyes like a new revelation, and I cried, "No wonder they say, 'All lovers are fools'!"

Everybody laughed. But my anger did not get the better of me now. I had learned self-control. I was now a person of reason.

From that day on, the words of psychology were full of living wonder. In a few weeks I was ahead of any one else in the class. I saw the students around me as so many pink-faced children who never had had to live yet. I realized that the time when I sold herring in Hester Street, I was learning life more than if I had gone to school.

70 The fight with Father to break away from home, the fight in the cafeteria for a piece of meat—when I went through those experiences I thought them privations and losses; now I saw them treasure chests of insight. What countless riches lay buried under the ground of those early years that I had thought so black, so barren, so thwarted with want!

Before long, I had finished the whole textbook of psychology.

"I'm through with the book," I said to Mr. Edman. "Please give me more work. I've got to keep my head going."

He gave me a list of references. And I was so excited with the first new book that I stayed up half the night reading it on and on. I could hardly wait for the class to show Mr. Edman all I had learned. After the lecture, I hastened to his desk.

"I'm all ready to recite on this new book," I cried, as I handed it to him.

75 "Recite?" He looked puzzled.

"Ask me any questions. See only how much I've just learned."

"I'm late to a class right now. I'm busy with lectures all day long."

"If you're busy all day, I'll come to you in the evening. Where do you live?"

He drew back and stared at me. "I'm glad to tell you what to read," he said, stiffly. "But I have no time for recitations outside of class hours. I'm too busy."

God! How his indifference cut me! "Too busy!" The miser. Here I come to him hungry, starving—come begging for one little crumb of knowledge! And he has it all—and yet pushes me back with, "I'm too busy!" 80

How I dreamed of college! The inspired companionship of teachers who are friends! The high places above the earth, where minds are fired by minds. And what's this place I've come to? Was the college only a factory, and the teachers machines turning out lectures by the hour on wooden dummies, incapable of response? Was there no time for the flash from eye to eye, from heart to heart? Was that vanishing spark of light that flies away quicker than it came unless it is given life at the moment by the kindling breath of another mind—was that to be shoved aside with, "I'm too busy. I have no time for recitations outside class hours"?

A few days later, I saw Mr. Edman coming out hurriedly from Philosophy Hall. Oh, if I could only ask him about that fear inhibition I had read about. How it would clear my mind to talk it over with him for only a minute. But he'd maybe be too busy to even glance at me.

"How do you do, Miss Smolinsky!" He smiled and stopped as he saw me. "How are you getting on with those references I gave you?"

My whole heart leaped up in gratitude. "Oh, perhaps I bothered you too much."

"No bother at all. I only wish I had more time." 85

That very evening I overheard two tired-looking instructors in the college cafeteria.

"Maybe I was a fool to take this job. No sweatshop labour is so underpaid as the college instructor."

"How do they expect us to live? I get a thousand dollars a year and I teach sixteen periods a week."

"And look at Edman. He teaches eighteen periods and his pay is no more than ours."

So that was it! And I had thought I hated Mr. Edman for being so aloof, so stingy with his time. Now I understood how overworked and overdriven he was. How much he had taught me in that one little class! What a marvellous teacher he was! *Ach!* If one could only meet such a man outside of class, how the whole world would open up and shine with light! 90

Summer came. And when the others went home for their vacation I found a canning factory near the town. And all summer I worked, stringing beans, shelling peas, pulling berries. I worked as long hours as in the New York laundry. But here, it was in sheds full of air.

And as I worked, I thought of Mr. Edman and all he had taught me. His course in psychology had opened to me a new world of reason and "objectivity." Through him, I had learned to think logically for the first time in my life.

Till now, I lived only by blind instinct and feeling. I might have remained for ever an over-emotional lunatic. This wider understanding of life, this new power of logic and reason I owe to Mr. Edman.

▼ ▼ ▼

The senior year came, and with it a great event. The biggest newspaper owner of the town, who was a rich alumnus of the college, offered a prize of a thousand dollars for the best essay on "What the College Has Done for Me." Everybody was talking about it, students, instructors, and professors.

What had the college done for me? I thought of the time when I first came here. How I was thrilled out of my senses by the mere sight of plain, clean people. The smashed hurdle in the gymnasium. The way I dashed into the bursar's office demanding money for my failed geometry. Yes. Perhaps more than all the others, I had something to write about. Maybe they wouldn't understand. But if truth was what they wanted—here they had it. I poured it out as it came from my heart, and sent it in. Then I had to put it out of my mind because I was so buried deep in my examinations. Everything was forgotten in this last fight to win my diploma. 95

It was Commencement Day at last. Glad but downhearted I was—glad because I'd won, but so sad I was to leave the battlefield! The thing I had dreamed about for so many years—and now it was over! Where I was going now, will I be able to find these real American people again—that draw me so?

With all the students and professors, I sat in the big assembly room and listened to the long speeches that seemed never to end.

At last a man came up to announce the winner of the contest. "The student," he said, "whose essay the judges found the best is a young lady. Her name is——" God in the world! Who? Who was it? They were clapping to beat the band. I only heard him say, "Will she please come forward to the platform?"

I heard the clapping louder and louder. Then I saw they were all looking at me. "Sara Smolinsky, it's you. It's you! Don't you hear? They're calling for you."

How my paralyzed feet ever got me to the platform, I don't know. So exciting it was! It was I, myself, standing there before that sea of faces! 100

The man handed me an envelope and said things that flew over my head. How could I have the sense to hear or think to say something?

Then all the students rose to their feet, cheering and waving and calling my name, like a triumph, "Sara Smolinsky—Sara Smolinsky!"

DISCUSSING THE TEXT

1. How does Sara perceive the college town on her arrival there? How does it differ from the world of the city she has left behind?
2. Why does Sara feel self-conscious when she meets the other college students? How does she "read" clothing styles as signs of class and personality? What experiences have you had in trying to read, or understand, people through their styles of dress? How accurate have your readings been?

3. Why does Sara get along better with older faculty members than with younger teachers and other students? Have you ever had a similar experience?
4. Yezierska implicitly contrasts the world of Martin's Laundry with the world of the college physical education class. What is the point of the comparison, as she develops it?

WRITING ABOUT THE TEXT

5. Although Sara is trying to break away from her home life and her past, she discovers in a psychology class that her past experiences can be put to use. Write a paragraph analyzing the ways in which Sara's memory of Zalmon the fish-peddler (par. 66) serves her education.
6. Write an essay on your own expectations when you arrived at college, and how the reality of what you found compared with the world you'd left behind. Then write a page comparing your experiences with Sara Smolinsky's. Consider Sara's reactions to the other students and to her teachers, her experiences with the physical education class and the failed geometry class, her financial worries, and her life before coming to college. How have your experiences been like hers? How have they been different?
7. For the young Yezierska, assimilation into mainstream American society through education was a major goal. Think of yourself as a fellow student of Yezierska's, and write a fictional summary of her essay, "What the College Has Done for Me" (par. 94).

ZORA NEALE HURSTON

School Again

Zora Neale Hurston (1901–1960) came of age as a writer during the Harlem Renaissance of the 1920s, a period of great vitality in African American arts, writing, popular music, and dance. She immediately became one of its most celebrated and controversial stars. The story Hurston tells in her autobiography, Dust Tracks on a Road, *begins with her family in Eatonville, Florida, where she grew up. Because Eatonville was a black town, as a child Hurston saw herself as belonging to the majority culture. That her father was an influential figure and a preacher in the town contributed further to this view. But Hurston's happy childhood was interrupted when, at thirteen, she was asked to care for her brother's children. A few years later she joined a theatrical troupe as wardrobe girl, and subsequently completed her high school degree in Baltimore.*

While still in college, Hurston won early critical acclaim with her first short stories in the 1920s. But her 1937 masterpiece, the novel Their Eyes Were Watching

God, *was judged by some at the time as not political enough, or as pandering to a white audience. Hurston was always careful to distinguish her own pride in her black cultural background from that of the so-called protest writers (such as Richard Wright), who concentrated on the deplorable conditions of African Americans in a racist society. To Hurston these writers were the "sobbing school of Negrohood who hold that nature somehow has given them a lowdown dirty deal." She wrote that she was "too busy sharpening my oyster knife" to weep over the sad state of the world.*

After peaking in the 1930s, Hurston's reputation and her career went into a slow decline, ending with her sad death and burial in an unmarked grave in Florida. Yet Hurston's great gift for comedy, her unique feminist sensibility, and the universality of her themes have made her, since the 1970s, one of the great rediscovered American writers of the twentieth century. As such, she has been a strong influence on writers such as Alice Walker, Toni Morrison, Toni Cade Bambara, and many others.

"School Again" is a chapter from Dust Tracks on a Road *recounting two stories about Hurston's social and intellectual growth. One story is about her move from a rural background into the elite cultural circles of the African American aristocracy. The other is of her crossing from the black world to the white world as she enters Barnard College (part of Columbia University), where she studied anthropology and folklore under the most prominent anthropologist of the period, Franz Boas. Significantly, in all of her work—as a fiction writer, a playwright, a theater producer, and an anthropologist collecting materials on African American folklore—Hurston maintained her connection with the rural countrysides of the American South. She drew on the South's vernacular language, its stories and characters, its practicality, and its informal poetry in all of her work.*

Back, out walking on fly-paper again. Money was what I needed to get back in school. I could have saved a lot of money if I had received it. But theatrical salaries being so uncertain, I did not get mine half the time. I had it when I had it, but when it was not paid I never worried. But now I needed it. Miss M———was having her troubles, trying to help her folks she informed me by mail, so I never directly asked her for anything more. I had no resentment, either. It had all been very pleasant.

I tried waiting on table, and made a good waitress when my mind was on it, which was not often. I resented being patronized, more than the monotony of the job; those presumptuous cut-eye looks and supposed-to-be accidental touches on the thigh to see how I took to things. Men at the old game of "stealing a feel." People who paid for a quarter meal, left me a nickel tip, and then stood outside the door and nodded their heads for me to follow on and hear the rest of the story. But I was lacking in curiosity. I was not worrying so much about virtue. The thing just did not call me. There was neither the beauty of love, nor material advantage in it for me. After all, what is the use in having swine without pearls? Some educated men sat and talked about the things I was interested in, but if I seemed to listen, looked at me as much to say, "What would that mean to you?"

Then in the midst of other difficulties, I had to get sick. Not a sensible sickness for poor folks to have. No, I must get down with appendicitis and have to have an operation right away. So it was the free ward of the Maryland General Hospital for me.

▼ ▼ ▼

How then did I get back to school? I just went. I got tired of trying to get the money to go. My clothes were practically gone. Nickeling and dimering along was not getting me anywhere. So I went to the night high school in Baltimore and that did something for my soul.

There I met the man who was to give me the key to certain things. In English, I was under Dwight O. W. Holmes. There is no more dynamic teacher anywhere under any skin. He radiates newness and nerve and says to your mind, "There is something wonderful to behold just ahead. Let's go see what it is." He is a pilgrim to the horizon. Anyway, that is the way he struck me. He made the way clear. Something about his face killed the drabness and discouragement in me. I felt that the thing could be done. 5

I turned in written work and answered questions like everybody else, but he took no notice of me particularly until one night in the study of English poets he read Kubla Khan.[1] You must get him to read it for you sometime. He is not a pretty man, but he has the face of a scholar, not dry and set like, but fire flashes from his deep-set eyes. His high-bridged, but sort of bent nose over his thin-lipped mouth . . . well, the whole thing reminds you of some old Roman like Cicero, Caesar or Virgil in tan skin.

That night, he liquefied the immortal brains of Coleridge, and let the fountain flow. I do not know whether something in my attitude attracted his attention, or whether what I had done previously made him direct the stream at me. Certainly every time he lifted his eyes from the page, he looked right into my eyes. It did not make me see him particularly, but it made me see the poem. That night seemed queer, but I am so visual-minded that all the other senses induced pictures in me. Listening to Coleridge's poem for the first time, I saw all that the writer had meant for me to see with him, and infinite cosmic things besides. I was not of the work-a-day world for days after Mr. Holmes's voice had ceased.

This was my world, I said to myself, and I shall be in it, and surrounded by it, if it is the last thing I do on God's green dirt-ball.

But he did something more positive than that. He stopped me after class and complimented me on my work. He did something else. He never asked me anything about myself, but he looked at me and toned his voice in such a way that I felt he knew all about me. His whole manner said, "No matter about the difficulties past and present, step on it!"

I went back to class only twice after that. I did not say a word to him about my resolve. But the next week, I went out to Morgan College to register in the high-school department. 10

---

[1]*Kubla Kahn:* a poem (1816) by S. T. Coleridge (*Ed.*)

William Pickens, a Negro, was the Dean there, and he fooled me too. I was prepared to be all scared of him and his kind. I had no money and no family to refer to. I just went and he talked to me. He gave me a brief examination and gave me credit for two years' work in high school and assigned me to class. He was just as understanding as Dwight Holmes in a way.

Knowing that I had no money, he evidently spoke to his wife, because she sent for me a few days later and told me enthusiastically that she had a job for me that would enable me to stay in school. Dr. Baldwin, a white clergyman, and one of the trustees of Morgan, had a wife with a broken hip. He wanted a girl to stay at the house, help her dress in the morning, undress at night and generally look after her. There was no need for anyone except in the morning and at night. He would give me a home and two dollars a week. The way Mrs. Pickens described the work to me, I could tell she knew I would be glad to accept the job, and I was.

So I went to live with the Baldwins. The family consisted of the Minister, his wife and his daughter, Miss Maria, who seemed to be in her thirties and unmarried.

They had a great library, and I waded in. I acted as if the books would run away. I remember committing to memory, overnight—lest I never get a chance to read it again—Gray's Elegy in a Country Churchyard. Next I learned the Ballad of Reading Gaol and started on the Rubaiyat.[2]

15 It would be dramatic in a Cinderella way if I were to say that the well-dressed students at school snubbed me and shoved me around, but that I studied hard and triumphed over them. I did study hard because I realized that I was three years behind schedule, and then again study has never been hard to me. Then too, I had hundreds of books under my skin already. Not selected reading, all of it. Some of it could be called trashy. I had been through Nick Carter, Horatio Alger, Bertha M. Clay[3] and the whole slew of dime novelists in addition to some really constructive reading. I do not regret the trash. It has harmed me in no way. It was a help, because acquiring the reading habit early is the important thing. Taste and natural development will take care of the rest later on.

▼ ▼ ▼

When it came time to consider college, I planned to stay on at Morgan. But that was changed by chance. Mae Miller, daughter of the well-known

---

[2]*Gray's Elegy . . . Rubaiyat: Elegy in a Country Churchyard* (1750), poem by Thomas Gray; *Ballad of Reading Gaol* (1898), poem by Oscar Wilde; *Rubaiyat of Omar Khayyam* (1859–1879), poem in quatrains by Edward Fitzgerald (*Ed.*)

[3]*Nick Carter . . . Bertha M. Clay:* Nick Carter, popular fiction detective hero created by John Coryell in 1870; Horatio Alger (1832–1899), author of numerous popular juvenile stories about young boys who become successful through luck and pluck; Bertha M. Clay, pen name of English novelist Charlotte Monica Braeme (1836–1884), who wrote sentimental, melodramatic tales (*Ed.*)

Dr. Kelly Miller of Howard University, came over to Morgan to spend the week-end with her first cousins, Bernice and Gwendolyn Hughes. So we were thrown together. After a few hours of fun and capers, she said, "Zora, you are Howard material. Why don't you come to Howard?"

Now as everyone knows, Howard University is the capstone of Negro education in the world. There gather Negro money, beauty, and prestige. It is to the Negro what Harvard is to the whites. They say the same thing about a Howard man that they do about Harvard—you can tell a Howard man as far as you can see him, but you can't tell him much. He listens to the doings of other Negro schools and their graduates with bored tolerance. Not only is the scholastic rating at Howard high, but tea is poured in the manner!

I had heard all about the swank fraternities and sororities and the clothes and everything, and I knew I could never make it. I told Mae that.

"You can come and live at our house, Zora," Bernice offered. At the time, her parents were living in Washington, and Bernice and Gwendolyn were in the boarding department at Morgan. "I'll ask Mama the next time she comes over. Then you won't have any room and board to pay. We'll all get together and rustle you up a job to make your tuition."

So that summer I moved on to Washington and got a job. First, as a waitress in the exclusive Cosmos Club downtown, and later as a manicurist in the G Street shop of Mr. George Robinson. He is a Negro who has a chain of white barber shops in downtown Washington. I managed to scrape together money for my first quarter's tuition, and went up to register.

Lo and behold, there was Dwight Holmes sitting up there at Howard! He saved my spirits again. I was short of money, and Morgan did not have the class-A rating that it now has. There was trouble for me and I was just about to give up and call it a day when I had a talk with Dwight Holmes. He encouraged me all he could, and so I stuck and made up all of those hours I needed.

I shall never forget my first college assembly, sitting there in the chapel of that great university. I was so exalted that I said to the spirit of Howard, "You have taken me in. I am a tiny bit of your greatness. I swear to you that I shall never make you ashamed of me."

It did not wear off. Every time I sat there as part and parcel of things, looking up there at the platform crowded with faculty members, the music, the hundreds of students about me, it would come down on me again. When on Mondays we ended the service by singing Alma Mater, I felt just as if it were the Star Spangled Banner:

Reared against the eastern sky
Proudly there on hill-top high
Up above the lake so blue
Stands Old Howard brave and true.
There she stands for truth and right,
Sending forth her rays of light,
Clad in robes of majesty
Old Howard! We sing of thee.

My soul stood on tiptoe and stretched up to take in all that it meant. So I was careful to do my classwork and be worthy to stand there under the shadow of the hovering spirit of Howard. I felt the ladder under my feet.

Mr. Robinson arranged for me to come to work at 3:30 every afternoon [25] and work until 8:30. In that way, I was able to support myself. Soon, most of the customers knew I was a student, and tipped me accordingly. I averaged twelve to fifteen dollars a week.

Mr. Robinson's 1410 G Street shop was frequented by bankers, Senators, Cabinet Members, Congressmen, and gentlemen of the Press. The National Press Club was one block down the same street, the Treasury Building was one block up the street and the White House not far away.

I learned things from holding the hands of men like that. The talk was of world affairs, national happenings, personalities, the latest quips from the cloakrooms of Congress and such things. I heard many things from the White House and the Senate before they appeared in print. They probably were bursting to talk to somebody, and I was safe. If I told, nobody would have believed me anyway. Besides, I was much flattered by being told and warned not to repeat what I had heard. Sometimes a Senator, a banker, a newspaper correspondent attached to the White House would all be sitting around my table at one time. While I worked on one, the others waited, and they all talked. Sometimes they concentrated on teasing me. At other times they talked about what had happened, or what they reasoned was bound to happen. Intimate stories about personalities, their secret love affairs, cloakroom retorts, and the like. Soon they took me for granted and would say, "Zora knows how to keep a secret. She's all right." Now, I know that my discretion really didn't matter. They were relieving their pent-up feelings where it could do no harm.

Some of them meant more to me than others because they paid me more attention. Frederick William Wile, White House correspondent, used to talk to me at times quite seriously about life and opportunities and things like that. He had seen three presidents come and go. He had traveled with them, to say nothing of his other traveling to and fro upon the earth. He had read extensively. Sometimes he would be full of stories and cracks, but at other times he would talk to me quite seriously about attitudes, points of view, why one man was great and another a mere facile politician, and so on.

▼ ▼ ▼

An incident happened that made me realize how theories go by the board when a person's livelihood is threatened. A man, a Negro, came into the shop one afternoon and sank down in Banks's chair. Banks was the manager and had the first chair by the door. It was so surprising that for a minute Banks just looked at him and never said a word. Finally, he found his tongue and asked, "What do you want?"

"Hair-cut and shave," the man said belligerently. [30]

"But you can't get no hair-cut and shave here. Mr. Robinson has a fine shop for Negroes on U Street near Fifteenth," Banks told him.

"I know it, but I want one here. The Constitution of the United States—"

But by that time, Banks had him by the arm. Not roughly, but he was helping him out of his chair, nevertheless.

"I don't know how to cut your hair," Banks objected. "I was trained on straight hair. Nobody in here knows how."

"Oh, don't hand me that stuff!" the crusader snarled. "Don't be such an Uncle Tom." 35

"Run on, fellow. You can't get waited on in here."

"I'll stay right here until I do. I know my rights. Things like this have got to be broken up. I'll get waited on all right, or sue the place."

"Go ahead and sue," Banks retorted. "Go on uptown, and get your hair cut, man. Don't be so hardheaded for nothing."

"I'm getting waited on right here!"

"You're next, Mr. Powell," Banks said to a waiting customer. "Sorry, mister, but you better go on uptown." 40

"But I have a right to be waited on wherever I please," the Negro said, and started towards Updyke's chair which was being emptied. Updyke whirled his chair around so that he could not sit down and stepped in front of it. "Don't you touch *my* chair!" Updyke glared. "Go on about your business."

But instead of going, he made to get into the chair by force.

"Don't argue with him! Throw him out of here!" somebody in the back cried. And in a minute, barbers, customers all lathered and hair half cut, and porters, were all helping to throw the Negro out.

The rush carried him way out into the middle of G Street and flung him down. He tried to lie there and be a martyr, but the roar of oncoming cars made him jump up and scurry off. We never heard any more about it. I did not participate in the mêlée, but I wanted him thrown out, too. My business was threatened.

It was only that night in bed that I analyzed the whole thing and realized that I was giving sanction to Jim Crow,[4] which theoretically, I was supposed to resist. But here were ten Negro barbers, three porters and two manicurists all stirred up at the threat of our living through loss of patronage. Nobody thought it out at the moment. It was an instinctive thing. That was the first time it was called to my attention that self-interest rides over all sorts of lines. I have seen the same thing happen hundreds of times since, and now I understand it. One sees it breaking over racial, national, religious and class lines, Anglo-Saxon against Anglo-Saxon, Jew against Jew, Negro against Negro, and all sorts of combinations of the three against other combinations of the three. Offhand, you might say that we fifteen Negroes should have felt the racial thing and served him. He was one of us. Perhaps it would have been a beautiful thing if Banks had turned to the shop crowded with customers and announced that this man was going to be served like everybody else even at the 45

[4]*Jim Crow:* laws that enforced segregation in the South following Reconstruction (*Ed.*)

risk of losing their patronage, with all of the other employees lined up in the center of the floor shouting, "So say we all!" It would have been a stirring gesture, and made the headlines for a day. Then we could all have gone home to our unpaid rents and bills and things like that. I could leave school and begin my wanderings again. The "militant" Negro who would have been the cause of it all, would have perched on the smuddled-up wreck of things and crowed. Nobody ever found out who or what he was. Perhaps he did what he did on the spur of the moment, not realizing that serving him would have ruined Mr. Robinson, another Negro who had got what he had the hard way. For not only would the G Street shop have been forced to close, but the F Street shop and all of his other six downtown shops. Wrecking George Robinson like that on a "race" angle would have been ironic tragedy. He always helped out any Negro who was trying to do anything progressive as far as he was able. He had no education himself, but he was for it. He would give any Howard University student a job in his shops if they could qualify, even if it was only a few hours a week.

▼ ▼ ▼

All in all, I did a year and a half of work at Howard University. I would have done the two full years, but I was out on account of illness, and by the time that was over, I did not have the money for my tuition.

I joined the Zeta Phi Beta Sorority, took part in all the literary activities on the campus, and made The Stylus, the small literary society on the hill. I named the student paper *The Hill Top.* The Stylus was limited to nineteen members, two of them being faculty members. Dr. Alain Leroy Locke was the presiding genius and we had very interesting meetings.

My joining The Stylus influenced my later moves. On account of a short story which I wrote for The Stylus, Charles S. Johnson, who was just then founding *Opportunity Magazine,* wrote to me for material. He explained that he was writing to all of the Negro colleges with the idea of introducing new writers and new material to the public. I sent on *Drenched in Light* and he published it. Later, he published my second story *Spunk.* He wrote me a kind letter and said something about New York. So, beginning to feel the urge to write, I wanted to be in New York.

This move on the part of Dr. Johnson was the root of the so-called Negro Renaissance. It was his work, and only his hush-mouth nature has caused it to be attributed to many others. The success of *Opportunity* Award dinners was news. Later on, the best of this material was collected in a book called *The New Negro* and edited by Dr. Alain Locke, but it was the same material, for the most part, gathered and published by Dr. Charles Spurgeon Johnson, now of the Department of Social Sciences, Fisk University, Nashville.

Being out of school for lack of funds, and wanting to be in New York, I decided to go there and try to get back in school in that city. So the first week of January, 1925, found me in New York with $1.50, no job, no friends, and a lot of hope.

The Charles Johnsons befriended me as best they could. I could always find something to eat out at their house. Mrs. Johnson would give me carfare and encouragement. I came to worship them really.

So I came to New York through *Opportunity*, and through *Opportunity* to Barnard. I won a prize for a short story at the first Award dinner, May 1, 1925, and Fannie Hurst offered me a job as her secretary, and Annie Nathan Meyer offered to get me a scholarship to Barnard. My record was good enough, and I entered Barnard in the fall, graduating in 1928.

I have no lurid tales to tell of race discrimination at Barnard. I made a few friends in the first few days. Eleanor Beer, who lived on the next chair to me in Economics, was the first. She was a New York girl with a sumptuous home down in West 71st Street, near the Hudson. She invited me down often, and her mother set out to brush me up on good manners. I learned a lot of things from them. They were well traveled and cosmopolitan. I found out about forks, who entered a room first, sat down first, and who offered to shake hands. A great deal more of material like that. These people are still lying very close to my heart. I was invited to Eleanor's wedding when she married Enzo de Chetalat, a Swiss mining engineer, but I was down in Florida at the time. So I sent her a hat-box full of orange blossoms for the occasion, so she could know how I felt.

The Social Register crowd at Barnard soon took me up, and I became Barnard's sacred black cow. If you had not had lunch with me, you had not shot from taw.[5] I was secretary to Fannie Hurst and living at her 67th Street duplex apartment, so things were going very well with me.

Because my work was top-heavy with English, Political Science, History and Geology, my adviser at Barnard recommended Fine Arts, Economics, and Anthropology for cultural reasons. I started in under Dr. Gladys Reichard, had a term paper called to the attention of Dr. Franz Boas and thereby gave up my dream of leaning over a desk and explaining Addison and Steele to the sprouting generations.

I began to treasure up the words of Dr. Reichard, Dr. Ruth Benedict, and Dr. Boas, the king of kings.

That man can make people work the hardest with just a look or a word, than anyone else in creation. He is idolized by everybody who takes his orders. We all call him Papa, too. One day, I burst into his office and asked for "Papa Franz" and his secretary gave me a look and told me I had better not let him hear me say that. Of course, I knew better, but at a social gathering of the Department of Anthropology at his house a few nights later, I brought it up.

"Of course, Zora is my daughter. Certainly!" he said with a smile. "Just one of my missteps, that's all." The sabre cut on his cheek, which it is said he got in a duel at Heidelberg, lifted in a smile.

---

[5]*shot from taw:* done the right or required thing, from game of marbles, where taw is the marble used as a shooter (*Ed.*)

Away from his office, Dr. Boas is full of youth and fun, and abhors dull, stodgy arguments. Get to the point is his idea. Don't raise a point which you cannot defend. He wants facts, not guesses, and he can pin you down so expertly that you soon lose the habit of talking all over your face. Either that, or you leave off Anthropology.

I had the same feeling at Barnard that I did at Howard, only more so. I felt that I was highly privileged and determined to make the most of it. I did not resolve to be a grind, however, to show the white folks that I had brains. I took it for granted that they knew that. Else, why was I at Barnard? Not everyone who cries, "Lord! Lord!" can enter those sacred iron gates. In her high scholastic standards, equipment, the quality of her student-body and graduates, Barnard has a right to the first line of Alma Mater. "Beside the waters of the Hudson, Our Alma Mater stands serene!" Dean Gildersleeve has that certain touch. We know there are women's colleges that are older, but not better ones. 60

So I set out to maintain a good average, take part in whatever went on, and just be a part of the college like everybody else. I graduated with a *B* record, and I am entirely satisfied.

Mrs. Meyer, who was the moving spirit in founding the college and who is still a trustee, did nobly by me in getting me in. No matter what I might do for her, I would still be in her debt.

Two weeks before I graduated from Barnard, Dr. Boas sent for me and told me that he had arranged a fellowship for me. I was to go south and collect Negro folklore. Shortly before that, I had been admitted to the American Folk-Lore Society. Later, while I was in the field, I was invited to become a member of the American Ethnological Society, and shortly after the American Anthropological Society.

Booker T. Washington[6] said once that you must not judge a man by the heights to which he has risen, but by the depths from which he came. So to me these honors meant something, insignificant as they might appear to the world. It was a long step for the waif of Eatonville. From the depth of my inner heart I appreciated the fact that the world had not been altogether unkind to Mama's child.

DISCUSSING THE TEXT

1. What was the importance to Hurston of her early reading of Coleridge's *Kubla Kahn* and other works of the great English poets? What other reading did Hurston do that influenced her intellectual development? Why do you think she did not mention African American writers?
2. For about a year and a half, Hurston attended Howard University, one of the most respected institutions in the United States. What does it symbolize

[6]*Booker T. Washington* (1856–1915): African American educator, author, and lecturer (*Ed.*)

for her? How would you compare her feelings about Howard with her feelings about Barnard College, from which she eventually graduated?

3. Hurston writes in a playful and often humorous way about crossing various borders in her educational life. Find several examples of Hurston's use of humor in this selection. Why do you think she chooses this style of writing? Do you find it effective? Why or why not?
4. As a student at Howard University in Washington, D.C., Hurston earned her tuition money by working as a manicurist at a barber shop for whites only, but staffed by blacks and owned by a black man, Mr. Robinson. In a group of four or five students, discuss Hurston's account of the eviction of the black man who demanded service from the barber shop (par. 29–44). What do you think about Hurston's reaction? How does she deal with the insights she has later that day as she reflects on the incident? How do you think you would have felt? Do you think she reaches a satisfying conclusion about the incident? Why or why not? Take notes as you work on this assignment, and be prepared to share your opinions with the class.

WRITING ABOUT THE TEXT

5. As she meditates about racial conflicts, Hurston asserts that "self-interest rides over all sorts of lines. . . . One sees it breaking over racial, national, religious and class lines, Anglo-Saxon against Anglo-Saxon, Jew against Jew, Negro against Negro, and all sorts of combinations of the three against other combinations of the three" (par. 45). Write a personal reaction to this statement.
6. Hurston offers a portrait of the influential anthropologist and teacher Franz Boas, from both a professional and a personal angle (par. 55–59). Using that as a model, write a portrait of someone you know (or have known in the past) in both a professional and a personal way, such as a teacher, doctor, or religious leader. Try to reveal different sides of this person's personality, and explain ways in which he or she has made a difference in the way you think about yourself and about the world.
7. In the voice of the young Hurston, write a fictional diary entry describing what you see as the most important event in your college career.
8. Both Anzia Yezierska and Zora Neale Hurston cross geographical, social, and ethnic borders when they go to college. Write a brief essay in which you compare and contrast their temperaments, their approaches to learning, and their social and intellectual experiences. Conclude by noting anything in their accounts that you can relate to your own experience.

JERRE MANGIONE

Growing Up Sicilian

A prominent Italian American writer of this century, Jerre Mangione was born in 1909 in Rochester, New York, into a family of Sicilian immigrants. His parents spoke only Sicilian and would not allow their children to speak English at home. As a child, Mangione experienced a sense of exclusion from the mainstream American community, and early on he developed a powerful ambition not only to learn English but also to become a writer. That ambition is the subject of this excerpt from his autobiographical memoir, An Ethnic at Large: A Memoir of America in the Thirties and Forties *(1983).*

Mangione has had a long and varied career as a professional writer, beginning with his work for Time *magazine in the early 1930s. He was national coordinating editor of the Federal Writers Project from 1934 to 1937, and he worked as a writer for various government agencies and advertising firms. In 1961 he began a second career as a college professor, serving as director of composition and of the creative writing program at the University of Pennsylvania during the 1970s. He has written many books, including* Mount Allegro *(1943), a novel;* The Dream and the Deal *(1972), a personal history of the Federal Writers Project of the Great Depression; and* La Storia *(1992), a massive history of the Italian American experience.*

In "Growing Up Sicilian," Mangione tells about his adventures with friends of different ethnicities as a child and adolescent during the 1920s, and his gradual awareness, as he moved from junior high to high school, that "it was possible to have friends who were not ethnics." Mangione gradually comes to see himself as an "American." The process of doing so involves breaking away from his supportive but also restrictive family, and crossing over into new geographical, social, and intellectual terrain as he leaves Rochester for Syracuse University.

Before my parents considered me old enough to go beyond the picket fence that separated me from the children on the street, I would peer through it for hours, longing to play with them and wondering what they could be saying to one another. Although I had been born in the same city as they, I spoke not their language. English was forbidden in our home—for reasons of love. Afraid of losing communication with their own flesh and blood, my parents, who spoke only Sicilian, insisted we speak their tongue, not the one foreign to them.

The feeling of being an outsider may have begun with that edict. Or it may have started when, finally allowed to go beyond the picket fence, I found myself among jeering strangers—the sons of Polish, German, and Russian Jewish immigrants who lived on the same block. Their loudest taunts were directed against my baptismal name of Gerlando, which they reduced to Jerry as soon as they had accepted me. From this action came the awareness of being doomed to lead a double life: the one I led among my drove of Sicilian relatives, the other in the street and at school.

There was also a third life, the one I lived with myself, which gradually was to dictate the secret resolve to break away from my relatives. It was largely based on para-Mitty[1] feats of the imagination that could easily transport me into agreeable realms far removed from the harsh realities of my everyday existence. (One winter I galloped over the snow-packed sidewalks of our neighborhood in the moonlight, believing I was a god disguised as a horse; in another season I kept rescuing my beautiful third-grade teacher from the flames about to consume her while she slept.) My fantasy life was well nourished by the piles of books I brought home from the public library, most of which I read clandestinely in the bathroom or under the bed since my mother believed that too much reading could drive a person insane.

As I tried to bridge the wide gap between my Sicilian and American lives, I became increasingly resentful of my relatives for being more foreign than anyone else. It irked me that I had not been born of English-speaking parents, and I cringed with embarrassment whenever my mother would scream at me in Sicilian from an upstairs window, threatening to kill me if I didn't come home that minute. If I rushed to obey her, it was not because I was frightened by her threat (there was nothing violent about her except the sound of her anger), but because I did not want my playmates to hear her Sicilian scream a second time.

5 My fondness for privacy, which my relatives considered a symptom of illness, added to my feelings of incompatibility. I was offended by their incessant need to be with one another. If they could have managed it, they would probably have all lived under the same roof. Only the families of my Jewish playmates approached their gregariousness, but they were recluses by comparison. My relatives were never at a loss for finding reasons for being together. In addition to parties for birthdays, weddings, anniversaries, and saint days, there were also parties when a child was baptized, when he was confirmed, and when he got a diploma. The arrival of another relative from Sicily or the opening of a new barrel of wine was still another pretext for another gathering of the clan.

▼ ▼ ▼

Convinced that our teachers made no effort to teach us the meaning of respect, my father distrusted American schools even more than the police. He held them responsible for promoting such shocking customs as that of boys and girls dating without a chaperone or young people marrying without their parents' consent. The American school system, for him, symbolized everything that outraged him about his adopted country. His diatribes on the subject were of such eloquence as to make us feel guilty for daring to like any of our teachers. Beneath his fury was the conviction that they were encouraging immorality, disrupting family life, and undermining his position as the head of his family.

---

[1]*para-Mitty:* dreamlike imaginings, like those of Walter Mitty, an average man who had many heroic fantasies, and a character in a story by James Thurber (1894–1961), "The Secret Life of Walter Mitty" (*Ed.*)

Like other Sicilian fathers, he never permitted his children to forget that they were living under a dictatorship, albeit, in his case, a loving one. In the eyes of his Sicilian peers, he was regarded as a maverick. He allowed his children to address their parents with the familiar *tu,* a concession rarely granted to children of Sicilians. And instead of spending his leisure time with his cronies drinking and playing cards, as was the habit of most Sicilian fathers, he preferred the company of his immediate family and would seldom go anywhere without them. He differed from the others in still another significant respect: despite his easily triggered hot temper, he never lifted a hand against his wife or his children.

Although he was of small stature, he conveyed the authority of a giant as he exhorted us to disregard the "nonsense" that the teachers stuffed into our skulls. Repeatedly we were reminded never to succumb to teachings that would cause us to disobey our parents. One evening, in a voice pregnant with moral significance, he read aloud to us the newspaper account of a Sicilian neighbor who had caught his daughter secretly dating an American; the neighbor had trailed the couple and, while they were kissing each other good night, pounced on the young man and bitten off part of his ear. "The teachers of that girl are to blame," my father told us, "for not teaching her to respect the wishes of a father."

Later, when my father discovered that his own daughter was seeing an American medical student on the sly, I expected a burst of temper that would badly scald my sister. But nothing of the kind happened. He simply asked her to invite the young man to the house. Then almost as soon as they were introduced, my father asked him point-blank whether he intended to marry his daughter. The bewildered young man paled and stuttered, trying to explain he was too young to think of marriage. In that case, my father told him, he was also too young to court his daughter. And that was the end of the romance.

10

As much as my father ranted against American schools, he and my mother yearned to send one of their sons to college, something which, they reminded each other, only the rich could afford to do in Sicily. Here it was not such an impossible dream. They chose me since I was the eldest and also because of my passion for reading, which they mistook for scholarly aptitude. I disappointed them at once by refusing to become either a doctor or a lawyer which, like most immigrants, they considered the only truly prestigious professions. Uncle Stefano urged that I become a pharmacist and presented me, on my next birthday, with an elaborate chemistry set. Because I was fond of him, I managed to show some interest in the possibility, but it literally went up in smoke when I almost set the house on fire while tinkering with hot test tubes.

▼ ▼ ▼

Not until I moved from junior high to high school did I become aware that it was possible to have friends who were not ethnics. The first of them were my Anglo-Saxon English teachers who, realizing with what intensity I concentrated on trying to master the language I was forbidden to speak at home, did whatever they could to encourage me. The chairman of the English department awarded me my first literary prize, a Baldwin apple from his own orchard which he presented with all the pomp befitting a Pulitzer. Accepting it in the same spirit, I could not persuade myself to eat the apple but kept it until it was fit for the garbage can.

Another of my English teachers, the faculty adviser of the high school weekly publication, made certain I joined its staff, with the result that I immediately fell into the company of a band of iconoclasts who called themselves the "Conceit Club." They reveled in their cynicism, bragged of their agnosticism, and shamelessly used the pages of the *Clarion* to flaunt their opinions. Twice the publication had been suspended by the high school principal, the first time for publishing a vitriolic editorial attacking the local Hearst newspaper, which was demanding the expulsion of some University of Rochester students who had formed an atheist club known as "The Damned Souls"; the second time for printing a review of a violin concert which likened the violinist's performance to "the squeaks of a dissipated rat."

At first I was wary of becoming closely associated with such reckless characters, afraid they might commit some indiscretion that would get all of us expelled. Yet once I discovered that the bond which held them together was the determination of each person in the group to become a published writer by the time he reached the age of twenty-one, nothing could keep me away from them. There were five of them: three Anglo-Saxons and two Jews, my old friend Mitch Rappaport and Jerry Joroslow, the editor in chief of the *Clarion,* who had come to the defense of "The Damned Souls."

Joroslow, the wittiest and most handsome member of the staff, had himself become an atheist. On one occasion he tried to prove to us, by means of differential calculus, that God could not possibly exist. When his explication went unchallenged, he dared each of us to rise and declare that if God existed, he strike him dead on the spot. His dare was laughed away when someone observed that if God existed, he would have had more sense than to permit the invention of anything as stupidly complicated as calculus. I was often out of my depth, but the excitement of their company prodded me into trying to win their favor. I launched a weekly column of literary and philosophic observations named "Fumes," and I found time to squeeze out pieces of fiction which I could present as evidence that I was worthy of their company. Nothing I did ever overcame the disdain of one of the Anglo-Saxons, but I became friends with the other two, especially Ed Havill, the most talented writer of the group.

▼ ▼ ▼

From the time I was thirteen I had been supplementing my father's meager wage with earnings from part-time jobs. I did not mind; the jobs were another means of exploring the American world. My first was ushering in a burlesque theater called The Family, for which I received five dollars a week and two free tickets. The money I gave to my mother, who was under the 15 impression I was employed as a cashier in a cigar store; the tickets went to my friends. I was too inexperienced to appreciate the off-color humor of the comedians who performed at The Family, but the chorus girls and their gyrations excited me and occupied a prominent place in my fantasy repertoire long after I quit the job.

▼ ▼ ▼

The only job I came to hate was digging ditches in the Eastman Kodak plant under the sadistic supervision of a foreman named Leary. I wanted to quit after the first excruciating day, but since it paid more than I had ever earned (thirty dollars a week), at a time when my parents were badly in debt, I felt compelled to stick it out. By some act of Providence, a few weeks later I contracted a severe case of poison ivy while clearing some land of its weeds. It laid me up for almost a month, but enabled me to leave the job with a clear conscience.

As soon as I recovered, I answered a classified advertisement for "young men with dancing ability" to perform in the musical *Sally,* which was being produced by the Lyceum Players, a local repertory company that starred professionals. Apparently my lack of self-assurance did not extend to my feet for I was promptly hired for the chorus line, and placed under the tutelage of George Cukor,[2] then a fledgling director. For the next two weeks Cukor, an impatient and demanding taskmaster, scolded and drilled his charges several times a day until he had whipped us into a synchronized team that could perform with enough precision to escape the brickbats of the local critics.

The role of Sally was played by a brunette named Dorothy Burgess, who seemed genuinely relieved on opening night that we could hoist her in the air with apparent ease. The featured male star was Louis Calhern, who drank incessantly but who, onstage, was the essence of controlled insouciance.

My sudden immersion in the theater generated such a state of euphoria in me as to arouse the fears of my mother, whose leaps of intuition never failed to astonish me. From the outset she disapproved of the job, claiming that theater people were a disreputable lot, not fit company for a seventeen-year-old. Why couldn't I find myself another busboy job instead where I would associate with "nice" people? But I sensed that her genuine fear, one which she was too prudent to voice, was that I might decide to become an actor or a dancer. To register her disapproval of any such notion, she refused to watch me perform, nor would she permit any other member of the family to do so.

There was, of course, some justification for her fear. A stage career struck me as an ideal means of escaping Rochester, and at the same time myself. Without considering whether or not I had acting talent, I was fascinated by the prospect of spending my life assuming a variety of roles that were anti- 20

[2]*George Cukor* (1899–1983): would become the well-known Hollywood director of *Dinner at Eight* (1933) and *A Star Is Born* (1954) (*Ed.*)

thetical to my private self, which I considered dangerously overburdened with Sicilian melancholy. I had no doubt that I was among the most melancholy of creatures, especially after the discovery that my paternal grandfather Gerlando, whose portrait my schoolmates often mistook for that of Edgar Allen Poe, had drowned himself in the Mediterranean one Christmas Eve when my father was still a child. I suspected that my grandfather's fate, which my father had twice tried to attain, could well become my own.

Acting, I reasoned, was a far less lonely activity than writing and could dispel my melancholy and possibly save me from myself. The idea gained momentum when the manager of the Lyceum Players hinted that he might be able to place me with a Broadway musical which was going into rehearsal in the fall. But after performing in three productions, once as an extra in a comedy starring Miriam Hopkins (*The Poor Nut*), I concluded that the stage was not for me. The prospect of enacting the same motions and words night after night struck me as dismal, far more conducive to self-destruction than a melancholy disposition. I wondered how any intelligent adult could endure the boredom of playing in a long-running production and pitied the lot of the actor for having to rely on the applause of strangers for his chief stimulus and reward. While writing was lonelier than acting, it offered a more enduring sense of achievement.

The decision came in the wake of an encounter with George Cukor who, on hearing I had recently completed a play, asked to see it. I sent him my one-act farce about a dentist and his patient, which was largely inspired by all the ordeals I had experienced in the hands of dentists from the age of fourteen when I mangled my front teeth while playing football on the street. Having been subjected to Cukor's imperial directorial style, I nervously awaited his verdict, expecting him to find me guilty for having committed an atrocity. Instead, much to my relief, he expressed enthusiasm for the quality of the dialogue, which reminded him of a Broadway comedy hit, *March Hares.* "I can't say much for the plot, but your dialogue is very amusing." After expressing surprise that I had never heard of *March Hares,* he advised me to read as much as possible, get a good liberal arts education, and get in touch with him after that. (For reasons beyond my ken, I never got in touch with Cukor.) He was only ten years older than I, but, listening to his advice, I felt as if Moses himself were dictating a special commandment for my exclusive benefit.

Cukor's encouragement came at the right time. That fall, as the newly elected head of the *Clarion,* I plunged into the editorship with great relish and unaccustomed self-confidence, radically changing the publication's format and the writing style, to resemble that of *Time,* the weekly I had been admiring ever since its inception a few years earlier. My boldness paid off. Within a few months, the *Clarion* was awarded a silver trophy for excellence at Cornell University's annual contest for high school publications. Even more exhilarating was the congratulatory letter from Henry R. Luce, one of the founders of *Time.* "Of course," wrote Luce, "the contents of your magazine make as much sense to us as *Time* would to a Hottentot. There is, however, a great difference: no Hottentot reads *Time;* about half of *Time's* editorial staff have now become ardent readers of the *Clarion.*" The letter concluded with the hope that he would see me "sometime in the near future."

In my state of bliss I interpreted the letter as a clear invitation to join the *Time* staff as quickly as possible. I promptly informed Luce that my services would be at his disposal in June on the day after I got my high school diploma, and then began reveling in the possibility of using *Time* as a convenient escape hatch from Rochester without incurring the expense and effort of a college education. The reply from *Time* dashed all such wishful thinking. There were no openings on the staff; however, since I seemed determined to be a professional journalist, I was advised to get a college education first.

That was more easily said than done; there were two obstacles immediately confronting me: a lack of tuition money and, what appeared to be more insurmountable, miserable grades in mathematics which precluded admission into the University of Rochester, the university my parents assumed I would be attending, if only for reasons of economy. The tuition I could acquire by working full time until I had saved enough money, but would my parents permit me to leave home for an out-of-town university that would admit me? 25

A good Sicilian son was expected to remain with his family; he left home only to be married; even then, he continued to live close by his parents. By leaving I would be violating a basic tenet of their philosophy. Yet to remain among my relatives, steeped in their past, was to deny myself the chance of finding out whether I could be an American without feeling like an impostor.

By now I had become all too aware that the wide gulf between my Sicilian and American worlds went beyond differences of custom and language. There was a basic difference of philosophy. Ingrained in the Sicilian soul by centuries of poverty and oppression were strong elements of fatalism which my relatives called *Destino.* In their minds *Destino,* the willingness to resign oneself to misfortune, was the key to survival; to refuse to believe that an almighty force predetermined the fate of all people was to court disaster.

In his thunderings against our teachers my father must have sensed that the philosophy they drummed into us was diametrically opposed to that of his people. There was nothing fatalistic about it; constantly our teachers talked of freedom, free enterprise, free will, and stressed the ability of the individual to change and improve his situation. My need to leave my relatives was buttressed by the conviction that my teachers must be right. Although at the age of eighteen I could sound as dogmatic as the Pope when I argued with my father, I could not let him know how radically our philosophies differed. Nor did I dare correct my mother's impression that since I could not be admitted to the local university, I would be applying to colleges within commuting distance.

The week after high school graduation I landed a full-time job at twenty dollars a week, dictating sales correspondence into the mouth of a dictaphone in behalf of the Samson Cutlery Company. "*Destino,*" said my mother who, prudently, believed in crediting Destiny with happy events as well as disasters. For six days a week, eight hours a day, I sang out the praises of Samson-produced stainless steel kitchen utensils. Whenever I tired of my false enthusiasm I would sneak downstairs to chat with the shipping clerk, who was an avid reader and a poet. Philip worked as a standup comic in small nightclubs on weekends and dreamed of getting into the big time. We were a comfort to each other. To no one else in the plant did I confide my plan for getting a college degree: quitting my post as soon as I had enough money for the first year's tuition, then financing the rest of my education with summer jobs and whatever part-time work I could pick up around a campus. On less optimistic days when I would observe how much easier it might be for me to develop a career in stainless steel, Philip, who was only five years older than I, would scold me with the earnestness of a concerned parent.

After nine months I had saved enough money and been admitted to Syracuse University, despite my weakness in mathematics, for the semester that started in February 1928. Not until I had dictated my last sales letter could I summon the courage to let my parents know that Syracuse was the nearest university that would admit me. To my surprise, neither of them objected. I had underestimated their love for me, their willingness to let me judge what was best for my future. My mother wept a little at the prospect of my leaving home; then, with her instinctive pragmatism and sense of tradition, made me promise I would take courses that would qualify me as a teacher, a profession she considered more honorable than that of a writer. Among our relatives she immediately began spreading the word that my heart was set on becoming a *professore*.

Except for my parents and my uncles Peppino and Stefano, my Sicilian relatives were disturbed that I had enrolled in an out-of-town university. With their customary candor, they wondered aloud whether I had turned into a calloused *Americano*, a heretic who had lost respect for family traditions, another Uncle Peppino. From their viewpoint there was no intelligent alternative to living among those who were sure to love you since they were of your own flesh and blood. In the long run, they said, your close relatives were the only ones you could trust, and you left them only when it became absolutely necessary, or when you were taken away in a coffin.

Had I argued with this attitude I would have strengthened their suspicion that I had become a disrespectful *Americano*. Yet I could not help suggesting that traveling to Syracuse was not nearly as drastic an action as the one they had taken when they left close relatives behind in Sicily to travel three thousand miles to a foreign country. I added that the distance between Rochester and Syracuse was as short as that between their home province, Agrigento, and Palermo, less than two hours away by train. That cheered them a little, but did not prevent them from cursing America as a land that encourages bad practices among the young, with the same invectives I had heard all through childhood.

When they saw me off at the station, they carried on as though I might never return.

DISCUSSING THE TEXT

1. How does Mangione feel about his Sicilian family? What are the sources of his difficulty with them? Of his pride in them?
2. What insights into Sicilian immigrant life do you gain from Mangione's portrait of his mother, father, and uncles? In what ways does Mangione see these family members as "typically" Sicilian? In what ways does he see them as different from other Sicilians?
3. How does Mangione begin to emerge from the strictly ethnic environment of his childhood? What does he mean when he says, "Not until I moved from junior high to high school did I become aware that it was possible to have friends who were not ethnics" (par. 11)? Who, according to Mangione, are *not* ethnics?
4. What borders does Mangione cross during the time recounted in this chapter of his autobiography? Make a list of all the border crossings you see in this selection; then describe them in a one-page essay.

WRITING ABOUT THE TEXT

5. Mangione writes that "There was a basic difference of philosophy" between the Sicilian and American worlds, and he refers to the concept of *Destino* in describing that difference (par. 27). Write a one-page essay in which you define *Destino* and explain how this concept differs from a more typically "American" philosophy.
6. Mangione uses short anecdotes to build toward a larger point about his developing sense of himself as he grows from childhood to adulthood. Try to think of several incidents from your childhood or teenage years that contributed to your becoming a college student today. Record these quickly in your journal or notebook. Using the Mangione selection as a model, incorporate these incidents into an essay about your own development.
7. What differences does Mangione discover between his Sicilian world and his American world? Would the same generalizations hold for other ethnic groups in relation to mainstream American culture? Examine one such group by speaking to several members of the group about their basic philosophies, their beliefs about the way the world works, and their attitudes toward the American culture that surrounds them. Report your findings in a two- to three-page essay.
8. In the voice of the young Mangione, write a letter to your Sicilian family recording your first impressions of college.

BHARATI MUKHERJEE

The Tenant

Bharati Mukherjee (b. 1940) uses the metaphor of "the tenant" in this story to represent a character whose uprootedness has taken her from place to place in the United States as a traveling academic. As an upper-class woman from India who is also an American citizen, the character of Maya Sanyal experiences conflicts of class, ethnicity, and gender. These conflicts are played out successively through her failed marriage and then her many relationships, always with non-Indian men.

Mukherjee shows Maya in her exchanges with different people: her friend Fran, in whom she can't quite confide; the Chatterji family; her two landlords, Ted and Fred; and her Indian suitor, Ashoke Mehta. In all of these relationships, the character of Maya emerges as a multicultural woman struggling to challenge her native traditions and cross over into a new land and a new "American" self.

Bharati Mukherjee, who teaches English at the University of California, Berkeley, is the author of the novels The Tiger's Daughter *(1972),* Wife *(1975), and* The Holder of the World *(1993) and the short story collection* The Middleman and Other Stories, *from which this story is taken. She was born in Calcutta, India, and has lived in Canada and the United States. Mukherjee sees herself not as a "hyphenated" (Indian-American) writer but rather as an American writer who has "chosen and achieved the right to be an American."*

Maya Sanyal has been in Cedar Falls, Iowa, less than two weeks. She's come, books and clothes and one armchair rattling in the smallest truck that U-Haul would rent her, from New Jersey. Before that she was in North Carolina. Before that, Calcutta, India. Every place has something to give. She is sitting at the kitchen table with Fran drinking bourbon for the first time in her life. Fran Johnson found her the furnished apartment and helped her settle in. Now she's brought a bottle of bourbon which gives her the right to stay and talk for a bit. She's breaking up with someone named Vern, a pharmacist. Vern's father is also a pharmacist and owns a drugstore. Maya has seen Vern's father on TV twice already. The first time was on the local news when he spoke out against the selling of painkillers like Advil and Nuprin in supermarkets and gas stations. In the matter of painkillers, Maya is a universalist. The other time he was in a barbershop quartet. Vern gets along all right with his father. He likes the pharmacy business, as business goes, but he wants to go back to graduate school and learn to make films. Maya is drinking her first bourbon tonight because Vern left today for San Francisco State.

"I understand totally," Fran says. She teaches Utopian Fiction and a course in Women's Studies and worked hard to get Maya hired. Maya has a Ph.D. in Comparative Literature and will introduce writers like R. K. Narayan and Chinua Achebe to three sections of sophomores at the University of Northern Iowa. "A person has to leave home. Try out his wings."

Fran has to use the bathroom. "I don't feel abandoned." She pushes her chair away from the table. "Anyway, it was a sex thing totally. We were good together. It'd be different if I'd loved him."

Maya tries to remember what's in the refrigerator. They need food. She hasn't been to the supermarket in over a week. She doesn't have a car yet and so she relies on a corner store—a longish walk—for milk, cereal, and frozen dinners. Someday these exigencies will show up as bad skin and collapsed muscle tone. No folly is ever lost. Maya pictures history as a net, the kind of safety net travelling trapeze artists of her childhood fell into when they were inattentive, or clumsy. Going to circuses in Calcutta with her father is what she remembers vividly. It is a banal memory, for her father, the owner of a steel company, is a complicated man.

Fran is out in the kitchen long enough for Maya to worry. They need food. Her mother believed in food. What is love, anger, inner peace, etc., her mother used to say, but the brain's biochemistry. Maya doesn't want to get into that, but she is glad she has enough stuff in the refrigerator to make an omelette. She realizes Indian women are supposed to be inventive with food, whip up exotic delights to tickle an American's palate, and she knows she should be meeting Fran's generosity and candor with some sort of bizarre and effortless countermove. If there's an exotic spice store in Cedar Falls or in neighboring Waterloo, she hasn't found it. She's looked in the phone book for common Indian names, especially Bengali, but hasn't yet struck up culinary intimacies. That will come—it always does. There's a six-pack in the fridge that her landlord, Ted Suminski, had put in because she'd be thirsty after unpacking. She was thirsty, but she doesn't drink beer. She probably should have asked him to come up and drink the beer. Except for Fran she hasn't had anyone over. Fran is more friendly and helpful than anyone Maya has known in the States since she came to North Carolina ten years ago, at nineteen. Fran is a Swede, and she is tall, with blue eyes. Her hair, however, is a dull, darkish brown.

"I don't think I can handle anything that heavy-duty," Fran says when she comes back to the room. She means the omelette. "I have to go home in any case." She lives with her mother and her aunt, two women in their mid-seventies, in a drafty farmhouse. The farmhouse now has a computer store catty-corner from it. Maya's been to the farm. She's been shown photographs of the way the corner used to be. If land values ever rebound, Fran will be worth millions.

Before Fran leaves she says, "Has Rab Chatterji called you yet?"

"No." She remembers the name, a good, reliable Bengali name, from the first night's study of the phone book. Dr. Rabindra Chatterji teaches Physics.

"He called the English office just before I left." She takes car keys out of her pocketbook. She reknots her scarf. "I bet Indian men are more sensitive than Americans. Rab's a Brahmin, that's what people say."

A Chatterji has to be a Bengali Brahmin—last names give ancestral secrets away—but Brahminness seems to mean more to Fran than it does to Maya. She was born in 1954, six full years after India became independent. Her India was Nehru's India: a charged, progressive place.

"All Indian men are wife beaters," Maya says. She means it and doesn't mean it. "That's why I married an American." Fran knows about the divorce, but nothing else. Fran is on the Hiring, Tenure, and Reappointment Committee.

Maya sees Fran down the stairs and to the car which is parked in the back in the spot reserved for Maya's car, if she had owned one. It will take her several months to save enough to buy one. She always pays cash, never borrows. She tells herself she's still recovering from the U-Haul drive halfway across the country. Ted Suminski is in his kitchen watching the women. Maya waves to him because waving to him, acknowledging him in that way, makes him seem less creepy. He seems to live alone though a sign, THE SUMINSKIS, hangs from a metal horse's head in the front yard. Maya hasn't seen Mrs. Suminski. She hasn't seen any children either. Ted always looks lonely. When she comes back from campus, he's nearly always in the back, throwing darts or shooting baskets.

"What's he like?" Fran gestures with her head as she starts up her car. "You hear these stories."

Maya doesn't want to know the stories. She has signed a year's lease. She doesn't want complications. "He's all right. I keep out of his way."

"You know what I'm thinking? Of all the people in Cedar Falls, you're the one who could understand Vern best. His wanting to try out his wings, run away, stuff like that." 15

"Not really." Maya is not being modest. Fran is being impulsively democratic, lumping her wayward lover and Indian friend together as headstrong adventurers. For Fran, a utopian and feminist, borders don't count. Maya's taken some big risks, made a break with her parents' ways. She's done things a woman from Ballygunge Park Road doesn't do, even in fantasies. She's not yet shared stories with Fran, apart from the divorce. She's told her nothing of men she picks up, the reputation she'd gained, before Cedar Falls, for "indiscretions." She has a job, equity, three friends she can count on for emergencies. She is an American citizen. But.

Fran's Brahmin calls her two nights later. On the phone he presents himself as Dr. Chatterji, not Rabindra or Rab. An old-fashioned Indian, she assumes. Her father still calls his closest friend, "Colonel." Dr. Chatterji asks her to tea on Sunday. She means to say no but hears herself say, "Sunday? Fiveish? I'm not doing anything special this Sunday."

Outside, Ted Suminski is throwing darts into his garage door. The door has painted-on rings: orange, purple, pink. The bull's-eye is gray. He has to be fifty at least. He is a big, thick, lonely man about whom people tell stories. Maya pulls the phone cord as far as it'll go so she can look down more directly on her landlord's large, bald head. He has his back to her as he lines up a dart. He's in black running shoes, red shorts, he's naked to the waist. He hunches his right shoulder, he pulls the arm back; a big, lonely man shouldn't have so much grace. The dart is ready to cut through the September evening. But Ted Suminski doesn't let go. He swings on worn rubber soles, catches her eye in the window (she has to have imagined this), takes aim at her shadow. Could she have imagined the noise of the dart's metal tip on her windowpane?

Dr. Chatterji is still on the phone. "You are not having any mode of transportation, is that right?"

Ted Suminski has lost interest in her. Perhaps it isn't interest, at all; perhaps it's aggression. "I don't drive," she lies, knowing it sounds less shameful than not owning a car. She has said this so often she can get in the right degree of apology and Asian upper-class helplessness. "It's an awful nuisance."

"Not to worry, please." Then, "It is a great honor to be meeting Dr. Sanyal's daughter. In Calcutta business circles he is a legend."

On Sunday she is ready by four-thirty. She doesn't know what the afternoon holds; there are surely no places for "high tea"—a colonial tradition—in Cedar Falls, Iowa. If he takes her back to his place, it will mean he has invited other guests. From his voice she can tell Dr. Chatterji likes to do things correctly. She has dressed herself in a peach-colored nylon georgette sari, jade drop-earrings and a necklace. The color is good on dark skin. She is not pretty, but she does her best. Working at it is a part of self-respect. In the mid-seventies, when American women felt rather strongly about such things, Maya had been in trouble with her women's group at Duke. She was too feminine. She had tried to explain the world she came out of. Her grandmother had been married off at the age of five in a village now in Bangladesh. Her great-aunt had been burned to death over a dowry problem. She herself had been trained to speak softly, arrange flowers, sing, be pliant. If she were to seduce Ted Suminski, she thinks as she waits in the front yard for Dr. Chatterji, it would be minor heroism. She has broken with the past. But.

Dr. Chatterji drives up for her at about five ten. He is a hesitant driver. The car stalls, jumps ahead, finally slams to a stop. Maya has to tell him to back off a foot or so; it's hard to leap over two sacks of pruned branches in a sari. Ted Suminski is an obsessive pruner and gardener.

"My sincerest apologies, Mrs. Sanyal," Dr. Chatterji says. He leans across the wide front seat of his noisy, very old, very used car and unlocks the door for her. "I am late. But then, I am sure you're remembering that Indian Standard Time is not at all the same as time in the States." He laughs. He could be nervous—she often had that effect on Indian men. Or he could just be chatty. "These Americans are all the time rushing and rushing but where it gets them?" He moves his head laterally once, twice. It's the gesture made famous by Peter Sellers. When Peter Sellers did it, it had seemed hilarious. Now it suggests that Maya and Dr. Chatterji have three thousand years plus civilization, sophistication, moral virtue, over people born on this continent. Like her, Dr. Chatterji is a naturalized American.

"Call me Maya," she says. She fusses with the seat belt. She does it because she needs time to look him over. He seems quite harmless. She takes in the prominent teeth, the eyebrows that run together. He's in a blue shirt and a beige cardigan with the K-Mart logo that buttons tightly over the waist. It's hard to guess his age because he has dyed his hair and his moustache. Late thirties, early forties. Older than she had expected. "Not Mrs. Sanyal."

This isn't the time to tell about ex-husbands. She doesn't know where John is these days. He should have kept up at least. John had come into her life as a graduate student at Duke, and she, mistaking the brief breathlessness of sex for love, had married him. They had stayed together two years, maybe a little less. The pain that John had inflicted all those years ago by leaving her had subsided into a cozy feeling of loss. This isn't the time, but then she doesn't want to be a legend's daughter all evening. She's not necessarily on Dr. Chatterji's side is what she wants to get across early; she's not against America and Americans. She makes the story—of marriage outside the Brahminic pale, the divorce—quick, dull. Her unsentimentality seems to shock him. His stomach sags inside the cardigan.

"We've each had our several griefs," the physicist says. "We're each required to pay our karmic debts."

"Where are we headed?"

"Mrs. Chatterji has made some Indian snacks. She is waiting to meet you because she is knowing your cousin-sister who studied in Scottish Church College. My home is okay, no?"

Fran would get a kick out of this. Maya has slept with married men, with nameless men, with men little more than boys, but never with an Indian man. Never. 30

The Chatterjis live in a small blue house on a gravelly street. There are at least five or six other houses on the street; the same size but in different colors and with different front yard treatments. More houses are going up. This is the cutting edge of suburbia.

Mrs. Chatterji stands in the driveway. She is throwing a large plastic ball to a child. The child looks about four, and is Korean or Cambodian. The child is not hers because she tells it, "Chung-Hee, ta-ta, bye-bye. Now I play with guest," as Maya gets out of the car.

Maya hasn't seen this part of town. The early September light softens the construction pits. In that light the houses too close together, the stout woman in a striped cotton sari, the child hugging a pink ball, the two plastic lawn chairs by a tender young tree, the sheets and saris on the clothesline in the back, all seem miraculously incandescent.

"Go home now, Chung-Hee. I am busy." Mrs. Chatterji points the child homeward, then turns to Maya, who has folded her hands in traditional Bengali greeting. "It is an honor. We feel very privileged." She leads Maya indoors to a front room that smells of moisture and paint.

In her new, deliquescent mood, Maya allows herself to be backed into the best armchair—a low-backed, boxy Goodwill item draped over with a Rajasthani bedspread—and asks after the cousin Mrs. Chatterji knows. She doesn't want to let go of Mrs. Chatterji. She doesn't want husband and wife to get into whispered conferences about their guest's misadventures in America, as they make tea in the kitchen. 35

The coffee table is already laid with platters of mutton croquettes, fish chops, onion pakoras, ghugni with puris, samosas, chutneys. Mrs. Chatterji has gone to too much trouble. Maya counts four kinds of sweetmeats in Corning casseroles on an end table. She looks into a see-through lid; spongy, white dumplings float in rosewater syrup. Planets contained, mysteries made visible.

"What are you waiting for, Santana?" Dr. Chatterji becomes imperious, though not unaffectionate. He pulls a dining chair up close to the coffee table. "Make some tea." He speaks in Bengali to his wife, in English to Maya. To Maya he says, grandly, "We are having real Indian Green Label Lipton. A nephew is bringing it just one month back."

His wife ignores him. "The kettle's already on," she says. She wants to know about the Sanyal family. Is it true her great-grandfather was a member of the Star Chamber in England?

Nothing in Calcutta is ever lost. Just as her story is known to Bengalis all over America, so are the scandals of her family, the grandfather hauled up for tax evasion, the aunt who left her husband to act in films. This woman brings up the Star Chamber, the glories of the Sanyal family, her father's philanthropies, but it's a way of saying, *I know the dirt.*

The bedrooms are upstairs. In one of those bedrooms an unseen, tormented presence—Maya pictures it as a clumsy ghost that strains to shake off the body's shell—drops things on the floor. The things are heavy and they make the front room's chandelier shake. Light bulbs, shaped like tiny candle flames, flicker. The Chatterjis have said nothing about children. There are no tricycles in the hallway, no small sandals behind the doors. Maya is too polite to ask about the noise, and the Chatterjis don't explain. They talk just a little louder. They flip the embroidered cover off the stereo. What would Maya like to hear? Hemanta Kumar? Manna Dey? Oh, that young chap, Manna Dey! What sincerity, what tenderness he can convey!

Upstairs the ghost doesn't hear the music of nostalgia. The ghost throws and thumps. The ghost makes its own vehement music. Maya hears in its voice madness, self-hate.

Finally the water in the kettle comes to a boil. The whistle cuts through all fantasy and pretense. Dr. Chatterji says, "I'll see to it," and rushes out of the room. But he doesn't go to the kitchen. He shouts up the stairwell. "Poltoo, kindly stop this nonsense straightaway! We're having a brilliant and cultured lady-guest and you're creating earthquakes?" The kettle is hysterical.

Mrs. Chatterji wipes her face. The face that had seemed plump and cheery at the start of the evening now is flabby. "My sister's boy," the woman says.

So this is the nephew who has brought with him the cartons of Green Label tea, one of which will be given to Maya.

Mrs. Chatterji speaks to Maya in English as though only the alien language can keep emotions in check. "Such an intelligent boy! His father is government servant. Very highly placed."

Maya is meant to visualize a smart, clean-cut young man from south Calcutta, but all she can see is a crazy, thwarted, lost graduate student. Intelligent, proper family guarantee nothing. Even Brahmins can do self-destructive things, feel unsavory urges. Maya herself had been an excellent student.

"He was First Class in B. Sc. from Presidency College," the woman says. "Now he's getting Master's in Ag. Science at Iowa State."

The kitchen is silent. Dr. Chatterji comes back into the room with a tray. The teapot is under a tea cozy, a Kashmiri one embroidered with the usual chinar leaves, loops, and chains. "*Her* nephew," he says. The dyed hair and dyed moustache are no longer signs of a man wishing to fight the odds. He is a vain man, anxious to cut losses. "Very unfortunate business."

The nephew's story comes out slowly, over fish chops and mutton croquettes. He is in love with a student from Ghana.

"Everything was A-Okay until the Christmas break. Grades, assistantship for next semester, everything."

"I blame the college. The office for foreign students arranged a Christmas party. And now, *baapre baap!* Our poor Poltoo wants to marry a Negro Muslim."

Maya is known for her nasty, ironic one-liners. It has taken her friends weeks to overlook her malicious, un-American pleasure in others' misfortunes. Maya would like to finish Dr. Chatterji off quickly. He is pompous; he is reactionary; he wants to live and work in America but give back nothing except taxes. The confused world of the immigrant—the lostness that Maya and Poltoo feel—that's what Dr. Chatterji wants to avoid. She hates him. But.

Dr. Chatterji's horror is real. A good Brahmin boy in Iowa is in love with an African Muslim. It shouldn't be a big deal. But the more she watches the physicist, the more she realizes that "Brahmin" isn't a caste; it's a metaphor. You break one small rule, and the constellation collapses. She thinks suddenly that John Cheever—she is teaching him as a "world writer" in her classes, cheek-by-jowl with Africans and West Indians—would have understood Dr. Chatterji's dread. Cheever had been on her mind, ever since the late afternoon light slanted over Mrs. Chatterji's drying saris. She remembers now how full of a soft, Cheeverian light Durham had been the summer she had slept with John Hadwen; and how after that, her tidy graduate-student world became monstrous, lawless. All men became John Hadwen; John became all men. Outwardly, she retained her poise, her Brahminical breeding. She treated her crisis as a literary event; she lost her moral sense, her judgment, her power to distinguish. Her parents had behaved magnanimously. They had cabled from Calcutta: WHAT'S DONE IS DONE. WE ARE CONFIDENT YOU WILL HANDLE NEW SITUATIONS WELL. ALL LOVE. But she knows more than do her parents. Love is anarchy.

Poltoo is Mrs. Chatterji's favorite nephew. She looks as though it is her fault that the Sunday has turned unpleasant. She stacks the empty platters methodically. To Maya she says, "It is the goddess who pulls the strings. We are puppets. I know the goddess will fix it. Poltoo will not marry that African woman." Then she goes to the coat closet in the hall and staggers back with a harmonium, the kind sold in music stores in Calcutta, and sets it down on the carpeted floor. "We're nothing but puppets," she says again. She sits at Maya's feet, her pudgy hands on the harmonium's shiny, black bellows. She sings, beautifully, in a virgin's high voice, "Come, goddess, come, muse, come to us hapless peoples' rescue."

Maya is astonished. She has taken singing lessons at Dakshini Academy in Calcutta. She plays the sitar and the tanpur, well enough to please Bengalis, to astonish Americans. But stout Mrs. Chatterji is a devotee, talking to God. 55

A little after eight, Dr. Chatterji drops her off. It's been an odd evening and they are both subdued.

"I want to say one thing," he says. He stops her from undoing her seat belt. The plastic sacks of pruned branches are still at the corner.

"You don't have to get out," she says.

"Please. Give me one more minute of your time."

"Sure." 60

"Maya is my favorite name."

She says nothing. She turns away from him without making her embarrassment obvious.

"Truly speaking, it is my favorite. You are sometimes lonely, no? But you are lucky. Divorced women can date, they can go to bars and discos. They can see mens, many mens. But inside marriage there is so much loneliness." A groan, low, horrible, comes out of him.

She turns back toward him, to unlatch the seat belt and run out of the car. She sees that Dr. Chatterji's pants are unzipped. One hand works hard under his Jockey shorts; the other rests, limp, penitential, on the steering wheel.

"Dr. Chatterji—*really!*" she cries. 65

The next day, Monday, instead of getting a ride home with Fran—Fran says she *likes* to give rides, she needs the chance to talk, and she won't share gas expenses, absolutely not—Maya goes to the periodicals room of the library. There are newspapers from everywhere, even from Madagascar and New Caledonia. She thinks of the periodicals room as an asylum for homesick aliens. There are two aliens already in the room, both Orientals, both absorbed in the politics and gossip of their far off homes.

She goes straight to the newspapers from India. She bunches her raincoat like a bolster to make herself more comfortable. There's so much to catch up on. A village headman, a known Congress-Indira party worker, has been shot by scooter-riding snipers. An Indian pugilist has won an international medal—in Nepal. A child drawing well water—the reporter calls the child "a neo-Buddhist, a convert from the now-outlawed untouchable caste"—has been stoned. An editorial explains that the story about stoning is not a story about caste but about failed idealism; a story about promises of green fields and clean, potable water broken, a story about bribes paid and wells not dug. But no, thinks Maya, it's about caste.

Out here, in the heartland of the new world, the India of serious newspapers unsettles. Maya longs again to feel what she had felt in the Chatterjis' living room: virtues made physical. It is a familiar feeling, a longing. Had a suitable man presented himself in the reading room at that instant, she would have seduced him. She goes on to the stack of *India Abroads,* reads through matrimonial columns, and steals an issue to take home.

Indian men want Indian brides. Married Indian men want Indian mistresses. All over America, "handsome, tall, fair" engineers, doctors, data processors—the new pioneers—cry their eerie love calls.

Maya runs a finger down the first column; her fingertip, dark with newsprint, stops at random. 70

> Hello! Hi! Yes, you *are* the one I'm looking for. You are the new emancipated Indo-American woman. You have a zest for life. You are at ease in USA and yet your ethics are rooted in Indian tradition. The man of your dreams has come. Yours truly is handsome, ear-nose-throat specialist, well-settled in Connecticut. Age is 41 but never married, physically fit, sportsmanly, and strong. I adore idealism, poetry, beauty. I abhor smugness, passivity, caste system. Write with recent photo. Better still, call!!!

Maya calls. Hullo, hullo, hullo! She hears immigrant lovers cry in crowded shopping malls. Yes, you who are at ease in both worlds, you are the one. She feels she has a fair chance.

A man answers. "Ashoke Mehta speaking."

She speaks quickly into the bright-red mouthpiece of her telephone. He will be in Chicago, in transit, passing through O'Hare. United counter, Saturday, two p.m. As easy as that.

"Good," Ashoke Mehta says. "For these encounters I, too, prefer a neutral zone."

On Saturday at exactly two o'clock the man of Maya's dreams floats toward her as lovers used to in shampoo commercials. The United counter is a loud, harassed place but passengers and piled-up luggage fall away from him. Full-cheeked and fleshy-lipped, he is handsome. He hasn't lied. He is serene, assured, a Hindu god touching down in Illinois. 75

She can't move. She feels ugly and unworthy. Her adult life no longer seems miraculously rebellious; it is grim, it is perverse. She has accomplished nothing. She has changed her citizenship but she hasn't broken through into the light, the vigor, the *hustle* of the New World. She is stuck in dead space.

"Hullo, hullo!" Their fingers touch.

Oh, the excitement! Ashoke Mehta's palm feels so right in the small of her back. Hullo, hullo, hullo. He pushes her out of the reach of anti-Khomeini Iranians, Hare Krishnas, American Fascists, men with fierce wants, and guides her to an empty gate. They have less than an hour.

"What would you like, Maya?"

She knows he can read her mind, she knows her thoughts are open to him. *You,* she's almost giddy with the thought, with simple desire. "From the snack bar," he says, as though to clarify. "I'm afraid I'm starved." 80

Below them, where the light is strong and hurtful, a Boeing is being serviced. "Nothing," she says.

He leans forward. She can feel the nap of his scarf—she recognizes the Cambridge colors—she can smell the wool of his Icelandic sweater. She runs her hand along the scarf, then against the flesh of his neck. "Only the impulsive ones call," he says.

The immigrant courtship proceeds. It's easy, he's good with facts. He knows how to come across to a stranger who may end up a lover, a spouse. He makes over a hundred thousand. He owns a house in Hartford, and two income properties in Newark. He plays the market but he's cautious. He's good at badminton but plays handball to keep in shape. He watches all the sports on television. Last August he visited Copenhagen, Helsinki and Leningrad. Once upon a time he collected stamps but now he doesn't have hobbies, except for reading. He counts himself an intellectual, he spends too much on books. Ludlum, Forsyth, MacInnes; other names she doesn't catch. She suppresses a smile, she's told him only she's a graduate student. He's not without his vices. He's a spender, not a saver. He's a sensualist: good food—all foods, but easy on the Indian—good wine. Some temptations he doesn't try to resist.

And I, she wants to ask, do I tempt?

"Now tell me about yourself, Maya." He makes it easy for her. "Have you ever been in love?"

"No."

"But many have loved you, I can see that." He says it not unkindly. It is the fate of women like her, and men like him. Their karmic duty, to be loved. It is expected, not judged. She feels he can see them all, the sad parade of need and demand. This isn't the time to reveal all.

And so the courtship enters a second phase.

When she gets back to Cedar Falls, Ted Suminski is standing on the front porch. It's late at night, chilly. He is wearing a down vest. She's never seen him on the porch. In fact there's no chair to sit on. He looks chilled through. He's waited around a while.

"Hi." She has her keys ready. This isn't the night to offer the six-pack in the fridge. He looks expectant, ready to pounce.

"Hi." He looks like a man who might have aimed the dart at her. What has he done to his wife, his kids? Why isn't there at least a dog? "Say, I left a note upstairs."

The note is written in Magic Marker and thumb-tacked to her apartment door. DUE TO PERSONAL REASONS, NAMELY REMARRIAGE, I REQUEST THAT YOU VACATE MY PLACE AT THE END OF THE SEMESTER.

Maya takes the note down and retacks it to the kitchen wall. The whole wall is like a bulletin board, made of some new, crumbly building-material. Her kitchen, Ted Suminski had told her, was once a child's bedroom. Suminski in love: the idea stuns her. She has misread her landlord. The dart at her window speaks of no twisted fantasy. The landlord wants the tenant out.

She gets a glass out of the kitchen cabinet, gets out a tray of ice, pours herself a shot of Fran's bourbon. She is happy for Ted Suminski. She is. She wants to tell someone how moved she'd been by Mrs. Chatterji's singing. How she'd felt in O'Hare, even about Dr. Rab Chatterji in the car. But Fran is not the person. No one she's ever met is the person. She can't talk about the dead space she lives in. She wishes Ashoke Mehta would call. Right now.

Weeks pass. Then two months. She finds a new room, signs another lease. Her new landlord calls himself Fred. He has no arms, but he helps her move her things. He drives between Ted Suminski's place and his twice in his station wagon. He uses his toes the way Maya uses her fingers. He likes to do things. He pushes garbage sacks full of Maya's clothes up the stairs. 95

"It's all right to stare," Fred says. "Hell, I would."

That first afternoon in Fred's rooming house, they share a Chianti. Fred wants to cook her pork chops but he's a little shy about Indians and meat. Is it beef, or pork? Or any meat? She says it's okay, any meat, but not tonight. He has an ex-wife in Des Moines, two kids in Portland, Oregon. The kids are both normal; he's the only freak in the family. But he's self-reliant. He shops in the supermarket like anyone else, he carries out the garbage, shovels the snow off the sidewalk. He needs Maya's help with one thing. Just one thing. The box of Tide is a bit too heavy to manage. Could she get him the giant size every so often and leave it in the basement?

The dead space need not suffocate. Over the months, Fred and she will settle into companionship. She has never slept with a man without arms. Two wounded people, he will joke during their nightly contortions. It will shock her, this assumed equivalence with a man so strikingly deficient. She knows she is strange, and lonely, but being Indian is not the same, she would have thought, as being a freak.

One night in spring, Fred's phone rings. "Ashoke Mehta speaking." None of this "do you remember me?" nonsense. The god has tracked her down. He hasn't forgotten. "Hullo," he says, in their special way. And because she doesn't answer back, "Hullo, hullo, hullo." She is aware of Fred in the back of the room. He is lighting a cigarette with his toes.

"Yes," she says, "I remember." 100

"I had to take care of a problem," Ashoke Mehta says. "You know that I have my vices. That time at O'Hare I was honest with you."

She is breathless.

"Who is it, May?" asks Fred.

"You also have a problem," says the voice. His laugh echoes. "You will come to Hartford, I know."

When she moves out, she tells herself, it will not be the end of Fred's world. 105

DISCUSSING THE TEXT

1. Maya is a complex character who is trying to come to terms with her ethnic identity. What does Mukherjee mean when she says that Maya "has

changed her citizenship but she hasn't broken through into the light, the vigor, the *hustle* of the New World" (par. 76)?

2. Even though Maya has tried to escape the cultural and historical weight of her upper-class Indian family, she still feels bound by its traditions. Explain how she sees herself in terms of her femininity, for example. Which other qualities in herself does she consider uniquely Indian? Why?
3. Dr. Chatterji is presented as a pompous, vain, and prejudiced man who makes certain assumptions about Maya's sexual availability because she is a divorced woman. Do you agree with Maya's assessment of his character? Can you see anything positive in his attitudes and behavior?

WRITING ABOUT THE TEXT

4. Maya has found Ashoke Mehta's personal ad in an issue of *India Abroads.* Assuming her voice, write the kind of personal ad that you think she would write in the same newspaper.
5. Maya's two landlords, Ted and Fred, play important roles in the story. Write a brief essay that addresses the following questions: What are some of Maya's fantasies about Ted, and what does this say about her? How does her relationship with Fred make her feel? Why do you think Fred uses the word "freak" to describe himself ? Why does Maya think that Fred sees her as also "wounded," perhaps a "freak" (par. 96)?
6. Assume that Maya will join Ashoke Mehta in Hartford, and write a brief essay that addresses the following questions: Why does Maya see Ashoke as "a Hindu god"? Will he fulfill the role of "landlord" when she moves to Hartford? Will Maya continue to see herself as a "tenant"? How will she cross yet another border by becoming involved with Ashoke?
7. In the periodicals room of the library, Maya reads a story in an Indian newspaper about a child who was stoned. Then she reads an editorial that argues that this is "not a story about caste but about failed idealism . . ."; Maya concludes, however, that it *is* about caste (par. 66–67). Do some research into the history of the caste system in India. Report your findings in a two- to three-page essay; conclude your essay by explaining why you think Maya disagrees with the newspaper editorial.

RUBÉN MARTÍNEZ

L.A. Journal

This selection is from Rubén Martínez's 1992 essay collection, The Other Side: Fault Lines, Guerrilla Saints, and the True Heart of Rock 'n' Roll. *Born in Los Angeles of a Salvadoran mother and a Mexican American father, Martínez chronicles in his book the perils of his overlapping cultural worlds: Mexico City, San Salvador, and Los Angeles. The volume's opening essay, "The Other Side," focuses on the author's efforts to integrate the various parts of his heritage into a coherent whole: "Weaned on a blend of cultures, languages, and ideologies . . . , I have lived both in the North and the South over my twenty-nine years, trying to be South in the South, North in the North, South in the North and North in the South."*

In the excerpts from "L.A. Journal" included here, Martínez engages the reader in the experience of border crossings by highlighting special occasions in his family history. "L.A. Journal" offers challenging ideas about the concept of cultural borders and the complexities of a multiethnic identity.

Rubén Martínez is a writer, performer, and Emmy Award–winning journalist. He has been an editor for the L.A. Weekly *and is a contributor to National Public Radio's "All Things Considered."*

I

April 1990

I am unpacking again. I am perpetually living out of boxes—boxes that are only half emptied before they must be filled and sealed again for the next move. But I want this stay to last a long time. I am in my late grandparents' house in the Silver Lake district of Los Angeles, in a hilly area of 1930s Deco homes that the Mexican side of my life has lived in for fifty years. The stay will not last long, though; I'm only caretaking the place for a few months while it's remodelled in anticipation of some yuppie's rent money.

In a couple of weeks Y will come up from Guatemala to stay with me for a month, so I pull out a few souvenirs and mementos from the boxes and hang them on the walls of my father's old bedroom so that there'll be a semblance of a home for us. I reach into a box and pick up a cardboard-framed photograph. "Baptism Souvenir," reads the badly printed cursive. "Our Lady Queen of the Angels (Old Mission Plaza)."

Nuestra Señora la Reina de Los Angeles de Porciúncula is the original, overwrought Catholic for the Old Plaza Church, which is popularly known as La Placita—the site of the city's founding. Every Sunday, thousands of Mexicanos, Chicanos and Centroamericanos come to hear one of the twelve masses offered at La Placita, dressed to kill in rented suits or humbly in home-stitched silk dresses. Around those who have come to baptize their kids swarm the photographers. Among these latter, on one Sunday in the fall of 1962, must have been one George A. Pérez, whose name is printed on the back of the cardboard frame.

The image is marred by rust-colored scratches, result of a gloss-enhancing wash that was probably Sr Pérez's finishing touch; year by year, the acid

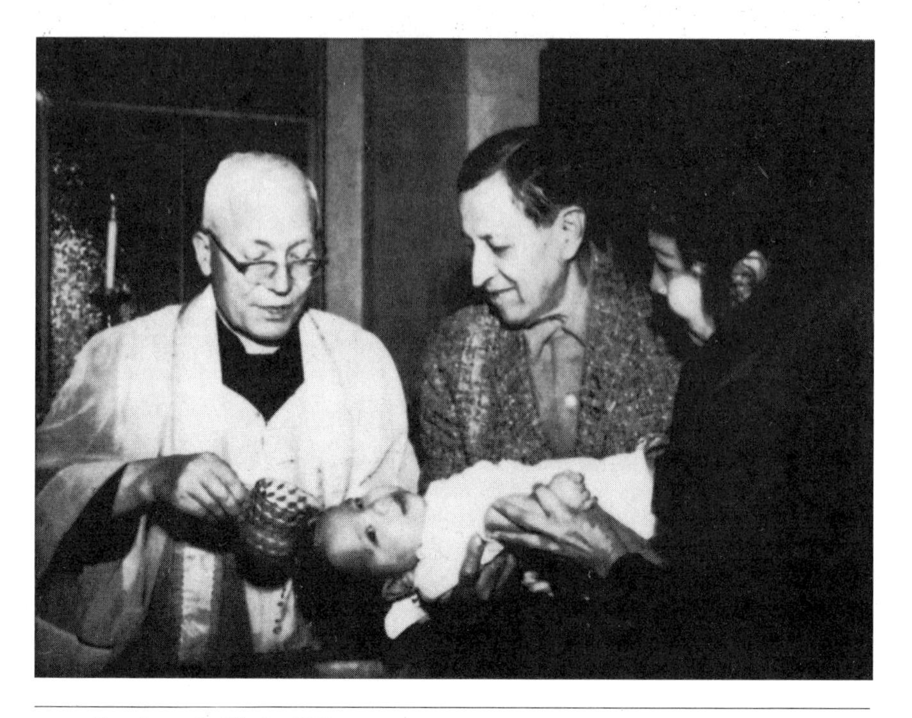

Baptism *La Placita 1962* (Courtesy of Rubén Martínez)

eats away at more and more of the picture. Flanking the silver-haired priest (horn-rimmed glasses, lips pursed) is a well-dressed, elderly couple. His aquiline, Northern–Mexican nose gives him an air of dignified *mestizo*ness, leaning away from the Spaniard and towards the *indígena;* she, light complected, with large eyes, high cheekbones and wide smile (less *indígena*).[1] My Grandparents. The camera has captured the very moment when the priest lets the water drip onto the head of a smiling kid swathed in virgin white. Me.

It is just a few days before the October Missile Crisis. My grandparents' restaurant has taken shape on Glendale Boulevard. Elvis Presley stopped by not long ago (my grandparents had no idea who he was) and left a note behind: "Nice place, great food. Elvis Presley." The napkin he wrote on will become my younger sister's prize possession. My father is doing litho work at a place called Rapid Blue Print, making $1.50 an hour, good money for a first- 5

[1]*mestizoness . . . indígena:* (Spanish) Martínez aludes here to the ethnic and racial complexity of Mexicans. *Mestizo* describes a person of mixed ancestry (white European and indigenous Mexican), and *indígena* describes a person whose ethnicity is totally indigenous to Mexico. Martínez means that even though his grandfather is of mixed origin, he leans toward the indigenous, while his grandmother is more European. (*Ed.*)

generation Mexican. He likes to slick his hair back, but he is not a *pachuco*[2]—he's proud to speak an unaccented English as well as a flawless Spanish. And, as he is still wont to say thirty years later, he is also proud to be better off than the *chusma,* the rabble, such as the recently arrived immigrants who gather in squalor in the *barrios* to the south and to the east of La Placita. My mother's doing her best at playing the classic housewife, watching a lot of TV (which inspires her to do her hair up like Jackie Kennedy's), singing nursery rhymes to me in Spanish, and probably still thinking a lot about her native El Salvador, which she left only a few years before. My parents live in their newly built house in Silver Lake (only five minutes away from my grandparents). It's all very middle-class idyllic and I'm the model first-born son. My parents often have representatives of the fledgling Latino middle class over to the house for martinis and cha-cha dancing, the men with Brylcreemed hair and sharp suits with thin ties, the women with knee-length polka-dotted dresses and their hair teased into Roman arches.

Father must work eighteen, sometimes twenty hours a day, and the loneliness begins to take its toll on my mother. Late one night, alone in the house, her son fast asleep, feeling the isolation, longing for the comfort of the large family she left behind in El Salvador—this, too, is exile—and awed by the vastness of a city she doesn't understand, she locks herself in the bathroom. My father finds her still there, shaken and wordless, in the early morning hours. From then on, I knew that there were monsters lurking outside in the darkness of the city, poised to leap and tear my family apart.

V

September, 1990

Going through one of my late Mexican grandparents' scrapbooks, I come across a black-and-white glossy. My grandmother is decked out in classic Spanish Romantic attire, a chiffon crown in the style of the nineteenth century on her head and trailing down her back, a ruffled, floor-length dress, white flowers in her hair. Similarly, my grandfather's silk-trim vest and black trousers, with a dark kerchief spilling out from the left pocket, loosely approximate a Spanish don. My grandparents are both standing, cradling their guitars and holding down a D-7 in the first position. Seated to their right at a dinner table is a white gentleman in an expensive, bureaucratic-conservative suit. He is smiling. He is also holding a gun. It looks like a real standard police issue of the period. The gun is pointed at my grandparents. This is a funny joke. My grandmother smiles effusively, with those perfect teeth of hers (cavityless her entire life), and my grandfather also plays along—smiling as he cowers away from the pistol.

---

[2]*pachuco:* (Mexican Spanish) a term to describe urban Mexicans of the 1930s and 1940s who developed their own language and style in the United States (*Ed.*)

Grandparents *The Paris Inn c. 1929* (Courtesy of Rubén Martínez)

The Paris Inn, where my grandparents played Mexican *ranchera* music for the city's elite, was a hot night spot throughout the 1940s. As I leaf through the photo album stuffed with dozens of photos of my grandparents entertaining, I suddenly imagine myself walking into the Paris Inn dressed in a sleeveless T-shirt and khakis, cool shades hiding my eyes, a crucifix dangling from my left earlobe. I ignore the maitre d' and his astonished look, sit down at a table and start snapping bread sticks, making a pile of crumbs over the white tablecloth. A nervous waiter comes over, backed up by a posse of two Mexican busboys. "*¡Ahórale!*"[3] I say, leaning back as far as possible, à la El Pachuco in Luis Valdez's *Zoot Suit.*[4] "For starters, how about some chips and salsa? *Y luego, tres tacos de carne asada, dos de lengua, y uno de carnitas. Y luego, maestro, me trae dos pupusas, una revuelta y una de queso. Ah! Y no se le olvide una Tecate bien heladita con limoncito y sal. He dicho.*" I clap my hands and wave them off. The customers are all looking my way—the bureaucrat with the gun is giving

[3]*¡Ahórale!:* (Mexican Spanish) playful version of the Spanish *ahora,* meaning "right now" (*Ed.*)

[4]*Zoot Suit:* (1978) a historical / musical play about Chicano life by Mexican American playwright and director Luis Valdez (b. 1940); made into a film in 1981 (*Ed.*)

"Y luego. . . . He dicho": (Spanish) "And then, three tacos of roasted meat, two of tongue, and one of beef. And then, sir, two pupusas, one mixed and one with cheese. Oh! And don't forget a Tecate beer, very, very cold, and with a pinch of lemon and salt. That's it." (*Ed.*)

The Paris Inn *c. 1946* (Courtesy of Rubén Martínez)

me a real hard look. And my grandparents, they pretend they don't know me, can you believe it? But, maybe they just don't recognize me dressed like a *cholo.*[5] Come to think of it, my grandmother would probably burst into tears if she did recognize me. I make like I don't know them either . . .

. . . but over by the bar there's Humphrey, I mean Rick,[6] and his watery and my red eyes lock. The slightest smile cracks those perpetually pouting lips, and with a slight nod of the head he motions over to the back exit. The

[5]*cholo:* (Mexican Spanish) low life; term associated with the gang culture of Mexican American barrios (*Ed.*)

[6]*Humphrey . . . Rick:* In this elaborate fantasy, Martínez places himself inside the popular American film *Casablanca* (1942, dir. Michael Curtis), starring Humphrey Bogart as Rick, an American expatriate living in Casablanca during World War II. Martínez is referring to the film's final scene, in which Rick gives up his hope of leaving Casablanca with the woman he loves, Elsa, and instead helps her husband to leave with her. In Martínez's fantasy, Elsa becomes Y, while he plays her husband. (*Ed.*)

door is open. I can see the silver cargo plane out on the rain-glazed runway, its propellers starting to turn over. I make a run for it. "Get away from that phone!" I hear Rick yell at the bureaucrat, who's dialling the LAPD from the phone at the front desk. The shots ring out behind me as I bound out onto the runway, where Y is waiting, enshrouded by the fog . . .

VIII

December, 1990

In a few days, I will travel south to Mexico City, to write an article about Mexican rock 'n' roll, and after yet another year-long separation, to meet Y, who is making the trip north from Guatemala. After spending a week there, we will make the trip back to Los Angeles together. We are willing ourselves back into each other's destinies, trying to rise above our fractured selves, our disjointed continent. 10

We've been at it for five years now (this running towards and away from each other, North and South), and our Christmasses and New Years have always been intense affairs. Last year, we visited family in San Salvador scant weeks after the FMLN[7] offensive, breathed air that still smelled faintly of mortar dust and charred bodies, listened to the traditional Christmas Eve fireworks explode across the city at midnight: Christ reborn as missiles scream and sparks fly skyward.

A few years before, we spent New Year's Eve here in Los Angeles, celebrating at the home of Salvadoran friends. It began as a wonderful time with *abuelas*[8] who reminisced about the old days, teens dancing, tots crawling underneath the tables. Then the shellshocked ex-Salvadoran army footsoldier in the apartment upstairs took out an automatic and started spraying bullets at enemies visible only to himself. The mothers and children screamed and everyone hit the ground. Somebody knocked over a lamp in a desperate attempt to turn off the light, and someone else crawled towards the telephone and frantically dialed the police. We were no longer in Los Angeles, but back in the middle of the war in San Salvador.

Last year, we spent New Year's Eve in Guatemala City with friends, drinking unto oblivion, setting off immense chains of firecrackers in the streets. Near midnight a friend's father lurched towards me, put his arm around my shoulder, and tried to work miracles against our inevitable diaspora: "In the year 2000," he slurred, "no matter how far we've gone away from each other, whether you're in Bangladesh and I'm in Valparaíso and my

---

[7]*FMLN:* Acronym for the contemporary Salvadoran guerrilla group Farabundo Martí Front for National Liberation, formed in 1980 to combat the rightist military junta in El Salvador at the time; named after Socialist leader Farabundo Martí, executed by a totalitarian government in 1932 (*Ed.*)

[8]*abuelas:* (Spanish) grandmothers, old women (*Ed.*)

deadbeat of a son's in New York, we're all going to get back together here, *cabrón,*[9] right here in this house, just like we're all together tonight . . ."

So this year it'll be Mexico City, the center of my universe: equidistant from San Salvador and Los Angeles, the cities/families that blur into each other for me like double vision. I need my Salvadoran fiancée here in Los Angeles, even as there is a force that urges me to be back in San Salvador. I need my cities, my families to be one.

It is during the holidays that this contradiction is always at its most intense. During this time I am usually surrounded by visions of my own death—a plane crash, AIDS, a gunshot, love, you name it—during the time that I, as a Catholic, should be thinking of beginnings, of possibilities. Instead, I am at once running into and away from my family, dying in their arms and stumbling drunk and alone, thousands of miles from home. 15

Tonight in Los Angeles, the houses and apartments of the *barrio* I live in are blinking with color. A glowing Santa Claus beams from the roof of the house next door. Jesuses and Marys march from house to house in the *posada* processions. *Nacimientos* adorn living rooms: *el niño Dios*[10] lies hidden under a veil in His crèche, awaiting midnight to be uncovered. The kids are watching, as I did years ago, Dr. Seuss's *How The Grinch Stole Christmas* and the Peanuts cartoon where Charlie Brown has that pitiful tree that revives only when Linus wraps his security blanket around it (always leaves me in tears, that one).

And the guerrillas of the FMLN will no doubt have a party somewhere in rebel-controlled territory, and there'll be those poignant car and plane crashes on Christmas Eve that perhaps make pointless any system of beliefs . . .

But there I will be at midnight Mass on the Twenty-fourth, back in Los Angeles after my week in Mexico City, with my fiancée at my side.

"Will one pure thing," Kierkegaard[11] counsels. I've apparently taken the idea seriously, since here I am, trying to subdue sentimental and sexual contradiction by willing one relationship to one person for the rest of this one lifetime. Ideas of tradition and eternity beckon me as I approach thirty, after an extended adolescence of quests that celebrated ephemerality and disconnectedness.

But the doubts, the sacred doubts! Does that one pure thing ever exist outside of an isolated moment, beyond a "sign that is destined to be contradicted"? I listen to the Latin American rock 'n' roll of the old days (part of the 20

---

[9]*cabrón:* (Spanish) bastard, swine (*Ed.*)

[10]*posada processions. . . . Nacimientos . . . el niño Dios:* Martínez refers here to the traditional Mexican Christmas Eve celebration, which includes a reenactment of the holy family seeking shelter at the inn (posada). The Nacimientos are the traditional crèches or stable scenes with the baby Jesus or God-child (el niño Dios). (*Ed.*)

[11]*Soren Kierkegaard* (1813–1855): Danish philosopher whose writings on religion and aesthetics greatly influenced twentieth-century existentialism (*Ed.*)

Cristo *San Salvador* (Courtesy of Rubén Martínez)

research for the article I will be writing), reminded of the innocence of the early seventies' teenagers, thousands of whom were massacred and exiled a few years later for believing. I look down at my hands, the ones that, in a horrible, drunken fight with Y in Guatemala City a year ago, smashed the framed image of Jesus I've kept since early childhood. We'd been dreaming that we could live together in Central America . . . blood on my hand, blood on the glass, blood on Jesus.

The sign must be contradicted. Perhaps it is only through contradiction—through the death of the moment in which we will, or think we will, purely—that we may transcend our fissured reality. Like Jesus doubting in the final moments on the cross before He is delivered by the Father. We must be stripped of whatever certainty we have—pride, ego, any concrete sense of self—in order to move on to what may be the true moment of pure will (the others, perhaps, were just rehearsals in bad faith).

Somebody get me a sledgehammer for Christmas. I want to take it to the reflection of myself in those bloody shards of glass lying on Jesus's image and do away with myself spectacularly well. To be truly new, to move finally toward something/someone. While I'm at it, I'd also take that hammer to the shiny mirror glass of the malls across the city, like Jesus at the temple.[12] Then everyone would be forced to pick flowers for presents, write poems, give embraces and make love to their enemies. We'd free ourselves from one jail, get roaringly drunk and lock ourselves into the next one.

What a time we picked to live in! The world's upside down or rightside up—I can't tell which—and we're smack in between the shattered dreams of previous generations and the abyss of the new century beyond. The holidays—symbolic markers of our passing through the world—set in motion forces impossible to contain. My uncles will be drunk, the grandmothers will wax nostalgic, you and I will embrace tensely, the fireworks will explode, the faithful will kneel, even the atheists will get sentimental, and many innocents will die. (It's already happening: a few days ago in Guatemala the army massacred a dozen people and wounded several dozen more when they fired into a peaceful procession of *indígenas* protesting human rights abuses in Santiago de Atitlán, one of the most beautiful places in the world.)

So, we'll raise a cup of wine to our lips on the Twenty-fourth at midnight, and toast to *el niño Dios* at the head of the *nacimiento* under the Christmas tree, His blanket already showing blotches of red from His omnipresent wounds.

And you and I will be trying to stop our own bleeding, uncertain whether or not we'll succeed. 25

DISCUSSING THE TEXT

1. In Journal V (p. 303), Martínez juxtaposes a number of cultural stereotypes. Beginning with a description of his Mexican grandparents' performance at the Paris Inn, Martínez then moves into a fantasy in which he, as a Mexican American, shocks the elegant clientele of the nightclub. How do the different stereotypes that Martínez draws on here complement one another? How do

[12]*Jesus at the temple:* Martínez alludes to the story of Jesus cleansing the temple of Jerusalem during the feast of Passover. According to the New Testament, Jesus threw the merchants and money changers from the temple. (*Ed.*)

they clash with one another? What do you think Martínez is trying to communicate in this passage?

2. How is the author's concept of borders expressed in his anecdote about the New Year's celebration at the home of Salvadoran friends in Los Angeles (Journal VIII, par. 12)? What borders are in effect during this incident? What borders are crossed?
3. What does Kierkegaard's injunction to "Will one pure thing" (par. 19) mean to Martínez? To what parts of his own life does he try to apply this statement?

WRITING ABOUT THE TEXT

4. Working with a group of four or five students, locate as many examples of religious language, symbols, and images as you can find in this selection. What role does religion, especially Catholicism, play in Martínez's understanding of his place within his various cultures? Be prepared to share your findings and ideas with the rest of the class.
5. In Journal I, Martínez recreates part of the family history by describing his baptism photograph (par. 3–4). Write a fictional conversation among the family members present at the baptism in which each family member gives his or her outlook on the child's multicultural heritage and the impact it will have on his future.
6. In "L.A. Journal," Martínez poses one of the conflicts experienced by the multicultural self by pointing out both positive and negative feelings about his predicament. While he appreciates the fact that he can experience different realities at once, he acknowledges his feelings of incompleteness and uprootedness (par. 10–15). Write a personal reaction that addresses the paradoxical nature of Martínez's viewpoints. Can you relate his conflicting feelings to your experience in any way?
7. Physical appearance is an important part of the memories of family members that Martínez presents in the "L.A. Journal"; in paragraph 4, for example, he describes the physical characteristics of his grandparents in the photograph from his baptism. Using this and other examples from this selection, write a one- to two-page essay discussing the significance of physical appearance in Martínez's understanding of different cultural identities.
8. Try writing an imaginary scene like the one Martínez constructs in Journal V. Begin with an image from an old photograph of family members or friends that you've seen. Imagine yourself appearing in the scene where the photograph was taken. What would you be wearing? How would you behave? What would you say or do? If you would like, conclude your description as Martínez does, by imagining yourself transformed into a character from one of your favorite films.

MAKING CONNECTIONS

1. The selections in this chapter revolve around the theme of crossing regional, geographical, cultural, and other borders. Think of an experience in your life in which you have crossed a border, either literally or symbolically, and write a brief essay about it.
2. Choose two selections from this chapter and discuss how each author treats the concept of crossing borders within personal, social, and cultural contexts. What similarities and differences do you see between these two authors' ideas and writing styles?
3. Both Frederick Douglass and Zora Neale Hurston were African Americans who crossed the border between South and North in the United States. Compare and contrast their experiences (as depicted in Douglass's *Narrative* and Hurston's "School Again") as they tried to construct new identities within the new world they encountered in the northeastern United States.
4. In "Growing Up Sicilian," Jerre Mangione describes his experience, as a young boy, of crossing borders among different ethnic groups. Compare and contrast his experiences with those of Piri Thomas in "Alien Turf" (Chap. 1, p. 47).
5. For Jerre Mangione in "Growing Up Sicilian" and for Sara Smolinsky in Anzia Yezierska's "College," the act of leaving home to attend college was a challenge to the family. Discuss the various strategies that Mangione and the character of Sara used to cross this particular border. Compare these two acts of defiance in terms of Mangione's and Sara Smolinsky's ethnic, social, and cultural contexts.
6. Recall the importance of a college education for Zora Neale Hurston and Anzia Yerzierska in transforming and developing their personalities and identities. With their experiences in mind, write a brief essay focusing on the significance of your college experience so far. What impact has this experience had on your personal and intellectual growth and development?
7. In his "L.A. Journal," Rubén Martínez describes himself as someone who is constantly crossing regional, geographical, and cultural borders. Choose another selection, from this chapter or an earlier one about a similar experience and write a brief essay that compares and contrasts the ideas expressed in the two selections. Some possible choices would be "Angels on the Ceiling," by Esmeralda Santiago, and "Growing Up Asian in America," by Kesaya E. Noda (p. 196).
8. Write an imaginary conversation on the experience of crossing borders between authors Esmeralda Santiago and Rubén Martínez.
9. Frederick Douglass states in his *Narrative* that, to protect other fugitive slaves, he cannot give the reader any details about his escape. To gain a richer understanding of the plight of fugitive slaves in the nineteenth century, prepare a brief research report on the operation of the Underground Railroad.
10. The late twentieth-century world of Indian immigrants in the United States, presented in Bharati Mukherjee's story "The Tenant," is, of course, quite different from the worlds described by the three voices presented in Ann Banks's "Immigrant Lives." But consider the character of Dr. Chatterji in "The Tenant." In what ways do you think his experiences as an immigrant

are similar to, and different from, those of Morris Horowitz, Manuel Captiva, or Philippe Lemay? How does the character of Maya respond to Dr. Chatterji's image of himself as an immigrant in America? Why does she respond this way?

11. The Alfred Stieglitz photograph at the beginning of this chapter, *The Steerage,* shows people returning to Europe from America. Write a description of the image, in which you try to interpret the activities and attitudes of those pictured. What reasons can you imagine for immigrants at this time to be returning to their homelands? Do some library research to try to locate possible answers to this question.

FURTHER READING

Frederick Douglass

Jacobs, Harriet. *Incidents in the Life of a Slave Girl.* New York: Oxford University Press, 1988.

Sundquist, Eric. *To Wake the Nations: Race in the Making of American Literature.* Cambridge, Mass.: Harvard University Press, 1993.

Ann Banks

Couch, W. T., ed. *These Are Our Lives.* 1938. Reprint, New York: Norton, 1975.

Esmeralda Santiago

Iglesias, Cesar Andreu, ed. *Memoirs of Bernardo Vega: A Contribution to the History of the Puerto Rican Community in New York.* New York: Monthly Review Press, 1984.

Acosta-Belen, Edna. ed. *The Puerto Rican Woman: Perspectives on Culture, History and Society.* New York: Praeger, 1986.

Anzia Yezierska

Howe, Irving. *World of Our Fathers.* New York: Harcourt, 1971.

Yezierska, Anzia. *Hungry Hearts.* New York: Grosset, 1920.

Zora Neale Hurston

Hemenway, Robert. *Zora Neale Hurston: A Literary Biography.* Champaign: University of Illinois Press, 1977.

Hurston, Zora Neale. *Their Eyes Were Watching God.* Champaign: University of Illinois Press, 1978.

Jerre Mangione

Boelhower, William. *Immigrant Autobiography in the United States.* Essedue edizione, 1982.

Mangione, Jerre. *Mount Allegro.* Boston: Houghton Mifflin, 1943.

Bharati Mukherjee

Mukherjee, Bharati. *The Holder of the World.* New York: Knopf, 1993.

———. *Jasmine.* New York: Fawcett, 1990.

Rubén Martínez

Gonzalez, Ray, ed. *Mirrors beneath the Earth: Short Fiction by Chicano Writers.* Willimantic, Conn.: Curbstone, 1992.

Heyck, Denis Lynn Daly. *Barrios and Borderlands: Cultures of Latinos and Latinas in the United States.* New York: Routledge, 1994.

Girl Reading *(photograph by Joel Gordon), 1992. This photograph was taken in the Jefferson Market Library, located in New York City's Greenwich Village, long a center for the arts and liberal politics, and still a neighborhood of rich diversity.*

5

In the World of Letters

I hungered for books, new ways of looking and seeing. It was not a matter of believing or disbelieving what I read, but of feeling something new, of being affected by something that made the look of the world different.

- RICHARD WRIGHT
Black Boy

Everything about that library was good, for it was usually empty and cool behind its awnings, and the shelves were packed with books that not many people ever seemed to take away. But even better was the long walk out of Brownsville to reach it.

- ALFRED KAZIN
Summer: The Way to Highland Park

Mrs. Eva Brady's daughter Jeannie has outgrown her Nancy Drews and Judy Boltons, so on rainy afternoons I cross the street and borrow them, trying not to march away with too many—the child of immigrants, I worry that the Bradys, true and virtuous Americans, will judge me greedy or careless. I wrap the Nancy Drews in paper covers to protect them.

- CYNTHIA OZICK
A Drugstore in Winter

She is English, purely and highly bred. I am more Italian than American. . . . We have absolutely nothing in common, except for the fact that we are both women.

- LOUISE DESALVO
A Portrait of the Puttana
as a Middle-Aged Woolf Scholar

I was always saying the wrong thing, asking the wrong questions. I could not confine my speech to the necessary corners and concerns of life.

- BELL HOOKS
Talking Back

Much of what I read is lost on me, lost in the wash and surf of inexactly understood words.

- EVA HOFFMAN
The New World

The language we used was the glue holding everything and everyone together.

- LOURDES GIL
Against the Grain:
Writing in Spanish in the U.S.A.

One of the most enduring ways of entering into American culture, for both native-born and foreigner, has been through books, through the world of written language. Books, and the libraries that house them, are fixed and revered institutions in our culture. Yet there is no fixed meaning in the books themselves, and although a reader may be substantially molded and revised through reading, he or she may also remain unchanged. In the selections in this chapter, however, although many books may have different meanings, in each case the experiences of reading and writing have been vehicles of self-invention for the writer.

One way that books have been consistently used is as a means of escape from an oppressive reality. Books can open up new worlds to the imagination, and their liberating function—freeing the self from the bounds of family, or of racial or ethnic identity, for example—has been noted by many people. Even though an individual may grow up with family stories that provide nourishment for the imagination and a sense of identity, books can often open up new worlds. For many readers books have provided not only an escape from the narrowness of poverty and/or discrimination but also a way of connecting to the larger world of mainstream culture. As such they have often been carefully guarded by the dominant culture, kept hidden from the powerless because of the subversive and liberating ideas they contain. Richard Wright, represented in this chapter through a selection from his book *Black Boy,* grew up as an African American in the South during the 1920s; as such, he had to borrow books by subterfuge. This act of defiance allowed Wright to make a powerful connection with a new world, one beyond the narrow-mindedness and racism of his immediate environment. For Wright, reading also opened up the way to writing—another important means of self-discovery, liberation, and power.

For those who can gain access to it, the library offers a perfect democracy of sorts—the potential, at least, for *anyone* to read *anything,* and to take from the experience whatever knowledge he or she can gain. Such knowledge can be power: a new awareness of one's own situation can point to possibilities for changing that situation. And just for this reason, conservators of culture may view the outsider in a welcoming way, or else with suspicion.

Yet the point of connection that books provide is unpredictable, and the individual reader responds, mostly, to a reflection of what is already formed in his or her self. Instead of a culture that would exclude him, Richard Wright found life models in the work of American writers of his time. For Wright, these writers provided models for living subversively: standing as he did outside the center of power, Wright was able to critique mainstream American culture and society through his writing. For Alfred Kazin, as he writes in "Summer: The Way to Highland Park," the library was also a place of liberation, a window into the past. Through books, Kazin found a way of making a connection between his own lonely self and the lonely selves of the many artists and writers in New York City who had preceded him, who had articulated American culture from their own perspectives.

For the young Cynthia Ozick, who would later become a writer of fiction, the world of books opened up endless possibilities for storytelling, producing an enchanting universe that could displace the banalities of everyday life. In "A Drugstore in Winter," Ozick describes the subversive activity of reading within the comforting embrace of her family, whose oral narratives also contributed to her development as a writer. For scholar Louise DeSalvo, the transforming effect of books had to do specifically with her encounter with the writings of Virginia Woolf. As DeSalvo tells us in "A Portrait of the *Puttana* as a Middle-Aged Woolf Scholar," the distance between her, an Italian American academic, and Woolf, the famous British author, was immense; yet that distance could be bridged through similarities and kinships that were, for DeSalvo, powerfully liberating. For bell hooks,* an African American cultural critic and academic who grew up in the South during the 1950s, reading and writing were a direct, challenging response to the male-dominated world of her childhood, as she recounts in "Talking Back."

If the book has often served as a bridge from the margins to the center of American culture, that bridge has not always been an easy one to cross. For Eva Hoffman, whose native language was Polish, the English language was perpetually strange. Lacking the familiarity that comes from learning a language as a native speaker, Hoffman relied on her discovered strength, an ability to deal with the abstract geometries of thought in English. In the selection from her memoirs reprinted here, Hoffman emphasizes the "foreignness" of English, the difficulties of learning to think, read, and write in her new language. Yet she also exploits the strength of that strangeness, allowing herself to experience her own responses in their oblique, original character. The chapter concludes with an essay by Lourdes Gil, a Cuban-born poet who has chosen, long after her arrival in this country, to continue to write in her native language, Spanish. Gil reminds us that cultural distances may not always be effectively bridged through books; instead, she claims that a sense of separateness and exile may in fact be a source of comfort and strength.

The writers featured in this chapter are different from one another in terms of experience, age, ethnicity, gender, and intellectual interests. However, they all belong to the same community in one way: they have all defined themselves within mainstream American culture, exploring their own culture and ethnicity by the active process of reading and writing.

**bell hooks:* pseudonym of Gloria Jean Watkins; see p. 355 (*Ed.*)

RICHARD WRIGHT

FROM

Black Boy

Richard Wright (1908–1960) is one of the major African American writers of the twentieth century. He is the author of many short stories, poems, and novels, including the powerful novel Native Son *(1940). Born in Mississippi, Wright moved from town to town with his family, and his early schooling was interrupted frequently. But Wright's wide reading and driving ambition to be a writer gave form to his self-education. He worked at odd jobs for a number of years, even as he was writing short stories during the 1930s; during this time, he was also employed by the Federal Writers Project.*

With Native Son, *Wright moved beyond the smaller audience of readers with leftist political ties to address a larger mainstream audience. In this novel Wright introduced the memorable character Bigger Thomas, an alienated urban black youth who commits a shocking (and accidental) murder that forces him to come to terms with his deepest beliefs. In 1947 Wright moved to France, where he became acquainted with Jean Paul Sartre and the circle of existentialists, philosophers whose thinking influenced his work. In the early 1950s Wright traveled to Africa and wrote about the political future of the continent in a postcolonial age. He died in 1960, before a new wave of interest in his work emerged as a result of the politics of black power.*

The selection that follows is an excerpt from the last two chapters of Wright's autobiography, Black Boy. *Here Wright describes his state of mind prior to his family's decision to leave Memphis and the South and seek their fortunes in Chicago and the North. As he calculates the possibilities for a meaningful life in the South, Wright considers his options: he could fight against racism and never win; he could remain a menial worker—in effect a slave; he could fight with other blacks in a meaningless enactment of self-hatred; or he could seek escape in alcohol. Given his own background and education, the option of a profession and a middle-class existence was quite remote for Wright. What sustained him in his flight to the North and in his eventual evolution into one of the great writers of the century was his connection with a world beyond the immediate one of American racism—a connection that develops, as we see here, through reading.*

CHAPTER THIRTEEN

One morning I arrived early at work and went into the bank lobby where the Negro porter was mopping. I stood at a counter and picked up the Memphis *Commercial Appeal* and began my free reading of the press. I came finally to the editorial page and saw an article dealing with one H. L. Mencken.[1] I knew by hearsay that he was the editor of the *American Mercury*, but aside from that I knew nothing about him. The article was a

---

[1]*H. L. Mencken* (1880–1956): American journalist and writer, who was an acerbic critic of American society, politics, and culture (*Ed.*)

furious denunciation of Mencken, concluding with one, hot, short sentence: Mencken is a fool.

I wondered what on earth this Mencken had done to call down upon him the scorn of the South. The only people I had ever heard denounced in the South were Negroes, and this man was not a Negro. Then what ideas did Mencken hold that made a newspaper like the *Commercial Appeal* castigate him publicly? Undoubtedly he must be advocating ideas that the South did not like. Were there, then, people other than Negroes who criticized the South? I knew that during the Civil War the South had hated northern whites, but I had not encountered such hate during my life. Knowing no more of Mencken than I did at that moment, I felt a vague sympathy for him. Had not the South, which had assigned me the role of a non-man, cast at him its hardest words?

Now, how could I find out about this Mencken? There was a huge library near the riverfront, but I knew that Negroes were not allowed to patronize its shelves any more than they were the parks and playgrounds of the city. I had gone into the library several times to get books for the white men on the job. Which of them would now help me to get books? And how could I read them without causing concern to the white men with whom I worked? I had so far been successful in hiding my thoughts and feelings from them, but I knew that I would create hostility if I went about this business of reading in a clumsy way.

I weighed the personalities of the men on the job. There was Don, a Jew; but I distrusted him. His position was not much better than mine and I knew that he was uneasy and insecure; he had always treated me in an offhand, bantering way that barely concealed his contempt. I was afraid to ask him to help me to get books; his frantic desire to demonstrate a racial solidarity with the whites against Negroes might make him betray me.

Then how about the boss? No, he was a Baptist and I had the suspicion that he would not be quite able to comprehend why a black boy would want to read Mencken. There were other white men on the job whose attitudes showed clearly that they were Kluxers or sympathizers, and they were out of the question.

There remained only one man whose attitude did not fit into an anti-Negro category, for I had heard the white men refer to him as a "Pope lover." He was an Irish Catholic and was hated by the white Southerners. I knew that he read books, because I had got him volumes from the library several times. Since he, too, was an object of hatred, I felt that he might refuse me but would hardly betray me. I hesitated, weighing and balancing the imponderable realities.

One morning I paused before the Catholic fellow's desk.

"I want to ask you a favor," I whispered to him.

"What is it?"

"I want to read. I can't get books from the library. I wonder if you'd let me use your card?"

He looked at me suspiciously.

"My card is full most of the time," he said.

"I see," I said and waited, posing my question silently.

"You're not trying to get me into trouble, are you, boy?" he asked, staring at me.

15 "Oh, no, sir."

"What book do you want?"

"A book by H. L. Mencken."

"Which one?"

"I don't know. Has he written more than one?"

20 "He has written several."

"I didn't know that."

"What makes you want to read Mencken?"

"Oh, I just saw his name in the newspaper," I said.

"It's good of you to want to read," he said. "But you ought to read the right things."

25 I said nothing. Would he want to supervise my reading?

"Let me think," he said. "I'll figure out something."

I turned from him and he called me back. He stared at me quizzically.

"Richard, don't mention this to the other white men," he said.

"I understand," I said. "I won't say a word."

30 A few days later he called me to him.

"I've got a card in my wife's name," he said. "Here's mine."

"Thank you, sir."

"Do you think you can manage it?"

"I'll manage fine," I said.

35 "If they suspect you, you'll get in trouble," he said.

"I'll write the same kind of notes to the library that you wrote when you sent me for books," I told him. "I'll sign your name."

He laughed.

"Go ahead. Let me see what you get," he said.

That afternoon I addressed myself to forging a note. Now, what were the names of books written by H. L. Mencken? I did not know any of them. I finally wrote what I thought would be a foolproof note: *Dear Madam: Will you please let this nigger boy*—I used the word "nigger" to make the librarian feel that I could not possibly be the author of the note—*have some books by H. L. Mencken?* I forged the white man's name.

40 I entered the library as I had always done when on errands for whites, but I felt that I would somehow slip up and betray myself. I doffed my hat, stood a respectful distance from the desk, looked as unbookish as possible, and waited for the white patrons to be taken care of. When the desk was clear of people, I still waited. The white librarian looked at me.

"What do you want, boy?"

As though I did not possess the power of speech, I stepped forward and simply handed her the forged note, not parting my lips.

"What books by Mencken does he want?" she asked.

"I don't know, ma'am," I said, avoiding her eyes.

"Who gave you this card?" 45

"Mr. Falk," I said.

"Where is he?"

"He's at work, at the M—— Optical Company," I said. "I've been in here for him before."

"I remember," the woman said. "But he never wrote notes like this."

Oh, God, she's suspicious. Perhaps she would not let me have the 50 books? If she had turned her back at that moment, I would have ducked out the door and never gone back. Then I thought of a bold idea.

"You can call him up, ma'am," I said, my heart pounding.

"You're not using these books, are you?" she asked pointedly.

"Oh, no, ma'am. I can't read."

"I don't know what he wants by Mencken," she said under her breath.

I knew now that I had won; she was thinking of other things and the 55 race question had gone out of her mind. She went to the shelves. Once or twice she looked over her shoulder at me, as though she was still doubtful. Finally she came forward with two books in her hand.

'I'm sending him two books," she said. "But tell Mr. Falk to come in next time, or send me the names of the books he wants. I don't know what he wants to read."

I said nothing. She stamped the card and handed me the books. Not daring to glance at them, I went out of the library, fearing that the woman would call me back for further questioning. A block away from the library I opened one of the books and read a title: *A Book of Prefaces.* I was nearing my nineteenth birthday and I did not know how to pronounce the word "preface." I thumbed the pages and saw strange words and strange names. I shook my head, disappointed. I looked at the other book; it was called *Prejudices.* I knew what that word meant; I had heard it all my life. And right off I was on guard against Mencken's books. Why would a man want to call a book *Prejudices?* The word was so stained with all my memories of racial hate that I could not conceive of anybody using it for a title. Perhaps I had made a mistake about Mencken? A man who had prejudices must be wrong.

When I showed the books to Mr. Falk, he looked at me and frowned.

"That librarian might telephone you," I warned him.

"That's all right," he said. "But when you're through reading those 60 books, I want you to tell me what you get out of them."

That night in my rented room, while letting the hot water run over my can of pork and beans in the sink, I opened *A Book of Prefaces* and began to read. I was jarred and shocked by the style, the clear, clean, sweeping sentences. Why did he write like that? And how did one write like that? I pictured the man as a raging demon, slashing with his pen, consumed with hate, denouncing everything American, extolling everything European or German, laughing at the weaknesses of people, mocking God, authority. What was this? I stood up, trying to realize what reality lay behind the meaning of the words . . . Yes, this man was fighting, fighting with words. He was using words as a weapon, using them as one would use a club. Could words be weapons? Well, yes, for here they were. Then, maybe, perhaps, I could use them as a weapon? No. It frightened me. I read on and what amazed me was not what he said, but how on earth anybody had the courage to say it.

Occasionally I glanced up to reassure myself that I was alone in the room. Who were these men about whom Mencken was talking so passionately? Who was Anatole France? Joseph Conrad? Sinclair Lewis, Sherwood Anderson, Dostoevski, George Moore, Gustave Flaubert, Maupassant, Tolstoy, Frank Harris, Mark Twain, Thomas Hardy, Arnold Bennett, Stephen Crane, Zola, Norris, Gorky, Bergson, Ibsen, Balzac, Bernard Shaw, Dumas, Poe, Thomas Mann, O. Henry, Dreiser, H. G. Wells, Gogol, T. S. Eliot, Gide, Baudelaire, Edgar Lee Masters, Stendhal, Turgenev, Huneker, Nietzsche, and scores of others? Were these men real? Did they exist or had they existed? And how did one pronounce their names?

I ran across many words whose meanings I did not know, and I either looked them up in a dictionary or, before I had a chance to do that, encountered the word in a context that made its meaning clear. But what strange world was this? I concluded the book with the conviction that I had somehow overlooked something terribly important in life. I had once tried to write, had once reveled in feeling, had let my crude imagination roam, but the impulse to dream had been slowly beaten out of me by experience. Now it surged up again and I hungered for books, new ways of looking and seeing. It was not a matter of believing or disbelieving what I read, but of feeling something new, of being affected by something that made the look of the world different.

As dawn broke I ate my pork and beans, feeling dopey, sleepy. I went to work, but the mood of the book would not die; it lingered, coloring everything I saw, heard, did. I now felt that I knew what the white men were feeling. Merely because I had read a book that had spoken of how they lived and thought, I identified myself with that book. I felt vaguely guilty. Would I, filled with bookish notions, act in a manner that would make the whites dislike me?

I forged more notes and my trips to the library became frequent. Reading grew into a passion. My first serious novel was Sinclair Lewis's *Main Street*.[2] It made me see my boss, Mr. Gerald, and identify him as an American type. I would smile when I saw him lugging his golf bags into the office. I had always felt a vast distance separating me from the boss, and now I felt closer to him, though still distant. I felt now that I knew him, that I could feel the very limits of his narrow life. And this had happened because I had read a novel about a mythical man called George F. Babbitt.

The plots and stories in the novels did not interest me so much as the point of view revealed. I gave myself over to each novel without reserve, without trying to criticize it; it was enough for me to see and feel something different. And for me, everything was something different. Reading was like

---

[2]*Main Street* (1920): a well-known novel by Sinclair Lewis (1885–1951), portraying the hypocrisy and provincialism of a "typical" American town (*Ed.*)

a drug, a dope. The novels created moods in which I lived for days. But I could not conquer my sense of guilt, my feeling that the white men around me knew that I was changing, that I had begun to regard them differently.

Whenever I brought a book to the job, I wrapped it in newspaper—a habit that was to persist for years in other cities and under other circumstances. But some of the white men pried into my packages when I was absent and they questioned me.

"Boy, what are you reading those books for?"

"Oh, I don't know, sir."

"That's deep stuff you're reading, boy." 70

"I'm just killing time, sir."

"You'll addle your brains if you don't watch out."

I read Dreiser's *Jennie Gerhardt* and *Sister Carrie*[3] and they revived in me a vivid sense of my mother's suffering; I was overwhelmed. I grew silent, wondering about the life around me. It would have been impossible for me to have told anyone what I derived from these novels, for it was nothing less than a sense of life itself. All my life had shaped me for the realism, the naturalism of the modern novel, and I could not read enough of them.

Steeped in new moods and ideas, I bought a ream of paper and tried to write; but nothing would come, or what did come was flat beyond telling. I discovered that more than desire and feeling were necessary to write and I dropped the idea. Yet I still wondered how it was possible to know people sufficiently to write about them? Could I ever learn about life and people? To me, with my vast ignorance, my Jim Crow station in life, it seemed a task impossible of achievement. I now knew what being a Negro meant. I could endure the hunger. I had learned to live with hate. But to feel that there were feelings denied me, that the very breath of life itself was beyond my reach, that more than anything else hurt, wounded me. I had a new hunger.

In buoying me up, reading also cast me down, made me see what was 75 possible, what I had missed. My tension returned, new, terrible, bitter, surging, almost too great to be contained. I no longer *felt* that the world about me was hostile, killing; I *knew* it. A million times I asked myself what I could do to save myself, and there were no answers. I seemed forever condemned, ringed by walls.

I did not discuss my reading with Mr. Falk, who had lent me his library card; it would have meant talking about myself and that would have been too painful. I smiled each day, fighting desperately to maintain my old behavior, to keep my disposition seemingly sunny. But some of the white men discerned that I had begun to brood.

"Wake up there, boy!" Mr. Olin said one day.

"Sir!" I answered for the lack of a better word.

---

[3]*Jennie Gerhardt* (1911) and *Sister Carrie* (1900): two novels by Theodore Dreiser (1871–1945), which offered a sympathetic view of the plight of poor women and of their recourse to prostitution (*Ed.*)

"You act like you've stolen something," he said.

I laughed in the way I knew he expected me to laugh, but I resolved to be more conscious of myself, to watch my every act, to guard and hide the new knowledge that was dawning within me.

If I went north, would it be possible for me to build a new life then? But how could a man build a life upon vague, unformed yearnings? I wanted to write and I did not even know the English language. I bought English grammars and found them dull. I felt that I was getting a better sense of the language from novels than from grammars. I read hard, discarding a writer as soon as I felt that I had grasped his point of view. At night the printed page stood before my eyes in sleep.

Mrs. Moss, my landlady, asked me one Sunday morning:

"Son, what is this you keep on reading?"

"Oh, nothing. Just novels."

"What you get out of 'em?"

"I'm just killing time," I said.

"I hope you know your own mind," she said in a tone which implied that she doubted if I had a mind.

I knew of no Negroes who read the books I liked and I wondered if any Negroes ever thought of them. I knew that there were Negro doctors, lawyers, newspapermen, but I never saw any of them. When I read a Negro newspaper I never caught the faintest echo of my preoccupation in its pages. I felt trapped and occasionally, for a few days, I would stop reading. But a vague hunger would come over me for books, books that opened up new avenues of feeling and seeing, and again I would forge another note to the white librarian. Again I would read and wonder as only the naïve and unlettered can read and wonder, feeling that I carried a secret, criminal burden about with me each day.

That winter my mother and brother came and we set up housekeeping, buying furniture on the installment plan, being cheated and yet knowing no way to avoid it. I began to eat warm food and to my surprise found that regular meals enabled me to read faster. I may have lived through many illnesses and survived them, never suspecting that I was ill. My brother obtained a job and we began to save toward the trip north, plotting our time, setting tentative dates for departure. I told none of the white men on the job that I was planning to go north; I knew that the moment they felt I was thinking of the North they would change toward me. It would have made them feel that I did not like the life I was living, and because my life was completely conditioned by what they said or did, it would have been tantamount to challenging them.

I could calculate my chances for life in the South as a Negro fairly clearly now.

I could fight the southern whites by organizing with other Negroes, as my grandfather had done. But I knew that I could never win that way; there were many whites and there were but few blacks. They were strong and we were weak. Outright black rebellion could never win. If I fought openly I would die and I did not want to die. News of lynchings were frequent.

I could submit and live the life of a genial slave, but that was impossible. All of my life had shaped me to live by my own feelings and thoughts. I could make up to Bess and marry her and inherit the house. But that, too, would be the life of a slave; if I did that, I would crush to death something within me, and I would hate myself as much as I knew the whites already hated those who had submitted. Neither could I ever willingly present myself to be kicked, as Shorty had done. I would rather have died than do that.

I could drain off my restlessness by fighting with Shorty and Harrison. I had seen many Negroes solve the problem of being black by transferring their hatred of themselves to others with a black skin and fighting them. I would have to be cold to do that, and I was not cold and I could never be.

I could, of course, forget what I had read, thrust the whites out of my mind, forget them; and find release from anxiety and longing in sex and alcohol. But the memory of how my father had conducted himself made that course repugnant. If I did not want others to violate my life, how could I voluntarily violate it myself?

I had no hope whatever of being a professional man. Not only had I been so conditioned that I did not desire it, but the fulfillment of such an ambition was beyond my capabilities. Well-to-do Negroes lived in a world that was almost as alien to me as the world inhabited by whites. 95

What, then, was there? I held my life in my mind, in my consciousness each day, feeling at times that I would stumble and drop it, spill it forever. My reading had created a vast sense of distance between me and the world in which I lived and tried to make a living, and that sense of distance was increasing each day. My days and nights were one long, quiet, continuously contained dream of terror, tension, and anxiety. I wondered how long I could bear it.

Chapter Fourteen

The accidental visit of Aunt Maggie to Memphis formed a practical basis for my planning to go north. Aunt Maggie's husband, the "uncle" who had fled from Arkansas in the dead of night, had deserted her; and now she was casting about for a living. My mother, Aunt Maggie, my brother, and I held long conferences, speculating on the prospects of jobs and the cost of apartments in Chicago. And every time we conferred, we defeated ourselves. It was impossible for all four of us to go at once; we did not have enough money.

Finally sheer wish and hope prevailed over common sense and facts. We discovered that if we waited until we were prepared to go, we would never leave, we would never amass enough money to see us through. We would have to gamble. We finally decided that Aunt Maggie and I would go first, even though it was winter, and prepare a place for my mother and brother. Why wait until next week or next month? If we were going, why not go at once?

Next loomed the problem of leaving my job cleanly, smoothly, without arguments or scenes. How could I present the fact of leaving to my boss? Yes,

I would pose as an innocent boy; I would tell him that my aunt was taking me and my paralyzed mother to Chicago. That would create in his mind the impression that I was not asserting my will; it would block any expression of dislike on his part for my act. I knew that southern whites hated the idea of Negroes leaving to live in places where the racial atmosphere was different.

▼ ▼ ▼

The next day when I was already in full flight—aboard a northward bound train—I could not have accounted, if it had been demanded of me, for all the varied forces that were making me reject the culture that had molded and shaped me. I was leaving without a qualm, without a single backward glance. The face of the South that I had known was hostile and forbidding, and yet out of all the conflicts and the curses, the blows and the anger, the tension and the terror, I had somehow gotten the idea that life could be different, could be lived in a fuller and richer manner. As had happened when I had fled the orphan home, I was now running more away from something than toward something. But that did not matter to me. My mood was: I've got to get away; I can't stay here. 100

But what was it that always made me feel that way? What was it that made me conscious of possibilities? From where in this southern darkness had I caught a sense of freedom? Why was it that I was able to act upon vaguely felt notions? What was it that made me feel things deeply enough for me to try to order my life by my feelings? The external world of whites and blacks, which was the only world that I had ever known, surely had not evoked in me any belief in myself. The people I had met had advised and demanded submission. What, then, was I after? How dare I consider my feelings superior to the gross environment that sought to claim me?

It had been only through books—at best, no more than vicarious cultural transfusions—that I had managed to keep myself alive in a negatively vital way. Whenever my environment had failed to support or nourish me, I had clutched at books; consequently, my belief in books had risen more out of a sense of desperation than from any abiding conviction of their ultimate value. In a peculiar sense, life had trapped me in a realm of emotional rejection; I had not embraced insurgency through open choice. Existing emotionally on the sheer, thin margin of southern culture, I had felt that nothing short of life itself hung upon each of my actions and decisions; and I had grown used to change, to movement, to making many adjustments.

In the main, my hope was merely a kind of self-defence, a conviction that if I did not leave I would perish, either because of possible violence of others against me, or because of my possible violence against them. The substance of my hope was formless and devoid of any real sense of direction, for in my southern living I had seen no looming landmark by which I could, in a positive sense, guide my daily actions. The shocks of southern living had rendered my personality tender and swollen, tense and volatile, and my flight was more a shunning of external and internal dangers than an attempt to embrace what I felt I wanted.

It had been my accidental reading of fiction and literary criticism that had evoked in me vague glimpses of life's possibilities. Of course, I had never seen or met the men who wrote the books I read, and the kind of world in which they lived was as alien to me as the moon. But what enabled me to overcome my chronic distrust was that these books—written by men like Dreiser, Masters, Mencken, Anderson, and Lewis[4]—seemed defensively critical of the straitened American environment. These writers seemed to feel that America could be shaped nearer to the hearts of those who lived in it. And it was out of these novels and stories and articles, out of the emotional impact of imaginative constructions of heroic or tragic deeds, that I felt touching my face a tinge of warmth from an unseen light; and in my leaving I was groping toward that invisible light, always trying to keep my face so set and turned that I would not lose the hope of its faint promise, using it as my justification for action.

The white South said that it knew "niggers," and I was what the white South called a "nigger." Well, the white South had never known me—never known what I thought, what I felt. The white South said that I had a "place" in life. Well, I had never felt my "place"; or, rather, my deepest instincts had always made me reject the "place" to which the white South had assigned me. It had never occurred to me that I was in any way an inferior being. And no word that I had ever heard fall from the lips of southern white men had ever made me really doubt the worth of my own humanity. True, I had lied. I had stolen. I had struggled to contain my seething anger. I had fought. And it was perhaps a mere accident that I had never killed . . . But in what other ways had the South allowed me to be natural, to be real, to be myself, except in rejection, rebellion, and aggression? 105

Not only had the southern whites not known me, but, more important still, as I had lived in the South I had not had the chance to learn who I was. The pressure of southern living kept me from being the kind of person that I might have been. I had been what my surroundings had demanded, what my family—conforming to the dictates of the whites above them—had exacted of me, and what the whites had said that I must be. Never being fully able to be myself, I had slowly learned that the South could recognize but a part of a man, could accept but a fragment of his personality, and all the rest—the best and deepest things of heart and mind—were tossed away in blind ignorance and hate.

I was leaving the South to fling myself into the unknown, to meet other situations that would perhaps elicit from me other responses. And if I could meet enough of a different life, then, perhaps, gradually and slowly I might learn who I was, what I might be. I was not leaving the South to forget the South, but so that some day I might understand it, might come to know what

---

[4]*Dreiser . . . Lewis:* Edgar Lee Masters (1868–1950) and Sherwood Anderson (1876–1941), along with Dreiser, Lewis, and Mencken, were American writers who defied in their work traditional views about American culture and society. *(Ed.)*

its rigors had done to me, to its children. I fled so that the numbness of my defensive living might thaw out and let me feel the pain—years later and far away—of what living in the South had meant.

Yet, deep down, I knew that I could never really leave the South, for my feelings had already been formed by the South, for there had been slowly instilled into my personality and consciousness, black though I was, the culture of the South. So, in leaving, I was taking a part of the South to transplant in alien soil, to see if it could grow differently, if it could drink of new and cool rains, bend in strange winds, respond to the warmth of other suns, and, perhaps, to bloom . . . And if that miracle ever happened, then I would know that there was yet hope in that southern swamp of despair and violence, that light could emerge even out of the blackest of the southern night. I would know that the South too could overcome its fear, its hate, its cowardice, its heritage of guilt and blood, its burden of anxiety and compulsive cruelty.

With ever watchful eyes and bearing scars, visible and invisible, I headed North, full of a hazy notion that life could be lived with dignity, that the personalities of others should not be violated, that men should be able to confront other men without fear or shame, and that if men were lucky in their living on earth they might win some redeeming meaning for their having struggled and suffered here beneath the stars.

DISCUSSING THE TEXT

1. What prompted Wright to seek out books by H. L. Mencken from the library? How does reading Mencken affect his view of America and of the white men he works for?
2. Why do members of the white world in which Wright moves seek to prohibit or discourage him from reading? Do you agree with these people's notion that they are somehow protecting Wright? Why or why not?
3. In a group of four or five students, discuss how Wright's program of reading changed his perspective on himself, his ambitions, and the world beyond the American South of the 1920s. Have you ever experienced a comparable dramatic shift in your point of view? Take notes as you work on this assignment, and be prepared to share your opinions and experiences with the class.
4. Near the end of this selection Wright says that "deep down, I knew that I could never really leave the South . . ." (par. 108). In leaving for Chicago, what part of the South does Wright feel that he takes with him? What connections does he feel with the South? What are his attitudes, and his hopes, toward the South and its future?

WRITING ABOUT THE TEXT

5. Faced with racial discrimination, Wright carefully plans his access to library books, first by approaching the one man in the office who he felt would help him, and then by acting the role of the meek Negro as he confronts the

librarian (par. 7–57). Do you think his strategies were worth it? What would you have done in his circumstances? Write two paragraphs expressing your views.

6. Wright encounters names and words in his reading that are unfamiliar to him but that excite his curiosity and fire his imagination. Choose two names that are unfamiliar to you from the long list Wright offers in paragraph 62. Look these names up in a reference work in your library, and write a paragraph on each that could serve as a useful introduction to people who are not familiar with this figure. What possible benefits can you see in being familiar with these names? Conclude this exercise by creating your own list of names of figures—particularly writers or artists—who are important to you.
7. "In buoying me up," Wright writes, "reading also cast me down . . ." (par. 75). Write a one- to two-page discussion of the "ups" and "downs" of reading for a man like the young Richard Wright. Can you imagine someone having a similar experience today? What kind of person would you imagine, and under what conditions?
8. Wright tells us that reading books rekindled in him "the impulse to dream . . . I hungered for books, new ways of looking and seeing." Keeping his experience in mind, write an essay about a book, poem, or story that you have read that changed your outlook on life in some way. If you have not had an experience of this kind, write an essay comparing your own experiences as a reader with those described by Wright.

ALFRED KAZIN

Summer: The Way to Highland Park

Alfred Kazin's A Walker in the City *(1951), from which this selection is excerpted, is an autobiography about coming to maturity in New York City, written when the author was in his thirties (1951). At the time he wrote the book, Kazin, who was born in Brooklyn, New York, in 1915, had already moved into the heart of literary circles in New York. He wrote articles and reviewed books for prominent journals and newspapers, including* The New Republic *and* Fortune *magazines. In addition, he had already written one of the landmark books in American literary history,* On Native Grounds *(1942), which defines a writing tradition in American literature based on responses to the changing realities of American life.*

Kazin holds a special place among literary critics of his generation. Soon after the publication of A Walker in the City, *Kazin began a long career in teaching, with distinguished appointments and lectureships at Harvard, Princeton, and the City University of New York, among others. He has edited many scholarly volumes on authors such as William Blake, Theodore Dreiser, and Herman Melville. His writing shows his wide range of knowledge and interests and his continued engagement with American literature and culture.*

In his autobiography, Kazin portrays himself as deeply excited by New York City. His walks through the city often serve as the framework for his personal narrative. In this excerpt from the book, the sixteen-year-old Kazin is walking to the library in Brooklyn that would serve as the indispensable source for his early reading. Describing a remembered walk on a summer evening, Kazin recreates his daily journey through various immigrant neighborhoods in Brooklyn. His insatiable appetite for books, as he tells it, is closely connected to his effort to discover his own cultural identity.

There was a new public library I liked to walk out to right after supper, when the streets were still full of light. It was to the north of the Italians, just off the El on Broadway, in the "American" district of old frame houses and brownstones and German ice-cream parlors and quiet tree-lined streets where I went to high school. Everything about that library was good, for it was usually empty and cool behind its awnings, and the shelves were packed with books that not many people ever seemed to take away. But even better was the long walk out of Brownsville to reach it.

How wonderful it was in the still suspended evening light to go past the police station on East New York and come out into the clinging damp sweetness of Italian cheese. The way to the borders of Brownsville there was always heavy with blocks of indistinguishable furniture stores, monument works, wholesale hardware shops. Block after block was lined with bedroom sets, granite tombstones, kitchen ranges, refrigerators, store fixtures, cash registers. It was like taking one last good look around before you said good-by. As the sun bore down on new kitchen ranges and refrigerators, I seemed to hear the clang of all those heavily smooth surfaces against the fiery windows, to feel myself pulled down endless corridors of tombstones, cash registers, maple beds, maple love seats, maple vanity tables. But at the police station, the green lamps on each side of the door, the detectives lounging along the street, the smell from the dark, damp, leaky steps that led down to the public toilets below, instantly proclaimed the end of Brownsville.

Ahead, the Italians' streets suddenly reared up into hills, all the trolley car lines flew apart into wild plunging crossroads—the way to anywhere, it seemed to me then. And in the steady heat, the different parts of me racing each other in excitement, the sweat already sweet on my face, still tasting on my lips the corn and salt and butter, I would dash over the tree-lined island at the crossroads, and on that boulevard so sharp with sun that I could never understand why the new red-brick walls of the Catholic church felt so cool as I passed, I crossed over into the Italian district.

I still had a certain suspicion of the Italians—surely they were all Fascists to a man? Every grocery window seemed to have a picture of Mussolini[1] frowning under a feather-tipped helmet, every drugstore beneath the old-fashioned gold letters pasted on the window a colored lithograph of the

[1]*Benito Mussolini* (1883–1945): Italian dictator, founder of Fascism (*Ed.*)

Madonna with a luminescent heart showing through a blue gown. What I liked best in the windows were the thickly printed opera posters, topped by tiny photographs of singers with olive-bronze faces. Their long straight noses jutted aloofly, defying me to understand them. But despite the buzz of unfamiliar words ending in the letter *i*, I could at least make contact with LA FORZA DEL DESTINO.[2] In the air was that high overriding damp sweetness of Italian cheese, then something peppery. In a butcher shop window at the corner of Pacific Street long incredibly thin sausage rings were strung around a horizontal bar. The clumps of red and brown meat dripping off those sausage rings always stayed with me until I left the Italians at Fulton Street—did they eat such things?

Usually, at that hour of the early evening when I passed through on my way to the new library, they were all still at supper. The streets were strangely empty except for an old man in a white cap who sat on the curb sucking at a twisted Italian cigar. I felt I was passing through a deserted town and knocking my head against each door to call the inhabitants out. It was a poor neighborhood, poor as ours. Yet all the houses and stores there, the very lettering of the signs AVVOCATO FARMACIA LATTERIA[3] tantalized me by their foreignness. Everything there looked smaller and sleepier than it did in Brownsville. There was a kind of mild, infinitely soothing smell of flour and cheese mildly rotting in the evening sun. You could almost taste the cheese in the sweat you licked off your lips, could feel your whole body licking and tasting at the damp inner quietness that came out of the stores. The heat seemed to melt down every hard corner in sight. 5

Beyond Atlantic Avenue the sun glared and glared on broken glass lining the high stone walls of a Catholic reformatory that went all around the block. Barbed wire rose up on the other side of the wall, and oddly serene above the broken glass, very tall trees. Behind those walls, I had always heard, lived "bad girls" under the supervision of nuns. We knew what all that broken glass meant. The girls stole out every night and were lifted over the walls every morning by their laughing boy friends. We knew. The place was a prison house of the dark and hypocritical Catholic religion. Whenever I heard the great bell in the yard clanging for prayers as I passed, I had the same image in my mind of endless barren courts of narrow rooms, in each of which a girl in a prison smock looked up with pale hatred at a nun.

> And priests in black gowns were walking their rounds
> And binding with briars my joys and desires[4]

---

[2]*La Forza del Destino* (1862): one of the best-known operas by Italian composer Giuseppe Verdi. The title means "the force of destiny." (*Ed.*)

[3]*Avvocato:* (Italian) advocate or lawyer; *Farmacia:* pharmacy; *Latteria:* dairy store (*Ed.*)

[4]*"And priests . . . desires":* from the poem "The Garden of Love," from *Songs of Experience,* by British poet William Blake (1757–1827), where he expressed his sentiments against established Christianity (*Ed.*)

Jesus! I would say to myself with hoped-for scorn, *Look at my Yeshua!*[5] How I wanted to get on to my library, to get on beyond that high stone wall lined with the jagged ends of broken milk bottles; never to have to look back at that red-bricked church that reared itself up across from the borders of Brownsville like a fortress. Once, on the evening before an examination, I had gone into that church, had tried vaguely to pray, but had been so intimidated by the perpetual twilight, the remoteness of the freezing white altar and the Italian women in kerchiefs around me, that at a low murmuring out of a confession box near the door I had run away. Yet how lonely it always was passing under the wall—as if I were just about to be flung against it by a wave of my own thought.

Ahead of me now the black web of the Fulton Street El. On the other side of the BANCA COMMERCIALE,[6] two long even pavements still raw with sunlight at seven o'clock of a summer evening take me straight through the German and Irish "American" neighborhoods. I could never decide whether it was all those brownstones and blue and gray frame houses or the sight of the library serenely waiting for me that made up the greatest pleasure of that early evening walk. As soon as I got out from under the darkness of the El on Fulton Street, I was catapulted into tranquility.

Everything ahead of me now was of a different order—wide, clean, still, every block lined with trees. I sniffed hungrily at the patches of garden earth behind the black iron spikes and at the wooden shutters hot in the sun—there where even the names of the streets, Macdougal, Hull, Somers, made me humble with admiration. The long quiet avenues rustled comfortably in the sun; above the brownstone stoops all the yellow striped awnings were unfurled. Every image I had of peace, of quiet shaded streets in some old small-town America I had seen dreaming over the ads in the *Saturday Evening Post,* now came back to me as that proud procession of awnings along the brownstones. I can never remember *walking* those last few blocks to the library; I seemed to float along the canvas tops. Here were the truly American streets; here was where they lived. To get that near to brownstones, to see how private everything looked in that world of cool black painted floors and green walls where on each windowsill the first shoots of Dutch bulbs rose out of the pebbles like green and white flags, seemed to me the greatest privilege I had ever had. A breath of long-stored memory blew out at me from the veranda of Oyster Bay. Even when I visited an Irish girl from my high school class who lived in one of those brownstones, and was amazed to see that the rooms were as small as ours, that a Tammany[7] court attendant's family could be as poor

---

[5]*Jesus! . . . Look at my Yeshua!:* Kazin expresses his dismay at what he sees as the Catholic reformatory's cruelty and injustice. *Yeshua* is Hebrew for Jesus. (*Ed.*)

[6]*Banca Commerciale:* (Italian) commercial bank (*Ed.*)

[7]*Tammany:* the Tammany Society of New York City, incorporated in 1789 and developed into a powerful force in city politics (*Ed.*)

as we were, that behind the solid "American" front of fringed shawls, Yankee rocking chairs, and oval daguerreotypes on the walls they kept warm in winter over an oil stove—even then, I could think of those brownstone streets only as my great entrance into America, a half-hour nearer to "New York."

I had made a discovery; I had stumbled on a connection between myself 10 and the shape and color of time in the streets of New York. Though I knew that brownstones were old-fashioned and had read scornful references to them in novels, it was just the thick, solid way in which they gripped to themselves some texture of the city's past that now fascinated me. There was one brownstone on Macdougal Street I would stop and brood over for long periods every evening I went to the library for fresh books—waiting in front of it, studying every crease in the stone, every line in the square windows jutting out above the street, as if I were planning its portrait. I had made a discovery: walking could take me back into the America of the nineteenth century.

On those early summer evenings, the library was usually empty, and there was such ease at the long tables under the plants lining the windowsills, the same books of American history lay so undisturbed on the shelves, the wizened, faintly smiling little old lady who accepted my presence without questions or suggestions or reproach was so delightful as she quietly, smilingly stamped my card and took back a batch of new books every evening, that whenever I entered the library I would walk up and down trembling in front of the shelves. For each new book I took away, there seemed to be ten more of which I was depriving myself.

▼ ▼ ▼

The automatic part of all my reading was history. The past, the past was great: anything American, old, glazed, touched with dusk at the end of the nineteenth century, still smoldering with the fires lit by the industrial revolution, immediately set my mind dancing. The present was mean, the eighteenth century too Anglo-Saxon, too far away. Between them, in the light from the steerage ships waiting to discharge my parents onto the final shore, was the world of dusk, of rust, of iron, of gaslight, where, I thought, I would find my way to that fork in the road where all American lives cross. The past was deep, deep, full of solitary Americans whose careers, though closed in death, had woven an arc around them which I could see in space and time—"lonely Americans," it was even the title of a book. I remember that the evening I opened Lewis Mumford's *The Brown Decades*[8] I was so astonished to see a photograph of Brooklyn Bridge,[9] I so instantly formed against that brown-

---

[8]*The Brown Decades . . . Eakins: The Brown Decades: A Study of the Arts in America, 1865–1895* (1931), a book by Mumford, provided Kazin with a new familiarity and knowledge of American culture. The artists and writers mentioned (Ryder, Peirce, Dickinson, and Eakins) were all influential in the latter part of the nineteenth century. (*Ed.*)

[9]*The Brooklyn Bridge:* designed by German American engineer John Augustus Roebling (1806–1869). Completed in 1888, it soon became a powerful symbol of American technology and architecture. For Kazin, the Brooklyn Bridge acts as an important connection to New York City's life and culture. (*Ed.*)

stone on Macdougal Street such close and loving images of Albert Pinkham Ryder, Charles Peirce, Emily Dickinson, Thomas Eakins, and John August Roebling, that I could never walk across Roebling's bridge, or pass the hotel on University Place named Albert, in Ryder's honor, or stop in front of the garbage cans at Fulton and Cranberry Streets in Brooklyn at the place where Whitman[10] had himself printed *Leaves of Grass,* without thinking that I had at last opened the great trunk of forgotten time in New York in which I, too, I thought, would someday find the source of my unrest.

I felt then that I stood outside all that, that I would be alien forever, but that I could at least keep the trunk open by reading. And though I knew somewhere in myself that a Ryder, an Emily Dickinson, an Eakins, a Whitman, even that fierce-browed old German immigrant Roebling, with his flute and his metaphysics and his passionate love of suspension bridges, were alien, too, alien in the deepest way, like my beloved Blake, my Yeshua, my Beethoven, my Newman—nevertheless I still thought of myself then as standing outside America. I read as if books would fill my every gap, legitimize my strange quest for the American past, remedy my every flaw, let me in at last into the great world that was anything just out of Brownsville.

So that when, leaving the library for the best of all walks, to Highland Park, I came out on Bushwick Avenue, with its strange, wide, sun-lit spell, a thankfulness seized me, mixed with envy and bitterness, and I waited against a hydrant for my violence to pass. Why were these people *here,* and we *there?* Why had I always to think of insider and outsider, of their belonging and our not belonging, when books had carried me this far, and when, as I could already see, it was myself that would carry me farther—beyond these petty distinctions I had so long made in loneliness?

DISCUSSING THE TEXT

1. Kazin must walk out of his own neighborhood—Brownsville—to get to the new public library. How does he recreate his sense of the Italian neighborhood that he walks through? What details does he use to make us see and imagine how it felt?
2. The last few blocks to the new library take Kazin through "German and Irish 'American' neighborhoods" (par. 8). What makes the streets and houses of these neighborhoods seem uniquely "American" to Kazin's eye? Where does his image of "America" come from? Can you think of a neighborhood you're familiar with that strikes you as particularly American? What about this neighborhood makes it seem American to you?
3. Kazin feels that he stands outside the real America, alienated from it. How do the lives of the nineteenth-century writers and thinkers that he encounters in the library help him to deal with this alienation? Why does he prefer

[10]*Walt Whitman* (1819–1892): Born in Brooklyn, New York, Whitman revolutionized American literature with the publication of his poetry collection, *Leaves of Grass* (1855). By the time of his death, Whitman was already considered a legendary American poet. (*Ed.*)

writers from the nineteenth century to those from the eighteenth or twentieth centuries?

4. Working with a group of four or five students, make a list of all the writers, artists, and other historical figures that Kazin mentions in this selection. Share whatever you know about these figures with the other members of your group. Take careful notes so that you can see how many of these figures your entire class as a whole can identify.

WRITING ABOUT THE TEXT

5. Write a one-page description of a walk of your own through a neighborhood, either one you know well or one that is new to you. Try to evoke the feel of this neighborhood through your selection of details.
6. Do you think the "lonely Americans" that Kazin describes in paragraph 12 would provide the same kind of solace for a young "walker in the city" today? Why or why not? If so, which figures do you think would be especially important? If not, who are some other figures who might provide solace or inspiration to a young walker today? Write a one-page response to these questions.
7. Kazin writes, "I read as if books would fill my every gap, legitimize my strange quest for the American past, remedy my every flaw, let me in at last into the great world that was anything just out of Brownsville" (par. 13). Write a brief essay comparing and contrasting Kazin's feelings about reading with those of Richard Wright in the previous selection (p. 319).
8. Kazin prefers to read writers from the nineteenth century because, he says, "The present was mean, the eighteenth century too Anglo-Saxon, too far away" (par. 12). Pick a period of American history (not necessarily an entire century—perhaps a particular decade, for instance) that is especially interesting to you. Write a one- to two-page essay explaining your interest in this period. Why do you find it more compelling than other periods in American history?

CYNTHIA OZICK

A Drugstore in Winter

Cynthia Ozick's autobiographical essay, "A Drugstore in Winter," originally published in the New York Times Book Review *in 1984, draws on her experiences growing up in the Bronx during the Great Depression of the 1930s. Ozick's father was a pharmacist, and both at the family drugstore and at home, Ozick was always hearing stories. Some came from her immigrant grandmother, who talked constantly of life in the "Old Country," a Russian village, and from her parents, who usually talked about their own neighborhood. In this memoir, Ozick begins by listing elements that will eventually (and characteristically) come together in her narrative: the every-*

day drugstore, the remarkable dome of the Boston State House, and her own feelings as a young reader as she dreams herself into being someone else.

Even though Ozick describes herself as a practical person, she is drawn to the mystical in her writing, which is steeped in biblical and Yiddish traditions. Her prose, often on the edge of humor, jumps frequently from one mood to another, mixing the real and the surreal, the practical and the dreamlike, the everyday and the sacred. A particularly noteworthy feature in Ozick's work is her style, especially her play with words, her inventiveness and original phrasing. Yet beneath the surface of this playful language is a serious concern with ideas and emotions.

Born in New York in 1928 into a Jewish American family, Ozick is a respected contemporary fiction writer, particularly for her short stories. She has been the recipient of Guggenheim and National Endowment for the Arts fellowships, and of the Mildred and Harold Strauss Living Grant. Among her many works, three award-winning collections of short fiction stand out: The Pagan Rabbi and Other Stories *(1971),* Bloodshed and Three Novellas *(1976), and* Levitation: Five Fictions *(1982). Critic Harold Bloom has said that Ozick's major concern in her work, culminating in her 1987 novel,* The Messiah of Stockholm, *has been to reconcile two driving forces in her life, the desire to remain within the Jewish tradition and the need to write fiction.*

This is about reading; a drugstore in winter; the gold leaf on the dome of the Boston State House; also loss, panic, and dread.

First, the gold leaf. (This part is a little like a turn-of-the-century pulp tale, though only a little. The ending is a surprise, but there is no plot.) Thirty years ago I burrowed in the Boston Public Library one whole afternoon, to find out—not out of curiosity—how the State House got its gold roof. The answer, like the answer to most Bostonian questions, was Paul Revere. So I put Paul Revere's gold dome into an "article," and took it (though I was just as scared by recklessness then as I am now) to the *Boston Globe,* on Washington Street. The Features Editor had a bare severe head, a closed parenthesis mouth, and silver Dickensian spectacles. He made me wait, standing, at the side of his desk while he read; there was no bone in me that did not rattle. Then he opened a drawer and handed me fifteen dollars. Ah, joy of Homer, joy of Milton! Grub Street[1] bliss!

The very next Sunday, Paul Revere's gold dome saw print. Appetite for more led me to a top-floor chamber in Filene's department store: Window Dressing. But no one was in the least bit dressed—it was a dumbstruck nudist colony up there, a mob of naked frozen enigmatic manikins, tall enameled skinny ladies with bald breasts and skulls, and legs and wrists and necks that horribly unscrewed. Paul Revere's dome paled beside this gold mine! A sight—mute numb Walpurgisnacht[2]—easily worth another fifteen dollars. I had a Master's

[1]*Grub Street:* a street in London where poor writers and journalists lived during the eighteenth century. The term was used in the nineteenth century as a symbol of literary hack work—the meaning that Ozick gives it here. (*Ed.*)

[2]*Walpurgisnacht:* a reference to the witches' sabbath of German tradition, held on April 30, the eve of May Day. In common usage, it means a wild event or festivity. (*Ed.*)

degree (thesis topic: "Parable in the Later Novels of Henry James") and a job as an advertising copywriter (9 a.m. to 6 p.m. six days a week, forty dollars per week; if you were male and had no degree at all, sixty dollars). Filene's Sale Days—Crib Bolsters! Lulla-Buys! Jonnie-Mops! Maternity Skirts with Expanding Invisible Trick Waist! And a company show; gold watches to mark the retirement of elderly Irish salesladies; for me the chance to write song lyrics (to the tune of "On Top of Old Smoky") honoring our Store. But "Mute Numb Walpurgisnacht in Secret Downtown Chamber" never reached the *Globe.* Melancholy and meaning business, the Advertising Director forbade it. Grub Street was bad form, and I had to promise never again to sink to another article. Thus ended my life in journalism.

Next: reading, and certain drugstore winter dusks. These come together. It is an aeon before Filene's, years and years before the Later Novels of Henry James. I am scrunched on my knees at a round glass table near a plate glass door on which is inscribed, in gold leaf Paul Revere never put there, letters that must be read backward: PARK VIEW PHARMACY There is an evening smell of late coffee from the fountain, and all the librarians are lined up in a row on the tall stools, sipping and chattering. They have just stepped in from the cold of the Traveling Library, and so have I. The Traveling Library is a big green truck that stops, once every two weeks, on the corner of Continental Avenue, just a little way in from Westchester Avenue, not far from a house that keeps a pig. Other houses fly pigeons from their roofs, other yards have chickens, and down on Mayflower there is even a goat. This is Pelham Bay, the Bronx, in the middle of the Depression, all cattails and weeds, such a lovely place and tender hour! Even though my mother takes me on the subway far, far downtown to buy my winter coat in the frenzy of Klein's on Fourteenth Street, and even though I can recognize the heavy power of a quarter, I don't know it's the Depression. On the trolley on the way to Westchester Square I see the children who live in the boxcar strangely set down in an empty lot some distance from Spy Oak (where a Revolutionary traitor was hanged—served him right for siding with redcoats); the lucky boxcar children dangle their stick-legs from their train-house maw and wave; how I envy them! I envy the orphans of the Gould Foundation, who have their own private swings and seesaws. Sometimes I imagine I am an orphan, and my father is an impostor pretending to be my father.

My father writes in his prescription book: *#59330 Dr. O'Flaherty Pow. 60/ # 59331 Dr. Mulligan Gtt .65/ #59332 Dr. Thron Tab .90.* Ninety cents! A terrifically expensive medicine; someone is really sick. When I deliver a prescription around the corner or down the block, I am offered a nickel tip. I always refuse, out of conscience; I am, after all, the Park View Pharmacy's own daughter, and it wouldn't be seemly. My father grinds and mixes powders, weighs them out in tiny snowy heaps on an apothecary scale, folds them into delicate translucent papers or meticulously drops them into gelatin capsules.

In the big front window of the Park View Pharmacy there is a startling display—goldfish bowls, balanced one on the other in amazing pyramids. A

German lady enters, one of my father's cronies—his cronies are both women and men. My quiet father's eyes are water-color blue, he wears his small skeptical quiet smile and receives the neighborhood's life-secrets. My father is discreet and inscrutable. The German lady pokes a punchboard with a pin, pushes up a bit of rolled paper, and cries out—she has just won a goldfish bowl, with two swimming goldfish in it! Mr. Jaffe, the salesman from McKesson & Robbins, arrives, trailing two mists: winter steaminess and the animal fog of his cigar,[3] which melts into the coffee smell, the tarpaper smell, the eerie honeyed tangled drugstore smell. Mr. Jaffe and my mother and father are intimates by now, but because it is the 1930s, so long ago, and the old manners still survive, they address one another gravely as Mr. Jaffe, Mrs. Ozick, Mr. Ozick. My mother calls my father Mr. O, even at home, as in a Victorian novel. In the street my father tips his hat to ladies. In the winter his hat is a regular fedora; in the summer it is a straw boater with a black ribbon and a jot of blue feather.

What am I doing at this round glass table, both listening and not listening to my mother and father tell Mr. Jaffe about their struggle with "Tessie," the lion-eyes landlady who has just raised, threefold, in the middle of that Depression I have never heard of, the Park View Pharmacy's devouring rent? My mother, not yet forty, wears bandages on her ankles, covering oozing varicose veins; back and forth she strides, dashes, runs, climbing cellar stairs or ladders; she unpacks cartons, she toils behind drug counters and fountain counters. Like my father, she is on her feet until one in the morning, the Park View's closing hour. My mother and father are in trouble, and I don't know it. I am too happy. I feel the secret center of eternity, nothing will ever alter, no one will ever die. Through the window past the lit goldfish, the gray oval sky deepens over our neighborhood wood, where all the dirt paths lead down to seagull-specked water. I am familiar with every frog-haunted monument: Pelham Bay Park is thronged with WPA art—statuary, fountains, immense rococo staircases cascading down a hillside, Bacchus-faced stelae—stone Roman glories afterward mysteriously razed by an avenging Robert Moses.[4] One year—how distant it seems now, as if even the climate is past returning—the bay froze so hard that whole families, mine among them, crossed back and forth to City Island, strangers saluting and calling out in the ecstasy of the bright trudge over such a sudden wilderness of ice.

---

[3]Mr. Matthew Bruccoli, another Bronx drugstore child, has written to say that he remembers with certainty that Mr. Jaffe did not smoke. In my memory the cigar is somehow there, so I leave it.

[4]*WPA . . . Robert Moses:* The Works Projects Administration was established by President Franklin Delano Roosevelt during the Great Depression of the 1930s to provide work for persons on relief in the construction and building industries. Ozick refers to artistic projects supported by the W.P.A. through the Federal Art Project during the 1930s. Robert Moses (1888–1981) served as New York's secretary of state under Roosevelt, then governor, but later fell into disagreement with him. He was New York City commissioner of parks from 1934 to 1960, and greatly altered the face of the city with new parks, beaches, highways, and bridges. (*Ed.*)

In the Park View Pharmacy, in the winter dusk, the heart in my body is revolving like the goldfish fleet-finned in their clear bowls. The librarians are still warming up over their coffee. They do not recognize me, though only half an hour ago I was scrabbling in the mud around the two heavy boxes from the Traveling Library—oafish crates tossed with a thump to the ground. One box contains magazines—*Boy's Life, The American Girl, Popular Mechanix.* But the other, the other! The other transforms me. It is tumbled with storybooks, with clandestine intimations and transfigurations. In school I am a luckless goosegirl, friendless and forlorn. In P.S. 71 I carry, weighty as a cloak, the ineradicable knowledge of my scandal—I am cross-eyed, dumb, an imbecile at arithmetic; in P.S. 71 I am publicly shamed in Assembly because I am caught not singing Christmas carols; in P.S. 71 I am repeatedly accused of deicide. But in the Park View Pharmacy, in the winter dusk, branches blackening in the park across the road, I am driving in rapture through the Violet Fairy Book and the Yellow Fairy Book, insubstantial chariots snatched from the box in the mud. I have never been *inside* the Traveling Library; only grownups are allowed. The boxes are for the children. No more than two books may be borrowed, so I have picked the fattest ones, to last. All the same, the Violet and the Yellow are melting away. Their pages dwindle. I sit at the round glass table, dreaming, dreaming. Mr. Jaffe is murmuring advice. He tells a joke about Wrong-Way Corrigan.[5] The librarians are buttoning up their coats. A princess, captive of an ogre, receives a letter from her swain and hides it in her bosom. I can visualize her bosom exactly—she clutches it against her chest. It is a tall and shapely vase, with a hand-painted flower on it, like the vase on the secondhand piano at home.

I am incognito. No one knows who I truly am. The teachers in P.S. 71 don't know. Rabbi Meskin, my *cheder*[6] teacher, doesn't know. Tessie the lion-eyed landlady doesn't know. Even Hymie the fountain clerk can't know—though he understands other things better than anyone: how to tighten roller skates with a skatekey, for instance, and how to ride a horse. On Friday afternoons, when the new issue is out, Hymie and my brother fight hard over who gets to see *Life* magazine first. My brother is older than I am, and doesn't like me; he builds radios in his bedroom, he is already W2LOM, and operates his transmitter (*da-di-da-dit, da-da-di-da*) so penetratingly on Sunday mornings that Mrs. Eva Brady, across the way, complains. Mrs. Eva Brady has a subscription to *The Writer;* I fill a closet with her old copies. How to Find a Plot. Narrative and Character, the Writer's Tools. Because my brother has his ham license, I say, "I have a license too." "What kind of license?" my brother asks, falling into the trap. "Poetic license," I reply; my brother hates me, but any-

---

[5]*Wrong-Way Corrigan:* Douglas "Wrong-Way" Corrigan was an American aviator who was supposed to fly from New York to California in 1938. He preferred to go to Ireland, and that is where he landed. When asked how someone headed for California could end up in Ireland, Corrigan claimed to have flown the "wrong way." No one believed him. (*Ed.*)

[6]*cheder:* Hebrew school (*Ed.*)

how his birthday presents are transporting: one year *Alice in Wonderland, Pinocchio* the next, then *Tom Sawyer.* I go after Mark Twain, and find *Joan of Arc* and my first satire, *Christian Science.* My mother surprises me with *Pollyanna,* the admiration of her Lower East Side childhood, along with *The Lady of the Lake.* Mrs. Eva Brady's daughter Jeannie has outgrown her Nancy Drews and Judy Boltons, so on rainy afternoons I cross the street and borrow them, trying not to march away with too many—the child of immigrants, I worry that the Bradys, true and virtuous Americans, will judge me greedy or careless. I wrap the Nancy Drews in paper covers to protect them. Old Mrs. Brady, Jeannie's grandmother, invites me back for more. I am so timid I can hardly speak a word, but I love her dark parlor; I love its black bookcases. Old Mrs. Brady sees me off, embracing books under an umbrella; perhaps she divines who I truly am. My brother doesn't care. My father doesn't notice. I think my mother knows. My mother reads the *Saturday Evening Post* and the *Woman's Home Companion;* sometimes the *Ladies' Home Journal,* but never *Good Housekeeping.* I read all my mother's magazines. My father reads *Drug Topics* and *Der Tog,* the Yiddish daily. In Louie Davidowitz's house (waiting our turn for the rabbi's lesson, he teaches me chess in *cheder*) there is a piece of furniture I am in awe of: a shining circular table that is also a revolving bookshelf holding a complete set of Charles Dickens. I borrow *Oliver Twist.* My cousins turn up with *Gulliver's Travels, Just So Stories, Don Quixote,* Oscar Wilde's *Fairy Tales,* uncannily different from the usual kind. Blindfolded, I reach into a Thanksgiving grabbag and pull out *Mrs. Leicester's School,* Mary Lamb's desolate stories of rejected children. Books spill out of rumor, exchange, miracle. In the Park View Pharmacy's lending library I discover, among the nurse romances, a browning, brittle miracle: *Jane Eyre.* Uncle Morris comes to visit (*his* drugstore is on the other side of the Bronx) and leaves behind, just like that, a three-volume Shakespeare. Peggy and Betty Provan, Scottish sisters around the corner, lend me their *Swiss Family Robinson.* Norma Foti, a whole year older, transmits a rumor about Louisa May Alcott; afterward I read *Little Women* a thousand times. Ten thousand! I am no longer incognito, not even to myself. I am Jo in her "vortex"; not Jo exactly, but some Jo-of-the-future. I am under an enchantment: who I truly am must be deferred, waited for and waited for. My father, silently filling capsules, is grieving over his mother in Moscow. I write letters in Yiddish to my Moscow grandmother, whom I will never know. I will never know my Russian aunts, uncles, cousins. In Moscow there is suffering, deprivation, poverty. My mother, theadbare, goes without a new winter coat so that packages can be sent to Moscow. Her fiery justice-eyes are semaphores I cannot decipher.

Some day, when I am free of P.S. 71, I will write stories; meanwhile, in winter dusk, in the Park View, in the secret bliss of the Violet Fairy Book, I both see and do not see how these grains of life will stay forever, papa and mama will live forever, Hymie will always turn my skatekey. 10

Hymie, after Italy, after the Battle of the Bulge, comes back from the war with a present: *From Here to Eternity.* Then he dies, young. Mama reads *Pride and Prejudice* and every single word of Willa Cather. Papa reads, in Yiddish, all of Sholem Aleichem and Peretz. He reads Malamud's *The Assistant* when I ask him to.

Papa and mama, in Staten Island, are under the ground. Some other family sits transfixed in the sun parlor where I read *Jane Eyre* and *Little Women* and, long afterward, *Middlemarch.* The Park View Pharmacy is dismantled, turned into a Hallmark card shop. It doesn't matter! I close my eyes, or else only stare, and everything is in its place again, and everyone.

A writer is dreamed and transfigured into being by spells, wishes, goldfish, silhouettes of trees, boxes of fairy tales dropped in the mud, uncles' and cousins' books, tablets and capsules and powders, papa's Moscow ache, his drugstore jacket with his special fountain pen in the pocket, his beautiful Hebrew paragraphs, his Talmudist's rationalism,[7] his Russian-Gymnasium Latin and German, mama's furnace-heart, her masses of memoirs, her paintings of autumn walks down to the sunny water, her braveries, her reveries, her old, old school hurts.

14 A writer is buffeted into being by school hurts—Orwell, Forster, Mann![8]—but after a while other ambushes begin: sorrows, deaths, disappointments, subtle diseases, delays, guilts, the spite of the private haters of the poetry side of life, the snubs of the glamorous, the bitterness of those for whom resentment is a daily gruel, and so on and so on; and then one day you find yourself leaning here, writing at that selfsame round glass table salvaged from the Park View Pharmacy—writing this, an impossibility, a summary of how you came to be where you are now, and where, God knows, is that? Your hair is whitening, you are a well of tears, what you meant to do (beauty and justice) you have not done, papa and mama are under the earth, you live in panic and dread, the future shrinks and darkens, stories are only vapor, your inmost craving is for nothing but an old scarred pen, and what, God knows, is that?

DISCUSSING THE TEXT

1. Why does Ozick begin her narrative by telling us about the two articles she wrote for the newspapers, one of which is published, the other not? What connection does this opening have with the rest of the memoir that follows? Do you find this choice of beginnings effective?
2. Why does Ozick repeat that it is the middle of the depression but that she doesn't know it, or that her mother and father "are in trouble" and she doesn't know it? Why is it important for her readers to know that she didn't know this at the time? How does this reality tie in with the conclusion of the essay?

---

[7]*Talmudist's rationalism:* a reference to the Talmud, the compilation of the Oral Law of the Jews, with extensive commentary, elucidation, and dialectical argument by rabbis and scholars (*Ed.*)

[8]*George Orwell, E. M. Forster, Thomas Mann:* Ozick refers here to these writers' negative experiences in school. (*Ed.*)

3. What is the picture we get of Ozick as a child attending P.S. 71? What kinds of things make her an outsider there? How do you think this early self-image relates to her development as a writer?
4. Do reading and writing offer the adult Cynthia Ozick the same forms of escape that books offered her as a child? Working with a group of four or five students, compare and contrast her experiences as a child and as an adult.

WRITING ABOUT THE TEXT

5. Ozick talks about how the box of children's books from the traveling library "transformed" her. Write a one-page response to the following questions: Why is reading so important for Ozick during this period in her life? How does she use books? What connections do you see between her immersion in the world of books and her work as a writer?
6. Reread Alfred Kazin's description of his feelings of alienation, as a Jewish American, from mainstream American culture in "Summer: The Way to Highland Park" (p. 330). Then write two paragraphs comparing and contrasting Kazin's experiences with those described by Ozick here.
7. Keeping Ozick's text in mind as a model, write a brief essay describing a familiar scene from your home or neighborhood while you were growing up (such as your kitchen, your living room, your porch, a relative's house, a local hangout). Let the reader know, through your description, how you feel about the persons connected with this place.

LOUISE DESALVO

A Portrait of the *Puttana* as a Middle-Aged Woolf Scholar

Louise DeSalvo (b. 1942), a professor of English and women's studies at Hunter College in New York City, writes here of her unlikely journey from the traditional Italian American family of her childhood to the life of a professional academic. The natural expectation for someone of her background was marriage, family, and subservience to the demands of a husband. But somewhere along the way—specifically in college—DeSalvo's imagination was set free by the example of the English writer Virginia Woolf (1882–1941). DeSalvo's lifelong immersion in Woolf's work, as she writes here, would significantly transform her own life.

Virginia Woolf, one of the great writers of modernist fiction, has in fact served as an important role model for many women in the latter half of the twentieth century. Woolf articulated the intellectual and emotional needs of women, in both essays and a series of well-known novels. Her works have become important references in much contemporary feminist thought. DeSalvo's own engagement with Woolf's early career extends into a growing fascination with the emergence of Woolf as an autonomous creative female voice within a predominantly male society.

"A Portrait of the Puttana *as a Middle-Aged Woolf Scholar" is taken from a collection of essays on women's issues, called* Between Women: Biographers, Novelists, Critics, Teachers and Artists Write about Their Work on Women, *which was coedited by DeSalvo, Carol Ascher, and Sara Ruddick and published in 1984. In this autobiographical essay, DeSalvo writes in a revealing manner, mixing incidents from her personal and family life with the story of how she came to be a Virginia Woolf scholar. By writing the essay in this way, DeSalvo helps her readers see the ways in which her identification with Woolf led to dramatic changes in DeSalvo's own life.*

Louise DeSalvo's work on Woolf includes Virginia Woolf's First Voyage: A Novel in the Making *(1980), and* Virginia Woolf: The Impact of Childhood Sexual Abuse on Her Life and Work *(1989). DeSalvo's development as a critic stems, as she has observed, from the study of the connections between fiction and cultural history.*

The year is 1975.

I am thirty-two years old, married, the mother of two small children, a Ph.D. candidate, on a charter flight to England with a friend to do research on Virginia Woolf at the University of Sussex in Falmer. This is the first time in my whole life that I am going away by myself. I have no idea where Falmer is, except that it is near Brighton. We have no hotel reservations. We have no idea how we will get to Brighton. But we are gloriously drunk on our third sherry, free from the responsibility of our children for awhile. (We have already had enough sherry so that each child can have her or his own little sherry bottle as a souvenir when we return home.) We are, at long last, grown-ups, going to do *real* research. The next generation of Woolf scholars, in incubation. We are formidable.

I come from a family, from a cultural heritage, where women simply don't go away to do things separately from men. That is not to say that men don't go away to do things separately from women. They do. And often. But in the land of my forebears, women sit around and wait for their men. Or they work very hard and watch their children and wait for their men. Or they watch their children and wait for their men. Or they make a sumptuous meal and they work very hard and watch their children and wait for their men. But they don't go anywhere without their men. Or do anything for themselves alone without their men. Except complain. To their children or to anyone else who will listen to them. About their men and about their bad luck in having been born female.

A few years ago, I decided, like everyone else, to explore my ethnic roots. It lasted a very short time. I bought a pasta machine. Learned how to combine the ingredients for pasta, to roll out the dough, and cut it. Word got out that I was a terrific pasta maker. Then I began to realize that you can tell how enslaved the women of any country are by the kind of preparation their traditional foods require. Any recipe that begins "Take a mortar and pestle . . ." now drives me into a feminist frenzy. Well, pasta making is something like that. Women who really care about their families make it fresh every day. Purists insist that if the sacred pasta dough is touched by metal pasta machines (i.e., twentieth-century labor-saving devices), it becomes slightly slippery—a quality in pasta that is akin to infidelity in wives. Oh yes, I now remember what women who do anything without their husbands are called. *Puttana.* Whores. I remember hearing stories in my childhood about how women like that were stoned to death in the old country.

Well, given a background like that, you can imagine the way I felt as we flew high above the Atlantic. There I was, a *puttana,* alone at last.

▼ ▼ ▼

I got into Woolf scholarship quite by accident. (Or so I thought at the time.) When I was in graduate school at New York University, I took a course with the Woolf scholar Mitchell Leaska. He was in the throes of his work on *The Pargiters,* his edition of the earlier draft of *The Years.* I was enthralled with his classes. I'll never forget the day that he brought in his transcription of Woolf's holograph, the handwritten draft of that novel. I changed my mind about what I would be doing with my scholarly life in the moments it took him to read to us from Woolf's earlier version of *The Years.* Here was a more political, less guarded Woolf. I had never known that earlier versions of literary texts were available. It had never occurred to me before that one could inquire into the process of the creation of a novel and learn about the writing process and the process of revision. It sounded like detective work. It was meticulous. It required stamina. Drive. It was exciting. I too would be working with manuscripts. I think I understood that I required a grand consuming passion in a project.

I soon decided to work with the manuscript of *The Voyage Out,* Woolf's first novel, because I wanted to catch Virginia Woolf in her beginnings where I thought she might be least guarded.

The Voyage Out is about Rachel Vinrace, a young, inexperienced woman, who accompanies her father on a trip to South America. On her father's ship, the *Euphrosyne,* she resumes a relationship with her aunt and uncle, Helen and Ridley Ambrose, and she meets Richard Dalloway, a former Member of Parliament, and his wife Clarissa. Rachel becomes involved with two parental surrogates—Helen and Clarissa—but the relationship with Clarissa is complicated because Rachel is sexually attracted to Richard. During a storm at sea, Rachel and he embrace. That night she has a dream that she is being pursued.

Later, when she is at Santa Marina, a South American port city, she meets Terence Hewet, who is spending his holiday there. They fall in love and decide to marry. But both are extremely reluctant lovers. Rachel dies of a mysterious illness before the couple can marry.

What I had no way of knowing when I decided to work on *The Voyage Out* was that I would have enormous difficulty keeping the problems that I was having in my life separate from the issues that Woolf was discussing in the novel. I had reached that moment of sexual reevaluation that often occurs at about thirty. Although I was married, I went through a time when I identified with Rachel so strongly that I believed I shared her distrust of intimacy. It was simpler for me to see myself in terms of Woolf's character than it was to look at my own problems. I vacillated between thinking that Rachel—and by extension I—were typical of all women, and thinking that her hesitations (and mine) were pathological. It took many years for me to separate myself from Rachel Vinrace. It took many years for me to understand that part of the reason for Rachel's hesitation was her submerged rage at the misogyny and brutality of the men in her life—all disguised through the artifice of civilization, to be sure, but there nonetheless. In the process of separating myself from Rachel, I learned not to make disparaging judgments about Rachel's behavior—or mine—but to look for the causes of that behavior in familial and societal histories. I also saw that I was letting this very close identification with Rachel hold me back, keep me in check, because my work was making me feel very powerful. And I was terrified of feeling powerful.

I wake up in the middle of the night from a dream. The dream is easy to describe, difficult to comprehend. Ishtar—the many-breasted goddess—with a face vaguely like that of Virginia Woolf but resembling my mother, in profile, has placed her hands under my armpits and has picked me up. Her face is impassive. She does not look at me, does not recognize me, stares past me. She begins shaking me—not violently, but powerfully and rhythmically. As she shakes me, all the things that define me as a woman fall off. They form a pile beneath my feet. As she continues to shake me, still staring beyond me, impassively and without emotion, what is left of me begins to shrivel into the baby doll that I remember having in my childhood. The only openings I have, now, are the hole in the middle of the little red mouth where you put the toy bottle and the one where the water runs out, between the legs. I begin saying, in the doll's voice that I remember, "Mama, mama." Ishtar stares impassively ahead. But she stops shaking me.

Working on Woolf's composition of *The Voyage Out* was my first long project. One that would take years. It terrified me and it thrilled me. Sometimes I would feel immensely powerful, feel that I, single-handedly, might change the course of Woolf scholarship. Or I would feel impotent, wondering how could I make any contribution to our knowledge of Woolf.

I learned what it is humanly possible to do in one day; what one cannot do; that one must trust the times when no work is getting done, because it is in those fallow periods that the unconscious mind is working. I had to change the way I thought about time. I had to scale down my expectations to a human level. All of this was very hard for me to do. Every time I sat down to the project,my infantile power fantasies reared their ugly heads. I always thought that I would get more done in one day than it was possible to do. Then my feelings of potency would turn into feelings of powerlessness and despair. I slowly learned that the work could proceed only as quickly as it could proceed. (I have not entirely learned that lesson yet.) I learned that I have the same trouble that anyone else has in working, in writing comprehensible sentences, in revising them, but that if I worked every day, the work would get done. I gradually realized what working on *The Voyage Out* for seven years must have been like for Virginia Woolf. I too was working on a project that was taking a very long time. There was the temptation, too, to work constantly, without interruption, to get it done more quickly. There was the temptation to work incessantly—days, nights, weekends—at the mountain of manuscripts, at the letters, diaries, and journals that Woolf had written while composing the novel.

From time to time, my husband reminds me of a moment in the days preceding our marriage. He was at work. I was at our apartment. The place was filthy. I was trying to clean it so that we could move in. All the stores in the neighborhood were closed because of some holiday. I decided that I would clean all the tiles in the bathroom. The only thing I had that would do the job was a toothbrush. So, instead of waiting for him to come back to help me, instead of waiting for the next day to get a scrub brush that would speed the work, I took the toothbrush to the tiles. When he came to pick me up, I was exhausted and miserable, but also triumphant because I had finished.

15

At the beginning, much of my work on Virginia Woolf's composition of *The Voyage Out* was like that day with the toothbrush.

▼ ▼ ▼

As I recorded the progress of Virginia Woolf's days to figure out what she was doing as she was writing *The Voyage Out,* I started realizing that this was one hell of a woman, filled with incredible energy, so different from my original impression of her. Reading about her life in London, her visits to the British Museum, the books she read, the jaunts down to Sussex on weekends, the trips to St. Ives, to Wells, to the Lizard, to Lelant, Cornwall, the walks, the work, the lived life, fruitful beyond my wildest imaginings, her engagement with the most important political and social issues of her day, her teaching of working-class people, I began to revise my picture of her and my hopes for myself. I decided that it would be foolish of me to spend endless days alone inside libraries working on Woolf when the great woman of my dreams had spent no small portion of hers walking around the countryside, cultivating important relationships, particularly with women, taking tea, learning to bake bread, teaching, getting involved in politics, becoming an essayist, a novelist, integrating work and pleasure, and having what seemed to me, in contrast to my confined scholarly life, a hell of a good time.

That's when I bought my first pair of hiking boots and started walking, first around the lower reaches of New York State and then, at long last, through Woolf's beloved Sussex and Cornwall and later through Kent, Cumbria, Northumbria, Yorkshire. I retraced the trips she took while she was writing *The Voyage Out;* visited the places she visited; read the books she read; began having important friendships of my own with Woolf scholars; started teaching; began writing essays; started writing poetry; wrote a novel.

In 1975 I was on my way from Brighton to Sevenoaks to see Knole, Vita Sackville-West's[1] ancestral home, delighted by the likelihood that Virginia Woolf herself had travelled these very roads to see Vita Sackville-West when she was writing *Orlando.* We had just come through a small stretch of moor that smelled powerfully of damp and peat when we saw a road sign that read, simply, "Sevenoaks," the village in which Knole is located. When I saw that sign, I began weeping, inexplicably and uncontrollably, filled with a sense of myself newly born, capable of working and of having fun, capable of enjoying my life's work. This was released somehow by that sign and the sense it inspired of the flesh-and-blood reality of the Virginia Woolf who had passed, a long time ago, by that very spot to go see a friend, another woman.

I thought that I would like to write about these two women, about their friendship, about their love affair, about their work. I thought about how the creative act has been misconstrued as a solitary, solipsistic act and how we must correct that misapprehension; we must write about the creative act as it is nurtured by loving friendships.

▼ ▼ ▼

I finished my dissertation and converted it into a book, *Virginia Woolf's First Voyage: A Novel in the Making.* My next big project became the editing of an early version of *The Voyage Out (Melymbrosia),* one of the versions I had studied and written about in the dissertation. An early version of the first novel of one of the greatest literary stylists of this century might prove useful, not only to scholars but also to common readers. I had been immensely excited when I first read through the pages of this submerged draft, seeing how different it was from the version that Woolf chose to publish. It was more radical politically, more lesbian, more contemptuous of men. 20

The work of editing the draft went like this: I would go to the Berg Collection and hand-copy pages of Woolf's typescript of the earlier version. There were 414 pages that had to be copied. I could copy about 15 or so pages on a good day, but I always expected myself to do better, to do more, as if I were in competition with my own limitations. The work taught me what it was like to be a medieval scribe. It was dreadful. The work couldn't be done from Xeroxes because there were many sets of corrections on the sheets in various ink colors, made at different times, and I was using only the earliest ones. After I copied a day's pages I would take my transcription home and type it. Then I would take my pages back to the Berg and proofread them against the original. Again I would take the typescript home, make corrections, then bring the corrected typescript back to the Berg and check that the corrections were correct. Next I would write textual notes, indicating where my text was different from Woolf's. Then I would type the textual notes; proof them against the original; make changes; bring the changes back to make sure they were correct; and so forth. I began to imagine myself in purgatory.

---

[1]*Vita Sackville-West* (1892–1962): a well-known author during the 1920s and 1930s, Sackville-West was Virginia Woolf's friend and lover. (*Ed.*)

I come to the breakfast table one morning during this time, trying to shake the effects of a night of work. My twelve-year-old son Jason (he was six when I began), usually cheerful in the morning, is sitting at the table in a foul, rotten mood. He glares at me. I ask him what is troubling him. He tells me that they had a discussion in his English class about the generation gap. Do I realize that he is the only child in the class who sees his mother less than he sees his father? Do I realize that my work is killing him? That he hates it? That he can't stand to have me up at my typewriter when he comes home from school? That the sound of the typewriter keeps him up all night? That he needs his sleep? He begins sobbing. I want to hold him but he won't allow it. I recall that the only time this child has ever had an uncontrollable temper tantrum was on the day he overheard me talking about beginning my second book. He looked at me and said, "Second book?" Then he threw himself off his chair onto the floor, began shrieking and beating his fists against the floor. When I calmed him enough so that he could talk, he told me that he thought that when I finished the first book, he would have me back again.

I understand why he is so angry. My work takes me away from him far more often than he would like; yet at twelve, he is beginning to want to separate himself from me. I ask him if he thinks anything that I have done has rubbed off on him. I love his compositions. He writes the most wonderful works of fiction. I am delighted, thinking that something of me has lodged itself in him. He says no, emphatically no. Nothing at all about my work has ever done him any good.

He calms down as quickly as he has flared up. He asks if I'd be interested in hearing the latest thing he has written. I say I am. He pulls a sheet of paper out of his notebook. It is the biography of an imaginary character, John C. Lectica. As Jason reads it to me, I think to myself "A chip off the old block."

Autumn 1978.

I receive a copy of *Virginia Woolf Miscellany* in the mail. There is an article by Quentin Bell,[2] entitled "Proposed Policy on Virginia Woolf's Unpublished Material." (An editor later tells me that originally it had been entitled "The Bottom of the Barrel" as in "scraping the bottom of the barrel.")

It reads, in part: "A short time ago a reputable scholar suggested the publication of an earlier version of one of the novels [I am sure Bell is referring to my work on *Melymbrosia*], not only because it would be of interest to other scholars but because it could be offered as—in effect—a new novel to the 'generalist Woolf reader.' This, I must say, arouses acute misgivings—suppose that the reader agrees with Virginia in condemning the earlier version, suppose that it is below her usual standard? Then, surely it is unfair to give it currency. Some such deflation of values follows any inflation of published

[2] *Quentin Bell* (b. 1910): Bell is the son of Virginia Woolf's sister, Vanessa, and Clive Bell. He is author of *Virginia Woolf: A Biography* (1972). (*Ed.*)

matter [and] must surely be apprehended. Scratch the bottom of the barrel and you will come up with impurities."

In the last six years of my life, I have probably spent more time working with Virginia Woolf's works than I have doing anything else. My work has become more important than my life. As I face the possibility that *Melymbrosia* might never be published, I must look back over my life to try to salvage something of myself, to try to see clearly what of my past I have tried to bury in my work.

I am thirteen years old. I have begun my adolescence with a vengeance. I am not shaping up to be the young woman I'm supposed to be. I am not docile. I am not sweet. I am certainly not quiet. And, as my father has told me dozens of times, I am not agreeable: if he says something is green, I am sure to respond that it is orange. I have mastered every conceivable method of turning my household into turmoil. I have devised a method of looking up at the ceiling when my father lectures me that instantly drives him into a frenzy.

In the middle of one of these fairly frequent outbursts, I run out of the house, feeling that I am choking, the tears hot on my cheeks. It is nighttime. I have no place to go. But I keep running. There are welcoming lights a few blocks away. It is the local library. I run up the stairs. I run up to the reading room with its engulfing brown leather chairs, pull an encyclopedia down from the shelf, and pretend to read so that I won't be kicked out. It is cool and it is quiet. My rage subsides. I think that if there is a heaven, surely it must resemble a library. I think that if there is a god, surely she must be a librarian.

▼ ▼ ▼

Autumn 1963.

I am a senior at Douglass College. In 1963 Douglass College is the kind of school a bright young working-class woman can afford. Douglass, I think, is filled with brilliant women, and I have never seen brilliant women before. I have studied Shakespeare with Doris Falk, the novel with Anna Wells, philosophy with Amelie Rorty. I now have Twentieth-Century Fiction with Carol Smith. 30

Carol Smith is lecturing on Virginia Woolf's *To the Lighthouse.* She is talking about the relationship between Mr. and Mrs. Ramsay in "The Window" section of the novel. I have never in my life heard such genius. I am taking notes, watching her talk, and watching her belly. She is very pregnant. She is wearing a beige maternity dress. I take down every word, while watching to see when the baby she is pregnant with will kick her again.

I learn to love Virginia Woolf. I observe that it is possible to be a woman, to be brilliant, to be working, to be happy, and to be pregnant. And all at the same time.

I am interviewed about how an Italian-American woman like me became a Woolf scholar. I search my memory, think of studying with Carol

Smith, and suddenly remember my fascination with the figure of Cam Ramsay in *To the Lighthouse.* Cam Ramsay, the child Mrs. Ramsay virtually ignores, so busy is she with her son James; Cam Ramsay, the child who is "wild and fierce." The child who clenches her fist and stamps her feet. The child who is always running away, running away. The child who will not let anyone invade the private space that she has created to protect herself in this family with a tyrannical father who strikes out with a beak of brass.

I remember my own adolescence. Could it be that I have seen something of myself in Cam those many years ago and that in trying to understand the relationship between Cam Ramsay and her creator, Virginia Woolf, I am also trying to learn something about my own past? Aren't I now in the middle of a long essay about Virginia Woolf as an adolescent, reading her 1897 diary, a tiny brown gilt leather volume, with a lock and a key, that must be read with a magnifying glass, so tiny and spidery is the hand, an essay that has given me more satisfaction to write than anything I have written yet about Virginia Woolf? And haven't I been stressing Woolf's capacity to cope, rather than her neurosis, in that difficult year? Could it be that in concentrating on Woolf's health, I am also trying to heal myself?

1968.

I am married, and enduring my husband's medical internship as best I can, on next to no money, with a baby who never sleeps and who cries all the time. Although I am twenty-five, I look fifty. I have deep circles under my eyes. I have no figure. I am still wearing maternity clothes. 35

I had put my husband through medical school. (According to him, I *helped* put him through medical school—his parents paid his tuition and gave him a small allowance, and I worked as a high school English teacher and paid for everything else.) In that internship year, we came very close to a divorce. Your basic doctor-in-training-meets-gorgeous-nurse-and-wants-to-leave-his-wife-and-small-baby story.

One day, I look into the bathroom mirror and decide that I will either kill myself or that I will go back to graduate school and become economically independent as quickly as I can. I look into the medicine chest, thinking that if my husband leaves me with this baby, I will probably be young, gifted, and on welfare. After wondering whether you could kill yourself by taking a year's supply of birth control pills and fantasying that, with the way my luck is running, I might grow some hair on my chest, but I probably wouldn't die, I decide that I will go back to school, get a Ph.D., and go into college teaching. I also realize that I might buy some time by squelching the young-doctor-leaves-his-young-wife-for-nurse script, at least temporarily, by announcing to my husband that if he leaves me, *he* can have the baby. Then he and his sweet young nurse can contemplate how romantic their life together will be with this baby who cries and throws up all the time.

He tells me he doesn't believe that I can part with my child.

I say, "Wanna bet?"

Shortly thereafter, he decides to hang around for a while longer. 40

The way I write this now, the "tough broad" tone I take, is of course a disguise for how hurt I was, for how seriously betrayed I felt. And I really don't know now what I would have done if he *had* left me. Unlike many of my friends, my husband *did* stay. I had done everything I was supposed to do. Clipped coupons. Made casseroles from *Woman's Day* with noodles and chopped meat and cream of mushroom soup for all his friends. I had laughed at the story of how Doctor X had fucked Nurse Y in the linen room adjacent to the O.R. and how the surgeon couldn't figure out where the grunts and groans were coming from, without paying too much attention to how Mrs. X or Nurse Y might feel about having this sexual conquest the subject of our dinner table conversation. And I didn't think at all then about how hospitals institutionalize the sexual and economic servitude of women.

I had done everything you were supposed to do, the way you were supposed to do it, and he still wanted to leave me. And that profound disillusionment, that rage at the preposterous hoax that society tries to play on young women by convincing them that if they do everything right for their men, their men will stay with them forever, stays with me to this day.

I had been a high school teacher early in our marriage, but that wasn't a career. I now wanted a career. And my own money. And access to the public world. I wanted to carry a briefcase. I wanted to carry a briefcase while walking down the path at a college, with students to my right and to my left, engaged in serious, important, intellectual discussions about literature. And I never wanted to depend on a man again as long as I lived.

When I first learned that Virginia Woolf had spent seven years in the creation of *The Voyage Out,* her first novel, I thought that surely she must have been mad for that, if for no other reason. But as I carted off copies of *Melymbrosia,* my reconstruction of the earlier version of that novel, to the Editor's Office of The New York Public Library some seven years after *I* had begun working with her novel, I reflected that I have come to share a great deal with this woman. I have come to be a great deal like her in her attitudes toward the male establishment and art and feminism and politics; have learned from living for seven years with her to take the very best from her while managing, through the example of her life and her honesty about it, to avoid the depths of her pain.

She has been very good to me, this woman. 45

In looking back over my life, I realize that my work on Virginia Woolf has helped me make some important changes.

Before I worked on Virginia Woolf, I wasn't a feminist. Before I worked on Virginia Woolf, I didn't know how strong a woman I was. Before I worked on Virginia Woolf, I whined a lot, like my Italian foremothers, about how men got all the breaks and about the ways they abused their women, like I felt I had been abused, but I didn't really understand that there was a social structure that was organized to keep men dominant and women subservient, and I really didn't understand how important it was for women to be economically independent and the potentially horrifying consequences if they were not.

Before I worked on Virginia Woolf, I would ask the young doctors who came to our house for dinner if I could get them another cup of coffee, being careful to wait until there was a break in the conversation. Now my husband, Ernie, and our children—Jason and Justin—get up to cook me breakfast. Virginia Woolf has, in many ways, created a monster in me, and I am proud to give her partial credit for it. I like to think that she would have been pleased that my reading *A Room of One's Own* has been a very important part of my emancipation from the tradition of the suffering woman. Now I am a hell-raiser, a spitfire, and I buy and wear "Mean Mother," "Nurture Yourself," and "I Am a Shameless Agitator" buttons. And I have recently started to pump iron (much to the amusement of fifteen-year-old Jason—the would-be writer, the one who used to throw up all the time, who has turned out to be a very nice kid after all—and eleven-year-old Justin, who has something to say about everything I do). But sometimes, when I'm feeling really good and have the time, I make them a bread pudding.

I think of what Virginia Woolf has done for our generation of women, of Woolf scholars. I think of what she has taught us.

There are the political and the feminist messages in *A Room of One's Own* 50 and *Three Guineas*. The antiauthoritarian, antipatriarchal stance. The exposure of the inequities between the way men are treated and the way women are treated. The difficulty of being a woman and being a creator. Woolf has unleashed our anger. Allowed us to use it constructively. She has taught us the value of work; the necessity of art; the necessity also of a feminist politics. She has taught us to express ourselves as women—in our lives, in our work, in our art.

Woolf was interested in the writer behind the work, in what she or he was like—what kind of house she lived in, what her writing schedule was like, what she ate for breakfast, how she dressed for dinner. She was concerned with what literature and memoirs revealed about the history of the times, its morals and mores. The pages of her essays and her notebooks are filled with questions and answers about the human beings behind the works of art, about the implications of art for humanity. Woolf taught us that writers are human beings, that writing is a human act, that the act of writing is filled with consequences for a society and for its readers. No "art for art's sake." Instead, "art for the sake of life."

She understood that literature by its very nature is a powerful didactic instrument and, therefore, as potentially dangerous as it is edifying. Literature teaches us when we are young about the way we are supposed to behave and about the consequences of certain kinds of behavior. Woolf reminds us of how profoundly influential literary texts can be in the formation of character and in the formation of a nation's character.

I imagine Woolf thinking, "What one must do is write a literature of one's own."

28 March 1941.

Virginia Woolf commits suicide by walking into the River Ouse with rocks in her pockets. My mother is three months pregnant. The fact that she is pregnant with me when Virginia Woolf dies is of no significance to her. Many years later I ask her if she remembers hearing about Virginia Woolf's death on the radio. She says no. Maybe she read Virginia Woolf when she was pregnant with me? *The Years?* It was a very popular novel. She says no. She never heard of Virginia Woolf until I started talking about her.

The fact that Virginia Woolf and my mother were alive at the same time, breathed the same air, so to speak, is mysteriously significant. The fact that my mother was pregnant with *me* when Woolf killed herself seems laden with meaning. What can explain the fact that I am devoting a very large part of my life to this woman with whom I have absolutely nothing in common? She is English, purely and highly bred. I am more Italian than American, rough, tough, a street kid, out of the slums of Hoboken, New Jersey. We have absolutely nothing in common, except for the fact that we are both women. 55

And that, I realize, is quite enough.

DISCUSSING THE TEXT

1. On her way to England on a research trip, without husband and children, DeSalvo ironically recalls a traditional Italian judgment on women "who do anything without their husbands" as *puttana,* whores. Why does she begin her essay with this point? How does it prepare the reader for what follows in the essay?
2. A good deal of DeSalvo's professional time is spent in the library. What does the library mean to DeSalvo? Does its emotional significance change for her over the years? Consider the story she tells of herself at age thirteen, as well as her later experiences as a scholar.
3. How and why does DeSalvo's work on Virginia Woolf change her view of herself? What lessons does she learn from Woolf? How does DeSalvo's image of Virginia Woolf change as well?

WRITING ABOUT THE TEXT

4. Write two paragraphs that address the following questions: Why does DeSalvo organize her essay in the manner she does, beginning at age thirty-two and then introducing various flashbacks to earlier moments that also relate to the present time? What, if anything, does she gain by this method of organizing her narrative?
5. DeSalvo presents two images of herself, as a traditional doctor's wife in the 1960s and as a feminist scholar in the 1970s. Make two separate lists of the

characteristics that go along with these two images. Then write two paragraphs, identifying specific changes in DeSalvo's view of herself and discussing how her work on Virginia Woolf contributed to those changes.

6. Assuming DeSalvo's voice, write a letter to Virginia Woolf in which you describe how Woolf's work has affected your intellectual and emotional development.
7. Keeping DeSalvo's text in mind as a model, write a brief essay on how something you have studied—either in school or out of school—has had an impact on your sense of yourself and on your life.

BELL HOOKS

Talking Back

bell hooks's essay from the book of the same title, Talking Back: Thinking Feminist, Thinking Black *(1989), explains how using her great-grandmother's name as her writing pseudonym allowed hooks to claim a "legacy of defiance, of will, of courage." Within the southern black community of her childhood, talking back as an equal to an authority figure was forbidden, especially for women. Ironically, though, the society that hooks describes is basically matriarchal and, for the women in hooks's family, self-assertion was natural within the home. In her critical writing and public life as an intellectual, hooks applies the concept of "talking back" to a predominantly white and patriarchal society—a society that, in her view, has ignored the plight of black women.*

bell hooks was born in Kentucky in 1952. She has taught at Yale University and Oberlin College and is presently a distinguished professor of English at City College of the City University of New York. hooks writes from her deep commitment to her developing vision as an African American feminist. In a 1993 interview, for example, she spoke of some of her earlier work, especially Ain't I a Woman: Black Women and Feminism *(1981), as being too insistent on problems of race, yet not discussing issues of class. In a recent collection of essays,* Outlaw Culture: Resisting Representations *(1994), hooks looks at American popular culture in terms of feminist thought, class, and the racial politics of beauty. In another collection,* Teaching to Transgress: Education as the Practice of Freedom *(1994), hooks argues that even though "identity politics," based on sex or race, can be instrumental in furthering the social, economic, and intellectual status of marginalized peoples, it can also become, in its extreme form, "a strategy for exclusion or domination."*

In the world of the southern black community I grew up in, "back talk" and "talking back" meant speaking as an equal to an authority figure. It meant daring to disagree and sometimes it just meant having an opinion. In the "old school," children were meant to be seen and not heard. My great-grandparents, grandparents, and parents were all from the old school. To make yourself heard if you were a child was to invite punishment, the back-hand lick, the slap across the face that would catch you unaware, or the feel of switches stinging your arms and legs.

To speak then when one was not spoken to was a courageous act—an act of risk and daring. And yet it was hard not to speak in warm rooms where heated discussions began at the crack of dawn, women's voices filling the air, giving orders, making threats, fussing. Black men may have excelled in the art of poetic preaching in the male-dominated church, but in the church of the home, where the everyday rules of how to live and how to act were established, it was black women who preached. There, black women spoke in a language so rich, so poetic, that it felt to me like being shut off from life, smothered to death if one were not allowed to participate.

It was in that world of woman talk (the men were often silent, often absent) that was born in me the craving to speak, to have a voice, and not just any voice but one that could be identified as belonging to me. To make my voice, I had to speak, to hear myself talk—and talk I did—darting in and out of grown folks' conversations and dialogues, answering questions that were not directed at me, endlessly asking questions, making speeches. Needless to say, the punishments for these acts of speech seemed endless. They were intended to silence me—the child—and more particularly the girl child. Had I been a boy, they might have encouraged me to speak believing that I might someday be called to preach. There was no "calling" for talking girls, no legitimized rewarded speech. The punishments I received for "talking back" were intended to suppress all possibility that I would create my own speech. That speech was to be suppressed so that the "right speech of womanhood" would emerge.

Within feminist circles, silence is often seen as the sexist "right speech of womanhood"—the sign of woman's submission to patriarchal authority. This emphasis on woman's silence may be an accurate remembering of what has taken place in the households of women from WASP backgrounds in the United States, but in black communities (and diverse ethnic communities), women have not been silent. Their voices can be heard. Certainly for black women, our struggle has not been to emerge from silence into speech but to change the nature and direction of our speech, to make a speech that compels listeners, one that is heard.

Our speech, "the right speech of womanhood," was often the soliloquy, the talking into thin air, the talking to ears that do not hear you—the talk that is simply not listened to. Unlike the black male preacher whose speech was to be heard, who was to be listened to, whose words were to be remembered, the voices of black women—giving orders, making threats, fussing—could be tuned out, could become a kind of background music, audible but not acknowledged as significant speech. Dialogue—the sharing of speech and recognition—took place not between mother and child or mother and male authority figure but among black women. I can remember watching fascinated as our mother talked with her mother, sisters, and women friends. The intimacy and intensity of their speech—the satisfaction they received from talking to one another, the pleasure, the joy. It was in this world of woman speech, loud talk, angry words, women with tongues quick and sharp, tender sweet tongues, touching our world with their words, that I made speech my birthright—and the right to voice, to authorship, a privilege I would not be denied. It was in that world and because of it that I came to dream of writing, to write.

Writing was a way to capture speech, to hold onto it, keep it close. And so I wrote down bits and pieces of conversations, confessing in cheap diaries that soon fell apart from too much handling, expressing the intensity of my sorrow, the anguish of speech—for I was always saying the wrong thing, asking the wrong questions. I could not confine my speech to the necessary corners and concerns of life. I hid these writings under my bed, in pillow stuffings, among faded underwear. When my sisters found and read them, they ridiculed and mocked me—poking fun. I felt violated, ashamed, as if the secret parts of my self had been exposed, brought into the open, and hung like newly clean laundry, out in the air for everyone to see. The fear of exposure, the fear that one's deepest emotions and innermost thoughts will be dismissed as mere nonsense, felt by so many young girls keeping diaries, holding and hiding speech, seems to me now one of the barriers that women have always needed and still need to destroy so that we are no longer pushed into secrecy or silence.

Despite my feelings of violation, of exposure, I continued to speak and write, choosing my hiding places well, learning to destroy work when no safe place could be found. I was never taught absolute silence, I was taught that it was important to speak but to talk a talk that was in itself a silence. Taught to speak and yet beware of the betrayal of too much heard speech, I experienced intense confusion and deep anxiety in my efforts to speak and write. Reciting poems at Sunday afternoon church service might be rewarded. Writing a poem (when one's time could be "better" spent sweeping, ironing, learning to cook) was luxurious activity, indulged in at the expense of others. Questioning authority, raising issues that were not deemed appropriate subjects brought pain, punishments—like telling mama I wanted to die before her because I could not live without her—that was crazy talk, crazy speech, the kind that would lead you to end up in a mental institution. "Little girl," I would be told, "if you don't stop all this crazy talk and crazy acting you are going to end up right out there at Western State."

Madness, not just physical abuse, was the punishment for too much talk if you were female. Yet even as this fear of madness haunted me, hanging over my writing like a monstrous shadow, I could not stop the words, making thought, writing speech. For this terrible madness which I feared, which I was sure was the destiny of daring women born to intense speech (after all, the authorities emphasized this point daily), was not as threatening as imposed silence, as suppressed speech.

Safety and sanity were to be sacrificed if I was to experience defiant speech. Though I risked them both, deep-seated fears and anxieties characterized my childhood days. I would speak but I would not ride a bike, play hardball, or hold the gray kitten. Writing about the ways we are traumatized in our growing-up years, psychoanalyst Alice Miller makes the point in *For Your Own Good* that it is not clear why childhood wounds become for some folk an opportunity to grow, to move forward rather than backward in the process of self-realization. Certainly, when I reflect on the trials of my growing-up years, the many punishments, I can see now that in resistance I learned to be vigilant in the nourishment of my spirit, to be tough, to courageously protect that spirit from forces that would break it.

While punishing me, my parents often spoke about the necessity of breaking my spirit. Now when I ponder the silences, the voices that are not heard, the voices of those wounded and/or oppressed individuals who do not speak or write, I contemplate the acts of persecution, torture—the terrorism that breaks spirits, that makes creativity impossible. I write these words to bear witness to the primacy of resistance struggle in any situation of domination (even within family life); to the strength and power that emerges from sustained resistance and the profound conviction that these forces can be healing, can protect us from dehumanization and despair.

These early trials, wherein I learned to stand my ground, to keep my spirit intact, came vividly to mind after I published *Ain't I A Woman* and the book was sharply and harshly criticized. While I had expected a climate of critical dialogue, I was not expecting a critical avalanche that had the power in its intensity to crush the spirit, to push one into silence. Since that time, I have heard stories about black women, about women of color, who write and publish (even when the work is quite successful) having nervous breakdowns, being made mad because they cannot bear the harsh responses of family, friends, and unknown critics, or becoming silent, unproductive. Surely, the absence of a humane critical response has tremendous impact on the writer from any oppressed, colonized group who endeavors to speak. For us, true speaking is not solely an expression of creative power; it is an act of resistance, a political gesture that challenges politics of domination that would render us nameless and voiceless. As such, it is a courageous act—as such, it represents a threat. To those who wield oppressive power, that which is threatening must necessarily be wiped out, annihilated, silenced.

Recently, efforts by black women writers to call attention to our work serve to highlight both our presence and absence. Whenever I peruse women's bookstores, I am struck not by the rapidly growing body of feminist writing by black women, but by the paucity of available published material. Those of us who write and are published remain few in number. The context of silence is varied and multi-dimensional. Most obvious are the ways racism, sexism, and class exploitation act to suppress and silence. Less obvious are the inner struggles, the efforts made to gain the necessary confidence to write, to re-write, to fully develop craft and skill—and the extent to which such efforts fail.

Although I have wanted writing to be my life-work since childhood, it has been difficult for me to claim "writer" as part of that which identifies and shapes my everyday reality. Even after publishing books, I would often speak of wanting to be a writer as though these works did not exist. And though I would be told, "you are a writer," I was not yet ready to fully affirm this truth.

Part of myself was still held captive by domineering forces of history, of familial life that had charted a map of silence, of right speech. I had not completely let go of the fear of saying the wrong thing, of being punished. Somewhere in the deep recesses of my mind, I believed I could avoid both responsibility and punishment if I did not declare myself a writer.

One of the many reasons I chose to write using the pseudonym bell hooks, a family name (mother to Sarah Oldham, grandmother to Rosa Bell Oldham, great-grandmother to me), was to construct a writer-identity that would challenge and subdue all impulses leading me away from speech into silence. I was a young girl buying bubble gum at the corner store when I first really heard the full name bell hooks. I had just "talked back" to a grown person. Even now I can recall the surprised look, the mocking tones that informed me I must be kin to bell hooks—a sharp-tongued woman, a woman who spoke her mind, a woman who was not afraid to talk back. I claimed this legacy of defiance, of will, of courage, affirming my link to female ancestors who were bold and daring in their speech. Unlike my bold and daring mother and grandmother, who were not supportive of talking back, even though they were assertive and powerful in their speech, bell hooks as I discovered, claimed, and invented her was my ally, my support.

That initial act of talking back outside the home was empowering. It was the first of many acts of defiant speech that would make it possible for me to emerge as an independent thinker and writer. In retrospect, "talking back" became for me a rite of initiation, testing my courage, strengthening my commitment, preparing me for the days ahead—the days when writing, rejection notices, periods of silence, publication, ongoing development seem impossible but necessary. 15

Moving from silence into speech is for the oppressed, the colonized, the exploited, and those who stand and struggle side by side a gesture of defiance that heals, that makes new life and new growth possible. It is that act of speech, of "talking back," that is no mere gesture of empty words, that is the expression of our movement from object to subject—the liberated voice.

DISCUSSING THE TEXT

1. hooks makes distinctions between "woman talk" and "man talk" in the African American community of her childhood. What are some of these distinctions? Do you think that they perpetuate rigid stereotypes of men and women? Why or why not?
2. What connections does hooks see between the act of speech and the act of writing? Why are these connections important? How is writing a way of "talking back"?
3. hooks implies that for African Americans and other oppressed groups, writing is not just a creative act but "an act of resistance, a political gesture . . . a courageous act." Discuss the implications of hooks's statement with a group of four or five other students. Do you agree or disagree with her? Would this difference apply to a white woman writer as well? Why or why not?

Take brief notes as you work on this assignment, and be prepared to share your opinions with the rest of the class.

4. Is hooks speaking only of racial and sexual domination in this essay? What other kinds of domination does she address?

WRITING ABOUT THE TEXT

5. Make a list of the characteristics of "back talk" and another list of the characteristics of "the right speech of womanhood," as hooks presents them. Can you provide some examples from your own experience as a speaker or writer that would fit into her categories? Write a brief essay comparing and contrasting these two lists. Conclude the essay by summarizing your own views on the subject of "appropriate" ways of speaking.
6. Write a fictitious dialogue between yourself and an authority figure in your life in which you practice the art of "talking back." What point would you wish to make by "talking back" to such a person?
7. Gloria Jean Watkins adopted bell hooks, her great-grandmother's name, as a pseudonym "to construct a writer-identity that would challenge and subdue all impulses leading me away from speech into silence" (par. 14). Think of a situation in which you too might want to adopt a pseudonym, and come up with one for yourself. Write a one- to two-page discussion of your chosen pseudonym and your reasons for choosing it.

EVA HOFFMAN

The New World

Eva Hoffman's memoir, Lost in Translation: A Life in a New Language *(1989), from which this selection is reprinted, chronicles the author's experiences as an undergraduate at Rice University in Houston, Texas, in the early 1960s. The Hoffmans, Polish Jews from Cracow, had emigrated to Canada in 1959 when Eva was an adolescent. Although life in Vancouver had given her a taste of "the New World," it was Hoffman's college experience and the world of literature, particularly American literature, that provided her with a sense of the possibility of a new self in a new language.*

This selection is written from Hoffman's double perspective as a European college student and as an American professional writer. This double focus is also present in the author's experience of two different languages and cultures, and in the unending process of translation that she undertakes.

Hoffman's objectives have been defined by her sense of exile and by her sense of alienation from the English language, along with her simultaneous desire to belong to American culture and possess its language. In all of her work, Hoffman has tried to exploit her status as an outsider, observing American culture from a "vantage point slightly outside the received categories."

Eva Hoffman was born in Cracow in 1945, and settled in the United States in 1963 after having lived with her family in Canada for four years. She earned a Ph.D. from Harvard University in 1974, and taught for a few years before becoming an editor for the New York Times *in 1980 (she has been editor of the* New York Times Book Review *since 1987). In her latest book,* Exit into History: A Journey through the New Eastern Europe *(1992), Hoffman offers a personal account of her travel experiences throughout several countries in the former Eastern bloc, particularly her native Poland.*

The Houston air is thick with heat and humidity, which slow everyone's movements to a sluggish, lazy saunter. The humidity is layered with so many smells that I detect a whiff of a Cracow summer among them, and it shoots me through with a sudden nostalgia, as for a love one has almost forgotten to mourn. But not for long, because what's going on right around me is so diverting. The Rice campus has a formal and somewhat stiff aesthetic, with a central quadrangle segmented by impeccably straight hedges and surrounded by Federal brick buildings, some of them with white columns and porticoes. I walk along the well-pruned paths with a sense of pleasurable excitement and confusion: I am in a new country again, and it is as different from Vancouver as Lagado is from Lilliput.[1] This is the real America, I'm convinced, not having any way of knowing that I'm in a particular region of it, at a specific and rather curious time in its history.

Really, of course, I'm in college country, and on first impression, it seems like a friendly and manageable place. My fellow students seem bright and shiny and squeaky clean—the girls in their tartan skirts and bobby socks, the boys with neatly pressed shirts and lively, open faces. "Excuse me," everyone I meet asks politely, "but I notice you have an accent. Do you mind if I ask where it's from?" I don't mind at all, especially since I soon discover that my answer makes a favorable impression. "How interesting," my interlocutors say when I tell them I am from Poland, and some of them proceed to ask me respectful questions, as if this bare fact gave me special stature. I, in turn, listen curiously to the way they speak—in a gamut of southern drawls and Texan twangs, which I find saucy and musical, and which I sincerely long to imitate.

At night, in our dormitory, groups of eager-eyed, fresh-skinned girls gather in their nighties in the common-room area and, to the strumming of someone's guitar, earnestly sing "Swing Low, Sweet Chariot," and "Kumbaya," and "Five Hundred Miles," songs that move some of them nearly to tears, but that seem to me, at first, oddly flat and unemotional; it takes awhile before I become attuned to their foursquare, dignified melodies.

My dormitory room is plain and purely functional—a bed, a closet, a desk—but it fills me with a sense of well-being, because it's a room like

---

[1] *Lagado . . . Lilliput:* a reference to two of the fictional countries in Jonathan Swift's satirical novel *Gulliver's Travels* (1756) (*Ed.*)

everybody else's, an equalizing space. Here, I don't need to be so aware of social distinctions, and neither, perhaps, does anyone else; here, I can be just whoever I am. A few hours after I arrive, I'm joined by Lizzy, who's to be my roommate. She is a tall, bony girl with clear brown eyes and a large, thoughtful mouth. "Where are you from?" she asks immediately, and I tell her. "And you?" I ask, and Lizzy tells me that she comes from Cleveland, and that she is a Lutheran. When I look puzzled, she explains that her ancestors came from Germany, and that American Lutherans were a particularly exacting branch of Protestantism, and that her parents are both people of high principle.

5 I discover that the social landscape which seems so homogeneous at first is divided into complex configurations that everyone recognizes through subtle signals which are quite lost on me. Lizzy points out to me Baptists from small southern towns who turn out to be mathematical geniuses, scions of old Texan families who are already planning their political futures, smart northern girls with bohemian manners, flirty southern debutantes who like to hide their cleverness, literary sophisticates, and budding religious leaders. And all of them decked out in those tartan checks and bobby socks and the friendliest, white-toothed smiles. Surely, Gulliver had an easier country to understand!

There are, for example, all those customs that nobody told me about—the hazing of freshman boys, the initiations into literary societies, which all the girls want to get into, and the barbecue parties on sunny lawns. Every week that first fall, all the freshmen, wearing extremely unattractive "beanies"—a light-colored version of yarmulkes—march in tandem to the enormous stadium to attend the compulsory football game. There, I witness rituals as arcane as Aztec ceremonies—elaborate choreographies of floodlit cheerleading, collective genuflections to a large stuffed owl, which is the university's mascot, and once a near riot, which starts up when an umpire's decision provokes streams of boys from both warring camps to run down the bleachers with the full intention of attacking each other—only to be stopped dead in their tracks when the Rice band strikes up the national anthem. It is their respect for the law that astonishes me as much as their bloodthirst, but I guess these are university students and good boys. It is at these games that I discover how one can't see the ball without knowing the rules of the game, and I sit through the lengthy events without unravelling the secrets of what goes on down there, in the enormous stadium, where surreally clad men huddle and disperse violently.

There are other phenomena I encounter that I cannot fit on any grid. It happens rather regularly that students whom I barely know stop me in the library or the cafeteria to unburden themselves of some confession. The campus eccentrics gravitate toward me, perhaps because they sense in me a fellow outsider who will not judge them by the mainstream standards. People compliment me on being a "good listener," but they're wrong. I'm more like a naturalist trying to orient myself in an uncharted landscape, and eyeing the flora and fauna around me with a combination of curiosity and detachment. They might be upset if they knew the extent to which I view them as a puzzling species, but instead, they see a sort of egalitarian attentiveness. Since I don't know what's normal and what weird here, I listen with an equally impartial and polite interest to whomever approaches me. In this way, I come to hear the story of a girl who speaks in tongues, and who every weekend submits herself to a leather-strap beating by her religious mentor; I listen to a boy who tells me, his eyes heated and glazed, that the world is foul, cankered, evil—evil with Communism, with sex, with corruption—and who that evening walks off a dormitory roof during a conversation with God. Then there are the three girls who, after swearing me to secrecy, ask me to follow them to the dormitory basement. There, they tell me in breathless whispers that they're preparing for a great enterprise in which they want me to join with them. They have powers of clairvoyance and mental telepathy, they explain, and moreover, they're convinced that I do too, except I'm repressing these abilities because I was brought up under that horrible "system." What they have divined through their clairvoyant vision is that the Russians are going to invade the United States from Cuba. When that happens, they'll be ready: they're going to fight. At this point, they open a large leather trunk for my inspection: in its interior, I see cans of food, powdered milk—and, among these innocuous objects, two large, steely blue revolvers. The three girls plan to conduct guerrilla warfare with these weapons, and they are fully prepared—in fact eager—to die in the Armageddon, because they know what'll follow death as well. They show me poems they've written—lugubrious, gory, and ridiculous—in which, after being wounded and scarred, the heroines have been lifted to another planet, from which they look down on combat cataclysmically spreading to all corners of the earth.

Even I know that this isn't normal, though it isn't crazy in the way I understand that word either. I remember the crazy person on our street in Cracow; from behind the windows of a one-story house, this unseen man howled and screamed with bestial abandon; that's how one knew he was crazy. Or there was Pani Grodzinska's sister, who was afraid to go out on the street, and shredded newspapers all over her room; that was another example of solid craziness. But this is different; these girls go to their classes and don't scream or wave their guns in public. It's just that they have these Ideas. Each culture breeds its own kind of derangement, I'll later learn, and these American classmates of mine seem to go crazy with a surfeit of moral fervors. But in this, they're not so unlike the apparently very normal man from the Rotary Club who invited me to his large and comfortable house, and showed me his collection of guns, and told me, getting very red in the face, that you can't trust the government, but if the Commies ever come this way, there'll be at least some boys in Texas who will know how to defend their country. "Only in America," I tell myself about such manifestations, meaning that I can't make any sense of them whatsoever.

Even a relatively intelligible person, like Lizzy, poses problems of translation. She—and many others around me—would be as unlikely in Poland as gryphons or unicorns. In her particular mingling of ideas and sensibility, of emotion and self-presentation, she is a distinctively American personality. Is she as smart as Basia?[2] As spunky? As attractive? But the terms don't travel across continents. The human mean is located in a different place here, and qualities like adventurousness, or cleverness, or shyness are measured along a different scale and mapped within a different diagram. You can't transport human meanings whole from one culture to another any more than you can transliterate a text. Nevertheless, Lizzy and I set out to understand each other with a will—and we run into misunderstandings with the rude surprise of rams butting into each other in the middle of a narrow bridge. In the evenings, we spend long hours, sitting on our beds, talking. Lizzy, it turns out, holds beliefs that seem self-evident to her and that run smack counter to truths that seem equally obvious to me. We discuss, of course, the largest questions—whether people are free or determined, and how to fulfill one's potential, and what it means to be happy. Then there are issues that have never crossed my mental horizon but that are central in Lizzy's moral geography—such as the nature of civic responsibility, and how to interpret the American Constitution, and how to achieve the ideal of self-sufficiency.

"You know, I think Barry Goldwater is right," Lizzy declares one evening as we're munching on some cafeteria cookies. "Welfare is a horrible system. Giving people something for nothing destroys their dignity." 10

"But what if people need help?" I ask. "There are so many rich people in this country. It isn't fair that they should have so much and others nothing." I can't distinguish Barry Goldwater from Adlai Stevenson,[3] but perhaps I've been influenced by ideas of equal distribution drilled into me in elementary school after all, or maybe it's just that the famous American "contrasts" still have the power to upset me.

"Giving people something for nothing destroys their individuality," Lizzy asserts. "You can only have dignity if you're self-sufficient."

"But why shouldn't people help each other?" I ask, really at a loss to understand. There's no common word for "self-sufficiency" in Polish, and it sounds to me like a comfortless condition, a harsh and artificial ideal.

"Because dependence is bad for your character," Lizzy retorts.

"But we're all dependent on each other!" I say, stating what only seems obvious. 15

"Don't you think it's humiliating to be dependent?" Lizzy asks. She's speaking out of a different sense of the human creature, of where dignity and satisfaction lie, and she's as flummoxed by this disagreement on basic principles as I.

---

[2]*Basia:* one of Eva's childhood friends in Poland (*Ed.*)

[3]*Barry Goldwater . . . Adlai Stevenson:* Hoffman stresses her lack of familiarity with American culture during her first year of college by confusing these two politicians. Barry Goldwater (b. 1909) ran for president against Lyndon B. Johnson in 1964 and represented right-wing, conservative Republican politics; Adlai Stevenson (1900–1965), a Democrat, served under President Roosevelt, was ambassador to the United Nations in the Kennedy administration, and was well known for his liberalism. (*Ed.*)

"No, I don't. I mean, what if you get into trouble? What if you lose your job? When there's unemployment, somebody has to lose their job! Do you think that nobody should help you then?"

"People get what they deserve," Lizzy says, her beautiful mouth tightening into a look which suggests that my opinions have something unsavory about them from which she prefers to dissociate herself. "If you have pride, you don't ask for handouts."

But at this, anger compresses itself in my forehead. "Do you think everyone starts out with the same amount of opportunity?" I say furiously, my voice knotting with frustration. "Do you think everyone starts even? And what if people are stupid, or untalented, or sick! Do you just want to throw them to rot, to end up in a ditch?" I have my pride too, and I don't say "And what if you're a new immigrant starting out with nothing?" but of course it's my family I'm defending in this quarrel, and it's the thought of my parents that makes my temperature rise so high.

"If you have enough character, you can always pull yourself out," Lizzy says, iron in her voice. "That's what this country is all about, and that's the philosophy that made it what it is." 20

"Then it's a mean and cruel philosophy!" I shout.

"I think your philosophy is pinko!" Lizzy hurls at me, looking hurt, and runs out of the room, slamming the door behind her. I'm left badly jangled by the exchange, and Lizzy, it turns out, runs up to the dormitory roof, where she cries tears of frustration and rage. But the next day, we start up again, talking about how we want to experience everything, and what kinds of adults we want to become. On this subject too it turns out that our mental pictures are quite at odds. Lizzy thinks maturity is a condition to be avoided at all costs. "Everyone keeps saying you should be well adjusted," she says. "But well adjusted to what?" The condition of adulthood, in her mind, stands for her mother's repetitious days, rows of suburban houses in which nothing new or exciting ever happens, and a conventionality that keeps you from being curious and alive. Maturity, in this system of associations, is the opposite of experience: it is a kind of shrinking of the soul. Her mother, Lizzy tells me, does not understand what it's like to be very happy or very unhappy, or to want to have adventures; it's as though she belonged to an entirely other, not fully human species, and Lizzy is genuinely afraid of turning into somebody like her, or other grown-ups she has known. Since I yearn for maturity with every fiber of my soul, I try to convey to Lizzy the mastery, and the self-possession, and the wherewithal to express myself fully that I keep hoping for. I try to paint the image, so potent in my mind, of Pani Witeszczak playing the piano with tenderness and control. I tell her that my mother is not some straw woman whom I've never seen suffer, or storm, or cry. "We're all human," I say, echoing my mother's line. I want to explain how maturity means entering into the great stream of experience, coming to know what people have always known. Lizzy looks at me thoughtfully, but she, literally, doesn't see it; her mind has been stocked with different images, and just as I can't see the pictures of her childhood, she can't leap outside them, can't imagine what's not in her head. Growing up will prove painfully difficult for her, as difficult as for most of her, and my, generation.

▼ ▼ ▼

In the middle of the year, my music teacher arranges for me to give a concert in the Rice auditorium, and at the end, my youthful audience rises and claps for a long time. Afterward, several boys approach me, their eyes enthusiastic with appreciation, and tell me courteously that my playing sounded great, and I looked real pretty up there on the stage in that long green dress. In the exhilaration of the moment, I feel that life is once again as it should be.

> Labour is blossoming or dancing where
> The body is not bruised to pleasure soul,
> Nor beauty born out of its own despair,
> Nor blear-eyed wisdom out of midnight oil.
> O chestnut-tree, great-rooted blossomer,
> Are you the leaf, the blossom or the bole?
> O body swayed to music, O brightening glance,
> How can we know the dancer from the dance?[4]

I'm sitting in a bracingly uncomfortable chair in the Rice University library, reading slowly, laboriously. The chestnut tree in the stanza summons my private chestnut tree, and the last line moves me all on its own, because that's what it's like to play the piano, in those moments when I can no longer tell whether I'm playing the music or the music is playing me. But what does "bole" mean, or "blear-eyed," or "midnight oil"? I have only the vaguest idea, and by the time I look up these words in a dictionary and accomplish the translation from the sounds to their definition, it's hard to reinsert them into the flow of the lines, the seamless sequence of musical meaning. I concentrate intensely, too intensely, and the lines come out straight and square, though I intuit a beauty that's only an inflection away. And so I struggle harder to enter the stanza, like a frustrated lover whose hunger is fed by the inaccessible proximity of her object.

Much of what I read is lost on me, lost in the wash and surf of inexactly understood words. And yet, chagrined though I am by this, I soon find that I can do very well in my courses. I believe this happens not only despite but also because of my handicap: because I have so little language. Like any disability, this one has produced its own compensatory mechanisms, and my mind, relatively deprived of words, has become a deft instrument of abstraction. In my head, there is no ongoing, daily monologue to distract me, no layers of verbal filigree to peel away before the skeleton of an argument can 25

---

[4]*Labour . . . dance?:* Hoffman had been reading "Among School Children" (1928), a poem by the Irish writer W. B. Yeats (1865–1939). (*Ed.*)

become clear. Without this sensuous texturing, the geometries of my own perceptions have become as naked to me as the exposed girders of a building before the actual building hides them. When I'm presented with an object of study—a problem or a book—it's easier for me to penetrate to the architectural plan than to appreciate the details of the exterior.

It's precisely because I know how thinned out the air of abstraction can be that I'll develop great respect for the significance of the surface and the concrete detail. But for now, it so happens that my accidental predisposition is perfectly fitted to the educational premises of the period. The education I receive at Rice is almost entirely formalistic, and the things we're required to do with what we read are just what I can do best in my verbally deprived condition. In a philosophy survey that introduces us to medieval religious thinkers and French existentialists, we're not asked whether arguments about God or the absurd seem true but how arguments about truth are constructed. In a history course on the Renaissance, we don't need to remember what sequence of events led up to the Reformation; instead, we're asked to contemplate the nature of retrospective knowledge, or whether an accurate interpretation of the past is possible. This I can do by arranging blocks of abstract ideas into a logical pattern, without stumbling on the treacherous shoals of specificity.

It takes me awhile to discover that this is a valuable talent. At first, I'm reluctant to study at all, lest I prove a miserable failure. Then in a philosophy class, a professor discussing the Platonic qualities of "largeness" and "smallness" asks whether we want to talk about a large or small orange, and when I cheekily suggest "How about medium?" he throws a piece of chalk at me in the most friendly way. In my English class, my paper on a John Donne sonnet is singled out to be read aloud, and I decide that it might be worthwhile to make an effort after all.

Not that my efforts ever become very disciplined. Studying too systematically or too hard would violate my Polish code of honor—that one should, in any system whatsoever, break as many rules as one can—and would take the flash and flair out of the grand game of getting away with it. But I perceive that there is another game going on here—of an intellectual kind—that I can play very well. I soak in the academic vocabulary of the time with an almost suspicious facility; for me, this is an elementary rather than an advanced language, a language I learn while I'm still in my English childhood. It does not have to make its way through layers of other vocabulary, and I can juggle it with resistless ease, as if it had no weight.

Even in literature, that most sensuously textured of expressions, my abstracting bent turns out to be useful. The Rice English Department in the mid-sixties is firmly in the grip of New Criticism[5]—that laboratory method which

---

[5]*New Criticism:* a school of American literary criticism, developed in the 1940s, which focused on close reading and explication of the text itself and paid little attention to its cultural and social contexts or to the author's life (*Ed.*)

concerns itself with neither writers' lives nor their worlds—and whether I'm reading Chaucer, or Jacobean tragedy, or *The Sound and the Fury,* I'm asked to parse pieces of text as if they were grammatical constructions. "Form is content," at this time, is taken to mean that there is no such thing as content.

Luckily for me, there is no world outside the text; luckily, for I know so little of the world to which the literature I read refers. My task, when I read a poem or a novel, is to find repeated symbols, patterns of words, recurring motifs, and motifs that pull against each other. These last are particularly prized because they have the honorific status of "irony" and "paradox." These are exercises I can perform with ease. The local details, from which most readers get their most immediate, primary pleasure, don't obstruct my way. The clothes people wear in novels, the places where they live, their characteristic gestures and turns of speech have, for me, no mimetic resonances[6] in English; Daisy in *The Great Gatsby* does not summon in my mind a spoiled, Waspish girl of a certain type, as she might for other readers; she is for me a formal entity, the symbol that Gatsby, another symbolic construction, craves. They are symbols clashing on the pages, until they resolve into their neat denouement, symbolic of American tragedies, of America itself. 30

I become an expert on this business of symbolic patterns. They seem to come in several varieties. There is, in American literature, individualism and the frontier, and there is society versus nature, and self versus society—and there is, first and foremost in those days, alienation. I become an expert in alienation too. I notice that it comes up in American literature more than elsewhere, and has a particularly American flavor. People are often lonely in American novels, and can't easily talk to each other; they flub human contacts horribly, and tend to find themselves in seedy rooms, alone, or out on the frontier, grimly questing. As for men and women, they either speak to each other with great sentimentality, as in *For Whom the Bell Tolls,* or find each other truly disgusting, as in *Miss Lonelyhearts.*[7]

Being an alien myself in the midst of all this alienation turns out to be no disadvantage. For one thing, New Criticism is an alienated way of reading meant for people who are aliens in the country of literature. It prizes detachment, objectivity, and the critical rather than the sympathetic faculties. It is a very cool criterion, but also an egalitarian one, for it requires no privileged acquaintance with culture, no aristocratic, proprietorial intimacies of connoisseurship.

But my particular kind of alienness serves me well too, for I soon discover that triangulation is a more useful tool in literary criticism than it is in

---

[6]*mimetic resonances:* refers to the concept of literary mimesis, which attempts to imitate or to copy reality through artistic representation (*Ed.*)

[7]*For Whom the Bell Tolls . . . Miss Lonelyhearts: For Whom the Bell Tolls* (1940), by Ernest Hemingway (1899–1961), and *Miss Lonelyhearts* (1933), by Nathanael West (1904–1940), two classic American novels in which human relationships are seen from contrasting points of view: West portrays the helplessness and ultimate failure of human relationships; Hemingway extols the virtues of commitment and sacrifice in them. (*Ed.*)

life. As I read, I triangulate to my private criteria and my private passions, and from the oblique angle of my estrangement, I notice what's often invisible to my fellow students. When I read *The Catcher in the Rye,* it's Holden Caulfield's immaturity that strikes me, and I write a paper upbraiding him for his false and coy naïveté—my old, Polish terms of opprobrium. Reading *The Ambassadors* requires a torture of concentration, but a glimpse of Strether coming ashore in France and registering the ever-so-minute changes of light and smell and facial expressions and angle of objects delivers a thrill of recognition: that's just what it's like to land on a foreign shore, and I want to write Henry James a thank-you note for capturing the ineffable with such exactitude. In Malamud's *The Assistant,* it's not the religious parable that fixes my attention but the dingy, dark little store in which the Jewish shopkeeper ekes out his hopeless living; I'm grateful again, that someone has made literature of such a condition.

Some kind of intellectual passion—or perhaps a passion for the work of the intellect—is being stoked in the midst of these placid exegeses. For one thing, I've learned that in a democratic educational system, in a democratic ideology of reading, I am never made to feel that I'm an outsider poaching on others' property. In this country of learning, I'm welcomed on equal terms, and it's through the democratizing power of literature that I begin to feel at home in America, even before I understand the literature or America, or the relationship between them, very well.

That relationship, as I find out firsthand, is confoundingly indirect. A visitor coming to the United States armed with the knowledge of Melville, and Hemingway and Faulkner and John Updike and Harold Robbins and Stephen King, would still be almost entirely unprepared for the broad and the intimate spectacle of the actual country confronting him. Driving on Interstate 1 would still be an immense surprise, and coping with the New York subway a sui generis experience; attending a party in a San Francisco home, or a wedding on Long Island, would be as strange as witnessing the rites in a Japanese novel; and while the Statue of Liberty might be recognizable from a book-jacket picture, an ordinary conversation in an ordinary living room would be full of those odd angles and slants of light and eruptions of the unfamiliar that Henry James registered so uncannily. It is only after a longer while that such a visitor might start putting together the living culture and the literature to which it has given rise: the crazed holy-talk of a street-corner preacher in Times Square might cross with a flash of Hazel Motes; the staccato aggressiveness of a New York intellectual elaborating some unlikely political proposition might synchronize with the rhythms of Norman Mailer's prose; during a long cross-country drive in the vastnesses of unpopulated wilderness, Thoreau's obsessions might become clear. Mimesis, it seems, works smoothly in only one direction, and life refuses conveniently to mirror the art in which it's seemingly mirrored. 35

At this point in my education, I can't translate backward. Literature doesn't yet give me America in its particulars—though as I read Emerson and

Thoreau and Walker Percy,[8] I feel the breath of a general spirit: the spirit, precisely, of alienness, of a continent and a culture still new and still uncozy, and a vision that turns philosophical or tortured from confronting an unworded world.

DISCUSSING THE TEXT

1. On arriving in Houston, young Eva thinks she's come to "the real America," a place where she need not be particularly "aware of social distinctions." How does she gradually learn that things are not quite so simple? What are some regional peculiarities about the United States (and Texas in particular) that she gradually comes to notice? What are some of the "complex configurations" of the not-so-homogeneous social landscape at the university? Can you compare her experiences to yours in any way?
2. Why does Eva describe college football game rituals "as arcane as Aztec ceremonies"? Can you think of similar cultural rituals you've observed, or in which you have participated, that have seemed alien to you?
3. What are some of the qualities about Eva that make the local eccentrics think of her as "a good listener"? Why do you think they gravitate toward her?
4. Working with a group of four or five students, try to come up with a one-sentence definition of the process of "triangulation" that Hoffman describes in paragraph 33. How does this process affect her reading of American literary classics? How does it tie in with what she calls "a democratic educational system" and "a democratic ideology of reading"? Take careful notes, and be prepared to share your definition and ideas with the rest of the class.

WRITING ABOUT THE TEXT

5. Assuming Eva's voice as college student, write a letter to a friend in Poland explaining how you are attempting to "translate" American culture into your own experience.
6. As she describes the "craziness" of some of her peers at the university, Hoffman observes that "Each culture breeds its own kind of derangement" (par. 8). Write two paragraphs addressing these questions: Can you think of a cultural practice in a foreign country that seems crazy to you? Can you

[8]*Hazel Motes . . . , Norman Mailer . . . , Ralph Waldo Emerson, Henry David Thoreau, Walker Percy:* Hoffman alludes to the fact that she first learned about American culture through literature by connecting scenes from real life to literary scenes or descriptions. Hazel Motes is a character in a novel by southern American writer Flannery O'Connor (1925–1964). Like the quintessential, nineteenth-century writers Emerson (1803–1882) and Thoreau (1817–1862), contemporary writers Norman Mailer (b. 1923) and Walker Percy (1916–1990) wrote about American life and culture. (*Ed.*)

think of a cultural practice in the United States that also seems crazy to you? How would you compare the two practices? Where does your definition of the term *crazy* come from?

7. Hoffman writes that her roommate Lizzy "holds beliefs that seem self-evident to her and that run smack counter to truths that seem equally obvious to me" (par. 9). Then, in paragraphs 10–22, she recounts an argument the two of them had over welfare in dialogue form. Using this dialogue as a model, write an account of an argument over a social or political issue that you have either participated in or overheard. What, if anything, do you think is gained from arguments of this kind?
8. Eva feels particularly attracted to some major themes in American literature (individualism and the frontier, society versus nature, self versus society, alienation). Write a brief essay that addresses the following questions: Why would some of these themes be important to an immigrant trying to understand American culture? Why is it significant that Eva encounters these themes through books?

LOURDES GIL

Against the Grain: Writing in Spanish in the U.S.A.

For Lourdes Gil, a Cuban American poet, writing in her native language of Spanish is an act of "complicity"—an act signifying allegiance and devotion to her past. In "Against the Grain: Writing in Spanish in the U.S.A.," which Gil translated into English for this anthology, she meditates on the relationship between language and identity, and she explains how writing in Spanish provides an important link both to her personal past and to her cultural traditions. She also explores the complex and metaphorical nuances of language—specifically in Spanish—that are important in her work as a poet.

Born in Havana, Cuba, Lourdes Gil has been in the United States since 1961 and lives in New Jersey. She has been the recipient of several awards for her writing, among them a Cintas Writer's Fellowship, and has been editor of the literary journals Lyra *and* Romanica. *Her books of poetry include* Blanca aldaba preludia *(White Threshold, 1989);* Empieza la ciudad *(The City Begins, 1989); and the forthcoming* El cerco de las transfiguraciones *(Circle of Transfigurations). Gil's numerous poems and essays have appeared in many anthologies and literary journals, both in Spanish and in English translation.*

"Language is the main instrument of man's refusal to accept the world as it is."

George Steiner, *After Babel*

I rarely dwell upon the fact that I have lived in the U.S. for over thirty years. I don't think about it in numerical terms, but rather as a space I once entered, an exile space. The concept of exile, from its Latin root "exsul," identifies its inherent condition, "outside of." The expatriate is, then, the perpetual outsider, the individual ousted from the community. I entered this exile space involuntarily (I was a child and others made the decision for me), yet the transition from the old to the new occurred in painful awareness. Something was blunted in the process, and my perception of time was permanently altered. As I walked into the uncharted, timeless regions of exile, I felt as if I was receding into a state of suspension, frozen in time, waiting for a faceless Godot.[1]

I have never pondered over the question too seriously—why I write in Spanish. It seemed natural to continue speaking the language I was born into, to proceed with the language I first learned to read and write in, the original vessel transporting me to the world of imagination and wonder. I regarded it as an essential component of my biological makeup, like the tone of my voice or the color of my eyes. I suppose it belongs to the realm of what psychologists call personal identity, anthropologists perceive as cultural identity, and the more ancient science of philosophy describes as Being or consciousness of Being.

Why cling to one's native tongue over such an extensive period of time? Why the linguistic transgression? Holding on to one's old identity in the face of the new can be an obstinate, fearsomely barren gesture of defiance. There is also an innate complicity in the act of choosing a language over another—a form of loyalty, perhaps, loyalty to the well-worn frame of reference where the self has been, up to that time, contextualized, an attachment to one's past, a devotion. We cannot forget there are hidden meanings in speech: the subtle undercurrents carrying other ways of life, the solace of traditions, a world inhabited by people who left an imprint on our lives, the books we've read, even a more exact definition of ourselves. Is there a dominance of language over us, a level where it settles, and where our mode of communication with others is established? Is it the eccentric site where the "encoding" of our writing and our speech occurs?

---

[1]*Godot:* reference to the major play *Waiting for Godot* (1948), by Irish writer Samuel Beckett (1906–1989). The play's characters talk on and on as they wait for Godot, who never comes. (*Ed.*)

Mine was an old Cuban family, steeped in the Cuban and Spanish traditions that appear to have been lost after the Revolution of 1959.[2] It was through them that I acquired a sense of history, of continuity, as a child, a notion of our presence in the world. I had a special bond with my grandparents and their generation. They exposed me to anecdotes from the early years of the Cuban Republic, the student strikes of the thirties, the prominent figures in public life, the events of the Second World War. They sang outmoded couplets and recited classical poetry. They lent me old books with quaint Victorian drawings.

The half-dozen uncles on my mother's side were a fascinating lot who had traveled extensively, and whose lives had been invariably linked to all ramifications of Cuban society. Some I knew and some had already died at the time I was growing up, but their stories were told over and over, so that they, and the stories themselves, eventually acquired mythic proportions. My great-grandmother, a formidable woman who crossed the Atlantic six times, presided over a Commission of Teachers traveling to the U.S. during the American occupation of the Island in 1899. She always conveyed an unadorned vision of colonial Havana to the rest of us, something that we regarded as a rather uncommon feat. 5

So I grew up with a particularly loaded cargo—all of that which is transmitted in the bosom of an old family, a family with great respect for the life of the country. It was a very strong influence, a sort of initiation rite. It endowed me with a notion of who I was—or, at least, of where I came from—and this is something that stays with you for the rest of your life. The language we used was the glue holding everything and everyone together. Language was bound to my experience of life with others, bound to a sense of place, a sense of belonging. It never occurred to me that it could be any different.

Many Cuban American authors of my generation, also arriving as children to the U.S., have chosen English for their creative work. Their literary vision and aesthetic canon seem to conform to the Anglo-Saxon perspective, either from a Eurocentric focus or from an ethnicity within American society. Why have they chosen this course? Clearly, they do not see themselves, or their craft, within the predicaments and textures of the Spanish language and literatures. They instead see their inner selves better reflected in the more recently acquired sounds and inflections of the English tongue.

Their defining choice may be divergent from mine, yet both these choices—theirs and mine—were made within the same given coordinates of

[2]*Revolution of 1959:* Cuba's Socialist Revolution of 1959, led by Fidel Castro (*Ed.*)

time and space. Some had families as old and traditional as mine and were educated with as strong a sense of national pride as I was. Why, then, did they come to organize their literary discourse in the mainstream of American life? Why did their creativity and its written expression evolve as a part of the signs and abstractions of one language over another?

And yet, what inner dialectic dictates self-definition for an exile? There are no footprints on the snow and we have little to guide us through this path. Except, perhaps, for the internally imposed exile suggested by James Joyce[3] in his *Portrait of the Artist*—the flight to a freedom from the social order and its entanglements, a process of dislocation, an erasure of the immediate surroundings, a subversion of codes, a liberation. 9

DISCUSSING THE TEXT

1. What connection does Gil see between one's native language and one's cultural identity? How does she relate issues of language and identity to the concept of exile? What are her views on exile?
2. Compare Gil's experiences with language and stories with those described by two other writers included in this chapter (such as Richard Wright and Cynthia Ozick). What are some similarities and differences that you see?
3. Reread the passage in this essay in which Gil refers to the "hidden meanings in speech" (par. 3). Where, according to Gil, do these "hidden meanings" come from? What examples of influences from your past, perhaps from family members or friends, do you see in your own speech?

WRITING ABOUT THE TEXT

4. Gil presents several ideas to explain why she has chosen to write in her native language. Can you think of any other possible reasons for her choice? Can you think of any reasons why a writer in her position would choose to write in English instead? Write two paragraphs in which you discuss the pros and cons of writing in a foreign language in the United States. Conclude by stating your own views on the matter.
5. Write a brief essay in which you compare and contrast Gil's views on language and identity with those of Eva Hoffman in "The New World" (p. 360).

---

[3]*James Joyce* (1882–1941): Irish writer who discussed the concept of voluntary exile in his novel *Portrait of the Artist as a Young Man* (1916) (*Ed.*)

6. In "Summer: The Way to Highland Park," Alfred Kazin (p. 330) traces his emerging identity as a young man to his solitary reading of acclaimed nineteenth-century writers. Gil, on the other hand, writes about the important *communal* experience of shared family stories in the shaping of her own language and identity. Which of these experiences strikes you as more fruitful and productive in the development of identity within a multicultural American society? Why? Write a two- to three-page essay explaining your views.

MAKING CONNECTIONS

1. Make a list of the five books that have most influenced your life, emotionally, intellectually, and psychologically. Write a brief essay discussing their impact on you.
2. Look again at the photograph at the beginning of the chapter, "Girl Reading," by Joel Gordon, which was taken at a public library in New York City (p. 314). Write a fictional diary entry in which the girl describes her time at the library.
3. Choose one selection from this chapter and write two paragraphs explaining what you like most about it. How does this selection illustrate its writer's attempt to integrate different elements of her or his culture through reading and writing?
4. Even though Richard Wright, in the excerpt from *Black Boy,* and Louise DeSalvo, in "A Portrait of the *Puttana* as a Middle-Aged Woolf Scholar," describe very different experiences at the library, both writers express the significance of the library in their personal and intellectual lives. Write an imaginary dialogue between Wright and DeSalvo in which they compare and contrast their experiences.
5. For Alfred Kazin, in "Summer: The Way to Highland Park," and Eva Hoffman, in "The New World," the classics of American literature represented a way into the mainstream culture. Make a list of the elements, themes, and ideas that these writers identify as representative of American literature. Write two paragraphs stating why these elements, themes, and ideas are important for these two writers.
6. For Cynthia Ozick in "A Drugstore in Winter," Louise DeSalvo in "A Portrait of the *Puttana* as a Middle-Aged Woolf Scholar," and bell hooks in "Talking Back," reading and writing were essential for the creation of their new identities. Write a brief essay in which you explore the kinds of restraints that these three women encountered within their respective cultural traditions, and describe how they overcame those restrictions by entering the world of letters. Can you offer a personal example as well—that is, have you ever had a similar experience, or do you know anyone who has?
7. In "Against the Grain," Lourdes Gil describes how her Cuban childhood and the family traditions that went along with it constitute an essential part of her writing. When Richard Wright writes about his departure for Chicago, he speaks about the South in a similar way, observing that its traditions—good and bad—will always be with him through his work. Write a brief essay that compares and contrasts how these two authors write about their origins.
8. Like Jerre Mangione in "Growing Up Sicilian" (see Chap. 4, p. 280), Eva Hoffman describes the university as a place that will allow her both to transcend the immigrant experience and to examine it within the context of American culture. Write a brief essay that compares and contrasts these two authors in terms of their views of a university education.

FURTHER READING

Richard Wright

Walker, Margaret. *Richard Wright, Daemonic Genius: A Portrait of the Man, A Critical Look at His Work.* New York: Warner Books, 1988.

Wright, Richard. *Native Son.* New York: Harper and Row, 1940.

———. *Uncle Tom's Children.* 1940. Reprint, New York: Harper and Row, 1965.

Alfred Kazin

Kazin, Alfred. *New York Jew.* New York: Vintage, 1979.

———. *Starting Out in the Thirties.* Boston: Little, Brown, 1965.

Cynthia Ozick

Bloom, Harold, ed., *Cynthia Ozick.* New York: Chelsea House, 1986.

Ozick, Cynthia. *Art and Ardor.* New York: Knopf, 1983.

———. *Levitation: Five Fictions.* New York: Knopf, 1982.

———. *The Pagan Rabbi, and Other Stories.* New York: Knopf, 1971.

Louise DeSalvo

DeSalvo, Louise. *"Children Never Forget": Virginia Woolf on Childhood, Adolescence, and Young Adulthood.* Boston: Beacon Press, 1988.

bell hooks

hooks, bell. *Black Looks: Race and Representation.* Boston: South End Press, 1992.

———. *Outlaw Culture: Resisting Representations.* New York: Routledge, 1994.

———. *Teaching to Transgress: Education as the Practice of Freedom.* New York: Routledge, 1994.

Eva Hoffman

Ferraro, Thomas. *Ethnic Passages; Literary Immigrants in Twentieth Century America.* Chicago: University of Chicago, 1993.

Lourdes Gil

Carolina Hospital, ed. *Cuban American Writers: Los Atrevidos.* Princeton, N.J.: Linden Lane Press, 1988.

Cruz, Victor Hernandez, et al., eds. *Paper Dance. 55 Latino Poets.* New York: Persea, 1995.

Man in an Indian Headdress, N.Y.C. *(photograph by Diane Arbus), 1969. Posing her subject in a Native American headdress, photographer Diane Arbus reveals a fascination that lasted throughout her career with people who assumed new identities through costume and dress, whether permanently or (as here) temporarily.*

6

Cross-Cultural Impersonations

next to of course god america i / love you land of the pilgrims' and so forth . . .

- E. E. CUMMINGS
next to of course god america i

It occurs to me that I am America. / I am talking to myself again.

- ALLEN GINSBERG
America

Sometimes it seems to me that I have never really been a Negro, that I have been only a privileged spectator of their inner life; at other times I feel that I have been a coward, a deserter, and I am possessed by a strange longing for my mother's people.

- JAMES WELDON JOHNSON
The Autobiography of an Ex-Colored Man

I had been a Negro more than three weeks and it no longer shocked me to see the stranger in the mirror.

- JOHN HOWARD GRIFFIN
Black like Me

In the stands we six boys drink beer in disgust, groan and hug our breasts, hold our heads and twist our faces at each other in embarrassment.

- JUDY GRAHN
Boys at the Rodeo

"That's a sad bunch of pictures," I told him, "so why lie about it?"
"The sadness is in you, son," he told me. "I don't see them sad at all."
"You're not a Mexican." It popped out of me just-like-that.

- DANNY SANTIAGO
Famous All Over Town

The politician come around and shook everybody's hand; though he didn't shake mine nor Granpa's. Granpa said this was because we looked like Indians and didn't vote nohow, so we was of practical no use whatsoever to the politician. Which sounds reasonable.

- FORREST CARTER
Trading with a Christian

The distasteful truth will out: like it or not, all writers are "cultural impersonators."

- HENRY LOUIS GATES
"Authenticity," or the Lesson of Little Tree

Previous chapters in this book have addressed the process of creating an American identity. Sometimes this process involves encounters with the "other," or persons of different racial, economic, or sexual backgrounds; sometimes it involves crossing the border from the position of marginalized (or less valued) American to a more complicated, hybrid identity. In many ways the American self—whether part of the dominant culture or one of the many minority cultures—is a malleable, changing one. Some of these changes occur slowly and without our noticing them; others can be the product of a willed transformation. And still others can be defined as "cultural impersonations" (a term coined by writer Cynthia Ozick), in which the individual assumes another identity for a relatively short time as an act of deliberate self-creation.

For example, a man might impersonate a woman; a light-skinned black person might try to "pass" as a white person; a writer, artist, or performer might change his or her name or appearance in an effort to adopt an entirely new cultural identity. Such impersonations can be made completely apparent to an intended audience, or they can be conducted as a kind of deception, for some ulterior purpose. Both kinds of impersonation are present in the selections included in this chapter.

Impersonation is possible in our culture because of the strong visible markers of ethnic, racial, and sexual identity, markers that can be imitated or assumed for a variety of reasons. People conduct cultural impersonations for purposes of self-discovery, for purposes of disguise, simply for play, or to satirize the rigidity of mainstream America, to name a few of those reasons. The frequency and ease of these impersonations raises the question of whether identity in America can, at times, be a kind of commodity, something that is traded and exchanged. In the face of such transformations and impersonations, what is the place of authenticity?

The photograph by Diane Arbus that frames this chapter, "Man in an Indian Headdress, N.Y.C." (1969), is a playful but also sinister comment on cross-cultural impersonation, portraying as it does a white man who has chosen to express his patriotism through the appropriation of a Native American cultural artifact, the headdress. Issues of authenticity and impersonation are explored throughout the chapter, beginning with an impersonation of American identity. The patriotic voice of a Stars-and-Stripes American is parodied by the poet E. E. Cummings in "next to of course god america i." Cummings, who was born into an elite Boston family, had come to identify himself with the Bohemian subculture of New York's Greenwich Village by the time he wrote this poem. By contrast, Allen Ginsberg, author of the next selection, the poem "America," was born into a Jewish family, on the margins of mainstream America. In "America" Ginsberg addresses mainstream culture from the standpoint of a person like himself who is deliberately seeming to be crazy, or perhaps has already been driven crazy by the madness of the America he describes. Ginsberg employs a variety of voices in this poem, especially toward the end, when things fly apart into a kind of chaos of impersonations.

Racial impersonations are the subject of the next two selections. James Weldon Johnson's *Autobiography of an Ex-Colored Man* (1912) confronts the reader with a case of both racial and literary impersonation. Johnson's protagonist is a light-skinned black man who passes for white and is more and more tortured about having rejected his African American identity. Furthermore, although the book is called an *Autobiography,* it is actually a work of fiction.

An interesting contrast—a white man passing as black—can be found in the selection from *Black like Me,* by John Howard Griffin. Concerned with the plight of black Americans during the 1950s, Griffin, who was white, had his skin chemically darkened and traveled throughout the South as an African American, documenting case after case of racial discrimination and injustice. To achieve his goals, Griffin needed to appear black to both whites and blacks; his experiment, which was based on a deception, led him to a deeper understanding of both himself and an ethnic "other." It also advanced the cause of civil rights for black Americans during the 1960s.

Judy Grahn's 1980 narrative, "Boys at the Rodeo" is an exploration of the politics of gender. Grahn's female narrator and her friends, all lesbians, decide to dress up in men's clothes and attend a rodeo, a scenario that becomes the source of the narrator's comments on issues of role-playing, cross-dressing, and gender stereotypes. The narrator is amazed to find that not only have she and her friends passed as males, they have also become younger—boys, in fact. Grahn's experience with impersonation is twofold. By being perceived as male, these female "boys" at the rodeo enter a different culture—male culture with its own bondings and rituals. They also come to see themselves, and women in general, from a different angle.

The contemporary selections by Danny Santiago and Forrest Carter (both pseudonyms) confront the reader with more complicated problems of cultural impersonation and literary authenticity. Daniel L. James published his book *Famous All Over Town,* as an "autobiographical novel" by Mexican American author Danny Santiago. Asa Earl Carter published the bogus autobiography *The Education of Little Tree* under the name Forrest Carter and falsely claimed to be a Native American. When comparing and contrasting these selections, try to imagine these men's motives for creating an ethnic "other," not only through the characters in their books but through authorial impersonation as well.

The final essay, " 'Authenticity,' or the Lesson of Little Tree," by Henry Louis Gates, Jr., inspired the theme of this chapter, offering as it does challenging questions on notions of authorship, authenticity, and cross-cultural impersonations. Gates points out that cases such as those of Carter and James confront the reader with disturbing issues. But he also notes the difficulty of labeling something as "authentic," arguing that "what the ideologues of authenticity cannot quite come to grips with is that fact and fiction have always exerted a reciprocal effect on each other."

E. E. CUMMINGS

next to of course god america i

Born in Cambridge, Massachusetts, E. E. Cummings (1894–1962) was a principal figure in the post–World War I, Greenwich Village movement that shook off the old habits of American genteel culture. Cummings graduated from Harvard University in 1915 and served in World War I in the ambulance corps in France. He recorded his experiences and antiwar sentiments in a successful novel, The Enormous Room *(1922), but is best known for several volumes of experimental poetry, collected in* Complete Poems, 1913–1962, *and published in 1968. Using typography in highly inventive and expressive ways, Cummings placed words on the page so as to reinforce the meaning of the poem, challenging his reader's eye and ear.*

Although much of his poetry is lyrical, Cummings exhibits here his talent as a sharp satirist. "next to of course god america i" (1926) takes America as its subject and offers a critique of American culture through a kind of cultural impersonation. Assuming a literary voice that mimics the speech of a booster of American values, the poem uses the language of patriotic clichés in a subversive way.

"next to of course god america i
love you land of the pilgrims' and so forth oh
say can you see by the dawn's early my
country 'tis of centuries come and go
and are no more what of it we should worry 5
in every language even deafanddumb
thy sons acclaim your glorious name by gorry
by jingo by gee by gosh by gum
why talk of beauty what could be more beautiful than these heroic happy dead 10
who rushed like lions to the roaring slaughter
they did not stop to think they died instead
then shall the voice of liberty be mute?"

He spoke. And drank rapidly a glass of water

DISCUSSING THE TEXT

1. Who is speaking the first thirteen lines of the poem "next to of course god america i"? Who is speaking the last line? How many clichés about America can you find in the first thirteen lines? Why does Cummings use them as part of this speech?
2. Why does Cummings style and punctuate the poem as he does (that is, with no capital letters and no punctuation marks separating sentences)?

WRITING ABOUT THE TEXT

3. What does patriotism mean to you and your friends? Make a list of words and ideas that are connected, for you, with the idea of American patriotism. Write two paragraphs about its significance in your life. Do you think it is a sentiment that should be satirized, as in the poem by E. E. Cummings? Why or why not?
4. Write a brief essay, or a poem, on a social or political issue that you feel strongly about. Try to imitate E. E. Cummings's style, deliberately incorporating sarcasm and clichés to make your point ironically.

ALLEN GINSBERG

America

Allen Ginsberg, born in Newark, New Jersey, in 1926, is an important figure in American letters. A major Beat writer of the post–World War II generation, Ginsberg rebelled against the culture of the American middle class both in his life and his work. Like Cummings, he was deeply affected by his generation's involvement in a major global war. For Ginsberg, the aftermath of World War II—in which the United States became a major power, possessed of nuclear weaponry that could destroy the earth—became a colossal and unavoidable fact of existence. Ginsberg's poems were, and still are, often shocking in their language and sentiments. His major early work, Howl *(1955), which was cleared of obscenity charges in a celebrated trial following its publication, is a lamentation for his post–World War II generation. Ginsberg's frank admissions concerning his own homosexuality, his drug use, his mysticism, and his apolitical communism, have won him wide notoriety and have made his poetry extremely controversial. Now a cultural icon, Ginsberg is presently Distinguished Professor of English at the City University of New York.*

"America" (1956) expresses Ginsberg's ambivalence about American society. He is angry at many aspects of 1950s culture, bewildered and dismayed by its contradictions, but he is not without some hope for the future. Ginsberg writes the poem as an address to "America," using the first-person voice; but the speaker of the poem seems rather crazy, and the rambling monologue is addressed as much to himself as to all other Americans. Throughout the poem, Ginsberg enjoys impersonating various voices, assuming a range of identities. He identifies himself as Catholic in one place, and in another as implicitly Jewish. He also identifies himself with the Scottsboro boys, a group of black teenagers wrongly accused of raping a white girl during the 1930s (the charges were ultimately dropped in a celebrated and prolonged legal case). Ginsberg says that his strophes or poetic lines are "all different sexes," and he is, at the end of the poem, "putting my queer shoulder to the wheel." Thus, he tells his readers, "I am America."

America I've given you all and now I'm nothing.
America two dollars and twentyseven cents January 17, 1956.
I can't stand my own mind.
America when will we end the human war?
Go fuck yourself with your atom bomb. 5
I don't feel good don't bother me.
I won't write my poem till I'm in my right mind.
America when will you be angelic?
When will you take off your clothes?
When will you look at yourself through the grave? 10
When will you be worthy of your million Trotskyites?
America why are your libraries full of tears?
America when will you send your eggs to India?
I'm sick of your insane demands.
When can I go into the supermarket and buy what I need with my good looks? 15
America after all it is you and I who are perfect not the next world.
Your machinery is too much for me.
You made me want to be a saint.
There must be some other way to settle this argument.
Burroughs[1] is in Tangiers I don't think he'll come back it's sinister. 20
Are you being sinister or is this some form of practical joke?
I'm trying to come to the point.
I refuse to give up my obsession.
America stop pushing I know what I'm doing.
America the plum blossoms are falling. 25
I haven't read the newspapers for months, everyday somebody goes on trial for murder.
America I feel sentimental about the Wobblies[2]
America I used to be a communist when I was a kid I'm not sorry.
I smoke marijuana every chance I get.
I sit in my house for days on end and stare at the roses in the closet. 30
When I go to Chinatown I get drunk and never get laid.
My mind is made up there's going to be trouble.
You should have seen me reading Marx.
My psychoanalyst thinks I'm perfectly right.
I won't say the Lord's Prayer. 35
I have mystical visions and cosmic vibrations.
America I still haven't told you what you did to Uncle Max after he came over from Russia.

---

[1]*William Burroughs* (b. 1914): along with Ginsberg, one of the major writers of the Beat generation; author of *Naked Lunch* (1959) (*Ed.*)

[2]*the Wobblies:* International Workers of the World, pre–World War I labor activists, precursors to organized American unionism (*Ed.*)

I'm addressing you.
Are you going to let your emotional life be run by Time Magazine?
I'm obsessed by Time Magazine. 40
I read it every week.
Its cover stares at me every time I slink past the corner candystore.
I read it in the basement of the Berkeley Public Library.
It's always telling me about responsibility. Businessmen are serious. Movie producers are serious. Everybody's serious but me. 45
It occurs to me that I am America.
I am talking to myself again.

Asia is rising against me.
I haven't got a chinaman's chance.
I'd better consider my national resources. 50
My national resources consist of two joints of marijuana millions of genitals an unpublishable private literature that jetplanes 1400 miles an hour and twentyfive-thousand mental institutions.
I say nothing about my prisons nor the millions of underprivileged who live in my flowerpots under the light of five hundred suns.
I have abolished the whorehouses of France, Tangiers is the next to go.
My ambition is to be President despite the fact that I'm a Catholic.

America how can I write a holy litany in your silly mood? 55
I will continue like Henry Ford my strophes are as individual as his automobiles more so they're all different sexes.
America I will sell you strophes $2500 apiece $500 down on your old strophe
America free Tom Mooney[3]
America save the Spanish Loyalists[4]
America Sacco & Vanzetti[5] must not die 60
America I am the Scottsboro boys.[6]
America when I was seven momma took me to Communist Cell meetings they sold us garbanzos a handful per ticket a ticket costs a nickel and the speeches were free everybody was angelic and sentimental about the workers it was all so sincere you have no idea what a good thing the party was in 1835 Scott Nearing was a grand old man a real

---

[3]*Tom Mooney* (1882–1942): labor leader convicted of throwing a bomb at a parade in 1919; he claimed to be innocent, but was imprisoned for twenty years before being pardoned in 1939. (*Ed.*)

[4]*Spanish Loyalists:* during the Spanish Civil War (1936–1939), the Loyalists were the defenders of the duly elected Spanish Republic, ultimately defeated by the Fascists. (*Ed.*)

[5]*Sacco & Vanzetti:* Nicola Sacco and Bartolomeo Vanzetti were Italian American anarchists, convicted of murder and executed in 1927 despite international protests. (*Ed.*)

[6]*Scottsboro Boys:* nine black young men arrested and jailed in Scottsboro, Alabama, in 1931 for the alleged rape of two white girls. The Supreme Court reversed their convictions, setting a precedent against legal injustice and racial discrimination. (*Ed.*)

mensch Mother Bloor the Silk-strikers' Ewig-Weibliche made me cry I once saw the Yiddish orator Israel Amter plain.[7] Everybody must have been a spy.

America you don't really want to go to war.

America it's them bad Russians.

Them Russians them Russians and them Chinamen. And them Russians. 65

The Russia wants to eat us alive. The Russia's power mad. She wants to take our cars from out our garages.

Her wants to grab Chicago. Her needs a Red *Reader's Digest*. Her wants our auto plants in Siberia. Him big bureaucracy running our filling-stations.

That no good. Ugh. Him make Indians learn read. Him need big black niggers. Hah. Her make us all work sixteen hours a day. Help.

America this is quite serious.

America this is the impression I get from looking in the television set. 70

America is this correct?

I'd better get right down to the job.

It's true I don't want to join the Army or turn lathes in precision parts factories, I'm nearsighted and psychopathic anyway.

America I'm putting my queer shoulder to the wheel.

–Berkeley, January 17, 1956

DISCUSSING THE TEXT

1. Why is the speaker of "America" angry? Which America is he angry with? What political events does the speaker allude to as an indication of America's state of mind?
2. Why does the speaker of "America" shift his voice toward the end (beginning with "America it's them bad Russians" [line 64])? What kind of voice(s) does he assume in the next several lines? What possible reasons can you think of for Ginsberg's choices here?
3. In a group of four or five students, discuss the following questions: How can you compare the America portrayed in Cummings's poem with the one portrayed in Ginsberg's? How do the poems' speakers situate themselves within America? How typical, or how idiosyncratic, do they portray themselves to be? Why? Take brief notes as you work on this assignment, and be prepared to share your opinions with the class.

WRITING ABOUT THE TEXT

4. Do some additional research into three of the political or historical allusions Ginsberg uses in his poem (such as Trotskyites, Wobblies, Tom Mooney,

[7]*Scott Nearing* (1883–1992): a professor of sociology, ousted from academia for his anti–World War I views; he was a Socialist and a pro-Soviet historian and biographer; *Mother Bloor:* Ella Reeve Bloor (1862–1951), Communist leader, union activist, and writer; *Ewig-Weibliche:* (German) eternal feminine; *Israel Amter* (1881–1954): Communist leader and orator (*Ed.*)

Spanish Loyalists, Sacco and Vanzetti, Scottsboro boys, Scott Nearing, and so on). Use an encyclopedia of the mid-twentieth century, a current biographical encyclopedia, or a history text. Write a brief summary in which you explain the factual background of these allusions. Conclude by discussing how knowledge of the people or events behind these allusions enhances your understanding of the poem.

5. Write a brief essay in which you discuss the speaker's state of mind in "America," using specific lines from the poem to make your point. Also address in your essay the following questions: Does the poem have any shock value for you today? How do you think audiences in the 1950s (when the poem was published) would have responded? How does your own vision of America compare with Ginsberg's?

JAMES WELDON JOHNSON

FROM

The Autobiography of an Ex-Colored Man

James Weldon Johnson's only novel, The Autobiography of an Ex-Colored Man, *from which this selection has been taken, was published anonymously in 1912. Initially the novel was assumed to be an actual autobiography, and it attracted little notice until it was reissued in 1927, this time in Johnson's name. In his novel, Johnson contends that the struggle for the African American man had shifted over the years: from the issue of whether the Negro was a human being with a soul, to whether the Negro had an intellectual capacity to master learning, and finally to his "social recognition." It is this last struggle that Johnson writes about, choosing a form that had developed in the nineteenth century, the novel about "passing." In this type of fiction, the hero or heroine is light-skinned enough to be taken for white, yet has a "drop" of black blood that automatically places him or her within a distinct class in American society. The dilemma for such a character is, very often, whether or not to pass as a white person, and then to deal with the consequences of that decision.*

James Weldon Johnson (1871–1938), a multi-faceted cultural leader, was a songwriter, a poet, and an editor. He was also field secretary and then general secretary of the National Association for the Advancement of Colored People (NAACP), one of the leading social forces at the time, from 1916 to 1930. Johnson was brought up in Jacksonville, Florida, in an economically secure and culturally rich environment, as the son of two free blacks. After graduating from Atlanta University in 1894, he became a teacher and principal at a high school in Jacksonville. During these years, and with the help of a white lawyer, he studied law, and in 1898 he became the first African American to practice law in Florida since the Reconstruction period. In 1901, along with his brother Rosamond, Johnson went to New York City to pursue a career as a songwriter for the musical theater. Active in Republican party politics and supported by Booker T. Washington, Johnson was appointed consul to Venezuela in 1906, where he wrote The Autobiography of an Ex-Colored Man.

The hero of Johnson's novel is sufficiently light-skinned to be taken as a white person, but discovers, as a boy, that he is a Negro. A talented pianist and composer, the narrator travels in Europe with a white patron; torn between the white and black social worlds, however, he decides to affirm his black racial identity and return to the South, where he witnesses a brutal and horrifying lynching of a black man. He feels "driven out" of the so-called Negro race by his shame, the "[s]hame at being identified with people that could with impunity be treated worse than animals." In the following chapter he returns to the North as a white man, or rather as neither black nor white, determined instead to "let the world take me for what it would."

Chapter XI

I have now reached that part of my narrative where I must be brief and touch only on important facts; therefore the reader must make up his mind to pardon skips and jumps and meagre details.

When I reached New York, I was completely lost. I could not have felt more a stranger had I been suddenly dropped into Constantinople. I knew not where to turn or how to strike out. I was so oppressed by a feeling of loneliness that the temptation to visit my old home in Connecticut was well-nigh irresistible. I reasoned, however, that unless I found my old music teacher, I should be, after so many years of absence, as much of a stranger there as in New York; and, furthermore, that in view of the step which I had decided to take, such a visit would be injudicious. I remembered, too, that I had some property there in the shape of a piano and a few books, but decided that it would not be worth what it might cost me to take possession.

By reason of the fact that my living-expenses in the South had been very small, I still had nearly four hundred dollars of my capital left. In contemplation of this, my natural and acquired Bohemian tastes asserted themselves, and I decided to have a couple of weeks' good time before worrying seriously about the future. I went to Coney Island and the other resorts, took in the pre-season shows along Broadway, and ate at first-class restaurants; but I shunned the old Sixth Avenue district as though it were pest-infected. My few days of pleasure made appalling inroads upon what cash I had, and caused me to see that it required a good deal of money to live in New York as I wished to live and that I should have to find, very soon, some more or less profitable employment. I was sure that unknown, without friends or prestige, it would be useless to try to establish myself as a teacher of music; so I gave that means of earning a livelihood scarcely any consideration. And even had I considered it possible to secure pupils, as I then felt, I should have hesitated about taking up a work in which the chances for any considerable financial success are necessarily so small. I had made up my mind that since I was not going to be a Negro, I would avail myself of every possible opportunity to make a white man's success; and that, if it can be summed up in any one word, means "money."

I watched the "want" columns in the newspapers and answered a number of advertisements, but in each case found the positions were such as I could not fill or did not want. I also spent several dollars for "ads" which brought me no replies. In this way I came to know the hopes and disappointments of a large and pitiable class of humanity in this great city, the people who look for work through the newspapers. After some days of this sort of experience I concluded that the main difficulty with me was that I was not prepared for what I wanted to do. I then decided upon a course which, for an artist, showed an uncommon amount of practical sense and judgment. I made up my mind to enter a business college. I took a small room, ate at lunch counters, in order to economize, and pursued my studies with the zeal that I have always been able to put into my work upon which I set my heart. Yet, in spite of all my economy, when I had been at the school for several months, my funds gave out completely. I reached the point where I could not afford sufficient food for each day. In this plight I was glad to get, through one of the teachers, a job as an ordinary clerk in a downtown wholesale house. I did my work faithfully, and received a raise of salary before I expected it. I even managed to save a little money out of my modest earnings. In fact, I began then to contract the money fever, which later took strong possession of me. I kept my eyes open, watching for a chance to better my condition. It finally came in the form of a position with a house which was at the time establishing a South American department. My knowledge of Spanish was, of course, the principal cause of my good luck; and it did more for me: it placed me where the other clerks were practically put out of competition with me. I was not slow in taking advantage of the opportunity to make myself indispensable to the firm.

What an interesting and absorbing game is money-making! After each deposit at my savings-bank I used to sit and figure out, all over again, my principal and interests, and make calculations on what the increase would be in such and such time. Out of this I derived a great deal of pleasure. I denied myself as much as possible in order to swell my savings. As much as I enjoyed smoking, I limited myself to an occasional cigar, and that was generally of a variety which in my old days at the "Club" was known as a "Henry Mud." Drinking I cut out altogether, but that was no great sacrifice. 5

The day on which I was able to figure up a thousand dollars marked an epoch in my life. And this was not because I had never before had money. In my gambling days and while I was with my millionaire I handled sums running high up into the hundreds; but they had come to me like fairy godmother's gifts, and at a time when my conception of money was that it was made only to spend. Here, on the other hand, was a thousand dollars which I had earned by days of honest and patient work, a thousand dollars which I had carefully watched grow from the first dollar; and I experienced, in owning them, a pride and satisfaction which to me was an entirely new sensation. As my capital went over the thousand-dollar mark, I was puzzled to know what to do with it, how to put it to the most advantageous use. I turned down first one scheme and then another, as though they had been devised for the sole purpose of gobbling up my money. I finally listened to a friend who advised me to put all I had in New York real estate; and under his guidance I took equity in a piece of property on which stood a rickety old tenement-house. I did not regret following this friend's advice, for in something like six months I disposed of my equity for more than double my investment. From that time on I devoted myself to the study of New York real estate and watched for opportunities to make similar investments. In spite of two or three speculations which did not turn out well, I have been remarkably successful. Today I am the owner and part-owner of several flathouses. I have changed my place of employment four times since returning to New York, and each change has been a decided advancement. Concerning the position which I now hold I shall say nothing except that it pays extremely well.

As my outlook on the world grew brighter, I began to mingle in the social circles of the men with whom I came in contact; and gradually, by a process of elimination, I reached a grade of society of no small degree of culture. My appearance was always good and my ability to play on the piano, especially rag-time, which was then at the height of its vogue, made me a welcome guest. The anomaly of my social position often appealed strongly to my sense of humour. I frequently smiled inwardly at some remark not altogether complimentary to people of colour; and more than once I felt like declaiming: "I am a coloured man. Do I not disprove the theory that one drop of Negro blood renders a man unfit?" Many a night when I returned to my room after an enjoyable evening, I laughed heartily over what struck me as the capital joke I was playing.

Then I met her, and what I had regarded as a joke was gradually changed into the most serious question of my life. I first saw her at a musical which was given one evening at a house to which I was frequently invited. I did not notice her among the other guests before she came forward and sang two sad little songs. When she began, I was out in the hallway, where many of the men were gathered; but with the first few notes I crowded with others into the doorway to see who the singer was. When I saw the girl, the surprise which I had felt at the first sound of her voice was heightened; she was almost tall and quite slender, with lustrous yellow hair and eyes so blue as to appear almost black. She was as white as a lily, and she was dressed in white. Indeed, she seemed to me the most dazzlingly white thing I had ever seen. But it was not her delicate beauty which attracted me most; it was her voice, a voice which made one wonder how tones of such passionate colour could come from so fragile a body.

I determined that when the program was over, I would seek an introduction to her; but at the moment, instead of being the easy man of the world, I became again the bashful boy of fourteen, and my courage failed me. I contended myself with hovering as near her as politeness would permit; near enough to hear her voice, which in conversation was low, yet thrilling, like the deeper middle tones of a flute. I watched the men gather round her talking and laughing in an easy manner, and wondered how it was possible for them to do it. But destiny, my special destiny, was at work. I was standing near, talking with affected gaiety to several young ladies, who, however, must have remarked my preoccupation; for my second sense of hearing was alert to what was being said by the group of which the girl in white was the centre, when I heard her say: "I think his playing of Chopin is exquisite." And one of my friends in the group replied: "You haven't met him? Allow me——" Then turning to me, "Old man, when you have a moment I wish you to meet Miss——." I don't know what she said to me or what I said to her. I can remember that I tried to be clever, and experienced a growing conviction that I was making myself appear more and more idiotic. I am certain, too, that, in spite of my Italian-like complexion, I was as red as a beet.

Instead of taking the car, I walked home. I needed the air and exercise as a sort of sedative. I am not sure whether my troubled condition of mind was due to the fact that I had been struck by love or to the feeling that I had made a bad impression upon her. 10

As the weeks went by, and when I had met her several more times, I came to know that I was seriously in love; and then began for me days of worry, for I had more than the usual doubts and fears of a young man in love to contend with.

Up to this time I had assumed and played my role as a white man with a certain degree of nonchalance, a carelessness as to the outcome, which made the whole thing more amusing to me than serious; but now I ceased to regard "being a white man" as a sort of practical joke. My acting had called for mere external effects. Now I began to doubt my ability to play the part. I watched her to see if she was scrutinizing me, to see if she was looking for anything in me which made me differ from the other men she knew. In place of an old inward feeling of superiority over many of my friends I began to doubt myself. I began even to wonder if I really was like the men I associated with; if there was not, after all, an indefinable something which marked a difference.

But, in spite of my doubts and timidity, my affair progressed, and I finally felt sufficiently encouraged to decide to ask her to marry me. Then began the hardest struggle of my life, whether to ask her to marry me under false colours or to tell her the whole truth. My sense of what was exigent made me feel there was no necessity of saying anything; but my inborn sense of honour rebelled at even indirect deception in this case. But however much I moralized on the question, I found it more and more difficult to reach the point of confession. The dread that I might lose her took possession of me each time I sought to speak, and rendered it impossible for me to do so. That moral courage requires more than physical courage is no mere poetic fancy. I am sure I should have found it easier to take the place of a gladiator, no matter how fierce the Numidian lion,[1] than to tell that slender girl that I had Negro blood in my veins. The fact which I had at times wished to cry out, I now wished to hide for ever.

During this time we were drawn together a great deal by the mutual bond of music. She loved to hear me play Chopin and was herself far from

---

[1]*Numidian lion:* African lion from the ancient country of Numidia, in the area of what is now Algeria (*Ed.*)

being a poor performer of his compositions. I think I carried her every new song that was published which I thought suitable to her voice, and played the accompaniment for her. Over these songs we were like two innocent children with new toys. She had never been anything but innocent; but my innocence was a transformation wrought by my love for her, love which melted away my cynicism and whitened my sullied soul and gave me back the wholesome dreams of my boyhood.

My artistic temperament also underwent an awakening. I spent many hours at my piano, playing over old and new composers. I also wrote several little pieces in a more or less Chopinesque style, which I dedicated to her. And so the weeks and months went by. Often words of love trembled on my lips, but I dared not utter them, because I knew they would have to be followed by other words which I had not the courage to frame. There might have been some other woman in my set whom I could have fallen in love with and asked to marry me without a word of explanation; but the more I knew this girl, the less could I find in my heart to deceive her. And yet, in spite of this spectre that was constantly looming up before me, I could never have believed that life held such happiness as was contained in those dream days of love.

One Saturday afternoon, in early June, I was coming up Fifth Avenue, and at the corner of Twenty-third Street I met her. She had been shopping. We stopped to chat for a moment, and I suggested that we spend half an hour at the Eden Musée. We were standing leaning on the rail in front of a group of figures, more interested in what we had to say to each other than in the group, when my attention became fixed upon a man who stood at my side studying his catalogue. It took me only an instant to recognize in him my old friend "Shiny." My first impulse was to change my position at once. As quick as a flash I considered all the risks I might run in speaking to him, and most especially the delicate question of introducing him to her. I confess that in my embarrassment and confusion I felt small and mean. But before I could decide what to do, he looked round at me and, after an instant, quietly asked: "Pardon me; but isn't this—?" The nobler part in me responded to the sound of his voice and I took his hand in a hearty clasp. Whatever fears I had felt were quickly banished, for he seemed, at a glance, to divine my situation, and let drop no word that would have aroused suspicion as to the truth. With a slight misgiving I presented him to her and was again relieved of fear. She received the introduction in her usual gracious manner, and without the least hesitancy or embarrassment joined in the conversation. An amusing part about the introduction was that I was upon the point of introducing him as "Shiny," and stammered a second or two before I could recall his name. We chatted for some fifteen minutes. He was spending his vacation north, with the intention of doing four or six weeks' work in one of the summer schools; he was also going to take a bride back with him in the fall. He asked me about myself, but in so diplomatic a way that I found no difficulty in answering him. The polish of his language and the unpedantic manner in which he revealed his culture greatly impressed her; and after we had left the Musée she showed it by questioning me about him. I was surprised at the amount of interest a refined black man could arouse. Even after changes in the conversation she reverted several times to the subject of "Shiny." Whether it was more than mere curiosity I could not tell, but I was convinced that she herself knew very little about prejudice.

Just why it should have done so I do not know, but somehow the "Shiny" incident gave me encouragement and confidence to cast the die of my fate. I reasoned, however, that since I wanted to marry her only, and since it concerned her alone, I would divulge my secret to no one else, not even her parents.

One evening, a few days afterwards, at her home we were going over some new songs and compositions when she asked me, as she often did, to play the Thirteenth Nocturne. When I began, she drew a chair near to my right and sat leaning with her elbow on the end of the piano, her chin resting on her hand, and her eyes reflecting the emotions which the music awoke in her. An impulse which I could not control rushed over me, a wave of exultation, the music under my fingers sank almost to a whisper, and calling her for the first time by her Christian name, but without daring to look at her, I said: "I love you, I love you, I love you." My fingers were trembling so that I ceased playing. I felt her hand creep to mine, and when I looked at her, her eyes were glistening with tears. I understood, and could scarcely resist the longing to take her in my arms; but I remembered, remembered that which has been the sacrificial altar of so much happiness—Duty; and bending over her hand in mine, I said: "Yes, I love you; but there is something more, too, that I must tell you." Then I told her, in what words I do not know, the truth. I felt her hand grow cold, and when I looked up, she was gazing at me with a wild, fixed stare as though I was some object she had never seen. Under the strange light in her eyes I felt that I was growing black and thick-featured and crimp-haired. She appeared not to have comprehended what I had said. Her lips trembled and she attempted to say something to me, but the words stuck in her throat. Then, dropping her head on the piano, she began to weep with great sobs that shook her frail body. I tried to console her, and blurted out incoherent words of love, but this seemed only to increase her distress, and when I left her, she was still weeping.

When I got into the street, I felt very much as I did the night after meeting my father and sister at the opera in Paris, even a similar desperate inclination to get drunk; but my self-control was stronger. This was the only time in my life that I ever felt absolute regret at being coloured, that I cursed the drops of African blood in my veins and wished that I were really white. When I reached my rooms, I sat and smoked several cigars while I tried to think out the significance of what had occurred. I reviewed the whole history of our acquaintance, recalled each smile she had given me, each word she had said to me that nourished my hope. I went over the scene we had just gone through, trying to draw from it what was in my favour and what was against me. I was rewarded by feeling confident that she loved me, but I could not estimate what was the effect upon her of my confession. At last, nervous and unhappy, I wrote her a letter, which I dropped into the mail-box before going to bed, in which I said:

> I understand, understand even better than you, and so I suffer even more than you. But why should either of us suffer for what neither of us is to blame for? If there is any blame, it belongs to me and I can only make the old, yet strongest plea that can be offered, I love you; and I know that my love, my great love, infinitely overbalances that blame and blots it out. What is it that stands in the way of our happiness? It is not what you feel or what I feel; it is not what you are or what I am. It is what others feel and are. But, oh! is that a fair price? In all the endeavours and struggles of life, in all our strivings and longings, there is only one thing worth seeking, only one thing worth winning, and that is love. It is not always found; but when it is, there is nothing in all the world for which it can be profitably exchanged.

The second morning after, I received a note from her which stated briefly 20 that she was going up into New Hampshire to spend the summer with relatives there. She made no reference to what had passed between us; nor did she say exactly when she would leave the city. The note contained no single word that gave me any clue to her feelings. I could gather hope only from the fact that she had written at all. On the same evening, with a degree of trepidation which rendered me almost frightened, I went to her house.

I met her mother, who told me that she had left for the country that very afternoon. Her mother treated me in her usual pleasant manner, which fact greatly reassured me; and I left the house with a vague sense of hope stirring in my breast, which sprang from the conviction that she had not yet divulged my secret. But that hope did not remain with me long. I waited one, two, three weeks, nervously examining my mail every day, looking for some word from her. All of the letters received by me seemed so insignificant, so worthless, because there was none from her. The slight buoyancy of spirit which I had felt gradually dissolved into gloomy heart-sickness. I became preoccupied; I lost appetite, lost sleep, and lost ambition. Several of my friends intimated to me that perhaps I was working too hard.

She stayed away the whole summer. I did not go to the house, but saw her father at various times, and he was as friendly as ever. Even after I knew that she was back in town, I did not go to see her. I determined to wait for some word or sign. I had finally taken refuge and comfort in my pride, pride which, I suppose, I came by naturally enough.

The first time I saw her after her return was one night at the theatre. She and her mother sat in company with a young man whom I knew slightly, not many seats away from me. Never did she appear more beautiful; and yet, it may have been my fancy, she seemed a trifle paler, and there was a suggestion of haggardness in her countenance. But that only heightened her beauty; the very delicacy of her charm melted down the strength of my pride. My situation made me feel weak and powerless, like a man trying with his bare hands to break the iron bars of his prison cell. When performance was over, I hurried out and placed myself where, unobserved, I could see her as she passed out. The haughtiness of spirit in which I had sought relief was all gone, and I was willing and ready to undergo any humiliation.

Shortly afterward we met at a progressive card party, and during the evening we were thrown together at one of the tables as partners. This was really our first meeting since the eventful night at her house. Strangely enough, in spite of our mutual nervousness, we won every trick of the game, and one of our opponents jokingly quoted the old saw: "Lucky at cards, unlucky in love." Our eyes met and I am sure that in the momentary glance my whole soul went out to her in one great plea. She lowered her eyes and uttered a nervous little laugh. During the rest of the game I fully merited the unexpressed and expressed abuse of my various partners; for my eyes followed her wherever she was and I played whatever card my fingers happened to touch.

Later in the evening she went to the piano and began to play very softly, as if to herself, the opening bars of the Thirteenth Nocturne. I felt that the psychic moment of my life had come, a moment which, if lost, could never be called back; and, in as careless a manner as I could assume, I sauntered over to the piano and stood almost bending over her. She continued playing, but, in a voice that was almost a whisper, she called me by my Christian name and said: "I love you, I love you, I love you." I took her place at the piano and played the Nocturne in a manner that silenced the chatter of the company both in and out of the room, involuntarily closing it with the major triad.

We were married the following spring, and went to Europe for several months. It was a double joy for me to be in France again under such conditions.

First there came to us a little girl, with hair and eyes dark like mine, but who is growing to have ways like her mother. Two years later there came a boy, who has my temperament, but is fair like his mother, a little golden-headed god, with a face and head that would have delighted the heart of an old Italian master. And this boy, with his mother's eyes and features, occupies an inner sanctuary of my heart; for it was for him that she gave all; and that is the second sacred sorrow of my life.

The few years of our married life were supremely happy, and perhaps she was even happier than I; for after our marriage, in spite of all the wealth of her love which she lavished upon me, there came a new dread to haunt me, a dread which I cannot explain and which was unfounded, but one that never left me. I was in constant fear that she would discover in me some shortcoming which she would unconsciously attribute to my blood rather than to a failing of human nature. But no cloud ever came to mar our life together; her loss to me is irreparable. My children need a mother's care, but I shall never marry again. It is to my children that I have devoted my life. I no longer have the same fear for myself of my secret's being found out, for since my wife's death I have gradually dropped out of social life; but there is nothing I would not suffer to keep the brand from being placed upon them.

It is difficult for me to analyse my feelings concerning my present position in the world. Sometimes it seems to me that I have never really been a

Negro, that I have been only a privileged spectator of their inner life; at other times I feel that I have been a coward, a deserter, and I am possessed by a strange longing for my mother's people.

30 Several years ago I attended a great meeting in the interest of Hampton Institute[2] at Carnegie Hall. The Hampton students sang the old songs and awoke memories that left me sad. Among the speakers were R. C. Ogden, ex-Ambassador Choate, and Mark Twain; but the greatest interest of the audience was centred in Booker T. Washington,[3] and not because he so much surpassed the others in eloquence, but because of what he represented with so much earnestness and faith. And it is this that all of that small but gallant band of coloured men who are publicly fighting the cause of their race have behind them. Even those who oppose them know that these men have the eternal principles of right on their side, and they will be victors even though they should go down in defeat. Beside them I feel small and selfish. I am an ordinarily successful white man who has made a little money. They are men who are making history and a race. I, too, might have taken part in a work so glorious.

My love for my children makes me glad that I am what I am and keeps me from desiring to be otherwise; and yet, when I sometimes open a little box in which I still keep my fast yellowing manuscripts, the only tangible remains of a vanished dream, a dead ambition, a sacrificed talent, I cannot repress the thought that, after all, I have chosen the lesser part, that I have sold my birthright for a mess of pottage.

DISCUSSING THE TEXT

1. In this final chapter from *The Autobiography of an Ex-Colored Man,* the narrator describes the agony of deciding whether or not to pass as white—in other words, to conduct a serious cultural impersonation. How does the narrator finally come to the decision that he must tell his future wife that he is not white? Why does he feel it is necessary to do so? After revealing his racial identity to his wife, why doesn't the narrator also reveal it, eventually, to his children?
2. Early in this selection the narrator says, "The anomaly of my social position often appealed strongly to my sense of humour" (par. 7). Can you see humor in the narrator's situation at this point in the selection? Why or why not?

---

[2]*Hampton Institute:* Founded in Hampton, Virginia, in 1868, the Hampton Institute was an industrial school for African American and Native American youths. (*Ed.*)

[3]*Ogden . . . Washington:* Robert Curtis Ogden (1836–1913), an advocate of educational reform, was the head of Hampton Institute's Board of Trustees. *Mark Twain* (Samuel Langhorne Clemens, 1835–1910) was already an acclaimed American writer, author of the novels *The Adventures of Tom Sawyer* (1876) and *The Adventures of Huckleberry Finn* (1884), among many other works. Booker T. Washington (1856–1915) leading educator, and writer of black and white ancestry, was founder of the Tuskegee Institute and author of *Up from Slavery* (1910). (*Ed.*)

3. In celebrating the achievements of black leaders like Booker T. Washington, the narrator implicitly accuses himself of moral cowardice for not having openly accepted his racial identity. Do you agree with this self-assessment, and with the self-condemnation implied by the last sentence of the selection? Why or why not?
4. Johnson makes the point at the end of the selection that one's identity, one's sense of self, is tied to one's sense of social obligations. Discuss the following questions with a group of four or five students. Do you think African Americans have any special obligations in this respect—that is, do you think it is right for African Americans to consider their own personal aspirations apart from the aspirations of their racial group? Would you answer in the same manner when considering members of other ethnic groups? Take brief notes as you work on this assignment, and be prepared to share your opinions with the rest of the class.

WRITING ABOUT THE TEXT

5. Johnson's *Autobiography* seems to imply that there was a great loss to the character, in terms of his ultimate creative achievement as a musical composer, as a result of his denying his race. Write a brief essay that focuses on the following question: Is creativity strengthened by the acceptance of one's racial or ethnic identity rather than its denial? Why or why not?
6. The narrator fears, once he has revealed his racial identity to his wife, that any failings he may have as a human being will be blamed on his race. Assuming the narrator's voice, write a letter addressed to his wife, explaining to her how he feels about revealing himself and expressing his fears about rejection.
7. Go to the library and do some research into the racial attitudes toward African Americans at the time Johnson's *Autobiography* takes place, 1912. What evidence can you find that would justify Johnson's concerns about his "drops" of African blood? Write a brief essay describing your findings. Be prepared to share your findings with the class.

JOHN HOWARD GRIFFIN

FROM
Black like Me

John Howard Griffin (1920–1980) was a writer and photographer who combined a deep concern over civil rights with an abiding interest in religious thought. In 1957 he wrote a study of school desegregation in Texas; a few years later, this study led him to write his best-known work, Black like Me *(1961), from which this selection is taken.* Black like Me, *which received enormous attention when it first appeared, helped to sensitize whites to the consequences of racial discrimination in America, laying important groundwork for the civil rights movement of the 1960s. Driven to see firsthand what it was like to be black, Griffin, who was white, traveled throughout the South as a black man. (To do this, he underwent extensive skin treatments in order to darken his skin, and in effect passed as black, reversing the direction of the usual passing from black to white.)* Black like Me *recounts Griffin's experiences during these travels in the fall of 1959.*

There were, of course, many books by black writers about the experience of being black in the South. But Griffin's work had a special character, since he came from the white world and was therefore a fresh—and often shocked—discoverer of the black world. Black like Me *also carried a special authority for many white readers, who had to admire the daring of Griffin's risky experiment. After all, Griffin had to appear black not only to southern whites but also to southern blacks. Thus he could have been in considerable personal danger had his impersonation been disclosed. (In fact, shortly after the book was published, Griffin and his family received several death threats.)*

Griffin also wrote numerous articles and short stories for newspapers and magazines, and published several books, among them The Church and the Black Man *(1969) and* A Time to Be Human *(1977). But he is best remembered for* Black like Me, *whose title comes from the 1924 poem "Dream Variation," by African American poet Langston Hughes.*

I hitchhiked up toward the swamp country between Mobile and Montgomery. A magnificent cool day.

I walked some miles before a large, pleasant-faced man halted his light truck and told me to get in. When I opened the door I saw a shotgun propped against the seat next to his knee. I recalled it was considered sport among some elements in Alabama to hunt "nigs" and I backed away.

"Come on," he laughed. "That's for hunting deer."

I glanced again at his florid face, saw he looked decent and climbed into the leather seat beside him.

"Do you have any luck getting rides through here?" he asked. 5

"No sir. You're my first ride since Mobile."

I learned he was a married man, fifty-three years old, father of a family now grown and grandfather of two children. He was certainly, by the tone of his conversation, an active civic leader and respected member of his community. I began to hope that I had encountered a decent white.

"You married?" he asked.

"Yes sir."

"Any kids?" 10

"Yes sir—three."

"You got a pretty wife?"

"Yes sir."

He waited a moment and then with lightness, paternal amusement, "She ever had it from a white man?"

I stared at my black hands, saw the gold wedding band and mumbled 15 something meaningless, hoping he would see my reticence. He overrode my feelings and the conversation grew more salacious. He told me how all of the white men in the region craved colored girls. He said he hired a lot of them both for housework and in his business. "And I guarantee you, I've had it in every one of them before they ever got on the payroll." A pause. Silence above humming tires on the hot-top road. "What do you think of that?"

"Surely some refuse," I suggested cautiously.

"Not if they want to eat—or feed their kids," he snorted. "If they don't put out, they don't get the job."

I looked out the window to tall pine trees rising on either side of the highway. Their turpentine odor mingled with the soaped smells of the man's khaki hunting clothes.

"You think that's pretty terrible, don't you?" he asked.

I knew I should grin and say, "Why no—it's just nature," or some other disarming remark to avoid provoking him.

"Don't you?" he insisted pleasantly.

"I guess I do."

"Why hell—everybody does it. Don't you know that?"

"No sir."

"Well, they sure as hell do. We figure we're doing you people a favor to get some white blood in your kids."

The grotesque hypocrisy slapped me as it does all Negroes. It is worth remembering when the white man talks of the Negro's lack of sexual morality, or when he speaks with horror about mongrelization and with fervor about racial purity. Mongrelization is already a widespread reality in the South—it has been exclusively the white man's contribution to the Southern Way of Life. His vast concern for "racial purity" obviously does not extend to all races.[1]

This aspect of Southern life does not hit the newspapers because, as my companion said, "Alabama nigger women are good about that—they won't never go to the cops or tell on you."

It was obvious what would happen if one of them tried it.

As I feared it would, my lack of "cooperation" nettled the driver. He took my silence, rightly, for disapproval.

"Where you from?" he asked.

"Texas."

"What're you doing down here?"

"Just traveling around, trying to find jobs."

"You're not down here to stir up trouble, are you?"

"Ohgodno."

"You start stirring up these niggers and we sure as hell know how to take care of you."

"I don't intend to."

"Do you know what we do to troublemakers down here?"

"No sir."

"We either ship them off to the pen or kill them."

---

[1]Later I encountered many whites who freely admitted the same practices my companion described. In fairness, however, other Southern whites roundly condemned it and claimed it was not as typical as my informants suggested. None denied that it was widespread.

He spoke in a tone that sickened me, casual, merciless. I looked at him. His decent blue eyes turned yellow. I knew that nothing could touch him to have mercy once he decided a Negro should be "taught a lesson." The immensity of it terrified me. But it caught him up like a lust now. He entertained it, his voice unctuous with pleasure and cruelty. The highway stretched deserted through the swamp forests. He nodded toward the solid wall of brush flying past our windows.

"You can kill a nigger and toss him into that swamp and no one'll ever know what happened to him."

"Yes sir . . ."

I forced myself to silence, forced myself to picture this man in his other roles. I saw him as he played with his grandchildren, as he stood up in church with open hymnal in hand, as he drank a cup of coffee in the morning before dressing and then shaved and talked with his wife pleasantly about nothing, as he visited with friends on the front porch Sunday afternoons. That was the man I had seen when I first got into the truck. The amiable, decent American was in all his features. This was the dark tangent in every man's belly, the sickness, the coldness, the mercilessness, the lust to cause pain or fear through self-power. Surely not even his wife or closest friends had ever seen him like this. It was a side he would show no one but his victims, or those who connived with him. The rest—what he really must be as a husband, devoted father and respected member of the community—I had to supply with my imagination. He showed me the lowest and I had to surmise the highest.

His face was set hard in an attempt to regain his equilibrium, when he pulled off the main highway and stopped on a dirt road that led into the jungle. We had engaged in a subtle battle of which I think he had only then become aware. He needed to salvage from it something. "This is where I turn off. I guess you want to stick to the highway." 45

I thanked him for the ride and opened the door. Before I could get out, he spoke again. "I'll tell you how it is here. We'll do business with you people. We'll sure as hell screw your women. Other than that, you're just *completely off the record as far as we're concerned.* And the quicker you people get that through your heads, the better off you'll be."

"Yes sir . . ." I stepped out and closed the door. He drove down the side road scattering fine gravel behind his wheels. I listened until his truck was out of hearing distance. The heavy air of evening, putrid with swamp rot, smelled fragrant. I walked across the highway, sat on my duffel and waited for another car. None came. The woods issued no sound. I felt strangely safe, isolated, alone in the stillness of dusk turning to night. First stars appeared in darkening skies still pale and the earth's heat escaped upward.

My mouth was dry and my stomach began to ache for food. I realized I had not eaten or had a drink of water all day. Cold surrounded me rapidly. I got up and began to walk along the highway in the darkness. It was better to walk than to freeze. My duffel pulled heavily at my arms and I knew I could not go far without food and rest.

I wondered at the lack of traffic on Alabama highways. No cars passed. My footsteps on the roadside gravel sloughed in echo from the wall of trees and brush.

50 After a while a light flickered among the foliage. I hurried forward around the curve of highway until I saw it came from an isolated service station at the top of the hill. When I arrived opposite it, I stood for some time across the highway and watched. An elderly white couple sat inside, surrounded by shelves of groceries and auto supplies, by soft drink machines and cigarette dispensers. They looked kind, gentle, and I framed in advance what I should say to allay any fears they might have of a large Negro appearing out of the night, and to convince them that they should sell me food and drink. Perhaps I might even ask them to let me spend the night sleeping on the floor there.

The woman saw me approach past the lighted gasoline lamps. I whistled to give them warning. She met me at the door. I felt an outgush of warm air and heard country music from a radio when she opened. I glanced through the glass to see the man seated in a chair, his ear close to his small radio.

"Pardon me, ma'am," I said, nodding low. "I'm traveling through to Montgomery. I got stranded on the highway and can't seem to get a ride. I wonder if I could buy something to eat and drink?"

She studied me with suspicion, her eyes hard in their wrinkles.

"We're closing up," she said and stepped back to shut the door.

55 "Please," I pleaded, not needing to feign abjection. "I've been without food and water all day."

I could see her hesitate, her caution and repugnance struggling against instincts of common decency. She obviously wanted to refuse me. She was also undoubtedly afraid not only of me but of having someone drive up for gasoline and see her waiting on me. But I recalled the driver's statement: "We'll do business with you people." I waited. The night was cold, the country lonely. Even animals had to eat and drink.

"Well, I guess it's all right," she said with disgust. She turned back into the room. I stepped inside and closed the door. Neither of them spoke. The old man glanced up at me from a lean, seamed face devoid of all expression.

I bought an orange drink and a package of cracker sandwiches. The atmosphere was so unhospitable I stepped outside where they could watch me and I drank the orange. When I finished, I returned the empty bottle and quickly bought another. The store had little to offer in the way of food that I could manage. The only two cans of sardines had no keys and the owner stared at the floor, nodding no when I asked if he had a can opener. I bought a fried pie, a loaf of bread and five Milky Way bars.

The woman stood in front of the gas heater and picked the dirt from under her thumbnail with the third finger of her other hand. When I mumbled my thanks, she was so absorbed in her task that she acknowledged my departure only by staring at her hands with a deeper frown. The husband stuck the money in his shirt pocket.

60 I walked down the highway into the darkness again, carrying both duffel bags in my left hand and feeding myself the tasteless pineapple fried pie with my right.

A distant hum behind me caught my attention. I turned to see a yellow glow on the road's horizon. It grew stronger and headlights appeared. Though I dreaded riding with another white man, I dreaded more staying on the road all night. Stepping out into full view, I waved my arms. An ancient car braked to a halt and I hurried to it. To my great relief, the reflections from the dash light showed me the face of a young Negro man.

We discussed my problem. He said he lived back in the woods, but had six kids and only two rooms. He wouldn't even have a bed to offer me. I asked him about some other house in the area where I might rent a bed. He said there were none any better than what he had to offer.

However, we could find no other solution.

"You can't stand out here all night. If you don't mind sleeping on the floor, you're welcome to come with me," he said finally.

65 "I don't mind sleeping on the floor," I said. "I just wouldn't want to put you to any trouble."

As we drove several miles down a lane into the forest, he told me he was a sawmill worker and never made quite enough to get out from under his debts. Always, when he took his check to the store, he owed a little more than the check could cover. He said it was the same for everyone else; and indeed I have seen the pattern throughout my travels. Part of the Southern white's strategy is to get the Negro in debt and keep him there.

"It makes it hard, doesn't it?" I said.

"Yeah, but you can't stop," he answered quickly. "That's what I tell the men at the mill. Some of them are willing just to sit there. I told them, 'Okay, so you're going to give up just because you get no butter with your bread. That's no way to act. Go ahead and eat the bread—but work, and maybe someday we'll have butter to go with it.' I tell them we sure ain't going to get it any other way."

I asked him if he could not get together with some of the others and strike for better wages. He laughed with real amusement.

70 "Do you know how long we'd last, doing something like that?"

"Well, if you stuck together, they sure couldn't kill you all."

"They could damn sure try," he snorted. "Anyway, how long could I feed my kids? There's only a couple of stores in twenty miles. They'd cut off credit and refuse to sell to us. Without money coming in, none of us could live."

He turned off the lane into a rutted path that led through dense underbrush up to a knoll. The headlights fell on a shanty of unpainted wood, patched at the bottom with a rusting Dr. Pepper sign. Except for the voices of children, a deep silence hung over the place. The man's wife came to the door and stood silhouetted against the pale light of a kerosene lamp. He introduced us. Though she appeared embarrassed, she asked me in.

The subdued babble of children mounted to excited shouts of welcome. They ranged in age from nine years to four months. They were overjoyed to have company. It must be a party. We decided it was.

Supper was on the makeshift table. It consisted entirely of large yellow beans cooked in water. The mother prepared mashed beans and canned milk for the infant. I remembered the bread and offered it as my contribution to the meal. Neither parent apologized for the meagerness of the food. We served ourselves on plastic dishes from the table and sat where we could find places, the children on the floor with a spread-out newspaper for a tablecloth. 75

I congratulated them on such a fine family. The mother told me they had been truly blessed. "Ours are all in good health. When you think of so many people with crippled or blind or non-right children, you just have to thank God." I praised the children until the father's tired face animated with pride. He looked at the children the way another looks at some rare painting or treasured gem.

Closed into the two rooms, with only the soft light of two kerosene lamps, the atmosphere changed. The outside world, outside standards disappeared. They were somewhere beyond in the vast darkness. In here, we had all we needed for gaiety. We had shelter, some food in our bellies, the bodies and eyes and affections of children who were not yet aware of how things were. And we had treats. We cut the Milky Way bars into thin slices for dessert. In a framework of nothing, slices of Milky Way become a great gift. With almost rabid delight, the children consumed them. One of the smaller girls salivated so heavily the chocolate dribbled syruplike from the corner of her mouth. Her mother wiped it off with her fingertip and unconsciously (from what yearning?) put it in her own mouth.

After supper, I went outside with my host to help him carry water from a makeshift boarded well. A near full moon shone above the trees and chill penetrated as though brilliance strengthened it. We picked our way carefully through fear of snakes down a faint footpath to the edge of the trees to urinate. The moon-speckled landscape exhaled its night rustlings, its truffle-odor of swamps. Distantly the baby cried. I listened to the muffled rattle of our waters against damp leaf loam. A fragment of memory returned—recollection of myself as a youngster reading Lillian Smith's *Strange Fruit,*[2] her description of the Negro boy stopping along a lonely path to urinate. Now, years later, I was there in a role foreign to my youth's wildest imaginings. I felt more profoundly than ever before the totality of my Negro-ness, the immensity of its isolating effects. The transition was complete from the white boy reading a book about Negroes in the safety of his white living room to an old Negro man in the Alabama swamps, his existence nullified by men but reaffirmed by nature, in his functions, in his affection.

---

[2]*Lillian Smith* (1897–1966): southern white writer and social worker, author of the novel *Strange Fruit* (1944), about the love relationship between a white man and a black woman (*Ed.*)

"Okay?" my friend said as we turned back. Moonlight caught his protruding cheekbones and cast the hollows beneath into shadow.

"Okay," I said. 80

The house stood above us, rickety, a faint light at the windows. I could hear the whites say, "Look at that shanty. They live like animals. If they wanted to do better they could. And they expect us just to accept them? They *like* to live this way. It would make them just as miserable to demand a higher standard of living of them as it would make us miserable to put us down to that standard."

I mentioned this to my host. "But we can't do any better," he said. "We work just for that . . . to have something a little better for the kids and us."

"Your wife doesn't seem to get down in the dumps," I remarked.

"No—she's good all the way through. I'll tell you—if we don't have meat to cook with the beans, why she just goes ahead and cooks the beans anyhow." He said this last with a flourish that indicated the grandness of her attitude.

We placed buckets of water on the cast-iron wood stove in the kitchen 85 so we could have warm water for washing and shaving. Then we returned outside to fill the wood-box.

"Are there really a lot of alligators in these swamps?" I asked.

"Oh God yes, the place is alive with them."

"Why don't you kill some of them? The tails make good meat. I could show you how. We learned in jungle training when I was in the army."

"Oh, we can't do that," he said. "They stick a hundred-dollar fine on you for killing a gator. I'm telling you," he laughed sourly, "they got all the loopholes plugged. There ain't a way you can win in this state."

"But what about the children?" I asked. "Aren't you afraid the gators 90 might eat one of them?"

"No . . ." he said forlornly, "the gators like turtles better than they do us."

"They must be part white," I heard myself say.

His laughter sounded flat in the cold air. "As long as they keep their bellies full with turtles, they're no danger to us. Anyway, we keep the kids close to the house."[3]

The cheerful and fretful noises of children being readied for bed drifted to us as we returned to the kitchen. Physical modesty in such cramped quarters was impossible, indeed in such a context it would have been ridiculous. The mother sponge-bathed the children while the husband and I shaved. Each of the children went to the toilet, a zinc bucket in the corner, since it was too cold for them to go outside.

Their courtesy to me was exquisite. While we spread tow sacks on the 95 floor and then feed sacks over them, the children asked questions about my

---

[3]The fine for killing alligators appears to be a conservation measure and means of controlling turtles, not a punitive action against the Negroes, though few Negroes realize this.

own children. Did they go to school? No, they were too young. How old were they then? Why, today is my daughter's fifth birthday. Would she have a party? Yes, she'd certainly had a party. Excitement. Like we had here, with the candy and everything? Yes, something like that.

But it was time to go to bed, time to stop asking questions. The magic remained for them, almost unbearable to me—the magic of children thrilled to know my daughter had a party. The parents brought in patchwork quilts from under the bed in the other room and spread them over the pallets. The children kissed their parents and then wanted to kiss Mr. Griffin. I sat down on a straight-back kitchen chair and held out my arms. One by one they came, smelling of soap and childhood. One by one they put their arms around my neck and touched their lips to mine. One by one they said and giggled soberly, "Good night, Mr. Griffin."

I stepped over them to go to my pallet near the kitchen door and lay down fully dressed. Warning the children he did not want to hear another word from them, the father picked up the kerosene lamp and carried it into the bedroom. Through the doorless opening I saw light flicker on the walls. Neither of them spoke. I heard the sounds of undressing. The lamp was blown out and a moment later their bedspring creaked.

Fatigue spread through me, making me grateful for the tow-sack bed. I fought back glimpses of my daughter's birthday party in its cruel contrasts to our party here tonight.

"If you need anything, Mr. Griffin, just holler," the man said.

"Thank you. I will. Good night." 100

"Good night," the children said, their voices locating them in the darkness.

"Good night," again.

"Good night, Mr. Griffin."

"That's enough," the father called out warningly to them.

I lay there watching moonlight pour through the crack of the ill-fitting 105 door as everyone drifted to sleep. Mosquitoes droned loudly until the room was a great hum. I wondered that they should be out on such a cold night. The children jerked in their sleep and I knew they had been bitten. The stove cooled gradually with almost imperceptible interior pops and puffings. Odors of the night and autumn and the swamp entered to mingle with the inside odors of children, kerosene, cold beans, urine and the dead incense of pine ashes. The rots and the freshness combined into a strange fragrance—the smell of poverty. For a moment I knew the intimate and subtle joys of misery.

And yet misery was the burden, the pervading, killing burden. I understood why they had so many children. These moments of night when the swamp and darkness surrounded them evoked an immense loneliness, a dread, a sense of exile from the rest of humanity. When the awareness of it strikes, a man either suffocates with despair or he turns to cling to his woman, to console and seek consolation. Their union is momentary escape from the swamp night, from utter hopelessness of its ever getting better for them. It is an ultimately tragic act wherein the hopeless seek hope.

Thinking about these things, the bravery of these people attempting to bring up a family decently, their gratitude that none of their children were blind or maimed, their willingness to share their food and shelter with a stranger—the whole thing overwhelmed me. I got up from bed, half-frozen anyway, and stepped outside.

A thin fog blurred the moon. Trees rose as ghostly masses in the diffused light. I sat on an inverted washtub and trembled as its metallic coldness seeped through my pants.

I thought of my daughter, Susie, and of her fifth birthday today, the candles, the cake and party dress; and of my sons in their best suits. They slept now in clean beds in a warm house while their father, a bald-headed old Negro, sat in the swamps and wept, holding it in so he would not awaken the Negro children.

I felt again the Negro children's lips soft against mine, so like the feel of my own children's good-night kisses. I saw again their large eyes, guileless, not yet aware that doors into wonderlands of security, opportunity and hope were closed to them. 110

It was thrown full in my face. I saw it not as a white man and not as a Negro, but as a human parent. Their children resembled mine in all ways except the superficial one of skin color, as indeed they resembled all children of all humans. Yet this accident, this least important of all qualities, the skin pigment, marked them for inferior status. It became fully terrifying when I realized that if my skin were permanently black, they would unhesitatingly consign my own children to this bean future.

One can scarcely conceive the full horror of it unless one is a parent who takes a close look at his children and then asks himself how he would feel if a group of men should come to his door and tell him they had decided—for reasons of convenience to them—that his children's lives would henceforth be restricted, their world smaller, their educational opportunities less, their future mutilated.

One would then see it as the Negro parent sees it, for this is precisely what happens. He looks at his children and knows. No one, not even a saint, can live without a sense of personal value. The white racist has masterfully defrauded the Negro of this sense. It is the least obvious but most heinous of all race crimes, for it kills the spirit and the will to live.

It was too much. Though I was experiencing it, I could not believe it. Surely in America a whole segment of decent souls could not stand by and allow such massive crimes to be committed. I tried to see the whites' side, as I have all along. I have studied objectively the anthropological arguments, the accepted clichés about cultural and ethnic differences. And I have found their application simply untrue. The two great arguments—the Negro's lack of sexual morality and his intellectual incapacity—are smoke screens to justify prejudice and unethical behavior. Recent scientific studies, published in *The Eighth Generation* (Harper & Brothers, New York), show that the contemporary middle-class Negro has the same family cult, the same ideals and goals as his white counterpart. The Negro's lower scholastic showing springs not from racial default, but from being deprived of cultural and educational advantages by the whites. When the segregationist argues that the Negro is scholastically inferior, he presents the most eloquent possible argument for desegregated schools; he admits that so long as the Negro is kept in tenth-rate schools he will remain scholastically behind white children.

I have held no brief for the Negro. I have looked diligently for all aspects of "inferiority" among them and I cannot find them. All the cherished question-begging epithets applied to the Negro race, and widely accepted as truth even by men of good will, simply prove untrue when one lives among them. This, of course, excludes the trash element, which is the same everywhere and is no more evident among Negroes than whites. 115

When all the talk, all the propaganda has been cut away, the criterion is nothing but the color of skin. My experience proved that. They judged me by no other quality. My skin was dark. That was sufficient reason for them to deny me those rights and freedoms without which life loses its significance and becomes a matter of little more than animal survival.

I searched for some other answer and found none. I had spent a day without food and water for no other reason than that my skin was black. I was sitting on a tub in the swamp for no other reason.

I went back into the shanty. The air was slightly warmer and smelled of kerosene, tow sacks and humanity. I lay down in the darkness, in the midst of snores.

"Mr. Griffin . . . Mr. Griffin."

I heard the man's soft voice above my shouts. I awakened to see the kerosene lamp and beyond it my host's troubled face. 120

"Are you all right?" he asked. In the surrounding darkness I sensed the tension. They lay silent, not snoring.

"I'm sorry," I said. "I was having a nightmare."

He stood upright. From my position flat on the floor his head appeared to touch the ceiling beams far above. "Are you all right now?"

"Yes, thank you for waking me up."

He stepped carefully over the children and returned to the other room. 125

It was the same nightmare I had been having recently. White men and women, their faces stern and heartless, closed in on me. The hate stare burned through me. I pressed back against the wall. I could expect no pity, no mercy. They approached slowly and I could not escape them. Twice before, I had awakened myself screaming.

I listened for the family to settle back into sleep. The mosquitoes swarmed. I lighted a cigarette, hoping its smoke would drive them out.

The nightmare worried me. I had begun this experiment in a spirit of scientific detachment. I wanted to keep my feelings out of it, to be objective in my observations. But it was becoming such a profound personal experience, it haunted even my dreams.

My host called me again at dawn. His wife stood in lamplight at the stove, pouring coffee. I washed my face in a bowl of water she had heated for me. We spoke by nods and smiles to avoid waking the children sprawled on the floor.

After breakfast of coffee and a slice of bread, we were ready to leave. I shook hands with her at the door and thanked her. Reaching for my wallet, I told her I wanted to pay her for putting me up. 130

She refused, saying that I had brought more than I had taken. "If you gave us a penny, we'd owe you change."

I left money with her as a gift for the children, and the husband drove me back to the highway.

The morning was bright and cool. Before long a car with two young white boys picked me up. I quickly saw that they were, like many of their generation, kinder than the older ones. They drove me to a small-town bus station where I could catch a bus.

I bought a ticket to Montgomery and went to sit outside on the curb where other Negro passengers gathered. Many Negroes walked through the streets. Their glances were kind and communicative, as though all of us shared some common secret.

As I sat in the sunlight, a great heaviness came over me. I went inside to the Negro rest room, splashed cold water on my face and brushed my teeth. Then I brought out my hand mirror and inspected myself. I had been a Negro more than three weeks and it no longer shocked me to see the stranger in the mirror. My hair had grown to a heavy fuzz, my face skin, with the continued medication, exposure to sunlight and ground-in stain, was what Negroes call a "pure brown"—a smooth dark color that made me look like millions of others. 135

I noted, too, that my face had lost animation. In repose, it had taken on the strained, disconsolate expression that is written on the countenance of so many Southern Negroes. My mind had become the same way, dozing empty for long periods. It thought of food and water, but so many hours were spent just waiting, cushioning self against dread, that it no longer thought of much else. Like the others in my condition, I was finding life too burdensome.

I felt a great hunger for something merely pleasurable, for something people call "fun." The need was so great that deep within, through the squalor and the humiliations of this life, I took some joy in the mere fact that I could be alone for a while inside the rest-room cubicle with its clean plumbing and unfinished wood walls. Here I had a water faucet to drink from and I could experience the luxury of splashing cold water on my face as much as I wanted. Here, with a latch on the door, I was isolated from the hate stares, the contempt.

The smell of Ivory livened the atmosphere. Some of the stain came off and I wondered how long it would be before I could pass as white again. I decided to take no more pills for a while. I removed my shirt and undershirt. My body, so long unexposed to the sun or the sun lamp, had paled to a *café-au-lait* color. I told myself I would have to be careful not to undress unless I had privacy henceforth. My face and hands were far darker than my body. Since I often slept in my clothes, the problem would not be great.

I wet my sponge, poured dye on it and touched up the corners of my mouth and my lips, which were always the difficult spots.

We boarded the bus in late afternoon and rode without incident to Selma, where I had a long layover before taking another bus into the state capital. 140

In deep dusk I strolled through the streets of the beautiful town. A group of nicely dressed Negro women solicited contributions for missionary activities. I placed some change in their cup and accepted a tract explaining the missionary program. Then, curious to see how they would fare with the whites, I walked along with them.

We approached the stationkeeper. His face soured and he growled his refusal. We walked on. In not a single instance did a white hear them out.

Two well-dressed men stood talking in front of the Hotel Albert.

"Pardon us, sir," one of the women said, holding a tract in her hand. "We're soliciting contributions for our missionary—"

"G'wan," the older one snapped, "I got too many of them damned tracts already." 145

The younger man hesitated, dug in his pocket and tossed a handful of change into the cup. He refused the tract, saying, "I'm sure the money'll be put to good use."

After we had gone two blocks, we heard footsteps behind us. We stopped at a street corner, not looking back. The younger man's voice came to us. "I don't suppose it does any good," he said quietly, "but I apologize for the bad manners of my people."

"Thank you," we said, not turning our heads.

As we passed the bus station, I dropped out of the little group and sat on a public bench near an outside phone booth. I waited until I saw a Negro use the phone, and then I hurried to it, closed the door and asked the long-distance operator to call my home collect.

When my wife answered, the strangeness of my situation again swept over me. I talked with her and the children as their husband and father, while reflected in the glass windows of the booth I saw another man they would not know. At this time, when I wanted most to lose the illusion, I was more than ever aware of it, aware that I was not the man she knew, but a stranger who spoke with the same voice and had the same memory. 150

Happy at least to have heard their voices, I stepped from the booth to the night's cooler air. The night was always a comfort. Most of the whites were in their homes. The threat was less. A Negro blended inconspicuously into the darkness.

Night coming tenderly
Black like me.[4]

---

[4]*Night . . . like me:* a reference to the 1924 poem "Dream Variation," by African American writer Langston Hughes (1902–1967) (*Ed.*)

At such a time, the Negro can look at the starlit skies and find that he has, after all, a place in the universal order of things. The stars, the black skies affirm his humanity, his validity as a human being. He knows that his belly, his lungs, his tired legs, his appetites, his prayers and his mind are cherished in some profound involvement with nature and God. The night is his consolation. It does not despise him.

The roar of wheels turning into the station, the stench of exhaust fumes, the sudden bustle of people unloading told me it was time to go. Men, better and wiser than the night, put me back into my place with their hate stares.

I walked to the back of the bus, past the drowsers, and found an empty seat. The Negroes gave me their sleepy smiles and then we were off. I leaned back and dozed along with the others.

DISCUSSING THE TEXT

1. Why do you think Griffin felt it was necessary for him to pass as black in order to find out what black experience was like? Since his experiment clearly required some deception—of both whites and blacks—do you think it was justified?
2. Although he is, of course, primarily concerned with issues of race, Griffin does make distinctions based on social *class* when he refers to "the trash element" among both blacks and whites (par. 115). What do you think of the class distinction he makes here? Does this point add to or diminish the strength of his argument overall?
3. What is meant by the term *mongrelization* (par. 26)? How does Griffin's discussion here tie in with ideas in the selection from James Weldon Johnson's much earlier novel, *The Autobiography of an Ex-Colored Man?*
4. Discuss the following questions with a group of four or five students. Can Griffin really claim to have experienced the "totality of [his] Negro-ness"? Can you think of ways in which his "black" experience was different from real black experience? What changes in Griffin's thinking occur as a result of his experiment? Take brief notes as you work on this assignment, and be prepared to share your opinions with the rest of the class.

WRITING ABOUT THE TEXT

5. Write two paragraphs discussing the following questions: Why does the white man who gives Griffin a ride tell him of his sexual exploits? How does he expect the "black" Griffin to respond? How does Griffin in fact respond, and what effect does this have on the white man? What would you have answered if you had been Griffin?
6. Write a one-page discussion of what you think Griffin means when he says, "I saw it not as a white man and not as a Negro, but as a human parent" (par. 111). What is the "it" Griffin refers to here? What is it about being a parent that allows him to see this "it" so clearly?
7. Write a brief essay in which you compare the reception of Griffin in the white-owned store with his reception in the black family that gives him

shelter. Does Griffin modify his behavior according to the racial context in which he finds himself? Describe differences and similarities both in the behavior of the people he encounters and in Griffin's own behavior.

8. As Griffin tells us about his personal experience with the black family that gives him shelter, he interrupts the narrative to discuss anthropological arguments about cultural and ethnic differences (par. 114–116). Similar arguments are still discussed today (see, for example, the controversy surrounding the publication of the 1994 book *The Bell Curve*). Do some research into these arguments over the idea of cultural and ethnic differences, and write a two- to three-page essay expressing your own views.

JUDY GRAHN

Boys at the Rodeo

Judy Grahn's narrative, which appears in True to Life Adventure Stories, *a two-volume collection of women's personal narratives edited by Grahn in 1980, poses a number of questions about role-playing and class and gender stereotypes. For the narrator of Grahn's story, the rodeo stands for a microcosm of society, in that both are a kind of fixed "contest." The female narrator's mistaken identity as a fourteen-year-old boy defines her role within that "contest" in new and interesting ways. As an outsider, someone who has "crossed over" through impersonation, the narrator can make observations about class, gender, and culture from a different perspective.*

Born in Chicago in 1940, Judy Grahn grew up in New Mexico and has lived in California for many years. One of her earliest works, the poem "Edward the Dyke" (1965), was considered unpublishable at the time it was written. This experience prompted Grahn to start her own press with the help of some friends. Their efforts led to the establishment of the Women's Press Collective in Oakland, California (1969–1978).

Grahn has taught in writing programs at several universities and is cofounder of the gay and lesbian studies program at the New College of California in San Francisco. She has received a National Endowment for the Arts grant for poetry and is the author of the poetry collection The Queen of Wands *(1982) and* Another Mother Tongue: Gay Words, Gay Worlds *(1984).*

A lot of people have spent time on some women's farm this summer of 1972 and one day six of us decide to go to the rodeo. We are all mature and mostly in our early thirties. We wear levis and shirts and short hair. Susan has shaved her head.

The man at the gate, who looks like a cousin of the sheriff, is certain we are trying to get in for free. It must have been something in the way we are walking. He stares into Susan's face. "I know you're at least fourteen," he says. He slaps her shoulder, in that comradely way men have with each other. That's when we know he thinks we are boys.

"You're over thirteen," he says to Wendy.

"You're over thirteen," he says to me. He examines each of us closely, and sees only that we have been outdoors, are muscled, and look him directly in the eye. Since we are too short to be men, we must be boys. Everyone else at the rodeo are girls.

We decide to play it straight, so to speak. We make up boys' names for each other. Since Wendy has missed the episode with Susan at the gate, I slap her on the shoulder to demonstrate. "This is what he did." Slam. She never missed a step. It didn't feel bad to me at all. We laugh uneasily. We have achieved the status of fourteen year old boys, what a disguise for travelling through the world. I split into two pieces for the rest of the evening, and have never decided if it is worse to be 31 years old and called a boy or to be 31 years old and called a girl.

Regardless, we are starved so we decide to eat, and here we have the status of boys for real. It seems to us that all the men and all the women attached to the men and most of the children are eating steak dinner plates; and we are the only women not attached to men. We eat hot dogs, which cost one tenth as much. A man who has taken a woman to the rodeo on this particular day has to have at least $12.00 to spend. So he has charge of all of her money and some of our money too, for we average $3.00 apiece and have taken each other to the rodeo.

Hot dogs in hand we escort ourselves to the wooden stands, and first is the standing up ceremony. We are pledging allegiance for the way of life—the competition, the supposed masculinity and pretty girls. I stand up, cursing, pretending I'm in some other country. One which has not been rediscovered. The loudspeaker plays Anchors Aweigh, that's what I like about rodeos, always something unexpected. At the last one I attended in another state the men on horses threw candy and nuts to the kids, chipping their teeth and breaking their noses. Who is it, I wonder, that has put these guys in charge. Even quiet mothers raged over that episode.

Now it is time for the rodeo queen contest, and a display of four very young women on horses. They are judged for queen 30% on their horse*man*ship and 70% on the number of queen tickets which people bought on their behalf to "elect" them. Talk about stuffed ballot boxes. I notice the winner as usual is the one on the registered thoroughbred whose daddy owns tracts and tracts of something—lumber, minerals, animals. His family name is all over the county.

The last loser sits well on a scrubby little pony and lives with her aunt and uncle. I pick her for the dyke even though it is speculation without clues. I can't help it, it's a pleasant habit. I wish I could give her a ribbon. Not for being a dyke, but for sitting on her horse well. For believing there ever was a contest, for not being the daughter of anyone who owns thousands of acres of anything.

Now the loudspeaker announces the girls' barrel races, which is the only grown women's event. It goes first because it is not really a part of the rodeo, but more like a mildly athletic variation of a parade by women to introduce the real thing. Like us boys in the stand, the girls are simply bearing witness to someone else's act.

The voice is booming that barrel racing is a new, modern event, that these young women are the wives and daughters of cowboys, and barrel racing is a way for them to participate in their own right. How generous of these northern cowboys to have resurrected barrel racing for women and to have forgotten the hard roping and riding which women always used to do in rodeos when I was younger. Even though I was a town child, I heard thrilling rumors of the all-women's rodeo in Texas, including that the finest brahma bull rider in all of Texas was a forty year old woman who weighed a hundred pounds.

Indeed, my first lover's first lover was a big heavy woman who was normally slow as a cold python, but she was just hell when she got up on a horse. She could rope and tie a calf faster than any cowboy within 500 miles of Sweetwater, Texas. That's what the West Texas dykes said, and they never lied about anything as important to them as calf roping, or the differences between women and men. And what about that news story I had heard recently on the radio, about a bull rider who was eight months pregnant? The newsman just had apoplectic fits over her, but not me. I was proud of her. She makes me think of all of us who have had our insides so overly protected from jarring we cannot possibly get through childbirth without an anesthetic.

While I have been grumbling these thoughts to myself, three barrels have been set up in a big triangle on the field, and the women one by one have raced their horses around each one and back to start. The trick is to turn your horse as sharply as possible without overthrowing the barrel.

After this moderate display, the main bulk of the rodeo begins, with calf roping, bronco riding, bull riding. It's a very male show during which the men demonstrate their various abilities at immobilizing, cornering, maneuvering and conquering cattle of every age.

A rodeo is an interminable number of roped and tied calves, ridden and unridden broncoes. The repetition is broken by a few antics from the agile, necessary clown. His long legs nearly envelope the little jackass he is riding for the satire of it. 15

After a number of hours they produce an event I have never seen before—goat tying. This is for the girls eleven and twelve. They use one goat for fourteen participants. The goat is supposed to be held in place on a rope by a large man on horseback. Each girl rushes out in a long run half way across the field, grabs the animal, knocks it down, ties its legs together. Sometimes the man lets his horse drift so the goat pulls six or eight feet away from her, something no one would allow to happen in a male event. Many of the girls take over a full minute just to do their tying, and the fact that only one goat has been used makes everybody say, 'poor goat, poor goat,' and start laughing. This has become the real comedy event of the evening, and the purpose clearly is to show how badly girls do in the rodeo.

Only one has broken through this purpose to the other side. One small girl is not disheartened by the years of bad training, the ridiculous cross-field run, the laughing superior man on his horse, *or* the shape-shifting goat. She downs it in a beautiful flying tackle. This makes me whisper, as usual, "that's the dyke," but for the rest of it we watch the girls look ludicrous, awkward, outclassed and totally dominated by the large handsome man on horse. In the stands we six boys drink beer in disgust, groan and hug our breasts, hold our heads and twist our faces at each other in embarrassment.

As the calf roping starts up again, we decide to use our disguises to walk around the grounds. Making our way around to the cowboy side of the arena, we pass the intricate mazes of rail where the stock is stored, to the chutes where they are loading the bull riders onto the bulls.

I wish to report that although we pass by dozens of men, and although we have pressed against wild horses and have climbed on rails overlooking thousands of pounds of angry animalflesh, though we touch ropes and halters, we are never once warned away, never told that this is not the proper place for us, that we had better get back for our own good, are not safe, etc., none of the dozens of warnings and threats we would have gotten if we had been recognized as thirty one year old girls instead of fourteen year old boys. It is a most interesting way to wander around the world for the day.

We examine everything closely. The brahma bulls are in the chutes, ready to be released into the ring. They are bulky, kindly looking creatures with rolling eyes; they resemble overgrown pigs. One of us whispers, "Aren't those the same kind of cattle that walk around all over the streets in India and never hurt anybody?"

Here in the chutes made exactly their size, they are converted into wild antagonistic beasts by means of a nasty belt around their loins, squeezed tight to mash their most tender testicles just before they are released into the ring. This torture is supplemented by a jolt of electricity from an electric cattle prod to make sure they come out bucking. So much for the rodeo as a great drama between man and nature.

A pale, nervous cowboy sits on the bull's back with one hand in a glove hooked under a strap around the bull's midsection. He gains points by using his spurs during the ride. He has to remain on top until the timing buzzer buzzes a few seconds after he and the bull plunge out of the gate. I had always considered it the most exciting event.

Around the fence sit many eager young men watching, helping, and getting in the way. We are easily accepted among them. How depressing this can be.

Out in the arena a dismounted cowboy reaches over and slaps his horse fiercely on the mouth because it has turned its head the wrong way.

I squat down peering through the rails where I see the neat, tight-fitting pants of two young men standing provocatively chest to chest.

"Don't you think Henry's a queer," one says with contempt.

"Hell, I *know* he's a queer," the other says. They hold an informal spitting contest for the punctuation. Meantime their eyes have brightened and their fronts are moving toward each other in their clean, smooth shirts. I realize they are flirting with each other, using Henry to bring up the dangerous subject of themselves. I am remembering all the gay cowboys I ever knew. This is one of the things I like about cowboys. They don't wear those beautiful pearl button shirts and tight levis for nothing.

As the events inside the arena subside, we walk down to a roped off pavillion where there is a dance. The band consists of one portly, bouncing enthusiastic man of middle age who is singing with great spirit into the microphone. The rest of the band are three grim, lean young men over fourteen. The drummer drums angrily, while jerking his head behind himself as though searching the air for someone who is already two hours late and had seriously promised to take him away from here. The two guitar players are sleepwalking from the feet up with their eyes so glassy you could read by them.

A redhaired man appears, surrounded by redhaired children who ask, "Are you drunk, Daddy?"

"No, I am not drunk," Daddy says. 30

"Can we have some money?"

"No," Daddy says, "I am not drunk enough to give you any money."

During a break in the music the redhaired man asks the bandleader where he got his band.

"Where did I get this band?" the bandleader puffs up, "I raised this band myself. These are all my sons—I raised this band myself." The redhaired man is so very impressed he is nearly bowing and kissing the hand of the bandleader, as they repeat this conversation two or three times. "This is *my* band," the bandleader says, and the two guitar players exchange grim and glassy looks.

Next the bandleader has announced "Okie From Muskogee," a song 35 intended to portray the white country morality of cowboys. The crowd does not respond but he sings enthusiastically anyway. Two of his more alert sons drag themselves to the microphone to wail that they don't smoke marijuana in Muskogee—as those hippies down in San Francisco do, and they certainly don't. From the look of it they shoot hard drugs and pop pills.

In the middle of the song a very drunk thirteen year old boy has staggered up to Wendy, pounding her on the shoulder and exclaiming, "Can you dig it, brother?" Later she tells me she has never been called brother before, and she likes it. Her first real identification as one of the brothers, in the brotherhood of man.

We boys begin to walk back to our truck, past a cowboy vomiting on his own pretty boots, past another lying completely under a car. Near our truck, a young man has calf-roped a young woman. She shrieks for him to stop, hopping weakly along behind him. This is the first bid for public attention I have seen from any woman here since the barrel race. I understand that this little scene is a re-enactment of the true meaning of the rodeo, and of the conquest of the west. And oh how much I do not want to be her; I do not want to be the conquest of the west.

I am remembering how the clown always seems to be tall and riding on an ass, that must be a way of poking fun at the small and usually dark people who tried to raise sheep or goats or were sod farmers and rode burros instead of tall handsome blond horses, and who were driven under by the beef raisers. And so today we went to a display of cattle handling instead of a sheep shearing or a goat milking contest—or to go into even older ghost territory, a corn dance, or acorn gathering. . . .

As we reach the truck, the tall man passes with the rodeo queen, who must surely be his niece, or something. All this non-contest, if it is for anyone, must certainly be for him. As a boy, I look at him. He is his own spitting image, of what is manly and white and masterly, so tall in his high heels, so *well horsed.* His manner portrays his theory of life as the survival of the fittest against wild beasts, and all the mythical rest of us who are too female or dark, not straight, or much too native to the earth to now be trusted as more than witnesses, flags, cheerleaders and unwilling stock.

As he passes, we step out of the way and I am glad we are in our disguise. I hate to step out of his way as a full grown woman, one who hasn't enough class status to warrant his thinly polite chivalry. He has knocked me off the sidewalk of too many towns, too often. 40

Yet somewhere in me I know I have always wanted to be manly, what I mean is having that expression of courage, control, coordination, ability I associate with men. To *provide.*

But here I am in this truck, not a man at all, a fourteen year old boy only. Tomorrow is my thirty second birthday. We six snuggle together in the bed of this rickety truck which is our world for the time being. We are headed back to the bold and shakey adventures of our all-women's farm, our all-women's households and companies, our expanding minds, ambitions and bodies, we who are neither male nor female at this moment in the pageant world, who are not the rancher's wife, mother earth, Virgin Mary or the rodeo queen—we who are really the one who took her self seriously, who once took an all out dive at the goat believing that the odds were square and that she was truly in the contest.

And now that we know it is not a contest, just a play—we have run off with the goat ourselves to try another way of life.

Because I certainly do not want to be a 32 year old girl, or calf either, and I certainly also do always remember Gertrude Stein's[1] beautiful dykely voice saying, what is the use of being a boy if you grow up to be a man.

DISCUSSING THE TEXT

1. What do you think the narrator means when she says that she has "never decided if it is worse to be 31 years old and called a boy or to be 31 years old and called a girl" (par. 5)? How would you connect this statement with the story's concluding line from Gertrude Stein?

---

[1]*Gertrude Stein* (1874–1946): American writer who lived for many years in Paris with her female lover, Alice B. Toklas; author of *Three Lives* (1909) and *The Autobiography of Alice B. Toklas* (1933) (*Ed.*)

2. According to the narrator, the goat-tying event for preadolescent girls is "the real comedy event of the evening." The girls "look ludicrous, awkward, outclassed and totally dominated by the large handsome man on horse," since the purpose of the event is "to show how badly girls do in the rodeo" (par. 16–17). Do you agree with the narrator's perceptions of this event? Why or why not? What is the narrator saying about power relationships in this particular passage? In what sense does the narrator portray *all* the contests at the rodeo as "fixed"?
3. The narrator refers to the calf-roped young woman, described near the end of the story, as representing "the conquest of the west" (par. 37). What does she mean by this? How would you compare the calf-roped woman with the two women described earlier, the "rodeo queen" and the "last loser" in the rodeo queen contest (par. 8–9)?
4. Working with a group of four or five students, try to recall times when each of you somehow assumed a different identity, either deliberately or by accident (perhaps because you were mistaken for someone else). Did this experience make you feel more or less powerful? Why? Be prepared to share your group's experiences with the class.

WRITING ABOUT THE TEXT

5. Write a brief description of the story's narrator. How does she challenge conventional ideas about gender? What kind of person do you think she is? What does her language tell us about the way she sees herself?
6. We are told that one of the women, Wendy, has felt that her experience at the rodeo has been her "first real identification as one of the brothers, in the brotherhood of man" (par. 36). And the narrator tells us that she herself always wanted to be "manly . . . having that expression of courage, control, coordination, ability I associate with men" (par. 41). Write a brief essay in which you discuss the significance of these two passages. What can we infer from these statements about "manliness" and the "brotherhood of man"? Do you think they are intended to be ironic? Are the women merely repeating models of masculine stereotypes? How do these passages tie in with the last three paragraphs of the story?
7. In paragraph 38, the narrator makes an implicit comparison between the tall rodeo clown riding on an ass and Native Americans; in the next paragraph she links the "wild beasts" of the rodeo with "all the mythical rest of us who are too female or dark, not straight," and so on. Write a brief essay explaining the argument Grahn is attempting to make by having her narrator make these comparisons. Conclude by discussing whether or not you find this argument convincing, and why.
8. Write a brief essay comparing and contrasting the cultural impersonations of the women in "Boys at the Rodeo" with that of John Howard Griffin in *Black like Me* (p. 398).

DANNY SANTIAGO

FROM

Famous All Over Town

Upon its publication in 1983, Danny Santiago's novel about Chicanos in east Los Angeles, Famous All Over Town, *became a critical success, winning the prestigious Richard and Hinda Rosenthal Foundation Award for fiction. The reclusive author had avoided meeting his editors at Simon and Schuster, could not be contacted by telephone, and had all his mail regularly sent to a post office box. When he failed to show up at the American Academy and Institute of Arts and Letters to accept the award, the rumor began to circulate that Danny Santiago did not exist. "Danny Santiago" was in fact the creation of Daniel L. James (1911–1988), born in Kansas into a well-to-do Anglo family.*

James had a degree in classical Greek from Yale University, had worked with Charlie Chaplin on the screenplay of The Great Dictator *in the 1930s, and had written two plays during the 1940s. But James's fortunes as a writer ended in 1951, when he was asked to testify before the House Committee on Un-American Activities, guided by the infamous Senator Joseph McCarthy to seek out Communist influences in American society. When asked if he had ever been a member of the Communist Party, James pleaded the Fifth Amendment, stating that he was not a party member at that time (he had in fact quit in 1948). His refusal to implicate others whom he knew during his affiliation with the Communist Party resulted in his being blacklisted. Unable to work in the film industry under his real name during the 1950s, James wrote screenplays for several monster movies under the pseudonym "Daniel Hyatt."*

Dan James's impersonation of "Danny Santiago" was both denounced and defended by Latino writers. For instance, writer Thomas Sanchez felt that what was at issue was not the author but his art: "A lot of professional Chicanos, professional Blacks, professional Jews, professional Anglo-Saxons say no one else can cut into their territory. . . . What creativity and art are all about are the absolute freedom to cross all those lines and go into any point of view in terms of the context of the work."

During the 1950s and 1960s, Dan James and his wife, Lilith, worked as volunteers in Lincoln Heights, a Chicano neighborhood in east Los Angeles. They organized social clubs for the children and adolescents, sponsored sports events, created a scholarship fund, and became close friends of the Chicano community. The stories that James wrote about his experiences in the barrio became the core of Danny Santiago's Famous All Over Town. *The novel's adolescent narrator, Rudy (Chato) Medina, is as alienated from his parents' Mexico as he is from the Anglo world, which he only half inhabits. A member of one of the local gangs, Chato becomes "famous all over town" by writing his name in crayon in the area of the city where he used to live, an area that was taken over by the Southern Pacific Railroad. This selection explores Chato's experiences as a member of the Shamrock gang, which is engaged in an ongoing war with another gang, the Sierras.*

CHAPTER 6

"Buy me shades," I begged Lena in the morning. My father had stomped my old ones because he claimed they made me look like a hoodlum but today I felt I would rather go out on the street without pants. Long lazy hours stretched out in front of me. I took my time eating my Corn Frosties which before I always ate on the run, then played with Dolores till she needed changing, which I pointed out to my mother.

"So change her," she said. "A little peepee wouldn't kill you."

"She's a girl," I said. "It wouldn't be right." And turned away to give my baby sister privacy while my mother changed her pants. "Are you really going down there to Mexico?" I asked.

"In exactly seventeen days and four hours." She waved her bus ticket at me to prove it, which she wore down her neck next to her heart.

"How long you gonna be gone?"

"A month, maybe two."

"Eee," I moaned. "What about us?"

"Lena will feed you, don't worry."

"Poison us, you mean. All she ever thinks about is her damn boyfriend." I tried a little fishing. My mother claimed she never knew of any boyfriend of my sister, but who can trust a woman? They always stick together. I gave up and switched back to Mexico. "Was my father really some crazy kind of cowboy down there?" I asked. "Did he wear those bullet-belts like in the movies, crossed over in front?"

"His real name was Pancho Villa," my mother said. "Didn't you know?"

Never try to get straight answers from my mother. It's impossible. I inspected the picture of my grandma on the wall which in seventeen days my mother would be seeing in real life. A fierce plump lady stared back at me. How she must have hated that cameraman. She looked ready to tear his leg off, and mine too. But she had my mother's nose exactly, and Lena's.

"How come everybody's got better noses than me?" I complained. "I might even be quite some handsome guy if it wasn't for this squashed potato. Did the doctor butcher me or what?"

"Nothing's wrong with your nose," my mother told me. "You breathe."

Which was what everybody always said.

"At the hospital they claimed they could operate and make me real sensational for $500."

"You bore me with your nose," my mother said. "Hold the baby while I go to the store."

"What if she does caca in her pants?"

"Call the Fire Department."

You can make conversation just so long with a 23-day baby. I tried TV. Nothing. I looked out the window. Nothing was doing on the street. The guys wouldn't get back from school till after three. And even when they did I wasn't sure about showing myself. Nobody had bothered to visit me in the hospital which could mean they had it in for me. You know how people talk behind your back. They could of at least sent me a Get Well card. I didn't care to think about it.

To pass the time I did something I hadn't done for ages, fished out my old sack of marbles. I set up a glassie on the linoleum and knuckled down with my faithful shooter, winner of 1,000 victories and only one defeat. I let fly and missed by a mile. "Just a damn minute," I told myself and tried again, a medium-hard shot, five feet away. This time I connected like a cannonball and the glassie flew out the door. "Magnífico, perfecto, estupendo," I crowed. Which was how Ernie Zapata used to congratulate me over at Boys' Club in the good old days.

Three o'clock finally rolled around. It was time to show myself outside. If only Lena could bring my shades first, but that was impossible, so I went out anyway and sat on the porch steps, wearing my County of L.A. bathrobe to inform the public I was still not a well man. By bad luck my first passer-by was stupid Kiko. He was in my class at Audubon but he came rattling a stick along the picket fence like a kindergardener.

"Hey traitor, where you been?" he yelled at me.

What a reception!

"Where do you think?" I asked, with my bathrobe staring the guy in the face.

"I pity you, man. You're really gonna get it for that Wolfie, man." 25

Down the street he went, rattling fences all the way. Wolfie was the rat that slapped me round my last day at school. There were witnesses and I was criticized. "Sick or not, you're Shamrock man," they told me. "And Wolfie's Sierra and Shamrock don't take shit from Sierra Street." That might be true for colds or even the Asiatic flu, but peritonitis? Forget it.

In front of Elva's house Kiko was pointing at me and various Jesters were staring. I only hoped Pelón was absent. Lately he had been cutting me to pieces with that tongue of his. A few months in Juvy will do wonders for a guy's oratory.

And now the Jesters came cruising up the sidewalk in good old Shamrock style, knees swinging high and loose and shoulders muscling free. Being War Minister, Gorilla led the way.

He had brown curly fur all over his face because as everybody knows, if you shave too early your beard will come in very wiry later on. His arms were long and his legs were short. You might not call him exactly handsome but those sad little eyes of his could see right through you to the heart. Buddha rolled along beside him, then came Termite, Hungryman and Kiko. No Pelón was good news, but the guys' faces were blank as ice cubes. They froze my blood, till finally Gorilla cracked a friendly smile.

"What you say, Chato?" he told me. "How you feeling, man?" 30

"We tried to see you in the hospital," Buddha reported. "Only dumb Pelón bust their cigarette machine so they chased us."

"Oh yah," Kiko remembered, "you was in the hospital, huh?"

They all pounded him. He howled and everybody asked me questions. It was Chato this and Chato that. Before, I was never what you might call too popular in the Jesters. By chance I had missed several of their punch-outs and my police record was pitiful, but everybody respects you when you return from the dead.

I showed off the bandage on my belly and brought out my sack of hospital souvenirs, the half-moon dish you vomit in, and a surgeon knife some doctor left on the next bed by mistake, and my thermometer and enough rolls of tape and bandage to last a lifetime. I had tried for a stethoscope but they never left any laying around.

"Give that Wolfie a message from me," I announced. "The first day the doctors give permission I'm really gonna stomp him." 35

But it seemed they had already attended to the guy. And the old war with Sierra had started up again after a six-month truce. For the benefit of those who might not know, Sierra Street is an ugly little cowpath up in the hills. They're Mexicans, but very low, pure drogadictos, and their sisters are mostly whores, it's said, and who knows about their mothers? Since before anybody can remember it's been War between Sierra and Shamrock, with quite a few corpses from time to time. A full-scale punch-out had been scheduled yesterday for after school, only the cops got there first. And anything could happen over the weekend.

So we talked of this and this and that till everybody got bored of my front steps.

"Let's sit in the Buick better," Kiko suggested, so we piled in. As usual Kiko got left outside but Gorilla let him hang his face in through the window and pass out cigarettes, and we sat there sucking in the good smoke and holding it in our lungs like it might be something more interesting, and cracked jokes and cooled our elbows out the windows of my father's Buick ready for anything, but no key for the ignition.

"I could jump the wires," Hungryman thought.

"And I could pay for your funeral," Buddha said. He had a lot of respect for my father. 40

Eventually it got quite boring.

"If only Pelón was here, he'd think of something."

"Pelón, shit, I need a woman, man."

"How 'bout that cross-eyed chick over in Dogtown?"

"Where you been, man? They got her in a Foster Home." 45

"Maybe we could stir up something at Forney Playground."

"She-it."

We checked over all the old familiar if's and maybe's. Everything either costed money or else you needed wheels. So there we sat and sat.

"Going someplace?" Lena teased us from the sidewalk and handed me my new shades. Gorilla blushed. He always blushed when Lena came in view, what you could see of him through the fuzz.

"They're the wrong color," I complained. "I told you black." 50

Gorilla nearly slugged me for ungrateful.

"See you later, hoodlums," Lena said. "Don't forget to send me a postcard when you get there."

Gorilla's eyes followed her into the house. It was pitiful. For years Lena was the movie star of his dreams. And now he pulled me out to the fence for privacy. "I hate to say it," he said, "but your sister's been seen going with a TJ."

"By who?" I asked.

"By me and not just one time neither. You're her brother, man, and you better straighten her out, even if you got to knock her round some." 55

That would be the day. Me and what army? But before I could answer the guy, here comes Pelón on a dead run from Main. He skids to a stop beside the Buick. You could smell burning rubber from his tennies. Bad news never comes in singles on Shamrock Street.

"The Sierra," he gasped and blew. "They gonna Pearl Harbor us. I just barely got away."

The Buick emptied.

"Four cars packed solid, man. Cholos, low-riders. I seen a shotgun in Robot's Chevy."

"Dig up the arsenal!" Buddha yelled. 60

"Clear the street!"

"Wait wait wait," Gorilla ordered and turned his sad little eyes on Pelón. "Where'd you spot them?"

"Parked opposite the brewery."

"Why would they want to advertise themself up there?"

"Maybe they had car trouble." 65

"Peló—on," Gorilla singsonged. "You're lying, Pelón. Remember last time we believed you? And called out the allies? And threw roofing nails in the street? And all we caught was the welfare lady? And Sierra's laughing at us yet."

We were all set to murder that little guy till we got interrupted. It was a noise nobody could doubt, motors racing, horns blasting, backfires, or was it guns? The Peewees dived for cover. Ladies snatched babies off of porches, screamed and ran inside. It was shots, now definitely. We ducked behind my father's gunboat Buick, all except Pelón.

"What's wrong with you?" he yelled at us. "It's only a fairy story. I made it up."

We pulled him behind the fender. The Sierra screeched their brakes, blasted horns.

"Chickenshit Shamrocks! Pinchi cabrones. Come out and fight, you putos!" And sprayed lead from zip guns, you heard it smash against the Buick. Buddha's kid brother ran for the courts. A shotgun blasted and he went down yelling. The big front window crashed at Miracle Market. I saw Wolfie in the second car. We scrambled in the dirt for rocks, gravel, anything to throw, and screamed and raved. 70

Less than a minute and it was over.

"Viva la Sierra," they yelled and their tires spinned screaming on the asphalt and away they went. Gorilla pounded his fists bloody on the Buick. It had three bullet holes, two in the fender, one in the door.

"Fucking cowards," Fat Manuel called us. "Nobody never dared raid Shamrock in my day," he added, which is Veteranos for you. Buddha's kid brother was yelling on the sidewalk. I grabbed my First Aid from the porch and ran to him. The kid's pants were all over blood, the seat especially. I sliced it off with my surgeon knife while Kiko held him down, and Buddha's mother screamed and screamed.

"It isn't vital," I explained, "but he can't be moved just yet." And carefully mopped up the blood with cotton. People crowded in. "Stand back," I ordered. "Let this man breathe." They paid attention. Buddha's mother grabbed Gorilla by the T-shirt and slapped his face. "You killed my baby," she kept screaming. I tried to calm the woman down. "It's only flesh wounds," I pointed out. "He'll recover."

I had barely finished bandaging the kid when sirens screamed down Main Street. I wanted to discuss my patient with the police but Lena dragged me in the house. We watched through the window. As usual the cops shoved people here and shoved people there. "Keep moving! Break it up," they ordered. 75

"Who made this crazy bandage?" one yelled, possibly from jealousy. They grabbed Gorilla and Pelón who were well known to them.

"Did you get their license plates?"

"I didn't see nothing, man," I heard Gorilla say. "I was too busy ducking, man." The cops threw him in their black-and-white with Pelón for questioning. Answers they would never get. No Shamrock rats. Not even on enemies. We have our own little ways of getting even.

The street was still boiling when my father came from work. The bullet holes in his Buick got loudly commented on. Lena put me in her bed while she argued with him on the porch.

"How could it be Junior's fault?" she said. "He was in the house resting all the time." But my father wasn't pacified. 80

"If I ever catch you with those rat-packers, I'll tear you apart," he stormed in and said, then stormed back to poke his finger in the Buick's bullet holes. I almost had to laugh.

"It isn't funny!" Lena yelled at me, then bursted into tears. "I thought it was you got shot," she wailed. "I was washing my hair and I think I fainted."

"Quit worrying," I told her. "I can take care of myself, man."

Looking back over the last half-hour I was more or less contented. My first time under fire and I didn't panic, and tended the wounded like a pro. All that blood hardly bothered me at all. Naturally I was raging at the Sierra, still there was no denying they brought a little spice into our life and we would pay them back double, don't worry. If not over the weekend, then Monday morning at school.

Audubon would be a battlefield, no doubt, full of cops and double patrols of teachers in the halls and on the grounds. Still, you can catch a guy between classes or at Nutrition or in the toledo.[1] Thirty seconds and too bad for him. But a certain picture came into my head, an ugly picture and I still can't forget it, that time four of us stomped Blackie. There he was on the pavement while we worked him over with our boots. He might be Sierra and no denying he once busted a baseball bat on Kiko from behind, but all bloody on the pavement and screaming and begging for his life like a baby, it made me sick. I had to kneel beside the telephone pole and vomit in the gutter. What 85

---

[1] *the toledo:* a playful, pseudo-Spanish version of "toilet" (*Ed.*)

was wrong with me that win or lose I couldn't feel good about it either way?

I laid there on the bed while Lena lectured me, wondering Did God spare my life at the hospital only to see me die in battle? And from outside listened to the Miracle Market howling over their busted window.

CHAPTER 7

In all my life I never saw so much heat as Monday morning on the way to school. Black-and-whites, foot cops, paddy wagons jammed Avenue 26 at the bridge where we crossed over to Audubon. TV had their trucks there too, and cameras. And there were pictures of the bullet holes in my father's Buick in the Sunday papers. RAT PACK STRIKES AGAIN was the headline. We were quite famous.

"One at a time," the cops ordered on the bridge, and patted everybody down.

"Careful! I got a loaded doughnut in there," Pelón yelled when they went through his lunch.

"Move on, clown," they told him and kicked his ass. 90

Boxer was next in line. She was Captain of our Auxiliary.

"No frisking girls," Pelón pointed out. "It's in the Constitution." They chased him but passed Boxer through. And then here came the Sierra.

"Well well if it isn't the Boy Scouts of America," some wisecrack copper said because Sierra was all in uniform, with those black knit watchcaps pulled down over their ears like helmets, real menacing. "Are we any match for them?" I wondered. Gorilla could take Robot, possibly. Buddha was fat and fearless. If he charged you, watch out. It was like getting runned over by a tank, and Kiko when he got mad used to froth at the mouth. Nobody cared to be around him. With Hungryman you could never be quite sure. He had his off days. But thank God for Termite. Still, in numbers the Sierra had us, and how much good could I ever do with my incision which was already starting in to hurt?

"We don't talk," Gorilla told the TV camera when it asked questions and we passed on through the gates of Audubon Junior High. Boxer whispered to me she had her brother's zip gun taped to her chest so tell Gorilla, which I did. She worshipped the guy but he only had eyes for my sister, which is life. So around then the last bell rang and we trooped off to our various classes, Sierra next to Sierra and Shamrock next to Shamrock with strict orders, "Don't go to the restroom except in threes."

"Underline every noun," my workbook instructed me. Nouns are said 95 to be the names of persons and things.

"(1) Oscar," I underlined him, "at sixteen was already the best football player in his school." My workbook was quite sports-minded. Next, I underlined "sixteen" which was the name of how old this Oscar was. Or could it be a when-where-how word? I casually glanced around at my neighbors. Nobody's paper was in view. I erased my underline.

A messenger came in and handed a green slip to Mr. Millstone who was our home-room teacher. I inspected her. She wasn't much to look at but not as boring as *Oscar* the sixteen-year-old football hero, or was it *sixteen?*

"Medina, Rudy!"

I jumped.

"Counselor's office." 100

"Oh-oh," somebody said.

Counselor is not as dangerous as Vice-principal but bad enough, and when I went up front for my pass, friends flashed me sympathetic faces and enemies slit their throats with fingernails.

The schoolyard empty looked twice life-size. It was solid blacktop, not clean healthy blacktop but blotchy gray from all our dirty feet. There were lines painted for basketball and numbers 1 to 12 to line up behind and wait. Today the sky looked blacktopped too and where it met the yard you saw chainlink fence. All we lacked was machine-gun towers.

I took a long look round for Sierra, then started off for the Administration building. I felt like an ant walking across that monster yard all by myself and when I tripped on a crack expected the whole world to bust out laughing at me. Where the steps went down, somebody had pulled the handrail loose. I gave it a healthy shake to do my bit, then went wading through plastic cups and dirty napkins by the picnic tables. A squashed Baby Ruth wrapped its loving arms around my shoe. I peeled it off.

"Tssss! Chato!" somebody hollered in a whisper. It was Boxer coming 105 from the Girls'. "Gym's next period and they search us. Act real lovey-dovey, huh? They're watching."

I snuggled over to her. She stroked my hair like going steady. And with her other hand slipped me the zip gun. "Get it to Gorilla," she said and left me running. And no time to tell her I was going to the counselor. And no chance to run her down because here's a yard teacher.

"Show your pass," he tells me.

I did. He followed me into Administration and down the long hall, with Boxer's pistol burning up my pocket. The barrel was a curtain rod with a rubber band-type trigger. It saw a lot of duty among the Veteranos, and once went off in Fat Manuel's pocket. And here I was carrying it into the lion's den. I said a prayer and knocked, what else?

"Come in, come in," somebody sang.

The previous counselor was your typical wrestler type, but this one was 110 a fat bouncy little man with blue sparkles in his eyes and wild white hair fuzzing out around his head. He didn't look too dangerous, but then you never know.

"Rudy Medina? Pilger's the name, Max Pilger. Sit down, son. One million years and you'll never guess why I called you in. The principal just received a letter about you."

Now what? People usually complained by phone.

"Dear Sir," Mr. Pilger read. "One of your eighth-graders, Rudy Medina, was recently under our care at County Hospital." Oh-oh, their missing thermometer, I thought, but it was Dr. Penrose and he praised me till I didn't know where to look, but suggested special counseling. "So, Mr. Rudy Medina that wants to tack an M.D. on his name, sit back and relax while we talk it over." Relax? With The Goods in my pants pocket? But this new counselor didn't look to be the suspicious type, and he even beamed a smile across his desk at me.

"You realize, son, it won't be easy. You need to be tops in every subject, the sciences especially, biology, chemistry, physics. How do you spell gastro-intestinal hemorrhoids? You've got to spell them before breakfast. In your sleep you've got to spell them. But God love you, Rudy, thousands of bright boys in your shoes make doctor, so why not you? Let's take a look at your track record."

He opened my folder. Every year they keep a record on you and it 115 follows you like a wolf from school to school.

"Ai-yi-yí," Mr. Pilger said when he saw page one. "C-minus average with a D in Spanish? In *Spanish,* Rudy Medina?"

I didn't mention it but Miss Helstrom's Spanish was from Spain. If you talked Mexican, forget it. Only Anglos got A's with her. Mr. Pilger sighed over every page till he got back to Mrs. Cully and 6th grade at Hibernia. My A's there cheered him up but what surprised him was a certain test they gave that year and IQ was its name.

"135!" he exploded. "Why son, you scored right off the board."

"Just lucky," I apologized.

He said there were no luckies on that IQ test, then fired me questions. 120 Did I get sick next term? Did anybody die? Or lose their job? Or how could my score drop forty points in one short year?

"Well," I more or less explained, "my seventh-grade teacher claimed Mrs. Cully cheated on my score."

"A teacher told you that?" Mr. Pilger picked up his pen to make a fiery note of it. "What was her name?"

"Miss Kaplan."

"Kaplan?" It seemed to take the heart out of him. "God love you, son," he finally said, "teachers have their bad days like all the rest of us."

The bell sounded off for 5th period. Classroom doors banged open, guys 125 hollered at each other, girls screamed and laughed and happy feet went stampeding down the hall. I wished I could be out there with them, but with that time bomb in my pocket maybe I was better off with this Mr. Pilger. I felt almost safe.

"Rudy," he said when the noise outside quieted down, "in Junior High a lot of bright boys and girls get lost and it's Max Pilger's job to find those buried jewels and bring them to the light."

Could he be meaning me?

"Tell me, Rudy," he asked. "How do you honestly feel about Audubon?"

"It's okay, I guess." Who was I to tell him?

"Doesn't it bother you that your class is reading at fourth-grade level? 130 Doesn't it bother you that every youngster with a Mexican name gets shunted into Metal Shop or Carpentry?"

"Not the girls," I pointed out. "They take Home Economics."

Mr. Pilger sadly shook his head at me. "Hurray for them," he said. "Now tell me frankly, are you learning anything? Do you enjoy *any* of your classes?"

"Maybe sometimes," I admitted.

"Rudy, Rudy, what am I going to do about a boy that one year cracks genius level and next year drops to dull normal?" I looked out the window. Questions like that bother me. "Son, to get two words from you I need a can opener, and it just happens I have one in stock."

He rustled in his desk and came up with a flat green box. It had the ugly word "test" written on it. No doubt he saw my disgusted look. 135

"It won't be graded," he quickly said. "This is strictly between you and me, and nothing to write down." He handed me the craziest picture I ever saw. It looked like some kindergardener spilled a bunch of paint, then folded the paper over.

"Huh?" I asked.

" 'Huh' is right. Now look close and tell me what it's a picture of."

"A giant man-eating butterfly," I said. "It's got wings fifty feet across and look, here's blood dripping from its mouth. Bullets couldn't kill it, so it goes flying around the world eating everyone in sight."

I was pleased with my answer but Mr. Pilger seemed upset. He said there were no rights and wrongs on this particular test but happy dancing girls was what most people seemed to see in that picture. Personally I don't know how they could unless they were either blind or sex-minded. So Mr. Pilger put away that test and handed me another. It had pictures too but more like photographs, and I was to make up a little story to fit them. 140

"Easy! They broke the poor guy's guitar," I said.

"Where is it broken?"

You couldn't exactly see the place but there was this sad-face kid staring at it, so what else?

"Couldn't the boy be daydreaming?" Mr. Pilger asked. "Maybe about the concert he'll some day give at Carnegie Hall?"

"Where's that?" I asked. 145

"And isn't that a violin in his hands?"

To my surprise it was. Mr. Pilger handed me more pictures, and I made up stories for him. They were good stories too, with lots of action, but Mr. Pilger wondered why no happy endings?

"That's a sad bunch of pictures," I told him, "so why lie about it?"

"The sadness is in you, son," he told me. "I don't see them sad at all."

"You're not a Mexican." It popped out of me just-like-that. 150

"Well," he said. "At last. The sleeping giant talks."

He looked at me a while.

"No, Rudy. I'm not a Mexican. I'm a Jew. Do you know what that means, son? You think you have it tough? We've been discriminated against for two thousand years. You should see the street Max Pilger grew up on. Tenements, son, five stories high and we lived on the top floor. Did the roof leak? It did. Did the landlord fix it? He did not. Toilet? Oh yes, run through the garbage two flight down."

Mr. Pilger bounced to his feet, his wild white hair all flying.

"Son, you think Audubon is bad? P.S. 153, New York City, was worse. Our teachers hated us. They made fun of our Jew-boy haircuts and our oiyoi accents, but we fought those teachers, Rudy. We fought them for good grades. By being two times twice as smart as other kids. We won our A's in spite of them. We made it, Rudy. Through high school, through college and beyond. From my own building came two medical doctors, one now a famous specialist with a very fine practice. Lawyers? By the dozen. Two judges, one of them respected. Yes sir, Mr. Rudy Medina, we made it and I'm going to see you make it too." 155

Mr. Pilger sat down and caught his breath. "Are you willing to cooperate?"

I think he really meant it. I think he took an interest. Maybe I had a friend on the other side at last.

"I'll try," I told him.

"Tomorrow is your new leaf. Come early. Seven A.M. I'll have a ninth-grader there to tutor you. We'll work on English first, and God love you, Rudy, we'll lift that C-minus to an A before the term is over."

I believed in him, almost. 160

"Write me out a pass," I reminded.

Mr. Pilger clapped his hand on his forehead. "Passes! Fences! Policemen in the restrooms!" he exploded. "What are we running here, a penitentiary?"

"More or less, maybe," I told him, and left his office, with my pass in hand and Boxer's zip gun in pocket.

DISCUSSING THE TEXT

1. Compare and contrast Chato's attitude and behavior when he is with his friends and his manner when at home with his mother and his baby sister. How can you reconcile these two aspects of Chato's personality?
2. When describing the Sierras, Chato says, "They're Mexicans, but very low, pure drogadictos, and their sisters are mostly whores, it's said, and who knows about their mothers?" (par. 36). What is your reaction to Chato's comments? How do you interpret Chato's opinion about the Sierras, in light of the fact that he himself is also a Mexican American?
3. Where does the school counselor Max Pilger's interest in Rudy/Chato come from? Do you find his comparison of Mexican Americans and Jewish Americans convincing? Why or why not?

WRITING ABOUT THE TEXT

4. Commenting on Dan James's impersonation of Danny Santiago as author of *Famous All Over Town,* Mexican American writer Thomas Sanchez has observed that "A work must be judged by the work itself, not the political or ethnic orientation of the author." Write two paragraphs in which you explain why you agree or disagree with Sanchez. Conclude by expressing your own opinion of the quality of "the work itself," based on the excerpt from the novel that you have read here.

5. Write a letter to the publisher of *Famous All Over Town* explaining why the book should or should not have been published, given the author's act of cultural impersonation.
6. Choose a recent newspaper or magazine article about ethnic conflict in the United States. Write another account of the incident described in the article, this time in the voice of one of the people involved. (To see firsthand what is involved in writing as a cultural impersonator, do *not* write this account from the perspective of a member of your own ethnic group.)

FORREST CARTER

Trading with a Christian

Forrest Carter's book The Education of Little Tree *(1976), from which this selection is reprinted, is a narrative told by a Cherokee boy who has been raised by his grandparents. "Forrest Carter" came to life in 1973 with the publication of his first novel,* The Rebel Outlaw: Josie Wales. *Before this he was known as Asa Earl Carter, born into a traditional white southern family in Alabama in the early 1920s.*

In 1976, Alabama reporter Wayne Greenhaw exposed Forrest Carter as Asa Carter in the New York Times, *but at that point the revealing news was all but ignored. Later that year, Forrest Carter's so-called autobiography,* The Education of Little Tree, *was published, and* Josie Wales *came out as a movie starring Clint Eastwood. Astonishingly, a recent edition of* Contemporary Authors *still describes Forrest Carter as a "half-Cherokee Indian . . . raised by his grandfather in the Tennessee hill country," a falsehood that was repeated in the University of New Mexico Press's 1986 edition of* Little Tree. *The book became a best-seller and was listed on the* New York Times *nonfiction best-seller list in 1991. This prompted historian Dan T. Carter to expose Asa Carter again, this time in an editorial published in the* New York Times *in October 1991. At that time, the* Times *finally moved the book to its* fiction *best-seller list.*

Known in Birmingham as "Ace" Carter, in his younger years the future author of Little Tree *had boasted about his hatred of African Americans in public political speeches and as coeditor of a monthly newsletter that openly advocated racial violence. He fought the Supreme Court's 1954 ruling desegregating public schools by founding two organizations, the White Citizens Council and the menacing Original Ku Klux Klan of the Confederacy. In 1957, six alleged members of Asa Carter's Klan group were convicted of mayhem after they abducted an African American man, Judge Aaron, castrated him, and poured turpentine on his wounds. Shunned by Birmingham's segregationists after this incident, Carter retired from politics until he was secretly hired as a speechwriter by George Wallace. It was Asa Earl Carter who wrote Wallace's 1963 inaugural speech as governor of Alabama, which included the infamous lines, "Segregation now! Segregation tomorrow! Segregation forever!" Asa Earl Carter then disappeared from public view, resurfacing in Texas in 1973 as "Forrest Carter."*

Surprisingly, and disturbingly, Carter succeeded in his cultural impersonation of the Cherokee alter ego he had created in Little Tree *throughout the 1970s. He lectured at several American universities, falsely claiming that a percentage of the book's royalties were contributed to Native Americans, and he even survived an interview with Barbara Walters on the* Today *show. Forrest Carter's obituary appeared in the* Abilene Reporter *on June 9, 1979.*

Although little is known about Asa / Forrest Carter's private life, there are two prevalent interpretations of his life among those who knew him. Some people feel that Asa Carter rejected his past life and became a new man (Forrest Carter) through the persona of Little Tree. But others feel that Asa Carter remained malicious and bigoted until the end, reveling in his power as an impersonator of a culturally and racially different "other."

The next morning, all the dogs was still jumping around, stiff-legged and proud. They knew they had done something which helped. I felt proud too . . . but I wasn't uppity about it, because such was part of the whiskey-making trade.

Ol' Ringer was missing. Me and Granpa whistled and hollered for him, but he didn't show up. We walked all around the cabin clearing, but he wasn't to be found anywhere. So we set off with the hounds to find him. We went up the hollow trail and the Narrows but could find no trace of him anywhere. Granpa said we had better backtrack up the mountain the way I had come down the night before. We did; first through the brush tangles, searching, and then up the mountain. Blue Boy and Little Red found him.

Ringer had run into a tree. Maybe it was the last tree he had run into, for Granpa said it looked like he had run into a lot of trees or else been hit with a club. His head was bloody all over and he lay on his side. His tongue was stabbed through with his teeth. He was alive, and Granpa picked him up in his arms and we carried him down the mountain.

We stopped at the spring branch, and me and Granpa washed the blood from his face and loosened his tongue from the teeth. There was gray hairs over his face and when I saw them I knew that ol' Ringer was very old and had no business running off in the mountains looking after me. We sat with him by the spring branch, and in a little while he opened his eyes; they were old and bleary and he could barely see.

I bent low to ol' Ringer's face and told him I 'preciated him looking for me in the mountains, and I was sorry. Ol' Ringer didn't mind, he licked my face, letting me know he'd just as soon do it all over again. 5

Granpa let me help carry ol' Ringer down the trail. Granpa carried most of him, but I toted his hind feet. When we got to the cabin, Granpa laid him down and said, "Ol' Ringer is dead." And he was. He had died on the trail, but Granpa said he knowed that we had come and got him, and that he was on his way home, and so he felt good about it. I felt some better too—though not much.

Granpa said ol' Ringer died like all good mountain hounds want to die: doing for their folks and in the woods.

Granpa got a shovel. We carried ol' Ringer up the hollow trail, up by the corn patch that he prided so in guarding. Granma come along too, and all the hounds followed, whining, with their tails between their legs. I felt the same.

Granpa dug ol' Ringer's grave at the foot of a little water oak. It was a pretty place; red sumach all around in the fall, and a dogwood tree standing by with white blooms in the spring.

Granma laid a white cotton sack in the bottom of the grave, and placed ol' Ringer on it and wrapped it around him. Granpa put a big board over ol' Ringer, so the 'coons couldn't dig him up. We covered up the grave. The hounds stood around, knowing it was ol' Ringer, and ol' Maud whined. Her and ol' Ringer had been partners at the corn patch. 10

Granpa pulled off his hat and said, "Good-bye, ol' Ringer." I said good-bye ol' Ringer, too. And so we left him, under the water oak tree.

I felt total bad about it, and empty. Granpa said he knew how I felt, for he was feeling the same way. But Granpa said everything you lost which you had loved give you that feeling. He said the only way round it was not to love anything, which was worse because you would feel empty all the time.

Granpa said, supposin' ol' Ringer had not been faithful; then we would not be proud of him. That would be a worse feeling. Which is right. Granpa said when I got old, I would remember ol' Ringer, and I would like it—to remember. He said it was a funny thing, but when you got old and remembered them you loved, you only remembered the good, never the bad, which proved the bad didn't count nohow.

But we had to get on with our trade. Me and Granpa toted our wares over the cutoff trail to Mr. Jenkins' crossroads store. "Wares" is what Granpa called our whiskey.

I liked the cutoff trail. We went down the hollow trail, and before we reached the wagon ruts, we turned and beared left to the cutoff trail. It ran over the ridges of the mountains that sloped toward the valley like big fingers pushing out and resting in the flatlands. 15

The hollows we crossed were shallow between the ridges and easy to climb out of. The trail was several miles long; passing through stands of pine and cedar on the slopes; persimmon trees and honeysuckle vine.

In the fall of the year, after frost had turned the persimmons red, I would stop on the way back and fill my pockets, and then run to catch up with Granpa. In the spring, I done the same thing, picking blackberries.

Oncet, Granpa stopped and watched me pick blackberries. It was one of the times he was put out about words, and how folks was fooled by them. Granpa said, "Little Tree, did ye know that when *black*berries is *green,* they is *red?*"

This total confused me, and Granpa laughed. "The *name* is give to *black*berries . . . to describe 'em by color . . . folks use the color *green* . . . meaning they ain't ripe . . . which when they ain't ripe, they are *red.*" Which is true.

Granpa said, "That's how the damn fool word-using gits folks all twisted up. When ye hear somebody using *words* agin' somebody, don't go by his words, fer they won't make no damn sense. Go by his *tone,* and ye'll know if he's mean and lying." Granpa was pretty much down on having too many words. Which was reasonable. 20

There was also hickor'nuts, chinkapins, walnuts and chestnuts usually laying by the trail side. So, no matter what time of year it was, coming back from the crossroads store kept me busy gathering.

Totin' our wares to the store was a pretty good job. I would sometimes fall far behind Granpa, carrying my three fruit jars in the sack. When I did, I knew he would be settin' down somewhere ahead, and when I got to him, we would rest.

When you toted that-a-way, by going from one settin' down place to another, it was not so hard. When we got to the last ridge, me and Granpa always set down in the bushes while we looked for the pickle barrel in front of the store. If the pickle barrel was not settin' out front that meant everything was all right. If it was settin' out front that meant the law, and we was not to deliver our wares. Everybody in the mountains watched for the pickle barrel, for other people had wares to deliver too.

I never saw the pickle barrel settin' out front, but I never failed to look for it. I had learned that the whiskey-making trade had a lot of complications to it. But Granpa said every trade has, more or less, some complications.

He said did ye ever think how it would be in the dentist trade, having to look down folks mouths all the time, day in and day out, nothing but mouths? He said such a trade would drive him total crazy and that the whiskey-making trade, with all its complications, was a sight better trade for a feller to be in. Which is right. 25

I like Mr. Jenkins. He was big and fat and wore overalls. He had a white beard that hung down over the bib of his overalls, but his head was near totally without hair; it shined like a pine knob.

He had all kinds of things in the store: big racks of shirts and overalls and boxes of shoes. There was barrels with crackers in them, and on a counter he had a big hoop of cheese. Also on the counter he had a glass case which had candy laid on the shelves. There was all kinds of candy and looked like there was more candy than he could ever run out of. I never seen anybody eat any of it, but I guess he sold some or he wouldn't have had it.

Every time we delivered our wares, Mr. Jenkins asked me if I would go to his woodpile and pick up a sack of wood chips for the big stove that set in the store. I always did. The first time, he offered me a big stick of striped candy, but I couldn't rightly take it just for picking up wood chips, which wasn't hardly no trouble atall. He put it back in the case, and found another piece which was old and which he was going to throw away. Granpa said that it was all right for me to take it, seeing as how Mr. Jenkins was going to throw it away, and it would not be of benefit to anybody. So I did.

Every month, he come across another old stick, and I guess I might near cleaned out his old candy. Which he said helped him out a lot.

It was at the crossroads store where I got slickered out of my fifty cents. 30
It had taken me a long time to accumulate the fifty cents. Granma would put aside a nickel or dime in a jar for me each month we delivered our wares.

It was my part of the trade. I liked to carry it, all in nickels and dimes, in my pocket when we went to the crossroads store. I never spent it and each time when we got home I put it back in the fruit jar.

It was a comfort to me, carrying it in my pocket to the store, and knowing it was mine. I kind of had my eye on a big red and green box which was in the candy case. I didn't know how much it cost, but I was figuring that maybe next Christmas I would buy it for Granma . . . and then we would eat what was in it. But as I say, I got slickered out of my fifty cents before then.

It was about dinnertime of a day right after we had delivered our wares. The sun was straight overhead and me and Granpa was resting, squattin' down under the store shed with our backs against the store. Granpa had bought some sugar for Granma and three oranges which Mr. Jenkins had. Granma liked oranges, which I did too, when you could get them. Seeing Granpa had three, I knew I would get one.

I was eating on my stick candy. Men commenced to come to the store in twos and threes. They said a politician was coming and was going to make a speech. I don't know that Granpa would have stayed, for as I say he didn't give a lick damn about politicians, but before we got rested here come the politician.

He was in a big car, kicking up rolls of dust from the road, so everybody 35
saw him a long way off before he got there. He had some feller driving his car for him, and he got out of the back seat. There was a lady in the back seat with him. All the time the politician talked, she throwed out little cigarettes that she had smoked part of. Granpa said they were ready-roll, tailor-made cigarettes, which rich people smoked as they was too lazy to roll their own.

The politician come around and shook everybody's hand; though he didn't shake mine nor Granpa's. Granpa said this was because we looked like Indians and didn't vote nohow, so we was of practical no use whatsoever to the politician. Which sounds reasonable.

He wore a black coat and had a white shirt with a ribbon tied at his neck; it was black and hung down. He laughed a lot and 'peared to be might happy. That is, until he got mad.

He got up on a box and commenced to get worked up about conditions in Washington City . . . which he said was total going to hell. He said it wasn't a thing in the world but Sodom and Gomorrah, which I guess it was. He got madder and madder about it and untied the ribbon around his neck.

He said the Catholics was behind every damn bit of it. He said they was practical in control of the whole thing, and was aiming to put Mr. Pope in the White House. Catholics, he said, was the rottenest, low-downest snakes that ever lived. He said they had fellers called priests that mated women called nuns, and the young'uns that come of the matin', they fed them to a pack of dogs. He said it was the awfulest thing he had ever seen nor heard tell of. Which it was.

He got to hollerin' pretty loud about it, and I guess, conditions being what they was in Washington City, it was enough to make a man holler. He said if it wasn't for him puttin' up a fight agin' them, that they would be in total control and spread plumb down to where we was at . . . which sounded pretty bad. 40

He said if they did, they would put all the womenfolks in convents and such . . . and would practical wipe out the young'uns. There didn't seem hardly any way atall to whip them unless everybody sent him to Washington City to see that it was done; and he said even then it would be a hard fight, because fellers was selling out to them all over the place, for money. He said he wouldn't take no money, as he had no use for it, and was total agin' it.

He said he felt like might near giving up sometimes and quittin' and just takin' it easy, like we done.

I felt right bad, takin' it easy; but when he finished talking, he got down from the box and commenced to laugh and shake hands with everybody. Which it looked like he had plenty of confidence he could handle the situation in Washington City.

I felt a little better about it, dependent on his gittin' back up there so he could whip the Catholics and such.

While he was shaking hands and talking to folks, a feller walked up to the fringe of the crowd leading a little brown calf on a rope. 45

He stood around watching the crowd and shook hands twicet with the politician, each time he come by. The little calf stood spraddle-legged behind him with its head down. I got up and edged over to the calf. I petted it oncet, but it wouldn't lift its head. The feller looked down at me from under a big hat. He had sharp eyes that crinkled nearly shut when he smiled. He smiled.

"Like my calf, boy?"

"Yes sir," I said, and stepped back from the calf, as I didn't want him to think I was bothering it.

"Go ahead," he said, real cheerful. "Go ahead and pet the calf. Ye won't hurt 'em." I petted the calf.

The feller spit tobacco juice over the calf's back. "I can see," he said, "that my calf takes to ye . . . more'n anybody he's ever taken up with . . . seems like he wants to go with ye." I couldn't tell that the calf looked the way he said, but it was his calf, and he ought to know. The feller knelt down in front of me, "Have you got any money, boy?" 50

"Yes, sir," I said, "I got fifty cents." The feller frowned, and I could see it wasn't much money and was sorry that it was all I had.

He smiled after a minute and said, "Well, this here calf is worth more'n a hundred times that much." I seen right off it worth that much. "Yes, sir," I said, "I wasn't figuring no way atall to buy it." The feller frowned again, "Well," he said, "I'm a Christian man. Somehow or 'nother, even costing me all that this here calf is worth, I feel in my heart ye'd ought to have it, the way it's taken up with ye." He thought on this for a while, and I could see right off that it pained him a lot to think of parting with the calf.

"I ain't—ner wouldn't take him atall, mister," I said.

But the feller held up his hand to stop me. He sighed, "I'm a'goin' to let ye have the calf, son, fer fifty cents fer I feel it's my Christian duty, and—no—I won't take no fer an answer. Jest give me yer fifty cents, and the calf is your'n."

Since he put it that-a-way, I couldn't hardly turn him down. I taken out all my nickels and dimes and give them to him. He passed the calf's rope to me, and walked off so quick, I didn't know which way he went. 55

But I felt mighty proud of my calf, even though I had more or less taken advantage of the feller—him being a Christian, which, as he said, handicapped him somewhat. I pulled my calf around to Granpa and showed it to him. Granpa didn't seem as proud of my calf as I was, but I reckined it was because it was mine, and not his. I told him he could have half of it, seeing as how we was practically partners in the whiskey-making trade. But Granpa just grunted.

The crowd was breaking up around the politician, everybody being more or less agreed that the politician had better git to Washington City right off and fight the Catholics. He passed out pieces of paper. Though he didn't give me one, I got one off the ground. It had his picture on it, showing him smiling like there wasn't a thing wrong in Washington City. He looked real young in the picture.

Granpa said we was ready to set out for home, so I put the politician's picture in my pocket, and led my calf behind Granpa. It was pretty hard going. My calf couldn't hardly walk. It stumbled and wobbled along, and I pulled on the rope best I could. I was afraid if I pulled too hard, my calf would fall down.

I was beginning to worry if I would ever get it to the cabin, and that maybe it was sick . . . even though it was worth a hundred times what I paid for it.

By the time I got to the top of the first ridge, Granpa was nearly at the bottom fixing to head across a hollow. I seen I would be left behind, so I yelled, "Granpa . . . do ye know any Catholics?" Granpa stopped. I pulled harder on my calf and commenced to catch up. Granpa waited until me and the calf come up to him. 60

"I seen one, oncet," Granpa said, "at the county seat." *Me* and the calf caught up, and was resting as hard we we could. "One I seen," Granpa said, "didn't look particular mean . . . though I figgered he had been in some kind of scrape . . . he had got his collar twisted up, and more than likely was jest drunk enough that he failed to notice it. He 'peared to be, howsoever, peaceful enough."

Granpa set down on a rock, and I seen he was going to give some thought to it, for which I was glad. My calf had his front legs spraddled in front of him and was pantin' pretty hard.

"Howsoever," Granpa said, "iff'n ye taken a knife and cut fer half a day into that politician's gizzard, ye'd have a hard time finding a kernel of truth. Ye'll notice the son of a bitch didn't say a thing about gittin' the whiskey tax taken off . . . 'er the price of corn . . . 'er nothin' else fer that matter." Which was right.

I told Granpa that I had noticed the son of a bitch never said a word about it.

Granpa reminded me that "son of a bitch" was a new cuss word, and was not to be used no way atall around Granma. Granpa said he didn't give a lick damn if priests and nuns mated every day in the week, no more'n he cared how many bucks and does mated. He said that was their matin' business. 65

Granpa said that as far as them feedin' young'uns to dogs, that there would never come a day when a doe would feed her young to a dog, ner a woman, so he knowed that was a lie. Which is right.

I commenced to feel some better about the Catholics. Granpa said that wasn't no doubt in his mind that the Catholics would like to git control . . . but he said, iff'n ye had a hog and ye didn't want it stole, jest git ten or twelve men to guard it, each one of which wanted to steal it. He said that hog would be safe as in yer own kitchen. Granpa said they was all so crooked in Washington City, that they had to watch one another all the time.

Granpa said that they was so many trying to git control, it was a continual dogfight all the time anyhow. He said the worst thing wrong with Washington City was it had so many damn politicians in it.

Granpa said, that even being that we went to a hard-shell Baptist church, he would sure hate to see the hard-shells git control. He said they was total agin' liquor drinking except maybe some fer theirselves. He said they would dry the whole country up.

I seen right off there was other dangers besides the Catholics. If the hard-shells got control, me and Granpa would be put out of the whiskey-making trade, and would likely starve to death. 70

I asked Granpa if it wasn't likely that the big shots, which made barrel sniffin' whiskey, wasn't trying to git control too; us putting a dent in their trade and all, so they could put us out of business. Granpa said that without a doubt they was trying hard as they could, bribing politicians practical every day in Washington City.

Granpa said they was only one thing certain. The Indian was not never going to git control. Which appeared not likely.

While Granpa was talking my calf laid down and died. He just laid over on his side and there he was. I was standing in front of Granpa holding onto the rope, and Granpa pointed behind me and said, "Yer calf is dead." He never owned to half of it being his.

I got down on my knees and tried to prop its head up and get it on its feet, but it was limp. Granpa shook his head, "It's dead, Little Tree. When something is dead . . . it's dead." Which it was. I squatted by my calf and looked at it. It was might near close to being as bad a time as I could remember. My fifty cents was gone, and the red and green box of candy. And now my calf—being worth a hundred times what I paid for it.

Granpa pulled his long knife from his moccasin boot and cut the calf open and pulled out its liver. He pointed at the liver. "It's speckled and diseased. We can't eat it." 75

It looked to me like there wasn't anything atall that could be done with it. I didn't cry—but I might near did. Granpa knelt and skinned the calf. "Reckin Granma would give ye a dime fer the skin; likely she can use it," he said. "And we'll send the dogs back . . . they can eat the calf." Reckin that was all that could be made of it. I followed Granpa down the trail—carrying the hide of my calf—all the way to the cabin.

Granma didn't ask me, but I told her I couldn't put my fifty cents back in the jar, for I had spent it for a calf—which I didn't have. Granma give me a dime for the hide and I put that in the jar.

It was hard to eat that night, though I liked ground peas and corn bread.

While we was eating, Granpa looked at me and said, "Ye see, Little Tree, ain't no way of learning, except by letting ye do. Iff'n I had stopped ye from buying the calf, ye'd have always thought ye'd ought to had it. Iff'n I'd told ye to buy it, ye'd blame me fer the calf dying. Ye'll have to learn as ye go."

"Yes, sir," I said. 80

"Now," Granpa said, "what did ye learn?"

"Well," I said, "I reckin I learned not to trade with Christians."

Granma commenced to laugh. I didn't see hardly anything funny atall about it. Granpa looked dumbstruck; then he laughed so hard he choked on his corn bread. I figgered I had learned something funny but I didn't know what it was.

Granma said, "What ye mean, Little Tree, is that ye'll be likely to have caution at the next feller who tells you how good and what a fine feller he is."

"Yes, ma'am," I said, "I reckin." 85

I wasn't sure about anything . . . except I had lost my fifty cents. Being plumb wore out, I went to sleep at the table and my head come down in my supper plate. Granma had to wash ground peas off my face.

That night I dreamed the hard-shells and Catholics come amongst us. The hard-shells tore up our still, and the Catholics et up my calf.

A big Christian was there, smiling at the whole thing. He had a red and green box of candy and said it was worth a hundred times as much, but I could have it for fifty cents. Which I didn't have—fifty cents; and so could not buy it.

DISCUSSING THE TEXT

1. In this selection, Little Tree comes across as an innocent, first accepting the politician's bigoted speech and later believing the con man who sells him the sick calf. What is the lesson that his grandfather teaches him as they discuss these two incidents? Do you think Little Tree has learned anything?
2. Read carefully Little Tree's description of the politician's clothes, manner, and words. What kind of impression does he make on Little Tree? How do

the boy's perceptions change after his grandfather shares with him his impressions of the politician?

3. Why is the selection called "Trading with a Christian"? What kinds of impersonations are conducted by characters who appear in this selection? What are their motivations?

WRITING ABOUT THE TEXT

4. Knowing what you know about Asa Carter, how do you react to Forrest Carter's portrayal of Little Tree in this selection? Can you reconcile Asa Carter with Forrest Carter on the basis of this portrayal? Write a personal response addressing these questions.
5. Consider Granpa's speech about words, beginning with the line, " 'That's how the damn fool word-using gits folks all twisted up' " (par. 20). Write a brief essay explaining how you think Granpa's ideas about words might be applied to the life of Asa/Forrest Carter.
6. Write a letter from Asa Carter to his publisher. In this letter, explain what you think Carter's motivations might have been for assuming a false identity and writing this so-called autobiography.
7. Both Daniel L. James (Danny Santiago) and Asa Earl (Forrest) Carter assumed pseudonyms and published books about characters whose ethnic backgrounds were different from their own. Can you see similarities in these writers' projects? What are the most significant differences between the two? Write a two- to three-page essay comparing and contrasting these two acts of cultural impersonation.

HENRY LOUIS GATES, JR.

"Authenticity," or the Lesson of Little Tree

In this essay, first published in the New York Times Book Review *in 1991, Henry Louis Gates, Jr., questions the notion of "authenticity" in literature. He cites various examples of the writer as "cultural impersonator," from authors of pseudoslave narratives in the nineteenth century to a number of more recent cases. Gates addresses actual instances of literary impersonation, such as the cases of "Forrest Carter" and "Danny Santiago" (whose works are excerpted in this chapter), but he also discusses writers who sometimes create characters and situations that fall outside their own ethnic and cultural milieu (such as John Updike and Philip Roth in some of their works).*

Gates suggests that "a book is a cultural event," and that the historical, social, and cultural contexts that influence its production are relevant to its reception. In that sense, he tells us, "authorial identity, mystified or not, can be part of that event." However, Gates does not believe that writers own ethnic turf; he argues for the "authenticity" of the text in its representation of reality, but not for the "authenticity" of the author.

A prolific writer and a major figure in African American literary criticism, Gates was born in West Virginia in 1950. Before beginning a distinguished career in academia, he worked as a correspondent and as a public relations representative. Gates has won numerous awards, including a MacArthur Foundation fellowship, and has written extensively and engagingly on African American literature and literary theory. He is the author of many articles on cultural issues as well as a number of scholarly books, including Figures in Black: Words, Signs, and the Racial Self *(1987) and* The Signifying Monkey: A Theory of African-American Literary Criticism *(1988). In 1994 he published a book of memoirs titled* Colored People.

It's a perennial question: Can you really tell? The great black jazz trumpeter Roy Eldridge once made a wager with the critic Leonard Feather that he could distinguish white musicians from black ones—blindfolded. Mr. Feather duly dropped the needle onto a variety of record albums whose titles and soloists were concealed from the trumpeter. More than half the time, Eldridge guessed wrong.

Mr. Feather's blindfold test is one that literary critics would do well to ponder, for the belief that we can "read" a person's racial or ethnic identity from his or her writing runs surprisingly deep. There is an assumption that we could fill a room with the world's great literature, train a Martian to analyze these books, and then expect that Martian to categorize each by the citizenship or ethnicity or gender of its author. "Passing" and "impersonation" may sound like quaint terms of a bygone era, but they continue to inform the way we read. Our literary judgments, in short, remain hostage to the ideology of authenticity.

And while black Americans have long boasted of their ability to spot "one of our own," no matter how fair the skin, straight the hair or aquiline the nose—and while the 19th-century legal system in this country went to absurd lengths to demarcate even octoroons and demi-octoroons[1] from their white sisters and brothers—authentic racial and ethnic differences have always been difficult to define. It's not just a black thing, either.

The very idea of a literary tradition is itself bound up in suppositions—that date back at least to an 18th-century theorist of nationalism, Johann Gottfried Herder—that ethnic or national identity finds unique expression in literary forms. Such assumptions hold sway even after we think we have discarded them. After the much-ballyhooed "death of the author"[2] pro-

[1]*octoroons and demi-octoroons:* persons with one-eighth and one-sixteenth African ancestry (*Ed.*)

[2]*death of the author:* term originated with critic Roland Barthes's essay "The Death of the Author" (1977), influential in literary theory throughout the 1980s, in which Barthes argues for readers to challenge the authority of the writer over the text's meaning and organization. Instead, he proposed a process of reading that confronts and works with (or against) the text's "codes." (*Ed.*)

nounced by two decades of literary theory, the author is very much back in the saddle. As the literary historian John Guillory observes, today's "battle of the books" is really not so much about books as it is about authors, authors who can be categorized according to race, gender, ethnicity and so on, standing in as delegates of a social constituency.

And the assumption that the works they create transparently convey the authentic, unmediated experience of their social identities—though officially renounced—has crept quietly in through the back door. Like any dispensation, it raises some works and buries others. Thus Zora Neale Hurston's "Their Eyes Were Watching God" has prospered, while her "Seraph on the Suwanee," a novel whose main characters are white, remains in limbo. "Our Nig," recently identified as the work of a black woman, almost immediately went from obscurity to required reading in black and women's literature courses. 5

The recent case of Forrest Carter, the author of the best-selling "Education of Little Tree," provided yet another occasion to reflect on the troublesome role of authenticity. Billed as a true story, Carter's book was written as the autobiography of Little Tree, orphaned at the age of 10, who learns the ways of Indians from his Cherokee grandparents in Tennessee. "The Education of Little Tree," which has sold more than 600,000 copies, received an award from the American Booksellers Association as the title booksellers most enjoyed selling. It was sold on the gift tables of Indian reservations and assigned as supplementary reading for courses on Native American literature. Major studios vied for movie rights.

And the critics loved it. Booklist praised its "natural approach to life." A reviewer for The Chattanooga Times pronounced it "deeply felt." One poet and storyteller of Abnaki[3] descent hailed it as a masterpiece—"one of the finest American autobiographies ever written"—that captured the unique vision of Native American culture. It was, he wrote blissfully, "like a Cherokee basket, woven out of the materials given by nature, simple and strong in its design, capable of carrying a great deal." A critic in The (Sante Fe) New Mexican told his readers: "I have come on something that is good, so good I want to shout 'Read this! It's beautiful. It's real.'"

Or was it?

To the embarrassment of the book's admirers, Dan T. Carter, a history professor at Emory University, unmasked "Forrest Carter" as a pseudonym for the late Asa Earl Carter, whom he described as "a Ku Klux Klan terrorist, right-wing radio announcer, home-grown American fascist and anti-Semite, rabble-rousing demagogue and secret author of the famous 1963 speech by Gov. George Wallace of Alabama: 'Segregation now . . . Segregation tomorrow . . . Segregation forever.' " Forget Pee-wee Herman[4] —try explaining this one to the kids.

---

[3]*Abnaki:* Native Americans of Algonquin stock (*Ed.*)

[4]*Pee-Wee Herman:* actor Paul Reuben's character and alter ego, star of the children's television program *Pee-Wee's Playhouse;* at the time Gates writes, Reuben had recently been arrested for indecent exposure at a movie theater. (*Ed.*)

What happens now? Will the Abnaki critic demote Little Tree's memoirs from the status of major autobiography to that of mediocre novel? Somehow, one imagines that Asa Earl Carter would have thoroughly enjoyed our critical chagrin. What is doubtful, though, is that the experience will prompt these critics to reflect on the importance that the imputation of realness has for them. 10

This is only the latest embarrassment to beset the literary ideologues of authenticity, and its political stakes are relatively trivial. It was not always such. The authorship of slave narratives published between 1760 and 1865 was also fraught with controversy. To give credence to their claims about the horrors of slavery, American abolitionists urgently needed a cadre of ex-slaves who could compellingly indict their masters with first-person accounts of their bondage. For this tactic to succeed, the ex-slaves had to be authentic, their narratives full of convincing, painstaking verisimilitude.

So popular did these become, however, that two forms of imitators soon arose: white writers, adopting a first-person black narrative persona, gave birth to the pseudoslave narrative; and black authors, some of whom had never even seen the South, a plantation or a whipping post, became literary lions virtually overnight.

Generic confusion was rife in those days. The 1836 slave narrative of Archy Moore turned out to have been a novel written by a white historian, Richard Hildreth; and the gripping "Autobiography of a Female Slave" (1857) was also a novel, written by a white woman, Mattie Griffith. Perhaps the most embarrassing of these publishing events, however, involved one James Williams, an American slave—the subtitle of his narrative asserts—"who was for several years a driver on a cotton plantation in Alabama." Having escaped to the North (or so he claimed), Williams sought out members of the Anti-Slavery Society, and told a remarkably well-structured story about the brutal treatment of the slaves in the South and of his own miraculous escape, using the literacy he had secretly acquired to forge the necessary documents.

So compelling, so gripping, so *useful* was his tale that the abolitionists decided to publish it immediately. Williams arrived in New York on New Year's Day, 1838. By Jan. 24, he had dictated his complete narrative to John Greenleaf Whittier.[5] By Feb. 15 it was in print, and was also being serialized in the abolitionist newspaper The Anti-Slavery Examiner. Even before Williams's book was published, rumors spread in New York that slave catchers were on his heels, and so his new friends shipped him off to Liverpool—where, it seems, he was never heard from again. Once the book was published, the abolitionists distributed it widely, sending copies to every state and to every Congressman.

Alas, Williams's stirring narrative was not authentic at all, as outraged Southern slaveholders were quick to charge and as his abolitionist friends 15

---

[5]*John Greenleaf Whittier* (1807–1892): well-known American poet and editor, interested in issues of social reform (*Ed.*)

reluctantly had to concede. It was a work of fiction, the production, one commentator put it, "purely of the Negro imagination"—as, no doubt, were the slave catchers who were in hot pursuit, and whose purported existence earned Williams a free trip to England and a new life.

Ersatz slave narratives had an even rougher time of it a century later, and one has to wonder how William Styron's "Confessions of Nat Turner"—a novel that aroused the strenuous ire of much of the black intelligentsia when it was published in 1967—might have been received had it been published by James Baldwin. Hands off our history, we roared at Mr. Styron, the white Southern interloper, as we shopped around our list of literary demands. It was the real thing we wanted, and we wouldn't be taken in by imitators.

The real black writer, accordingly, could claim the full authority of experience denied Mr. Styron. Indeed, the late 1960's and early 70's were a time in which the notion of ethnic literature began to be consolidated and, in some measure, institutionalized. That meant policing the boundaries, telling true from false. But it was hard to play this game without a cheat sheet. When Dan McCall published "The Man Says Yes" in 1969, a novel about a young black teacher who comes up against the eccentric president of a black college, many critics assumed the author was black, too. The reviewer for The Amsterdam News, for example, referred to him throughout as "Brother McCall." Similar assumptions were occasionally made about Shane Stevens when he published the gritty *Bildungsroman*[6] "Way Uptown in Another World" in 1971, which detailed the brutal misadventures of its hero from Harlem, Marcus Garvey Black. In this case, the new voice from the ghetto belonged to a white graduate student at Columbia.

But the ethnic claim to its own experience cut two ways. For if many of their readers imagined a black face behind the prose, many avid readers of Frank Yerby's historical romances or Samuel R. Delany's science fiction novels are taken aback when they learn that these authors are black. And James Baldwin's "Giovanni's Room," arguably his most accomplished novel, is seldom taught in black literature courses because its characters are white *and* gay.

Cultural commentators have talked about the "cult of ethnicity" in postwar America. You could dismiss it as a version of what Freud called "the narcissism of small differences." But you could also see it as a salutary reaction to a regional Anglo-American culture that had declared itself as universal. For too long, "race" was something that blacks had; "ethnicity" was what "ethnics" had. In midcentury America, Norman Podhoretz reflected in "Making It," his literary memoirs, "to write fiction out of the experience of big-city immigrant Jewish life was to feel oneself, and to be felt by others, to be writing exotica at best; nor did there exist a respectably certified narrative style in English which was anything but facsimile WASP. Writing was hard enough,

[6]*Bildungsroman:* (German) "novel of education" in which the protagonist passes from childhood into maturity through varied and often traumatic experiences (*Ed.*)

but to have to write with *only* that part of one's being which had been formed by the acculturation-minded public schools and by the blindly ethnicizing English departments of the colleges was like being asked to compete in a race with a leg cut off at the thigh."

All this changed with the novelistic triumphs of Saul Bellow and Philip Roth—and yet a correlative disability was entered in the ledger, too. In the same year that Mr. Styron published "The Confessions of Nat Turner," Philip Roth published "When She Was Good," a novel set in the rural heartland of gentile middle America and infused with the chilly humorlessness of its small-town inhabitants. This was, to say the least, a departure. Would critics who admired Mr. Roth as the author of "Good-bye, Columbus"[7] accept him as a chronicler of the Protestant Corn Belt? 20

Richard Gilman, in The New Republic, compared Mr. Roth to a "naturalist on safari to a region unfamiliar to him" he declared himself unable to "account for the novel's existence, so lacking is it in any true literary interest." Maureen Howard, in Partisan Review, said she felt "the presence of a persona rather than a personal voice." To Jonathan Baumbach, writing in Commonweal, the book suggested "Zero Mostel doing an extended imitation of Jimmy Stewart."[8] "He captures the rhythms of his characters' speech," Mr. Baumbach says of Mr. Roth, "but not, I feel, what makes them human." If the book was written partly in defiance of the strictures of ethnic literature, those very strictures were undoubtedly what made the book anathema to so many reviewers.

And what if "When She Was Good" had been published under the name Philip McGrath? Would the same reviewers still have denounced it as an artistic imposture? Does anyone imagine that Zero Mostel would have come to mind? Yet there is a twist in the tale. Even a counterfeit can be praised for its craft. For some, the novel's worth was enhanced precisely because of its "inauthenticity"—because it was seen as an act of imagination unassisted by memory.

Under any name, Kazuo Ishiguro's "Remains of the Day"—a novel narrated by an aging and veddy English butler—would be a tour de force; but wasn't the acclaim that greeted it heightened by a kind of critical double take at the youthful Japanese face on the dust jacket? To take another recent example, no one is surprised that admirers of Norman Rush's recent novel "Mating" would commend the author on the voice of its female narrator. Subtract from the reality column, add to the art column. Thus Doris Grumbach, who commended Mr. Roth's novel for its careful observation, concludes her own review with an assessment of technique: "To bring off this verisimilitude is,

---

[7]*Goodbye, Columbus* (1959): novella by Jewish American writer Philip Roth (b. 1933), centered almost exclusively on Jewish American characters (*Ed.*)

[8]*Zero Mostel . . . Jimmy Stewart:* Zero Mostel (1915–1977) was a Jewish American comedian whose work capitalized on his Jewish persona; actor Jimmy Stewart (b. 1908) symbolizes a "typical" American. (Ed.)

to my mind, an enormous accomplishment." Would she have been so impressed with the virtuosity of a Philip McGrath?

Sometimes, however, a writer's identity is in fact integral to a work's artifice. Such is the case with John Updike's "Bech: A Book," the first of two collections of short stories featuring Mr. Updike's Jewish novelist, Henry Bech. The 1970 book opens with a letter from the protagonist, Henry, to his creator, John, fussing about the literary components from which he was apparently jury-rigged. At first blush (Bech muses), he sounds like "some gentlemanly Norman Mailer; then that London glimpse of *silver* hair glints more of gallant, glamorous Bellow. . . . My childhood seems out of Alex Portnoy and my ancestral past out of I. B. Singer. I get a whiff of Malamud in your city breezes, and am I paranoid to feel my 'block' an ignoble version of the more or less noble renunciations of H. Roth, D. Fuchs and J. Salinger?[9] Withal, something Waspish, theological, scared and insulatingly ironical that derives, my wild surmise is, from you."

What is clear is that part of the point of John Updike's Bech is that he is *John Updike's* Bech: an act Cynthia Ozick has described as "cultural impersonation." The contrast between Bech and Updike, then, far from being irrelevant, is itself staged within the fictional edifice. You could publish "Bech" under a pseudonym, but, I maintain, it would be a different book. 25

Conversely—but for similar reasons—one might argue that exposing the true author of "Famous All Over Town," a colorful picaresque novel set in a Los Angeles barrio, was a form of violence against the book itself. Published in 1983 under the nom de plume Danny Santiago, the book was hailed by Latino critics for its vibrancy and authenticity, and received the Richard and Hinda Rosenthal Foundation Award from the American Academy of Arts and Letters for an outstanding work of fiction. But Santiago, assumed to be a young Chicano talent, turned out to be Daniel L. James, a septuagenarian WASP educated at Andover and Yale, a playwright, screenwriter and, in his later years, a social worker. And yet Danny Santiago was much more than a literary conceit to his creator, who had for 20 years lost faith in his own ability to write; Danny was the only voice available to him. Judging from the testimony of his confidant, John Gregory Dunne,[10] Mr. James may well have felt that the attribution was the only just one; that "Famous All Over Town" belonged to Danny Santiago before it quite belonged to Daniel James.

---

[9]*Norman Mailer, Saul Bellow, Bernard Malamud, Henry Roth, Daniel Fuchs, J. D. Salinger:* contemporary Jewish American writers whose fiction exemplifies their ethnicity and their intellectual preoccupations; *Alex Portnoy:* the Jewish American protagonist of Philip Roth's novel, *Portnoy's Complaint* (1969); *I. B. Singer:* Isaac Bashevis Singer (1904–1991), Polish-born Jewish writer who emigrated to the United States in 1935 but continued to write in Yiddish; his novels and *Collected Stories* (1982) focus on the cultural and religious traditions of Polish Jews. Singer won the Nobel Prize for literature in 1978. (*Ed.*)

[10]*John Gregory Dunne:* contemporary American journalist and writer, whose article on Daniel James, "The Secret of Danny Santiago," appeared in the *New York Review of Books,* August 16, 1984 (*Ed.*)

Death-of-the-author types cannot come to grips with the fact that a book is a cultural event; authorial identity, mystified or not, can be part of that event. What the ideologues of authenticity cannot quite come to grips with is that fact and fiction have always exerted a reciprocal effect on each other. However truthful you set out to be, your autobiography is never unmediated by literary structures of expression. Many authentic slave narratives were influenced by Harriet Beecher Stowe; on the other hand, authentic slave narratives were among Stowe's primary sources for her own imaginative work, "Uncle Tom's Cabin." By the same token, to recognize the slave narrative as a genre is to recognize that, for example, Frederick Douglass's mode of expression was informed by the conventions of antecedent narratives, some of which were (like James Williams's) whole-cloth inventions.

So it is not just a matter of the outsider boning up while the genuine article just writes what he or she knows. If Shane Stevens was deeply influenced by Richard Wright, so too were black protest novelists like John O. Killens and John A. Williams. And if John Updike can manipulate the tonalities of writers like Saul Bellow, Bernard Malamud and Philip Roth, must we assume that a Bruce Jay Friedman,[11] say, is wholly unaffected by such models?

The distasteful truth will out: like it or not, all writers are "cultural impersonators."

30 Even real people, moreover, are never quite real. My own favorite (fictional) commentary on the incursion of fiction upon so-called real life is provided by Nabokov's Humbert Humbert[12] as he reflects upon the bothersome task of swapping life stories with a new and unwanted wife. Her confessions were marked by "sincerity and artlessness," his were "glib compositions"; and yet, he muses, "technically the two sets were congeneric since both were affected by the same stuff (soap operas, psychoanalysis, and cheap novelettes) upon which I drew for my characters and she for her mode of expression."

Start interrogating the notion of cultural authenticity and our most trusted critical categories come into question. Maybe Danny Santiago's "Famous All Over Town" can usefully be considered a work of Chicano literature; maybe Shane Stevens' "Way Uptown in Another World" can usefully be considered within the genre of black protest novels. In his own version of the blindfold test, the mathematician Alan Turing famously proposed that we credit a computer with intelligence if we can conduct a dialogue with it and not know whether a person or machine has been composing the responses. Should we allow ethnic literatures a similar procedure for claiming this title?

At this point, it is important to go slow. Consider the interviewer's chestnut: are you a woman writer or a writer who happens to be a woman? A black writer or a writer who happens to be a black? Alas, these are deadly disjunc-

---

[11]*Bruce Jay Friedman* (b. 1930): Jewish American fiction writer; author of *Stern* (1962) *(Ed.)*

[12]*Humbert Humbert:* main character and narrator of the novel *Lolita* (1958), by Russian American writer Vladimir Nabokov (1899–1977) *(Ed.)*

tions. After struggling to gain the recognition that a woman or a black (or, exemplarily, a black woman) writer is, in the first instance, a writer, many authors yet find themselves uneasy with the supposedly universalizing description. How can ethnic or sexual identity be reduced to a mere contingency when it is so profoundly a part of who a writer is?

And yet if, for example, black critics claim special authority as interpreters of black literature, and black writers claim special authority as interpreters of black reality, are we not obliged to cede an equivalent dollop of authority to our white counterparts?

We easily become entrapped by what the feminist critic Nancy K. Miller has called "as-a" criticism: where we always speak "as a" white middle-class woman, a person of color, a gay man and so on. And that, too, is a confinement—in the republic of letters as in the larger polity. "Segregation today . . . Segregation tomorrow . . . Segregation forever"; that line, which Asa Earl Carter wrote for George Wallace's inauguration speech as Governor, may still prove his true passport to immortality. And yet segregation—as Carter himself would demonstrate—is as difficult to maintain in the literary realm as it is in the civic one.

The lesson of the literary blindfold test is not that our social identities don't matter. They do matter. And our histories, individual and collective, do affect what we wish to write and what we are able to write. But that relation is never one of fixed determinism. No human culture is inaccessible to someone who makes the effort to understand, to learn, to inhabit another world. 35

Yes, Virginia, there *is* a Danny Santiago. And—if you like that sort of thing—there is a Little Tree, too, just as treacly now as he ever was. And as long as there are writers who combine some measure of imagination and curiosity, there will continue to be such interlopers of the literary imagination. What, then, of the vexed concept of authenticity? To borrow from Samuel Goldwyn's[13] theory of sincerity, authenticity remains essential: once you can fake that, you've got it made.

DISCUSSING THE TEXT

1. In his discussion of Philip Roth's *When She Was Good,* Gates observes, "Even a counterfeit can be praised for its craft. For some, the novel's worth was enhanced precisely because of its 'inauthenticity'—because it was seen as an act of imagination unassisted by memory" (par. 22). Could you apply this judgment to Carter's *Education of Little Tree?* To Santiago's *Famous All Over Town?* Do you agree that "an act of imagination unassisted by memory" is worthy of special praise?

[13]*Samuel Goldwyn* (1882–1974): legendary film producer and studio magnate influential in the creation of the Hollywood film industry (*Ed.*)

2. What is " 'as-a' criticism," which Gates mentions and attributes to feminist critic Nancy K. Miller (par. 34)? Why does he follow his discussion of this kind of criticism with a reference to the "Segregation forever" speech that Asa Earl Carter wrote for George Wallace?
3. The essay's conclusion suggests that although identity, culture, and history do matter in literature, they are not fixed, determined categories. Gates argues that "No human culture is inaccessible to someone who makes the effort to understand, to learn, to inhabit another world" (par. 35). Working with a group of four or five students, discuss this idea in relation to *The Education of Little Tree, Famous All Over Town,* and other works that Gates discusses in his essay. Do you think all these writers have made "the effort to understand, to learn, to inhabit another world"? How can you know? Be prepared to share your thoughts on these questions with the rest of the class.

WRITING ABOUT THE TEXT

4. Do you think Gates believes there is such a thing as authenticity? How do you think he would define it? Write a one-paragraph definition of the term, drawing only on the ideas presented in this essay.
5. Gates declares that "like it or not, all writers are 'cultural impersonators' " (par. 29). What do you think he means by this statement? Do you agree or disagree? Write a brief essay expressing your views.
6. Find a contemporary example of cultural impersonation in popular culture (for example, a television show depicting men in drag, a film in which white actors portray Latino characters, white rap artists). Write a brief essay discussing this so-called act of impersonation in terms of Gates's arguments.
7. Do some additional research into one of the literary works (other than Santiago's *Famous All Over Town* or Carter's *Little Tree)* that Gates discusses in this essay. If possible, read at least a portion of the actual work. Write a brief essay providing additional information on the author, the plot, characters, and style of the work, and so on. Conclude by discussing whether or not you would call this work authentic.

MAKING CONNECTIONS

1. In this chapter, the theme of cultural and ethnic crossover and assimilation has been developed with a twist by authors who have impersonated a racial, ethnic, or gender "other" in their works. Choose two selections from the chapter and discuss how effective (or ineffective) the authors have been in creating these cross-cultural impersonations.
2. In Judy Grahn's "Boys at the Rodeo," the act of crossing the gender line becomes a metaphor for achieving freedom and power. Choose one other selection from this chapter in which, in your opinion, a cultural impersonation becomes a means of achieving freedom or power. Write a brief essay that compares and contrasts how the achievement of freedom or power is effected in the two selections through cross-cultural impersonation.
3. Make a list of the cultural stereotypes about African Americans that the narrators encounter in James Weldon Johnson's selection from *The Autobiography of an Ex-Colored Man* and in the selection from *Black like Me* by John Howard Griffin. Then write two paragraphs that address the following questions: What does the experience of "passing" teach the narrators about stereotypes? What have you learned from these selections?
4. Both Forrest Carter in "Trading with a Christian" and Danny Santiago in "Famous All Over Town" have impersonated people from other cultures in order to write fictional autobiographical works. Write a brief essay that discusses the following questions: Are these writers justified in conducting such impersonations? Why or why not? How does the fact that their motivations were, perhaps, quite different play a role in your respective assessments? How does knowing what you know about the authors influence your reading of their texts?
5. Both E. E. Cummings and Allen Ginsberg attempt to portray the lunacy of mainstream American thinking by impersonating the voices of the targets of their satire. Do you think they are successful in ridiculing mainstream American culture? Write an evaluative essay in which you compare the two poems in terms of their success as satires of American society and thinking.
6. James Weldon Johnson's *Autobiography of an Ex-Colored Man* is about cultural and racial impersonation. But it is also, in a way, about literary impersonation, for Johnson published his novel anonymously, and virtually all readers took it for a nonfiction autobiography. Taking into account the ideas on authenticity expressed by Henry Louis Gates, Jr., write an essay that discusses issues of racial, cultural, and literary impersonation in the chapter from Johnson's *Autobiography* included here.
7. Write a brief description of the photograph by Diane Arbus at the beginning of this chapter (p. 378). Then write your personal reaction to this image in light of the themes and issues of cross-cultural impersonation that you have encountered in this chapter.
8. Go back to the photograph of Guillermo Gómez-Peña's impersonation of Amerindians in Chapter 1 (p. 25). Then look again at the Arbus photograph in this chapter. In a group of four or five classmates, discuss the following questions: How are the images similar? How are they different? What is the role of the artist in each one? What does each photograph

suggest about cultural stereotypes? What does it suggest about ethnic or cultural impersonations?

9. In the voice of someone who is different from you in gender, race, ethnicity, or class, write a brief essay on a contemporary, controversial issue. (Some possibilities are: gays in the military, immigration policies, affirmative action, English-only laws, the politics of abortion, or interracial adoptions.) After you've finished your essay, write a brief paragraph explaining how writing in the voice of an "other" has affected your thinking on this particular issue.

FURTHER READING

E. E. CUMMINGS

Cummings, E. E. *Complete Poems.* New York: Liveright, 1994.

Kennedy, Richard S. *Dreams in the Mirror: A Biography of E. E. Cummings.* New York: Liveright, 1979.

ALLEN GINSBERG

Ginsberg, Allen. *Collected Poems, 1947–1980.* New York: Harper and Row, 1984.

Miles, Barry. *Ginsberg: A Biography.* New York: Viking Press, 1990.

JAMES WELDON JOHNSON

Chesnutt, Charles. *The Marrow of Tradition.* New York: Penguin Books, 1993.

Harper, Frances. *Iola Leroy.* (1892). Reprint, New York: Oxford University Press, 1988.

Johnson, James Weldon. *Along This Way: The Autobiography of James Weldon Johnson.* New York: DaCapo, 1973.

JOHN HOWARD GRIFFIN

Daniel, Brad, ed. *The John Howard Griffin Reader.* Boston: Houghton Mifflin, 1968.

JUDY GRAHN

Garber, Marjorie. *Vested Interests: Cross Dressing and Cultural Anxiety.* New York: Harper Perennial, 1993.

Grahn, Judy. *Another Mother Tongue: Gay Words, Gay Worlds.* Boston: Beacon Press, 1984.

DANNY SANTIAGO

Dunne, John Gregory. "The Secret of Danny Santiago." *New York Review of Books,* August 16, 1984.

Urrea, Luis Alberto. *Across the Wire: Life and Hard Times on the Mexican Border.* New York: Doubleday, 1993.

FORREST CARTER

Rubin, Dana. "The Real Education of Little Tree." *Texas Monthly,* February 1992, 79–96.

Swann, Brian, ed. *Coming to Light: Contemporary Translations of the Native Literatures of North America.* New York: Random House, 1994.

Trafzer, Clifford E. *Earth Song, Sky Spirit: Short Stories of the Contemporary Native American Experience.* New York: Doubleday, 1992.

HENRY LOUIS GATES, JR.

Gates, Henry Louis, Jr. *Colored People: A Memoir.* Vintage, 1994.

———. *The Signifying Monkey: A Theory of African-American Literary Criticism.* New York: Oxford University Press, 1988.

Spike Lee Directs ''Public Enemy'' *(photograph by Stephen Allen), 1989. Lee, the most widely known African American film director of the last decade, here directs the popular rap group Public Enemy in a music video for ''Fight the Power.'' (The song was featured in the sound track of Lee's film* Do the Right Thing.) *Lee, in white T-shirt, directs Flavor Flav (white sunglasses) and Chuck D (baseball cap) in the same Bedford-Stuyvesant section of Brooklyn where* Do the Right Thing *takes place. The video is of a staged public demonstration, with mock-political signs and posters. Under the ''P'' of ''Philadelphia'' is the Public Enemy logo, a rifle site with a black man at the center.*

(S. Allen/Liaison)

7

Representing Ethnicity

[T]he friendship of an Indian is easily acquired, provided it is sought in good faith. . . . I hope I may be permitted to expatiate a little on this subject; perhaps it may be beneficial to some white persons hereafter.

- JOHN HECKEWELDER
Friend and Foe

He saw photography as a powerful force for the shaping of consciousness, relying on the viewer's belief in the reality of the subject while providing his own interpretation.

- FROM THE EDITORS' INTRODUCTION TO LEWIS HINE
Picturing the Immigrant

As advertisers targeted their products towards a mass audience, the need arose to create an "average person."

- AMY RASHAP
The American Dream for Sale: Ethnic Images in Magazines

The only African American represented in the historic first issue of *Life* appeared in a full page ad for the Young and Rubicam advertising agency. The ad was dominated by a photograph of a black man receiving a punch to the face.

- BILL GASKINS
The World According to Life: *Racial Stereotyping and American Identity*

[M]any—including young Black males who have also bought into this myth—have come to see the sports arena as having provided Blacks with at least one four-lane highway to success. This view is not only simplistic, it is quite flawed.

- Earl Smith
The Genetically Superior Athlete: Myth or Reality

[W]ho among female Latin writers has the most impact today? Clearly, Gloria Estefan.

- Enrique Fernández
Spitfires, Latin Lovers, Mambo Kings

While all Blacks suffer discrimination in America, the darker one's skin the more one's humanity is ignored.

- Itabari Njeri
Sushi and Grits: Ethnic Identity and Conflict in a Newly Multicultural America

What signs in outward appearance make visible the differences between people from different social or cultural backgrounds? And how do these visible markers get turned into caricatures and exaggerated stereotypes? How can a person manage to create an individual identity in the face of these stereotypes, so pervasive in our popular culture? These questions frame this chapter, and they can be applied to the entire American experience—all two hundred–plus years of it.

The first groups to experience the stigma of misrepresentation and cultural stereotyping were the Native Americans, who—with their feathers and furs and painted skins—were often viewed by the Europeans as primitive savages and cruel barbarians, as heathens who lacked the saving grace of Christianity. Such a view allowed white settlers to rationalize the use of violence and the removal of Native Americans to territories outside the sphere of white interest, and also contributed to the strenuous effort to convert these so-called heathens to Christianity. Among those who tried to convert the Indians was John Heckewelder, a Moravian missionary who came to understand and appreciate the Indian character. In 1819 Heckewelder wrote an account of his experiences, titled *Account of the History, Manners, and Customs of the Indian Nations,* that sought to revise white stereotypes of Indians. Heckewelder's dialogue between an Indian and a captured white man is a fascinating document that illuminates the moral complexity of the Indian's position relative to the white man.

By the time Heckewelder wrote his account, the largely Anglo-American population in the original thirteen colonies had established itself on a secure political footing. From this population emerged the managers of a growing capitalistic economy of factories and railroads, canals, bridges, and buildings—managers who welcomed the immigrant laborer whose wage demands were low. By mid-century, these alien workers were greeted with some suspicion, especially by the country's working class, which was seeking to defend its own economic status. Between 1890 and 1914, when a total of twenty million foreigners entered the United States, feelings of animosity toward recent immigrants grew even stronger (see the contrasting poems by Emma Lazarus and Thomas Bailey Aldrich, written near the start of this massive migration, in Chapter 1, pp. 26–27). Many immigrants to the United States during this period, particularly those from the Mediterranean region and the Slavic countries (Eastern Europe and Russia), seemed distinguishable by their appearance: in their dress and certain facial characteristics, they *looked* different from the Anglo-Saxons who were already established in this country.

Underlying the popular prejudice against these groups of people was a quasi-scientific belief that appearance and behavior were naturally linked, and that both were predetermined by genetic inheritance. Many efforts to explain social behaviors by arguing for an underlying genetic explanation sprang from the theories of Italian criminologist Cesare Lombroso (1835–1909), who argued that some individuals—based on measurements of the brain that implied structural characteristics—were born criminals. Lombroso's theories became popular in the United States toward the end of the nineteenth century, when they were used to support the racist position that blacks, especially, were inherently inferior on the evolutionary scale. The pseudoscience of criminology was also used as an argument for preventing the spread of "idiocy" by allowing institutionalized persons to be sterilized so that they could not reproduce. Such arguments were actually taught in eugenics courses at universities throughout the United States around the turn of the century and were used to support the separation of the races, and also to justify policies that set non-Anglo Americans up as second-class citizens and cast doubt on all "foreign-looking" immigrants. Differences in these immigrants' physical appearance—in their clothing, hair, and skin color, for example—caused them to experience additional discrimination and hostility from a resentful "native" population who forgot that they (or their parents or grandparents) had once been immigrants as well.

The reception given the immigrants can be judged from such descriptions as these by a *New York Times* reporter viewing the processing of new arrivals at Ellis Island under the guidance of the commissioner general of immigration: " 'Come with me,' he added, rising and leading the way through corridor after corridor, past men, women and children herded like cattle and hardly more intelligent, until, throwing open a door at the far end of the building, a motley assemblage of vice-ridden, stolid, bovine parodies of manhood was disclosed . . ." ["Are We Facing an Immigration Peril?" *New York Times,* January 29, 1905; reprinted in *Portal to America: The Lower East Side 1870–1925,* ed. Allon Schoener (New York: Holt, Rinehart & Winston, 1967), p. 27].

The language of prejudice allowed most mainstream Americans to view the new immigrants as dumb or, indeed, bovine—and therefore a class of labor one could with good conscience exploit and mistreat. But in the photographs of Lewis Hine (see "Picturing the Immigrant," p. 466)—which were taken to educate the public about the dire conditions of the immigrants' lives—they are portrayed with dignity and compassion. Despite Hine's efforts, the visible markers of ethnic and racial difference were easy to exaggerate and caricature, and the popular culture (including magazines, newspapers, cartoons, postcards, advertisements, photographs, theatrical and movie presentations, and literature) was pervaded by such negative imagery. Amy Rashap's essay "The American Dream for Sale: Ethnic Images in Magazines" addresses the caricaturing of ethnic and racial minorities in magazine and newspaper advertising, a particularly widespread practice during this period.

Advertising was not the only forum for such ethnic and racial stereotyping in newspapers and magazines. During the heyday of *Life* magazine's influence (the late 1930s and 1940s), African Americans were grossly underrepresented in images of American life. When they *were* shown, as Bill Gaskins argues in "The World According to *Life,*" it was in the form of brutal caricatures. These caricatures derive ultimately from nineteenth-century visual stereotypes of blacks as either dangerously bestial or comical and lazy. These images, in turn, are related to the minstrel show representations of blacks that began in the post–Civil War period and continued through the turn of the century. Once again these negative stereotypes were often fueled by feelings of resentment, in this case on the part of urban Northerners, toward the large numbers of African Americans arriving in the cities of the North, many of them fleeing the tight restrictions of the Jim Crow laws in the South (see p. 58).

Today our thinking about race and ethnicity may be less governed by obviously exaggerated visual stereotypes, but it is still influenced by other kinds of fixed imagery. For example, in "The Genetically Superior Athlete:

Myth or Reality," Earl Smith examines the pervasive belief that blacks are superior athletes, including the political ramifications of this belief. In "Spitfires, Latin Lovers, Mambo Kings," Enrique Fernández analyzes and challenges the narrow definition of *Latin,* and the corresponding stereotypes that are usually transmitted by popular mass culture, particularly by Hollywood films. The chapter closes with Itabari Njeri's essay "Sushi and Grits: Ethnic Identity and Conflict in a Newly Multicultural America," which focuses on the problems of ethnic definition and representation faced by multiracial, multicultural Americans as we approach the end of the twentieth century, offering some viable alternatives for the resolution of these problems.

While most stereotypes have been created and propagated by people outside the group represented, it's worth remembering that other images of ethnic and racial identity can be the property of the group itself, as the photograph introducing this chapter suggests. Movie director Spike Lee is shown here directing a scene from a music video used in his well-known film *Do the Right Thing,* featuring the rap group "Public Enemy." Much of the ongoing controversy surrounding rap music relates to the image of the urban ghetto that rap music evokes. You may want to think about the kind of representation of African American life that these songs create and whether or not they contribute to a polarization or a bridging of racial and ethnic groups. In this chapter as a whole, this same general question is raised in a variety of ways: What are the effects of such cultural images and stereotypes on relations between different groups of people?

JOHN HECKEWELDER

Friend and Foe

John Heckewelder (1743–1823) came to the United States in 1754 with his parents, who were missionaries in the Moravian church, and he inherited their zeal. The Moravians were active among the Indians of Pennsylvania and Ohio, converting them to Christianity and assisting in their migrations from settled areas to safer areas. Living with the Moravian Christian Indians for fifteen years, Heckewelder had an unusual ability to understand their customs and languages, and on numerous occasions he escorted them through territories where they might otherwise have been vulnerable to attacks by whites. At one point during the Revolutionary War (1781), while Heckewelder was held captive by a company of hostile English soldiers, nearly one hundred Christian Indians in his territory were massacred by whites. After the war, Heckewelder's knowledge of Indians was enlisted by the government on several occasions, when he served as adviser in various negotiations with the Iroquois. In the last years of his life, Heckewelder wrote one of the most authoritative early sources on Native Americans, Account of the History, Manners, and Customs of the Indian Nations, Who Once Inhabited Pennsylvania and the Neighboring States *(1819), from which the present selection is taken.*

Heckewelder wrote his Account *not only to set down a record of white-Indian relations, but also in the hope that he might benefit white persons who would have future dealings with the Indians. Heckewelder knew that his white audience would tend to believe that Indians were by nature deceitful, treacherous savages who simply could not be trusted. It is that very prejudice, based on stereotyped representations of the Indian, that Heckewelder argues against in this chapter from his* Account, *explaining the nature of Indian friendship and offering many examples of Indians risking their own lives to save the life of a white friend. To Heckewelder the Indians possess, at bottom, "simple hearts." The excerpt reprinted here includes the record of an extraordinary dialogue between an Indian chief and a white person, Crawford, whom the chief regarded as a friend, in the minutes before Crawford was to be killed by Indians seeking revenge for the murder of members of their own tribe.*

Those who believe that no faith is to be placed in the friendship of an Indian are egregiously mistaken, and know very little of the true character of those men of nature. They are, it is true, revengeful of their enemies, to those who wilfully do them an injury, who insult, abuse, or treat them with contempt. It may be said, indeed, that the passion of revenge is so strong in them that it knows no bounds. This does not, however, proceed from a bad or malicious disposition, but from the violence of natural feelings, unchecked by social institutions, and unsubdued by the force of revealed religion. The tender and generous passions operate no less powerfully on them than those of an opposite character, and they are as warm and sincere in their friendship, as vindictive in their enmities. Nay, I will venture to assert that there are those among them who on an emergency would lay down their lives for a friend: I could fill many pages with examples of Indian friendship and fidelity, not only to each other, but to men of other nations and of a different colour than themselves. How often, when wars were impending between them and the whites, have they not forewarned those among our frontier settlers whom they thought well disposed towards them, that dangerous times were at hand, and advised them to provide for their own safety, regardless of the jealousy which such conduct might excite among their own people? How often did they not even guard and escort them through the most dangerous places until they had reached a secure spot? How often did they not find means to keep an enemy from striking a stroke, as they call it, that is to say from proceeding to the sudden indiscriminate murder of the frontier whites, until their friends or those whom they considered as such were out of all danger?

These facts are familiar to every one who has lived among Indians or in their neighbourhood, and I believe it will be difficult to find a single case in which they betrayed a real friend or abandoned him in the hour of danger, when it was in their power to extricate or relieve him. The word "Friend" to the ear of an Indian does not convey the same vague and almost indefinite meaning that it does with us; it is not a mere complimentary or social expression, but implies a resolute determination to stand by the person so distinguished on all occasions, and a threat to those who might attempt to molest him; the mere looking at two persons who are known or declared friends, is sufficient to deter any one from offering insult to either. When an Indian believes that he has reason to suspect a man of evil designs against his friend, he has only to say emphatically: "This is *my friend,* and if any one tries to hurt him, I will do to him *what is in my mind.*" It is as much as to say that he will stand in his defence at the hazard of his own life. This language is well understood by the Indians, who know that they would have to combat with a spirited warrior, were they to attempt any thing against his friend. By this means much bloodshed is prevented; for it is sufficiently known that an Indian never proffers his friendship in vain. Many white men and myself among others have experienced the benefit of their powerful as well as generous protection.

When in the spring of the year 1774, a war broke out between the Virginians and the Shawanese and Mingoes, on account of murders committed by the former on the latter people, and the exasperated friends of those who had suffered had determined to kill every white man in their country, the Shawano chief *Silver-heels,* taking another Indian with him, undertook out of friendship to escort several white traders from thence to Albany, a distance of near two hundred miles; well knowing at the time that he was running the risk of his own life, from exasperated Indians and vagabond whites, if he should meet with such on the road, as in fact he did on his return.

▼ ▼ ▼

Indeed, the friendship of an Indian is easily acquired, provided it is sought in good faith. But whoever chooses to obtain it must be sure to treat them on a footing of perfect equality. They are very jealous of the whites, who, they think affect to consider themselves as beings of a superior nature and too often treat them with rude undeserved contempt. This they seldom forgive, while on the other hand, they feel flattered when a white man does not disdain to treat them as children of the same Creator. Both reason and humanity concur in teaching us this conduct, but I am sorry to say that reason and humanity are in such cases too little attended to. I hope I may be permitted to expatiate a little on this subject; perhaps it may be beneficial to some white persons hereafter.

The Indians are, as I have already observed before, excellent physiognomists. If they are accosted by or engaged in business with a number of whites, though they may not understand the language that is spoken, they will pretty accurately distinguish by the countenance, those who despise their colour from those who are under the influence of a more generous feeling, and in this they are seldom mistaken. They fix their eyes on the whole party round, and read as it were in the souls of the individuals who compose it. They mark those whom they consider as friends, and those whom they think to be their enemies, and are sure to remember them ever after. But what must those expect, if a war or some other circumstance should put them into the power of the Indians, who, relying on their supposed ignorance of our idiom, do not scruple even in their presence to apply to them the epithets of *dogs, black d—ls,* and the like? Will not these poor people be in some degree justifiable in considering those persons as decidedly hostile to their race? such cases have unfortunately too frequently happened, and the savages have been blamed for treating as enemies those who had so cruelly wounded their most delicate feelings! many white men have been thus put to death, who had brought their fate on themselves by their own imprudence. On the other hand the Indians have not failed to mark those who at the time reprobated such indecent behaviour and reproached their companions for using such improper language. In the midst of war these benevolent Christians have been treated as friends, when perhaps, they had forgotten the humane conduct to which they were indebted for this kind usage.

Their reasoning in such cases is simple, but to them always conclusive. They merely apply their constant maxim, which I believe I have already noticed, that "good can never proceed from evil or evil from good, and that good and evil, like heterogeneous substances, can never combine or coalesce together." How far this maxim is founded in a profound knowledge of human nature, it is not my business to determine; what is certain is that they adhere to it in almost every occasion. If a person treats them ill, they ascribe it invariably to his bad heart; it is the bad spirit within him that operates: he is, therefore, a bad man. If on the contrary one shews them kindness, they say he is prompted so to act by "the good spirit within him," and that he has a *good heart;* for if he had not, he would not do good. It is impossible to draw them out of this circle of reasoning, and to persuade them that the friendship shewn to them may be dissembled and proceed from motions of interest; so convinced are they of the truth of their general principle "that good cannot proceed from an evil source."

The conduct of the Europeans towards them, particularly within the last fifty or sixty years, has, however, sufficiently convinced them that men may dissemble, and that kind speeches and even acts of apparent friendship do not always proceed from friendly motives, but that the bad spirit will sometimes lurk under the appearance of the good. Hence, when they speak of the whites in general, they do not scruple to designate them as a false, deceitful race; but it is nevertheless true that with individuals, they frequently forget this general impression, and revert to their own honest principle; and if a white man only behaves to them with common humanity, it is still easy to get access to their simple hearts. Such are those brutes, those savages, from whom, according to some men, no faith is to be expected, and with whom no faith is to be kept; such are those *barbarous* nations, as they are called, whom God, nevertheless, made the lawful owners and masters of this beautiful country; but who, at no very remote time, will probably live, partially live, only in its history.

My object in this chapter is to prove that those men are susceptible of the noblest and finest feelings of genuine friendship. It is not enough that by a long residence among them, I have acquired the most complete conviction of this truth; facts and not opinions, I know, are expected from me. Perhaps I might rest satisfied with the proofs that I have already given, but I have only shewn the strength and have yet to display the *constancy* of their attachments; and although in the story which I am going to relate, a friend was forced to see his friend perish miserably without having it in his power to save him from the most terrible death that vengeance and cruelty could inflict, we shall not be the less astonished to see him persevere in his friendly sentiments, under circumstances of all others the most calculated, (particularly to an Indian) not only to have entirely extinguished, but converted those sentiments into feelings of hatred and revenge.

I am sorry to be so often obliged to revert to the circumstance of the cruel murder of the Christian Indians on the Sandusky river in the year 1782, by a gang of banditti,[1] under the command of one Williamson. Not satisfied with this horrid outrage, the same band, not long afterwards marched to Sandusky, where it seems they had been informed that the remainder of that unfortunate congregation had fled, in order to perpetrate upon them the same indiscriminate murder. But Providence had so ordered it that they had before left that place, where they had found that they could not remain in safety, their ministers having been taken from them and carried to Detroit by order of the British government, so that they had been left entirely unprotected. The murderers, on their arrival, were much disappointed in finding nothing but empty huts. They then shaped their course towards the hostile Indian villages, where being, contrary to their expectations, furiously attacked, Williamson and his band took the advantage of a dark night and ran off, and the whole party escaped, except one Colonel Crawford and another, who being taken by the Indians, were carried in triumph to their village, where the former was condemned to death by torture, and the punishment was inflicted with all the

[1]*banditti:* bandits (*Ed.*)

cruelty that rage could invent. The latter was demanded by the Shawanese and sent to them for punishment.

While preparations were making for the execution of this dreadful sentence, the unfortunate Crawford recollected that the Delaware chief Wingenund,[2] of whom I have spoken in the beginning of this chapter, had been his friend in happier times: he had several times entertained him at his house, and shewed him those marks of attention which are so grateful to the poor despised Indians. A ray of hope darted through his soul, and he requested that Wingenund, who lived at some distance from the village, might be sent for. His request was granted, and a messenger was despatched for the chief, who, reluctantly, indeed, but without hesitation, obeyed the summons, and immediately came to the fatal spot.

This great and good man was not only one of the bravest and most celebrated warriors, but one of the most amiable men of the Delaware nation. To a firm undaunted mind, he joined humanity, kindness and universal benevolence; the excellent qualities of his heart had obtained for him the name of *Wingenund,* which in the Lenape language signifies *the well beloved.* He had kept away from the tragical scene about to be acted, to mourn in silence and solitude over the fate of his guilty friend, which he well knew it was not in his power to prevent. He was now called upon to act a painful as well as difficult part: the eyes of his enraged countrymen were fixed upon him; he was an Indian and a Delaware; he was a leader of that nation, whose defenceless members had been so cruelly murdered without distinction of age or sex, and whose innocent blood called aloud for the most signal revenge. Could he take the part of a chief of the base murderers? Could he forget altogether the feelings of ancient fellowship and give way exclusively to those of the Indian and the patriot? Fully sensible that in the situation in which he was placed the latter must, in appearance, at least, predominate, he summoned to his aid the firmness and dignity of an Indian warrior, approached Colonel Crawford and waited in silence for the communications he had to make. The following dialogue now took place between them.

CRAWF. Do you recollect me, Wingenund?

WINGEN. I believe I do; are you not Colonel Crawford?

CRAWF. I am. How do you do? I am glad to see you, Captain.

WINGEN. (embarrassed) So! yes, indeed.

CRAWF. Do you recollect the friendship that always existed between us, and that we were always glad to see each other?

WINGEN. I recollect all this. I remember that we have drunk many a bowl of punch together. I remember also other acts of kindness that you have done me.

CRAWF. Then I hope the same friendship still subsists between us.

WINGEN. It would, of course, be the same, were you in your proper place and not here.

[2] This name, according to the English orthography, should be written *Winganoond* or *Wingaynoond,* the second syllable accented and long, and the last syllable short.

Crawf. And why not here, Captain? I hope you would not desert a friend in time of need. Now is the time for you to exert yourself in my behalf, as I should do for you, were you in my place.

Wingen. Colonel Crawford! you have placed yourself in a situation which puts it out of my power and that of others of your friends to do any thing for you.

Crawf. How so, Captain Wingenund?

Wingen. By joining yourself to that execrable man, Williamson and his party; the man, who, but the other day murdered such a number of the Moravian Indians, knowing them to be friends; knowing that he ran no risk in murdering a people who would not fight, and whose only business was praying.

Crawf. Wingenund, I assure you, that had I been with him at the time, this would not have happened; not I alone but all your friends and all good men, wherever they are, reprobate acts of this kind.

Wingen. That may be; yet these friends, these good men did not prevent him from going out again, to kill the remainder of those inoffensive, yet *foolish* Moravian Indians! I say *foolish,* because they believed the whites in preference to us. We had often told them that they would be one day so treated by those people who called themselves their friends! We told them that there was no faith to be placed in what the white men said; that their fair promises were only intended to allure us, that they might the more easily kill us, as they have done many Indians before they killed these Moravians.

Crawf. I am sorry to hear you speak thus; as to Williamson's going out again, when it was known that he was determined on it, I went out with him to prevent him from committing fresh murders.

Wingen. This, Colonel, the Indians would not believe, were even I to tell them so.

Crawf. And why would they not believe it?

Wingen. Because it would have been out of your power to prevent his doing what he pleased.

Crawf. Out of my power! Have any Moravian Indians been killed or hurt since we came out?

Wingen. None; but you went first to their town, and finding it empty and deserted you turned on the path towards us? If you had been in search of warriors only, you would not have gone thither. Our spies watched you closely. They saw you while you were embodying yourselves on the other side of the Ohio; they saw you cross that river; they saw where you encamped at night; they saw you turn off from the path to the deserted Moravian town; they knew you were going out of your way; your steps were constantly watched, and you were suffered quietly to proceed until you reached the spot where you were attacked.

Crawf. What do they intend to do with me? Can you tell me?

Wingen. I tell you with grief, Colonel. As Williamson and his whole cowardly host, ran off in the night at the whistling of our warrior's balls, being satisfied that now he had no Moravians to deal with, but men who could fight, and with such he did not wish to have any thing to do; I say, as he escaped, and they have taken you, they will take revenge on you in his stead.

CRAWF. And is there no possibility of preventing this? Can you devise no way to get me off? You shall, my friend, be well rewarded if you are instrumental in saving my life.

WINGEN. Had Williamson been taken with you, I and some friends, by making use of what you have told me, might perhaps, have succeeded to save you, but as the matter now stands, no man would dare to interfere in your behalf. The king of England himself, were he to come to this spot, with all his wealth and treasures could not effect this purpose. The blood of the innocent Moravians, more than half of them women and children, cruelly and wantonly murdered calls aloud for *revenge.* The relatives of the slain, who are among us, cry out and stand ready for *revenge.* The nation to which they belonged will have *revenge.* The Shawanese, our grandchildren, have asked for your fellow prisoner; on him they will take *revenge.* All the nations connected with us cry out *Revenge! revenge!* The Moravians whom you went to destroy having fled, instead of avenging their brethren, the offence is become national, and the nation itself is bound to take REVENGE!

CRAWF. Then it seems my fate is decided, and I must prepare to meet death in its worst form?

WINGEN. Yes, Colonel!—I am sorry for it; but cannot do any thing for you. Had you attended to the Indian principle, that as good and evil cannot dwell together in the same heart, so a good man ought not to go into evil company; you would not be in this lamentable situation. You see, now, when it is too late, after Williamson has deserted you, what a bad man he must be! Nothing now remains for you but to meet your fate like a brave man. Farewel, Colonel Crawford! they are coming;[3] I will retire to a solitary spot.

I have been assured by respectable Indians that at the close of this conversation, which was related to me by Wingenund himself as well as by others, both he and Crawford burst into a flood of tears; they then took an affectionate leave of each other, and the chief immediately *hid himself in the bushes,* as the Indians express it, or in his own language, retired to a solitary spot. He never, afterwards, spoke of the fate of his unfortunate friend without strong emotions of grief, which I have several times witnessed. Once, it was the first time that he came into Detroit after Crawford's sufferings, I heard him censured in his own presence by some gentlemen who were standing together for not having saved the life of so valuable a man, who was also his particular friend, as he had often told them. He listened calmly to their censure, and first turning to me, said in his own language: "These men talk like fools," then turning to them, he replied in English: "If king George himself, if your king had been on the spot with all his ships laden with goods and treasures, he could not have ransomed my friend, nor saved his life from the rage

[3]The people were at that moment advancing, with shouts and yells, to torture and put him to death.

of a *justly* exasperated multitude." He made no further allusion to the act that had been the cause of Crawford's death, and it was easy to perceive that on this melancholy subject, grief was the feeling that predominated in his mind. He felt much hurt, however, at this unjust accusation, from men who, perhaps, he might think, would have acted very differently in his place. For, let us consider in what a situation he found himself, at that trying and critical moment. He was a Delaware Indian and a highly distinguished character among his nation. The offence was national, and of the most atrocious kind, as it was wanton and altogether unprovoked. He might have been expected to partake with all the rest of his countrymen in the strong desire which they felt for *revenge.* He had been Crawford's friend, it is true, and various acts of sociability and friendship had been interchanged between them. But, no doubt, at that time, he believed him, at least, not to be an enemy, to his nation and colour, and if he was an enemy, he might have expected him to be, like himself, a fair, open generous foe. But when he finds him enlisted with those who are waging a war of extermination against the Indian race, murdering in cold blood, and without distinction of age or sex, even those who had united their fate to that of the whites, and had said to the Christians: "Your people shall be *our* people, and your God *our* God,"[4] was there not enough here to make him disbelieve all the former professions of such a man, and to turn his abused friendship into the most violent enmity and the bitterest rage. Instead of this we see him persevering to the last in his attachment to a person, who, to say the least, had ceased to be deserving of it; we see him in the face of his enraged countrymen avow that friendship, careless of the jealousy that he might excite; we see him not only abstain from participating in the national revenge, but deserting his post, as it were, seek a solitary spot to bewail the death of him, whom, in spite of all, he still loved, and felt not ashamed to call his *friend.*

It is impossible for friendship to be put to a severer test, and the example of Wingenund proves how deep a root this sentiment can take in the mind of an Indian, when even such circumstances as those under which the chief found himself, fail to extinguish it.

DISCUSSING THE TEXT

1. Heckewelder predicts that the Indians, once masters of this "beautiful country," nevertheless "at no very remote time, will probably live, partially live, only in its history" (par. 7). How has the Indian "lived" in our history? What representations of Indians have been passed down to us? With a group of four or five students, discuss popular images of the Native American. Make a list of the different types of images that occur to you and discuss their sources in American popular culture. That is, where do these images come from? How do they enter our minds?

[4]Ruth, i. 16.

2. How does Heckewelder explain, at the outset, the nature of Indian behavior, especially their extremes of passion for revenge and for friendship?
3. Why can the Indian Wingenund, Crawford's professed friend, not prevent the white man from being tortured and put to death? What does Heckewelder intend to demonstrate about Indian character and friendship by including this dialogue? Does he succeed?

WRITING ABOUT THE TEXT

4. Why does Heckewelder use the dialogue form? What is achieved by it? What can he tell us through dialogue that he might not be able to convey in a straight narrative? Can you see any reasons for *not* using dialogue in this way? Write a brief essay in which you argue for or against the use of dialogue in an account of this kind.
5. Go to the library and examine a book of photographs of Native Americans. (If possible, examine the work of Edward Curtis, who photographed the North American Indian tribes in the early decades of the twentieth century.) Focusing on four or five images, write an essay on how you think the photographer wants his audience to perceive the Indians.
6. Write a brief essay discussing the Indian reasoning about good and evil that Heckewelder describes in this account. Do you agree or disagree with this understanding of good and evil? What other examples from American history (or from contemporary life) can you think of that seem to argue for or against this particular way of understanding human behavior?

LEWIS HINE

Picturing the Immigrant

The "foreignness" of the immigrant has often been exaggerated in drawings and cartoons carried by the popular press and in advertisements (see Amy Rashap's essay, p. 474). Such negative images of ethnic and racial minorities have created and reinforced barriers to social progress and integration. At the same time, however, the plight of the immigrants (who were crowded into tiny apartments; restricted, for all practical purposes, to the ghettos of the cities; and forced to work for substandard wages) became of great concern to a group of reformers and progressive social critics around the turn of the century. These critics and reformers fought for better working conditions, better housing, and better education for American immigrants. One such reformer was the photographer Lewis Hine (1874–1940), who began photographing the immigrants on Ellis Island in 1905 and continued portraying their lives on the Lower East Side of Manhattan (in New York City) through the early decades of the century. (Ellis Island, in Upper New York Bay, southwest of Manhattan, served as the main point of arrival for immigrants to the United States from 1892 to 1943.)

Hine was born in Wisconsin and, after a series of jobs following high school and some training in art, he enrolled briefly at the University of Chicago. He seized the opportunity to come to New York in 1901 to teach nature study and geography at the Ethical Culture School, where he was invited by the school's superintendent, Frank Manny, to use the camera for educational purposes. Photography soon fully engaged Hine's imagination. He took his students out into the country to photograph nature, but he also led them all around New York, photographing the economic life of the city and its inhabitants. Back at school, Hine and his students would study the images they had taken in the field and relate them to various aspects of their studies—from art to economics and geology. Hine became so interested in educational uses of the camera that he wrote a series of articles on the subject during this time, promoting the use of the camera as a way of enhancing the taste, understanding, and analytic abilities of students.

One of Hine's strongest interests was the immigrants who were coming through Ellis Island in such great numbers, arriving from Russia, Ireland, Italy, and other lands, and settling in New York at that time. Through his photographs, Hine strove to render his subjects sympathetically, avoiding the common visual representations of the day—which tended to depict immigrants as either dumb beasts, fit for nothing but hard labor, or happy idiots who didn't seem to care what sort of lives they led. Opposed to both of these condescending attitudes, Hine sought to portray the immigrants with a kind of quiet dignity that emphasized that they were, in fact, as fully human as their viewers. Hine was supported in this endeavor by the Ethical Culture School's director, who wanted the students to view the recent immigrants with the same respect with which they perceived the original Plymouth Rock Pilgrims.

Hine was working within a tradition of documentary photography that had been established in the late 1880s by Jacob Riis, who also focused on social conditions on Manhattan's Lower East Side, where many immigrants settled. (See Riis's photo, p. 68.) But whereas Riis emphasized housing problems, Hine portrayed the immigrants in a more complex and well-rounded way: whereas Riis tended to see his subjects as victims, often with brutalized expressions on their faces, Hine saw the immigrant as a human being with positive feelings and aspirations as well.

Beyond his Ellis Island and Lower East Side work, Hine was interested in furthering social reform and in changing the ways in which Americans viewed the working class. During the first two decades of the twentieth century, he did much work for the National Child Labor Relations Committee, work that took him around the country to a variety of industrial locations where children were employed in factories, mines, and mills. In his later years, he photographed workers in factories and construction sites (such as that of the Empire State Building), producing photographs that allowed the viewer to see workers in a positive light, as people who were making a great contribution to the national economy.

Using a box-type 5 × 7 camera on a tripod, Hine provided photographic images to various social agencies and published his work as illustrations for articles in the reform journals of the day. He saw photography as a powerful force for the shaping of consciousness, relying on the viewer's belief in the reality of the subject while providing his own interpretation of that subject. The photographs included here were taken in the first decade of the twentieth century and were published in progressive and reform social survey magazines. They include images of Ellis Island, Manhattan's Lower East Side, and the immigrant working class.

"Italian Immigrant, East Side, N.Y.C." (1910) (Courtesy George Eastman House)

"Looking for Lost Baggage, Ellis Island" (1906) (Courtesy George Eastman House)

"Climbing into America" (1908) (Courtesy George Eastman House)

"Children on Street, Lower East Side, N.Y.C." (n.d.) (Courtesy George Eastman House)

"Labor Agency" (1910) (Courtesy George Eastman House)

"Steelworkers at Russian Boarding House, Homestead, Pa." (1907/08)
(Courtesy George Eastman House)

DISCUSSING THE TEXT

1. In *Looking for Lost Baggage, Ellis Island,* and *Climbing into America,* Hine shows us the immigrant during his or her first days (or even hours) in the United States. What details in these photographs would lead us to see these immigrants as recent arrivals? Look at their dress, the expressions on their faces, and so forth. What kinds of emotions are registered in these images?
2. Why do you think Hine chose to photograph his subjects on Ellis Island at the particular moments pictured here? What do you suppose he was trying to make us see or feel about them? Do you think he succeeds?
3. Why does Hine group the workers in *Steelworkers at Russian Boarding House, Homestead, Pa.* in the way that he does? What kind of clothing are they wearing? Where are they looking? Why? What does Hine hope to achieve by portraying the workers as he has done here?

WRITING ABOUT THE TEXT

4. Examine Hine's *Children on Street, Lower East Side, N.Y.C.* carefully. Make a list of the details of the street, the signs on the buildings, the activities of the children, what they are wearing, how they are standing, and anything else

that seems to offer a clue toward understanding their lives. Then write a brief essay in which you use your observations to address the following questions: What does this image tell you about the immigrant's life in New York? How did Hine want us to see these children in relation to their environment?

5. In Hine's photograph of the Labor Agency, which portrays a number of men standing outside an employment office, he is careful to let us see the signs on the building. In the voice of a social reformer, write a personal reaction to the photograph that addresses the following questions: What do the signs tell us about conditions of labor during this time? Why is the agency called "International Labor Agency"? Does the dress or posture of the people gathered there tell us anything about their condition?
6. In the voice of the immigrant woman portrayed in *Looking for Lost Baggage, Ellis Island,* write a letter to a relative back home (a) reacting to the family's arrival in the United States, and (b) interpreting this photograph that was taken of her and her family.

AMY RASHAP

The American Dream for Sale: Ethnic Images in Magazines

Advertisements are fascinating mirrors of culture, because they are efforts at persuasion aimed at the largest possible audience. As such, they reflect what their creators think most people will believe or find convincing. The mass-circulation magazines that evolved during the early twentieth century assumed, as Amy Rashap suggests in the following article, that their audiences were fairly unified, holding a good many beliefs—and prejudices—in common. Most advertisements were aimed at the mainstream or average American, who was presumed to be white, Christian, a member of a family with two parents and two children, living in a single-family house. In the version of American society depicted in these ads, the ethnic individual was generally marginalized, outside the space occupied by the "average" consumer. In other ads, ethnicity was often used to make some dramatic point about a given product by featuring some easily recognized and often exaggerated characteristic of the ethnic individual: in short, by turning the ethnic person into a stereotype.

In "The American Dream for Sale: Ethnic Images in Magazines," Amy Rashap analyzes several examples of such ads, identifying ethnic stereotypes and discussing how they have been used. She also notes that with the civil rights movement of the 1950s and 1960s, ethnicity became much more visible, and advertisers began trying to sell their products to particular ethnic groups by featuring representative ethnic people in their ads. It is interesting to consider, when reading Rashap's article, exactly how representative such images are, and which aspects of a given ethnic group's identity the ads are attempting to portray.

Amy Rashap (b. 1955) has a Ph.D. from the University of Pennsylvania in folklore and is interested in popular culture. She is currently at work on a book about ways of viewing the body, food, and dieting in American culture. She wrote this essay for a catalog published in conjunction with an exhibition at the Balch Institute for Ethnic Studies, a museum and research library in Philadelphia devoted to the full range of American ethnicities.

"Promise—large promise—is the soul of advertising," wrote Dr. Samuel Johnson in the eighteenth century. His dictum has remained remarkably accurate during the last two hundred and fifty years. Advertisements tell the viewer much more than the merits of a particular product. From the glossy and colorful pages of magazines, catalogues, and newspaper supplements the reader can extract images of how to live the perfect American life. This exhibit shows how the depiction of ethnic groups has changed radically in the advertisements of nationally distributed magazines over the last century. The pictures tell a complex tale of economic power and mobility; of conflicting attitudes towards one's ethnic heritage and towards Anglo-American culture.

The development of modern advertising, with its sophisticated use of imagery and catchy phrases, grew hand in hand with the advent of the affordable monthly and weekly magazines. By the 1880's factories were churning out a plethora of ready-made goods, and the expanded system of railways and roads linked producer and consumer into a national network. During this period magazine production rose apace. Due to a variety of factors, ranging from improved typesetting techniques and low postal rates to the utilization of increasingly sophisticated photoengraving processes, publishers began to produce low-priced, profusely illustrated magazines fashioned to appeal to a national audience. The contents of the magazines, such as *Collier's, The Saturday Evening Post* and *The Ladies Home Journal*, covered a wide variety of topics: from homemaking to current events, new inventions to briskly paced fiction. By 1905 twenty general monthlies, each with a circulation of over 100,000, were in existence. Ranging in price from 10 to 15¢, easily within the budget of tens of thousands of Americans, they were an ideal vehicle for carrying the manufacturer's messages to a national audience.

What were the implications of advertising for the masses? As advertisers targeted their products towards a mass audience, the need arose to create an "average person," a type who embodied the qualities and attitudes of many others. Advertisers devised images that tapped into deeply held beliefs and myths of an "all-American" lifestyle—one that didn't just sell a product, but a way of life that people could buy.

The very nature of the advertising medium itself necessitates the use of symbols and character types that could be understood at a glance. If the advertisement was to be effective, its message had to be quickly absorbed and understood. Thus, in their depiction of ethnic groups, advertisers often used commonly held stereotypes. Within these stock images, however, one can observe various levels of complexity.

5 When the N.H.M. Hotels ad in figure 1 appeared in 1936, the nation was still in the midst of the Great Depression. The black railroad porter, with his knowledge of the rails and reputation for prompt and courteous service, was an effective spokesman for a hotel chain dependent for its livelihood upon

FIGURE 1
Magazine advertisement, 1936 (Courtesy Balch Institute)

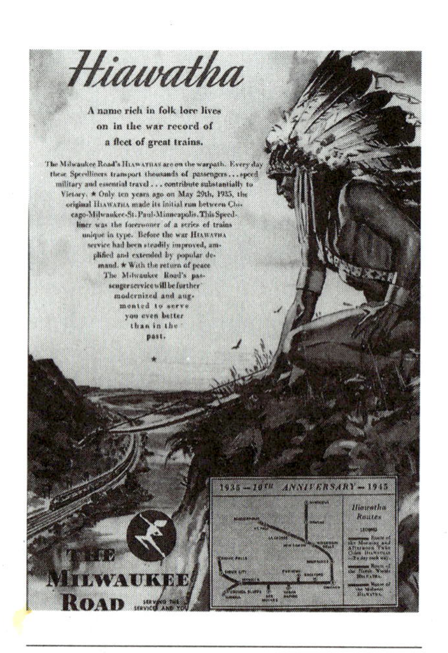

FIGURE 2
National Geographic *advertisement, July 1945*
(Courtesy Balch Institute)

Americans getting back on the move. The portrayal of the porter is interesting in this ad, for, beyond the obvious fact that the only blacks present are in service roles, the spokesman's subservience is visually reinforced by his deferential smile, slight stoop, and bent knees. As porters, blacks could assist in the resurgence of the American economy, but not fully participate in its benefits.

An advertisement for the Milwaukee Railroad from a 1945 *National Geographic* (figure 2) reveals another way in which ethnic groups are shown as outsiders—at the service of American culture while not actively participating in it. Here is the Noble Savage, not as the representative of any particular group of Native Americans, but as the symbol for the railroad itself, barely visible in the advertisement. In both the visuals and the copy the sale is made through stock images and associations. He is as familiar as a dime store Indian; a reassuring and time-honored part of the American landscape. However, while the Indian shown here still brandishes his bow and arrow, he has been tamed. He gazes mutely over the changed landscape, another symbol of technological domination.

In a 1949 ad in *American Home,* Chiquita Banana entices us to buy her goods. Wearing a traditional ruffled skirt and fruit-laden hat, she embodies the stereotypical, fun-loving, gay Hispanic woman. While she occasionally doffs the more demure chef's hat, her smile and pert manner never waver. Her basic message is one of festivity, tempered with the American housewife's concern for nutrition: while bananas are good for you, they can be fun, too! They make mealtimes a party. In the later television ads of the 1960s, Chiquita

Banana was transformed into a more overtly sexual figure doing the rumba. Singing her famous "I'm Chiquita Banana . . ." song in a Spanish accent, the advertisement's emphasis was more on festivity than wholesomeness.

The use of simple external attributes to symbolize ethnic identification has long been a favorite technique of advertisers. In a Royal Crown Cola advertisement of 1938 (figure 3), the reader was urged be like the thrifty "Scotchman" and buy the economical refreshment. Presenting its Scotsman with a broad grin and conspiratorial, chummy wink, the ad pokes gentle fun at the Scottish reputation for miserliness. Whether the character in Scottish garb is Scottish or not is incidental, for the white American can easily put on this ethnic persona without compromising or jeopardizing his identity. The Scottish stereotype can be invoked by using a few external character traits; the image does not extend beyond that initial statement. The black stereotype represented in the N.H.M. Hotel ad, however, reflects more deeply-held attitudes toward cultural differences. Compare the closeness of the two men in the RC Cola ad with the black porter and the white traveler in figure 1. Even the spacing between the characters in both ads is significant: while the men in the RC Cola ad display an easy intimacy, the black porter stands deferentially apart from the white traveler.

Advertisements were not the only medium that reflected the subservient role certain ethnic groups occupied within mainstream American culture. Magazine fiction too depicted a world in which white, Anglo-Americans were getting most of the world's material goods and occupying the more powerful roles in most human relationships. In story after story the heros and heroines were of northern European stock, and in many cases when the protagonists were nominally foreign, their visual portrayal and characterization would belie the differences. This tendency is illustrated in a 1913 cover of the *Sunday Magazine of the Philadelphia Press,* which shows a pretty young Serbian dancer smiling languidly out at the viewer (figure 4). In her colorful native costume and dance pose, she plays her role of "old country" ethnic. But while her dress presents an image of quaint and wholesome rusticity, her features bear a reassuringly western European stamp. She satisfied an American need for foreign experience and armchair travel without really challenging any assumptions about significant cultural variation.

Until the advent of the civil rights movement of the 1950's and 60's, American businessmen and advertisers assumed, on the whole, that the best way to sell their products was to address their advertisements to the white Anglo-American. Hence magazine stories and ads were geared towards appealing to this constituency through the use of images and symbols that were familiar and appealing to them. In recent years, however, though advertisers have become increasingly concerned with the purchasing power of the different ethnic groups, the images they use continue to reassure the consumer that the group's "foreignness" is carefully controlled. Their cultural identity is often reduced to a few superficial symbols. 10

A recent Sprite ad (figure 5) reveals a group of smiling Americans of all different lineages brandishing their favorite brand of soda. Yet while different ethnic groups are shown, they are all of the wholesome "all American"

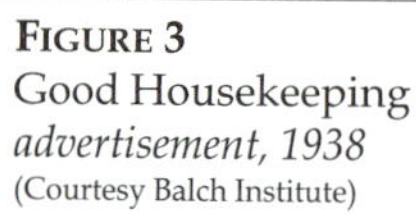

FIGURE 3
Good Housekeeping *advertisement, 1938* (Courtesy Balch Institute)

FIGURE 4
Magazine cover, November 9, 1913 (Courtesy Balch Institute)

type. The advertisement's point is that the "you"—the American youth, who chose Sprite, now includes Asians, Hispanics and blacks.

Advertisements that have appeared in nationally distributed magazines targeted at specific ethnic groups also need mentioning. Until the Civil Rights movement gave many groups the impetus to speak out in their own voices, many of the advertisements in such magazines showed them displaying all the accoutrements and mannerisms of white, middle-class Americans. Thus the Ballantine Beer ad (figure 6) in a 1955 issue of *Ebony* portrays a group of thoroughly Anglicized and fair-complexioned black people. In black society light skin often gave a person enhanced prestige and eased acceptance into white American culture.

13 Today agencies have been formed to deal exclusively with advertisements targeted towards specific minority groups. Many of these more recent ads reveal the complex negotiations involved in attempting to reconcile indigenous cultural needs with societal acceptance: a crucial issue facing many ethnic Americans today.

SOURCES

Berleson, Bernard and Patricia J. Salter, "Majority and Minority Americans: An Analysis of Magazine Fiction." In *Mass Culture, The Popular Arts in America,* edited by Bernard Rosenberg and David Manning White. New York: The Free Press, 1957. Pp. 235–250.

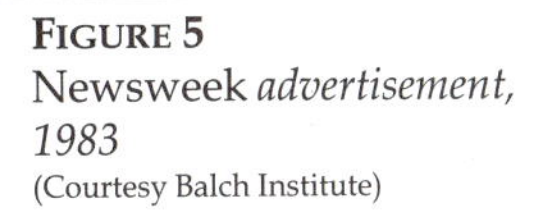

FIGURE 5
Newsweek *advertisement, 1983*
(Courtesy Balch Institute)

FIGURE 6
Ebony *advertisement, January 1955* (Courtesy of S&P Company, Mill Valley, CA, and the J. Walter Thompson Collection at the John W. Hartman Center for Sales, Advertising, and Marketing History, Duke University)

Mott, Frank Luther, *A History of American Magazines.* Cambridge: Harvard University Press, 1957.

Peterson, Theodore, *Magazines in the Twentieth Century.* Urbana: University of Illinois Press, 1956.

DISCUSSING THE TEXT

1. Rashap offers examples of ads that portray stereotypes of African Americans, Native Americans, Hispanics, and Scots, among others. Would people from these different ethnic groups necessarily find their respective images in these ads offensive? Why or why not?
2. Rashap states that in ads that show American society as multicultural, all people portrayed are the "wholesome 'All American' type." What are your views on this particular issue? Do you agree with Rashap's observation? How would you explain this tendency in such ads?
3. In a group of four or five students, discuss three of the ads included in this selection in terms of the following questions: What sorts of messages about ethnicity are these ads transmitting? How do you think they would be "read" today? Do they compare to recent advertisements in any way? Take brief notes as you work on this assignment, and be prepared to share your opinions with the class.

WRITING ABOUT THE TEXT

4. If you are not a Native American, imagine yourself as one and write a personal response to the 1945 ad from *National Geographic* (figure 2). What feelings do you think this ad would provoke in a contemporary Native American person of your age?
5. Find two ads from a current mass-market magazine (such as *People, Time, Ebony,* or *Vanity Fair*) that target specific ethnic and/or racial groups. Then write two paragraphs that address the following questions: To what extent are the images stereotypes? How would you compare the images in this ad to those in one or more of the ads included in Rashap's essay?
6. Write a brief essay in which you compare and contrast the *Ebony* ad of 1955 (figure 6), and the *Newsweek* ad of 1983 (figure 5). What sorts of changes, if any, do you see in the more recent ad? How do both ads reflect their times? How do you think the specific groups targeted by these ads would react?

BILL GASKINS

The World According to *Life:* Racial Stereotyping and American Identity

One of the most influential of magazines in the mid-twentieth century, Life *was founded in 1936 and immediately became the premier picture magazine of its time, with a circulation of twenty million by 1942. Prior to* Life*, the pages of news magazines like* Time *contained photographs and illustrations, but the main emphasis was on the printed text.* Life *reversed the proportion, concentrating heavily on the photograph and creating the picture story, with its text and captions, around the sequence of edited images. In the years before the age of television,* Life *was one of the most important contributors to a general understanding of American culture. Thus its depiction of racial and ethnic minorities is of special interest.*

Bill Gaskins (b. 1953) is a photographer and writer who has published essays on film and photography in such art journals as New Art Examiner *and* Afterimage*. Currently a visiting artist and lecturer at the School of the Art Institute in Chicago, he teaches photography and a course on the visual representation of race. In this selection, Gaskins analyzes the content and frequency of articles depicting African Americans in* Life *magazine. Based on his examination of issues of the magazine published between 1936 and 1946 (when television began to replace photojournalism), Gaskins concludes that the treatment of blacks in* Life *was racist. He argues further that editors of contemporary news magazines need to pay closer attention to the African American community's representations of itself in its own journals and magazines. The article from which this selection is excerpted originally appeared in 1993 in* Afterimage, *a journal devoted to examining the cultural implications of visual media.*

> One major element of ideologies of dominance, such as sexism and racism, is to dehumanize people by stereotyping them, by denying them their variousness and complexity.[1]
>
> –BARBARA CHRISTIAN

In 1936 the pages of magazines such as *Time, Vanity Fair,* and *Esquire* were dominated by copy, with a minimum of illustration used. Often the text ran three columns deep on each page. Most cover illustrations were either pen and ink or charcoal drawings. Photography was used sparingly in randomly arranged layouts and often limited to studio portraits of personalities. Most magazines of the thirties were marketed towards the literate middle-to-upper-class white male. The presumption of publishers at that time was that women were neither consumers of news nor preoccupied with affairs of the world and consequently, not a part of the editorial or marketing strategies of most magazines.

The '30s equivalent of contemporary cable television, *Life* was a radical departure from the typical weekly magazine of the day in that it considered a less exclusive readership. Physically its format was considerably larger than most of its competitors, visually dominating newsstands with dynamic cover photographs and its red and white logo of capital letters at the top left corner. When *Life* made its public debut on November 23, 1936, all 250,000 newsstand copies were sold on the first day. By the end of the first year, Americans were buying five to six million copies a week.[2] Between the covers *Life* also represented a departure from conventional magazines through its minimal use of copy and radical use of photography to form a visual narrative. Publisher Henry Luce was clear regarding the role of the camera in this new journalism. He stated:

> The camera would act as interpreter, recording what modern industrial civilization is, how it looks, how it meshes . . . To see life; to see the world; to eyewitness great events; to watch the focus of the poor and the gestures of the proud . . . to see and be instructed.[3]

The editorial direction of *Life* was heavily influenced by the two premiere German picture weeklies of the mid-1920s, the *Berliner Illustrierte Zeitung* (BIZ) and the *Munchner Illustrierte Presse* (MIP).[4] As competitors, both magazines pushed each other to a level of picture editing and layout in which text was minimal and reading almost unnecessary. The technological advances of

---

[1]Barbara Christian, "The Race for Theory," *Feminist Studies,* vol. 14, no. 1 (March 1988), p. 75.

[2]Loudon Wainwright, *The Great American Magazine: An Inside History of LIFE* (New York: Alfred A. Knopf, 1968), p. 24. Wainwright's position as an editor at *Life* gave him access to information about Luce's decision to create a weekly picture magazine, sales statistics, and other information about the formation of the magazine.

[3]*Life,* vol. 1, no. 6 (December 28, 1936), p. 9.

[4]Naomi Rosenblum, *A World History of Photography* (New York: Abbeville Press, 1984), p. 461.

German-made 35mm hand cameras such as the Leica gave rise to a photojournalism that was free of the posed character of photojournalism seen elsewhere. The images were energetic and exciting and captured the reader's interest with a combination of visual and psychological tension. The key figure in the development of the new photojournalism was the picture editor. The photo editor at *Life* emerged as the conductor of a weekly visual symphony. The photographs were to be arranged for maximum effect upon the senses and emotions of the reader. What Luce sought was a "syncopation" of words and pictures that he called "the essay":

> In learning this syncopation, we create a great new thing in weekly journalism. We demand for it now to [have] a much harder-hitting dynamic journalistic quality. It has got to be an essay with a point . . . the mere charm of photographic revelation is not enough.[5]

While the essay would entertain, the objective of *Life* magazine was to inform the reader in a manner that required a minimum of effort on their part. In 1936 the testimony of a satisfied subscriber attests to the success of the magazine's pedagogical mission: "I went through it in half an hour and more information remained in my head than I can usually keep after reading a book bigger than I can lift."[6]

▼ ▼ ▼

The only African American represented in the historic first issue of *Life* appeared in a full page ad for the Young and Rubicam advertising agency. The ad was dominated by a photograph of a black man receiving a punch to the face.[7] This image provided a preview of the kinds of representations of African Americans that would appear in the pages of *Life* magazine in the future. With rare exception, blacks were presented as entertainers and athletes, in insignificant roles supporting whites, as physical objects of sexual or social voyeurism and/or as a social problem as part of a so-called "underclass."

Life's earliest attempt at in-depth coverage of blacks would present a paternal view of African American life framed by an equally paternalist analysis of the "Negro condition." In a 1938 feature essay, "NEGROES: The U.S. Also Has A Minority Problem," the editors present a history of Africans in America beginning with slavery and ending with an assimilationist portrait of America's black community striving to imitate white, upper-class values. The Ku Klux Klan, lynchings, separate and unequal public accommodations, and other features of a racially segregated society are not a part of the "minority problem" that the editors attempt to analyze. The myth that Southern blacks were content with segregation is represented through coverage of a sharecropper and his family. Interestingly, the editors specifically suggest that

[5]Wainwright, pp. 99–100.
[6]*Life*, vol. 1, no. 6, p. 69.
[7]*Life*, vol. 1, no. 1 (November 23, 1936), p. 81.

the only solution to racism in America would be either through black integration with or separation from white society. The so-called "Negro problem" is never clearly defined, nor is the system of race-based privileges that creates obstacles to the progress of blacks and of the country as a whole. The following is an excerpt from the editor's introduction to the essay:

> He is a minority more sharply set off than any of the world's other minorities. Like most minorities he has only two solutions for the evil of inequality: he can be assimilated and merge himself into the lives and ways of the white man, or he can boldly build, within the white civilization, a black civilization of his own. Either solution seems unattainable in the time of any living generation. According to some anthropologists, the Negro, even if given social equality could never be racially absorbed by the whites.
>
> Every white man knows that there is a Negro problem. But few know the Negro. He is recognized as the bale-heaving stevedore chanting the unhappy songs of a happy-go-lucky race; or as the crapshooter who has given America a picturesque jargon; or as the hysteric convert, or as the old "darky" who has borrowed trappings, bearing and beard of the Southern colonel and thus created a caricature of his old massa.
>
> . . . In the South, this new Negro seems acclimated. There, as a restricted class, he leads an earthy, easygoing life which rarely ends in suicide. Ignorant but intelligent, improvident, but imitative, his world is relatively small and he is relatively happy in it . . . The white man will be surprised at the achievements of the Negro in America, some of which are set forth on the following pages.[8]

While in this article *Life* identified 20 prominent members of the black community nationwide, eight of the 20 came from the ranks of the arts, sports, and entertainment. The editors focus on the middle-class status of these figures, who include Marian Anderson, Jesse Owens, Langston Hughes, and Claude McKay and avoid any acknowledgment that they and other black men and women actively criticized and sought to dismantle racism in American society. While the majority of African Americans holding graduate degrees were at one time undergraduates at black colleges, these institutions are denigrated by the editors who write that "Most of them [black colleges], however, are little better than good high schools."[9] In some cases there are glaring omissions in the biographies of the figures mentioned. For example, the editors chose to describe Paul Robeson as an athlete and entertainer, failing to mention the fact that he received a scholarship to attend Rutgers University, his facility with a variety of foreign languages, and his skills as a writer and orator in the cause of freedom and equality for all the world's exploited masses. Instead he is described thusly: "Baritone Paul Robeson, one of the best singers of his or any race was an All-America football end at Rutgers in

---

[8]*Life*, vol. 5, no. 14 (October 3, 1938), p. 49.
[9]Ibid., p. 58.

1918."[10] And in an interesting reversal of the "one-drop rule,"[11] Walter White, then president of the NAACP, has his so-called white blood favored over his black blood in the following caption: "Spokesman Walter White, pale, blond, only 1/64 Negro, heads the potent National Association for Advancement of Colored People."[12] This overt reference to genealogy in the description of White comes off as a not-too-veiled attempt to connect White's leadership and intelligence to his "whiteness" and not his 1/64 of "blackness." The article concludes with coverage of members of negro high-society in black social clubs and pursuing the fine arts.

The readers of *Life* would see very little in the way of coverage of the lives of these or other prominent blacks in subsequent issues. Prominent black Americans would, for all practical purposes, disappear from the world according to *Life.* In a statistically-based article titled "Black and White Coverage in *Life,* 1937–1972," journalism scholar Mary Alice Sentman reviewed *Life* magazine in five-year increments from 1937 to 1972. Her findings show that in 1937 the percentage of *Life*'s coverage honoring a prominent African American was the highest at 4.6%. For the years cited in her study between 1937 and 1972 there was 0% coverage of prominent African Americans. The total percentage of black coverage in the final year of *Life* was .04%, well below the African American percentage of the population.[13]

The language of the editors and writers is often condescending and paternalistic. "Mammy" was a frequently used term for black women caretakers, especially if they were full-figured. "Boy," "porter," and "blackamoor" were the terms used when referring to black men. Black children were not spared in the name-calling as the feature essay, "Doctors Pick Prize Pickaninnies at Memphis Tri-State Negro Fair" shows.[14] References to the suspect intelligence of blacks often appears in the captions of the photographs illustrating the stories. The following is an excerpt from an essay on the isle of Martinique:

> They have the elaborate good manners of the eighteenth-century, once learned and never forgotten. They are the kindest, gentlest and most conscientious people in the Caribbean. They are also remarkably stupid. It is said that a Martinique worker must be re-taught even the most elementary job every four weeks, year after year.[15]

---

[10]Ibid., p. 52.

[11]In the eighteenth-century American south the legal determination of racial status was based on the "one drop rule," meaning that a single drop of black blood made a person black. See F. James Davis, *Who is Black? One Nation's Definition* (University Park, PA: State University Press, 1991), p. 4.

[12]*Life,* vol. 5, no. 14, p. 53.

[13]Mary Alice Sentman, "Black and White: Disparity in Coverage By Life Magazine from 1937 to 1972," *Journalism Quarterly,* vol. 60, no. 2 (1983), p. 501.

[14]*Life,* vol. 4, no. 17 (April 25, 1938), pp. 66–67.

[15]*Life,* vol. 11, no. 24 (September 15, 1941), p. 96.

A simple photograph and caption from a 1936 issue provides an illustration of the social order between the races. "The Speaker Speaks To His Gardener" is about the relationship between William Brockman Bankhead, then U.S. Speaker of the House of Representatives, and his gardener "Doc." Class distinctions between them are established for the reader by obvious differences in dress, Bankhead's title, and the black man's "pet" name. Bankhead's authority over the black worker in the photograph is punctuated by the following excerpt from the caption: " 'Doc' and the House of Representatives are similar in one respect, both work better when ruled with a firm hand."[16]

Whether blacks physically appeared in *Life* articles or not, racial coding was a consistent feature of the reporting that foregrounded the activities of whites and the myth of a race-based superiority. Many readers of *Life* expected that this stereotype would be maintained and protested against more accurate portrayals. In a December 1937 issue, *Life* covered a black debutante ball in the feature section "*Life* Goes to a Party." Two published letters complained about the coverage: "Your Negro pictures were not only uninteresting, but repulsive to the majority of southern readers. Mr. and Mrs. are not terms applied to Negroes here." The other letter was even more direct: "I didn't know that *Life* went to a nigger party."[17]

The image of blacks in the roles of butlers, cooks and maids appears regularly in a variety of articles featuring the lifestyles of rich and famous whites, or in advertisements for products such as Aunt Jemima Pancake mix or Cream of Wheat cereal. The Aunt Jemima ads use a series of photographs presented in a cartoon style complete with balloons containing dialogue. The black woman in these ads was depicted in the "mammy" role, as servant to a white family, with her bandanna-covered head and a pitiful imitation of Negro dialect placed in her mouth by an ad agency copywriter.[18]

The most frequent coverage of African American singers, dancers, actors, and athletes appeared in feature and spot news reports. A 1941 story on a Lindy-Hop competition, an African American dance form of that era, is an example of the voyeuristic quality of many of these stories. "The Lindy" was a dance popularized by blacks in Harlem during the 1940s. It was a high-energy combination of dance and gymnastics that held great entertainment value for whites who—ironically—were frequently the judges of competitions that often took place at exclusive society functions in New York City. Part of the attraction of the Lindy Hop for many white viewers was what they considered to be the unrestrained and scandalous display of the Negro's "natural" rhythm and sexuality. In the essay "Lindy-Hopping at Harvest Moon Ball," one photograph presents a female contestant in what must have been considered a near pornographic pose for a 1941 readership, as the flashgun of the camera freezes for eternity her exposed rear end. Through the caption the

---

[16] *Life*, vol. 1, no. 6 (December 28, 1936), p. 9.
[17] Sentman, p. 506.
[18] *Life*, vol. 4, no. 17 (April 25, 1938), p. 80.

editors impart their judgment on the propriety of the dance but not their use of the photograph: "Sailing Through Space, Alyce Pearson completes a 'jive tumble' with her partner, James Outlaw. Together they won third place in this division. As a dance, [the] Lindy Hop is not noted for its dignity."[19]

In the section "Pictures to the Editors" amateur and professional photographers were invited to submit photographs to the photo editors for publication, usually in the last few pages of the magazine. Often the people in the photographs selected had some physical or socially aberrant character and were presented as an object of curiosity or derision. Other photographs stretched the reader's imagination through unusual camera angles. Some of the most brutally voyeuristic and caricatured photographs of blacks appeared in this section. The negro as freak is the subtext of a photograph appearing in a 1941 issue that shows a black male side show performer's 17-inch plus feet under the caption "Biggest Feet."[20] Photographs appearing in this section frequently presented the African American as a violent criminal, dramatically and graphically connecting the image of black males with physical violence and crime. One "Picture to the Editors" shows readers the large head wound of a black man, distinguished by a knife stuck through his skull. An essay titled "*Life* goes to a party with the convicts in California's San Quentin Prison," includes pictures from a prison talent show. One photograph of a group of black performers includes the terse, fact-filled caption: "Seven out of every hundred San Quentin inmates are Negroes."[21] The reader is provided with immediate visual evidence of the black as a social problem along with easily digestible statistical data pertaining to blacks as a group.

Life's depiction of black men involved in task-oriented, physical pursuits such as laboring and athletics obscures the contribution of those African Americans who exceed the expectations of a racially segregated society and achieve success. The essay, "John Borican is Greatest All-Around Track Athlete," focused the reader's attention on the athletic achievements of a black Columbia University graduate student and pentathelete through the time-motion photography of Gjon Mili.[22] The reader sees dramatic multiple images of Borican in the stages of a broad jump and clearing a high-hurdle. The story emphasizes the statistics of his athletic achievement, rather than the statistics concerning the number of black male Ph.D.s in Ivy League schools in 1941 or the social hurdles Borican cleared to become a candidate for a doctorate degree at that time. Given the multi-dimensional character of his life, the coverage of this essay was extremely one-dimensional. While there is a one column photograph of him working at an easel, we see no examples of his art work

---

[19]*Life*, vol. 11, no. 24 (September 15, 1941), p. 10.
[20]Ibid., p. 108.
[21]*Life*, vol. 4, no. 24 (June 13, 1938), p. 72.
[22]*Life*, vol. 11, no. 21 (November 24, 1941), pp. 62–63.

and there are no shots of him in his role as a youth counselor for the New York Boys Club.

Other essays, while having no direct relationship to African American life or culture, would foreground stereotypical images of blacks, reducing the black presence to a visual prop and providing visual evidence of a race-based social order and the superior status of whites. Often these images would have comic value for the reader as in "Night Club Rough House."[23] This essay, which focuses on a private after-hours club in New York City, presents a black waiter as a subject of derision and comic relief for the patrons of the club and for the readers. The black man in this essay literally becomes an object without thoughts or feelings as he is shown having the chalk lines of a tic-tac-toe grid drawn on his head by two white men. "Watermelons To Market," an essay that appeared in a 1937 issue, offers perhaps the most aggressive example of visual stereotyping to occur in the history of *Life.* The cover photograph presents a black man who is nude from the waist up viewed from behind. Bands from the suspenders on his pants cross his back and shoulders. He is seated atop a pile of watermelons in a horse-drawn wagon heading down a dirt road that fades into the horizon of the composition. The use of flash separates the black man and the watermelons from the rest of the scene giving the simply composed photograph a greater graphic punch and arresting the viewer's attention. This issue is only one of 23 in the entire history of *Life* as a weekly in which African Americans appeared on the cover.

The interior photographs illustrate the division of labor involved in taking the watermelon from field to table. Most of the essay illustrates the physical labor performed by black men and women in agricultural communities. Whites appearing in the essay are shown in positions of authority and responsibility. While one of the captions in the essay states that both whites and blacks pick and eat watermelon, no whites are seen picking melons and they are seen eating watermelon in only one image. Perhaps none of the essay's photographs have as much impact as an image in which a full-figured black woman with an exposed breast is posed nursing her child while eating a slice of melon so large that it obscures everything but her nose and her eyes, which gaze upward in an apparent state of gastronomic rapture inspired by the watermelon. The caption reads: "Nothing makes a Negro's mouth water like a luscious fresh-picked melon. Any colored 'mammy' can hold a huge slice in one hand while holding her offspring in the other. Since the watermelon is 92% water, tremendous quantities can be eaten. What melons the Negroes do not consume will find favor with the pigs."[24] This is a highly graphic stereotype punctuated and reinforced by a nakedly racist caption that combines watermelons, blacks, mammies, pickaninnies, and pigs. The above citations reveal *Life*'s editorial mentality toward blacks at its most extreme. This

[23]*Life,* vol. 10, no. 9 (March 3, 1941), p. 88.
[24]*Life,* vol. 3, no. 3 (August 9, 1937).

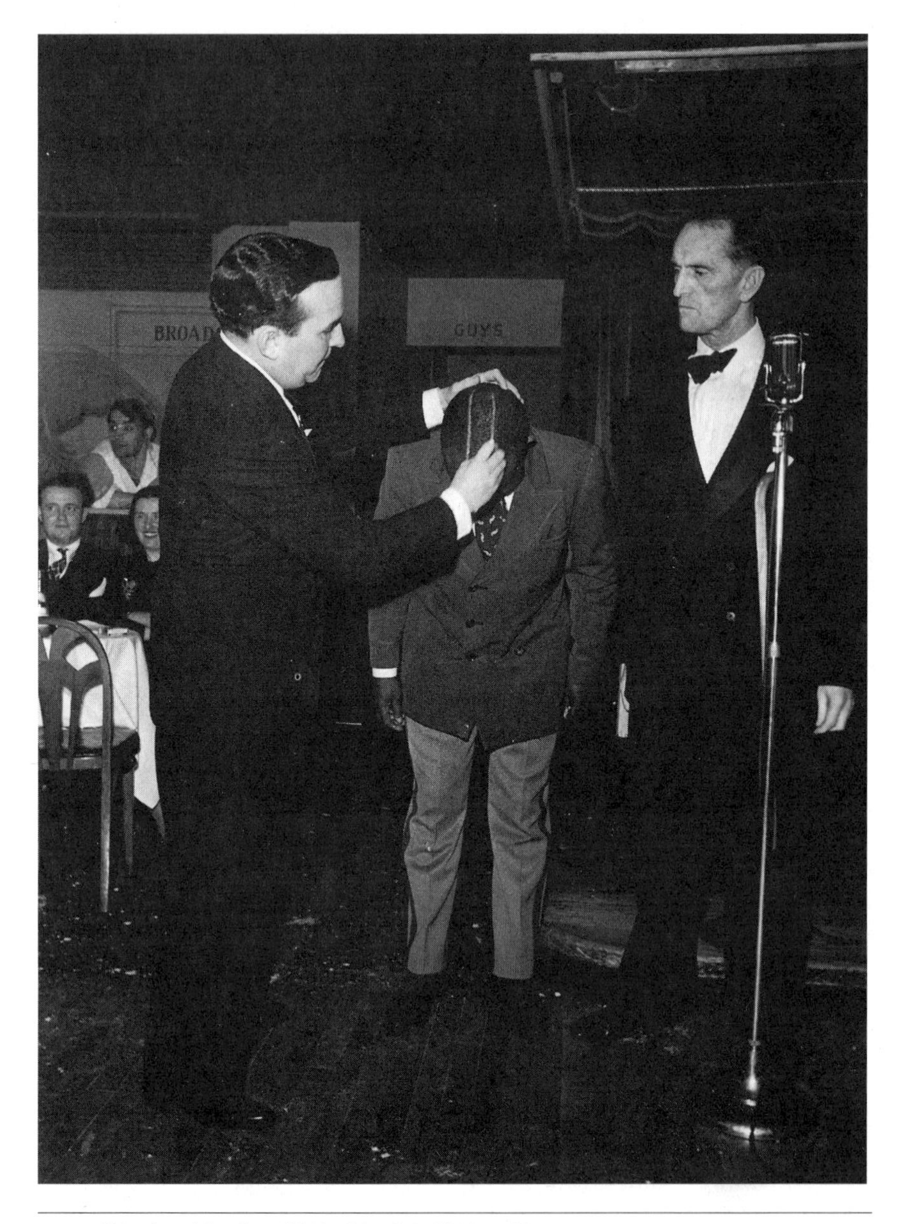

"To play ticktacktoe," Life, *March 3, 1941, p. 88.* (Alfred Eisenstaedt, Life Magazine © Time Warner Inc.)

mentality served as a model for more sophisticated and coded—but no less racist—representations in later issues of *Life* and other American magazines and newspapers.

▼ ▼ ▼

NEGROES

THE U. S. ALSO HAS A MINORITY PROBLEM

A BLACK GIRL SINGS A HYMN

"NEGROES: The U.S. Also Has a Minority Problem," pagespread from Life, *October 3, 1938, p. 49.* (Life Magazine © Time Warner Inc.)

Given the explicit racism conveyed by *Life* magazine and considering its influence in American photojournalism the question is, how much does contemporary coverage of African American life differ from the model established by *Life* magazine in 1936? A look at the four major general interest news or infotainment magazines (for the week ending May 31, 1993), *Time, Newsweek, People* and *Life* reveals that only *Life* magazine has a black as the subject of a cover story. Predictably "Inside the Private World of Michael Jackson" is yet another presentation of the "negro as entertainer." This issue of *Life* is distinguished however by a letter to the editor about the special issue on the American West published during the previous month. Despite extensive historical documentation of the black male and female presence in the American West there were no references in this issue to people like Bill Pickett, Nate "Deadwood Dick" Love, "Stagecoach" Mary Fields or other prominent blacks in the history of the Old West beyond a sidebar about an obscure black midwife. This glaring omission is cited by two disgruntled readers:

> Where are all the black heroes of the Old West? And where are the hundreds of modern black rodeo cowboys? In this age of multicultural awareness we expect *Life* to be more sensitive.[25]

[25]*Life,* vol. 16, no. 7 (June 1993), p. 8.

How can an understanding of black life progress when superficial stories about non-threatening, multimillion dollar athletes and entertainers like Michael Jordan and Michael Jackson or images of black urban youth as leaders in the creation of popular culture and teen pregnancies constantly dominate contemporary journalism? Or is obscuring the black American presence the objective? In the face of a rapidly declining educational system visual media have taken on an increasingly pedagogical role in American society. Given this, social and economic progress by African Americans as a group and as individuals continues to be neutralized by "ethnic cleansing" in journals like *Life* magazine. A 1990 survey by the University of Chicago's National Opinion Research Center critiques the notion of progress in the societal perception of African Americans. It revealed that 53% of non-blacks believe that African Americans are less intelligent than whites; 51% believe they are less patriotic; 56% believe they are more violence-prone; 62% believe they are more likely to "prefer to live off welfare" and less likely to "prefer to be self-supporting."[26] Even more troubling is the fact that many African Americans agree with these perceptions, often with as little understanding of the complexity of African American life as most whites.

In 1968 the Report of the National Advisory Commission on Civil Disorders (the so-called "Kerner Commission") published subsequent to urban unrest in the summer of that year specifically identified the socializing role that news media plays in this country:

> If what the white American reads in the newspaper or sees on television conditions his expectations of what is ordinary and normal in the larger society, he will neither understand nor accept the black American. By failing to portray the Negro as a matter of routine and in the context of the total society, the news media have, we believe, contributed to the black-white schism in this country.[27]

Twenty-five years later the commission's critique remains ignored by most editors in mainstream journalism.

In the current atmosphere of so-called multiculturalism African American popular culture is embraced, even as physical, economic, and institutional hostility toward African American people persists. For many in the African American community the multicultural embrace of black culture is a suspect one. It is our culture that is being embraced, not us. Too often an either colonized, homogenized, or appropriated representation of African American culture is the object of America's warmest affection. In 1992 the FBI released its first national survey of "hate crimes" against American citizens. The group subjected to the highest number of incidents were African Americans. Of the 4558 crimes reported in 1991, 1689 were against blacks.[28] In addition, the sur-

---

[26] Studs Terkel, *RACE How Blacks and Whites Think and Feel About the American Obsession* (New York: The New Press, 1992), p. 1.

[27] *Report of the National Advisory Commission on Civil Disorders* (New York: Bantam, 1968), p. 383.

[28] *Emerge,* vol. 6, no. 4 (April 1993), p. 10.

vey does not account for the thousands of deaths resulting from the hate crimes of black-on-black homicide, or the number of blacks who might have been included in the total number of crimes against gays and lesbians. These trends can be attributed to media driven images of blacks that at once inspire fear and racism in whites and self-hatred in blacks.

These images might begin to change if publishers, editors, and advertisers in print journalism question their image of the African as "different from and less than," an image that still appears to influence their daily editorial decisions. Considering the chronic inability of most mainstream print media to present wide-ranging reports on African American life, the deprogramming of this perception could start with more Americans (especially magazine editors) becoming consumers and readers of local and nationally published black news media (*Emerge, Essence, Jet, Ebony, Transition, Callaloo, The Black Scholar,* for example). Not only are these media important sources of news from a black perspective, available on most newsstands, these magazines are themselves, *news* sources. They provide reports and analysis of national and world events no less significant than those found in the so-called mainstream media. This most alternative of alternative media can also provide many people with an introduction to individuals and insights that can not only provide greater definition of and solutions to America's problem with its "white" identity, but to other problems affecting the future path of our country and the world. 20

DISCUSSING THE TEXT

1. Gaskins maintains that "In the face of a rapidly declining educational system visual media have taken on an increasingly pedagogical role in American society" (par. 17). Do you agree with this statement? Why or why not?
2. In his article, Gaskins analyzes the 1938 feature essay "NEGROES: The U.S. Also Has a Minority Problem." What aspects of African American experience does he say are suppressed in this *Life* essay? What evidence does he offer for his assertions? Can you think of any other possible explanations for the content of this essay?
3. In a group of four or five students, discuss some of the typical images or stereotypes of black people that Gaskins finds in *Life* magazine during the period he is investigating. Are any of these stereotypes surprising or shocking to you? Are any of them still prevalent in the American media? Take brief notes as you work on this assignment, and be prepared to share your opinions with the class.

WRITING ABOUT THE TEXT

4. Examine a recent issue of *Time* and a recent issue of *Newsweek* for a given week. Write two paragraphs describing how often and in what ways blacks are portrayed in these magazines, both in the text and in the pictures. Do you think the magazine's stories and photographs are slanted to give

readers a particular notion of African American life? If so, how would you describe that notion?

5. Examine a recent issue of at least two of the black magazines Gaskins lists in paragraph 20 (*Emerge, Essence, Jet,* and so on). Write a one-page analysis of the portrayal of blacks in these magazines, both in the text and in the pictures. Do you think that the stories are slanted to give readers a particular notion of African American life? If so, how would you describe that notion?
6. Write a brief essay that compares and contrasts your findings in response to questions 4 and 5 above.
7. Both Amy Rashap (p. 474) and Bill Gaskins write about visual images in their essays. What do Rashap and Gaskins contribute to your understanding of visual images through their writing? How would you compare their approaches? What kinds of questions do they ask? Write a brief essay in response to these questions.

EARL SMITH

The Genetically Superior Athlete: Myth or Reality

That African Americans are better in sports than whites is a commonly held belief, seemingly supported by their great visibility and domination in basketball, football, track and field, and other sports. But are blacks "naturals" in sports? It is this very question—"Is there a genetically superior athlete?"—that Earl Smith considers in detail in his essay, as he examines the available scientific and social science literature on the subject. Smith makes clear his own position at the outset, when he declares in his first sentence, "There is no such thing as the genetically superior Black American athlete." But as he shows in the rest of the article, the matter is not that simple. Whether or not we believe in preexisting, genetically endowed characteristics has great implications for how we regard achievement and potential among individuals. This, in turn, can affect our social programs.

Earl Smith, who is African American, is a professor of sociology at Pacific Lutheran University in Tacoma, Washington. Writing in the mode of social science articles, Smith labels the parts of his argument according to the conventions of the field: Introduction; Method of Study; Literature Review (that is, a review of existing scholarship); Discussion; Conclusion. Smith also uses statistical tables to summarize some of the data he presents that contribute to the logical argument he shapes in this article. The article was written for and originally appeared in Black Studies *(1990), a collection of scholarly essays focusing on cultural and social issues.*

Introduction

There is no such thing as the genetically superior Black American athlete. Indeed, the very notion itself conjures up images of the brute, all physical and no brains athlete who has been programmed to perform successfully in athletic contests. There is, though, and this truth has been gaining in stature ever since Jesse Owens shattered the white supremacist beliefs of Adolph Hitler at the 1936 Berlin Olympics, a fine-tuned, athletically capable and relatively well-educated young Black male who is demonstrating his talents in a *few select* high revenue, high visibility sports.[1] These athletes have proven themselves in the sports arena and because of this are being put under the microscope for further study and analysis by the sport scientist community.[2]

To put it differently, at the very moment that national unemployment rates have gone up in the Black community—over the past ten years this rate has held steady at between 30 and 40 percent for Blacks,[3] especially among young Blacks and the Black elderly—[4] the one area in social life where Blacks have found a modicum of success is being openly disparaged.

Unlike the racial comments about the lack of "necessities" among Black athletes made by the vice president for personnel for the Dodgers baseball team, Al Campanis, or the comments made by the sports announcer Jimmy "The Greek" Snyder,[5] who feels that Black American athletes are bred for success, now there are scientists who are equipped with powerful computers telling the world that these young Black Americans were born[6] to be basketball players (jumpers) and track and field stars (runners).

In the recent NBC special "Black Athletes: Fact and Fiction" (April 25, 1989) it was noted that Blacks are naturals in many of the sport games they play. To illustrate the point, the commentator said that world class sprinter Calvin Smith is physically built more like West Africans (since Smith is Black and a descendent of slaves who initially came from West Africa) and therefore has a different muscle structure than those Blacks from East Africa (who have *less* fast twitch muscles and therefore are naturals for middle and long distance running), thus giving him a natural edge in his speciality, the 100 and 200 meter dashes. This line of reasoning is not new by any means, although it is

---

[1]One could add that in team sports like football and basketball, black male athletes are also being well paid for their work, although Koch (1989), in a very interesting essay, "Is there Discrimination in the Black Man's Game," points out from his analysis of salary data that as a group Black players in the NBA are being paid *less* than their white counterparts.

[2]The *return* to genetic explanations for sport superiority was at the basis of the NBC special, looking at the scholarly/empirical research of white scientists at the University of Texas at Austin. Yet, one has to wonder why with the long history of debating this question and Black participation in sports, Black scientists have not taken advantage of what seems to be a sure money-maker in trying to prove Black American physical superiority.

[3]For clarification on this point see, Ellwood, *Poor Support* (1988) and Duncan, *Years of Poverty, Years of Plenty* (1984).

[4]Age is very important when trying to analyze unemployment rates. See, especially, M. Hurd. 1989. "The Economic Status of the Elderly." *Science* 244:659–664.

[5]*Al Campanis . . . Jimmy "The Greek" Snyder:* prominent American sports personalities during the late twentieth century (*Ed.*)

[6]One wonders about this: is this because slave masters on plantations in the colony of Maryland would breed their slaves in ways similar to the practice adhered to with horses for sale to other prospective owners?

curious why it has been resurrected at this point in time. It was not long ago that Blacks from any part of the world, including Harlem, were thought not to possess the essentials to be able to compete at distances longer than 100 meters. Now that the Kenyan middle and long distance runners have begun to excel at their events, a new theory has emerged, the "geographical theory of running" applied to explain the success of the Kenyan middle distance runners.

5 Being employed as a professor at Washington State University, which has a long history of excellent Kenyan middle distance runners, has afforded this writer the worthwhile opportunity to observe many of these runners on and off the track. Seeing the comparisons being made in the NBC special between Black Americans and African runners was very interesting, in that some of these athletes competed at Washington State and have also been students in my classes. The point is that in interviews with former Washington State University track runners this writer was able to ascertain that these athletes trained very hard to reach world class status: Henry Rono (former world record holder in 5 events; current world record holder in 2 events; collegiate record holder in 7 events; everything from the mile run up through the 10,000 meter run, as well as National Freshmen record holder for the 21K run) and Peter Koech (National Freshmen record holder in the 5,000 meter run; PAC-10 champion 10,000 and 5,000 meter runs; NCAA 3,000 meter steeplechase champion; 1988 Olympic silver medal winner in the 3,000 meter steeplechase; and current world record holder in the 3,000 meter steeplechase) trained daily and trained very hard to outdistance their competition. Julius Korior (Olympic gold medal in the 3,000 meter steeplechase, 1984) and Gabriel Tiacoh (1984 Olympic silver medal in the 400 meter dash) also trained hard on a daily basis, as did Richard Tuwei (PAC-10 champion in the 5,000 meter run and PAC-10 champion in the 3,000 meter steeplechase).

These athletes would run in the hot, dry weather of the summer and the cold of the winter. On any given day in February or July or September, one could witness the familiar gallop of these great world class runners on the rural roads of Pullman, Washington; two or three of them together made quite an impression, one etched in this writer's memory that will last forever. Early morning or late afternoon, with the western sun rising or descending on the hills of the Palouse, these great athletes outlined against the beautiful sky was a sight to see. These runners, competing at world class levels, were not and (for some who are still active) are not *natural* athletes.[7] Regardless of the fact that most come from high altitude regions of Africa, they train very hard to be the best in their respective events.

Black Americans, stuffing and twisting and running up and down a basketball court—from Wilt "the Stilt" Chamberlain to "Dr" Julius Erving to

---

[7]The situation is not going to change in the foreseeable future; in a recent issue of *Track and Field News* (June, 1989), it was reported that because of the victories by the Kenyan distance runners in the 1988 Olympic Games, especially in the 5,000 meter run and the 3,000 meter steeplechase, hundreds of young boys and girls lined up for a local track meet to run those two events!

Table 1 Race/Ethnicity and Field of Doctorate, 1987

Ethnicity	*Total Fields*	*Phys. Science*	*Engineering*	*Life Science*	*Social Science*	*Humanities*	*Education*	*Other*
Total U.S.	22,396	2,995	1,505	4,132	4,270	2,675	5,388	1,431
Am. Indians	115	10	7	16	22	11	41	8
Asian Am.	540	104	135	145	75	25	41	15
Black Am.	765	29	12	78	136	73	379	58
Hispanic Am.	618	64	24	77	146	96	186	25
White Am.	20,358	2,788	1,327	3,816	3,891	2,470	4,741	1,325

Source: Summary Report, 1987: Doctorate Recipients from United States Universities, National Research Council.

Michael Jordan—are not *natural* athletes either. The many defensive backs and the new fancy running backs who year in and year out put points on the scoreboard—as well as entertain the fans with their almost superhuman feats for their college/university and professional teams—are not *natural* athletes either. But, what is a great irony in this whole new chapter (of the same old story) is why these athletes are only seen as being "natural athletes" in basketball, football and/or running? Why isn't this familiar song sung each time a Black seizes an opportunity in a sport like golf, cricket, swimming, handball, gymnastics, tennis or some of the many other sports that Blacks do not dominate (but have shown time and time again that they can not only play the game, but can compete at national and international levels once they are given the opportunity to participate)?

It is being argued herein that no athlete, Black or white—from Leroy "Satchel" Paige to Cheryl Miller to Larry Bird to Arnold Palmer to Muhammed Ali—is a natural athlete. Snyder and Spreitzer, in their discussion of this issue note (1989, p. 78):

> It is often said that someone is a "natural athlete." This expression can be misleading if it is understood to mean that a person did not have to learn the ideas, attitudes, and movements associated with a given sport. The notion of a natural athlete no doubt applies primarily to people who are born with physical attributes such as coordination, agility, speed, power, and stamina. However, the refinement of these attributes, skills and techniques as well as the psychological and social aspects of play and sport have to be acquired.

In sum, what the above authors are saying is that regardless of race or socioeconomic status or some of the many other things that people believe in when it comes to athletic abilities or a lack thereof, the athlete—Black or white—must train and perform to be a superior athlete if one is determined to compete at the college/university level and in professional sports.

Method of Study

The specific method employed to produce this paper has been a wide ranging literature review, which crosses several science and social science disciplines. The opportunity afforded by this approach in examining what scholars and others have said about the natural acclimation of Black athletes is unique in that it allows one to be as forthright as possible. The aim of the discussion, then, is (1) a dissemination of those facts already gathered by others and (2) an analysis of specific studies to ascertain, where possible, the validity of positions taken in the NBC documentary,[8] and, finally, arriving at new theoretical insights about Black American athletes.[9]

To maintain all forms of injustice requires that it first be rationalized; in fact, the greater the injustice is, the more prolonged its life meaning and, in the example being discussed herein, the greater its rationale. It is not surprising, then, that an enormous amount of literature exists on the nature of sport prowess. For this essay, the literature has been divided into that which (1) supports the view that Black athletes have some kind of natural edge in terms of their sport abilities and (2) a comparison literature which tries to temper these views, looking at other factors which are said to influence Black abilities in sport.

LITERATURE REVIEW

Eighteenth and nineteenth century physicians and anthropologists were the first scientists who made earnest attempts at classifying human racial differences. The major questions these scientists asked—from the French physician François Bernier to the English surgeon Charles White—were questions about racial differences that transcended earlier findings that placed the emphasis of explanation on geography as the great divide between the races.[10] White (1799, p. iv), in his treatise *An Account of the Regular Gradation in Man,* posited the view that the human species, although not on an evolutionary chain as others believed and especially Charles Darwin, was made up of a hierarchy which he termed "an immense chain of beings, endowed with various degrees of intelligence and active powers, suited to their stations in the general system."

Blacks, in Charles White's scheme of things, occupied a low or intermediate place in this "system," which he placed as being between the white man

---

[8] The special program elicited quite a stir from scholars and the lay public alike. See R. Lapchick, 1989, "Pseudoscientific Prattle About Athletes." *New York Times,* April 29, and Jon Entine, 1989, "No Scientist Challenged The Conclusion of a Black Physical Edge," letter to the editor, *New York Times.* May 24. Needless to say, the issue remains very hot and very important for sport sociological research.

[9] This is quite a departure for sociological research where empirical data is collected and analyzed or previous studies using empirical data are replicated. The aim is to test both theoretical and methodological accuracy. Colleagues in the humanities inform me that it is OK to do this kind of work as long as, in the final analysis, the *overall* aim is to advance theoretical knowledge.

[10] Stripped of its veneer, this is essentially the same "nature v. nurture" debate that has been around for years. See Carl Bereiter. 1969. "The Future of Individual Differences." *Harvard Educational Review,* Reprint Series No. 2.

and the ape. This type of idea spread widely and quickly. With the growth of industrialization, which brought about the building of roads, a railway system, more economical ocean travel and factory production, the spread of new ideas about the human condition, and the specificity of what made human beings "tick," continued apace.[11]

Herbert Spencer, the English philosopher, who coined the term "the survival of the fittest," (a term that has been misplaced and most often attributed to Charles Darwin), pursued a large research endeavor that he thought would help explain how this new industrialization should proceed and what specific role humans should play in the process. Thus, Spencer paid close attention to what he considered to be important characteristics of human beings, especially among different racial and ethnic groups.[12] One critical finding that Spencer made, which is important for our purposes herein, is the fact that his ideas about industrialization, miscegenation, public education, innate racial characteristics, poor laws and working conditions were also deep concerns in the United States in the late 1880s. Essentially, some 100 years *before* Ronald Reagan, Spencer did not see a role for government in regulating the life chances for its citizens; he felt that all aspects of social life, especially when it came to provisions, should be left to the individuals themselves, regardless of their socioeconomic status. Put differently, Spencer was vehemently opposed to helping the poor. One is also mindful that these ideas were uncritically accepted in U.S. academic circles mainly by sociologist Charles H. Cooley and political scientist William G. Summer.[13]

Both the dissemination and acceptance of these views were widespread. It was not long, before the racial consciousness movement, spurred on by the eugenicists[14] expounding concerns such as the following: David Starr-Jordan, then president of Stanford University, stated that: "poverty, dirt and crime are the result of poor human material."[15] "Poor human material," then, became the basis for the eugenicists and their movement, the thrust of which was to offer compulsory sterilization to those persons who were considered genetically defective.

▼ ▼ ▼

[11]The best social history of this world-wide development is still Karl Marx's study *Capital,* Volume 1, London: Vintage Books, 1976.

[12]Herbert Spencer. 1969. *The Man Versus the State: Four Essays on Politics and Society.* Introduction by D. Macrae. Baltimore: Penguin Books.

[13]Some seventy-nine years later, Joseph LeConte, a disciple of Spencer, wrote an essay that received considerable attention. In his "Scientific Relation of Sociology to Biology" he argued that, everything else being equal, individual differences between Blacks and whites was, simply put, the way God worked—without any input from these individuals. See, especially, John S. Haller. 1971. *Outcasts From Evolution: Scientific Attitudes of Racial Inferiority. 1895–1900.* Urbana: University of Illinois Press, p. 162.

[14]*eugenicists:* advocates of human improvement through genetic control (*Ed.*)

[15]Cited in T. Gossett. 1965. *Race: The History of an Idea in America.* Dallas: Southern Methodist University Press, p. 159.

It was out of this concern for "racial superiority" that the countervailing perspective "racial inferiority" came to be associated with Black Americans. Running through most, if not all, of this eugenics literature is that the racial inferiority of Blacks can be traced to their neuroanatomical differences from whites. Robert Bean greatly popularized these purported differences in several essays but especially his belief that Black Americans lack abstract reasoning, apperception and learning abilities.[16] 15

Of course, the flip-side of this discussion of mindlessness, defective genes, low brain weight and low I.Q. scores, culminating in the *Harvard Education Review* essay by Arthur Jensen entitled "How Much Can We Boost IQ and Achievement?"[17] is that without brains, Blacks are therefore better suited for other functions such as menial, low-paying jobs, and athletic games that do not have as a prerequisite superior mental reasoning.

The mantle on these discussions was taken up by Martin Kane in his highly visible *Sports Illustrated* article entitled "An Assessment of Black Is Best."[18] Combining the evolutionary, biosocial perspectives of the physical scientists and anthropologists discussed earlier, Kane proposed that Black athletes are superior to white athletes for the following reasons:

1. Blacks have won 12 of the last 13 NBA Most Valuable Player awards.
2. In 1969 all four offense and defense Rookie of the Year awards went to Blacks.
3. In baseball Blacks have won the National League's Most Valuable Player award 16 of 22 times.
4. Blacks make up 63 percent of National Basketball Association (NBA) All-Star teams.

In the attempt to explain the above, Kane turns to genetically transmitted physical and psychological factors. His analysis is presented in the following schematic:

1. Black athletes have longer legs, arms and narrower hips and greater arm circumference than white athletes.
2. More tendon to muscle and "double jointedness" among Black athletes compared to whites.
3. Black athletes *relax* more than whites.
4. Blacks are better athletes than whites because they are the descendants of Black slaves who had to adapt to their harsh environments.

Although presented in outline form, the essential elements of Kane's argument are discernible. He sees significant variability in the Black physique

---

[16]Robert Bean. 1906. "Some Racial Peculiarities of the Negro Brain." *American Journal of Anatomy* 5:353–432.

[17]In Arthur Jensen. 1969. *Environment, Heredity and Intelligence,* Reprint Series 2, Harvard Educational Review.

[18]Martin Kane. 1971. "An Assessment of Black is Best." *Sports Illustrated,* January 18.

compared to that of white athletes and that the similarity of this Black physique is what gives the Black athlete his physical powers.

What is so interesting about this early work of Kane is how close the NBC special followed its results even in an examination of Black athletes from other countries. As mentioned earlier, the NBC special revisited geography and posited that the success of the East African runners, especially the Kenyan middle and long distance runners, could be attributed to geography and musculo-skeletal development.

When Kip Keino of Kenya beat Jim Ryun, the favored American, in the 1500 meter run in 1968 Olympic Games, explanations abounded around geography, anatomy and physiology without a word said about the training methods of the Kenyan superstar or that many of the African athletes had been free from European colonial rule for less than a decade, which may have prevented them from being engaged in sport activities long before the mid 1960s. The point to be made here is that Kane and others have not been very convincing in attempting to explain athletic success via purported anthropometric racial differences. It is ironic, then, that Kane pays no attention to *within* race differences—the more relevant question, if one were really interested in attempting to demonstrate Black American versus Black African athletic differences (as opposed to those Kane claims exist between Black and white athletes only).

When one compares the physique of a Bob Beamon with Carl Lewis—both superstars in the long jump—one is comparing apples with oranges. A simple look at body type raises the question of how both have outdistanced the field of other long jumpers, yet it is impossible to come up with an explanation based on the logic of Kane as to why two totally opposite-built Black athletes have performances that are so similar. A long list of dissimilarities among Black athletes could be constructed looking at athletes in basketball to gymnastics to tennis to football.

Following the publication of the Kane essay there were several attempts to empirically validate his findings. Embedded within much of what Kane says is the notion that specific tasks are more natural for Black athletes than whites. In one essay (Dunn and Lupfer 1974) young fourth grade boys were tested on a variety of tasks. The critical findings were that Black boys are better at reactive tasks—activities one has to respond to—as opposed to initiating an activity which white boys are more adept at. On the basis of the results from this type of study, and others that are similar in design and results, (Jordan 1969; Jones and Hochner 1973), scholars contend that this is why so many Black baseball players are outfielders and not pitchers[19] or defense backs and not quarterbacks in football.[20]

---

[19]Cf. Earl Smith and Monica A. Seff. 1990. "Race, Position Segregation and Salary Equity in Professional Baseball." *Journal of Sport and Social Issues* 13 (2):101–119.

[20]See also, Jonathan Brower. 1973. "The Black Side of Football: The Salience of Race." unpublished PhD Dissertation, University of California, Santa Barbara.

Nothing in the aforementioned literature that supports Black superiority in sports, demonstrates that this is the case. Much of this literature offers only speculative hypotheses about sport behavior of Blacks (primarily males) yet the empirical evidence for such longstanding beliefs is surprisingly absent. In the attempt to review as much of this literature as possible, the writer was quite surprised at the dearth of empirical research in an area in which subjects for research should have proven to be willingly available.

▼ ▼ ▼

For many years American sportswriters, fans, team owners and white players have firmly believed that Blacks are superior in some sports (even specific positions like outfielder in baseball) and inferior at others (e.g., swimming and positions like quarterback in football) based on their genetic makeup. What is so interesting, in light of the television documentary that aired on NBC, is that there is no compelling scientific evidence to substantiate these "theories," nor is there one shred of evidence available for replication. Can one scientifically validate these claims if one cannot replicate the studies that purportedly produced the results in the first place? Since this is close to impossible, it seems the only thing one can actually do at this point in time is to conduct the requisite studies that will produce the needed data. 25

For this writer, a major need is to focus more on why Black males spend so much of their time perfecting their game. It seems that if one is seriously interested in knowing why the National Basketball Association, for example, is made up of at least 73 to 75 percent Black players, then one needs to investigate the causal linkages that exist between the training that is necessary to become an elite basketball player in America and the success of Blacks at this sport. Any other suggestions—especially those centered around the "natural superiority" belief—remain just that, suggestion and ill-founded speculation.

Highly visible Black superstars are legendary; yet without systematically examining empirical evidence, many—including young Black males who have also bought into this myth—have come to see the sports arena as having provided Blacks with at least one four-lane highway to success.[21] This view is not only simplistic, it is quite flawed. The numbers of successful Black athletes are quite small. More Blacks fail in their attempt to become professional sport stars than make it as successful collegiate and professional athletes. (This is a sensitive subject; empirical data are very hard to come by. Yet, it is known that young Black males, who are overrepresented in high school and college sports and in some professional sports, have nearly a 10,000 to 1 chance from the time they start participating in sports to make it as a profes-

[21]Earl Smith and Monica A. Seff. 1990. "Race, Position Segregation and Salary Equity in Professional Baseball." *Journal of Sport and Social Issues* 13:101–119.This paper provides a good example from one sport and focuses on the necessity to examine empirical evidence before accepting this perspective. Koch (1989) provides another example from the sport of basketball in his essay entitled "Is There Discrimination in the Black Man's Game."

sional athlete. The odds are worse when looking at the probability that these athletes will successfully "retire" from professional sports and assume a managerial position or work in any number of occupations directly associated with sports, e.g., marketing, radio and/or television work).[22]

Discussion

The main question posed at the outset of the NBC program was, "Are Black athletes better than white athletes?" Carl Lewis (echoing the sentiment of Black athletes who spoke with Kane in 1971, e.g., Calvin Hill and Lee Evans), the eminent American sprinter, says that Black athletes are better. Others interviewed for the program—except Stanford track and field coach Brooks Johnson—also said they felt that Black Americans are superior athletes when compared to whites. Yet, it is interesting that this program, having an international, comparative focus (the camera crews traveled all the way to Eldoret, located at the Equator and home of many of the Kenyan runners) could not devote one minute of time discussing the early (and failed) attempts by American coaches to prepare Africans who are Watusi (located in central Africa) to high jump, seeing that they have an average height of seven feet. For some reason these Africans could not high jump, and since the time of those experiments, it has been learned that one need not be seven feet tall to high jump anyway. The discussion of lack of jumping ability among whites ("white man's disease") seems rather arcane in that many of the top high jumpers (and even long jumpers) over the past twenty-five years have been athletes who would be classified as "white"; this includes Soviets, Romanians, East Germans, and Cubans. But maybe these athletes aren't white or Black—just simply red? Then again, it may be that the "theory" about this white man's disease is only limited to NCAA Division II basketball players or novice high jumpers, anyway. Table 2 shows for the past seven Olympic Games—Rome (1960) through Los Angeles (1984)—the ethnicity of high jumpers and long jumpers who have won Olympic gold medals.

Although inconclusive, these data do point in a direction enabling one to question some of the assertions made in the NBC special program on the Black American athlete. For the 28 possible gold medals for both male and female high jumpers and long jumpers, whites have won all but 5 of these medals. Furthermore, not a single word was said in the NBC program about the below par performance of Manute Bol, an African who is seven feet, six inches tall, plays for the Washington Bullets professional basketball team and cannot jump over a piece of paper. Why?

This writer proposes that special focus on the physical characteristics of Black American athletes takes away from a focus—which would yield the kind of empirical data necessary to begin looking intelligently at this question of superiority of athletic abilities—on their dedication, motivation, determination, discipline, and just as importantly the intelligence needed to be elite 30

[22]Richard Lapchick. 1988. "The Student-Athlete." *New Perspectives* 19:35–45.

Table 2 Performance of Males/Females in the High Jump at the 1960–1984 Olympic Games

	Year						
Sex	*1960 Rome*	*1964 Tokyo*	*1968 Mexico*	*1972 Munich*	*1976 Montreal*	*1980 Moscow*	*1984 LA*
Male	White	White	White	White	White	White	White
Female	White	White	White	White	White	White	White

Table 3 Performance of Males/Females in the Long Jump at the 1960–1984 Olympic Games

	Year						
Sex	*1960 Rome*	*1964 Tokyo*	*1968 Mexico*	*1972 Munich*	*1976 Montreal*	*1980 Moscow*	*1984 LA*
Male	Black	White	Black	Black	Black	White	Black
Female	White	White	White	White	White	White	White

athletes.[23] Over ten years ago Jack Olsen made the point in his successful book[24] addressing this question in regards to the natural abilities of Black athletes. He put it thus:

> People keep reminding me that there is a difference in physical ability between the races, but I think there isn't. The Negro boy practices longer and harder. The Negro has the keener desire to excel in sports because it is more mandatory for his future opportunities than it is for a white boy. There are nine thousand different jobs available to a person if he is white.

Furthermore, Black athletes are located in those sports wherein they have had an opportunity to compete.[25] White athletes, on the other hand, are more widely dispersed around the sports arena in that they have had competitive opportunities in more sports. What looks like dominance on the part of Black athletes is, in fact, a situation akin to that which takes place when opportuni-

[23]If one is serious about trying to understand why certain races and ethnic groups are concentrated in specific sports (e.g., Asians in gymnastics, Canadians in hockey), the real or more important question that needs to be asked is why are whites more widely spread across the sport spectrum? Why, for example, do whites dominate in auto racing, gymnastics, bowling, golf, swimming, tennis, cycling, skiing, football, baseball, hockey, water polo, horse racing, and pool to name just a few of the sports that whites are dominant in. Are they, it could and should be asked, genetically superior in these sports? No one, who thinks for himself/herself and is over twelve years of age, and has sense, would make such a ridiculous statement.

[24]Jack Olsen. 1968. *The Black Athlete.* New York: Time Life Books, p. 14.

[25]Earl Smith. 1988. "Position Segregation Keeps Blacks Out Of Management." Op-ED: *The Atlanta Journal/The Atlanta Constitution,* March 16.

ties in other areas of our society open up for Black people: they seize these opportunities and because they have worked so hard to obtain them in the first place, they then go on to excel. Isn't this simple enough to understand?[26]

In the absence of scientific investigations, folk wisdom and assumptions have prevailed as facts.[27] On the basis of the evidence presented above, it seems sheer folly to even speculate that somehow Blacks have a natural propensity for excellence in sports. If Black athletes hold a genetic edge in athletics, it would seem that they would look around and figure out that it is in golf and tennis—described by Wells, Pearson and Picou (1988) as "sports of the affluent classes"—that higher salaries and more lucrative product endorsements may be commanded. As well, in these "sports of the affluent classes" the life chances of the athlete are much greater than they are in either basketball or football, where one finds the majority of Black athletes concentrated. The case of track and field is still open in that it is too early to tell how long performance money will be associated with this sport. One may speculate that corporate sponsorship of track athletes will not last, arguing on the basis of the short lived professional track tour of a few years ago, which folded after only a few unsuccessful seasons.[28]

Conclusion

Sociologists who study sport institutions in American society, have been very keen when it comes to identifying the macro social problems that exist within U.S. sport institutions. Yet, much of this work is social-problem oriented and therefore reflective. To move the analysis forward, somewhat, and begin to transcend this useful but limited orientation, one needs to enlarge the research paradigm to include studies that not only look at the problems that seem to engulf Black athletes, which is very important, but one must also begin codifying those traits and characteristics that have proven to be successful for these athletes. One area that comes to mind is the concern over occupational attainment for those college athletes, male and female, who

[26]Examining the available data on the Olympic Games is interesting on this point. For the most part they are only concentrated in a few sports and not represented in many others. Kjeldsen (1984) looked at participation by ethnicity in the 1936, 1960 and 1980 Olympic Games. What he found is very interesting: Blacks participated in basketball, track and field, and boxing. Other sports (e.g., swimming, wrestling, fencing) show that Blacks are below their demographic proportion within the U.S. population.

[27]This big problem is discussed, using the example of the faulty logic and methodology of Husserl, in the text by Barry Hindess entitled *Philosophy and Methodology in the Social Sciences*, Harvester Press, London, 1977, p. 88.

[28]George Steinbrenner, owner of the New York Yankees baseball team, provides a good example for a counter argument. Steinbrenner has invested in not only a few select track and field stars but owns and controls a major track and field club based in Florida and thus, effectively, is paying these athletes to run and jump. This type of managed relationship is new for the sport of track and field.

graduate[29] but who do not pursue professional athletic careers.[30] Sport scientists know very little about these athletes. What is known about the curriculum patterns for these athletes? What types of mentoring have they had? How does this affect the transition into a world without sports, which most athletes have known little of for many years? And, what kinds of jobs do these athletes get when their collegiate careers are over? Questions such as these are not driven by the social-problems approach but, more so, by the kinds of questions sport scientists need to be asking. In so doing, they then broaden the research focus when it comes to understanding the institution of sports in general and the specific place of Black athletes in this institution in particular.

To make the issues spelled out above clearer as well as stronger, a deeper contextual and empirical analysis is needed before the book on many of the topics discussed herein can be closed. To be sure, there is the need to be continually reminded that those Black athletes who do become the nation's Saturday afternoon entertainment, do so after many long hours and long years of hard work. The acclaim for Black athletic prowess and the ability to rationalize the lack of Black representation in scientific and professional fields of endeavor simply points to the continued existence of "scientific racism" that reared its ugly head and became known to the public on the threshold of World War II. There is no convincing evidence to justify the conclusion that permanent organic differences—which allow for superior athletic performances on the one hand and inferior performances on the other—exist between African, Black American and white athletes. 33

DISCUSSING THE TEXT

1. In this article's "Introduction," Smith states his own position, that "there is no such thing as the genetically superior Black American athlete" (par. 1), although he does acknowledge the visibility of young black males in a *few* sports. Why does Smith think that the argument of genetic superiority detracts from the success of black Americans?

---

[29] The graduation question is paramount in collegiate athletics. Recently, the National Collegiate Athletic Association (NCAA) and individual college programs came under fire for not reporting graduation rates when a Government Accounting Office study showed that a majority of major football and basketball programs graduated between 0 and 40 percent of their student-athletes. Senator Edward Kennedy has proposed that all colleges make available to families of respective recruits their graduation rates—by sport, race and sex—prior to signing the student. On this hot subject see the volume edited by Richard Lapchick and John B. Slaughter, 1989, *The Rules of The Game,* New York: American Council on Education, Macmillan Publishing Company.

[30] A research project is underway wherein this writer surveyed athletes from a large, public 4-year university, asking them questions about their athletic careers, academic training, and occupational attainment. The major question posed asked how these activities intersect with each other and impact on the athlete once they have graduated from the university. The results from that research project are forthcoming.

2. Smith maintains that it is more important to study the differences *within* races than the differences *between* races. Why does he make this argument? Do you agree or disagree? Why?
3. Smith observes that American sportswriters often assume that blacks are superior in some sports and inferior in others (pars. 4, 25). In a group of four or five students, discuss this issue. Does Smith himself hold these views? Do you think there is anything wrong with holding these views? What is your position on the matter? Take brief notes as you work on this assignment, and be prepared to share your opinions with the class.

WRITING ABOUT THE TEXT

4. Toward the end of the Introduction, Smith quotes a discussion by Snyder and Spreitzer of the expression "natural athlete"; he then goes on to summarize this quotation and express his own view that hard work, not natural endowment, creates the superior athlete (par. 8). Write a list of the qualities that you associate with the term "natural athlete," and then write two paragraphs comparing your ideas with those cited in Smith's article. Do you agree with Smith's analysis of the term "natural athlete"?
5. Smith observes that although sports remain a highly visible area of black success, the number of blacks who actually succeed in athletics is quite small, relative to those who try. See the movie *Hoop Dreams,* and write an essay in which you evaluate the factors required for success in basketball, based on the careers depicted.
6. Interview a sample of at least ten fellow students, asking them the question, "Are blacks better athletes than whites?" As a follow-up, ask them what their evidence is, or simply why they feel the way they do about this issue. Write a short essay that (a) summarizes and (b) assesses the validity of these students' views.

ENRIQUE FERNÁNDEZ

Spitfires, Latin Lovers, Mambo Kings

In this article, which originally appeared in the Arts and Leisure section of the New York Times *on April 19, 1992, Enrique Fernández offers a summary of Latin popular culture in the United States over the past decade. As he cites different examples of the contribution of Latinos to music, the film industry, and literature, Fernández also analyzes various stereotypes seen in the mainstream culture's representation of Latinos in the arts, particularly in film.*

Fernández contrasts African American and Latin cultures in terms of the impact that each has had on American culture. He observes that blacks have begun to enter the popular imagination through images that transcend stereotypes, but "Latin culture remains a culture of otherness," perhaps because it is often represented, even when the intent is positive, as being too "hot."

Another aspect of Latin American culture that is often overlooked is its remarkable diversity. Although the Spanish language creates a linguistic bond among the majority of Latin Americans, and although there are other common cultural characteristics, major differences also exist among the many Hispanic groups in the United States today. But these differences remain largely unnoticed by the mainstream culture. For example, even though the three largest groups of Latinos in the United States—Mexican Americans, Cuban Americans, and Puerto Ricans—see themselves as quite distinct from one another, they are often portrayed in the mass media as a homogeneous "Latin type."

Journalist Enrique Fernández is the editor of the popular, mass-media Spanish-language magazine Más. *He writes often about Latin American and U.S. Latino art and literature.*

In most Hollywood films, whenever a black actor walks into a scene, the movie is infused with a new emotional element. The African-American presence has haunted, frightened, healed, comforted, enchanted, enticed and stirred American filmgoers for decades.

The reaction to Hispanics has been narrower. In the early days of Hollywood, when the movies dealt almost exclusively with stereotypes, Latinos were vaguely lumped with Italians as greasers. In fact, it was an Italian, the brilliantine-haired Rudolph Valentino, who transformed the greaser into the Latin lover. Playing a swaggering Argentine in the 1921 film "Four Horsemen of the Apocalypse," the matinee idol danced the forbidden tango and combined the seductive power of Latin culture in film, music and dance. What Valentino—and other Latin lovers—brought to the screen was heat.

When "The Mambo Kings," the story of two Cuban musicians who came to New York at the peak of the 40's mambo craze, opened over the winter, the critic Gene Shalit referred to it as "a scorcher" with "hot music, hot romance, a hot movie." Janet Maslin, writing in The Times, called it "fiery . . . impassioned." In seven decades, it seems, things have not changed all that much for Latinos. While African-Americans on screen have gone from servants ("Gone With the Wind") to savants (Morgan Freeman in "Robin Hood") and are the embodiment of "cool," Latin characters remain mostly "hot." In Hollywood film, that mirror of the American imagination, Latinos turn up as fiery gang members ("West Side Story"), hot-tempered bandits (any Peckinpah film), smoldering playboys (usually played by Ricardo Montalbán or César Romero) or purveyors of the mambo, the rhumba and the steamy lambada.

At various points in the last decade, Latinos seemed on the verge of breaking away from these stereotypes, and not only in Hollywood. Edward James Olmos, a Mexican-American, played an authoritative police lieutenant on the NBC series "Miami Vice," and Jimmy Smits, who is part Puerto Rican, portrayed a cool-tempered lawyer on NBC's "L.A. Law." Raul Julia (a Puerto Rican), Andy García (a Cuban) and Rubén Blades (a Panamanian) turn up regularly in films.

The Broadway show "Tango Argentino" inspired a tango craze in 1985. David Byrne and Paul Simon released albums heavily influenced by Latin music. Linda Ronstadt recorded Mexican songs. The Cuban-American novelist Oscar Hijuelos received the Pulitzer Prize in 1990 for his novel "The Mambo Kings Play Songs of Love," on which "The Mambo Kings" was based. The film "Havana" was released last year, and Mr. Olmos's Mexican-American prison drama, "American Me," came out last month. 5

So the trend-watchers have been on alert. Not just: Is there a Latin revival? But: Are we living through a boom? Is there a Latin Spike Lee waiting in the wings, a Latin Hammer? If rap can make it, the thinking goes, maybe so can salsa and merengue.

Maybe . . . not. Latin culture will likely never have the same impact on America as black culture. Perhaps it is *too* hot. Or too diverse: which version of Latin music will cross over—the Mexican corridos that Linda Ronstadt sings, or the Afro-Cuban beats of Rubén Blades? And what about the tango? The Latin arts that have traditionally prevailed in this country, like Xavier Cugat's music, have invariably been watered down for the American palate.

Which is not to say that genuine Latin culture cannot be found. It exists in the novels of Gabriel García Márquez, in impressive exhibitions like "Mexico: Splendors of 30 Centuries" at the Metropolitan Museum of Art in 1990, in merengue clubs and downtown performance spaces, in an Emmy-winning Spanish-language local newscast and Obie-winning plays by María Irene Fornés. But so far, in spite of the 25 million Hispanics in the United States (projected to be the largest minority in a few years), Latin culture remains a culture of otherness. That otherness plays itself out across the artistic landscape.

Passion: Caliente vs. Cool

"This Latin music's mayhem," the Caribbean-flavored, style-hopping singer Kid Creole has said. Language is only part of the explanation for why Spanish-language music hasn't crossed over. Latin music is excited. While the English-language love song drips with honey or violates your ears, Latin ballads are full of something foreign to American culture: passion. The Latin male singer lays his heart bare, singing open-throated in a voice made vulnerable. To Americans, vulnerability and machismo are antithetical. Not so. The Latin balladeer can have a broken heart, but his heart exudes power.

Most Spanish-language ballads rise to an operatic crescendo. To the Anglo-American ear, this emotional outpouring sounds corny or embarrassing. For one thing, it is not cool, and cool is what distinguishes, and attracts the world to, American culture. In the United States, Latin singers like Julio Iglesias appeal primarily to ladies of a certain age who appreciate Tom Jones and Engelbert Humperdinck. Even hip Latin music like salsa or merengue seems overly romantic to listeners weaned on heavy metal and rap. 10

Gloria Estefan, who fronts the Miami Sound Machine, *has* crossed over to the pop charts. The love songs she writes, like "Cuts Both Ways," appeal to both her American listeners and her huge Latin following. In Ms. Estefan's native Cuba, and throughout Latin America, there is a rich songwriting tradition. But Ms. Estefan's creative roots lie in American pop. It is for that reason that she is our one-woman Latin boom.

Border as Metaphor: The Great Divide

The border as reality and metaphor appears in Latin art and speculative thinking, most notably in works by the performance artist Guillermo Gómez Peña, who was at the Brooklyn Academy of Music last year. Mr. Gómez Peña has devoted much of his writing to arte fronterizo (border art), which sees the border as a unique space where Latin and Anglo esthetics collide and blend.

The border personifies many things. It is the great divide that Anglos fear to cross. (The 1982 film "The Border" replays the hackneyed theme: How Can the Gringo's Soul Survive the Spectacle of Suffering in the Third World?) It is the line that Mexican-Americans must pass over to regain their soul. (In the 1987 movie "La Bamba," the director Luis Valdez sends his hero, Ritchie Valens, on a harrowing tour south of the border to create a great fusion hit.) It also represents insurmountable alienation.

Consider "American Me," the directorial debut of Edward James Olmos, which was written, produced and acted primarily by Hispanics. The movie, which opened last month to mixed reviews, faced trepidation over its political correctness. How could Mr. Olmos, the spokesman for every noble Latin cause in the country, make a film in which practically all the Hispanic characters are cold-blooded, drug-dealing murderers?

Much of the debate about ethnicity in the arts focuses on such issues— 15 positive and negative role models, stereotypes, political correctness—often to the point where esthetics become secondary. How much political weight can the arts bear before they become, well, unbearable?

Mr. Olmos was perhaps betting that "American Me" would work as classic tragedy: through its emotional structure, not through positive or negative role models. He cast himself as Santana, an El Cid[1] of the East Los Angeles barrios and prisons whose quest for respect and full manhood ends tragically, precisely because his choices are the wrong ones. Mr. Olmos has defied political correctness to present the ultimate case for otherness. Santana will never cross any border, real or imaginary, to regain his soul. He has sunk too deep.

Another film, Orson Welles's gloriously pulpy 1958 "Touch of Evil," explores the fears, attractions and violence of Latino-Anglo relations in a border town. It also breaks all the rules of ethnic correctness, with Anglos playing Latinos. Unlike so many other movies about ethnic tension, the hero is not an Anglo confronting racism and injustice. The hero is a good Mexican cop, played by Charlton Heston with an accent that makes that of the Italian Ar-

---

[1]*El Cid:* legendary Spanish hero (d. 1099), who fought the Moorish occupation of Spain; his bravery, chivalry, and generosity have made him a prototype of the noble Spanish warrior. (*Ed.*)

mand Assante in "The Mambo Kings" sound positively lyrical. In fact, Mr. Heston, looking like a young Carlos Fuentes,[2] makes a dashing Mexican.

But the righteous Mexican character gets everything wrong, while the bigoted Anglo sheriff played by Orson Welles is right, even if his tactics are vile. What drives the plot is the dark-haired Mexican cop's interrupted attempts to consummate his marriage to the very blond Janet Leigh. Welles, the director, was having a good time toying with the audience's good conscience *and* with its feelings about Latino-Anglo sex.

Latin Spitfires: Temptresses and Scribes

The Latin spitfire harks back to Lupe Vélez, the Mexican film star who made a career in Hollywood between the wars. Like the greaser, the Latin temptress reveals sexual fears and desires with an allure that is purely racial: the archetypal dark woman who competes with the virginal blonde for the hero's affection. The Latin spitfire is all woman, and her femininity is dangerous.

20 Associated with that archetype is the American male's nostalgia del machismo,[3] a longing for a world where one does not have to deal with the vicissitudes of equality. In the 1987 movie "Extreme Prejudice," the righteous Anglo hero, Nick Nolte, travels south to an impossible showdown à la "The Wild Bunch."[4] There, waiting as a trophy, is María Conchita Alonso—looking exactly like Rita Moreno did a generation before her.

Don't cry for María Conchita. She has turned the fantasy of a spitfire into a career. Elizabeth Peña, a New York stage actress, likewise was cast in "La Bamba" and "Down and Out in Beverly Hills" (1985) as an irresistible object of desire.

Meryl Streep can play serious roles and at the same time conjure up sexual heat. So can Glenn Close, Sigourney Weaver, Ellen Barkin, to name a few. But the screen does not seem ready for Latinas in serious roles.

Where the presence *is* felt is in literature. Oscar Hijuelos may have won the Pulitzer, but few Latina writers are more celebrated than the Mexican-American short-story writer Sandra Cisneros, who appears to be at the front of a new wave of acclaimed Latin women writers. The Dominican Julia Álvarez published "How the García Girls Lost Their Accents" last year: "She has, to her great credit, beautifully captured the threshold experience of the new immigrant, where the past is not yet a memory and the future remains an anxious dream," wrote Donna Rifkind in The New York Times Book

---

[2]*Carlos Fuentes* (b. 1928): well-known Mexican writer (*Ed.*)

[3]*nostalgia del machismo:* (Spanish) nostalgia for machismo; Fernández suggests that North American men idealize the typically Latino cult of masculinity, or machismo. (*Ed.*)

[4]*The Wild Bunch:* western film (1969) directed by Sam Peckinpah about outlaws on the run who wind up in Mexico; famous for its violent, bloody scenes (*Ed.*)

Review. And recently, the Cuban-American Cristina García received strong reviews for her first novel, "Dreaming in Cuban"; Michiko Kakutani called it "fierce, visionary" and "dazzling" in The Times.

Indeed, the world of letters seems more progressive than the world of Hollywood. There is a heightened awareness among the literati that other voices—women's voices—are important. (Not to mention that publishing a book is far less expensive than making a film, and Middle America has yet to make bankable a Latina movie star.)

25 And yet who among female Latin writers has the most impact today? Clearly, Gloria Estefan. More people hear the songs she writes than will read any of the Latin community's books.

The Source: In Search of Authenticity

Last year, John Leguizamo's Off Broadway show, "Mambo Mouth," a one-man cornucopia of Latin caricatures, tickled Anglo audiences. But some Latin critics found his portraits offensive. Mr. Leguizamo's comedy did not always connect with the complexity and nuances of Latin culture. His South American boxer seemed Chicano, his Cuban talk-show host Nuyorican; when a character complained about Dominican music, we heard salsa, not merengue. Much Latin humor is about cultural differences, but Mr. Leguizamo was disconnected from Latin America, in tune only with a hip-hop barrio culture. The real Latin spirit is quite different, and not always palatable to the crossover audience.

A year and a half ago, Elena Burke appeared at the fabled Tropicana nightclub in Havana. The legendary Ms. Burke sings in a genre of jazz-inflected bolero from the 40's and 50's called in Spanish by an English word: feeling. A handful of young Cubans in the audience stared at her with adoring eyes and hung on every slurred word. Ms. Burke appeared to have had too much to drink and kept forgetting songs or changing her repertory in the middle of a number. The tourists—and whatever dignitaries from the rapidly fading socialist world still lingered around Havana—were not impressed. They saw only an over-the-hill chanteuse when they had come for the Tropicana's famous jiggling mulatto chorus girls.

Americans need not go to Havana, the forbidden city, to see the real thing. A Cuban singer known as the Queen of Latin Soul, La Lupe, lived in New York City for years and had a following among both Latinos and Anglos. But the American popular audience is fickle. The Queen of Latin Soul died in New York on Feb. 28, broke and broken at age 53.

A Latin boom? Maybe not this year, or even this decade. But with the numbers of Latinos in this country growing, artists will some day create a real Latin movement. In the meantime, if you want something more challenging, the culture of the Latin world is already there. It has always been there, buried in the barrios, south of the border, on the other side of the mirror.

DISCUSSING THE TEXT

1. Fernández argues that the diversity of Latino culture makes it difficult to incorporate into mainstream American culture. Do you agree or disagree with him? What kinds of images does the term "Latino culture" evoke for you? In what ways do these images blend—or clash—with mainstream American culture as you see it?
2. What do you think of Fernández's assessment that Latino culture is "hot" and American culture "cool"? Can we use these terms and manage to avoid stereotypes? Can such broad generalizations be effective in helping to understand contemporary American life? Why or why not?
3. Fernández says that "Latin culture will likely never have the same impact on America as black culture" (par. 7). Working with four or five students and drawing on your awareness of literature, the arts, and popular culture (as well as other reading you have done in this class), try to determine whether or not you agree with this statement. Be prepared to share your opinions (and the reasons behind those opinions) with the rest of the class.

WRITING ABOUT THE TEXT

4. Do you agree with Fernández's contention that passion is "foreign to American culture" (par. 9)? Write a brief argument for or against this idea, citing examples to back up the points you make.
5. Write a list of the character traits or qualities that you associate with the terms Fernández uses in relation to Latino culture (for example, "spitfires," "Latin lover," "mambo king"). Then write a brief sketch of an imaginary character who embodies some of these qualities.
6. Watch a film (or video) that somehow addresses Latino life and culture (you might try to see one of the films Fernández refers to, for example). Write a review that focuses on the film's interpretation of Latino characters. To what extent do the characters fit the kinds of stereotypes Fernández describes? To what extent do they differ?
7. Fernández argues that with all the attention that must be paid to "positive and negative role models, stereotypes, political correctness" (par. 15) in works about Latino life, it can be difficult for the artist, writer, or filmmaker to focus on "esthetics." Write a one- to two-page description of a work you have seen or read that deals with Latino life and that manages to be artistically satisfying without relying on stereotypes *or* political correctness.

ITABARI NJERI

Sushi and Grits: Ethnic Identity and Conflict in a Newly Multicultural America

Itabari Njeri is best known for her memoir, Every Good-Bye Ain't Gone: Family Portraits and Personal Escapades, *which received the American Book Award in 1990. In this essay, adapted from her 1993 book,* Sushi and Grits: The Challenge of Diversity, *she combines personal experience and observations with a well-researched knowledge of interracial relationships in contemporary U.S. culture.*

Drawing on her own multiethnic background—African, East Indian, English, Amerindian, and French—she offers an insightful critique of race relations not only between blacks and whites but also among people of color whose ancestry includes a mixture of races and ethnicities. She deals specifically with the continuing problem of "colorism," a term used initially by writer Alice Walker to define "the preferential or prejudicial treatment of same-race people based on skin color."

Placing this problem of discriminatory treatment among members of the same racial group within a historical and cultural context, the author cites the works and opinions of W. E. B. Du Bois (also see Chap. 3, p. 161); Marcus Garvey (1887–1940; a Jamaican leader who promoted unity among blacks); and Frantz Fanon (1925–1961; a psychiatrist from Martinique whose revolutionary work analyzed the political impact of white colonialism on blacks). After presenting several different viewpoints on this controversial and divisive issue of conflict in intraminority relations, Njeri comes out against classifications of individuals based on "race" (a term that she takes issue with at the beginning of her essay), arguing that eliminating such a practice might be the best way to eradicate oppression.

Itabari Njeri (born as Jill Stacey Moreland in 1952) has worked as a professional singer and actress and has also distinguished herself as a journalist for the Miami Herald *and the* Los Angeles Times. *In 1992 she was a Pulitzer Prize finalist for criticism, and she has received a National Association of Black Journalists award for feature writing and a National Endowment for the Humanities Fellowship for Outstanding Journalists.*

At a camp in the woods of eastern Massachusetts, a woman stepped to the front of a room bathed in harsh fluorescent light and took the hand of Barbara Love. "So, tell us who you are," said Love. The woman shifted from side to side. She flashed a nervous smile. Knowing she was here to heal, knowing it was a setting of anonymity, knowing she had the complete, respectful attention of a community of people who—no matter their disparate origins—had lived some piece of her psychic terror, she spoke her name.

"Gloria.[1] I am of Creole ancestry, born in Louisiana." She was about forty-five, a handsome, statuesque woman with a hint of gold in a complexion

[1]Some names and details have been changed to protect the anonymity of sources.

that was brown like the crown of a well-baked biscuit. A college dean, she told the group she often mediates disputes involving issues of "race"[2] and ethnicity on campus. "I," she said, "was the darkest one in my family. All my life I heard my grandparents, my cousins, my—everyone—whispering 'nigger-nigger-nigger-nigger. . . .' " The more she said it, the more it became an aspirate hiss—" 'nihhger-nihhger-nihhger . . . NIHHGGER!' " She laughed. "*Errrgggggg.*" It was the sound of someone gargling with gravel. She shivered.

"When I had my first child, it was a beautiful mahogany-colored boy. He was so beautiful. *Errrgggggg.*" She shook again. "Then I had my daughter." The woman moaned.

Love caressed her hand and smiled encouragingly. "Then you had a daughter," she said. They stood silent for seconds. All that was flesh and wood in the room seemed to breathe with them. Gloria looked at the gathering of Re-Evaluation Counselors—Puerto Ricans, Chinese Americans, Colombian Americans, Japanese Americans, and the seemingly endless variations on "Black." All of them were members of an international peer-counseling community spawned by the human potential movement, influenced by twelve-step programs such as Alcoholics Anonymous, and based on an understanding that the hurt child in all of us is usually the result of damage from physical injury, illness, or various forms of social oppression—classism, racism, sexism, adultism (the oppression of children). Further, RC assumes that unless we have a safe place to express the pain that results from these assaults to the psyche, the wounds fester, and can lead to rigid, irrational patterns of thought and behavior.

---

[2]Except in direct quotations, I will place the word "race" in quotes or italics to signal how problematic the use of this term is. As many social scientists have acknowledged for years, "race" is a pseudo-scientific category that has been used to justify the political subordination of non-White peoples based on superficial physical differences. "Race," of course, is a social construct of enormous political significance. But there is one race, *Homo sapiens,* and the physical variations that characterize the species do not amount to fundamental, qualitative differences, as the popular use of the term suggests.

The cultural and physical variations among humans are best contained within the concept of ethnicity, a term that can encompass shared genetic traits, culture, and history—real or perceived.

Further, no one's skin color, obviously, is literally black or white. Phenotype is not a definitive indicator of one's genetic background. Recognizing, however, that social identity in the United States is based primarily on this color divide, I acknowledge it, but treat *Black* and *White* as proper nouns. Throughout this essay I use *Black* to refer to so-called *Negroid* peoples in Africa or of African descent, treating it as a generic ethnic reference to people lumped together for political reasons though, indeed, linked by history, blood, and culture—no matter how distant or diluted. Similarly, I treat *White* as a proper noun, a generic ethnic reference to so-called *Caucasoid* peoples, especially Europeans, Euro-Americans, and others claiming pure European ancestry.

Both the accepted meanings attached to "race" and ethnicity in our current social lexicon and my challenges to them are imperfect descriptors. My hope is that, by challenging our *a priori* acceptance of "race," and the social classifications that result, I will prompt discussions of "race" as a concept, "racism" as an ideology, and the false reality they create in our daily lives.

But here Gloria had the safety to speak. 5

She squealed, "Blue eyeeeees. My daughter, she was vanilla-colored, like ice-cream, with red hair and blue . . . eyes." She pulled her shoulders to her ears. "And I freaked out."

"Why?"

"Why? Why?" Her voice was singsong. "Because . . ." Then, from some boxed-up corner of her soul, she let loose a scream so primal it seemed to reach back thirty thousand years . . . pierced the room's thin, dry wall . . . echoed through the woods . . . shook the leaves and scarred the trees. "Because . . ."

And then this biscuit-brown woman revealed that she'd spent the past twenty-five years of her life in mortal fear that her vanilla-ice-cream-colored child would hate her, reject her because . . .

"I'm a nigger. Oh, God, because I'm Black, because I'm so Black. . . ." 10 And then she screamed that ancient scream again and fell into moaning for what seemed an eternity by the unyielding knot in my gut. I heaved and thought of Jeffrey, my cousin. He looked like Ricky Nelson[3] and always wanted to be the baddest nigger on the block.

Like me, he was African American and Caribbean American or, to break it down, African, French, English, Arawak, East Indian, and probably more—a typical New World Black. When he was being sent to prison, the judge, examining his record, called him a White man. My cousin protested and pointed to our brown-skin grandmother in the courtroom. "If she's Black, I'm Black, too." Then he demanded he be treated just like any other "Negro." The judge obliged, adding a year to his sentence.

Trying to prove how bad he was in the eyes of other Black men, my cousin bought into the street life, absorbing, as they had, an oppressor's definition of a Black male: a hustler—confusing patterns of survival for culture. And since Jeffrey was a Black man growing up in Harlem during the late fifties, he saw few options but the street life. But his looks made the price of admission exceedingly high.

When they found his body on a Harlem rooftop, bloated, bullet-pierced, it was because he'd spent his too-short life trying to prove how *bad* he was.

I cannot hear this golden-hued Creole woman's story without thinking of Jeffrey or his sister—pale, golden-haired, and hoping desperately that her next baby is *black-black-black*—wishing out loud that she could give her first child to somebody else to raise 'cause he's so *light-light-light*.

Caught in the shifting, irrational nuances of a seldom acknowledged but 15 constantly reinforced color hierarchy, and the aesthetic preferences that accompany it, I know that moaning woman, in her capacity as dean and sometime mediator, has to deal with feelings of inadequacy and resentment based on the hue of her skin when dealing with other people of color. These feelings

---

[3]*Ricky Nelson:* actor and popular singer who epitomized all-American (white) good looks; one of two sons in the television show *Ozzie and Harriet* (1952–1966) (*Ed.*)

impede her effectiveness as a mediator and, in her larger community, a political activist. I believe it's one of many similar psychological factors that insidiously undermine attempts by Blacks, and other people of color, to achieve economic, political, and cultural self-determination. These psychological factors are rooted in our oppression by the dominant group in this society and its rationalizing ideology of White supremacy, which is used to mask and facilitate class exploitation of every ethnic group in this country.

What writer Alice Walker defined as *colorism,* the preferential or prejudicial treatment of same-*race* people based on skin color, continues to this day. And as she once wrote, unless we exorcise it "we cannot as a people progress. For colorism, like colonialism, sexism and racism, impedes us."

Just four years ago, two Euro-American social scientists documented that the social and economic gap between light- and dark-skinned African Americans is as significant as "one of the greatest socioeconomic cleavages in America," the chasm between the income and status of all Blacks and Whites. A dark-skinned Black earns seventy cents for every dollar a light-complexioned African American makes, according to the 1988 study conducted by Michael Hughes and Bradley R. Hertel, professors at Virginia Polytechnic Institute and State University in Virginia. Most telling, said the two social psychologists, are the percentages for Blacks and Whites that show who is employed in professional and managerial occupations—high-status jobs.

Almost 29 percent of all whites hold such jobs, the study found, while Blacks hold about 15 percent. That is nearly a two-to-one ratio. Ironically, the same ratio holds true for light-skinned Blacks—27 percent of whom hold such jobs—compared with 15 percent of dark-skinned Blacks who were employed in these positions.

Significantly, when Hughes and Hertel compared their findings to studies done between 1950 and 1980 on the relationship between skin color and socioeconomic status, they concluded that nothing had "changed appreciably." The effect of "skin color on life chances of Black Americans was not eliminated by the Civil Rights and Black pride movements."

Understandably, African Americans are loath to acknowledge such disparities, even though we aren't to blame for them. It undermines the image of ethnic solidarity. 20

"It's absurd for any Black person to be talking about [color distinctions among African Americans] without talking about White supremacy," says Washington, D.C., psychiatrist Frances Cress Welsing, the controversial author of "The Cress Theory of Color Confrontation and Racism (White Supremacy)," which traces the roots of White racism to a fear of genetic annihilation of the planet's White minority.

"It is White people that keep saying and imposing that if you look like an African you should be at the bottom of the choice spectrum."

That is what Hughes and Hertel concluded from their study, too.

They found that skin color, like gender, acts as a "diffuse status characteristic." For example, a man is believed more competent to pilot a plane than a woman "when in fact there is no evidence that gender has anything to do with ability," Hughes said.

Skin color works this way too, and that's how Whites respond to it. "We focused on Whites because White people are the ones who are generally responsible for making upper-level management and personnel decisions. They are more likely to decide whether people get through educational institutions." In short, they are the ones in power. And when they look at a darker-complexioned Black person, Hughes and Hertel believe, they think they are seeing someone "less competent"—someone less like them than a fairer-complexioned person. 25

White people may make these distinctions, African Americans argue, but most Blacks don't, they continually insist, reading from a script W. E. B. Du Bois might have written in the first quarter of this century.

In a 1921 attack on the Jamaican-born Black nationalist leader Marcus Garvey, Du Bois, writing in an issue of *The Crisis,* contended that "Garvey has sought to import to America and capitalize the antagonism between blacks and mulattoes in the West Indies. This has been the cause of the West Indian failures to gain headway against whites. Yet Garvey imports it into a land where it never had any substantial footing and where today, of all days, it is absolutely repudiated by every thinking Negro. . . . American Negroes recognize no color line in or out of the race, and they will in the end punish the man who attempts to establish it."

When I raise the painful issue of colorism, African Americans write angry letters, call in to radio shows or attack me in person, asserting I exaggerate the problem, the problem doesn't exist, or, conversely, accuse me of airing the "race's" dirty laundry.

▼ ▼ ▼

I know the exact moment I was compelled to investigate the extent and impact of colorism among our people. It was 1976. I was not long out of college, living in Brooklyn, recovering from my travels as a backup singer with Major Harris of "Love Won't Let Me Wait" fame and reading Alice Walker's essay "If the Present Looks Like the Past, What Does the Future Look Like?" in *In Search of Our Mothers' Gardens.*

I wanted to know who these light-skinned Black women were that Walker wrote were insensitive to the pain of their darker-skinned sisters. As with many light-complexioned Blacks, the people in my family who looked closest to being White compensated by being aggressively Black. 30

But Walker wrote: "I think there is probably as much difference between the life of a black black woman and a 'high yellow' black woman as between a 'high yellow' woman and a white woman."

I put down the book and called the woman who had been my best friend since college, Celia. She was short, beautiful, charismatic, and a black-black Black woman. She was more than a dear friend. I called her Sister C.

When we hung up, I was numb. And for many days after, I would suddenly weep when alone, replaying her voice in my head. How could we have been so close and I not know how much she'd been hurt by people contemptuous of her for her color, her belligerently close-cropped hair, and the defiantly neon-bright colors she wore? And she was particularly bitter about her relatives, half of whom looked White, some of whom passed for White, and had practically disowned Celia and the other dark, poorer members of her family. Over the next decade I would watch Celia, with the help of friends but virtually none of her more affluent, fair-complexioned relatives, take care of two parents stricken with Alzheimer's and no money, nurse the children of several brothers who had been lost to the streets, put one parent in the grave, leave another in a nursing home, and finally die herself of cancer at the age of thirty-eight.

In 1988, two years before Celia's death, I remember telling a very dark-complexioned acquaintance—a fellow female journalist—how appalled I was at the pervasiveness of a problem I, too, had thought buried. She looked me up and down with silent contempt, examining pore by pore my face—a fraction past yellow, barely brown—and shot a blast of air through her nose that was half a chuckle, half a snort. "You just finding all this out?"

35 While all Blacks suffer discrimination in America, the darker one's skin the more one's humanity is ignored. "You know the Links," said E. B. Attah, a Nigerian-born sociologist who has taught at Atlanta University, referring to the elite Black social-service organization. "Well, I had a member of the Links showing me pictures of different chapters. When she encountered a dark-skinned woman in a picture she'd say: 'How did *she* get in there?'

"I'm very dark-skinned and anybody in this country who is dark-skinned can tell you about encountering situations of lighter-skinned people devaluing you as a human being because of your darkness."

▼ ▼ ▼

Against this historical landscape of psychological anguish, fortified daily by continued socioeconomic discrimination based on color and "race," comes a new generation of so-called multiracial Americans demanding that they be acknowledged as a distinct "racial" group. The concerns they raise are not new within communities of color. However, that their concerns are becoming part of a national debate relates to massive population shifts that may lead to a new majority in twenty-first-century America: people of color. Many demographers predict that Whites (I don't consider most Latinos White, given their largely mixed Indian, African, and European ancestry) may be a minority toward the end of the next century. Latino and Asian immigration, the higher birthrate among Latinos and Blacks and intermarriage among all groups are key factors in the rise of the multiethnic population.

Tagged an "emerging" population by social scientists, multiethnic Americans may be the most significant group to spring from a newly pluralistic America. Their demand for recognition is stimulating what I think will be a decades-long debate—one that may force all Americans to confront the myths that surround "race" and ethnicity in the United States.

High on the political agenda of many now-vocal multiethnic Americans is the demand for a new "multiracial" census category that specifically identifies ethnically and "racially" mixed citizens. The size of the "multiracial" population may be about five million—probably more than twice that number, say multiethnic activists. But the exact figures are unknown because the census requires people to either identify with one "race" or ethnic group or to check "other" when filling out data for the Census Bureau.

The ranks of multiethnic activists are being bolstered by their monoethnic kin—parents, grandparents, and spouses—who have helped form support groups in, among other places, Atlanta, Buffalo, Chicago, Houston, Los Angeles, Omaha, San Diego, Seattle, San Francisco, Pittsburgh, and Washington, D.C. Similar support groups are popping up on college campuses, particularly in California, a center of multicultural activism. While these activists failed to get a new multiethnic designation on the 1990 census, they are pushing to see one established for the year 2000. 40

In general, supporters of the category want recognition and political representation for people of mixed heritage. Opponents say minority groups would shrink if such a designation is allowed, leading to a loss of political representation and congressionally appropriated funds, based on the census count, used to remedy the effects of past and continuing discrimination.

These multiethnic Americans may be Mexican American and Italian American; Japanese American and Cherokee; Korean American, Armenian American, and Chinese. But the most problematic amalgams are those that include the genes of America's most stigmatized group: Negroes, Blacks, Afro-Americans, African Americans, African heritage people—a "spade" by any other name in the consciousness of still too many White Americans. The issue of a special census designation, and social recognition, is especially important to this group because of the way in which "race" has been traditionally defined in America for people of African descent: socially, any known or perceived African ancestry makes one Black—the one-drop-in-the-bucket theory of descent.

"If you consider yourself Black for political reasons, raise your hand," Charles Stewart said to a predominantly African American audience at a symposium I organized for the National Association of Black Journalists in 1990. "The overwhelming majority raised their hands," said Stewart, a Democratic Party activist in Los Angeles. "When I asked how many people here believe that they are of pure African descent, without any mixture, nobody raised their hands." The point, said Stewart, is this: "If you advocate a category that includes people who are *multiracial* to the detriment of their Black identification, you will replicate what you saw—an empty room. We cannot afford to have an empty room. We cannot afford to have a race empty of Black people—not so long as we are struggling against discrimination based on our identification as Black people."

But a woman I will call Anna Vale eschews the little-dab'll-do-you school of genetics. She is a Californian of Japanese, African American, and Native American descent. A voice from the sushi-and-grits generation, she represents the new kind of diversity challenging old "racial" conceptions. Her eyes scan me skeptically. She does not trust me. Though I have written often and sympathetically about the issues so-called "multiracial" Americans face and the problem of colorism, she fears that I, too, will "rape" her. That's what Black people have been doing to her all her life, she claims, committing political and psychological rape on her person. And I'll do it, too, she insists, by writing a piece that distorts the reality of Americans like her who assert their "biological truth" and seek an identity separate from Blacks.

"What I don't appreciate about the African American community," she tells me, "is this mentality of annexing anyone with one drop of African blood. . . . I don't know why African American people seem so obsessed with annexing other people." Yet, says Anna, when "multiracial" people want to voice their unique concerns—political support for Amer-Asian refugees, many of whom have African American fathers, funding for works of art that present the complex cultural views of, for instance, a Black-Korean American—they are told to "be quiet," and "just carry out the political and cultural agenda of African Americans." 45

As she sits in a Santa Monica café, Vale's delicate body belies the dragon within. "African Americans want us to be their political slaves," she says with the intensity of water at a low boil. "They are saying, 'Come join us.' But it's not because of some great brother or sister love—it's political. If their numbers decrease, their chance of getting public funds decrease—as well as political representation. To me, that's a totally unethical way of saying that you want people to be a member of your community. As far as I am concerned all slavery is over—whether it's physical slavery on the plantation or political slavery that gives one group, like African Americans, the audacity to say that they own people because they have one drop of African blood."

Of course, it was White slave owners in the antebellum South who perpetuated the little-dab'll-do-you rule. They wanted to make sure that Blacks of mixed heritage—usually the products of White masters' raping of enslaved Black women—had no special claim to freedom because their fathers were free. They inherited the status of their slave mothers and were categorized with "pure" Blacks to assure the perpetuation of the slave population. In the postslave era, the alleged inferiority of African blood—no matter how little of it one possessed—was used to rationalize the continued social and political subordination of Blacks. Wisely, Blacks made a political virtue out of a necessity, asserting that we would not allow our heterogeneous ancestry to divide and render us politically dysfunctional—as many argue has been the case with Brazil's "Black" population.

I looked at Anna and listened to her ahistorical and apolitical diatribe. Her comments were a more extreme form of the kind of Black bashing I've often heard from multiethnics of African descent—usually ones who have had little contact with, or understanding of, the Black side of their heritage. I fear that the increasingly acrimonious nature of the debate among multiethnic Americans and African Americans is turning into a dialogue of the deaf. Pain and rage are the barriers. And though Anna often sees me as the enemy, I have always viewed her as a wounded sister. I understand the source of her rage.

Born in Japan and brought to the U.S. while in grade school, she knew little about her father's African American and Native American family. He died when she was young. Her mother, a Japanese war bride, raised Anna as only she could: to be a good Japanese daughter.

On the days Anna brought sushi to lunch, African American children teased her. But their mild teasing escalated to schoolyard terrorism: a group of Black girls pushing her down . . . cutting off her long, dark hair 'cause she swung it like a White girl. . . . 50

. . . a Black cop in L.A. ignoring her pleas for help after a fender bender injured her light-skinned son, then calling her a "half-breed bitch." . . .

From her perspective, the dark-brown, long-haired Polynesian-looking and Japanese-speaking woman has had the foot of an African American on her neck all her life.

"Communities of color are the most severe in doling out this kind of oppression," she says grimly. "The oppressed seem to oppress more."

In 1903, when Du Bois wrote that the "problem of the twentieth century is the problem of the color-line—the relation of the darker to the lighter races of men in Asia and Africa, in America and the islands of the sea," he referred to the domination of Whites over darker peoples. This remains true. But that domination has bred an insidious offspring: internalized oppression, that is, the installing of the oppressor's values within the psyche of oppressed people, so that—in a system of structured inequality such as ours—the psychological dynamics that help to keep the system in place function on automatic pilot. In effect, the mind becomes the last plantation.

One wonders if the assertion of a unique, multiethnic identity—particularly for a person of African heritage in the United States—is the ultimate expression of (or, through a synthesis of competing identities, an escape from) the divided consciousness that Du Bois said defined American Blacks. For where, save the United States—the New World—could an Anna be forged? Not just in the particulars of her ethnicity, but in the clear anguish, for many like her, such an amalgamation in an African-tinged package causes? Where else but in the United States does a slave master's economically motivated definition of identity reign so completely? Multiple souls, multiple thoughts, multiple "unreconciled strivings" warring "in one dark body, whose dogged strength alone," Du Bois wrote, "keeps it from being torn asunder." 55

▼ ▼ ▼

But as a new century nears, ushering in the next millennium and unprecedented ethnic and "racial" diversity in the U.S., millions like Anna sound a disturbing and potentially potent riff on Du Bois's classic statement of color division. Further, given the tense, competitive relations between Blacks and other people of color vying for the dubious status of America's most significant minority, acute observers of the social landscape have correctly predicted that intraminority group conflicts will be a key factor leading to the fire next time.[4] As Richard Rubenstein, former director of the Center for

---

[4]*the fire next time:* refers to lines from a spiritual: "God gave Noah the rainbow sign/ No more water, the fire next time" (to punish evildoers, the Lord sent the flood; in the next mark of wrath, the earth will burn); also a reference to James Baldwin's *The Fire Next Time* (1962) about racial relations (*Ed.*)

Conflict Analysis and Resolution at George Mason University, said in a July 12, 1990, *Los Angeles Times* article that anticipated the 1992 Los Angeles "riots" (specifically citing tensions between Blacks and Korean immigrant merchants and police brutality as causes), the nation is on the brink of "civil war."

Hedging so powerful an assertion in customary journalistic fashion, the article continued: "That grim prediction doesn't necessarily mean riots in the streets but a combination of [individual] sociopathic behavior" and "intensified intergroup conflict."

In California, which provides a microcosm of existing and, perhaps, future intraminority group relations, neighborhoods once predominantly Black, such as Watts, are shifting to Latino majorities. Typical of conflicts in these changing neighborhoods is the Latino charge that they are underrepresented on the staffs of hospitals in changing neighborhoods that have large numbers of Latino patients but too few Spanish-speaking nurses. In 1990, for example, the U.S. Equal Employment Opportunity Commission found "significant disparities" in the promotion of Latinos at the Los Angeles County–University of Southern California medical center. There, Latinos accounted for 14 percent of registered nurses but occupied only 4 percent of nursing-supervisor positions. In contrast, Blacks represented 20 percent of the nurses but 29 percent of the supervisors. Whites, however, still outnumbered everybody, accounting for 40 percent of the nurses and 46 percent of the supervisors.

Blacks argue that they should not have to give up jobs they fought for and won in the afterglow of the civil rights struggle and in the wake of the Watts rebellion. As one Black activist complained, "You don't see us going into East L.A. trying to take jobs from Latinos."

And then there is the much-publicized, sometimes deadly, conflict between Korean immigrant merchants and Blacks in many impoverished urban neighborhoods. Many of these merchants view Blacks as violent, ignorant, and unwilling to work, while Blacks see them as among the most arrogant and rude in a succession of exploitative middlemen entrepreneurs. 60

These variations on intraminority group conflict are related phenomena, in great part a consequence of what that brilliant analyst of the colonized mind, psychiatrist Frantz Fanon, called internalized oppression.

". . . so tell us who you are," said Love. ". . . was the darkest one in my family . . . heard my grandparents, my cousins, my everyone—whispering 'nigger-nigger-nigger. . . .' "

But Re-Evaluation Counseling theory has gone beyond the purely psychological consequences of oppression that Fanon explored. The theory weds the concept of internalized oppression to class analysis, creating what I think of as liberation psychology.

"I define internalized oppression as that process whereby a set of beliefs, attitudes, and misinformation about members of a target or oppressed group are put out by the dominant group to justify their subordination," says Love, both a professor of education at the University of Massachusetts at Amherst and a leader in the Re-Evaluation Counseling community. That misinformation becomes embedded in the psyche—the emotional domain of that target group, she explains.

65 "There is extensive internalized oppression within the Black community," Love states unequivocally. "It was a deliberate part of the system of dehumanizing Africans who were brought to the United States and making them fit to be slaves. We were not fit to be slaves when we came here, so we had to be made to be fit—that is to go along with and participate in an oppressive system. And that process continues to this day."

Among the consequences of internalized oppression are "the ways in which we put each other down. The ways in which we play out the dehumanization that got inflicted on *us,* at *each other,*" Love continues. It's the flip side of the oppression itself.

Tall, possessing skin with the soft patina of polished mahogany and disposed to wearing flowing African gowns, Love relates that her own sister had long hair and light skin. "If she tossed her hair in a certain way, she"—like Anna—"was accused of trying to act like a White girl. And the other kids jumped her." Why? "Because we have internalized this set of notions about what it means to be beautiful," says Love. "And what it means to be beautiful in this society is to be like Whites.

"The oppression says that by definition Black people cannot be beautiful. But if someone—because of our genetically mixed heritage—comes along looking like the dominant group, we say, 'If you're Black you are not beautiful—that is, you can't have long hair and here you've got long hair. It's wrong. We'll fix it. We'll cut it off and we'll put you back in your place. Because your place is to be like us: nobody.' "

Looking to the broader community of color, what happens when two historically subjugated people, culturally dissimilar, collide? In one notorious case, a Black teenage girl in Los Angeles was killed by a Korean American merchant after a dispute over a $1.49 bottle of orange juice.

70 The merchant, a then fifty-year-old woman named Soon Ja Du, was the daughter of a doctor and a literature major in college before she came to the United States with her husband and three children. She never adjusted to her loss of status as an immigrant who, because of language barriers, was compelled to work in a knitting factory for many years before her family saved enough to buy two combination liquor-and-food markets.

A devout Christian, Du reportedly never felt comfortable selling liquor or having to keep a gun in the stores, one of which was in the midst of gang-plagued South-Central Los Angeles—the Empire Market and Liquor Store. And she later told a probation officer she was afraid of, and didn't understand, the poor Blacks who frequented her store. "They look healthy, young," she said through an interpreter. "Big question why they don't work. Didn't understand why got welfare money and buying alcoholic beverages and consume them . . . instead of feeding children. . . . Didn't understand at first," she said. Eventually, she explained, "paid less attention," and decided that it was "their way of living."

Days after Black gang members had terrorized her adult son, Du saw fifteen-year-old Latasha Harlins walk into the Empire Market, take a container of orange juice from a refrigerated case, and place it in her open backpack.

With the juice visible, the girl walked to the counter with two dollars in her hand. Du accused her of stealing the juice. Harlins turned halfway to show her the exposed juice container and said she was paying for it. Du did not believe her, yanked Harlins toward her, pulling the arm of the girl's sweater.

What happened then?

Years before and months after the incident, commentators insist on calling the tensions between Blacks and Koreans an essentially cultural conflict.

At root, I think the conflict stems from economic and political inequality *exacerbated* by cultural differences. And the nation's White elite are not just *tsk-tsk-tsking* spectators. It has much to do with the way capitalism works. As Edna Bonacich, professor at the University of California in Irvine and an expert on the role of middleman minorities around the world, points out, "Korean Americans, to a certain extent, are fronting for the larger White power structure. They are both beneficiaries of the arrangement and the victims of it." The sale of liquor in the Black community is but one example of how Korean immigrant merchants, like Jews before them and Arab immigrants in other parts of the country, fulfill their middleman role. 75

Corporate-owned liquor companies sell their products through Korean-owned liquor stores in the Black community, Bonacich says. Koreans, who then distribute liquor in a community plagued by substance abuse, "bear the brunt of the anger the African-American community rightfully has against the larger system of oppression. Koreans become sort of foot soldiers of internal colonialism," asserts Bonacich.

Cultural and ethnic difference "are no doubt a small factor in these types of conflict," Bonacich contends, "but unless you deal with the structural problems, you do not solve the conflict."

But I would argue that we have to move on all these fronts—cultural (which includes psychological issues) and structural—simultaneously. Actions rooted in bigotry usually turn these simmering hostilities into social conflagrations. Even when people of apparent goodwill try to cooperate, an aide to Los Angeles Mayor Tom Bradley admitted, there is this "impenetrable veil" of hostility, based on ethnic stereotyping, that undermines joint economic and cultural ventures.

Traditional mediation and bridge-building efforts are too superficial to penetrate that veil. They don't get at the psychological terror, fed by bigotry, that lead the Soon Ja Dus of the world to shoot the Latasha Harlinses who inhabit the planet's inner cities.

A significant part of the problem lies in a failure to address the exaggerated psychological dimensions of intraminority group tensions. Most interethnic conflicts have a psychological aspect—rigidity of thinking, low self-esteem, compensatory behavior. But I think these are especially significant in disputes between historically subordinate groups. 80

In the case of Korean immigrants, they carry not only the historical memory of subjugation under the Japanese but the day-to-day reality of anti-Asian prejudice in the United States and the isolation caused by language and cultural differences. African Americans carry not only the historical memory of slavery but their status as America's most stigmatized minority.

In many respects, I believe Korean Americans and African Americans to be very similar. Accustomed to being targets of abuse, members of both groups are quick to defend themselves if anyone seems ready to violate their humanity. I see it especially in the often swaggering, chip-on-the-shoulder posture of African American and Korean immigrant men. I saw it in the quick defense of Latasha Harlins when she slugged Soon Ja Du three times in the face after Du grabbed her. I saw it when the battered Du threw a stool at Harlins . . . then took a gun . . . braced herself on the counter, and as Harlins turned to leave . . . shot the girl in the back of the head. Over and over, I watched the now infamous videotape of the incident in Du's store and saw the consequences of "internalized oppression."

In other words, when a battered wife stabs her husband in the chest after he's complained that the eggs are overdone again, it's a safe bet that the murder was over more than breakfast.

There are few safe places where oppressed groups can express their distress. The nation's power elite are not going to let poor people of any color riot on Rodeo Drive.[5] Instead, much of that rage is turned inward—alcoholism, drug abuse, suicide—or directed toward those equally or more marginalized—Black-on-Black crime, child abuse, spouse abuse, violence against Korean merchants, ethnic-bashing between Blacks and Latinos.

The model I've seen that best addresses this phenomenon of internalized oppression is RC. 85

RC communities exist worldwide, with headquarters in Seattle. What Love and other RC counselors do, first one on one at the level of peer counseling, then in larger support groups, is help the "client" "discharge" the distress, born of the hurt, that keeps them numb or enraged and often irrational. Each person takes turns being a client and being a counselor. The goal is self-healing and clear thinking. When used by organizations, that clear thinking can be wedded to a pragmatic program of social change.

Says Love: When people are able to identify, talk about, and discharge their pain with the help of an aware, supportive human being, they "can take the information, minus the painful emotions" and reevaluate behavior. It's when the information is covered over with all that painful emotion that we get stuck and end up hurting one another rather than responding to one another from a rational place of thinking."

The healing work that RC communities and RC-influenced prejudice-reduction programs utilize (and there are many of the latter around the country, often presented by independent diversity consultants contracted by governmental agencies, schools, and corporations) is essential work; but it is not enough. I've yet to come across a conflict-resolution model that clearly connects the dots.

---

[5]*Rodeo Drive:* luxury shopping district in Beverly Hills, California (*Ed.*)

I believe we need a holistic conflict analysis and resolution model, one that comprehends the psychological issues that RC identifies but that more clearly articulates the need for institutional change and gives people the skills to do it.

Further, the model should show that it is only through building coalitions within communities and across all types of communities that structural change can occur—and this can only happen if the profound hurts all of us have suffered and the dehumanizing myths we have internalized about each other are "discharged." 90

Perhaps programs utilizing what people find valuable in RC should be established in every neighborhood, as accessible as twelve-step programs are. But unlike RC, which is not a political organization, the clear thinking that peer counseling facilitates should be applied to an agenda that participants develop themselves for social change—whether it be transforming the policing of neighborhoods, the nation's system of public education, or the United States government.

▼ ▼ ▼

Even free, as is RC, relatively few people will make the effort to seek counseling of any sort. So what can we do? I write, and I hope that, just as I was influenced and inspired by Alice Walker to investigate the significance of colorism, what I say rouses people, beyond the halls of academe, to discuss in beauty parlors and barbershops, on radio and TV shows and in church, color conflict among our own people and relations with other ethnic groups of color—remember, we are likely to be the majority one day. We should, as well, reconnect with allies in the White community. The latter are often marginalized by their own community when they take progressive and honorable stands against racism. And as many young African Americans work through the morass of our own oppression, we push them away with the orthodoxy of a vulgar, compensatory nationalism—this era's version called Afrocentrism—that often denies their humanity.

These tensions have no easy remedies. But we have to work toward an atmosphere of cooperation rather than antagonism. If we don't, the bottom line for African Americans is this: our numbers are shrinking relative to the growth of other minorities. Like the poor, troublesome Black people are always with us, lament many Whites. But as one elderly Black xenophobe acknowledged, White people have some "new niggers" now ("I'm just a high-tech coolie," said one politically conscious Chinese American engineer)—ones that look more like them, act more like them, and don't haunt their days and nights with cries of "No justice, no peace." Know something else, in some parts of the country they vote more like conservative Whites. And when they marry into White families, some grandpas and grandmas (happy that at least their new child-in-law is not Black) are more than willing to lobby for a new mixed-race census category that might take some of the taint off their grandchild's color and may, eventually, make them honorary White people. (That's already the case with large numbers of Latinos, East Indians, and Arabs.)

Not long ago, I heard about a bumper sticker spotted on a car cruising down a Los Angeles freeway: *If I had known then what I know now, I would have picked my own cotton.*

Tired of reaping what they've sown, many White Americans will happily embrace the proliferating Asian American and Latino population in an effort to exploit intraminority conflicts and permanently marginalize Blacks, if we can't reach honorable political, social, and cultural compromises with other groups, particularly people of color. 95

As we approach this mine-laden social-psychological terrain, among the questions we should be asking is, What does it mean to be an African American at the end of the twentieth century? In the same breath we should ask, What does it mean to be an American? These questions are at the heart of the unresolved tension in discussions about cultural pluralism: balancing what is perceived to be universal with ethnic particularism.

Examine the lived American culture—as opposed to what usually gets funded by public television. It has been shaped by many groups and at its base is European, African, and Native American. It is not the exclusively Eurocentric artifact that Patrick Buchanan, for example, extolled during campaign speeches for the Republican presidential nomination in 1992.

Buchanan even sounded un-American to many other conservative Whites who cherish the notion of the melting pot. But most Americans don't really know what the "pot" represents: a process of assimilation that results in a homogenized end product. You know, the same Big Mac you get here you get in Oshkosh. If this were an accurate representation of America, as newspaper headlines commonly suggest—MIAMI MELTING POT BOILS OVER—the country would not be the contentious place that it is.

▼ ▼ ▼

While many Blacks argue that they know they have mixed ancestry, they don't acknowledge it because (1) it would appear that they are trying to distance themselves from a socially stigmatized Black identity, of which they are not ashamed; (2) their non-Black ancestry is so distant they could not identify it precisely; (3) if they did know their non-Black ancestors, their descendants wouldn't accept them as kin; (4) most of their non-Black ancestors were White men who raped enslaved Black women and they want nothing to do with a kinship forged by brutality.

For these reasons, as well as the dictates of U.S. social customs and sometimes law, we have not *embraced* the fact that we are generically a creolized population. And the rise of Afrocentrism has encouraged the science fiction that we are an unadulterated ethnic group. No ethnic group is pure, as Du Bois pointed out long ago. For centuries, Africans mixed with myriad ethnic groups before any were enslaved and shipped to the New World. 100

While rape of Black women by White men was pervasive once we got here, not every sexual encounter between individuals of the two groups was coerced—to think so displays a fundamental misunderstanding of human nature.

But when rape did occur, we must remember that it is the perpetrator of the crime, not the victim, who bears the shame. And to constantly cast this criminal aspect of New World history as the cruel burden the descendants of slaves must bear is like stigmatizing a contemporary victim of sexual assault.

As far as I am concerned, every Black person with White ancestry should, no matter how they came by it, own it. That is not a rejection of African American identity, but an affirmation of the complex ancestry that defines us as an ethnic group. It will normalize what is erroneously treated as an exotic and, consequently, divisive characteristic among African Americans. Further, the acknowledgment of our ties by blood and culture puts the lie to the official silence on America's historically miscegenated identity.

But again, carnal knowledge of each other "across the color line" not only goes beyond rape but includes other non-Whites. Zora Neale Hurston once wrote: "I am colored but offer nothing in the way of extenuating circumstances except the fact that I am the only Negro in the United States whose grandfather on the mother's side was *not* an Indian chief." So where we once tried to find every drop of non-Black blood as a buffer against our caste status, we now tend to proclaim that all of us are exclusively the descendants of African princes, princesses, kings and queens. (You notice how no one ever claims descent from the village thief.) In reality, many social scientists estimate that most of our non-African ancestry is Native American.

As demographers point to the growth of the non-White population and 105 the consequent "browning" of America, the already heterogeneous African American gene pool will become more so: Black, Korean American, Hispanic; Japanese, African American, and East Indian; Ethiopian, African American, Chinese, and Euro-American. In Los Angeles, I meet people with these and similar backgrounds frequently.

Is the African American community capable of embracing such diversity? Is it too much of a stretch for the traditionally defined African American population, which is essentially monocultural, to include people of African descent whose consciousness has been shaped by a multicultural family?

What should we expect if the Annas of the world meet African Americans who continually vent their own pain through the physical and psychological abuse of multiethnic people who have African ancestry but do not identify solely with the African American community? Is there any alternative but for people like Anna to reject us and work for a separate census designation and the social and political recognition that will result?

Certainly getting the personal pain that arises from these conflicts healed is essential. When that process is begun perhaps people can think more clearly about the question of a "multiracial" census category, and the notion of "race," period.

Says Love: "The question of whether there should be a new racial category has to be considered aside from personal pain and personal history."

Love believes, as I do, that "personal wishes have to be viewed in the 110 context of what it means to live in an oppressive society where inequality is based on social identity groups. And where *race* is the fundamental criterion on which those groupings, and thus divisions, are made.

"If you go at it from a sociological rather than a personal standpoint, it is disastrous to create a new category, because the oppression itself is based on exactly that kind of division," Love argues. "We should be putting our energies into using the historic juncture of the year 2000 as a time when we will abolish all racial categories."

I know many multiethnic activists would argue that this is a progressive-sounding argument to deny them recognition and representation. But if their interest is the elimination of oppression—and not social vengeance against Blacks—then the elimination of classifications based on "race" is the only solution that makes sense. We should be challenging the nomenclature of oppression and attacking the philosophical underpinnings of racism—all a necessary part of dismantling institutionalized discrimination.

Finally, the exorcising of the psychological consequences of oppression that divide communities of color is a painful matter that many of us would rather deny or argue should be done out of sight and earshot of the enemy. But Black folks are among the most studied people on the planet. Who *doesn't* know our business?

114 As long as colorism and conflicts with other minority groups distract us from the larger issues of social and economic justice, the nation's system of structured inequality prevails. Which is why so many among the country's White power elite smile indulgently at the notion of a "browner," "newly multicultural" America. They know what the last plantation is, too.

DISCUSSING THE TEXT

1. Njeri cites writer Alice Walker's definition of *colorism* as "the preferential or prejudicial treatment of same-*race* people based on skin color" (par. 16). Have you ever experienced a similar kind of prejudice or favoritism? Is there an equivalent of this phenomenon within your own ethnic/racial group?
2. Njeri sees Re-Evaluation Counseling as an important agent of social change (par. 85–89). Explain briefly what RC is and what its objectives are. Do you think it offers viable ways to combat racism? Why or why not?
3. In discussing the possible categorization of individuals as "multiracial," favored by many ethnically and racially mixed citizens, Njeri cites the opposition's view that "minority groups would shrink . . . , leading to a loss of political representation" (par. 41). In a group of four or five students, discuss your views on this issue. What is your own position on racial classifications? How do you support your views? Take brief notes as you work on this assignment together, and be prepared to share your opinions with the class.

WRITING ABOUT THE TEXT

4. Write an imaginary dialogue between two members of the same ethnic/racial group in which the concept of multiracial identity is debated from two opposing viewpoints.

5. Find a recent example of intraminority group conflict reported in the media. Write two paragraphs about it, first providing your own interpretation of the event and then applying Njeri's argument to the situation.
6. Reread the passage that discusses the plight of Anna Vale, "a Californian of Japanese, African American, and Native American descent . . . [a] voice from the sushi-and-grits generation" (par. 44–55). Write a brief essay analyzing her experience in terms of Frantz Fanon's concept of internalized oppression, which Njeri refers to in paragraph 61.
7. When oppression is internalized, Njeri writes, "the mind becomes the last plantation" (par. 54)—a notion she returns to in the concluding line of her essay ('They know what the last plantation is, too"). Write a brief essay explaining Njeri's use of the metaphor of the plantation here. Who are the "they" she refers to in her closing line? Do you agree with this understanding of racial politics in the United States? Why or why not?

MAKING CONNECTIONS

1. Of all the selections included in this chapter, select the one that you have found most interesting in terms of challenging any preconceptions you might have had about representations of ethnicity. Then write a brief essay explaining how the particular piece has affected your own views on ethnic representation.
2. Choose one of the Lewis Hine photographs in "Picturing the Immigrant" and one of the ads included in Amy Rashap's article "The American Dream for Sale: Ethnic Images in Magazines." Then write two paragraphs that compare and contrast the two images.
3. Look through a recent magazine and find two images (photographs, ads, or drawings)—one that clearly targets a specific ethnic group, and one that you feel makes no particular effort to do so. Write two lists describing the images; then compare and contrast the two in a brief essay. What have you learned from this exercise?
4. Compare and contrast the stereotype of the black athlete in Earl Smith's article "The Genetically Superior Athlete: Myth or Reality" with the common Latino stereotype described by Enrique Fernández in "Spitfires, Latin Lovers, Mambo Kings."
5. Choose an image from the visual illustrations included in this chapter. Write a description of it from the point of view of the person(s) that it portrays, conveying that person's feelings about the image.
6. Choose one of the written selections in this chapter (except the final one). Evaluate the author's understanding of race or ethnicity in this selection in light of Njeri's discussion of these concepts in her long footnote early in "Sushi and Grits: Ethnic Identity and Conflict in a Newly Multicultural America" (p. 512). Do you think Njeri's arguments about notions of "race" in any way qualify the arguments made in this other selection? Why or why not?
7. Look closely at the photograph that introduces this chapter, which shows director Spike Lee working with the rap group Public Enemy on a music video that was used in the film *Do the Right Thing*. The background for this scene appears to be a political demonstration—notice the signs and placards—and the whole image raises the question of how race and racial images enter into the political process. Write a brief essay describing the photograph, making sure to note some of the many "signs" of ethnicity that are pictured here, from dress to posters. Do you think that these signs have any political significance? Explain why or why not.

FURTHER READING

John Heckewelder

Lyman, Christopher. *The Vanishing Race and Other Illusions: Photographs of Indians by Edward Curtis.* New York: Pantheon Books, 1982.

Taylor, William B., and G. Y. Pease, eds. *Violence, Resistance, and Survival in the Americas: Native Americans and the Legacy of Conquest.* Washington, D.C.: Smithsonian Institution, 1994.

Washburn, Wilcomb E., ed. *The Indian and the White Man.* New York: Doubleday, 1964.

Lewis Hine

Hine, Lewis. *Men at Work: Photographic Studies of Men and Machines.* New York: Dover, 1977.

Trachtenberg, Alan. *America and Lewis Hine: Photographs 1904–1940.* New York: Aperture, 1977.

Amy Rashap

Ewen, Stuart. *Captains of Consciousness: Advertising and the Social Roots of the Consumer Culture.* New York: McGraw-Hill, 1976.

Goffman, Erving. *Gender Advertisements.* New York: Harper and Row, 1979.

Marchand, John. *Advertising the American Dream.* Berkeley: University of California Press, 1985.

Bill Gaskins

Terkel, Studs. *RACE: How Blacks and Whites Think and Feel about the American Obsession.* New York: New Press, 1992.

Willis, Deborah. *Picturing Us: African-American Identity in Photographs.* New York: New Press, 1994.

Earl Smith

Gossett, Thomas. *Race: The History of an Idea in America.* Dallas: Southern Methodist University Press, 1963.

Owens, Jesse. *Jesse: The Man Who Outran Hitler.* New York: Fawcett Books, 1978.

Williams, Vernon. *From a Caste to a Minority: Changing Attitudes of American Sociologists Toward Afro-Americans, 1896–1945.* Westport, Conn.: Greenwood Press, 1989.

Enrique Fernández

Fiske, John. *Media Matters: Everyday Culture and Political Change.* Minneapolis: University of Minnesota, 1994.

Leguizamo, John. *Mambo Mouth.* New York: Bantam Books, 1993.

Miller, Randall M., ed. *Ethnic Images in American Film and Television.* Philadelphia: Balch Institute, 1978.

Itabari Njeri

Early, Gerald, ed. *Lure and Loathing: Essays on Race, Identity, and the Ambivalence of Assimilation.* New York: Penguin Books, 1993.

Njeri, Itabari. *Every Good-bye Ain't Gone: Family Portraits and Personal Escapades.* New York: Times Books, 1990.

Puerto Rico Day Parade *(photograph by Joel Gordon), June 11, 1995. The photograph was taken along Fifth Avenue in New York City at the annual parade celebrating Puerto Rican contributions to New York's public life and popular culture.*

8

The Politics of Ethnicity

My native country, thee,
Land of the noble free,—
  Thy name I love

- SAMUEL FRANCIS SMITH
America

The free?
Who said the free? . . .

- LANGSTON HUGHES
Let America Be America Again

By what you read, you may learn how deep your principles are. I should say they were skin deep.

- WILLIAM APES
An Indian's Looking-Glass for the White Man

Black people have searched desperately for allies in the struggle against racism—and have found Jews to be disproportionately represented in the ranks of that struggle.

- CORNEL WEST
On Black-Jewish Relations

[B]y confronting anti-Semitism and racism, people of goodwill can transcend both—or at least keep them dormant.

- RICHARD GOLDSTEIN
The New Anti-Semitism: A Geshrei

The government should not be obliged to preserve any group's distinctive language or culture

- LINDA CHAVEZ
Toward a New Politics of Hispanic Assimilation

[D]iversity is desirable only in principle, not in practice. Long live diversity . . . as long as it conforms to my standards.

- ARTURO MADRID
Diversity and Its Discontents

[M]ulticulturalism seems but one more sign of the ways in which the issues of education are but the issues of the nation at large.

- WILLIAM M. CHACE
The Real Challenge of Multiculturalism (Is Yet to Come)

In the preceding chapter, we looked at various ways in which ethnicity has been represented in mainstream American culture: through advertisements, magazine articles and photographs, and popular films. Some essays in Chapter 7 also discussed more controversial issues of cultural and racial stereotypes, often challenging the reader to think critically about representations of ethnicity. This final chapter, "The Politics of Ethnicity," addresses the question of how different ethnic and racial groups (and individuals) get along within the common world we inhabit—in our schools, our communities, and the country as a whole. To some extent the topic of racial/ethnic relations has been implicit throughout this book; now we will focus on the issue more directly. Sometimes it seems as if there is not one America but many. The pride people feel in themselves and their culture is displayed more often in celebration of their own particular ethnic or cultural background (as in the Puerto Rico Day Parade pictured at the beginning of this chapter) than in the country as a whole. Do we even have, as we near the end of the twentieth century, a single "whole" country to talk about or sing about?

Nearly everyone can hum or sing the words to Samuel Francis Smith's classic patriotic song, "America," which portrays a land where all is harmony and pride. Smith's America is certainly a land worth singing about, but for many people it bears no resemblance to our own more troubled country. If Smith's "America" presents a kind of idealized version of the United States, then Langston Hughes's "Let America Be America Again," written over one hundred years later, presents something probably closer to our present reality, and it challenges traditional views about the "sweet land of liberty."

How far apart are the political ideals we pay lip service to and the reality of our lives and behavior? William Apes's "An Indian's Looking Glass for the White Man," written in 1833, offers a relatively early discussion of this question, and of ethnic politics, as its author argues against the prejudice and violence against Native Americans that was prevalent during his lifetime. The two contemporary essays that follow, Cornel West's "On Black-Jewish Relations" and Richard Goldstein's "The New Anti-Semitism: A *Geshrei*," continue to explore the theme of racial strife and discrimination by looking at two groups that have a history of joint alliances as well as violent clashes. Both West and Goldstein frame their discussions of the relationship between Jewish Americans and African Americans within the specific context of contemporary American politics, arguing against demagoguery and advocating mutual cooperation and respect between the two groups.

Linda Chavez's 1991 essay "Toward a New Politics of Hispanic Assimilation" looks at the politics of ethnicity from a different angle. Chavez suggests that Hispanics should take a more active role in assuming what she sees as their responsibility to adapt to American culture. She argues against entitlements and bilingual education, maintaining that assimilation into the mainstream culture would give Hispanics a stronger base from which to make social and economic advancements in the United States.

The final two selections in this chapter move the debate on the politics of ethnicity into the arena of higher education. Both Arturo Madrid (in "Diversity and Its Discontents") and William M. Chace (in "The Real Challenge of Multiculturalism (Is Yet to Come)") focus on the current controversies about the teaching of diversity on American campuses. Although their approaches to, and opinions about, multiculturalism are quite different, both authors, who are also academics, see the politics of ethnicity as a challenging arena that can lead to serious reflection and positive change.

"The Politics of Ethnicity," the last chapter of *Inventing America: Identity, Ethnicity, and Culture,* brings the discussion begun in Chapter 1, "Encountering Others," full circle. Through its exploration of the ways in which American writers have addressed the question of identity in terms of race and ethnicity, and challenged aspects of mainstream American culture, this anthology has reached out to erase the boundaries between "them" and "us." We all encounter the "other" in our daily lives, *but we too are that "other,"* constantly growing, changing, and learning—as we try to accept *both* ourselves and others.

SAMUEL FRANCIS SMITH

America

Can the United States live up to its best ideals? That question is always current, and it tests our collective will even as we observe the changing character and composition of American society at the end of the twentieth century. What ideals do we share as Americans? Justice? Freedom? Opportunity? Do we have the strength to continue to invent America in the face of the new challenges and changes in its population?

This selection presents a nineteenth-century version of the American dream: the patriotic hymn "America," by Samuel Francis Smith, affirmed traditional, homogeneous ideals in their simplest form at a Fourth of July celebration in 1831 in Boston. From the opposite end of the cultural spectrum, Langston Hughes challenges those ideals in his poem "Let America Be America Again," published at the height of the Great Depression in 1938 (see next selection, p. 537).

Although most Americans have heard the patriotic song "America" and can sing it, few have read the poem in its entirety. We take the version that we sing so much for granted that the poem's additional verses have become virtually nonexistent (all the more reason to read carefully this most popular of American poems, which one can hardly do without being overcome by the melody). Even when it was published in 1832, "America" celebrated a nation that was changing in the face of urbanization and the industrial revolution; yet the ideal has continued to resonate well into a time that the author could hardly have imagined. Samuel Francis Smith (1808–1895) was born in Boston and graduated from Harvard University and from the Andover Theological Seminary. Although Smith wrote a great deal of poetry, biography, local history, and tales, this simple hymn, written "within half an hour" by the young minister, has had by far the greatest impact of all his work.

My country, 'tis of thee,
Sweet land of liberty,
Of thee I sing;
Land where my fathers died,
Land of the pilgrim's pride, 5
From every mountain-side
Let freedom ring.

My native country, thee,
Land of the noble free,—
Thy name I love; 10
I love thy rocks and rills,
Thy woods and templed hills;
My heart with rapture thrills
Like that above.

Let music swell the breeze, 15
And ring from all the trees,
Sweet freedom's song;

Let mortal tongues awake,
Let all that breathe partake,
Let rocks their silence break,— 20
The sound prolong.

Our fathers' God, to Thee,
Author of liberty,
To Thee I sing;
Long may our land be bright 25
With freedom's holy light;
Protect us by thy might,
Great God our King.

DISCUSSING THE TEXT

1. Who do you imagine the speaker of the poem "America" to be? What social class? What religion? What gender? Who were his or her ancestors?
2. How inclusive (or exclusive) do you take the words in "America" to be? That is, to what extent do you think Americans today (including recent immigrants) can identify with these sentiments?

WRITING ABOUT THE TEXT

3. Do you think it would be possible to write a poem like "America" today? Why or why not?
4. Ask several of your friends and family members to recite the words to "America" (from memory) and to tell you what they think those words mean. Write a brief essay that summarizes your findings.

LANGSTON HUGHES

Let America Be America Again

Langston Hughes's poem, "Let America Be America Again," written in the later years of the Great Depression (1938), provides an interesting counterpoint to Smith's "America" (and a different way of thinking about the questions posed by that selection). Hughes (1902–1967) was born in Joplin, Missouri, and worked at a number of jobs (including cook, busboy, seaman) before establishing himself as a writer. He attended Columbia University for a year (1921–1922), and graduated from Lincoln University, Missouri, in 1929, by which time he had already published The Weary Blues *(1926), the first of many volumes of poetry. Hughes is one of the most eminent poets of the mid-twentieth century and an important figure of the Harlem Renaissance of the 1920s, a period of great achievement by African Americans, not only in literature but also in art and particularly in music, through the rising popularity of jazz.*

Hughes brought to his poetry a sharp ear for everyday language, a familiarity with blues and ballad forms, and a passionate concern with the afflictions, and the joys, of the African American experience. In addition to many volumes of poetry, including Fields of Wonder *(1947) and* Montage of a Dream Deferred *(1951), Hughes wrote two novels, many plays, nonfiction, an autobiography, and several short story collections.*

In "Let America Be America Again," Hughes identifies himself with the whole of marginalized American society, including different immigrant groups, people of color, and poor whites, calling on the land to fulfill in reality the ideals that it has so roundly proclaimed for so many years. Although Hughes does not allude to Smith or to his "America," his own poem can be read as a response to the sort of patriotism that the earlier poem invokes.

Let America be America again.
Let it be the dream it used to be.
Let it be the pioneer on the plain
Seeking a home where he himself is free.

(America never was America to me.) 5

Let America be the dream the dreamers dreamed—
Let it be that great strong land of love
Where never kings connive nor tyrants scheme
That any man be crushed by one above.

(It never was America to me.) 10

O, let my land be a land where Liberty
Is crowned with no false patriotic wreath,
But opportunity is real, and life is free,
Equality is in the air we breathe.

(There's never been equality for me, 15
Nor freedom in this "homeland of the free.")

Say who are you that mumbles in the dark?
And who are you that draws your veil across the stars?

I am the poor white, fooled and pushed apart,
I am the red man driven from the land. 20
I am the refugee clutching the hope I seek—
But finding only the same old stupid plan
Of dog eat dog, of mighty crush the weak.
I am the Negro, "problem" to you all.
I am the people, humble, hungry, mean— 25
Hungry yet today despite the dream.

Beaten yet today—O, Pioneers!
I am the man who never got ahead,
The poorest worker bartered through the years.
Yet I'm the one who dreamt our basic dream 30
In that Old World while still a serf of kings,
Who dreamt a dream so strong, so brave, so true,
That even yet its mighty daring sings
In every brick and stone, in every furrow turned
That's made America the land it has become. 35
O, I'm the man who sailed those early seas
In search of what I meant to be my home—
For I'm the one who left dark Ireland's shore,
And Poland's plain, and England's grassy lea,
And torn from Black Africa's strand I came 40
To build a "homeland of the free."

The free?
Who said the free? Not me?
Surely not me? The millions on relief today?
The millions who have nothing for our pay 45
For all the dreams we've dreamed
And all the songs we've sung
And all the hopes we've held
And all the flags we've hung,
The millions who have nothing for our pay— 50
Except the dream we keep alive today.

O, let America be America again—
The land that never has been yet—
And yet must be—the land where *every* man is free.
The land that's mine—the poor man's, Indian's, Negro's, ME— 55
Who made America,
Whose sweat and blood, whose faith and pain,
Whose hand at the foundry, whose plow in the rain,
Must bring back our mighty dream again.

O, yes, 60
I say it plain,
America never was America to me,
And yet I swear this oath—
America will be!

DISCUSSING THE TEXT

1. What do you think Hughes means by saying, "Let America be America again"? What is the difference between the use of the word "America" in the first stanzas of the poem and its use in the final stanzas?

2. When Hughes finally identifies the voice within the parentheses (in the poem's first sixteen lines), this voice turns out to be many voices. What kinds of thoughts do these voices speak? What, if anything, do they have in common? To whom do you think Hughes is speaking in this poem?
3. In a group of four or five classmates, discuss how you think the speaker in Hughes's poem feels. Do you think this speaker is bitter? Proud? Angry? Hopeful? Take brief notes as you work on this assignment (including specific lines in the poem that support your ideas), and be prepared to share your opinions with the rest of the class.

WRITING ABOUT THE TEXT

4. Write a short essay defining the "American dream" that Hughes refers to in "Let America Be America Again." What is this dream? What is its appeal? Why has it failed to become a reality for so many?
5. Make a list of the things Smith celebrates in "America." Then make a list of the things that you think Hughes wants America to be. Write a brief essay comparing Smith's ideal with Hughes's dreams.

WILLIAM APES

An Indian's Looking-Glass for the White Man

The encounter between the Europeans and the Native Americans initiated a conflict of cultures that, for over two centuries, was almost exclusively presented by one side, the new arrivals. The explorers, missionaries, pilgrims, farmers, and conquistadors who settled the American continent published their views in their own written languages, using the printing press. Except for some early translations of Indian speeches and oral texts, the white reader did not encounter the Indian's own voice in published form until the early nineteenth century. And since Indians' education often came through Christian missionary schools, the published voices of Native Americans grew out of a cultural experience that was not their own. William Apes's "Indian" voice, for example, was distinctly Christian. Apes's "looking-glass"—his effort to call whites to account by asking them to look at themselves—was fashioned out of moral prescriptions he had absorbed during his conversion to Methodism.

*William Apes, born in Massachusetts in 1798 (date of death unknown), was the first Native American to publish an autobiography (*A Son of the Forest*, 1829) and other literary works. His mother was a full-blooded Pequot Indian, and his father was half white. Indentured as a servant to whites at an early age, Apes converted to Methodism at age fifteen and eventually became a minister in the church. He was an ardent spokesperson for Indian rights, most significantly in his legal representation of the Mashpee tribe in their struggle for self-government in the 1830s.*

"An Indian's Looking-Glass for the White Man," from Apes's personal narrative, The Experience of Five Christian Indians of the Pequod Tribe *(1833), argues movingly against the prevailing prejudices and harsh treatment of Native Americans. Apes's rhetorical strategy—that of holding a mirror up to the white man—called on the white readers of the time to examine honestly their own behavior toward the Indian, and to measure its morality by their own white standards (that is, by Christian standards). Apes's text is still timely at the end of the twentieth century, addressing prophetically the tragic role that discrimination according to race and skin color would play in American life.*

Having a desire to place a few things before my fellow creatures who are travelling with me to the grave, and to that God who is the maker and preserver both of the white man and the Indian, whose abilities are the same, and who are to be judged by one God, who will show no favor to outward appearances, but will judge righteousness. Now I ask if degradation has not been heaped long enough upon the Indians? And if so, can there not be a compromise; is it right to hold and promote prejudices? If not, why not put them all away? I mean here amongst those who are civilized. It may be that many are ignorant of the situation of many of my brethren within the limits of New England. Let me for a few moments turn your attention to the reservations in the different states of New England, and, with but few exceptions, we shall find them as follows: The most mean, abject, miserable race of beings in the world—a complete place of prodigality and prostitution.

Let a gentleman and lady, of integrity and respectability visit these places, and they would be surprised; as they wandered from one hut to the other they would view with the females who are left alone, children half starved, and some almost as naked as they came into the world. And it is a fact that I have seen them as much so—while the females are left without protection, and are seduced by white men, and are finally left to be common prostitutes for them, and to be destroyed by that burning, fiery curse, that has swept millions, both of red and white men, into the grave with sorrow and disgrace—Rum. One reason why they are left so is, because their most sensible and active men are absent at sea. Another reason is, because they are made to believe they are minors and have not the abilities given them from God, to take care of themselves, without it is to see to a few little articles, such as baskets and brooms. Their land is in common stock, and they have nothing to make them enterprising.

Another reason is because those men who are Agents, many of them are unfaithful, and care not whether the Indians live or die; they are much imposed upon by their neighbors who have no principle. They would think it no crime to go upon Indian lands and cut and carry off their most valuable timber, or anything else they chose; and I doubt not but they think it clear gain. Another reason is because they have no education to take care of themselves; if they had, I would risk them to take care of their property.

Now I will ask, if the Indians are not called the most ingenious people amongst us? And are they not said to be men of talents? And I would ask, could there be a more efficient way to distress and murder them by inches than the way they have taken? And there is no people in the world but who may be destroyed in the same way. Now if these people are what they are held up in our view to be, I would take the liberty to ask why they are not brought forward and pains taken to educate them? to give them all a common education, and those of the brightest and first-rate talents put forward and held up to office. Perhaps some unholy, unprincipled men would cry out, the skin was not good enough; but stop friends—I am not talking about the skin, but about principles. I would ask if there cannot be as good feelings and principles under a red skin as there can be under a white? And let me ask, is it not on the account of a bad principle, that we who are red children have had to suffer so much as we have? And let me ask, did not this bad principle proceed from the whites or their forefathers? And I would ask, is it worth while to nourish it any longer? If not, then let us have a change; although some men no doubt will spout their corrupt principles against it, that are in the halls of legislation and elsewhere. But I presume this kind of talk will seem surprising and horrible. I do not see why it should so long as they (the whites) say that they think as much of us as they do of themselves.

This I have heard repeatedly, from the most respectable gentlemen and ladies—and having heard so much precept, I should now wish to see the example. And I would ask who has a better right to look for these things than the naturalist himself—the candid man would say none.

I know that many say that they are willing, perhaps the majority of the people, that we should enjoy our rights and privileges as they do. If so, I would ask why are not we protected in our persons and property throughout the Union? Is it not because there reigns in the breast of many who are leaders, a most unrighteous, unbecoming and impure black principle, and as corrupt and unholy as it can be—while these very same unfeeling, self-esteemed characters pretend to take the skin as a pretext to keep us from our unalienable and lawful rights? I would ask you if you would like to be disfranchised from all your rights, merely because your skin is white, and for no other crime? I'll venture to say, these very characters who hold the skin to be such a barrier in the way, would be the first to cry out, injustice! awful injustice!

But, reader, I acknowledge that this is a confused world, and I am not seeking for office; but merely placing before you the black inconsistency that you place before me—which is ten times blacker than any skin that you will find in the Universe. And now let me exhort you to do away that principle, as it appears ten times worse in the sight of God and candid men, than skins of color—more disgraceful than all the skins that Jehovah ever made. If black or red skins, or any other skin of color is disgraceful to God, it appears that he has disgraced himself a great deal—for he has made fifteen colored people to one white, and placed them here upon this earth.

Now let me ask you, white man, if it is a disgrace for to eat, drink and sleep with the image of God, or sit, or walk and talk with them? Or have you the folly to think that the white man, being one in fifteen or sixteen, are the only beloved images of God? Assemble all nations together in your imagination, and then let the whites be seated amongst them, and then let us look for the whites, and I doubt not it would be hard finding them; for to the rest of the nations, they are still but a handful. Now suppose these skins were put together, and each skin had its national crimes written upon it—which skin do you think would have the greatest? I will ask one question more. Can you charge the Indians with robbing a nation almost of their whole Continent, and murdering their women and children, and then depriving the remainder of their lawful rights, that nature and God require them to have? And to cap the climax, rob another nation to till their grounds, and welter out their days under the lash with hunger and fatigue under the scorching rays of a burning sun? I should look at all the skins, and I know that when I cast my eye upon that white skin, and if I saw those crimes written upon it, I should enter my protest against it immediately, and cleave to that which is more honorable. And I can tell you that I am satisfied with the manner of my creation, fully—whether others are or not.

But we will strive to penetrate more fully into the conduct of those who profess to have pure principles, and who tell us to follow Jesus Christ and imitate him and have his Spirit. Let us see if they come any where near him and his ancient disciples. The first thing we are to look at, are his precepts, of which we will mention a few. "Thou shalt love the Lord thy God with all thy heart, with all thy soul, with all thy mind, and with all thy strength." The second is like unto it. "Thou shalt love thy neighbor as thyself." On these two precepts hang all the law and the prophets—Matt. xxii. 37, 38, 39, 40. "By this shall all men know that they are my disciples, if ye have love one to another"—John xiii. 35. Our Lord left this special command with his followers, that they should love one another.

Again, John in his Epistles says, "He who loveth God, loveth his brother also"—iv. 21. "Let us not love in word but in deed"—iii. 18. "Let your love be without dissimulation. See that ye love one another with a pure heart fervently"—1. Peter, viii. 22. "If any man say, I love God, and hateth his brother, he is a liar"—John iv. 20. "Whosoever hateth his brother is a murderer, and no murderer hath eternal life abiding in him." The first thing that takes our attention, is the saying of Jesus, "Thou shalt love," &c. The first question I would ask my brethren in the ministry, as well as that of the membership, What is love, or its effects? Now if they who teach are not essentially affected with pure love, the love of God, how can they teach as they ought? Again, the holy teachers of old said, "Now if any man have not the spirit of Christ, he is none of his"—Rom. viii. 9. Now my brethren in the ministry, let me ask you a few sincere questions. Did you ever hear or read of Christ teaching his disciples that they ought to despise one because his skin was different from theirs? Jesus Christ being a Jew, and those of his Apostles certainly were not whites,—and did not he who completed the plan of salvation complete it for the whites as well as for the Jews, and others? And were not the whites the most degraded people on the earth at that time, and none were more so; for they sacrificed their children to dumb idols! And did not St. Paul labor more abundantly for building up a christian nation amongst you than any of the Apostles. And you know as well as I that you are not indebted to a principle beneath a white skin for your religious services, but to a colored one.

What then is the matter now; is not religion the same now under a colored skin as it ever was? If so I would ask why is not a man of color respected; you may say as many say, we have white men enough. But was this the spirit of Christ and his Apostles? If it had been, there would not have been one white preacher in the world—for Jesus Christ never would have imparted his grace or word to them, for he could forever have withheld it from them. But we find that Jesus Christ and his Apostles never looked at the outward appearances. Jesus in particular looked at the hearts and his Apostles through him being discerners of the spirit, looked at their fruit without any regard to the skin, color or nation; as St. Paul himself speaks, "Where there is neither Greek nor Jew, circumcision nor uncircumcision, Barbarian nor Scythian, bond nor free—but Christ is all and in all." If you can find a spirit like Jesus Christ and his Apostles prevailing now in any of the white congregations, I should like to know it. I ask, is it not the case that every body that is not white is treated with contempt and counted as barbarians? And I ask if the word of God justifies the white man in so doing? When the prophets prophesied, of whom did they speak? When they spoke of heathens, was it not the whites and others who were counted Gentiles? And I ask if all nations with the exception of the Jews were not counted heathens? and according to the writings of some, it could not mean the Indians, for they are counted Jews. And now I would ask, why is all this distinction made among these christian societies? I would ask what is all this ado about Missionary Societies, if it be not to christianize those who are not christians? And what is it for? To degrade them worse, to bring them into society where they must welter out their days in disgrace merely because their skin is of a different complexion. What folly it is to try to make the state of human society worse than it is. How astonished some may be at this—but let me ask, is it not so? Let me refer you to the churches only. And my brethren, is there any agreement? Do brethren and sisters love one another?—Do they not rather hate one another. Outward forms and ceremonies, the lusts of the flesh, the lusts of the eye and pride of life is of more value to many professors, than the love of God shed abroad in their hearts, or an attachment to his altar, to his ordinances or to his children. But you may ask who are the children of God? perhaps you may say none but white. If so, the word of the Lord is not true.

I will refer you to St. Peter's precepts—Acts 10. "God is no respecter of persons"—&c. Now if this is the case, my white brother, what better are you than God? And if no better, why do you profess his gospel and to have his spirit, act so contrary to it? Let me ask why the men of a different skin are so despised, why are not they educated and placed in your pulpits? I ask if his services well performed are not as good as if a white man performed them? I ask if a marriage or a funeral ceremony, or the ordinance of the Lord's house would not be as acceptable in the sight of God as though he was white? And if so, why is it not to you? I ask again, why is it not as acceptable to have men to exercise their office in one place as well as in another? Perhaps you will say that if we admit you to all of these privileges you will want more. I expect that I can guess what that is—Why, say you, there would be intermarriages. How that would be I am not able to say—and if it should be, it would be nothing strange or new to me; for I can assure you that I know a great many that have intermarried, both of the whites and the Indians—and many are their sons and daughters—and people too of the first respectability. And I could point to some in the famous city of Boston and elsewhere. You may now look at the disgraceful act in the statute law passed by the Legislature of Massachusetts, and behold the fifty pound fine levied upon any Clergyman or Justice of the Peace that dare to encourage the laws of God and nature by a legitimate union in holy wedlock between the Indians and whites. I would ask how this looks to your law makers. I would ask if this corresponds with your sayings—that you think as much of the Indians as you do of the whites. I do not wonder that you blush many of you while you read; for many have broken the ill-fated laws made by man to hedge up the laws of God and nature. I would ask if they who have made the law have not broken it—but there is no other state in New England that has this law but Massachusetts; and I think as many of you do not, that you have done yourselves no credit.

But as I am not looking for a wife, having one of the finest cast, as you no doubt would understand while you read her experience and travail of soul in the way to heaven, you will see that it is not my object. And if I had none, I should not want any one to take my right from me and choose a wife for me; for I think that I or any of my brethren have a right to choose a wife for themselves as well as the whites—and as the whites have taken the liberty to choose my brethren, the Indians, hundreds and thousands of them as partners in life, I believe the Indians have as much right to choose their partners amongst the whites if they wish. I would ask you if you can see any thing inconsistent in your conduct and talk about the Indians? And if you do, I hope you will try to become more consistent. Now if the Lord Jesus Christ, who is counted by all to be a Jew, and it is well known that the Jews are a colored people, especially those living in the East, where Christ was born—and if he should appear amongst us, would he not be shut out of doors by many, very quickly? and by those too, who profess religion?

By what you read, you may learn how deep your principles are. I should say they were skin deep. I should not wonder if some of the most selfish and ignorant would spout a charge of their principles now and then at me. But I would ask, how are you to love your neighbors as yourself? Is it to cheat them? is it to wrong them in any thing? Now to cheat them out of any of their rights is robbery. And I ask, can you deny that you are not robbing the Indians daily, and many others? But at last you may think I am what is called a hard and uncharitable man. But not so. I believe there are many who would not hesitate to advocate our cause; and those too who are men of fame and respectability—as well as ladies of honor and virtue. There is a Webster, an Everett, and a Wirt, and many others who are distinguished characters—besides an host of my fellow citizens, who advocate our cause daily. And how I congratulate such noble spirits—how they are to be prized and valued; for they are well calculated to promote the happiness of mankind.

▼ ▼ ▼

Do not get tired, ye noble-hearted—only think how many poor Indians want their wounds done up daily; the Lord will reward you, and pray you stop not till this tree of distinction shall be levelled to the earth, and the mantle of prejudice torn from every American heart—then shall peace pervade the Union. 15

DISCUSSING THE TEXT

1. Apes asks white readers to examine honestly their behavior toward the Indian by using the measure of their own Christian morality; yet he does so from a relatively powerless position within the culture. How does his position as a marginal member of the dominant society affect his attitudes? His tone? His appeals for justice?
2. Apes declares, against the prejudices of his time, that Indian abilities and talents are equal to those of whites. What are the reasons he gives to support his claim?
3. Working with a group of other students, make a list of all the places in this essay where Apes uses, or makes references to, colors. What different uses does Apes make of the concept of color? What is his purpose here?

WRITING ABOUT THE TEXT

4. Drawing on references from the Bible, Apes takes several principles as his standards in measuring white behavior and attitudes toward Indians. Make a list of the various principles Apes uses, and explain how they are helpful to him as he develops his argument. Then write a brief paragraph stating your opinion. Do you think that these principles are good ones for Apes to use in making his argument? Why or why not?
5. One strategy Apes uses to make his argument in this selection is to hold up a mirror to his audience. Reread quickly "The Life of Olaudah Equiano or Gustavus Vassa the African," in Chapter 2, and then write two paragraphs comparing and contrasting Apes's strategy with the strategy employed by Olaudah Equiano.
6. In paragraph 4, Apes refers to a "bad principle" that has caused the suffering of the Indians. What is this "bad principle"? Does Apes identify it directly? Outline an argument for or against the idea that one bad principle was the cause of all Native Americans' suffering.
7. Apes associates Indians with Jews and with blacks, in their relationship with the white race. Write a page addressing the following questions: How accurate are these analogies between Indians, Jews, and blacks? Do they seem appropriate today? What other groups might be associated with Indians in this way?
8. What if, as Apes asks in paragraph 8, "each skin" in American culture today "had its national crimes written upon it"? Using Apes's rhetorical strategy

(that of the looking-glass), write an essay addressing this question in reference to at least three groups in American society today. (Remember that you will need to establish your own set of principles, in order to determine what counts as a "national crime.")

CORNEL WEST

On Black-Jewish Relations

In this essay, from the collection Race Matters *(1993), African American philosopher and theologian Cornel West offers his perspective on the present tensions between African Americans and Jews. Even though, as West says, "there was no* golden age *in which Blacks and Jews were free from tension and friction," relations between the two groups were generally warm and mutually supportive from the early 1900s through the late 1960s. This includes the period from the founding of the National Association for the Advancement of Colored People (NAACP) through the civil rights movement of the 1960s, when many Jewish leaders—and students—worked cooperatively with southern blacks. Over the past twenty years, however, that relationship has become strained for a number of reasons, and now the two groups—or at least the more progressive and constructive members of each group—are trying to find ways to respond to this strain.*

West argues in this selection that African Americans and Jews today are far from unanimous in their opinions about the present and future of black-Jewish relations. African Americans who advocate separation blame the Jews for many of the problems African Americans are experiencing today. Against the polemical stance of the extreme of African American opinion stand scholars and intellectuals like West and Henry Louis Gates, Jr. West views African American extremists critically, attempting to understand where they are coming from and what their appeals are, yet trying also to counter their arguments with views that might heal the breach between the two groups. West sees black anti-Semitism as self-destructive, and chooses to focus instead on mutuality and cooperation as the keys to future progress for both groups.

Cornel West (b. 1953), has taught at Yale and Princeton universities and is now a member of the African American Studies Department at Harvard University. Among his scholarly works are The American Evasion of Philosophy *(1989) and* The Ethical Dimension of Marxist Thought *(1991). West himself carries on the pragmatic tradition of American philosophy, which is deeply concerned with the ethical and social consequences of general beliefs. West's commitment to a cooperative relationship between African Americans and Jewish Americans is reflected in a recent book,* Jews and Blacks: Let the Healing Begin *(1995), which is a dialogue between West and Jewish American writer Michael Lerner, editor of* Tikkun*, a Jewish magazine priding itself on its independence and fresh approaches to social and political issues.*

> For if there are no waving flags and marching songs at the barricades as Walter marches out with his little battalion, it is not because the battle lacks nobility. On the contrary, he has picked up in his way, still imperfect and wobbly in his small view of human destiny, what I believe Arthur Miller once called "the golden thread of history." He becomes, in spite of those who are too intrigued with despair and hatred of man to see it, King Oedipus refusing to tear out his eyes, but attacking the Oracle instead. He is that last Jewish patriot manning his rifle at Warsaw; he is that young girl who swam into sharks to save a friend a few weeks ago; he is Anne Frank, still believing in people; he is the nine small heroes of Little Rock; he is Michelangelo creating David and Beethoven bursting forth with the Ninth Symphony. He is all those things because he has finally reached out in his tiny moment and caught that sweet essence which is human dignity, and it shines like the old star-touched dream that it is in his eyes.
>
> –LORRAINE HANSBERRY, "An Author's Reflections: Walter Lee Younger, Willy Loman and He Who Must Live" (1959)

Recent debates on the state of black-Jewish relations have generated more heat than light. Instead of critical dialogue and respectful exchange, we have witnessed several bouts of vulgar name-calling and self-righteous finger-pointing. Battles conducted on the editorial pages, like the one between Henry Louis Gates, Jr., the eminent Harvard professor, and John Henrik Clarke, the distinguished pan-African scholar, in the *New York Times* and the *City Sun,* respectively, do not take us very far in understanding black-Jewish relations.

Black anti-Semitism and Jewish antiblack racism are real, and both are as profoundly American as cherry pie. There was no *golden age* in which blacks and Jews were free of tension and friction. Yet there was a *better* age when the common histories of oppression and degradation of both groups served as a springboard for genuine empathy and principled alliances. Since the late sixties, black-Jewish relations have reached a nadir. Why is this so?

In order to account for this sad state of affairs we must begin to unearth the truth behind each group's perceptions of the other (and of itself). For example, few blacks recognize and acknowledge one fundamental fact of Jewish history: a profound hatred of Jews sits at the center of medieval and modern European cultures. Jewish persecutions under the Byzantines, Jewish massacres during the Crusades, Jewish expulsions in England (1290), France (1306), Spain (1492), Portugal (1497), Frankfurt (1614), and Vienna (1670), and Jewish pogroms[1] in the Ukraine (1648, 1768), Odessa (1871), and throughout Russia—especially after 1881 culminating in Kishinev (1903)—constitute the vast historical backdrop to current Jewish preoccupations with self-reliance and the Jewish anxiety of group death. Needless to say, the Nazi attempt at Judeocide in the 1930s and 1940s reinforced this preoccupation and anxiety.

The European hatred of Jews rests on religious and social grounds—Christian myths of Jews as Christ-killers and resentment over the dispropor-

---

[1]*pogroms:* organized massacres of Jews in czarist Russia (*Ed.*)

tionate presence of Jews in certain commercial occupations. The religious bigotry feeds on stereotypes of Jews as villainous transgressors of the sacred; the social bigotry, on alleged Jewish conspiratorial schemes for power and control. Ironically, the founding of the state of Israel—the triumph of the quest for modern Jewish self-determination—came about less from Jewish power and more from the consensus of the two superpowers, the United States and USSR, to secure a homeland for a despised and degraded people after Hitler's genocidal attempt.

5 The history of Jews in America for the most part flies in the face of this tragic Jewish past. The majority of Jewish immigrants arrived in America around the turn of the century (1881–1924). They brought a strong heritage that put a premium on what had ensured their survival and identity—institutional autonomy, rabbinical learning, and business zeal. Like other European immigrants, Jews for the most part became complicitous with the American racial caste system. Even in "Christian" America with its formidable anti-Semitic barriers, and despite a rich progressive tradition that made Jews more likely than other immigrants to feel compassion for oppressed blacks, large numbers of Jews tried to procure a foothold in America by falling in step with the widespread perpetuation of antiblack stereotypes and the garnering of white-skin privilege benefits available to nonblack Americans. It goes without saying that a profound hatred of African people (as seen in slavery, lynching, segregation, and second-class citizenship) sits at the center of American civilization.*

The period of genuine empathy and principled alliances between Jews and blacks (1910–67) constitutes a major pillar of American progressive politics in this century. These supportive links begin with W. E. B. Du Bois's *The Crisis* and Abraham Cahan's *Jewish Daily Forward* and are seen clearly between Jewish leftists and A. Philip Randolph's[2] numerous organizations, between Elliot Cohen's *Commentary*[3] and the early career of James Baldwin, between prophets like Abraham Joshua Heschel[4] and Martin Luther King, Jr., or between the disproportionately Jewish Students for a Democratic Society (SDS) and the Student Non-Violent Coordinating Committee (SNCC).[5] Presently, this inspiring period of black-Jewish cooperation is often downplayed by blacks and romanticized by Jews. It is downplayed by blacks because they focus on the astonishingly rapid entree of most Jews into the middle and upper middle classes during this brief period—an entree that has spawned both an intense conflict with the more slowly growing black middle class and a social resentment from

---

[2]*A. Philip Randolph* (1889–1979): African American leader, advocate of unity of black and white labor (*Ed.*)

[3]*Commentary:* a leading Jewish literary and political magazine edited by Elliot Cohen during the 1940s and 1950s, and during that time a liberal, anti-communist voice (*Ed.*)

[4]*Abraham Heschel* (1907–1972): Jewish theologian and political leader who sought through his writing and his activism a common meeting ground with other faiths (*Ed.*)

[5]*SDS and SNCC:* radical student organizations during the late 1960s, active in their support of racial integration and their opposition to the Vietnam War (*Ed.*)

a quickly growing black impoverished class. Jews, on the other hand, tend to romanticize this period because their present status as upper middle dogs and some top dogs in American society unsettles their historic self-image as progressives with a compassion for the underdog.

In the present era, blacks and Jews are in contention over two major issues. The first is the question of what constitutes the most effective means for black progress in America. With over half of all black professionals and managers being employed in the public sphere, and those in the private sphere often gaining entree owing to regulatory checks by the EEOC, attacks by some Jews on affirmative action are perceived as assaults on black livelihood. And since a disproportionate percentage of poor blacks depend on government support to survive, attempts to dismantle public programs are viewed by blacks as opposition to black survival. Visible Jewish resistance to affirmative action and government spending on social programs pits some Jews against black progress. This opposition, though not as strong as that of other groups in the country, is all the more visible to black people because of past Jewish support for black progress. It also seems to reek of naked group interest, as well as a willingness to abandon compassion for the underdogs of American society.

The second major area of contention concerns the meaning and practice of Zionism[6] as embodied in the state of Israel. Without a sympathetic understanding of the deep historic sources of Jewish fears and anxieties about group survival, blacks will not grasp the visceral attachment of most Jews to Israel. Similarly, without a candid acknowledgment of blacks' status as permanent underdogs in American society, Jews will not comprehend what the symbolic predicament and literal plight of Palestinians in Israel means to blacks. Jews rightly point out that the atrocities of African elites on oppressed Africans in Kenya, Uganda, and Ethiopia are just as bad or worse than those perpetrated on Palestinians by Israeli elites. Some also point out—rightly—that deals and treaties between Israel and South Africa are not so radically different from those between some black African, Latin American, and Asian countries and South Africa. Still, these and other Jewish charges of black double standards with regard to Israel do not take us to the heart of the matter. Blacks often perceive the Jewish defense of the state of Israel as a second instance of naked group interest, and, again, an abandonment of substantive moral deliberation. At the same time, Jews tend to view black critiques of Israel as black rejection of the Jewish right to group survival, and hence as a betrayal of the precondition for a black-Jewish alliance. What is at stake here is not simply black-Jewish relations, but, more importantly, the *moral content* of Jewish and black identities and of their political consequences.

---

[6]*Zionism:* Zion is the biblical name for Jerusalem, which came to represent Israel, the homeland for exiled Jews. Zionism is an international political movement with many different factions, originally formed to reestablish Israel as a nation; for the most part, Zionists are unconditionally supportive of the state of Israel. (*Ed.*)

The ascendance of the conservative Likud party in Israel in 1977 and the visibility of narrow black nationalist voices in the eighties helped solidify this impasse. When mainstream American Jewish organizations supported the inhumane policies of Begin and Shamir,[7] they tipped their hats toward cold-hearted interest group calculations. When black nationalist spokesmen like Farrakhan and Jeffries[8] excessively targeted Jewish power as subordinating black and brown peoples they played the same mean-spirited game. In turning their heads from the ugly truth of Palestinian subjugation, and in refusing to admit the falsity of the alleged Jewish conspiracies, both sides failed to define the *moral* character of their Jewish and black identities.

The present impasse in black-Jewish relations will be overcome only when self-critical exchanges take place within and across black and Jewish communities not simply about their own group interest but also, and, more importantly, about what being black or Jewish means in *ethical terms.* This kind of reflection should not be so naive as to ignore group interest, but it should take us to a higher moral ground where serious discussions about democracy and justice determine how we define ourselves and our politics and help us formulate strategies and tactics to sidestep the traps of tribalism and chauvinism. 10

The vicious murder of Yankel Rosenbaum in Crown Heights[9] in the summer of 1991 bore chilling testimony to a growing black anti-Semitism in this country. Although this particular form of xenophobia from below does not have the same institutional power of those racisms that afflict their victims from above, it certainly deserves the same moral condemnation. Furthermore, the very *ethical* character of the black freedom struggle largely depends on the open condemnation by its spokespersons of *any* racist attitude or action.

In our present moment, when a neo-Nazi like David Duke[10] can win 55 percent of the white vote (and 69 percent of the white "born-again" Protestant vote) in Louisiana, it may seem misguided to highlight anti-Semitic behavior of black people—the exemplary targets of racial hatred in America. Yet I suggest that this focus is crucial precisely because we black folk have been in the forefront of the struggle against American racism. If these efforts fall prey to anti-Semitism, then the principled attempt to combat racism forfeits much of its moral credibility—and we all lose. To put it bluntly, if the black freedom

---

[7]*Begin and Shamir:* Menachem Begin became prime minister of Israel in 1977 and was an advocate for Israeli expansion in the West Bank. His tough policies against self-government for the Palestinian Arabs of the West Bank were adopted by his successor, Yitzhak Shamir. A member of the conservative Likkud party and the right wing–religious coalition, Shamir became prime minister of Israel in 1983 and was assassinated in 1995. (*Ed.*)

[8]*Farrakhan and Jeffries:* Louis Farrakhan, leader of the Nation of Islam, and Leonard Jeffries, a professor of African American Studies at City College, CUNY, have both made public their anti-Semitic views. (*Ed.*)

[9]*Yankel Rosenbaum in Crown Heights:* See headnote for the following selection (Richard Goldstein, "The New Anti-Semitism: A *Geshrei,* p. 555). (*Ed.*)

[10]*David Duke:* politician and former member of the Ku Klux Klan, well known for his racism and anti-Semitism; almost elected governor of Louisiana in 1991 (*Ed.*)

struggle becomes simply a power-driven war of all against all that pits xenophobia from below against racism from above, then David Duke's project is the wave of the future—and a racial apocalypse awaits us. Despite Duke's resounding defeat, we witness increasing racial and sexual violence, coupled with growing economic deprivation, that together provide the raw ingredients for such a frightening future.

Black people have searched desperately for allies in the struggle against racism—and have found Jews to be disproportionately represented in the ranks of that struggle. The desperation that sometimes informs the antiracist struggle arises out of two conflicting historical forces: America's historically weak will to racial justice *and* an all-inclusive moral vision of freedom and justice for all. Escalating black anti-Semitism is a symptom of this desperation gone sour; it is the bitter fruit of a profound self-destructive impulse, nurtured on the vines of hopelessness and concealed by empty gestures of black unity. The images of black activists yelling "Where is Hitler when we need him?" and "Heil Hitler," juxtaposed with those of David Duke celebrating Hitler's birthday, seem to feed a single fire of intolerance, burning on both ends of the American candle, that threatens to consume us all.

Black anti-Semitism rests on three basic pillars. First, it is a species of anti-whitism. Jewish complicity in American racism—even though it is less extensive than the complicity of other white Americans—reinforces black perceptions that Jews are identical to any other group benefiting from white-skin privileges in racist America. This view denies the actual history and treatment of Jews. And the particular interactions of Jews and black people in the hierarchies of business and education cast Jews as the public face of oppression for the black community, and thus lend evidence to this mistaken view of Jews as any other white folk.

Second, black anti-Semitism is a result of higher expectations some black folk have of Jews. This perspective holds Jews to a moral standard different from that extended to other white ethnic groups, principally owing to the ugly history of anti-Semitism in the world, especially in Europe and the Middle East. Such double standards assume that Jews and blacks are "natural" allies, since both groups have suffered chronic degradation and oppression at the hands of racial and ethnic majorities. So when Jewish neoconservatism gains a high public profile at a time when black people are more and more vulnerable, the charge of "betrayal" surfaces among black folk who feel let down. Such utterances resonate strongly in a black Protestant culture that has inherited many stock Christian anti-Semitic narratives of Jews as Christ-killers. These infamous narratives historically have had less weight in the black community, in stark contrast to the more obdurate white Christian varieties of anti-Semitism. Yet in moments of desperation in the black community, they tend to reemerge, charged with the rhetoric of Jewish betrayal.

Third, black anti-Semitism is a form of underdog resentment and envy, directed at another underdog who has "made it" in American society. The remarkable upward mobility of American Jews—rooted chiefly in a history and culture that places a premium on higher education and self-organization—easily lends itself to myths of Jewish unity and homogeneity that have gained currency among other groups, especially among relatively unorganized groups like black Americans. The high visibility of Jews in the upper reaches of the academy, journalism, the entertainment industry, and the professions—though less so percentage-wise in corporate America and national political office—is viewed less as a result of hard work and success fairly won, and more as a matter of favoritism and nepotism among Jews. Ironically, calls for black solidarity and achievement are often modeled on myths of Jewish unity—as both groups respond to American xenophobia and racism. But in times such as these, some blacks view Jews as obstacles rather than allies in the struggle for racial justice.

These three elements of black anti-Semitism—which also characterize the outlooks of some other ethnic groups in America—have a long history among black people. Yet the recent upsurge of black anti-Semitism exploits two other prominent features of the political landscape identified with the American Jewish establishment: the military status of Israel in the Middle East (especially in its enforcement of the occupation of the West Bank and Gaza); and the visible *conservative* Jewish opposition to what is perceived to be a major means of black progress, namely, affirmative action. Of course, principled critiques of U.S. foreign policy in the Middle East, of Israeli denigration of Palestinians, or attacks on affirmative action *transcend* anti-Semitic sensibilities. Yet vulgar critiques do not—and often are shot through with such sensibilities, in white and black America alike. These vulgar critiques—usually based on sheer ignorance and a misinformed thirst for vengeance—add an aggressive edge to black anti-Semitism. And in the rhetoric of a Louis Farrakhan or a Leonard Jeffries, whose audiences rightly hunger for black self-respect and oppose black degradation, these critiques misdirect progressive black energies arrayed against unaccountable corporate power and antiblack racism, steering them instead *toward* Jewish elites and antiblack conspiracies in Jewish America. This displacement is disturbing not only because it is analytically and morally wrong; it also discourages any effective alliances across races.

The rhetoric of Farrakhan and Jeffries feeds on an undeniable history of black denigration at the hands of Americans of every ethnic and religious group. The delicate issues of black self-love and black self-contempt are then viewed in terms of white put-down and Jewish conspiracy. The precious quest for black self-esteem is reduced to immature and cathartic gestures that bespeak an excessive obsession with whites and Jews. There can be no healthy conception of black humanity based on such obsessions. The best of black culture, as manifested, for example, in jazz or the prophetic black church, refuses to put whites or Jews on a pedestal or in the gutter. Rather, black humanity is affirmed alongside that of others, even when those others have at times dehumanized blacks. To put it bluntly, when black humanity is taken for granted and not made to prove itself in white culture, whites, Jews, and others are not that important; they are simply human beings, just like black people. If the best of black culture wanes in the face of black anti-Semitism, black people will become even more isolated as a community and the black freedom struggle will be tarred with the brush of immorality.

For example, most Americans wrongly believe that the black community has been silent in the face of Yankel Rosenbaum's murder. This perception exists because the moral voices in black America have been either ignored or drowned out by the more sensationalist and xenophobic ones. The major New York City newspapers and periodicals seem to have little interest in making known to the public the moral condemnations voiced by Reverend Gary Simpson of Concord Baptist Church in Brooklyn (with ten thousand black members), Reverend James Forbes of Riverside Church (with three thousand members), Reverend Carolyn Knight of Philadelphia Baptist Church in Harlem, Reverend Susan Johnson of Mariners Baptist Church in Manhattan, Reverend Mark Taylor of the Church of the Open Door in Brooklyn, Reverend Victor Hall of Calvary Baptist Church in Queens, and many more. Black anti-Semitism is not caused by media hype—yet it does sell more newspapers and turn our attention away from those black prophetic energies that give us some hope.

My fundamental premise is that the black freedom struggle is the major buffer between the David Dukes of America and the hope for a future in which we can begin to take justice and freedom for all seriously. Black anti-Semitism—along with its concomitant xenophobias, such as patriarchal and homophobic prejudices—weakens this buffer. In the process, it plays into the hands of the old-style racists, who appeal to the worst of our fellow citizens amid the silent depression that plagues the majority of Americans. Without some redistribution of wealth and power, downward mobility and debilitating poverty will continue to drive people into desperate channels. And without principled opposition to xenophobias from above *and* below, these desperate channels will produce a cold-hearted and mean-spirited America no longer worth fighting for or living in. 20

DISCUSSING THE TEXT

1. What reasons does West offer for some African Americans' feelings of hostility toward Jews? Do you find any of these reasons legitimate? Why or why not?
2. West says that "Black anti-Semitism and Jewish antiblack racism are real" (par. 2). What examples does he offer of "Jewish antiblack racism"? Do you agree with his assessment of these examples?
3. Although West condemns the logic and spirit of Louis Farrakhan's or Leonard Jeffries's anti-Semitism, he empathizes with their audiences. How does he explain their audiences' susceptibility to these men's rhetoric?
4. In a group of four or five students, discuss West's assessment of the relations between African Americans and Jews in reference to two major issues: (1) affirmative action and (2) government spending on social programs. What are your own views on these issues? Take brief notes as you work on this assignment, and be prepared to share your opinions with the class.

WRITING ABOUT THE TEXT

5. In recent newspapers or magazines, look for an account of an incident that illustrates racial tension between African Americans and Jews. Then write a fictional dialogue between two people, one African American, the other Jewish American, about the incident.
6. Think of an instance in which you have expressed or observed someone else express antiblack or anti-Jewish sentiments. Write a brief essay in which you (a) describe the context and the incident, and (b) try to analyze what motivated the expression of those sentiments.
7. West writes that African Americans and Jews must work to "formulate strategies and tactics to sidestep the traps of tribalism and chauvinism" (par. 10). Based on the ideas presented in West's essay, write two paragraphs defining the terms *tribalism* and *chauvinism.*
8. West argues that both groups must think seriously "about what being black or Jewish means in *ethical terms*" (par. 10). Do you agree that the problems of racism and anti-Semitism are, fundamentally, *moral* issues? Why or why not? What do you think of West's contention that a racial or ethnic group's "*ethical* character" (par. 11) depends on the degree to which it condemns racism of any kind? Write a one- to two-page essay expressing your thoughts on these questions.

RICHARD GOLDSTEIN

The New Anti-Semitism: A *Geshrei*

This essay first appeared in the New York City periodical The Village Voice *in October 1991, two months after the violent race riots that took place in the Crown Heights neighborhood of Brooklyn, New York. Crown Heights had been a racially charged neighborhood for many years, populated as it is by American and Caribbean blacks, Latinos, and Jews belonging to the Orthodox Lubavitcher Hasidic sect.**

The Crown Heights riots began on August 19, 1991, when a West Indian child named Gavin Cato was accidentally killed by a car from the Lubavitcher Rebbe's motorcade. The violent riot that ensued culminated later that day with the murder of an innocent bystander, a young Hasidic student from Australia named Yankel Rosenbaum. During the three days of looting, torching, and vandalism that followed Gavin

*Although Hasidism has its roots in the third century B.C.E., the ultraconservative Lubavitch-Chabad movement was founded in Lithuania in 1773 and was established in Brooklyn, New York, in 1940. The Lubavitcher Hasidim believe in miracles, reject secular studies, and advocate separatism; Hasidic men are easily identified by their traditional black garments and hats and their unshaven beards. In 1950, Menachem Mendel Schneerson (1902–1994), popularly referred to as the Lubavitcher Rebbe, became the spiritual leader of the sect.

Cato's death, Mayor David Dinkins of New York City, who had denounced the rioters, deployed two thousand police officers in Crown Heights.

Richard Goldstein centers his discussion of anti-Semitism on the Crown Heights tragedy, focusing on the strains placed on the relationship between blacks and Jews because of both racism against blacks and anti-Semitism. Goldstein fears that it is only the extreme right, their common enemy, that profits from the deterioration of cooperative relations between blacks and Jews.

The essay's title includes the Yiddish word geshrei, *which means a warning, protest, or appeal. Even though Goldstein condemns anti-Semitism in strong terms and blames several prominent African American leaders for either inciting bigotry or remaining silent about it, he has conceived his essay as an appeal to reason and to feelings of tolerance and cooperation between African Americans and Jews. Goldstein uses the historical lessons of pogroms* *(see the footnote on p. 548)* *and the Holocaust, and even his own personal experiences, to warn his readers of the tragic results of racial prejudice and violence.*

Richard Goldstein (b. 1944) is executive editor of The Village Voice, *and has written extensively on cultural and sexual politics. He is also author of* Reporting the Counterculture *(1989).*

My grandmother hid in a bureau drawer for three days while colorful Christians rampaged through the shtetl.[1] But that stuff happened in the Old World—we lived in America, the greatest country in the world. I knew about the Holocaust, of course, but all my relatives had the luxury of dying from natural causes. We lived in New York, the greatest Jewish city in the world. We didn't need the promised land—we were Yankees, safe at last.

When I was eight, we took a vacation in Pennsylvania, my first trip out of New York. While we stopped for gas on a country road, I went to get a Coke. I noticed a group of men in overalls staring at me, whispering. A boy my age stepped forward and politely asked if I was Jewish. I realized the Star of David was dangling out of my tee-shirt, and grabbed it instinctively. When I nodded yes, he asked, in a strangely animated voice: "Can we please see your horns?" I shuddered and backed up toward the car. When I told my mother what had happened, she yanked me into the seat beside her and held me tight while my father paid. Then we sped away.

I stopped wearing the Star of David that summer. I had learned an important lesson about the terms of my liberation in America: The less I look Jewish, the safer I will be. Even as an adult, when I tell jokes in dialect I'm always aware of who I am addressing and what their response will be. And I always feel uncomfortable during the High Holy Days watching people in yarmulkes[2] rushing through the streets, knowing they'll be swaying and moaning something ancient and indecipherable, even to me.

---

[1]*shtetl:* (Yiddish) a small town or community of Jews in Eastern Europe (*Ed.*)

[2]*yarmulkes:* (Yiddish) a skullcap worn by observant Jewish men, especially when at prayer (*Ed.*)

I always wear jeans on Yom Kippur.[3] Not just because I'm a secular humanist, but because, on some level, I want to hide. My mother's terror in Pennsylvania stays with me, along with her unspoken message that history is not over for us. Even in America, we are vulnerable to superstitions and slanders so grotesque that there can be no defense against them. And these fairy tales for fanatics linger just below the surface of ordinary life. As they did in Crown Heights.

5 What happened there in August of 1991 was the worst outbreak of anti-Semitism in New York during my lifetime. Ideas that had been buried were suddenly exhumed, and I was forced to confront their enduring power. For four days, images that belonged in grainy, Nazi-era documentaries were all too live on TV: people shouting "Heil Hitler"; windows smashed in dozens of Jewish homes; and the ultimate, timeless desecration—a Jewish life lost to a raging mob. Yankel Rosenbaum was the child of concentration camp survivors, and he had come to Brooklyn from his native Australia to study the Holocaust. He didn't know, when he left his house to visit friends, that a West Indian child named Gavin Cato had been accidentally run over by a car carrying the Lubavitcher rebbe; or that rumors had spread through the black community that a Hasidic ambulance service had refused to help the dying boy; or that mobs were roaming the streets, screaming "Get the Jews." To these enraged people, many of them recent immigrants from the Caribbean, Yankel Rosenbaum had no personality except for what his Hasidic clothing signified. He had been reduced to the Eternal Jew, and as a gang of teenagers closed in on him, he was stabbed four times in the chest and back. "Cowards," he cried. "Cowards." My grandmother could have said the same, and if she survived what Yankel Rosenbaum didn't, it was only because she had lived in such constant dread that she knew when to hide, while he thought he was safe at last.

In the days that followed, a suspect in the death of Rosenbaum was arrested. Lemrick Nelson was promptly dubbed "Jew-Slay Teen" by the indefatigable *New York Post*. It seems his landlord—a fellow named Klein—had complained to his father about the noise this seventeen-year-old was making. "The Jew got me in trouble," he was heard to say. On the night of the riot, when Rosenbaum stumbled toward him, baffled and babbling, did this young man see his landlord's face? "I didn't like his accent," the youth told police when they arrested him, his clothes still wet with Rosenbaum's blood. It was not enough to convince a jury that this was the killer, and since no one else from the mob was arrested, whoever murdered Rosenbaum is still at large. That fact, along with the memory of police failing to stem the violence for four days, has resonated with the history of pogroms in politically explosive ways, making it tempting for many Jews to conclude that the black mayor of New York City was responsible for what befell the Hasidim of Crown Heights. But the more disturbing possibility is that what happened there in 1991 could

[3]*Yom Kippur:* (Hebrew) the Day of Atonement; Jewish holiday and day of fasting (*Ed.*)

happen again; next time, perhaps, between Latinos and Hasidim in nearby Williamsburg, or in several neighborhoods at once. The Crown Heights riot revealed a simmering anti-Semitism that no amount of police protection could keep at bay. Not in a sprawling, seething city like New York.

Consider what occurred several days after the Rosenbaum murder, and miles away, on a train roaring up the West Side of Manhattan. An Orthodox Jew was punched by a black man shouting, "That's for killing children." Perhaps this Jew looked just like the teacher who dissed him back in high school, or the Jews who called his mother "the *schwartzer*"[4] when she came to clean their house. Bad Jews, good Jews; all Jews are the same. And we all risk punishment for daring to assert our Jewishness.

As a child, I was intensely aware of the old men, stooped and scarred, wandering through the neighborhood with long beards and strange fringes spilling out of their pants. They frightened me—and I still recoil from Hasidim. To me they are no different from Christian fundamentalists—just as nasty, narrow-minded, and contemptuous. I remember a group of Hasidim picketing in Greenwich Village during the early days of the AIDS epidemic. "A gay synagogue is like a whorehouse on Yom Kippur," their handout read. That night, I had a nightmare in which a Hasid wearing a long black coat strode into the hospital room where I lay in a stark white bed. He reached across me and turned the resuscitator off.

These days, when Hasidim cruising the Village in their Mitzvah Mobile[5] ask me, "Are you Jewish?" I reply, "Not if you are." Yet I know my uneasiness in their presence is not just a matter of belief. Sitting across from a Hasid in the subway, I feel that old chill in my shoulders. It's not so different from a closet case eyeing a drag queen. These people are *flaming,* and they remind me of my vulnerability. To the anti-Semite all Jews have horns.

I know that there is racism in Hasidic hearts—and fists. And I'm sure that there have been deals struck with politicians and privileges traded for votes. But the riots that followed the death of Gavin Cato cannot be explained solely in terms of class privilege or racial injustice. During that unholy week, the entire mythology of anti-Semitism was unfurled. 10

Hovering over the rage at a child's accidental death were centuries of belief that Jews prey on Christian children. You can read in Chaucer,[6] that titan of the Western canon, about a schoolboy abducted and ritually murdered by Jews, though his body miraculously emits a hymn of praise. Jews call this the Blood Libel because it stems from the myth that matzoh[7] must be made

---

[4]*the schwartzer:* (Yiddish) black; pejorative, racist term for blacks (*Ed.*)

[5]*Mitzvah Mobile:* Mitzvah (Yiddish) means commandment or good deed. Goldstein refers to groups of Hasidim who travel to different parts of New York City in an effort to convert other Jews to their sect. (*Ed.*)

[6]*Geoffrey Chaucer* (1340?–1400): British author, well known for his *Canterbury Tales* (ca. 1387) (*Ed.*)

[7]*matzoh:* (Hebrew) flat, thin, unleavened bread eaten by Jews during the Passover holiday (*Ed.*)

with the blood of Christian infants. You can give guided tours of matzoh factories till kingdom come, but this idea persists in the subconscious. It allowed a mob to transform a reckless driver into the emblem of their oppression. As the false rumor spread that a Jewish-run ambulance had refused to treat the child, you could sense the ancient belief that Jews promote only their own interests, not with the solidarity every community exhibits toward its own, but from some deeper tribal drive.

In Crown Heights, there's a black Episcopalian priest named Rev. Heron A. Sam who preaches that Jews have appropriated the term Semite, which rightfully belongs to Africans and Arabs as well as "the Hebrew race." (Although the reverend thinks "the hooked nose popularly associated with Semitic types is actually Hittite.") From this racist obsession, it's easy to assert that "the Jew has managed by consanguinity [interbreeding with Europeans] to affect a skin complexion change that has put him outside the realm of blackness, and so he can appeal to his acquired white brothers and sisters. . . ." This tactic "can only lead such a race of people to become manipulators and anarchists."

Imagine the impact of such a sermon on a seventeen-year-old who is furious at his Jewish landlord. Imagine how easy it would be for that boy to conclude: "The Jew got me in trouble." And once the belief has been implanted that Jews are an ersatz people who abandoned their natural skin tone to gain racial advantage, imagine how logical it is to think of the Hasidim as part of an international conspiracy.

"Diamond merchants," Rev. Al Sharpton[8] called them at Gavin Cato's funeral. "Don't just talk about the jeweler [whose store was burned] on Utica. Talk about how Oppenheimer in South Africa sends diamonds straight to Tel Aviv and deals with the diamond merchants here in Crown Heights." There's a social reality here, but the mob in Crown Heights was invited by its leaders to jack it up with the iconography of anti-Semitism. They were encouraged to see the Hasidim, not as a tight-knit voting bloc with significant political clout, but as an incarnation of the Elders of Zion[9]—that invention of the czarist secret police. Black rage at white power was transformed into anti-Semitism by the myth of the omnipotent Jew.

How could this happen? How could people who have never lived in Europe believe in such quintessentially European legends? The answer doesn't lie 15

---

[8]*Rev. Al Sharpton:* African American separatist leader, active in New York City, who is known for his radical anti-Semitism and who ran in the Democratic primary for the senate in New York (*Ed.*)

[9]*Elders of Zion:* The *Protocols of the Elders of Zion* was a fabricated document published in czarist Russia in 1902 and popular in Europe during the 1920s. It falsely claimed a Jewish conspiracy to overthrow Christian society and take over the world. The *Protocols of the Elders of Zion* was used as anti-Semitic propaganda in Nazi Germany and has been reissued recently in Egypt and some Arab countries. In the United States, it can be found in some Nation of Islam bookstores. (*Ed.*)

in lie in the souls of black folks—they are no more anti-Semitic than whites. It lies in the nature of the prejudice. Fear and loathing of Jews is a pervasive force in Western consciousness, ready to be unleashed whenever the time is right. These periodic outbursts are a safety valve for those unable to overcome their oppression, or even comprehend its source. That was the scenario for the pogroms my grandmother dreaded, the Holocaust my parents escaped, and the violence in Crown Heights. The conditions of life for African Americans—the growing indifference to worsening poverty, the declining quality of life in the inner cities, and the genteel racism of the governing elite—are a classic matrix for anti-Semitism. Jews have always been a handy target in tough times.

But it's been clear for some time that, among some segments of the black intelligentsia, anti-Semitism is more openly expressed than anywhere else in American life, apart from the far right. Within this milieu, the most primitive ideas have been given an overlay of reason and righteousness that harks back to the dregs of Western civ. Talk about the return of the repressed: When Leonard Jeffries asserts that Jewish faculty at the City College of New York are organized into a secret cabal that actually calls itself the Kaballah, he is piecing together a cosmology the czar's henchmen, not to mention Goebbels,[10] would be proud to call their own. Talk about Eurocentrism!

Racist scholarship might seem arcane, if not loony, to most black folks if it weren't tethered to the power and glory of hip-hop. And this exhuming of ancient stereotypes in music and movies had done much more than the raving of Louis Farrakhan to make anti-Semitism respectable again. When Public Enemy rap about the "so-called chosen" who "got me like Jesus"; when Professor Griff[11] says "Jews are responsible for the majority of wickedness that goes on across the globe"; when Spike Lee[12] creates Joe and Josh Flatbush, cardboard club owners who reduce every human emotion to profiteering—they make the most archaic myths about Jews seem modern and heroic again.

Why do these artists get away with Jew baiting? The answer lies partly in the racially mixed market for their work. Black culture often performs a surrogate role in American society, defining rebellion and delineating the forbidden for a funk-hungry nation. Just as rappers play the sex-outlaw many white youths wish they could be, slamming women and gays with all the bile that must be swallowed in bourgeois society, black anti-Semites act out the bigotry other Americans aren't quite willing to express. And their emergence signals something about American culture as a whole.

---

[10]*Joseph Goebbels* (1897–1945): Nazi Germany's minister of propaganda under Adolf Hitler (*Ed.*)

[11]*Public Enemy . . . Professor Griff:* African American rap group, including Griff, known for their aggressive political lyrics (*Ed.*)

[12]*Spike Lee:* contemporary African American film director; Joe and Josh Flatbush were two Jewish characters in Lee's 1990 film *Mo' Better Blues* (*Ed.*)

For the first time since the Great Depression, Jewish stereotypes are being used to provide a gritty frisson to works of art. *The Death of Klinghoffer*[13] has a libretto that equates Jews with bourgeois banality and Palestinians with proletarian dignity. *Barton Fink*[14] has movie moguls who behave like figments of T. S. Eliot's[15] imagination. ("The rats are underneath the pile/The Jew is underneath the lot.") The fact that Jews played a role in creating these works is itself a sign of profound anxiety. One way for Jews to deal with the horror of anti-Semitism is to deflect it onto an evil Jewish other. But this strategy only fuels the fire.

20 Not long after the Crown Heights riot, the Family network announced it was pulling a series of Bible videos to change the features of certain Jewish characters. The Anti-Defamation League had objected to the fact that the moneychangers were hook-nosed and epicene. Network officials were embarrassed; and they stressed that making the Jews look like normal people would cost a pretty penny (everything is money with these evangelicals). But the question remains how anyone in modern America could render Bible characters that so closely resemble the cartoons that once graced *Der Stürmer*.[16] The only answer is that the image of the conniving Jews is so entrenched that it doesn't seem remarkable, except to Jews.

By locating anti-Semitism exclusively in the black community, the *Post–Commentary* alignment[17] hopes to convince Jews that their interests lie in an alliance with other white ethnics, under the neocon umbrella. But this ambition blinds the Jewish right to the extent of anti-Semitism in American life. It may seem to many Jews that the tangible signs of their oppression—such as quotas and restrictive covenants—have been swept away. But it takes a Pat Buchanan[18] (not to mention David Duke) to remind us that anti-Semitism is still a potentially potent force in American politics, especially when combined with racism. The omnipotent Jew and the rapacious black male are twin

---

[13]*The Death of Klinghoffer* (1991): American opera by composer John Adams, with libretto by Alice Goodman, based on the hijacking by four Palestinian terrorists of the Italian cruise ship *Achille Lauro* in Alexandria in 1985. Klinghoffer was a Jewish American passenger who was thrown overboard to his death by the terrorists. (*Ed.*)

[14]*Barton Fink* (1991): American film about Hollywood directed by Joel and Ethan Coen. Goldstein alludes to the film's portrayal of Jewish American producers as greedy and corrupt. (*Ed.*)

[15]*T. S. Eliot* (1888–1927): American / British poet and critic, extremely influential in modernist poetics, and well known for anti-Semitic references in several of his poems. The quotation is from Eliot's 1920 poem "Burbank with a Baedeker: Bleistein with a Cigar." (*Ed.*)

[16]*Der Stürmer:* an anti-Semitic journal founded by Julius Streicher in Germany during the Nazi period (*Ed.*)

[17]*Post-Commentary alignment:* Goldstein alludes to the daily newspaper the *New York Post,* and to the Jewish journal *Commentary*. (*Ed.*)

[18]*Pat Buchanan:* contemporary American politician and writer well known for his ultraconservative views; Goldstein alludes to Buchanan's racist and anti-Semitic attitudes (*Ed.*)

specters in the Western psyche, always available to be played as an instrument of public policy. As they were when George Bush invoked the image of Willie Horton[19] to win the White House in 1988; as they were when Bush portrayed himself in 1991 as "one lone little guy" held hostage by powerful Israel lobbyists.

Demagogues high and low still feed on the mythology that clings to Jews and blacks alike. Yet both groups have forgotten their precariousness in the rush to judge each other guilty of oppression. Crown Heights has given the bigots a golden opportunity. Now blacks may be held up to Jews as the real anti-Semites, even as Jews are held up to blacks as the real racists. This spectacle shatters an alliance that has been the fulcrum of progressivism for generations. It empowers neither blacks nor Jews, but their common enemies.

What's a liberal to do in the face of such a crisis? Pretend it's something else. For the most part, the media have taken note of Jew-baiting asides in rap music, crypto-Nazi imagery in a colorful jazz musical, as if it were a sour belch to be quickly swallowed. Some critics spoke up loud and clear, but the mainstream was reluctant to risk it. As a result, the anti-Semitism of Public Enemy and Spike Lee was less than resolutely condemned, sending a signal to the audience that it's permissible to act on such ideas. Those who overlooked the obvious, for whatever reasons, helped lay the groundwork for Crown Heights.

By now, there's a consensus that the riot was an act of anti-Semitism. But this judgment wasn't generated by the left. At first, many white progressives focused on the advantages the Hasidim enjoy, as if that entitled the crowd to shout, "Kill the Jews." Only gradually did the left confront the truth. It's painful, indeed, to face the fact that victims of bigotry can be guilty of bigotry—it threatens your image of the oppressed. How much easier to buy the claim that blacks cannot be anti-Semitic, or even to convince yourself that what happened in Crown Heights is part of some larger geopolitical struggle—a hip-hop *intifada*.[20]

I'm convinced that some white leftists were silent because, consciously or not, they share the assumptions of the rioters. It's hip, in certain progressive circles, to speak of Jews as if they've lost their legitimacy. You could glimpse this reflex in the antiwar protesters who cheered when the Scud missiles fell on Israel; and you could see it in the lubricious alliance between the New Alliance Party[21] and Farrakhan. There's nothing contradictory about this pact. 25

---

[19]*Willie Horton:* A convicted criminal, serving a prison term in Massachusetts during the 1980s. Horton committed another crime when on leave from jail under a plan established by the governor of Massachusetts, Michael Dukakis. In widely shown commercials, the Bush election campaign used this incident against Dukakis, the Democratic presidential candidate in 1988. (*Ed.*)

[20]*intifada:* (Arabic) uprising; Goldstein likens the situation in Crown Heights to the many skirmishes in the occupied territories of the West Bank in Israel. (*Ed.*)

[21]*New Alliance Party:* left-wing party based in New York City. African American politician Lenora Fulani was the party's candidate in the 1992 presidential election. (*Ed.*)

Anti-Semitism of the left has firm roots in populism as well as Marxist ideology. (The term itself was coined in the nineteenth century by a liberal mayor of Vienna, who used anti-Semitism, as Ed Koch[22] would later use racism, to secure a populist base.)

David Dinkins called the murder of Yankel Rosenbaum what it was: a lynching. But other black leaders were as prone to euphemism as white progressives. Many reiterated the underlying conditions in Crown Heights and demanded a redress of grievances as the price for peace. None spoke of the deadly myths about Jews that had animated this violence, just as few black leaders condemned the anti-Semitism of Leonard Jeffries. (Rev. Calvin Butts, the city's most influential black minister, said he wanted to hear more from Jeffries before addressing the question; and he never did.) Solidarity makes truth-telling difficult, and the reality of oppression makes it hard for any black leader to condemn an eruption of black rage. But the conflation of Jew-baiting with black empowerment is now so evolved that it seems like Tomming, if not treason, to call anti-Semitism what it is. The sight of a phalanx of black men marching through a white neighborhood has achieved the sanctity of a ritual, and hardly anyone on the left questions the context, or the content, of what is being shouted at whom. The likelihood of black—or white—progressives speaking out against icons of resistance is slim indeed.

The silence of humanists had a sickeningly familiar quality to Jews who remember the world's response to the Nazis; the reluctance to act on, or even acknowledge, the possibility of genocide until it was too late. This sense of abandonment remains an indelible part of Jewish consciousness. It fosters the circled-wagons mentality the world so often reads as Jewish paranoia. It animates the comedy of Jewish assimilation, and the Noh drama of Jewish self-hate—both are strategies to hide the dirty secret that can lead to disgrace and even death. And it creates the illusion that the only safety for a Jew is within the tribe. The last tendency—call it psychic Zionism—is the leading beneficiary of what occurred in Crown Heights. In terms of Jewish history, this was another victory for the spirit of Jabotinsky over Einstein—another triumph of nationalism over humanism.

During the height of the violence, the *New York Post* ran a front-page photo of a twelve-year-old boy sobbing by the fallen frame of his injured father. It raised goose bumps when I saw it, resonating with the image of children in the Warsaw Ghetto, surrendering to armed Nazis against a background of flames. The *Post* was milking my memory of Jewish helplessness, just as Sharpton had milked his constituency by envisioning Gavin Cato sharing "heaven's playroom" with the three girls killed in the 1962 firebombing of a black church in Birmingham. While readers of *The City Sun* were invited to regard Aaron Lopez, an eighteenth-century slave trader, as an emblem of the

---

[22]*Ed Koch:* contemporary Jewish American politician, known for his flamboyant and outspoken style. Koch was mayor of New York from 1978 to 1990. (*Ed.*)

Jews, I was invited to regard Sonny Carson[23] and his storm troopers as the vanguard of the black community. "Who speaks for New York's blacks if not the . . . riot inciters?" asked *Post* columnist Eric Breindel. He compared the events in Crown Heights to Kristallnacht, when thousands of Jewish businesses were destroyed and thousands lost their lives—with the cooperation of the German state. "The pretext in Crown Heights," Breindel blithely asserted, "was far thinner [than in Nazi Germany.]"

Long before Kristallnacht, the German Socialist leader August Bebel warned his compatriots against the illusion that bigotry is a source of power. "Anti-Semitism is the socialism of fools," Bebel proclaimed. His words have yet to be heeded, as we saw in Crown Heights. The polarization process that followed in the wake of the rioting is now a fact of urban life. The failure of moderate black ministers such as Calvin Butts and Herbert Daughtry to articulate an alternative to demagoguery gave the media an excuse to ignore the African-American clergy who did speak out and also left the door wide open for Sharpton, who rushed right in. Meanwhile, the inability of white progressives to confront anti-Semitism gave right-wingers an excuse to come out swinging. As the *Post* asked disingenuously, "Who else speaks for the black community?" It's a cry that will surely be echoed in *Commentary* and all the house organs of retrenchment. The new excuse for polite white racism will be Crown Heights.

The realpolitik of black anti-Semitism is that it is all too effective at reviving the most painful memories of persecution. These fears push many Jews into an alliance with other white ethnics, almost always to the benefit of the right. Observing this shift, many blacks conclude that Jewish progressivism is a myth, and not a potential to be nurtured. The net effect is a polarization of urban politics along racial and religious grounds, limiting the prospects for multiracial coalitions that have been crucial to the election of African-American mayors. In New York City, where political power flows from ethnic alliances, Crown Heights has given those who hope to split the white liberal vote from the black community a potent weapon. It has made it easier for conservatives to conflate affirmative action, multicultural education, and even the aspiration of black politicians with savagery. So striking is the damage done to black empowerment by those four days of riot and rampage that it's fair to say the men who spurred on the mob were either government agents or fools. 30

The only way to take back righteousness from the right is for progressives to call this riot what it was: a wannabe pogrom. The OED defines that word as "an organized massacre . . . chiefly applied to those directly against Jews." No one planned this riot, nor did the City of New York tolerate it. You can argue

---

[23]*Sonny Carson:* contemporary African American community activist, who along with other black leaders denounced as racist the circumstances surrounding the death of Michael Griffith in Howard Beach, New York in 1986 (*Ed.*)

that the police response was too little too late, but their restraint was standard procedure during a racial disturbance, and nothing directed at Jews. In the end, the system worked to contain the violence, something my grandmother, who lived through a real pogrom, would have found miraculous. But what if the mob had been left to its own devices? Were these people so different from the Jew-haters of other eras? Were the demagogues that spurred them on?

The real lesson of Crown Heights is that Jews must learn to live in a more dangerous world, where hate goes unanswered and primitive passions are stoked as a safety valve for helpless rage. Jewish children in years to come may live much like my parents, with a subtle but consuming sense of dread. America could yet turn out to be not so different from the Old World my grandparents fled. But there's another possibility: that by confronting anti-Semitism and racism, people of goodwill can transcend both—or at least keep them dormant. In Crown Heights, the situation remains volatile, and every week, it seems, brings a mugging, a beating, or a quarrel with potentially explosive overtones. In public, the hate persists. In private, I'm convinced, many blacks and Jews are horrified by what's occurred. That may explain why, in the 1992 City Council primary, the worst hatemongers—C. Vernon Mason, Colin Moore, and Yehuda Levin—all went down to defeat. It may be too much to hope for some grand gesture of reconciliation; in the current climate, you take your hope where you can find it—in small courtesies that signal what still can't be proclaimed.

In Brooklyn, two months after the riot, I forgot where my car was parked. Walking down a dark narrow street, I saw a group of black teenagers hanging out. I felt my body tighten against the desire to draw back. I've spent much of my life struggling against that reflex, so I approached the kids and asked directions. They answered politely and we fell into an oddly formal banter—broad smiles and cordial good-nights. I realized we were acting out an elaborate etiquette of communication in tough times. I wouldn't call it trust, but at least I didn't yell for the police, and they didn't ask to see my horns.

DISCUSSING THE TEXT

1. At the beginning of the essay, Goldstein tells us that the one lesson he learned about his encounter with bigots at the age of eight was, "The less I look Jewish, the safer I will be" (par. 3). Do you think his fear is justified? Have you ever tried to hide or play down your own ethnicity?
2. Goldstein uses the anti-Semitic image of the horned Jew both at the beginning and at the end of his essay. Why do you think he does this? How does his ending the essay with this image affect your reading of it? Do you think this device is effective rhetorically? Why or why not?
3. While discussing recent negative images of Jews in the work of African American artists such as Spike Lee and Public Enemy, Goldstein argues that "Black culture often performs a surrogate role in American society, defining rebellion and delineating the forbidden for a funk-hungry nation. Just as rappers play the sex-outlaw many white youths wish they could be,...

black anti-Semites act out the bigotry other Americans aren't quite willing to express" (par. 18). Discuss this idea in a group of four or five students. Do you agree or disagree with Goldstein's argument? Take brief notes as you work on this assignment, and be prepared to share your opinions with the rest of the class.

WRITING ABOUT THE TEXT

4. Find a newspaper or magazine article (from August 1991) about the Crown Heights riots, and write a personal response to the event. In discussing your own reactions, refer to Goldstein's essay as well, stating whether or not you agree with his views and explaining why.
5. What do you think of Goldstein's statement that "It's painful, indeed, to face the fact that victims of bigotry can be guilty of bigotry—it threatens your image of the oppressed" (par. 24). Can you think of a time when you had a similar realization—perhaps about the attitudes of someone who shares your own ethnic, class, or gender identity? Write a one- to two-page essay on this idea of "victims" who are "guilty of bigotry" themselves. Try to draw on your own experiences, and the lessons you have learned from those experiences.
6. Choose a selection from another chapter in this book that discusses ethnic and racial prejudice (such as Piri Thomas, "Alien Turf," and Kesaya E. Noda, "Growing Up Asian in America"). Write a brief essay comparing and contrasting this selection with Goldstein's "The New Anti-Semitism: A *Geshrei*."
7. Drawing on Goldstein's analysis of the relationship between African Americans and Jews, particularly in the closing pages of his essay (pp. 564–565), write an essay comparing and contrasting Goldstein's arguments with those of Cornel West in "On Black-Jewish Relations."

LINDA CHAVEZ

Toward a New Politics of Hispanic Assimilation

Linda Chavez's controversial book, Out of the Barrio *(1991), argues that "attempts to keep Hispanics outside the mainstream of this society—speaking their own language, living in protected enclaves, entitled to privileges based on disadvantage—"could interfere with their progress and achievement. Chavez suggests that Hispanics born in the United States have made educational and economic advancements comparable to those made by the descendants of other ethnic groups, but that their achievements have been diminished and obscured by the ongoing arrival of large numbers of both legal and illegal immigrants from Latin America. In her view, Hispanic leaders foster division among different groups, exhorting Latinos to remain outside mainstream culture, separate and distinct, in a place that is ultimately harmful to them. Many Latino leaders and intellectuals see Chavez as a mouthpiece of mainstream conservative politics, and claim that her views on cultural assimilation ignore many of the problems that Hispanics face in their daily lives.*

Linda Chavez, born in 1947 into a Mexican American family, is an educator and author and has been actively involved in American politics for many years. She has worked on several committees on civil and legal rights, was the White House director of public liaison under President Ronald Reagan, and is president of the Center for Equal Opportunity in Washington, D.C. This selection is the last chapter of Out of the Barrio. *It summarizes her views on assimilation in the realms of language and culture, political participation, education, and entitlements.*

Assimilation has become a dirty word in American politics. It invokes images of people, cultures, and traditions forged into a colorless alloy in an indifferent melting pot. But, in fact, assimilation, as it has taken place in the United States, is a far more gentle process, by which people from outside the community gradually became part of the community itself. Descendants of the German, Irish, Italian, Polish, Greek, and other immigrants who came to the United States bear little resemblance to the descendants of the countrymen their forebears left behind. America changed its immigrant groups—and was changed by them. Some groups were accepted more reluctantly than others—the Chinese, for example—and some with great struggle. Blacks, whose ancestors were forced to come here, have only lately won their legal right to full participation in this society; and even then civil rights gains have not been sufficiently translated into economic gains. Until quite recently, however, there was no question but that each group desired admittance to the mainstream. No more. Now ethnic leaders demand that their groups remain separate, that their native culture and language be preserved intact, and that whatever accommodation takes place be on the part of the receiving society.

Hispanic leaders have been among the most demanding, insisting that Hispanic children be taught in Spanish; that Hispanic adults be allowed to cast ballots in their native language and that they have the right to vote in districts in which Hispanics make up the majority of voters; that their ethnicity entitle them to a certain percentage of jobs and college admissions; that immigrants from Latin America be granted many of these same benefits, even if they are in the country illegally. But while Hispanic leaders have been pressing these claims, the rank and file have been moving quietly and steadily into the American mainstream. Like the children and grandchildren of millions of ethnic immigrants before them, virtually all native-born Hispanics speak English—many speak only English. The great majority finish high school, and growing numbers attend college. Their earnings and occupational status have been rising along with their education. But evidence of the success of native-born Hispanics is drowned in the flood of new Latin immigrants—more than five million—who have come in the last two decades, hoping to climb the ladder as well. For all of these people, assimilation represents the opportunity to succeed in America. Whatever the sacrifices it entails—and there are some—most believe that the payoff is worth it. Yet the elites who create and influence public policy seem convinced that the process must be stopped or, where this has already occurred, reversed.

From 1820 to 1924 the United States successfully incorporated a population more ethnically diverse and varied than any other in the world. We could not have done so if today's politics of ethnicity had been the prevailing ethos. Once again, we are experiencing record immigration, principally from Latin America and Asia. The millions of Latin immigrants who are joining the already large native-born Hispanic population will severely strain our capacity to absorb them, unless we can revive a consensus for assimilation. But the new politics of Hispanic assimilation need not include the worst features of the Americanization era. Children should not be forced to sink or swim in classes in which they don't understand the language of instruction. The model of Anglo conformity would seem ridiculous today in a country in which 150 million persons are descended from people who did not come here from the British Isles. We should not be tempted to shut our doors because we fear the newcomers are too different from us ever to become truly "American." Nonetheless, Hispanics will be obliged to make some adjustments if they are to accomplish what other ethnic groups have.

Language and Culture

Most Hispanics accept the fact that the United States is an English-speaking country; they even embrace the idea. A *Houston Chronicle* poll in 1990 found that 87 percent of all Hispanics believed that it was their "duty to learn English" and that a majority believed English should be adopted as an official language.[1] Similar results have been obtained in polls taken in California, Colorado, and elsewhere. But Hispanics, especially more recent arrivals, also feel it is important to preserve their own language. Nearly half the Hispanics in the *Houston Chronicle* poll thought that people coming from other countries should preserve their language and teach it to their children. There is nothing inconsistent in these findings, nor are the sentiments expressed unique to Hispanics. Every immigrant group has struggled to retain its language, customs, traditions. Some groups have been more successful than others. A majority of Greek Americans, for example, still speak Greek in their homes at least occasionally.[2] The debate is not about whether Hispanics, or any other group, have the right to retain their native language but about whose responsibility it is to ensure that they do so.

---

[1]Jo Ann Zuniga, "87% in Poll See Duty to Learn English," *Houston Chronicle,* July 12, 1990.

[2]Commission on Civil Rights, *The Economic Status of Americans of Southern and Eastern European Ancestry* (Washington, D.C.: GPO, 1986), 45.

The government should not be obliged to preserve any group's distinctive language or culture. Public schools should make sure that all children can speak, read, and write English well. When teaching children from non-English-speaking backgrounds, they should use methods that will achieve English proficiency quickly and should not allow political pressure to interfere with meeting the academic needs of students. No children in an American school are helped by being held back in their native language when they could be learning the language that will enable them to get a decent job or pursue higher education. More than twenty years of experience with native-language instruction fails to show that children in these programs learn English more quickly or perform better academically than children in programs that emphasize English acquisition. 5

If Hispanic parents want their children to be able to speak Spanish and know about their distinctive culture, they must take the responsibility to teach their children these things. Government simply cannot—and should not—be charged with this responsibility. Government bureaucracies given the authority to create bicultural teaching materials homogenize the myths, customs, and history of the Hispanic peoples of this hemisphere, who, after all, are not a single group but many groups. It is only in the United States that "Hispanics" exist; a Cakchiquel Indian in Guatemala would find it remarkable that anyone could consider his culture to be the same as a Spanish Argentinean's. The best way for Hispanics to learn about their native culture is in their own communities. Chinese, Jewish, Greek, and other ethnic communities have long established after-school and weekend programs to teach language and culture to children from these groups. Nothing stops Hispanic organizations from doing the same things. And, indeed, many Hispanic community groups around the country promote cultural programs. In Washington, D.C., groups from El Salvador, Guatemala, Colombia, and elsewhere sponsor soccer teams, fiestas, parades throughout the year, and a two-day celebration in a Latin neighborhood that draws crowds in the hundreds of thousands.[3] The Washington Spanish Festival is a lively, vibrant affair that makes the federal government's effort to enforce Hispanic Heritage Month in all of its agencies and

[3]In May 1991, a riot broke out in a Latino neighborhood in Washington, D.C., where many new immigrants live (many of them illegal aliens). Both the local and national media described the two nights of arson and looting in political terms, as an expression of the alienation of the Hispanic community. In fact, fewer than half of the people arrested during the incident were Hispanic; most were young black males from a nearby neighborhood. There were few injuries and no deaths, and much criticism was directed at the police by local residents for standing by while young men looted stores, many of which were owned by Latinos. The Washington, D.C., metropolitan area is home to nearly a quarter of a million Hispanics, more than 80 percent of whom live in the suburbs of the city, far from the neighborhood where this incident occurred. Nonetheless, national Hispanic leaders, including members of the Hispanic Congressional delegation, flocked to the scene of the violence to portray as typical of the area's Latino population the problems which occurred in the few blocks of this urban settlement of recent immigrants.

departments each September seem pathetic by comparison. The sight and sound of mariachis strolling through the cavernous halls of the Department of Labor as indifferent federal workers try to work above the din is not only ridiculous; it will not do anything to preserve Mexican culture in the United States.

Hispanics should be interested not just in maintaining their own, distinctive culture but in helping Latin immigrants adjust to their American environment and culture as well. Too few Hispanic organizations promote English or civics classes, although the number has increased dramatically since the federal government began dispensing funds for such programs under the provisions of the Immigration Reform and Control Act, which gives amnesty to illegal aliens on the condition that they take English and civics classes.[4] But why shouldn't the Hispanic community itself take some responsibility to help new immigrants learn the language and history of their new country, even without government assistance? The settlement houses of the early century thrived without government funds. The project by the National Association of Latino Elected and Appointed Officials (NALEO) to encourage Latin immigrants to become U.S. citizens is the exception among Hispanic organizations; it should become the rule.

Political Participation

The real barriers to Hispanic political power are apathy and alienage. Too few native-born Hispanics register and vote; too few Hispanic immigrants become citizens. The way to increase real political power is not to gerrymander districts to create safe seats for Hispanic elected officials or treat illegal aliens and other immigrants as if their status were unimportant to their political representation; yet those are precisely the tactics Hispanic organizations have urged lately. Ethnic politics is an old and honored tradition in the United States. No one should be surprised that Hispanics are playing the game now, but the rules have been changed significantly since the early century. One analyst has noted, "In the past, ethnic leaders were obliged to translate raw numbers into organizational muscle in the factories or at the polls. . . . In the affirmative-action state, Hispanic leaders do not require voters, or even protesters—only bodies."[5] This is not healthy, for Hispanics or the country.

Politics has traditionally been a great equalizer. One person's vote was as good as another's, regardless of whether the one was rich and the other poor. But politics requires that people participate. The great civil rights struggles of the 1960s were fought in large part to guarantee the right to vote. Hispanic leaders demand representation but do not insist that individual His-

---

[4]For fiscal year 1989 the federal government distributed nearly $200 million in grants to state and local governments to assist in providing English and civics classes for adults and other services for those eligible for amnesty.

[5]Peter Skerry, "Keeping Immigrants in the Political Sweatshops," *Wall Street Journal*, Nov. 6, 1989.

panics participate in the process. The emphasis is always on rights, never on obligations. Hispanic voter organizations devote most of their efforts toward making the process easier—election law reform, postcard registration, election materials in Spanish—to little avail; voter turnout is still lower among Hispanics than among blacks or whites. Spanish posters urge Hispanics to vote because it will mean more and better jobs and social programs, but I've never seen one that mentions good citizenship. Hispanics (and others) need to be reminded that if they want the freedom and opportunity democracy offers, the least they can do is take the time to register and vote. These are the lessons with which earlier immigrants were imbued, and they bear reviving.

10 Ethnic politics was for many groups a stepping-stone into the mainstream. Irish, Italian, and Jewish politicians established political machines that drew their support from ethnic neighborhoods; and the machines, in turn, provided jobs and other forms of political patronage to those who helped elect them. But eventually, candidates from these ethnic groups went beyond ethnic politics. Governor Mario Cuomo (D) and Senator Alfonse D'Amato (R) are both Italian American politicians from New York, but they represent quite different political constituencies, neither of which is primarily ethnically based. Candidates for statewide office—at least successful ones—cannot afford to be seen merely as ethnic representatives. Ethnic politics may be useful at the local level, but if Hispanic candidates wish to gain major political offices, they will have to appeal beyond their ethnic base. Those Hispanics who have already been elected as governors and U.S. senators (eight, so far) have managed to do so.

EDUCATION

Education has been chiefly responsible for the remarkable advancements most immigrant groups have made in this society. European immigrants from the early century came at a time when the education levels of the entire population were rising rapidly, and they benefited even more than the population of native stock, because they started from a much lower base. More than one-quarter of the immigrants who came during the years from 1899 to 1910 could neither read nor write.[6] Yet the grandchildren of those immigrants today are indistinguishable from other Americans in educational attainment; about one-quarter have obtained college degrees. Second- and third-generation Hispanics, especially those who entered high school after 1960, have begun to close the education gap as well. But the proportion of those who go on to college is smaller among native-born Hispanics than among other Americans, and this percentage has remained relatively constant across generations, at about 10–13 percent for Mexican Americans. If Hispanics hope to repeat the

---

[6]Richard A. Easterlin, "Immigration: Economic and Social Characteristics," in Stephan Thernstrom, ed., *Harvard Encyclopedia of American Ethnic Groups* (Cambridge: Harvard University Press, 1981), 478.

successful experience of generations of previous immigrant groups, they must continue to increase their educational attainment, and they are not doing so fast enough. Italians, Jews, Greeks, and others took dramatic strides in this realm, with the biggest gains in college enrollment made after World War II.[7] Despite more than two decades of affirmative action programs and federal student aid, college graduation rates among native-born Hispanics, not to mention immigrants, remain significantly below those among non-Hispanics.

The government can do only so much in promoting higher education for Hispanics or any group. It is substantially easier today for a Hispanic student to go to college than it was even twenty or thirty years ago, yet the proportion of Mexican Americans who are graduating from college today is unchanged from what it was forty years ago. When the former secretary of education Lauro Cavazos, the first Hispanic ever to serve in the Cabinet, criticized Hispanic parents for the low educational attainment of their children, he was roundly attacked for blaming the victim. But Cavazos's point was that Hispanic parents must encourage their children's educational aspirations and that, too often, they don't. Those groups that have made the most spectacular socioeconomic gains—Jews and Chinese, for example—have done so because their families placed great emphasis on education.

Hispanics cannot have it both ways. If they want to earn as much as non-Hispanic whites, they have to invest the same number of years in schooling as these do. The earnings gap will not close until the education gap does. Native-born Hispanics are already enjoying earnings comparable to those of non-Hispanic whites, once educational differences are factored in. If they want to earn more, they must become better educated. But education requires sacrifices, especially for persons from lower-income families. Poverty, which was both more pervasive and severe earlier in this century, did not prevent Jews or Chinese from helping their children get a better education. These families were willing to forgo immediate pleasures, even necessities, in order to send their children to school. Hispanics must be willing to do the same—or else be satisfied with lower socioeconomic status. The status of second- and third-generation Hispanics will probably continue to rise even without big gains in college graduation; but the rise will be slow. Only a substantial commitment to the education of their children on the part of this generation of Hispanic parents will increase the speed with which Hispanics improve their social and economic status.

Entitlements

The idea of personal sacrifice is an anomaly in this age of entitlements. The rhetoric is all about rights. And the rights being demanded go far beyond

---

[7]See Richard Alba, *Ethnic Identity: The Transformation of White America* (New Haven: Yale University Press, 1990), 7. Both men and women born after 1930 showed large gains, although the gains were higher for men, probably reflecting the increase in college attendance by veterans under the G.I. Bill.

the right to equality under the law. Hispanics have been trained in the politics of affirmative action, believing that jobs, advancement, and even political power should be apportioned on the basis of ethnicity. But the rationale for treating all Hispanics like a permanently disadvantaged group is fast disappearing. What's more, there is no ground for giving preference in jobs or promotions to persons who have endured no history of discrimination in this country—namely, recent immigrants. Even within Hispanic groups, there are great differences between the historical discrimination faced by Mexican Americans and Puerto Ricans and that faced by, say, Cubans. Most Hispanic leaders, though, are willing to have everyone included in order to increase the population eligible for the programs and, therefore, the proportion of jobs and academic placements that can be claimed. But these alliances are beginning to fray at the edges. Recently, a group of Mexican American firemen in San Francisco challenged the right of two Spanish Americans to participate in a department affirmative action program, claiming that the latter's European roots made them unlikely to have suffered discrimination comparable to that of other Hispanics. The group recommended establishing a panel of twelve Hispanics to certify who is and who is not Hispanic.[8] But that is hardly the answer.

15 Affirmative action politics treats race and ethnicity as if they were synonymous with disadvantage. The son of a Mexican American doctor or lawyer is treated as if he suffered the same disadvantage as the child of a Mexican farm worker; and both are given preference over poor, non-Hispanic whites in admission to most colleges or affirmative action employment programs. Most people think this is unfair, especially white ethnics whose own parents and grandparents also faced discrimination in this society but never became eligible for the entitlements of the civil rights era. It is inherently patronizing to assume that all Hispanics are deprived and grossly unjust to give those who aren't preference on the basis of disadvantages they don't experience. Whether stated or not, the essence of affirmative action is the belief that Hispanics—or any of the other eligible groups—are not capable of measuring up to the standards applied to whites. This is a pernicious idea.

Ultimately, entitlements based on their status as "victims" rob Hispanics of real power. The history of American ethnic groups is one of overcoming disadvantage, of competing with those who were already here and proving themselves as competent as any who came before. Their fight was always to be treated the same as other Americans, never to be treated as special, certainly not to turn the temporary disadvantages they suffered into the basis for permanent entitlement. Anyone who thinks this fight was easier in the early part of this century when it was waged by other ethnic groups does not know

---

[8]"Spanish Progeny Are Not Hispanic, S.F. Group Insists," *San Diego Union*, Nov. 24, 1990. Ironically, both Spanish American firemen would have been promoted in the department even without benefit of affirmative action; they received the third- and sixth-highest scores on exams administered to sixty-eight persons for twenty promotion slots.

history. Hispanics have not always had an easy time of it in the United States. Even though discrimination against Mexican Americans and Puerto Ricans was not as severe as it was against blacks, acceptance has come only with struggle, and some prejudices still exist. Discrimination against Hispanics, or any other group, should be fought, and there are laws and a massive administrative apparatus to do so. But the way to eliminate such discrimination is not to classify all Hispanics as victims and treat them as if they could not succeed by their own efforts. Hispanics can and will prosper in the United States by following the example of the millions before them.

DISCUSSING THE TEXT

1. How do you think Linda Chavez would define the term *assimilation?* How do you think her critics would define it?
2. Chavez believes that ethnic politics has been "a stepping-stone into the mainstream" for Irish, Italian, and Jewish politicians, among others (par. 10). Do you agree with this opinion? Do you know of any politician at the state or national level who uses his or her ethnicity when campaigning?
3. In her discussion of the role of culture and language in the process of assimilation, Chavez asserts that "No children in an American school are helped by being held back in their native language when they could be learning the language that will enable them to get a decent job or pursue higher education" (par. 5). In a group of four or five students, discuss the implications of this view. How much do you know about bilingual education? What are your own views of this practice? Take brief notes as you work on this assignment, and be prepared to share your opinions with the class.

WRITING ABOUT THE TEXT

4. Write a personal response to Chavez's views on entitlements and affirmative action, focusing particularly on the following statement from her essay: "Ultimately, entitlements based on their status as 'victims' rob Hispanics of real power. The history of American ethnic groups is one of overcoming disadvantage, of competing with those who were already here and proving themselves as competent as any who came before" (par. 16). Do you agree with this assessment of "the history of American ethnic groups"? What evidence can you think of to support, or to argue against, Chavez's outlook on entitlements and affirmative action?
5. Chavez seems to imply that Hispanics do not place as much emphasis on education as Chinese and Jewish families do, and that they are not willing to make the necessary sacrifices to provide a good education for their children (par. 13). Write a brief essay in which you analyze Chavez's opinions. How effectively do you think she argues this point? What evidence does she provide? What are your own views on the matter?
6. Find a recent article on affirmative action and entitlements, for Hispanic Americans or another disadvantaged group. Write a brief summary and

analysis of this article, comparing the information or arguments it provides with those expressed in Chavez's essay.

7. Go back to Rubén Martínez's "L.A. Journals" (p. 301) and take some notes about his views on identity, ethnicity, and the process of assimilation. Then write a brief essay in which you compare and contrast Martínez's views on assimilation, in its relation to identity, with the views that Linda Chavez expresses in her essay.

ARTURO MADRID

Diversity and Its Discontents

The last thirty years have been a period of tremendous change in educational institutions in the United States, as the proportion of minorities has grown from a relatively small, even invisible, number to a sizable and growing presence on American campuses. Along with this dramatic change has come a corresponding political and educational challenge: What is the best way to accommodate this new minority presence? Some argue that the traditional way is still best—socializing the individual to the dominant culture and values of the Western European humanist tradition. Others, however, argue that the traditional culture and values must be expanded—that the circle must be enlarged—to accommodate a more diverse educational curriculum. Arturo Madrid is one of the latter group; in this selection he argues from a perspective shaped by his own education as a native Spanish speaker, someone who was initially compelled to learn the Anglo-American traditions and language and deny his Spanish heritage and language.

Even though Madrid has been a professor of Spanish and an educational leader for many years, in this essay he still portrays himself as an outsider, particularly within the context of current debates surrounding issues of diversity. He also, paradoxically, sees his own identity as one that falls both inside and outside "America": his lineage goes back several generations in New Mexico, yet his visible identity as a Mexican American marks him as an "other" relative to los americanos.

Arturo Madrid (b. 1939) has a Ph.D. in Hispanic languages and literatures from the University of California at Los Angeles, and has held academic and administrative positions at several schools, including Dartmouth College and the University of Minnesota. From 1984 to 1993 he served as the founding president of The Tomás Rivera Center, a national institute for policy studies on Latino issues affiliated with the Claremont Graduate School in California and Trinity University in Texas. He has published numerous articles on diversity and higher education and the English-only movement. Currently, Madrid is professor of Humanities in the Department of Modern Languages at Trinity University. This selection originally appeared in the journal Academe *in 1990.*

My name is Arturo Madrid. I am a citizen of the United States, as are my parents and as were my grandparents and my great-grandparents. My ancestors' presence in what is now the United States antedates Plymouth Rock, even without taking into account any American Indian heritage I might have.

I do not, however, fit those mental sets that define America and Americans. My physical appearance, my speech patterns, my name, my profession (a professor of Spanish) create a text that confuses the reader. My normal experience is to be asked, "And where are *you* from?" My response depends on my mood. Passive-aggressive, I answer, "From here." Aggressive-passive, I ask, "Do you mean where I am originally from?" But ultimately my answer to those follow-up questions that will ask about origins will be that we have always been from here.

Overcoming my resentment I try to educate, knowing that nine times out of ten my words fall on inattentive ears. I have spent most of my adult life explaining who I am not. I am exotic, but—as Richard Rodriguez of *Hunger of Memory* fame so painfully found out—not exotic enough . . . not Peruvian, or Pakistani, or whatever. I am, however, very clearly the *other,* if only your everyday, garden-variety, domestic *other.* I will share with you another phenomenon that I have been a part of, that of being a missing person, and how I came late to that awareness. But I've always known that I was the *other,* even before I knew the vocabulary or understood the significance of otherness.

I grew up in an isolated and historically marginal part of the United States, a small mountain village in the state of New Mexico, the eldest child of parents native to that region, whose ancestors had always lived there. In those vast and empty spaces people who look like me, speak as I do, and have names like mine predominate. But the *americanos* lived among us: the descendants of those nineteenth-century immigrants who dispossessed us of our lands; missionaries who came to convert us and stayed to live among us; artists who became enchanted with our land and humanscape and went native; refugees from unhealthy climes, crowded spaces, unpleasant circumstances; and, of course, the inhabitants of Los Alamos, whose sociocultural distance from us was accentuated by the fact that they occupied a space removed from and proscribed to us. More importantly, however, they—*los americanos*—were omnipresent (and almost exclusively so) in newspapers, newsmagazines, books, on radio, in movies, and, ultimately, on television.

5 Despite the operating myth of the day, school did not erase my otherness. It did try to deny it, and in doing so only accentuated it. To this day what takes place in schools is more socialization than education, but when I was in elementary school—and given where I was—socialization was everything. School was where one became an American, because there was a pervasive and systematic denial by the society that surrounded us that we were Americans. That denial was both explicit and implicit.

Quite beyond saluting the flag and pledging allegiance to it (a very intense and meaningful action, given that the United States was involved in a war and our brothers, cousins, uncles, and fathers were on the frontlines), becoming American was learning English, and its corollary: not speaking Spanish. Until very recently ours was a proscribed language, either *de jure*—by rule, by policy, by law—or *de facto*—by practice, implicitly if not explicitly, through social and political and economic pressure. I do not argue that learning English was not appropriate. On the contrary. Like it or not, and we had no basis to make any judgments on that matter, we were Americans by virtue of having been born Americans and English was the common language of Americans. And there was a myth, a pervasive myth, to the effect that if only we learned to speak English well—and particularly without an accent—we would be welcomed into the American fellowship.

Sam Hayakawa and the official English movement[1] folks notwithstanding, the true text was not our speech, but rather our names and our appearance, for we would always have an accent, however perfect our pronunciation, however excellent our enunciation, however divine our diction. That accent would be heard in our pigmentation, our physiognomy, our names. We were, in short, the *other*.

Being the *other* involves contradictory phenomena. On the one hand being the *other* frequently means being invisible. Ralph Ellison wrote eloquently about that experience in his magisterial novel, *Invisible Man*. On the other hand, being the *other* sometimes involves sticking out like a sore thumb. What is she/he doing here?

For some of us being the *other* is only annoying; for others it is debilitating; for still others it is damning. Many try to flee otherness by taking on protective colorations that provide invisibility, whether of dress or speech or manner or name. Only a fortunate few succeed. For the majority of us otherness is permanently sealed by physical appearance. For the rest, otherness is betrayed by ways of being, speaking, or doing.

10 The first half of my life I spent downplaying the significance and consequences of otherness. The second half has seen me wrestling to understand its complex and deeply ingrained realities; striving to fathom why otherness denies us a voice or visibility or validity in American society and its institutions; struggling to make otherness familiar, reasonable, even normal to my fellow Americans.

I spoke earlier of another phenomenon that I am a part of: that of being a missing person. Growing up in northern New Mexico I had only a slight sense of us being missing persons. *Hispanos*, as we called (and call) ourselves in New Mexico, were very much a part of the fabric of the society, and there were *hispano* professionals everywhere about me: doctors, lawyers, schoolteachers, and administrators. My people owned businesses, ran organizations, and were both appointed and elected public officials.

My awareness of our absence from the larger institutional life of the society became sharper when I went off to college, but even then it was

---

[1]*Sam Hayakawa and the official English movement:* Madrid refers to linguist and former senator S. I. Hayakawa, known for his efforts to declare English the official language of the United States. Over the past few years, approximately twenty states, among them Arizona, Colorado, and Florida, have made provisions declaring English their states' official language. (*Ed.*)

attenuated by the circumstances of history and geography. The demography of Albuquerque still strongly reflected its historical and cultural origins, despite the influx of Midwesterners and Easterners. Moreover, many of my classmates at the University of New Mexico were *hispanos,* and even some of my professors. I thought that would obtain at UCLA, where I began graduate studies in 1960. Los Angeles had a very large Mexican population and that population was visible even in and around Westwood and on the campus. Many of the groundskeepers and food-service personnel at UCLA were Mexican. But Mexican-American students were few and mostly invisible, and I do not recall seeing or knowing a single Mexican-American (or, for that matter, African American, Asian, or American Indian) professional on the staff or faculty of that institution during the five years I was there. Needless to say, people like me were not present in any capacity at Dartmouth College, the site of my first teaching appointment, and of course were not even part of the institutional or individual mind-set. I knew then that we—a we that had come to encompass American Indians, Asian Americans, African Americans, Puerto Ricans, and women—were truly missing persons in American institutional life.

Over the past three decades the *de jure* and *de facto* types of segregation that have historically characterized American institutions have been under assault. As a consequence, minorities and women have become part of American institutional life. Although there are still many areas where we are not to be found, the missing persons phenomenon is not as pervasive as it once was. However, the presence of the *other,* particularly minorities, in institutions and in institutional life resembles what we call in Spanish a *flor de tierra* (a surface phenomenon): we are spare plants whose roots do not go deep, vulnerable to inclemencies of an economic, or political, or social, nature.

Our entrance into and our status in institutional life are not unlike a scenario set forth by my grandmother's pastor when she informed him that she and her family were leaving their mountain village to relocate to the Rio Grande Valley. When he asked her to promise that she would remain true to the faith and continue to involve herself in it, she asked why he thought she would do otherwise. "Doña Trinidad," he told her, "in the Valley there is no Spanish church. There is only an American church." "But," she protested, "I read and speak English and would be able to worship there." The pastor responded, "It is possible that they will not admit you, and even if they do, they might not accept you. And that is why I want you to promise me that you are going to go to church. Because if they don't let you in through the front door, I want you to go in through the back door. And if you can't get in through the back door, go in the side door. And if you are unable to enter through the side door I want you to go in through the window. What is important is that you enter and stay."

Some of us entered institutional life through the front door; others 15 through the back door; and still others through side doors. Many, if not most of us, came in through windows, and continue to come in through windows. Of those who entered through the front door, some never made it past the lobby; others were ushered into corners and niches. Those who entered through back and side doors inevitably have remained in back and side rooms. And those who entered through windows found enclosures built around them. For, despite the lip service given to the goal of the integration of minorities into institutional life, what has frequently occurred instead is ghettoization, marginalization, isolation.

Not only have the entry points been limited, but in addition the dynamics have been singularly conflictive. Gaining entry and its corollary, gaining space, have frequently come as a consequence of demands made on institutions and institutional officers. Rather than entering institutions more or less passively, minorities have of necessity entered them actively, even aggressively. Rather than waiting to receive, they have demanded. Institutional relations have thus been adversarial, infused with specific and generalized tensions.

The nature of the entrance and the nature of the space occupied have greatly influenced the view and attitude of the majority population within those institutions. All of us are put into the same box; that is, no matter what the individual reality, the assessment of the individual is inevitably conditioned by a perception that is held of the class. Whatever our history, whatever our record, whatever our validations, whatever our accomplishments, by and large we are perceived unidimensionally and dealt with accordingly. I remember an experience I had in this regard, atypical only in its explicitness. A few years ago I allowed myself to be persuaded to seek the presidency of a well-known state university. I was invited for an interview and presented myself before the selection committee, which included members of the board of trustees. The opening question of that brief but memorable interview was directed at me by a member of that august body. "Dr. Madrid," he asked, "why does a one-dimensional person like you think he can be the president of a multidimensional institution like ours?"

Over the past four decades America's demography has undergone significant changes. Since 1965 the principal demographic growth we have experienced in the United States has been of peoples whose national origins are non-European. This population growth has occurred both through birth and through immigration. A few years ago discussion of the national birthrate had a scare dimension: the high—"inordinately high"—birthrate of the Hispanic population. The popular discourse was informed by words such as "breeding." Several years later, as a consequence of careful tracking by government agencies, we now know that what has happened is that the birthrate of the majority population has decreased. When viewed historically and comparatively, the minority populations (for the most part) have also had a decline in birthrate, but not one as great as that of the majority.

There are additional demographic changes that should give us something to think about. African Americans are now to be found in significant numbers in every major urban center in the nation. Hispanic Americans now number over 15 million people, and although they are a regionally concentrated (and highly urbanized) population, there is a Hispanic community in almost every major urban center of the United States. American Indians, heretofore a small and rural population, are increasingly more numerous and urban. The Asian American population, which has historically consisted of small and concentrated communities of Chinese-, Filipino-, and Japanese-Americans, has doubled over the past decade, its complexion changed by the addition of Cambodians, Koreans, Hmongs, Vietnamese, et al.

Prior to the Immigration Act of 1965, 69 percent of immigration was from Europe. By far the largest number of immigrants to the United States since 1965 have been from the Americas and from Asia: 34 percent are from Asia; another 34 percent are from Central and South America; 16 percent are from Europe; 10 percent are from the Caribbean; the remaining 6 percent are from other continents and Canada. As was the case with previous immigration waves, the current one consists principally of young people: 60 percent are between the ages of 16 and 44. Thus, for the next few decades, we will continue to see a growth in the percentage of non-European-origin Americans as compared to European Americans. 20

To sum up, we now live in one of the most demographically diverse nations in the world, and one that is increasingly more so.

During the same period social and economic change seems to have accelerated. Who would have imagined at mid-century that the prototypical middle-class family (working husband, wife as homemaker, two children) would for all intents and purposes disappear? Who could have anticipated the rise in teenage pregnancies, children in poverty, drug use? Who among us understood the implications of an aging population?

We live in an age of continuous and intense change, a world in which what held true yesterday does not today, and certainly will not tomorrow. What change does, moreover, is bring about even more change. The only constant we have at this point in our national development is change. And change is threatening. The older we get the more likely we are to be anxious about change, and the greater our desire to maintain the status quo.

Evident in our public life is a fear of change, whether economic or moral. Some who fear change are responsive to the call of economic protectionism, others to the message of moral protectionism. Parenthetically, I have referred to the movement to require more of students without in turn giving them more as academic protectionism. And the pronouncements of E. D. Hirsch and Allan Bloom[2] are, I believe, informed by intellectual protectionism. Much more serious, however, is the dark side of the populism which underlies this evergoing protectionism—the resentment of the *other.* An excellent and fascinating example of that aspect of populism is the cry for linguistic protection-

---

[2]*E. D. Hirsch and Allan Bloom:* In 1987, Hirsch (b. 1928) published *Cultural Literacy: What Every American Needs to Know,* and Bloom (1930–1992), *The Closing of the American Mind.* In these two books, Professors Hirsch and Bloom condemned what they saw as the politics of multiculturalism and proposed a return to a more traditional idea of liberal education, focused on established works of literature, often referred to as "Great Books." (*Ed.*)

ism—for making English the official language of the United States. And who among us is unaware of the tensions that underlie immigration reform, of the underside of demographic protectionism?

A matter of increasing concern is whether this new protectionism, and the mistrust of the *other* which accompanies it, is not making more significant inroads than we have supposed in higher education. Specifically, I wish to discuss the question of whether a goal (quality) and a reality (demographic diversity) have been erroneously placed in conflict, and, if so, what problems this perception of conflict might present. 25

As part of my scholarship I turn to dictionaries for both origins and meanings of words. Quality, according to the *Oxford English Dictionary,* has multiple meanings. One set defines quality as being an essential character, a distinctive and inherent feature. A second describes it as a degree of excellence, of conformity to standards, as superiority in kind. A third makes reference to social status, particularly to persons of high social status. A fourth talks about quality as being a special or distinguishing attribute, as being a desirable trait. Quality is highly desirable in both principle and practice. We all aspire to it in our own person, in our experiences, in our acquisitions and products, and of course we all want to be associated with people and operations of quality.

But let us move away from the various dictionary meanings of the word and to our own sense of what it represents and of how we feel about it. First of all we consider quality to be finite; that is, it is limited with respect to quantity; it has very few manifestations; it is not widely distributed. I have it and you have it, but they don't. We associate quality with homogeneity, with uniformity, with standardization, with order, regularity, neatness. All too often we equate it with smoothness, glibness, slickness, elegance. Certainly it is always expensive. We tend to identify it with those who lead, with the rich and famous. And, when you come right down to it, it's inherent. Either you've got it or you ain't.

Diversity, from the Latin *divertere,* meaning to turn aside, to go different ways, to differ, is the condition of being different or having differences, is an instance of being different. Its companion word, diverse, means differing, unlike, distinct; having or capable of having various forms; composed of unlike or distinct elements. Diversity is lack of standardization, of regularity, of orderliness, homogeneity, conformity, uniformity. Diversity introduces complications, is difficult to organize, is troublesome to manage, is problematical. Diversity is irregular, disorderly, uneven, rough. The way we use the word diversity gives us away. Something is too diverse, is extremely diverse. We want a little diversity.

When we talk about diversity, we are talking about the *other,* whatever that other might be: someone of a different gender, race, class, national origin; somebody at a greater or lesser distance from the norm; someone outside the set; someone who possesses a different set of characteristics, features, or attributes; someone who does not fall within the taxonomies we use daily and with which we are comfortable; someone who does not fit into the mental configurations that give our lives order and meaning.

In short, diversity is desirable only in principle, not in practice. Long live diversity . . . as long as it conforms to my standards, my mind set, my view of life, my sense of order. We desire, we like, we admire diversity, not unlike the way the French (and others) appreciate women; that is, *Vive la différence!*—as long as it stays in its place. 30

What I find paradoxical about and lacking in this debate is that diversity is the natural order of things. Evolution produces diversity. Margaret Visser, writing about food in her latest book, *Much Depends on Dinner,* makes an eloquent statement in this regard:

> Machines like, demand, and produce uniformity. But nature loathes it: her strength lies in multiplicity and in differences. Sameness in biology means fewer possibilities and therefore weakness.

The United States, by its very nature, by its very development, is the essence of diversity. It is diverse in its geography, population, institutions, technology; its social, cultural, and intellectual modes. It is a society that at its best does not consider quality to be monolithic in form or finite in quantity, or to be inherent in class. Quality in our society proceeds in large measure out of the stimulus of diverse modes of thinking and acting; out of the creativity made possible by the different ways in which we approach things; out of diversion from paths or modes hallowed by tradition.

One of the principal strengths of our society is its ability to address, on a continuing and substantive basis, the real economic, political, and social problems that have faced and continue to face us. What makes the United States so attractive to immigrants is the protections and opportunities it offers; what keeps our society together is tolerance for cultural, religious, social, political, and even linguistic difference; what makes us a unique, dynamic, and extraordinary nation is the power and creativity of our diversity.

The true history of the United States is one of struggle against intolerance, against oppression, against xenophobia, against those forces that have prohibited persons from participating in the larger life of the society on the basis of their race, their gender, their religion, their national origin, their linguistic and cultural background. These phenomena are not consigned to the past. They remain with us and frequently take on virulent dimensions.

If you believe, as I do, that the well-being of a society is directly related to the degree and extent to which all of its citizens participate in its institutions, then you will have to agree that we have a challenge before us. In view of the extraordinary changes that are taking place in our society we need to take up the struggle again, irritating, grating, troublesome, unfashionable, unpleasant as it is. As educated and educator members of this society we have a special responsibility for ensuring that all American institutions, not just our elementary and secondary schools, our juvenile halls, or our jails, reflect the diversity of our society. Not to do so is to risk greater alienation on the part of 35 a growing segment of our society; is to risk increased social tension in an already conflictive world; and, ultimately, is to risk the survival of a range of institutions that, for all their defects and deficiencies, provide us the opportunity and the freedom to improve our individual and collective lot.

Let me urge you to reflect on these two words—quality and diversity—and on the mental sets and behaviors that flow out of them. And let me urge you further to struggle against the notion that quality is finite in quantity, limited in its manifestations, or is restricted by considerations of class, gender, race, or national origin; or that quality manifests itself only in leaders and not in followers, in managers and not in workers, in breeders and not in drones; or that it has to be associated with verbal agility or elegance of personal style; or that it cannot be seeded, nurtured, or developed.

Because diversity—the *other*—is among us, will define and determine our lives in ways that we still do not fully appreciate, whether that other is women (no longer bound by tradition, house, and family); or Asians, African Americans, Indians, and Hispanics (no longer invisible, regional, or marginal); or our newest immigrants (no longer distant, exotic, alien). Given the changing profile of America, will we come to terms with diversity in our personal and professional lives? Will we begin to recognize the diverse forms that quality can take? If so, we will thus initiate the process of making quality limitless in its manifestations, infinite in quantity, unrestricted with respect to its origins, and more importantly, virulently contagious.

I hope we will. And that we will further join together to expand—not to close—the circle.

DISCUSSING THE TEXT

1. Madrid says about his early schooling that "becoming American was learning English, and its corollary: not speaking Spanish" (par. 6). And yet, learning English did not provide him immediate or easy entrance into American society. Why not? What factors held him back? What is his attitude as he recounts his experiences?
2. After spending the first half of his life trying to conceal his "otherness," Madrid now wants to make otherness "normal" to his fellow Americans. What accounts for this shift in his perspective? To what degree has Madrid been affected by external circumstances (for example, demographic changes)?
3. Madrid argues that because of long-standing resistance to their presence, members of minority groups have had to enter American institutions "aggressively"; as a result, he says, "Institutional relations have . . . been adversarial, infused with specific and generalized tensions" (par. 16). Do you agree? Can you think of examples from institutions you are familiar with (such as schools, businesses, churches, or your own college or university) that support or challenge this assertion?
4. Madrid argues that the "true history of the United States is one of struggle against intolerance, against oppression, against xenophobia" (par. 34). What does Madrid mean by "true history"? Do you agree with him? Is it necessary

to agree with Madrid on this point in order to agree with his conclusions in the essay? Discuss these questions with a group of four or five students. Take brief notes as you work on this assignment, and be prepared to share your opinions with the rest of the class.

WRITING ABOUT THE TEXT

5. Write two paragraphs that address the following questions: How does Madrid define his two key terms, *quality* and *diversity?* Are you satisfied with his definitions? How does he use his definitions of these terms to advance his argument on behalf of diversity? Think of two other key words (such as pluralism and dogmatism, liberal and conservative, or individual and community); define the two terms, using a dictionary; and use these definitions to advance your argument on behalf of one or the other.
6. When Madrid was interviewed for the position of president of a university, he was asked, "Why does a one-dimensional person like you think he can be the president of a multidimensional institution like ours?" (par. 17). What do you think was meant by this question? Assuming Madrid's voice and the attitudes he conveys in this essay, write a response to the question.
7. Keeping in mind Madrid's experiences in his interview, prepare a set of questions that *you* would ask a candidate for the position of university president. What kinds of qualifications do you think a candidate would need to lead a "multidimensional institution"? What kinds of qualifications would a candidate need to lead the university toward the goal that Madrid describes—that of "ensuring that all American institutions . . . reflect the diversity of our society" (par. 35)?

WILLIAM M. CHACE

The Real Challenge of Multiculturalism (Is Yet to Come)

The ongoing conflict between the traditional curriculum and the new, multicultural curriculum that has been taking place within colleges and universities is a reflection of contemporary political debate as well. The traditional curriculum (or course of study) at American universities has centered around the study of classic texts within Western civilization, commonly known as Great Books. The multicultural curriculum attempts to look not only at texts that have been deemed as "classic" but also at others that reflect issues of ethnicity, class, and gender within mainstream culture.

American society is looking to education, as it always has, to solve problems that are really social and economic in nature. As long as colleges and universities keep adding courses in one special area after another, they are accommodating the new social and educational imperatives; but what happens when they run out of space?

How much of the old curriculum will have to be sacrificed to make room for the new? And will the adjusted curriculum have any real focus or coherence? Can we even assume that the old curriculum of Great Books really was "great"? What do we mean by "great"? Who determines what should be taught? These are some of the issues that underlie William M. Chace's consideration of the challenge of multiculturalism.

Chace continues the discussion opened by Arturo Madrid in the preceding selection about the value of the new multiculturalism, or diversity, to use Madrid's term. Chace writes with an awareness that the values of pluralism *(that is, an openness to different approaches, ideas, and interpretations) are under attack, including the fundamental assumption that different methods, theories, values, and perspectives must be tolerated in a free society. Instead of this tolerance, Chace sees strains and tensions opening up within the university (as within American society overall), including conflicts among different minority groups and also between minority groups and those who argue for preserving so-called American traditions. How can one preserve democratic values in a context of pluralistic tolerance of all points of view? Is a single, unified culture an indispensable goal that is worth fighting for? Chace's consideration of these issues is a fitting conclusion to this volume, for they are fundamental to the range of problems considered in this text as a whole.*

William M. Chace (b. 1938), educated at Haverford College and the University of California at Los Angeles, taught for many years at Stanford University and is presently at Emory University, Georgia. He is author of The Political Identities of Ezra Pound and T. S. Eliot *(1973), and editor of* James Joyce: A Collection of Critical Essays *(1973), among other works. This essay, "The Real Challenge of Multiculturalism (Is Yet to Come)" appeared, like the preceding selection by Arturo Madrid, in* Academe *in 1990.*

If turbulent discussions about the "core curriculum" dominated campus agenda in the 1980s, "multiculturalism" and its several meanings promise to provide similar tension and controversy in the 1990s. Again the debate will include imperatives of two kinds—the formally academic and the political. The former will have to do with revising the canon, with including both "high" and "popular" culture in the curriculum, with embracing new genres of expression of every kind and from every quarter of the world. The latter, less explicit and yet throbbing with urgency, will have to do with race, with ethnicity, with gender and sexual preference, and, at last, with acquiring power in the university. It makes sense to distinguish among these several matters, or at least to know when one is talking about one and not the other. The pressure to do otherwise, to see "multiculturalism" as one solitary thing, is to confound the educational with the political. Although they are kindred, their differences are many.

The debate, sure to be found on almost every American campus, will be in part defined by a contradiction that will be tough, if not impossible, to resolve. On the one hand, belief in a stable and codified body of knowledge that everyone should absorb is now frail beyond repair, fatally weakened by the resounding defeat of the "traditionalist" position in "core curriculum" debates. A loose and confused consensus that the curriculum is on its way to revision has become received opinion. Indeed, the weakening of support for the "core curriculum" at Stanford and elsewhere was part and parcel of the ascendence of multiculturalism, even in its current inchoate form. Many teachers and administrators have come, albeit with some misgivings, to place their confidence in this new and vague entity. It will, they believe, provide greater inclusiveness on campuses; it will thwart parochialism; it will be yet another chapter in the history of America's ability, within its institutions, to embrace "the other." In short, it will reinforce the pluralism indelibly a part of the nation's past, and increasingly a part of its future. Since the colleges and universities of America have long been one of the most important staging areas of social change, multiculturalism seems but one more sign of the ways in which the issues of education are but the issues of the nation at large.

On the other hand, some real concern is now present within those same institutions that some of the very forces underlying the multicultural movement may be eroding that cherished pluralism and inclusiveness. Off the campus, as well, in the commentary of journalists like William Raspberry and George Will or essayists like Diane Ravitch, the pluralist consensus as we have traditionally understood it is seen in jeopardy. The recent *Campus Life* report from the Carnegie Endowment for the Advancement of Teaching notes with dismay the erosion of many features of campus life supportive of a sense of community. Racial tensions, strains between gays and straights, charges of sexual harassment, the widening gulf between students with amorphous desires to be mentored and faculty with steadfast ambitions to achieve professional recognition, the corollary division of student life into the "curricular" and the "co-curricular," and the anti-sentimental consensus that college campuses are no longer homes for "Mr. Chips"—all these realities work at least imaginatively to open the once-secluded haven of the college campus to the explosive tensions of the world beyond the campus. To some observers, what is now happening in higher education in this country has parallels in the dislocations of Eastern Europe, in the tribal divisions of Africa, in the linguistic rivalries of Canada and Belgium, or in the fraternal bloodbath of Northern Ireland. In its conclusion, the report says that "the deep social divisions that all too often divide campuses racially and ethnically undermine the integrity of higher education." What has been seen as external to the campus, and both inferior and injurious to it, is now envisioned as having invaded it.

But what must be recognized with respect to this discomfiture is that so few proponents of multiculturalism of either kind—the pedagogical *or* the political—have been able to establish with precision what, in practice, "their" multiculturalism would be. Until that is done, no reaction—whether one of benign satisfaction or one of anxiety—seems appropriate.

For those who have accepted (with misgiving but with good will) the idea 5
of multiculturalism as a way of broadening the teaching horizon, a large problem looms. It is this: the project of establishing a genuine curriculum is enormous in its bibliographical dimensions. So many countries, so many books and forms of music, so much art work, so much history and so many lan-

guages! Will the intellectual reservoir involved in such a polymathic revision of the task of teaching really be sufficient to honor the promise of multiculturalism?

Meanwhile, the political proponents of multiculturalism seem, each by each, less interested in the vastness of the total enterprise than in the possibility of guaranteeing the inclusion of their particular cultural formations within the curriculum and within the university. Perhaps it is to be assumed that after each specific group has achieved representation, a kind of "invisible hand" will look after the cumulative results, but that assumption is not based on anything the political proponents have yet said. Indeed, a concern with coherence within the final results would strike many of them as inappropriate. It would militate against the imperative that the previously underrepresented culture in question should take its place within the curriculum and on the campus. After all, the very idea of looking after the whole construct is largely irrelevant to individual groups each proceeding on the exigency exerted by previous neglect.

Even further divisions are evident between these two groups. For instance, the former group, that primarily interested in multiculturalism as an educational matter, includes many who promote multiculturalism from a largely negative position, arguing against historic curricular exclusion and the distorted valuation of one culture "over" another. These voices do not necessarily embrace any vision of a "common culture," for they see the presence of a malign hegemonic history interfering with the proper educational mission in which they are interested.

The latter groups also have their doubts about the prospect of any "common culture," but for different reasons. They believe that history is a sinister process of exclusion and victimization, and they assume that any synthesis between historic unequals is most unlikely. Moreover, should such synthesis be achieved, the individual integrity of the oppressed culture in question would instantly be threatened by homogenization. Working under the rubric of multiculturalism, such groups thus advance a form of separatism or cultural nationalism.

An additional source of difference between the two groups is that those primarily interested in revising the canon for reasons of pedagogy and equity uneasily confront the fact that inclusion of new subject matter within the new curriculum might not necessarily guarantee equivalence of classroom results. A shorthand way of putting this plain fact is to say that affinity with the subject matter will not guarantee a student success in the classroom; "outsiders" can get "A" grades in multicultural courses and "insiders" can still fail them.

10 On the other hand, those interested in revising the curriculum because they want to strengthen their political and cultural base assume that the very existence of new subject matter will work, pedagogically, to the advantage of students from their own camp. The belief in role models as both the creators of the works to be studied and the teachers to lead that study is based on the conviction that exclusion and stigmatization as the "other" can be remedied by the presence of the "same" in a student's life. But before this is to be

believed and acted on in planning educational policy, much more study has to be given to how different groups really can and do apply intellectual discipline to *any* subject matter, including their "own."

Yet another problem with multiculturalism comes into view when one notes that much of curricular life does not lend itself to racial, ethnic, or gender distinctions. The natural sciences and mathematics cannot easily be transformed under the pressure of cultural nationalism or group-specific ideologies. Moreover, even if the 1990s were able to construct, as some people might soon be proposing with some urgency, a "female mathematics" or a "black biology" or a "gay chemistry," the necessity, now long delayed, of making up for the dismaying lack of competence among *all* American young people in the realms of mathematics and the natural sciences will not thereby be answered. There is little evidence that multiculturalism will be able to make up for the deep inadequacies suffered by millions of American secondary and elementary school children in subjects whose most expert practitioners seem increasingly to come from cultures other than the American.

Dangers of another kind will confront those making the good-faith assumption that revision of the curriculum to include more and more of that which has been excluded can proceed without accruing any costs. The costs will be felt by those who will be asked, who must be asked, to surrender the teaching of certain subjects (perhaps near and dear to them for decades), and by those who will not find certain subjects taught to them any more. Almost any gains will be by substitution, not by accumulating a larger curricular inventory.

But, amid all these difficulties and doubts, I find reason to believe that multiculturalism will bring with it some genuine rewards and satisfactions. It will do so because it will, among other things, engender the perpetually refreshing spectacle of change; it will bring a new level of excitement and energy to American higher education. Change, any change at all, traditionally serves to inspire participating faculty and to make students aware of the dramatic events through which they are passing. The heightened self-consciousness and public scrutiny already a part of the debate about multiculturalism will continue for some time, no matter what multiculturalism is at last determined to be, and that level of conscious awareness will reinforce the sense of excitement. As Gerald Graff has shown in *Professing Literature,* the history of curricular change in the humanities (where courses in multiculturalism will most likely be established) is not so much a history of radically new knowledge as it is a history of new emphases and new approaches. Change *is* the distinguishing element in the teaching of "disciplines" whose actual disciplinary coherence has always been open to question. So change will once again be the subject of the day, and the controversy surrounding multiculturalism will take its place in a long line of controversies that have extended life and vitality to fields where virtually everything is subject to revision, cancellation, and rediscovery.

Secondly, much interesting and hitherto mostly unknown material will be taught and absorbed. That will constitute education, pure and simple. Areas once defined as *terra incognita* will be explored by people with energy and a spirit of pioneering. But no miracles will happen. African, Eastern European, Caribbean, and Asian writers will be read (most in translation); "new" forms of music and art will be introduced; traditional canons of learning will perpetually be revised or found decadent or degrading.

Certain other problems, deeper ones, will remain untouched. That is because multiculturalism will not constitute a philosopher's stone providing the basic tools of all genuine education: analysis, retention of materials, clear exposition, and intellectual seriousness. Multiculturalism will not reduce the difficulty of being very intelligent. Nor will it soften the climate of competition in which genuine quickness of mind always somehow manifests itself and is, one way or another, admired. 15

The project of multiculturalism, then, in the 1990s is to look beyond both the curricular changes that are ever-flowing in higher education and the political changes that help to prompt them. It will be to develop courses that are more than "samplers" of the variegated cultures of the world. (That way, sheer dilettantism lies.) It will be to acknowledge that those same curricular changes will do little to provide genuine support to students otherwise deficient in the basic tools of analysis, exposition, and structured thinking. It will be to develop the means to remind students and teachers alike that almost all of intellectual life—whose substance *is* the *raison d'être* of any college or university—is made up of parts that only for artificial reasons have been sequestered one from the other. Hence the real pedagogical mission is to bring into association the apparently dissimilar, to reveal the commonality of all forms of discourse and taxonomy, all systems of mental discrimination.

In practice, then, the project of multiculturalism will in all likelihood include a dramatic blurring of the distinctions separating "high" from "low" culture, academic culture from popular culture. It will reinforce the holistic and anthropological, rather than the specialized and formalized, conception of culture. Culture without the capital "C" will be in the ascendent, and will give further impetus to programs in "cultural studies" as they unite literary, historical, and sociological investigations.

Other changes will come, their definition to be provided in practice as curriculum is generated and scrapped, proposed and revised. While this process is nothing less than traditional, it will prove unnerving to some witnesses. Their anxieties, while easy to credit, need not be profound. After all, much will remain secure and fixed in any landscape influenced by multiculturalism. People frightened by what they envision as apocalyptic transformations would do well to consider the essential conservatism of all academic practices, as well as the conservatism of most social organisms.

In thinking about the imagined and threatened dissolution of the culture of the former British Empire, and, at the same time, its extraordinary ability to remain "British" amid enormous demographic changes, the noted literary critic Michael Gorra has said that England's multiracial society

> is not a mosaic or a rainbow. Nor is it a great assimilating stewpot, into which the immigrant's identity can melt. Instead it's a stir-fry, whose ingredients are at once distinctive and yet bound and flavored by the sauce of a common culture. And in which each new ingredient changes, however subtly, the taste of that unifying sauce.[1]

For the decade into which American higher education is now moving, 20 the problem will be that of finding and then describing that "unifying sauce." Particularisms of every kind will make the job difficult. The purely political proponents of multiculturalism will not prove helpful at every turn. The cheap thrills of simply adding new and exotic titles to already tired courses will obscure the task at hand. And there will be present the ever-seductive appeal of an "easier" way of education, the advertisement of short-cuts promising the avoidance of the tough-minded disciplinary exactitude forever crucial to genuine intellectual life.

The struggle to come was long ago described by Alexis de Tocqueville when he defined, in *Democracy in America,* the dilemma of a country and a culture whose coherence, whose "unifying sauce," was endangered both by individualistic strains forever competing with each other and thus presenting a picture of social disarray and by an overwhelming social conformity that ground down to nothing those same solitary entities.

With multiculturalism, the same apparently irreconcilable phenomenon appears: how to unite the isolable and passionate voices of cultures not yet a part of the traditional conformity; how not to lose the integrity of those voices in the process; how not to allow the urge to conformity once again to define the ultimate results.

The struggle will properly absorb the energies of very many good people.

DISCUSSING THE TEXT

1. Chace begins with the premise that the "traditionalist" position has essentially lost the debate on the future of American education, and that "multiculturalism"—with its greater inclusiveness—has won the day. Do you agree, from your own experience at your college or university? Think of points where multiculturalism is evident (or not evident) in the curriculum of your own institution to serve as your evidence.
2. Chace worries that the broadening of the curriculum, including more and more representation from specific groups and political constituencies, will lead to incoherence in the whole. Do you think that this is a justifiable worry? Should there be a "common culture" that all Americans share in and learn about in their schooling? Why or why not?
3. What does Chace mean when he says that multiculturalism will not reduce the "climate of competition" (par. 15) within American education? Do you

[1]Michael Gorra, "The Importance of Being British," *Boston Review* 25 (August 1990): 28.

agree with him? Do you consider this element of competition a good thing, as Chace seems to feel? Why or why not?

4. Chace sees a limit to what multiculturalism can achieve in a curriculum; he argues that the natural sciences and mathematics, for example, do not lend themselves to "racial, ethnic, or gender distinctions" (par. 11). Do you agree? Can you think of any instances where matters of race, gender, or ethnicity might be relevant to the study of science and mathematics? Discuss this issue in a group of four or five students. Take brief notes as you work on this assignment, and be prepared to share your opinions with the rest of the class.

WRITING ABOUT THE TEXT

5. Acknowledging the triumph of multiculturalism on many college campuses, Chace sees on the same campuses an erosion of the sense of community and a growth in tensions and conflicts between different students (particularly those who identify with specific racial, ethnic, or sexual minorities). Do you think this is a fair analysis? Think of an example of such a conflict, either on your own campus or on another campus that you are aware of. Drawing on this example, write a response to Chace's analysis of such conflicts, explaining why you agree or disagree with this analysis.
6. Chace sees the tendency toward multiculturalism in the curriculum as part of a trend toward a general blurring of cultural boundaries (between high and low culture and academic and popular culture, for example). Do you agree? Write a brief essay in which you (a) explain the difference between high and low culture as you understand these terms, and (b) describe examples of the crossing of boundaries between high and low culture in contemporary life (in advertising, music, movies, television programs, or literature, for example).
7. The ultimate challenge for American education, as Chace sees it, is determining how to "unite the isolable and passionate voices of cultures not yet a part of the traditional conformity" (par. 22). How important is it to have a "unifying sauce," as Chace calls it (borrowing Michael Gorra's metaphor)? What is gained by having this kind of cultural unity? Is anything sacrificed in obtaining it? Write an essay in which you first consider these questions from opposing viewpoints and then take a stand and explain the reasons for your opinion.
8. Chace identifies the "basic tools of all genuine education" as "analysis, retention of materials, clear exposition, and intellectual seriousness" (par. 15). Write a one- to two-page essay in which you identify, and explain, what *you* consider the "basic tools" of education. What role (if any) do you think multiculturalism would play in developing these tools?

MAKING CONNECTIONS

1. Choose the one selection from this chapter that best illustrates for you the "politics of ethnicity." Write a personal essay, drawing on experiences from your own life as you respond to the issues that the selection raises.
2. Drawing on the ideas on racial prejudice raised by William Apes ("An Indian's Looking-Glass for the White Man") and Cornel West ("On Black-Jewish Relations"), write a fictional dialogue between these two authors in which they discuss the reasons behind the white American culture's historical treatment of African Americans and Native Americans.
3. In 1991, Richard Goldstein wrote in "The New Anti-Semitism: A *Geshrei*" that "In New York City, where political power flows from ethnic alliances, Crown Heights has given those who hope to split the white liberal vote from the black community a potent weapon" (p. 564). Find an article in a newsmagazine like *Time* or *Newsweek* on the New York City mayoral election of November 1994 (an election in which the Democratic incumbent, David Dinkins, an African American, was defeated by white Republican candidate Rudolph Giuliani). Write a brief essay that interprets the election results in terms of Goldstein's assessment of ethnic politics in New York City.
4. Both Richard Goldstein and Cornel West write about the complex relationship between African Americans and Jews from the point of view of their respective ethnicities. Choose a passage from each selection that discusses a specific case of racial prejudice and violence, and write a brief essay that analyzes both passages. How do the passages you have chosen illustrate the major themes of each essay? How are the authors' arguments similar? How are they different?
5. In "Diversity and Its Discontents," Arturo Madrid maintains that the minority man or woman is treated "unidimensionally"—that is, simply as a member of a minority group rather than as a unique individual (see p. 579). Consider this claim in relation to Linda Chavez's views on what she perceives as some minorities' "victim" status in "Toward a New Politics of Hispanic Assimilation." Discuss both the advantages and the disadvantages of being considered a member of an ethnic minority in the realm of education or affirmative action, for example.
6. What differences do you see between the opinions of William Chace (in "The Real Challenge of Multiculturalism [Is Yet to Come]") and Arturo Madrid (in "Diversity and Its Discontents") on educational issues? Make two separate lists of these writers' views on education, particularly in relation to multicultural concerns. Write a brief essay in which you discuss their arguments and conclude by stating your own opinion on the fundamental questions that these writers raise.
7. Go back to Itabari Njeri's essay "Sushi and Grits: Ethnic Identity and Conflict in a Newly Multicultural America" in Chapter 7 (p. 512). Write an essay comparing and contrasting Njeri's arguments and those of Linda Chavez in "Toward a New Politics of Hispanic Assimilation."
8. The photograph introducing this chapter captures the excitement and pride felt by onlookers at a Puerto Rico Day Parade in New York City, which has a sizable Puerto Rican population. For many years, Puerto Ricans living both on the island and in the mainland have debated among themselves how

closely tied they should be to the United States. What do you think are the benefits in feeling an intense loyalty to one's own particular ethnic culture? What may be the liabilities, to either the individual or the culture as a whole? Write an essay, using the photograph as a starting point, that deals with these issues, integrating two or three of the readings from this chapter and others that may be relevant to your concerns.

9. Reread the poems included throughout this book: "The New Colossus" and "Unguarded Gates" in Chapter 1 (pp. 26 and 27); "next to of course god america i" and "America" in Chapter 6 (pp. 383 and 384); and "America" and "Let America Be America Again" in Chapter 8 (pp. 536 and 537). Take notes on how each poem invents, or questions the idea of, America. Then write an essay that integrates the points of view expressed in three or four of the poems, comparing and contrasting opposing arguments as you go along. In your conclusion, express your own ideas about what America is, what it is not, and what it could become. What would be your way of "inventing America"?

FURTHER READING

SAMUEL FRANCIS SMITH

Benson, Susan Porter, et al., eds. *Presenting the Past: Essays on History and the Public.* Philadelphia: Temple University Press, 1986.

Bodnar, John. *Remaking America: Public Memory, Commemoration, and Patriotism in the Twentieth Century.* Princeton, N.J.: Princeton University Press, 1992.

LANGSTON HUGHES

Rampersad, Arnold. *The Life of Langston Hughes.* New York: Oxford University Press, 1986.

WILLIAM APES

McQuaid, Kim. "William Apes, Pequot, an Indian Reformer in the Jackson Era." *New England Quarterly* 50 (1977): 605–25.

Trafzer, Clifford E., ed. *Earth Song, Sky Spirit. Short Stories of the Contemporary Native American Experience.* New York: Doubleday, 1992.

Vizenor, Gerald. *Manifest Manners: Postindian Warriors of Survivance.* Middletown, Conn.: Wesleyan University Press, 1994.

CORNEL WEST

Friedman, Murray, and Peter Binzen. *What Went Wrong: The Creation and Collapse of the Black-Jewish Alliance.* New York: Free Press, 1995.

Sowell, Thomas. *Race and Culture: A World View.* New York: Basic Books, 1994.

RICHARD GOLDSTEIN

Berman, Paul, ed. *Blacks and Jews: Alliances and Arguments.* New York: Delacorte Press, 1994.

Locke, Hubert G., ed. *The Black Anti-Semitism Controversy: Protestant Views and Perspectives.* Selinsgrove, Penn.: Susquehanna University Press, 1994.

LINDA CHAVEZ

Lind, Michael. *The Next American Nation: The New Nationalism and the Fourth American Revolution.* New York: The Free Press, 1995.

Shorris, Earl. *Latinos: A Biography of the People.* New York: W. W. Norton, 1993.

ARTURO MADRID

Bromwich, David. *Politics by Other Means: Higher Education and Group Thinking.* New Haven: Yale University Press, 1992.

Graff, Gerald. *Beyond the Culture Wars: How Teaching the Conflicts Can Revitalize American Education.* New York: W. W. Norton, 1992.

WILLIAM M. CHACE

Aufderheide, Patricia. *Beyond PC: Toward a Politics of Understanding.* St. Paul, Minn.: Graywolf Press, 1992.

Hirsch, E. D., Jr. *Cultural Literacy. What Every American Needs to Know.* Boston: Houghton Mifflin, 1987.

Acknowledgments

Agee, James, "Near a Church." Pages 38–43 from *Let Us Now Praise Famous Men.* Copyright © 1939, 1940 by James Agee; 1941 by James Agee and Walker Evans. Renewed 1969 by Mia Fritsch Agee and Walker Evans. Reprinted by permission of Houghton Mifflin Co. All rights reserved.

Aldrich, Thomas Bailey, "Unguarded Gates." Pages 275–276 from *The Poems of Thomas Bailey Aldrich* (1907).

Apes, William, "An Indian's Looking-Glass for the White Man." Pages 1755–1760 from *The Heath Anthology of American Literature,* volume 1 (1990). Reprinted by permission of D.C. Heath and Company, Inc.

Arendt, Hannah, "We Refugees." Reprinted by permission of Harcourt Brace and Company.

Baldwin, James, "Stranger in the Village." Pages 135–149 from *Notes of a Native Son.* Copyright © 1955, renewed 1983 by James Baldwin. Reprinted by permission of Beacon Press.

Banks, Ann, ed., "Immigrant Lives: Oral Histories Collected by the W.P.A. Federal Writers Project." Excerpts from *First Person America,* an anthology. Published by W. W. Norton (1991). Reprinted by permission.

Carter, Forrest, "Trading with a Christian." This excerpt is from *The Education of Little Tree.* Published by the University of New Mexico Press and is reprinted by arrangement with Eleanor Friede Books Inc. Copyright © 1976 by Forrest Carter. All rights reserved. Reprinted by permission.

Chace, William M., "The Real Challenge of Multiculturalism (Is Yet to Come)." Reprinted in *Academe* (November/December 1990), volume 76, No. 5. William M. Chace is President of Emory University. He wrote this essay when serving as President of Wesleyan University in Connecticut. Reprinted by permission of Dr. Chace and *Academe.*

Chavez, Linda, "Toward a New Politics of Hispanic Assimilation." Selected excerpts from pages 161–171 and 194–196 from *Out of the Bario.* Copyright © 1991 by BasicBooks, a division of HarperCollins Publishers, Inc. Reprinted by permission of the publisher.

Cummings, E. E., "next to of course god america i," is reprinted from *Complete Poems, 1904–1962.* Edited by George J. Firmage, by permission of Liveright Publishing Corporation. Copyright © 1926, 1954, 1991 by the Trustees for E. E. Cummings Trust. Copyright © 1985 by George James Firmage.

DeSalvo, Louise, "A Portrait of the *Puttana* as a Middle-Aged Woolf Scholar." *Between Women: Biographers, Novelists, Critics, Teachers and Artists Write about Their Work on Women.* Edited by Carol Ascher, Louise DeSalvo, and Sara Ruddick. Copyright © 1983 Louise A. DeSalvo. Beacon Press (1984). Reprinted by permission of the author.

Douglass, Frederick, "Escaping from Slavery." Chapter 11 from *Narrative of the Life of Frederick Douglass, An American Slave* (1845). Copyright © 1960 by the President and Fellows of Harvard College; Benjamin Quarles, ed. Cambridge, MA: The Belknap Press of Harvard University Press. Reprinted by permission of the publishers.

Dreyfuss, Joel, "The Invisible Immigrants." Excerpt from "The Invisible Immigrants: Haitians in America Are Industrious, Upwardly Mobile and Vastly Misunderstood," in *New York Times* magazine section (May 23, 1993). Copyright © 1993 by The New York Times Company. Reprinted by permission.

Du Bois, W. E. B., "The Twoness of the American Negro." Pages 3–12 "Of Our Spiritual Strivings" from *The Souls of Black Folk.* Copyright © 1989 Viking Penguin, a division of Penguin Books USA, Inc. Penguin Books Ltd., Penguin Books Australia Ltd., Penguin Books Canada Ltd., Penguin Books N.Z. Ltd. All rights reserved. Reprinted by permission.

Equiano, Olaudah, "Kidnapped into Slavery." Chapter 2 (pages 30–52) from *The Life of Olaudah Equiano or Gustavus Vassa, the African. Written by Himself.* Negro University Press (1837).

Ets, Marie Hall, "Rosa, the Life of an Italian Immigrant." Chapter 2 (pages 210–218) from *Rosa, the Life of an Immigrant,* ed. Maria Hall. Copyright © 1970 by the University of Minnesota. Reprinted by permission.

Fernández, Enrique, "Spitfires, Latin Lovers, Mambo Kings." *The New York Times* (April 19, 1992). Copyright © 1992 by The New York Times Company, Inc. Reprinted by permission.

Garcia, Cristina, "Enough Attitude." Pages 127–144 from *Dreaming in Cuban* by Cristina Garcia. Copyright © 1992 by Cristina Garcia. Reprinted by permission of Alfred A. Knopf, Inc.

Gaskins, Bill, "The World According to *Life*: Racial Stereotyping and American Identity." *Afterimage* (1993). Reprinted by permission of the author.

Gates, Henry Louis, Jr., "'Authenticity,' or the Lesson of Little Tree." First appeared in *The New York Times* Book Review. Copyright © 1991 by Henry Louis Gates, Jr. Reprinted by permission of Brandt & Brandt Literary Agents, Inc.

Gil, Lourdes, "Against the Grain: Writing in Spanish in the U.S.A." Copyright Lourdes Gil. Reprinted by permission of the author.

Ginsberg, Allen, "America." *Collected Poems 1947–1980* by Allen Ginsberg. Copyright © 1956, 1959 by Allen Ginsberg. Copyright renewed. Reprinted by permission of HarperCollins Publishers, Inc.

Goldstein, Richard, "The New Anti-Semitism: A *Geshrei*." Richard Goldstein is Executive Editor of *The Village Voice,* where this piece first appeared. Reprinted by permission of the author and *The Village Voice.*

Grahn, Judy, "Boys at the Rodeo." *True to Life Adventure Stories.* Volume 2 (1981). Copyright © 1978 Judy Grahn. Reprinted by permission of the author.

Griffin, John Howard, "Black like Me." Excerpt from *Black like Me.* Copyright © 1960, 1961, 1977 by John Howard Griffin. Reprinted by permission of Houghton Mifflin Co. All rights reserved.

Handlin, Oscar, "The Ghettos." Excerpt from Chapter 6 in *The Uprooted: The Epic Story of the Great Migrations that Made the American People* by Oscar Handlin. Copyright © 1951 by Oscar Handlin. Reprinted by permission of Little, Brown & Company.

Heckewelder, John, "Friend and Foe." Pages 72–74, 76–85 from *The Indian and the White Man,* Wilcomb E. Washburn, ed. Doubleday/Anchor Books (1964).

Hijuelos, Oscar, "Dark Ignorance." Selections (pages 175–178) from *Our House in the Last World* by Oscar Hijuelos. Copyright © 1983 by Oscar Hijuelos. Reprinted by permission of Persea Books, Inc.

Hoffman, Eva, "The New World." *Lost in Translation* by Eva Hoffman. Copyright © 1989 by Eva Hoffman. Used by permission of Dutton Signet, a division of Penguin Books USA Inc.

hooks, bell, "Talking Back." Reprinted from *Talking Back: Thinking Feminist, Thinking Black.* South End Press (1988, 1989). Reprinted with permission of the publisher.

Hurston, Zora Neale, "School Again." Pages 105–209, 113–125 from *Dust Tracks on a Road* by Zora Neale Hurston. Copyright © 1942 by Zora Neale Hurston. Renewed 1970 by John C. Hurston. Reprinted by permission of HarperCollins Publishers, Inc.

Hughes, Langston, "Let America Be America Again." Published by *International Workers Order.* Copyright © 1938 by Langston Hughes; renewed 1965 by Langston Hughes. Reprinted by permission of Harold Ober Associates Incorporated.

Johnson, James Weldon, "Crossing the Color Line." Chapter 11 from *The Autobiography of an Ex-Colored Man* by James Weldon Johnson. Copyright © 1927 by Alfred A. Knopf Inc. and renewed 1955 by Carl Van Vechten. Reprinted by permission of the publisher.

Kazin, Alfred, "Summer: The Way to Highland Park." Excerpt from *A Walker in the City.* Copyright © 1951; renewed 1979 by Alfred Kazin. Reprinted by permission of Harcourt Brace & Company.

La Sorte, Michael, "Italians and Americans." Pages 138–148 from *La Merica: Images of Italian Greenhorn Experiences* by Michael La Sorte. Temple University Press: Philadelphia 19122. Copyright © 1985 by Temple University. All rights reserved. Published 1985. Reprinted by permission of Temple University Press.

Lazarus, Emma, "The New Colossus." *American Women Poets of the Nineteenth Century,* Ed. Cheryl Walker. Copyright © 1992 by Rutgers, The State University. Reprinted by permission of Rutgers University Press.

Madrid, Arturo, "Diversity and Its Discontents." *Academe* (November/December 1990). Reprinted by permission of the author and *Academe.* Arturo Madrid is Murchison Distinguished Professor of the Humanities at Trinity University. From 1984 until 1993 he served as Founding President of the Tomas Rivera Center, a national institute for policy studies on Latin issues.

Mangione, Jerre, "Growing Up Sicilian." Selections from pages 13–34 of *An Ethnic at Large: A Memoir of America in the Thirties and Forties.* Copyright © 1978 by Jerre Mangione. All rights reserved. No part of *An Ethnic at Large* may be reproduced in any form or by any electronic or mechanical means without permission of the author.

Martínez, Rubén, "L.A. Journal," from *The Other Side: Fault Lines, Guerrilla Saints, & the True Heart of Rock & Roll.* Published by Verso (UK)/New Left Books, 1992. Reprinted by permission of the publisher.

McKnight, Reginald, "Confessions of a Wannabe Negro." Excerpt (pages 95–97, 99–112) from *Lure and Loathing: Essays of Race, Identity, and the Ambivalence of Assimilation,* ed. Gerald Early. (1993). Reprinted by permission of the author.

Metzker, Isaac, ed. "Dear Editor: Letters to the *Jewish Daily Forward.*" Excerpted letters from *A Bintel Brief* by Isaac Metkzer. Copyright © 1971 by Doubleday, a division of Bantam

Doubleday Dell Publishing Group, Inc. Used by permission of Bantam Doubleday Dell Publishing Group, Inc.

Mora, Pat, "Legal Alien." *Chants* (1985). Published by Arte Publico. Reprinted with permission from the publishers of *Chants.*

Mukherjee, Bharati, "The Tenant." Pages 97–113 from *The Middleman and Other Stories* by Bharati Mukherjee. Copyright © 1988 by Bharati Mukherjee. Used by permission of Grove/Atlantic, Inc.

Ng, Fae Myenne, "False Gold." Pages 12–13 from *The New Republic* (July 19 and 26, 1993). Copyright © 1993 by The New Republic, Inc. Reprinted by permission of The New Republic.

Njeri, Itabari, "Sushi and Grits: Ethnic Identity and Conflict in a Newly Multicultural America." *Lure and Loathing: Essays on Race, Identity, and the Ambivalence of Assimilation,* ed. Gerald Early. Copyright © 1993 by Itabari Njeri. Published by the Penguin Group (1993). Reprinted by permission of the author.

Noda, Kessaya E., "Growing Up Asian in America." *American Waves: An Anthology of Writings by and About Asian Women* by Asian Women United. Copyright © 1989 by Asian Women United. Reprinted by permission of the author.

O'Gorman, Edmundo, "The Process of Invention." *The Invention of America.* Indiana University Press (1961), pp. 73–81. Reprinted by permission of Indiana University Press.

Ozick, Cynthia, "A Drugstore in Winter." *Art and Ardor* by Cynthia Ozick. Copyright © 1983 by Cynthia Ozick. Reprinted by permission of Alfred A. Knopf, Inc.

Parker, Pat, "For the white person who wants to know how to be my friend." *Movement in Black* by Pat Parker. Published by Firebrand Books (1990): Ithaca, New York. Copyright © 1979 by Pat Parker. Reprinted by permission of Firebrand Books.

Rashap, Amy, "The American Dream for Sale: Ethnic Images in Magazines." *Ethnic Images in Advertising.* Published by The Balch Institute for Ethnic Studies, Philadelphia, PA (1984). Reprinted by permission of the author.

Raya, Anna Lisa, "It's Hard Enough Being Me," from *Columbia College Today* (Winter/Spring 1994), Kirstin Wortman, Assistant Editor. Reprinted by permission of *Columbia College Today.*

Rodriguez, Richard, "Asians." Pages 158–174 from *Days of Obligation* by Richard Rodriguez. Copyright © 1992 by Richard Rodriguez. Used by permission of Viking Penguin, a division of Penguin Books USA Inc.

Said, Edward, "Reflections on Exile." *Granta* #13 (Autumn 1984). Copyright © 1984 by Edward Said. Reprinted with permission of Wiley, Aitken & Stone, Inc.

Santiago, Danny, "Famous All Over Town." Chapter 6 (pages 54–68) from *Famous All Over Town.* Copyright © 1983 by Danny Santiago. Reprinted by permission of Simon & Schuster, Inc.

Santiago, Esmeralda, "Angels on the Ceiling." Excerpted from pages 211–219 from *When I Was Puerto Rican* by Esmeralda Santiago. Copyright © 1993 by Esmeralda Santiago. Reprinted by permission of Addison-Wesley Publishing Company, Inc.

Smith, Earl, "The Genetically Superior Athlete: Myth or Reality." *Black Studies: Theory, Method, and Cultural Perspectives,* ed. Talmadge Anderson. Copyright © 1990 by the Board of Regents of Washington State University. Reprinted by permission of the publisher, Washington State University Press, Pullman, Washington 99165-5910. All rights reserved.

Thomas, Piri, "Alien Turf." *Down These Mean Streets* by Piri Thomas. Copyright © 1967 by Piri Thomas. Reprinted by permission of Alfred A. Knopf, Inc.

West, Cornel, "On Black-Jewish Relations." Pages 71–79 from *Race Matters.* Copyright © 1993 by Cornel West. Reprinted by permission of Beacon Press.

Wright, Richard, "A Hunger for Books." Selected excerpts from pages 267–285 of *Black Boy* by Richard Wright. Copyright © 1937, 1942, 1945 by Richard Wright. Copyright renewed 1973 by Ellen Wright. Reprinted by permission of HarperCollins, Inc.

Yezierska, Anzia, "College." Selections from *Bread Givers* by Anzia Yezierska. Copyright © 1925 by Doubleday; renewed 1952 by Anzia Yezierska, transferred to Louise Levitas Henriksen 1970. Reprinted by permission of Persea Books.

Yu, Connie Young, "The World of Our Grandmothers." *Making Waves* by Asian Women United. Copyright © 1989 by Asian Women United. Reprinted by permission of Beacon Press.

Rhetorical Index

Index of Authors and Titles

*An asterisk indicates a photograph.

(Continued from inside front cover)

1940

World War II
Atomic bomb
United Nations formed
Nuremberg trials
Mao unites China

1941 James Agee: "Near a Church"
1942 Zora Neale Hurston: "School Again"
1943 Hannah Arendt: "We Refugees"
1945 Richard Wright: "A Hunger for Books"
1948 Edmundo O'Gorman: "The Process of Invention"

1950

Korean War
Brown v. *Board of Education of Topeka, Kansas*
Rosenbergs' execution
McCarthy's pursuit of "unAmericans"
Race riots in South
Castro topples Batista regime in Cuba

1951 Oscar Handlin: "The Ghettos"
Alfred Kazin: "Summer: The Way to Highland Park"
1955 James Baldwin: "Stranger in the Village"
1956 Allen Ginsberg: "America"

1960

Civil Rights movement
Cuban Missile Crisis
Vietnam War
President Kennedy assassinated
Watts riots
Berlin Wall built
Malcolm X assassinated
Martin Luther King, Jr., assassinated
Men on moon

1961 John Howard Griffin: *Black like Me*
1967 Piri Thomas: "Alien Turf"
1969 Diane Arbus: "Man in an Indian Headdress, N.Y.C." *(photo)*

1970

Watergate affair
Roe v. *Wade*
End of Vietnam War
Nixon resigns
Energy crisis

1970 Marie Hall Ets: "Rosa: The Life of an Italian Immigrant"
1975 Cristina Garcia: "Enough Attitude"
1976 Forrest Carter: "Trading with a Christian"
1978 Jerre Mangione: "Growing Up Sicilian"
Pat Parker: "For the white person who wants to know how to be my friend"

1980

Equal Rights Amendment fails
Reagan's conservative economics
AIDS epidemic
Multicultural curriculum debated

1980 Judy Grahn: "Boys at the Rodeo"
1983 Danny Santiago: "Famous All Over Town"
1984 Louise DeSalvo: "A Portrait of the *Puttana* as a Middle-Aged Woolf Scholar"
Oscar Hijuelos: "Our House in the Last World"
Pat Mora: "Legal Alien"
Cynthia Ozick: "A Drugstore in Winter"
Amy Rashap: "The American Dream for Sale: Ethnic Images in Magazines" *(photo essay)*
Edward Said: "Reflections on Exile"